THE LIFE AND TIMES
OF
WILLIAM HOWARD TAFT

CHIEF JUSTICE TAFT. FROM THE PORTRAIT BY ERNEST L. IPSEN

William Howard Taft

The Life and Times

By

HENRY PRINGLE

A Biography in Two Volumes
★ ★ Volume Two ★ ★

Published by American Political Biography Press

Newtown, CT

Published by
AMERICAN POLITICAL BIOGRAPHY PRESS

Library of Congress Catalog Card Number 97-74247
ISBN Number (13) 978-0-945707-20-2

by

AMERICAN POLITICAL BIOGRAPHY PRESS
39 Boggs Hill
Newtown, Connecticut
06470-1971
Tel: (203) 270-9777
E-Mail: APBPress@EarthLink.Net

www.apbpress.com

This is the third printing of the first edition.

All publications of
AMERICAN POLITICAL BIOGRAPHY PRESS
Are dedicated to my wife
Ellen and our two children
Katherine and William II

This particular book is
Dedicated to:

Richard Wolstoncroft, Bruce Ipe & Stuart Benedict

Henry Pringle
Dedicated his work
To
Dr. I.C. Rubin
WHO HAS SUPERVISED THE
PUBLICATION OF TWO
FAR MORE IMPORTANT EDITIONS
With Love and Gratitude

CONTENTS

CONTENTS

LIST OF ILLUSTRATIONS

THE LIFE AND TIMES
OF
WILLIAM HOWARD TAFT

CHAPTER XXX

DEFEAT IN NOVEMBER

OCCASIONALLY a friend would beseech the President to mend his ways. One of these was Guy W. Mallon, a boyhood companion. Mallon wrote from Cincinnati in January, 1910, of his distress that the Taft administration appeared to be so closely allied to Aldrich and Cannon. Did not his old friend realize, he pleaded, that "loyalty to party has passed from a virtue to a weakness, in general estimation, within the last few years?" [1]

Justifiable impatience over such doctrinaire views moved the President when he replied:

The difficulty of being president just at present is that the public asks a man to do something which he has not the power to do except by associating with the Republican party and those who lead it in the House and Senate. The general feeling which you seek to interpret would have me enact laws without any party, and reach affirmative results by my good right hand. The absurdity of the view involved in this will ultimately be recognized by the people— perhaps not until after the Republican party has been defeated two or three times— and the emptiness of the demagogues who are now trading on what they call "Cannonism" and "Aldrichism" will be shown.

It is my fate to be in office at a time when conditions suggest the illogical view which you think prevails, which may lead to party defeat. All I can do is to do the best I can to make the government as good as I can and secure as much legislation as I can in the right direction, and in doing so to use those instruments which are indispensable to the passage of laws.

Taft's acerbity was that of all the conscientious, well-intentioned men who have found themselves elevated to the White House by fate. The President was not lacking in realism, how-

[1] G. W. Mallon to Taft, Jan. 8, 1910.

ever. What he wanted, he said, was to "point back to things done and not to a record of wind and hypocritical demagogy." The trouble with such people as his friend, Mallon, he continued— and it is logical to suppose that Theodore Roosevelt was also in his mind, "is that you do not take into consideration the responsibilities that you would have if you were trying to do something . . . and were to look about to see how you could do a definite thing."

So annoyed was the President that he boiled over in a second letter to Mallon a few days later. He flatly refused to denounce either Cannon or Aldrich or "to be carried off my feet by yelling by a lot of demagogues in respect to men who have done a great deal for the country." True, the power of the speaker should be curbed. True, too, Aldrich was too conservative and too devoutly a high-tariff advocate. But Taft, who was supposed to be so serene and smiling, fairly snarled as he declared he would make no general attack on them.

". . . this reckless, violent, unmeasured abuse, without knowing on what ground, without definition or limit," he said, "ought not to be encouraged and certainly will get no help from me." [2]

Predictions of defeat in November continued, however, to pour into the White House and most of them, no doubt, reached Taft. The President's private secretary was informed in June that Anson Phelps Stokes, too, had been lamenting the sad plight of the administration. Mr. Stokes saw no solution save drastic changes in the President's Cabinet. Ballinger, Hitchcock, Knox, Wilson and Wickersham should all be removed, he believed. The President did not, it appears, reply to this sweeping suggestion. Had he done so, his phrases would have been even more violent. He remained unshaken in his determination to keep Ballinger. Certainly he had no intention whatever of asking any of the others to resign.

"Life is not worth living and office is not worth having," he had written with respect to Ballinger, "if, for the purpose of acquiring the popular support, we have to do a cruel injustice or acquiesce in it." [3]

[2] Taft to Mallon, Jan. 13, 17, 1910. [3] Taft to P. A. Baker, May 21, 1910.

—2—

The specific issue, meanwhile, which would bring Theodore Roosevelt back to public life, was taking form. Governor Hughes of New York, in January, 1907, started to urge a direct primary law and the abolition of the convention system for the nomination of state officials. The theory of the direct primary— it has not, unfortunately, been borne out fully— was that it would mean the end of control by party bosses. Among others, Speaker James W. Wadsworth, Jr., of the New York Assembly, opposed the change. He said, with some prophetic truth, that the bosses would still rule. Their leadership would continue. It would be more dangerous than in the past because it would be leadership without responsibility.[4] Speaker Wadsworth might safely have gone further and insisted that the voter with no personal interest in the outcome would rarely take part in a primary election; that the party hirelings would mark the ballots.

Direct primaries were to be very important to Roosevelt during his 1912 fight for the Republican nomination. Up to 1910, though, he had shown little, if any, interest in the reform. At first, he had no desire to help Governor Hughes, whom he did not really like, put it into effect in New York. Why he did so can be explained only on the ground that Roosevelt, insecure and bothered by the conflicting forces which pulled him, was not wholly aware of what he was doing. It all seems to have happened by accident. On June 28, 1910— just two days before he saw Taft at Beverly— the colonel arrived in Cambridge for a reunion of his class. On the following day he was seated on the platform in Sanders Theatre with Governor Hughes. One or two people in the commencement audience noticed that the governor and the ex-President were conversing earnestly at moments during the exercises.

"Our governor has a very persuasive way with him," said Roosevelt when he spoke at a luncheon an hour later. "I had intended to keep absolutely clear from any kind of public or political question after coming home, and I could carry my resolution out

[4] Holthusen, H. F., *James W. Wadsworth, Jr.*, pp. 55-61.

all right until I met the governor this morning, and he then explained to me that I had come back to live in New York now; and I had to help him out, and after a very brief conversation with him I put up my hands and agreed to help him."

Like Taft's praise of the Payne-Aldrich act at Winona, this must take its place among the fateful statements, born of too-hasty thinking, uttered by public men. That night, Roosevelt made a public appeal for passage of the direct primary. If he had only paused to learn the facts he would have discovered that the bill was almost certain to lose and that his prestige would be greatly damaged.[5]

President Taft had also placed his influence behind the primary bill. He told Roosevelt that defeat of the measure would surely jeopardize Republican success in the oncoming Congressional campaign.[6] The President, too, had been drawn into the New York contest against his will. He was not even a resident of the state. Besides, he did not agree with Governor Hughes that all nominees for office should be selected at a primary. He did not think the voters were competent to choose candidates for minor offices or judicial posts, because they would not familiarize themselves with their qualifications. On the other hand, he was inclined to favor popular selection of candidates for the state legislature and for Congress.[7]

Governor Hughes accepted this compromise and Taft thereupon ordered federal officeholders in New York state to use their influence on its behalf. He sent telegrams to postmasters and to others whose food and shelter depended on the government and instructed them to proceed to Albany on behalf of the reform. It was essential to the "interests of the party." The name of the President could be used with "discretion," if necessary.[8]

All the appeals were futile. The primary measure was decisively defeated on July 1.[9] To Taft, it was another cause for discouragement; he saw no chance that the party would win in the fall.[10] To Roosevelt, of course, the setback was a personal defeat which demanded vindication.[11] It was doubly impossible, now,

[5] New York *Times,* June 30, 1910. [6] Butt, Archie, *Taft and Roosevelt,* Vol. I, p. 420. [7] Taft to L. C. Griscom, June 23, 1910. [8] Taft to F. Greiner, A. J. Smythe *et al.,* June 29, 30, 1910. [9] New York *Times,* July 2, 1910. [10] Taft to W. L. Ward, July 3, 1910. [11] Dunn, A. W., *From Harrison to Harding,* Vol. II, p. 125.

for him to dwell quietly at Oyster Bay. Before many days had passed further appeals for his assistance in New York would be made. Surrender, then, would be less reluctant by far. Such would be the Roosevelt predicament during the two years ahead. He would announce that he was through with politics. He then would bow to necessity and plunge into some fight. He would be defeated and would retire again. And this would continue until that February day in 1912 when he told a reporter at Cleveland, Ohio, that his hat was in the ring.

—3—

The defeat on the primary bill in the New York legislature, so trivial save for its larger implications, might have brought Taft and Roosevelt closer had it not been for the buzz of activity at Oyster Bay. The situation was graphically presented in a contemporary cartoon bearing the caption, "Excursion Time." This showed two gates at a railroad station: one marked "Oyster Bay" and the other "Beverly." A crowd was jamming its way through the first. But no one at all was passing through the gate where a train for the summer White House waited.[12] Certainly Roosevelt made slight effort to protect the feelings of his one-time friend and protégé. Pinchot and LaFollette were not the only insurgents who were warmly received at Oyster Bay. The colonel saw nearly all of the men regarded by Taft as his most bitter enemies and as dangerous to the nation's welfare. The President could not believe that they had gone, uninvited, to Sagamore Hill. He remarked to Archie Butt that Jim Garfield and Pinchot had, in any event, spent the night and played tennis with Roosevelt.[13]

On July 2, 1910, the visitor at Oyster Bay was Senator Joseph L. Bristow of Kansas whom Taft listed among his adversaries. In due time he boarded a train for New York.

"Theodore Roosevelt," he told the reporters, "is a bigger and broader man today than ever before. When he speaks, he speaks the naked truth. His jaw has a new angle of determination."[14]

[12] New York *Times*, July 17, 1910. [13] Butt, Archie, *op. cit.*, Vol. I, p. 416. [14] New York *Times*, July 3, 1910.

On July 5, Representative Miles Poindexter of Washington appeared; "a more blatant demagogue and Democrat never existed" had been the President's description of Poindexter, who had intended to run for the Senate that fall.[15] Poindexter was a luncheon guest at Sagamore Hill. He was assured that Roosevelt favored his candidacy.

"What shall I tell the newspapermen?" Poindexter asked.

"Tell them we had a very pleasant conversation and found ourselves in entire agreement," said the colonel.

Poindexter did so and this was duly published. He was surprised, however, to see that the morning papers also contained a few lines to the effect that Roosevelt, although making no direct statement, would support his contest for the Senate.[16] President Taft saw the item too, and was further distressed.

"I do not see how I am going to get out of having a fight with President Roosevelt," he said. ". . . He seems to have thrown down the gauntlet . . . for what was given to the press he gave out himself. I have doubted up to the present time whether he really intended to fight my administration or not, but he sees no one but my enemies. . . . I confess it wounds me very deeply. I hardly think the prophet of the square deal is playing it exactly square with me now."

Later in the day, the President read the dispatch to Mrs. Taft. It confirmed, once again, that lady's innate distrust of Roosevelt.

"Well," she said, "I suppose you will have to fight Mr. Roosevelt for the nomination, and if you get it he will defeat you. But it can't be helped." [17]

Even Roosevelt, it would seem, felt that he had gone too far in the Poindexter matter. He specifically denied, on July 6, that he had ever agreed to give his support. But Taft found small comfort in this; he was now certain that the former President had formed an alliance with his foes.[18] The Sagamore visitor of July 7 offered additional proof. This was Beveridge of Indiana, whom Taft regarded as the worst of the whole insurgent tribe. To disapproval of Beveridge's views on the tariff was added a deep per-

[15] Taft to J. L. Wilson, May 16, 1910. [16] Poindexter to author, July 10, 1930; New York *Times,* July 6, 1910. [17] Butt, Archie, *op. cit.,* Vol. II, pp. 434-436. [18] *Ibid.,* Vol. II, p. 437; Poindexter to author, July 10, 1930.

sonal dislike of the man himself. He was, the President had written, "a liar and an egotist and so self-absorbed that he cannot be
depended on for anything, and I really am not particularly concerned whether he is elected in Indiana or not. I suppose I prefer
a Republican to a Democrat; but he has attempted to kill my legislation." [19]

Roosevelt, after the Oyster Bay conference, promised specifically that he would fight on Beveridge's behalf. The Indiana
senator, like Bristow and Poindexter and LaFollette and the rest,
emerged to sing the colonel's praises.

"I have had many talks with Mr. Roosevelt in the past few
years," he observed, "but never in my experience have I had one
more satisfactory than today's." [20]

The clouds grew darker as the summer progressed and the
distrust heightened. Reports were incessant, by August, that Roosevelt would seek the nomination in 1912. "I am hopeful that Mr.
Roosevelt will not take the course you fear," wrote the President
in a typical letter, "but of course I know nothing about it and I
could not do anything, if I would, on the subject. I don't understand his conduct." [21]

At this critical juncture, while his political future hung in
the balance, Taft blundered again. Roosevelt was still smarting
from the defeat on the direct primary measure. He was breathing
defiance to the Old Guard which had administered the chastisement. By now he had entirely forgotten his earlier resolution to
avoid politics and was declaring that he would take part in the
New York gubernatorial campaign. A friend advised against it.
All the portents indicated a Democratic victory. Why did he risk
a second setback?

"They made the fight on me and I've got to vindicate myself," he said.[22]

Two possible courses were open to Taft. The first was to be
careful and do nothing. The second was to use the vast powers of
his office on behalf of Roosevelt. Instead, the President merely
walked clumsily and he was soon in a trap. The Republican State
Committee was due to meet in New York on August 16 to recom-

[19] Taft to C. P. Taft, April 19, 1910. [20] New York *Times,* July 8, 1910. [21] Taft to
W. O. Bradley, Aug. 19, 1910. [22] Dunn, A. W., *op. cit.,* Vol. I, p. 125.

mend a temporary chairman for the forthcoming state convention at which a candidate for governor to succeed Hughes would be named. Roosevelt, some time previously, had agreed to act as temporary chairman on condition, as he recalled his statement, that the convention would nominate the "right kind of a man on a clearcut progressive program."[23] This was the opportunity for which the Old Guard had been waiting. It would reveal its opposition to Roosevelt. It would endorse Vice-president Sherman for temporary chairman instead. It circulated reports that the President, too, favored Sherman.

Taft protested, after a fashion. He telegraphed Sherman that a conference should be held with Roosevelt and friction avoided. On the following day, August 15, he was called to the telephone at Beverly. The vice-president was on the wire; he wanted to know whether Taft was aware that Roosevelt sought the post of temporary chairman. Taft said he had no objection whatever.

"Why, don't you know that he will make a speech against you and the administration, and will carry the convention . . . and take the machinery out of the hands of your friends?" Sherman asked.

Taft said that he did not so understand the situation. He again urged harmony. He told Sherman to "understand distinctly that you cannot involve me in a fight with Mr. Roosevelt over such a question."

But no conference with Roosevelt was held. The committee met on August 16 and promptly endorsed Sherman. The Rough Rider was astounded when the news reached him at the office of the *Outlook*. He would carry the fight to the floor of the convention itself, he intimated. The newspapers, next morning, emphasized the probability that Taft had been behind Sherman.[24]

Such was not the case. Taft had merely done too little. In truth, however, he was not entirely disappointed at the result. On the afternoon of the committee meeting he was motoring with his military aide and Norton, his secretary. The outcome had already been reported to the White House.

[23] New York *Times*, Aug. 19, 1910. [24] Taft to L. C. Griscom, Aug. 20, 1910; to C. D. Norton, Aug. 22, 23, 1910; New York *Times*, Aug. 17, 1910.

"Have you seen the newspapers this afternoon?" Taft asked. "They have defeated Theodore." [25]

If Taft considered it a victory— in his more reflective moments he really knew better— he must have known it was a costly one. Already there had been indications of the result in November. On August 3, at the state convention in Iowa, the progressives had shown marked strength. Senators Dolliver and Cummins had been endorsed for re-election. The Payne-Aldrich act had been condemned. Crashing cheers had greeted Roosevelt's name while Taft, President of the United States and the head of his party, had received but polite applause.[26] The lines were being formed for one of the strangest campaigns in all the annals of politics. Taft and Roosevelt were both to speak on behalf of the Republican party. But the statements to be made by Roosevelt would be heard with dismay, anger and alarm by the man in the White House. The ideas to be expressed would violate his most fundamental beliefs.

"My speeches," said Roosevelt as he started forth, "will represent myself entirely, nobody else." [27]

—4—

The President sent a long letter to Nicholas Longworth in mid-July setting forth his accomplishments.[28] A few weeks later, laboriously and again in his own hand, he started to draft a 6,000-word statement of the "reasons which should lead voters in the coming November election to cast their ballots for Republican candidates for Congress." Political exigency caused Taft to soften his condemnation of the insurgents. The question was no longer "what complexion of Republican one prefers . . . in the election such differences should be forgotten. . . .

"The only other alternative is a Democratic majority," he wrote. ". . . It is difficult, very difficult, to state all the principles that would govern such a majority in its legislative course. . . . We may reasonably assume, however, that a Democratic majority in the House would reject the Republican doctrine of protection." [29]

[25] Butt, Archie, *op. cit.*, Vol. II, p. 481. [26] New York *Times*, Aug. 4, 1910. [27] *Ibid.*, Aug. 20, 1910. [28] Taft to Longworth, July 15, 1910. [29] Taft to McKinley, Aug. 20, 1910.

This was hardly Taft at his best. No president in history has been at his best on the eve of an election. The appeal, duly published, was addressed to the conservative interests of the nation; these were the interests which had been appalled when Roosevelt succeeded to the presidency in 1901 and to whom, in due course, he had turned in the campaign of 1904. These were the interests which had elected Taft in 1908 and which had been violently displeased by his constructive accomplishments. Taft's misfortune was that he had to ask for a vote of confidence in the face of a vigorous and noisy opposition, of which Roosevelt became the leader, in his own party. His was a house divided. And so, during the summer of 1910, the credit side of the administration ledger was almost entirely forgotten.

The President had, during the past year, done a good deal to aggravate a bad situation. Stubborn honesty is an admirable quality— but often a disastrous one for the man whose fate depends on politics. Every newspaper publisher in the country and every magazine publisher as well had been dismayed or angered by a section of the President's annual message of December 7, 1909. This pointed to a $17,500,000 deficit in the Post Office Department. It had been caused, Taft said, by the low rates at which magazines and newspapers were carried. The rural free delivery was also being conducted at a loss. Second-class mail, said the President, was now transmitted at one cent a pound although the cost was over nine cents. The government paid out $63,000,000 more than it received. Only profits from first-class mail had prevented the department as a whole from showing a deficit far larger than $17,500,000:

The figures are startling, and show the payment by the government of an enormous subsidy to the newspapers, magazines and periodicals, and Congress may well consider whether radical steps should not be taken to reduce the deficit in the post office department caused by this discrepancy between the actual cost of transportation and the compensation exacted therefor. . . . I commend the whole subject to Congress, not unmindful of the spread of intelligence which a low charge for carrying newspapers and periodicals assists. I very much doubt, however, the wisdom of a policy which constitutes so large a subsidy and requires additional taxation to meet it.[30]

The issue was not to be settled until long after the November election. That it played an important part in the campaign is clear. In time, Taft would protest that his administration had been attacked by the nation's newspapers and periodicals because he had suggested this change. His hostility toward them, when their protests against an increase began early in 1910, was profound. He expressed this, first, when Senator Dolliver defended the publishers who, said the President, "use their magazines to cry out against the capitalists and the robber barons that they point to as deriving something out of the federal treasury from the federal system of protection which makes them fat, without realizing that they are doing exactly what they denounce." [31]

The magazines, he insisted, were getting "about $50,000,000 out of the government that they are not entitled to, and I am going to fight that thing through." The President's irritation had been heightened by the attacks in *Collier's* and other publications on Secretary Ballinger.

"If we wish to contribute a subsidy of $50,000,000 to the education of the country," he said, "I can find a good deal better method of doing it than by the circulation of *Collier's Weekly* and *Everybody's Magazine.*" [32]

This, too, was an old issue. The theory that the rate for second-class mail was actually a subsidy had been raised in 1905, when Roosevelt was president. Exhaustive investigations had been conducted by Congressional committees. Roosevelt, however, had been very careful not to embroil himself in this vexatious question. He mentioned it in his first message to Congress in 1901 and then was silent. He called for no change in the rates. It was typical of Taft to face it, just as he had also faced tariff revision. It was typical of certain publishers to declare that the administration, seeking to adjust the second-class rates, was attacking education. Their contention that an increase would mean bankruptcy was not wholly convincing.

[30] *Addresses,* Vol. XVII, p. 35. [31] Taft to R. L. O'Brien, Jan. 31, 1910. [32] Taft to Bannard, March 2, 1910.

In December, 1910— too late, of course, to have affected the Congressional canvass— Charles P. Taft refuted their arguments. He pointed out that A. W. Little, publisher of *Pearson's Magazine,* had just offered stock in his company for public sale. In his prospectus, Mr. Little had called magazine publishing "an immensely profitable industry." He said that $100 invested in *Munsey's Magazine* at its inauguration would now be worth $12,000. He said that *Everybody's Magazine,* the *Ladies' Home Journal* and others were "making surprising fortunes." [33]

Taft's courage was the greater, whatever may be said of his political sagacity, because he saw clearly the dangers. Only "a proper sense of duty," he pointed out, "would be likely to induce the Executive to bring this matter to the attention of the public." For it aroused the "hostility of a very influential element in forming public opinion . . . who control the news they give and the editorial opinions they express." [34]

The summer of 1910 was an unhappy one. The President attempted to rest at Beverly. But his waking hours were never free from the annoyances of politics. He added to the anger of the insurgents— surely this must have been stubbornness too— by playing golf with Henry C. Frick whose estate was at Pride's Crossing. Captain Butt protested to Mrs. Taft that this was unwise, that it would add to the belief that the President was in league with the ultraconservatives. She agreed. She said she would do her best to stop it, but the games went on. The President said that he liked Frick; he would not listen to arguments on the subject. He even played poker, one night, at the Frick palace. This, however, was accomplished with stealth. The President, his military aide and Secretary Norton stole past the secret-service guards and went, by themselves, to the home of the steel magnate.

A visit by J. P. Morgan to the summer White House on July 17 also was surrounded with the secrecy of some criminal conspiracy. The financier arrived at Beverly in a motorboat and was closeted with Taft for an hour. No word of his visit was published. Calls by Aldrich and Murray Crane of Massachusetts were equally stealthy. But secrecy is rarely permanent regarding a president's

[33] *Fourth Estate,* Dec. 24, 1910. [34] Taft to F. Lockley, Feb. 8, 1910.

activities; news of Frick and Morgan soon reached Roosevelt and his insurgent followers.[35]

—5—

The Roosevelt who journeyed westward in the summer of 1910 was pondering doctrines he would have rejected when in the White House. Two reasons lay behind the change. One was that he was out of office and unfettered by its responsibilities. The other was that Roosevelt had become definitely more radical since leaving the presidency. Political thinking, generally, had moved somewhat to the left. Bryan had been partly responsible. LaFollette's ideas had penetrated beyond the borders of Wisconsin; they had penetrated, it may be, even the minds of a few of the respectables. The new political thinking found expression, in November, 1909, in Herbert Croly's book, *The Promise of American Life*. Croly and Roosevelt held many views in common. They did not approve of Thomas Jefferson, for instance. Croly raised the heresy that the Constitution might be destructive of genuine democracy. Croly, like Roosevelt, believed in the moral aspects of reform.

"The principle of democracy *is* virtue," was one sentence from his book which Roosevelt must surely have regarded as "bully." [36]

An additional influence was tearing to shreds the remaining banners of laissez-faire. This was Woodrow Wilson who accepted the Democratic nomination for governor of New Jersey in the early fall of 1910. In a brief twenty-four months, this one-time pedagogue would impress the entire nation with his strength and his liberalism. Wilson asked for heavier railroad taxes, an eight-hour day on public works, the direct primary, criminal liability for corporation officers and a corrupt practices act. He effected some of these reforms in New Jersey. He called his gospel the New Freedom and it was actually not very different from the New Nationalism, the rival label adopted by Roosevelt.

Taft's tragedy was that he had no comparable label of his own. So he was branded, in a measure unfairly, the guardian of the Old Regime. He alienated the Bryan followers. He alienated men

[35] Butt, Archie, *op. cit.*, Vol. II, pp. 443-444, 457, 467. [36] Croly, Herbert, *The Promise of American Life*, pp. 29, 35-36, 454.

who believed in LaFollette, in Wilson and in Theodore Roosevelt. A scant few would remain true to the Old Regime in 1912. They would give Taft just eight votes in the Electoral College.

It is impossible to state with certainty why Roosevelt concluded to break all his good resolutions and campaign in the summer and fall of 1910. Cabot Lodge had uged him to "avert disaster and ruin" and to "unite the party." Roosevelt replied that he could hardly become a "thick and thin unflinching partisan of all that had been done"; in other words, come out in complete approval of Taft. He added, with accuracy, that "Taft, Cannon, Aldrich and the others have totally misestimated the character of the movement which we now have to face in American life." For a year, Roosevelt said, he had refused to admit that Taft could have been wrong. Then he had been forced to conclude "that he *had* gone wrong on certain points."

"The Taft people have been wild that I should come out in a flaming general endorsement of the Taft administration, which would be bitterly resented by most of my stanchest friends," he told Lodge, a month after he returned from Europe. "The greatest service I can render to Taft, the service which . . . will tend to secure his renomination . . . is to try to help the Republican party to win at the polls this fall, and that I am trying to do." [37]

So it must be assumed, other evidence lacking, that the colonel set forth to bring about Taft's renomination. His indictment of the President, it will be noted, had been vague in the extreme. But he chose, on this speaking tour, a strange way of aiding the administration. For what he did was to widen the breach between the left and right wings of the G.O.P. Even worse, he aroused bitterness and hostility in the President. Bewildered and on the defensive, Taft retreated still further into his shell of conservatism.

Roosevelt's first major speech was at Denver, Colorado, on August 29 and in it he reiterated the criticism of the courts which he had expressed in 1907 and 1908.[38] But this was only a curtain raiser for one of the most important, possibly one of the most disastrous, speeches of his career. This was at Osawatomie, in Kansas. The occasion for the address was a gathering of Civil War

[37] Lodge, H. C., *Selections from the Correspondence of Theodore Roosevelt and Henry Cabot Lodge*, Vol. II, pp. 377, 379-380, 386. [38] New York *Times*, Aug. 30, 1910.

veterans. Roosevelt began his address by referring to the dark days
of the war. Next, he quoted that phrase of Abraham Lincoln's
which— among all his utterances— has been regarded as most unfortunate by the respectables:

"Labor is prior to, and independent of, capital. Capital is only
the fruit of labor, and could never have existed if labor had not
first existed. Labor is the superior of capital, and deserves that much
higher consideration."

Had he uttered such radical sentiments, himself, Roosevelt
pointed out, he would be "even more strongly denounced as a communist agitator." Then came stirring statements which, borne by
the magic of telegraphy, greatly disturbed the large man in the
White House. Roosevelt said that he stood for the square deal but
"I mean not merely that I stand for fair play under the present
rules of the game, but that I stand for having those rules changed
so as to work for a more substantial equality of opportunity and
of reward." So he called for an end to the influence of special
interests in politics. Corporate affairs must be entirely public. Corporations must not contribute to campaign chests. The government
must supervise all corporate capitalization. It must fix railroad
rates. It must extend this control to such necessaries of life as
meat, oil and coal. Roosevelt did not criticize the Payne-Aldrich
act except to say that the "special interests are too influential" in
the drafting of tariff schedules. But big fortunes should be held
down through graduated inheritance and income taxes. Then came
the sections which sent a chill through the hearts of the respectables. Roosevelt pointed to the paradox of rigid states' rights in
an age when so much industry was interstate in character. It
was a paradox which would still be troubling his kinsman, Franklin
D. Roosevelt, after a quarter of a century had passed:

The state must be made efficient for the work which concerns
only the people of the state; and the nation for that which concerns
all the people. There must remain no neutral ground to serve as a
refuge for lawbreakers, and especially lawbreakers of great wealth,
who can hire the vulpine legal cunning which will teach them how
to avoid both jurisdictions. It is a misfortune when the national
legislature fails to do its duty in providing a national remedy, so

that the only national activity is the purely negative activity of the judiciary in forbidding the state to exercise power in the premises. . . .

The American people are right in demanding that New Nationalism, without which we cannot hope to deal with new problems. . . . This New Nationalism regards the executive power as the steward of the public welfare. It demands of the judiciary that it shall be interested primarily in human welfare, rather than in property, just as it demands that the representative body shall represent all the people rather than any one class or section.

One paragraph, though, was still worse. It reeked of utter socialism:

We are face to face with new conceptions of the relations of property to human welfare, chiefly because certain advocates of the rights of property against the rights of men have been pushing their claims too far. The man who wrongly holds that every human right is secondary to his profit must now give way to the advocate of human welfare, who rightly maintains that every man holds his property subject to the general right of the community to regulate its use to whatever degree the public welfare may require it.[39]

Even Theodore Roosevelt was a degree alarmed, in September, 1910, by these words. He protested that he had merely been quoting Lincoln. He admitted that it had been a "blunder of some gravity" to "take that position in the fashion that I did." [40]

Taft, of course, was shocked. At first he had been merely hurt by Roosevelt. "If I only knew what the President [*sic*] wanted . . ." had been his plaintive remark to Captain Butt, "I would do it, but you know he has held himself so aloof that I am absolutely in the dark. I am deeply wounded." [41] He knew now, all too well, what his predecessor wanted. He was certain that Roosevelt sought to destroy the Constitution.

"I don't know whither we are drifting," Taft wrote, "but I do know where every real thinking patriot will stand in the end, and that's by the Constitution." [42]

[39] Roosevelt, Theodore, *Works*, National Edition, Vol. XVII, pp. 5-22. [40] Bishop, J. B., *Theodore Roosevelt and His Time*, Vol. II, pp. 303-304. [41] Butt, Archie, *op. cit.*, Vol. II, p. 485. [42] Taft to Edward Colston, Sept. 8, 1910.

—6—

The President's nerves were on edge. He lost his temper on the golf links; once he swore explosively and tossed his club twenty-five feet after a bad shot. He talked too much about Roosevelt's sins and his remarks were not limited to his intimates.[43] The gist of what he said was repeated in a long report to Charles P. Taft who was abroad:

After you left Mr. Roosevelt came, and of his course you have certainly seen full accounts. He told Meyer [the secretary of the navy], as he has told others, that he intends to work for my re-nomination and election, but if this is true he has taken a peculiar course to bring it about. . . . He has made some speeches that indicate that he is going quite beyond anything that he advocated when he was in the White House, and has proposed a program which it is absolutely impossible to carry out except by a revision of the federal Constitution.

He has attacked the Supreme Court, which came like a bolt out of a clear sky, and which has aroused great indignation throughout the country on the part of the conservatives. His tour through the West has been one continual ovation, and his speeches have been of the same old kind—attacking corporations, corruption in politics, and setting forth his own views and his own actions as instances of proper conduct with reference to the wicked powers of evil in the Republic. I am bound to say that his speeches are fuller of the ego now than they ever were, and he allows himself to fall into a style that makes one think he considers himself still the President of the United States. In most of these speeches he has utterly ignored me. . . . His attitude toward me is one that I find difficult to understand and explain. . . .

It looks a little bit as if he were hunting reasons for criticizing me and justifying his attitude toward me. But I have made up my mind in regard to it— that the only course for me to pursue is to sit tight and let him talk. He is at the head of the insurgents, and for the time being the insurgents are at the top of the wave. They have carried Wisconsin and Kansas and California and Iowa, and they may carry Washington. . . .

[43] Butt, Archie, *op. cit.*, Vol. II, pp. 503, 499.

The only feasible policies that he advocates are those which I am trying to put through. Those which go beyond are . . . utterly impracticable because they could never be gotten through without a revolution or revision of the Constitution, either of which is impossible.

In searching for the reasons behind Roosevelt's enmity, the President told of rumors regarding his expressions of gratitude toward his brother. Roosevelt was reported to be bitter "because I dared to include you in the same class with him as assisting me in my canvass for the presidency. I venture to say that swelled-headedness could go no further than this." [44]

A week later Taft told Horace Taft that Roosevelt's receptions in the West "together . . . with the urgent appeals of Pinchot and Garfield, have prepared him to think that running for a third term is not objectionable, and that the demand for him is so great that he cannot resist it . . . especially when before him is so large a demand and opportunity for real reform in the shape of 'New Nationalism.'"

His present mental condition, therefore, rejects me entirely and I think he occupies his leisure time in finding reasons why he is justified in not supporting me. Roosevelt has no one to advise him of the conservative type, like Root or Moody or Knox or myself, as he did when he was in office. . . .

The thing of all others that I am not going to do is to step out of the way of Mr. Roosevelt when he is advocating such wild ideas as those in . . . the Osawatomie speech. I think the "New Nationalism" . . . speech frightened every lawyer in the United States, and has greatly stirred up the indignation and fear of the thinking part of New England and the middle states. It contained certainly a threat that would startle most conservative institutions. How far, if the contest were on and the issues were united in the far West, the extreme to which Mr. Roosevelt goes would drive away his support, one cannot tell. I should think that . . . he would carry all the western states.[45]

The most significant aspect of this communication was Taft's reference to the conservative interests and his intimation that he

[44] Taft to C. P. Taft, Sept. 10, 1910. [45] Taft to Horace D. Taft, Sept. 16, 1910.

was their champion. A brief two years before he would have rejected the role.

The newspapers were filled, of course, with accounts of the increasing friction. But the Republican leaders deluded themselves that Roosevelt and Taft could still be portrayed as Damon and Pythias. Such had been the reason for the meeting at Beverly. Another opportunity was provided at the National Conservation Congress at St. Paul on September 5. It was proposed that a dinner be given for them and thereby, as the president of the congress phrased it, "give two of the best men in the United States a chance to have a good, long talk at an *accidental* meeting." President Taft, however, vetoed the suggestion.[46] They spoke, instead, on consecutive days, and each paid a somewhat insincere tribute to the other. The President said that Roosevelt had started the conservation crusade ". . . and I rejoice in my heritage." [47] The ex-President was not to be outdone: "Much that I have to say will be but a repetition of what was so admirably said on this very platform by the President of the United States yesterday." [48]

A second Taft-Roosevelt meeting was finally arranged and it was, all in all, about as futile as the first. It was held on September 19, 1910, at New Haven where the President was attending a session of the Yale Corporation. Roosevelt's arrival was characteristically dramatic. He came across Long Island Sound from Oyster Bay in a speedboat, ran into rough weather, went ashore at Stamford and made the rest of the trip by motor. Having thus defied the winds and the waves, even as he had defied the African lions, the colonel was closeted— this time alone— with Taft for about an hour. Archie Butt noted, though, that "if they are not farther apart than ever, at least they are no nearer." They left in the same motor "and the colonel told stories and the President wreathed his face with a purely physical smile and laughed aloud, but it was all strained." The specific purpose of the conference was to discuss the approaching New York State Republican Convention at which Roosevelt would battle for vindication against the Old Guard. But Taft was rapidly approaching a point where Roosevelt's probable defection in 1912 obscured all else.

[46] P. N. Baker to C. D. Norton, Aug. 6, 1911. (Italics mine.) [47] *Addresses*, Vol. XXIX, p. 142. [48] New York *Tribune*, Sept. 8, 1910.

". . . if you were to remove Roosevelt's skull now," he declared the day of their meeting, "you would find written on his brain '1912.' But he is so purely an opportunist that should he find conditions changed materially in another year . . . you would not find there '1912,' and Roosevelt would deny that it was ever there." [49]

"It was perfectly characteristic that after having sought the interview, as he undoubtedly did," wrote the President to Mrs. Taft, "our friend should at once advertise that it was not at his instance but at Griscom's [Lloyd C. Griscom, a prominent New York Republican], or wearing [sic] around to the point of showing that it was at my instance. But this playing for position and small politics . . . all have no attraction for me. They only furnish me amusement in revealing his present character, which is a development of that I knew, but a development in a direction that I did not expect. . . .

"Roosevelt was very pleasant and I hope that I was. . . . We talked about a great many things, but did not come down to business until after the rest had left us, and Roosevelt and I sat alone. . . . I . . . told him just what my position was in respect to New York, to wit, that I wanted to stand by the cause that I had already upheld in my letter to Griscom; that I thought it was important if we were to carry New York at all, that the candidate should not be the result of a victory by the machine, and that the platform should not be dictated by the machine. He said he agreed with me, but I said I cannot use the federal patronage for the purpose, and he said he would not ask me to, but that what he wanted was the prestige of my support which this meeting . . . would give. . . . He was glad to secure my assistance in the fight; I was glad to give it, and that is all there is about it." [50]

Meanwhile, reports on Roosevelt's hostility continued to flood the White House. Frick transmitted one of them. It was only hearsay and Taft, as a lawyer, would have barred it. But Taft, as a politician, probably believed this account of a conversation between W. C. Reick, a correspondent of the New York *Times,* and the colonel. Roosevelt was quoted as saying that Taft had not

[49] Butt, Archie, *op. cit.,* Vol. II, pp. 518-524. [50] Taft to Helen H. Taft, Sept. 24, 1910.

carried out his policies; in consequence, it would be impossible to support the President for renomination in 1912 and he would take the nomination himself. Roosevelt had declared that the third term tradition had small weight with the voters. He was positive of carrying the entire West, some of the South and enough of the East to assure victory in November, 1912. The ex-President added that he would not oppose endorsement of the Taft administration at the New York State Republican Convention. Any attempt to boom Taft for 1912, on the other hand, would bring out his immediate opposition.[51]

Harmony of a sort was finally achieved at the gathering which assembled at Saratoga on September 27. Taft threw his support to Roosevelt and against Vice-president Sherman and the others of the Old Guard. He told Elihu Root that it was impossible for him to stand with Tim Woodruff, Barnes and the rest of the "dead lot" who were fighting Roosevelt. He again disclaimed that the friction was due to anything he had done.

"In other words," he said pathetically, "I don't think it is my fault. I am not conscious of having attempted to do anything except in the interests of the party and the country, and I must be content to abide the decision of those whose judgments ultimately make up public opinion." [52]

Root, finding his duty repugnant, went to Saratoga and opposed the Sherman forces. The convention opened with the usual prayer. "Bless this assembly, which is gathered to take sweet counsel together," intoned the Rev. Joseph Carey and the prayer very nearly caused an outburst of merriment. Roosevelt, despite his rejection by the New York County Committee, achieved the post of temporary chairman. Root was made permanent chairman.[53] Roosevelt's most important victory was the nomination of Henry L. Stimson, whom he had once appointed United States attorney, for governor. He was certain that "Harry" Stimson was a "man of my type." He campaigned lustily, if in vain, on his behalf.[54]

"I hope you saw the proceedings of the Saratoga convention and the very satisfactory resolution endorsing your husband," observed the President to Mrs. Taft. "Roosevelt made a speech praising

[51] J. C. Harper to H. C. Frick (a copy to Taft), Sept. 15, 1910. [52] Taft to Root, Sept. 24, 1910. [53] New York *Tribune,* Sept. 28, 1910. [54] *Ibid.,* Sept. 29, 1910.

578 THE LIFE AND TIMES OF WILLIAM HOWARD TAFT

me also, which must have gone a little hard with him, but which indicated that he found it necessary." [55]

In doing so, Roosevelt had injured the cause of the insurgents and had thereby added further confusion to a situation already chaotic. He had damaged, in particular, the election chances of Beveridge. Before long, in far-off Indiana, John Worth Kern, who was Beveridge's opponent, would be pointing with amused scorn to the vacillations of the prophet of the New Nationalism. By inference, he had endorsed the Payne-Aldrich act. Roosevelt, said Mr. Kern, had merely sought glory by achieving the temporary chairmanship of the New York meeting:

Having achieved this eminence, Roosevelt's strength departed, his valor oozed away, and the war-cry which struck terror to the hearts of the standpatters at Osawatomie died upon his lips and could no more be repeated. That temporary chairmanship apparently did for the mighty Roosevelt what the silly and seductive Delilah did for his valorous predecessor, the mighty Samson. While Samson slept, he lost his hair and his strength; while Roosevelt, intoxicated over his victory over the Old Guard, his power to serve the people departed.[56]

Events began to move more swiftly now. Maine's state election had already gone Democratic and the G.O.P. was hoping that its hitherto favorite slogan— As Maine Goes So Goes the Nation— would not this time be a true one.[57] Taft, hearing the result, was not greatly surprised. He said, again, that the House would probably be Democratic.[58] In New York, the campaign degenerated into a vitriolic debate on whether Roosevelt would seek the presidency in 1912; in the resulting clamor both Stimson and John A. Dix, his Democratic adversary, became unimportant.[59]

"We are living," sighed the President, "in a 'great and awful' time politically." [60]

Among other things, Taft was worried about Ohio where Warren G. Harding, whom the President called a "man of clean life, of great force as a public speaker and attractive in many

[55] Taft to Helen H. Taft, Sept. 28, 1910. [56] Bowers, Claude, *Beveridge and the Progressive Era*, p. 396. [57] New York *Tribune*, Sept. 13, 1910. [58] Taft to F. W. Cram, Sept. 15, 1910. [59] New York *World*, Nov. 1, 1910. [60] Taft to Horace D. Taft, Oct. 7, 1910.

TAFT WITH HIS SON, ROBERT, AND HIS DAUGHTER, MRS. HELEN TAFT MANNING

Photo by Raymoth

THE TRAVELING PRESIDENT; TAFT IN THE WEST

[See page 458

ways," was the gubernatorial nominee.[61] It was proving excessively difficult to raise campaign funds in Ohio. The President, out of his limited resources, sent $5,000 to the war chest.[62] So vital was it, Taft felt, to carry Ohio that he intervened to prevent an attack on Roosevelt by ex-Senator Foraker.[63] But Foraker still smarted from Roosevelt's onslaughts in 1908. He denounced the New Nationalism. He said it would make an autocrat of the president.[64]

On election eve, Taft predicted a "general Republican slump, with a majority against us of from twenty to twenty-five." [65]

This proved a too-optimistic prophecy. The Democrats had a majority of fifty in the House. They gained eight seats in the Senate; among others, Beveridge was defeated. Stimson lost to Dix in New York. The handsome Harding was consigned to private life by Judson Harmon but did not, unfortunately for his country, permanently remain there. In New Jersey, Woodrow Wilson would be the next governor.[66]

—7—

Both Roosevelt and Taft had lost. Both proved to be excellent losers. The colonel retired again to Oyster Bay; this time, he swore, he would really remain a country squire. "I think that the American people feel a little bit tired of me, a feeling with which I cordially sympathize," he said.[67] The aspect which gave him the most satisfaction, he told Cabot Lodge, was that "it will put a stop to the talk about my being nominated in 1912, which was beginning to make me very uneasy." [68] A fortnight after the balloting, M. Jules Jusserand, the French ambassador, was a guest at Sagamore Hill. He prided himself on his knowledge of American politics. At great length, with Gallic vehemence, he berated Roosevelt for the mistake he had made. At last the colonel pounded on the table.

"J'accuse, j'accuse!" he shrilled in the treble which marked

[61] Taft to Herrick, Oct. 11, 1910. [62] Taft to C. P. Taft, Oct. 18, 1910. [63] Taft to L. C. Laylin, Oct. 22, 1910. [64] New York *Tribune*, Oct. 23, 1910. [65] Taft to Horace D. Taft, Nov. 3, 1910. [66] New York *World*, Nov. 9, 1910. [67] Bishop, J. B., *op. cit.*, Vol. II, p. 390. [68] Lodge, H. C., *op. cit.*, Vol. II, p. 394.

his moments of high excitement. "You are fiercer than M. Zola! Of course I intended to stay out of local politics . . . but what was I to do when such old personal and political friends as Cabot Lodge and Henry Stimson were in danger? I am glad I tried to help them out." [69]

Nor did Taft reveal any signs of rancor. He reassured the defeated Harding that it would not take the Democrats long "to convince everybody of their incapacity." The outlook for 1912 was by no means hopeless.[70] Besides, there was work to be done. The President prepared to leave immediately on a trip of inspection in Panama. He began drafting his message to Congress. Taft was always happier when his eyes no longer smarted from the smoke of political battle. Now that the election was over, even if disastrously, his nerves became calm again. The explosions of temper subsided. He was, once more, the sweet-natured soul whom everybody loved.

Late in November a letter was addressed to the President by Miss Esther B. Fleming of Iowa. She requested a favor. Her brother, Cadet Philip B. Fleming of West Point, had been involved in a minor scrape at the Academy and might not be allowed to attend her wedding to Lieutenant Harding Polk of the United States cavalry. Would not the President order the superintendent of West Point to grant him a leave for that purpose? Taft must have chuckled as he dictated his reply:

You advise me that your brother is under discipline because he joined in a conspiracy of silence against some instructor or officer at the Academy, and that the privileges of himself and many other first-class men have been taken away from them. I greatly regret that under this rule you are to be denied the pleasure of having your brother present to witness the most interesting ceremony of your life, and I know what a disappointment it will be to you not to have him.

But that is the trouble with all human punishment; it usually falls a little heavier upon the innocent than upon the guilty. I have no doubt that your brother is a fine cadet. I believe that he leads the class, and I have no doubt that he will rise to distinction in the army; but I venture to think that when he is invited again to a breach of discipline, the fact that he was unable to be present at the wedding of a sweet sister will make him a good deal better officer and man than if I were to ignore the advantage of discipline to the whole school, and to him in particular, by granting him a privilege which under the just rules of the school has been withheld from him.

Now, my dear young lady, you will think I am a very severe, unappreciative, unromantic and priggish president; but after you have passed four or five years of your married life and have seen the good effect that this has had upon your brother, and have yourself, possibly, taken a lesson as to discipline in the army, you will write a note thanking me.

With good wishes, and with the earnest hope that both your husband and your brother will ultimately become major generals . . . [71]

The President returned from Panama in time for Christmas at the White House. Always generous, he sent out innumerable packages. Three days after the holiday a note of thanks arrived from Alice Roosevelt Longworth:

I have just got back from Christmas at Sagamore and found your adorable present! It was *too* dear of you to think of me and a cigarette holder is just the very thing I need.[72]

The normal Taft, relieved of the annoyances of political combat, was thus more than merely friendly and amiable. He was broad-minded to the point of radicalism. Ladies, except for possible exceptions among the fast embassy crowd, did not smoke in 1910. But Taft had a warm affection for Alice Longworth. If she wanted to smoke, he had no objection whatever.

[71] Taft to Esther Fleming, Dec. 16, 1910. [72] Alice Longworth to Taft, Dec. 28, 1910.

CHAPTER XXXI

UNLIKE THE WALLS OF JERICHO

AMONG THE voluminous documents in the private papers of William Howard Taft is a memorandum of a conversation between the President and Senator Reed Smoot of Utah. Senator Root and Charles D. Norton, the President's private secretary, were present. The memorandum bears no date but it was dictated by Taft, undoubtedly in the early spring of 1911, probably in March. It closes with a significant notation: "The above does not include words of emphasis that ought not to be repeated."

Clearly, Taft lost his temper during the session and uttered, as he was quite capable of doing, a lusty oath or two. For the subject under his discussion was as close to his heart as any issue which faced him in the presidential years. The Senate was debating the reciprocity agreement whereby Taft hoped to establish virtual free trade with Canada. The cautious and clever Smoot was among the politicians who had been warning the President that approval of free trade would bring down upon him the wrath of the nation's farmers. Why not, asked Smoot in substance, allow it to be quietly defeated? The transcript of the conversation was:

Senator Smoot: May I speak with you about reciprocity? Of course I know this is a tender subject with you, but I would like to say one thing.
The President: Say it.
Senator Smoot: Would you like to have reciprocity come up in the Senate and be beaten?
The President: Of course I would not.
Senator Smoot: Wouldn't it be better politically to have it come up and be defeated?
The President: I am not urging reciprocity on any political ground. I am urging it because I believe in it as a policy for the government

and the country, and believe that it is going to do good both to the United States and to Canada.

Senator Smoot: Well, you have no idea of the bitter opposition there is to it.

The President: I cannot help what they feel; the testing of reciprocity will dissipate all their fears, and I wish to push it through.

Senator Smoot: You have fifty votes for reciprocity now, but there are half a dozen Democratic senators who are anxious to avoid an extra session and will vote in any way in order to get away, and therefore we could get it up and vote on it and beat it, if you are willing.

Senator Root [interrupting]: I believe what Smoot says is right.

The President: I am not willing. I am not in favor of it on political grounds at all. It is said I am going to split the party, but it is mighty certain that the party will be split and defeated if they don't follow me in this regard. What I want to do is to get the bill through, and I am going to do everything possible to secure it.

Senator Smoot: Well, that is all I wanted to know, because I wanted to do exactly as you wished.[1]

So the fight for free trade with Canada went on. It was to be a gaudy battle and the principals were a varied lot. They included Sir Wilfrid Laurier, the white-haired premier of Canada and head of the Liberal party. Sir Wilfrid would crash to political defeat because he advocated reciprocity. There were tariff experts, lobbyists, American and Canadian Cabinet members and politicians. Champ Clark of Missouri was to jeopardize reciprocity's success with one of the most idiotic speeches in the long history of senatorial speeches. Rudyard Kipling would cable, when it seemed as though Canada might ratify: "It is her own soul that Canada risks today." Even Stephen Leacock, then known as an economist instead of the author of humorous stories, endorsed the myth that reciprocity was a Yankee scheme for the annexation of Canada.

"The Americans are a great people," said Leacock, "but fifty years ago we settled the question as to what our lot was to be with respect to them. We have decided once and for all that the British flag was good enough for us."[2]

[1] Undated memorandum marked "Dictated by the President two or three hours after the conversation," Taft papers, Library of Congress. [2] Poland, Eleanor, *Reciprocity Negotiations Between Canada and the United States: 1866-1911,* Radcliffe College Thesis, 1932.

Most commanding of all was the figure of William Howard Taft. True, he blundered and by an unfortunate phrase increased the apprehension of Canada regarding annexation; at least one unfortunate phrase seems to have been inevitable in every major campaign conducted by Taft. He fought for reciprocity with a splendid courage, though. He did not compromise. He did not falter. He believed— and in this he was clearly right— that only good would result from destruction of the American-Canadian tariff walls.

Charles D. Hilles described the opposition of Uncle Joe Cannon and the other Congressional nonbelievers.

"The other big hens like Hale [Senator Hale of Maine]," he reported, "look askance at the President, very much as if they found that they had hatched and bred a duck. He is happy over the prospects and sees well beyond the present discomforts." [3]

The President blew hard on his trumpets. Reciprocity was authorized by Congress in July, 1911. The fact that, in the end, the tariff walls trembled but did not fall was hardly Taft's fault.

"I believe this treaty is right," he wrote while the contest was on, "but I rather think its advocacy will eliminate me from the consideration of practical politicians. But I am not particularly troubled about that." [4]

Canadian reciprocity was part of an even rosier dream. Taft was pondering, in late 1909 and early 1910, whether a series of trade agreements could not be effected with the chief European countries whereby tariffs would be lowered. Negotiations were started with Germany to that end.[5] Tentative proposals were made, also, to Mexico.[6] The complexities in the path to such agreements were great, however, and in the end only Canadian reciprocity was seriously considered. But the mere fact that the President advocated these downward revisions is proof that he was not, as charged by the insurgents, an extreme protectionist. He had signed the Payne-Aldrich act in the belief that it was a step in the right direction. He agreed that the tariff cuts were not drastic enough.

[3] Hilles to Horace Taft, Feb. 9, 1911. [4] Taft to Horace D. Taft, Jan. 27, 1911. [5] Taft to von Bernstorff, Jan. 31, 1910; to H. C. Emery, Feb. 19, 1910. [6] Huntington Wilson to C. D. Norton, Aug. 22, 1910.

—2—

As the President drafted his December, 1910, message to Congress it seemed entirely possible to accomplish reciprocity with Canada. A long record of failure in previous trade agreements did not cause him to hesitate. Only one attempt had been successful. The Elgin-Marcy treaty of 1854 had lasted for ten years and then had been abrogated by the United States. In general, its provisions had been of greater benefit to Canada. Besides, protectionist sentiment in each country was growing.[7] By the start of 1910, however, the time had apparently arrived for another drive for free trade. Relations between the two countries were harmonious. Such troublesome questions as the Alaska boundary dispute and the North Atlantic fisheries controversy had been amicably settled. For ten years or more, Canada had been increasing her levies against United States imports and now the tide of opinion was beginning to favor lower duties.

Logical reasons existed for free trade. A boundary of three thousand miles, unfortified and without physical barriers, lay between two friendly powers. The people spoke the same language. Their customs did not differ greatly. The cost of living was about the same in each country and wages, too, were almost identical. The American manufacturer could not contend that he required protection from goods produced at starvation wages. The farmer should not have claimed— but he would do so— that the importation of Canadian products would injure his market.

"The farmers along the northern border of New York won't do a thing to Taft . . . in 1912 if his reciprocity agreement with Canada goes through," warned a constituent in January, 1910. "Just wait and see."[8]

Taft ignored this prediction. The Payne-Aldrich act contained a provision for minimum and maximum duties and required that the maximum was to be imposed against any country which discriminated unfairly in its trade relations with the United States. In 1907, Canada had signed a treaty with France whereby she could export certain products to that country at a lower rate. In return,

[7] Poland, Eleanor, *op. cit.* [8] J. A. Sleicher to C. D. Norton, Jan. 27, 1910.

she permitted the importation of French goods at duties below those for similar goods from the United States. This agreement was held to be discriminatory. It was announced at Washington that the higher rates permitted by the Payne-Aldrich act would be enforced on March 31, 1910, unless the French favoritism was terminated. The President was successful in averting a tariff war. Concessions were made on both sides.[9] During the year, representatives of the United States conferred with Canadian officials at Ottawa. By December, when he addressed Congress, the President was able to point to the possibility of further conferences leading to reciprocity.[10]

The President, himself, had taken part in the negotiations during the year. In March, 1910, he had conferred at Albany, New York, with W. S. Fielding, the Dominion finance minister. The visit was returned when Fielding arrived in Washington that same month and was entertained at the White House.[11]

During the preliminary negotiations with Canada in 1910, Taft was supported by powerful influences in the United States. The newspaper publishers had been outraged by the President's proposal to increase second-class postal rates. They were his enthusiastic supporters on Canadian reciprocity, though, because they saw in it the probability of cheaper newsprint. The Payne-Aldrich rates on wood pulp and paper had far from satisfied the publishers. Ordinary pulp wood was admitted free under the act, but levies were still made on pulp which had been chemically treated. Far more serious, the rates on newsprint had not been changed. The publishers contended that the cost of producing this vital product was $5.35 a ton lower in Canada than in the United States. They made the flat charge that the International Paper Company was levying monopoly prices. They said that both paper and pulp should be admitted free.

Thus Taft found himself— the experience must have seemed strange— the hero of the publishers. Their editorial support was augmented by the general dissatisfaction with the 1909 tariff rates. A third influence was a growing belief in the United States that trade with Canada would become very much more important. Charles M. Pepper, an expert in the State Department, predicted that it would

⁹ Taft to H. C. Emery, Feb. 19, 1910. ¹⁰ *Addresses*, Vol. XX, pp. 12-14. ¹¹ Taft to Horace D. Taft, March 28, 1910.

reach $400,000,000 "within a few years" and that the balance would be in favor of the United States. This was heartening to the nation's manufacturers. In 1907 the total had been $340,119,000; the exports to Canada had been over $100,000,000 in excess of the imports.[12] Mr. Pepper's estimate was decidedly conservative. Even without benefit of reciprocity, Canada's imports from the United States climbed to $331,000,000 by 1912. For Canada had prospered greatly in the decade after the turn of the century. American capital had penetrated the Dominion to a large extent. Free trade would make that capital more productive.

The summer of 1910 was occupied with further conferences among Canadian and American officials. It was agreed, generally, that agricultural products were to move across the border without duties. The United States argued on behalf of greatly cut levies, at the least, on manufactured products. This aroused hostility in Canadian manufacturing and industrial circles. Sir Wilfrid Laurier discovered, however, strong sentiment for reciprocity when he toured his western provinces that summer. On September 30, 1910, Finance Minister Fielding asked that the United States take the initiative in resuming official negotiations. Expert Pepper and Henry M. Hoyt, the counselor of the State Department, went to Ottawa in November. They were to obtain, if they could, free exchange of food and other commodities consumed by the mass of the people in the United States. Another factor behind Taft's advocacy of reciprocity, it is obvious, was the rising protest against the cost of living.

The bogey of annexation by the United States was one obstacle to agreement. The second important one was the opposition of Canada's vested interests. Progress was made, however, and on November 10, 1910, the Ottawa sessions adjourned with an understanding that they would be resumed at Washington in January, 1911. Fielding and his associates were Canada's representatives at the American capital. On January 21, 1911, a satisfactory plan was drafted. Reciprocity would be effected by concurrent legislation in both countries instead of by a treaty. Nearly all agricultural products except wool were to be admitted without duty. A few minerals, iron and steel plates and wire were also on the free list. Meats, lard, canned vegetables, flour, certain varieties of farm machinery and

[12] Poland, Eleanor, *op. cit.*

equipment, maple sugar and syrup, automobiles and innumerable other products would move in each direction at lowered, identical rates. The publishers of the United States were taken care of with free paper and free wood pulp; the latter as long as Canada refrained from limiting its shipment.[13]

The President, of course, was very much pleased. Facetiously, he told Horace Taft, who had always favored tariff cuts, that "your support of the reciprocity agreement makes me hesitate as to whether I ought to urge it; but I will chance that you are for once right." [14] Taft made up his mind that he would call a special session of Congress, if necessary, to obtain approval of the measure.[15] He was uncertain, as the battle began, where his support lay.

"Whatever happens," he confided to his brother, "it will be admitted, I think, that I have added considerably to the interest of the present session. LaFollette, who has been called and calls himself the 'defender of God's patient poor,' has not yet determined what God's patient poor wish in this regard. This is also the case with some others of the defenders of that part of humanity." [16]

It would be July, 1911, before Congress finally gave its endorsement to reciprocity. Meanwhile Taft, wholly innocently, was arousing opposition to it in Canada. In January, 1911, shortly before an agreement on reciprocity had been achieved with Canada, he explained the situation to Theodore Roosevelt:

. . . the amount of Canadian products we would take would produce a current of business between western Canada and the United States that would make Canada *only an adjunct of the United States.* It would transfer all their important business to Chicago and New York, with their bank credits and everything else, and it would increase greatly the demand of Canada for our manufactures. I see this is an argument made against reciprocity in Canada, and I think it is a good one.[17]

Realizing the potency of the argument— as yet advanced only in private— it is surprising that Taft did not take scrupulous care that the sensibilities of Canada were protected. His failing was that he simply could not appreciate the danger that a carelessly expressed

[13] Poland, Eleanor, *op. cit.* [14] Taft to Horace D. Taft, Feb. 8, 1911. [15] *Idem,* Feb. 16, 1911. [16] *Idem,* Jan. 30, 1911. [17] Taft to Roosevelt, Jan. 10, 1911. (Italics mine.)

phrase might be misinterpreted and twisted. He transmitted the reciprocity agreement to Congress on January 26, 1911, with a message in which he summarized the history of the negotiations. He told of the friendly relationship between the two nations. A trade agreement was the obvious next step. No violation of the protective principle lay in free trade with Canada.

"The Dominion," the President said, "has greatly prospered. It has an active, aggressive and intelligent people. *They are coming to the parting of the ways.* They must soon decide whether they are to regard themselves as isolated permanently from our markets by a perpetual wall or whether we are to be commercial friends. If we give them reason to take the former view, can we complain if they adopt methods denying access to certain of their natural resources except upon conditions quite unfavorable to us?" [18]

The more damaging phrase, "only an adjunct of the United States," was made in private and therefore caused no disturbance. The second, "They are coming to the parting of the ways," was not an irritant until Taft repeated it during the approaching weeks. Taken in its context it carried, of course, no aspersion against Canada and no hint whatever of a move for annexation. But on February 14, 1911, Champ Clark arose in the House and spoke on behalf of the agreement. He favored reciprocity "because I hope to see the day when the American flag will float over every square foot of the British North American possessions clear to the North Pole." Naturally, this sent cold shudders down Canadian spines. Once, this had been a familiar enough assertion by American politicians with an eye on the Irish vote. Even Theodore Roosevelt, in 1886, had hoped for a day "when not a foot of American soil will be held by any European power." And at the time of the Venezuelan friction with England in 1895 he had said that in a war with Great Britain "Canada would surely be conquered, and . . . it would never he returned." [19] Loyal Canadians had heard few such assertions during the decade of 1901 to 1910. It was alarming to hear them again now.

[18] *Addresses*, Vol. XX, pp. 135-142. (Italics mine.) [19] Pringle, H. F., *Theodore Roosevelt, a Biography*, pp. 166-167.

—3—

In January and February, Taft sought support for reciprocity wherever he could find it. Aldrich of Rhode Island, his "wicked partner" in other battles, was absent because of ill-health. Three days after sending his message to Congress, the President told Aldrich that reciprocity was the only way in which the American system of protection could be saved. Without it, the Democrats would win in 1912. Their tariff cuts would "play havoc with our industries and create chaos in business." [20] It was a shrewd appeal to the high priest of protection. Aldrich, from Georgia, described the insomnia from which he suffered and then attested his belief in the "most liberal trade arrangements with our neighbors. . . . As to the Canadian agreement, I have not seen the taxes and so cannot speak by the book. I am inclined to think it is more liberal in the concessions than I should have had the courage to make." Aldrich added that he would not criticize, however; he hoped that the Senate Finance Committee would act promptly on the measure. But he did not think that he should become its active proponent.[21] This was less than the President must have desired from Aldrich. Other pledges flooded in, however. Roosevelt forgot his bitterness of the fall long enough to say that reciprocity with Canada was excellent in every respect.[22] Boies Penrose of Pennsylvania was an ally.[23] William Randolph Hearst cabled his approval from London.[24] James J. Hill, who saw visions of augmented traffic for his transportation lines, promised to speak on behalf of the agreement.[25] Andrew Carnegie reported that even the Democrats were enthusiastically behind it.[26]

"The reciprocity agreement with Canada," said the historian, James Ford Rhodes, "is a measure of broad statesmanship which, if enacted by Congress, will, for its present accomplishment and future promise, glorify this administration." [27]

This was encouraging. But Taft, his heart so set on victory, was indignant when the New York *Evening Post,* always a low-tariff journal, published an editorial criticizing his qualities as a leader. He protested to the editor:

[20] Taft to Aldrich, Jan. 29, 1911. [21] Aldrich to Taft, Feb. 17, 1911. [22] Roosevelt to Taft, Jan. 12, 1911. [23] Penrose to Taft, July 27, 1911. [24] Hearst to J. T. Graves, Aug. 10, 1911. [25] Hill to Taft, Feb. 8, 1911. [26] Carnegie to Taft, Feb. 18, 1911. [27] Rhodes to Taft, March 7, 1911.

I am right in the midst of the fight for reciprocity, and I believe that you are very strongly in favor of it. What is the necessity for your writing such an article . . . ? Suppose you think that I am awkward and a blunderer in every cause that I sustain, what is the necessity for emphasizing it just at the time when I need all the force I can get in order to carry through the measure?

Now you think I am hurt by what you say, but you are mistaken about that. I have been schooled and my hide thickened in respect to your general attitude, of which this is only a part. But it is a mere psychological curiosity that prompts me to write this letter to ask why it is necessary, when a fight is on in which you are just as much as a sympathizer as anybody can be, for you to say things calculated to minimize the enthusiasm that you apparently would like to have me arouse. . . . You do not have to answer this, but the reading of your editorial just suggested the query.

Having thus relieved his feelings, Taft concluded not to mail this letter to Rollo Ogden.[28]

The President took his case to the people. He made three trips into the farm belt before summer was over in an attempt to quiet the fears of the agriculturalists. At Columbus, Ohio, in February, he said that anyone "who would initiate a policy to injure the farmer has much to answer for at the bar of public opinion." Reciprocity had been criticized, Taft said, "as an attack upon the farmer by depriving him of protection. . . . It is said to be a manufacturers' agreement; that is, in the interest of the manufacturing classes and adverse to the farmer." The President denied these allegations.

"How is the farmer to be hurt?" he demanded.

He discussed corn. The corn crop of Canada was but .6 per cent of that of the United States: "Certainly in respect of corn, the American farmer is king and will remain so, reciprocity or no reciprocity. Indeed, the change will greatly help him by increasing his supply [cattle were on the free list] of young and thin cattle, now very scarce, for feeding with his corn and making good beef." Nor was it true, Taft added, that the agreement would injure the wheat farmer. He pointed out that Canada had exported only 63,500,000 bushels in 1909 while production in the United States was

---

[28] Taft to Rollo Ogden, Feb. 14, 1911 (not mailed).

737,000,000 bushels out of which 92,000,000 went to the foreign markets. The price of wheat, Taft told his audience, was fixed at Liverpool. It did not matter, he accurately observed, whether Canada's small export quota was sold in the United States or abroad.

"The world supply is just the same in either case," he said, "and the world price, which governs the domestic price, is accordingly the same."

The President then proclaimed the general benefits certain to result from reciprocity. Trade with Canada would increase. The economic result would be comparable to the stimulus which came when the pioneers pushed into the West and settled the lands which had once been wilderness.

"We have with pioneer energy pushed on to the Pacific and taken up all the good land," he concluded. ". . . Should we not, by taking down a useless and unnecessary tariff wall, bring within our agricultural resources the great plains of the northwest?" [29]

He continued his argument at Springfield, Illinois, on the next day. The agreement "allows the admission into the United States free of duty . . . all lumber from Canada not further manufactured than sawed," the President explained. The rate under the Payne-Aldrich act was $1.25 per thousand feet. The duties on shingles and laths were reduced. Taft said that the timber resources of the United States had been greatly depleted and that $19,000,000 worth of lumber had been imported from Canada, despite the tariff, in 1910. Prices had been rising. The American farmer, who was the chief consumer of lumber, would be greatly benefited, he said. But then the President again used his unfortunate phrase.

". . . we have taken up those things that are involved in a Canadian reciprocity treaty," he said, "because opportunity offered. Now is the accepted time! Now Canada is in the mood! *She is at the parting of the ways!* Shall she be an isolated country, as much separated from us as if she were across the ocean, or shall her people and our people profit by the proximity that our geography furnishes and stimulate the trade across the border?" [30]

Three days later Champ Clark called for the annexation of British North America. The foes of reciprocity coupled this imperialistic outcry with Taft's malapropism, and the movement for

[29] *Addresses*, Vol. XX, pp. 163-169, [30] *Ibid.*, pp. 175-182. (Italics mine.)

its defeat began to accelerate. In April, the President attempted to undo the harm. "The talk of annexation is bosh," he declared. "Everyone who knows anything about it realizes that it is bosh. Canada is a great, strong youth, anxious to test his muscles, rejoicing in the race he is ready to run. The United States has all it can attend to with the territory it is now governing, and to make the possibility of the annexation of Canada by the United States a basis for objection to any steps toward their great economic and commercial union should be treated as one of the jokes of the platform." [31]

—4—

Meanwhile, the President was having troubles of his own in obtaining Congressional approval of the bill. The House, controlled by the Democratic party, passed the measure on February 14. But the Senate Finance Committee reported it out on February 24 without recommendation and it was not voted upon before adjournment. Taft had anticipated this outcome. He had reiterated his belief that he had "given the Republican party a path to victory if they will take it." [32] He was shocked when word reached him that Senator Bradley of Kentucky might vote in the negative.

"I regard this as the most important measure of my administration. The suggestion that it can have any effect upon Kentucky is utterly ridiculous. . . . I shall be very bitterly disappointed if I can't count on your support when I need it for a measure that I think would be of the highest importance to the welfare of the country. . . . I am striving to bring about what I think will be an epoch in our country's history." [33]

Immediately after the Senate's recess, the President determined to call a special session. This convened on April 4, 1911. Commands and appeals soon streamed from the White House. Senator McLean of Connecticut was wavering, Taft heard in May. He wondered whether this might be due to a friendship between the senator and Gifford Pinchot. It was "quite within the limits of Pinchot's possible activities to oppose reciprocity because I am in favor of it,"

[31] *Ibid.*, p. 289. [32] Taft to J. A. Sleicher, Feb. 17, 1911. [33] Taft to Bradley, Feb. 27, 1911.

he wrote.[34] Wetmore of Rhode Island was also reported to be apprehensive over the political effect of reciprocity. This, said the President, was due to the senator's "loyalty to the industries of his state . . . he feels there will be reprisals from those who oppose the measure. . . . In this he makes a great mistake. He will not attract any support for his interests at all, and by deserting the administration he will take away from me all control of the situation." [35] Even Elihu Root had offered amendments to the administration bill. Taft did not doubt that the New York senator was a genuine friend of reciprocity, "but the paper manufacturers in his district do not desire the bill to go as far as it does go." [36]

The allies of the President were a curiously mixed crew. Even now, although twenty-five years have passed, it is impossible to untangle the skeins of mixed motives which prompted certain of them to favor reciprocity. Among them— in addition to Hearst and J. J. Hill and Carnegie— were Senators Crane, Penrose, Wetmore and Smoot, all of them extreme standpatters. On the other hand, it was opposed by such insurgents as LaFollette and Cummins.[37]

The President fought for his bill by direct appeals to the members of Congress. He did his utmost to convince the public of its worth. In May he received a delegation from the National Grange at the White House and attempted to show them that their alarms were unfounded. "After it has been given one year's trial," he said, "neither side will think of reversing it." But if it was true that the farmer had been injured, he added, a single session of Congress could repeal it.[38] In Chicago in June, Taft said that opposition came from the nation's lumber interests and from the paper manufacturers. It also came from "those who claim to represent the farmers and agricultural interests of the country." He proceeded to deny the validity of all their contentions.[39]

"I have to talk out," he explained when he returned to Washington, "and while I will be hammered on the floor of the Senate, I am content to leave the matter to the public if only we can secure enough votes to pass the bill." [40]

The House approved reciprocity on April 21, 1911. The Senate

[34] Taft to C. H. Clarke, May 20, 1911. [35] Taft to Aldrich, May 20, 1911. [36] Taft to J. T. Graves, May 31, 1911. [37] Taft to R. A. Taft, Aug. 27, 1911. [38] *Addresses*, Vol. XX, p. 339. [39] *Ibid.*, Vol. XXI, pp. 54-55. [40] Taft to J. M. Dickinson, June 5, 1911.

continued to debate it until July 22 when it voted for the bill by
53 to 27. Affirmative ballots were cast by 31 Democrats and 22
Republicans; the negative ones by 24 Republicans and 3 Democrats.
So it was, strictly speaking, a Democratic victory; assisted by Penrose, Crane and the Senate standpatters.[41] The measure was signed
by the President four days later.

He was delighted with the outcome, so much so that he forgot
his detestation of the New York *World* long enough to telegraph to
that paper his appreciation of the support it had given.[42] He even
abandoned, for the moment, his detestation of the Democrats themselves. In a formal statement he called the bill "a nonpartisan measure" and acknowledged "the credit that belongs to the Democratic
majority in the House, and the Democratic minority in the Senate
. . . the Democrats did not 'play politics,' they followed the dictates
of a higher policy." [43] His pleasure, however, was short-lived. It was
ironical that Taft, often the loser in his own country, should now
win a major victory at home and suffer defeat in a land over which
floated another flag. The opposition was, as the summer grew,
heaping abuse on the white head of Sir Wilfrid Laurier of Canada.

Sir Wilfrid accepted the challenge. He dissolved Parliament on
July 29, 1911, and appealed to the people.[44] He took the stump
himself and in phrases worthy of a Roosevelt or a Bryan campaigned
for his cause. Laurier was a picturesque old gentleman who had been
chief of the Liberal party for more than twenty years. He wore his
white locks in the manner to be made famous by Lloyd George in
the years ahead. His arguments were a happy blend of emotionalism,
appeals for loyalty and some logic.

"Henry of Navarre, at the Battle of Ivry," he cried at Montreal
on July 12, "said 'Follow my white plume and you will find it
always in the forefront of honor.' Like Henry IV, I say to you young
men: 'Follow my white plume, the white hairs of sixty-nine years,
and you will . . . find it always in the forefront of honor.' "

[41] Taft to C. P. Taft, July 22, 1911. [42] Taft to New York *World,* July 22, 1911.
[43] Statement, July 23, 1911. [44] Poland, Eleanor, *op. cit.*

"Bet on the Old Cock," he commanded at Three Rivers, Quebec, on August 17. ". . . Soon I shall be seventy years old, and the rest which I have not known for so many years would be most grateful to me . . . but I should be ashamed of myself if I did not devote what talents I may have, and all my strength, to the service of my country. I do not know what the future holds. It is said that the most uncertain things in the world are horseraces, elections and cockfights. If I were a betting man, however, I would bet on the old cock which has been winning for the last fifteen years. I do not boast . . . they may defeat me; but they cannot take away the fifteen years of prosperity which the country has known under the Laurier government."

Sir Wilfrid, in other speeches, insisted that reciprocity would benefit the Dominion— "our young and growing Dominion"— more than it would the United States.

"They tell us that this reciprocity in natural products will lead us to annexation," he said. "I would like to know how it will do that. . . . How would it come about that this Canada of ours would be annexed by the United States? It could only be by two ways, by violence or by persuasion. No one has ever heard that it is the intention of the United States to conquer Canada. . . . Shall we then be seduced from our loyalty? . . . I don't understand that kind of logic which says that a man will lose his manhood by trading with a good neighbor. We stand upon our manhood. We will trade with our neighbors and make a good thing out of it. And if they will not trade with us later on, we can get along without them. This talk of annexation is simply beneath the contempt and beneath the attention of a serious people." [45]

The talk went on, none the less. Even before the United States Congress had approved reciprocity, the London *Observer* published a lengthy leader under the caption, "President Taft's Indiscretion." This cited his "parting of the ways" speeches. It mentioned Champ Clark's violent nonsense. What the United States really desired, said the *Observer,* was a towering Chinese wall of tariff restrictions which would hem all of North America. And where would John Bull, who also had goods to sell, be then? The editorial continued:

[45] Laurier campaign documents, Taft papers, Library of Congress.

The question for Canada— and Mr. Taft's speech will help her to appreciate it still better— is whether she shall jeopardize her whole national birthright for an immediate mess of pottage. We gladly agree that the violent annexation of the Dominion is not contemplated by the United States. We maintain . . . that by the vast majority of Americans, President Taft probably included, reciprocity is regarded as an agency which will lead by easy stages to the pacific absorption, though in the end the absolute absorption, of Canada.[46]

Hysteria dominated the debate. The Montreal *Star* hinted of a nefarious scheme whereby the Standard Oil Company would seize the Canadian Pacific Railway and, through it, the Dominion itself. But behind the excitement lay certain intelligent arguments against the agreement. It was apparent that reciprocity would cut down the flow of American capital. American factories would no longer be operated in Canada to avoid tariff payments. It was declared, with some truth, that the agreement was far too insecure with respect to duration; if either Congress or the Dominion Parliament could cancel it at will, the danger existed of business disruption. Moreover, Canada's railroads might be damaged. They had been constructed, through vast public grants, with the conception that traffic in Canada would move east and west. Now a north and south movement, to and from the United States, was to be substituted.

Effective, also, was the cry that Canada's future lay with the Empire and that this was a step disloyal to the home country. But Whitelaw Reid, the American ambassador at London, assured Secretary of State Knox that this came from a noisy minority.

Finally, it was really a struggle between the business interests of Canada and the people of her Northwest. Finance Minister Fielding told Secretary Knox, confidentially, of "the greatest campaign fund ever held by a political party in Canada" which had been behind the Conservatives. Fielding thought that the money had come from Dominion manufacturers and "powerful financial institutions." Possibly some of the funds had been contributed by the "English Tariff Reform people . . . and some of the big interests in your country, which, having failed to defeat the agreement at

[46] London *Observer*, April 30, 1911.

Washington, were quite ready to serve the same purpose by defeating it in Canada." [47]

The Canadian elections would be held on September 21, 1911. As the day approached, with defeat probable if not certain, appeals came from the friends of reciprocity for Taft to declare again that Uncle Sam was casting no lecherous eye toward Fair Canada. But the President felt there was no more that he could do. [48]

At Kalamazoo, Michigan, where he stopped on another of his unending tours, Taft heard the bad news. "Laurier government and reciprocity beaten," was the telegram received by one of the correspondents in the presidential party. [49] That night, the President addressed the Kalamazoo Commercial Club.

"I have just had news about reciprocity," he said. ". . . I presume that it falls upon an audience in which there may be a division of opinion as to whether it ought to cause rejoicing or not. For me, it is a great disappointment. I had hoped that reciprocity would go through and that it would prove the correctness of my judgment, but it takes two parties to make a contract. . . . I presume we can get along doing business at the same old stand." [50]

"I should like to have had this scalp dangling at my official belt even if I am to wear the belt only four years. I thought, and still think, that it would have been a beneficial measure for both countries, but now it is an exploded issue. Some of the alleged political wiseacres who follow in my train and on my train, and bombard the train by wire, try to comfort me by predicting that the defeat in Canada will give me an affirmative advantage politically. Their reasoning is that those in our country who favored reciprocity know that I was earnestly for it, and will not blame me for its failure, while the farmers who were averse to the measure for selfish reasons will have no real grievance, now that the threatening cloud has passed by."

This was the important paragraph in a letter addressed to Horace Taft and signed, in the President's hand, "Will." But there is a postscript, also in his handwriting, at the bottom of the final page. It throws light on Taft's real reaction to the blow from

[47] Poland, Eleanor, op. cit. [48] J. E. Jones to Hilles, Aug. 19, 1911; Hilles to Jones, Aug. 23, 1911. [49] Sept. 21, 1911, Taft papers, Library of Congress. [50] Addresses, Vol. XXII, pp. 156-157.

Ottawa. It proves that the biographer, groping amid masses of documents, can be certain of the authenticity of few of them.

"This letter was dictated by Hilles," said the postscript. "I am sorry about reciprocity on account of the real loss to both countries in its defeat. Its political effect I can't calculate and I don't care about." [51]

—6—

Most serious, in Taft's judgment, was the end of his hope that the reciprocity agreement would quiet the clamor for downward revision of the Payne-Aldrich act. The President did not oppose lower tariffs, but he insisted that investigation by the Tariff Board should be the first step.[52] During the special session called to approve reciprocity, however, the Democrats joined with the insurgents in making changes which, in the President's opinion, varied from nonscientific to absurd.

The Tariff Board was Taft's personal creation. It was the first major step to replace traditional tariff revision— marked by logrolling and ignorance— with a system based on accurate knowledge. The Payne-Aldrich act did not provide specifically for a Tariff Board. It merely permitted the President to engage expert assistants to advise him in applying the maximum and minimum rates of the act and provided $75,000 for the purpose. Taft appointed a board of three members with Henry C. Emery, professor of economics at Yale, as chairman. The other members were Alvin H. Sanders, editor of the *Breeders' Gazette* and a moderate protectionist, and James B. Reynolds, formerly assistant secretary of the treasury. That all three were selected from the Republican party was a tactical error on Taft's part. He vigorously denied that they were tainted by partisanship, however, and called them "trained economists" which, to a degree, they were.[53]

". . . at the first meeting which we had with the President," Chairman Emery recalled, "he gave us our instructions . . . to find out as rapidly as possible all essential facts regarding the effect of the tariff without reference to any party, any theory or any sectional

[51] Taft to Horace D. Taft, Sept. 26, 1911. [52] Taft to McKinley, Aug. 20, 1910. [53] *Addresses*, Vol. XXII, pp. 222-223; New York *World*, Sept. 1, 1911.

interest: I shall never forget the emphasis with which he told us that he wanted the facts and nothing but the facts." [54]

The Tariff Board, existing without specific authorization of Congress and depending for its existence wholly on Congressional appropriation of funds, was less than a satisfactory agency for the arduous work of tariff research. The President advocated, as Congress convened in December, 1910, a permanent body to be called the Tariff Commission.[55] Instead, however, additional funds were provided; these would allow the work to go on until July 1, 1911. The final session of the Sixty-first Congress also failed to approve a statutory commission of five experts. Again, however, an appropriation was passed. Taft added two Democrats— William M. Howard of Georgia and Professor Thomas W. Page of the economics staff at the University of Virginia— to the three Republicans on his own quasi-legal board. He ordered the board to investigate the operation of Schedule K, which related to wool, and Schedule I, on cotton, of the Payne-Aldrich act. It was to report by December, 1911, when the first session of the Sixty-second Congress would convene.[56]

By July, 1911, the President realized that his foes in Congress would not wait for this report and he was firm in his decision to reject any tariff revisions offered. The wool bill came first. It slashed duties by almost fifty per cent and the President insisted that no adequate investigation had been conducted to determine the effect of this on the woolen industry or the woolgrowers. The second measure, so called, was the "Farmers' Free List." This had been named with extraordinary sagacity; it was a chaotic mixture which abolished or cut the tariffs on many objects purchased by farmers. But Taft stood firm.

"I have no difficulty about either," he said, while Congress debated. "I shall veto both, no matter in which form they come to me; because the bills have been drawn without accurate knowledge." [57]

A bill to lower cotton duties seemed to Taft to be the "joke . . . of the whole session." [58] Certainly it was confusing enough. An

[54] Address, H. C. Emery, Jan. 11, 1911, Taft papers. [55] Taft to Lodge, Dec. 30, 1910. [56] Addresses, Vol. XXII, pp. 117, 223. [57] Taft to C. P. Taft, July 22, 1911. [58] Taft to R. A. Taft, Aug. 27, 1911.

amendment to the cotton bill reduced the duties on chemicals. Then came some amendments relating to metals.

"So hastily was the bill thrown together, so little attention was paid to the consideration of it in the Senate . . . ," observed the President, "that the most ludicrous results were reached."

Taft vetoed this bill, together with the wool schedule and the Farmers' Free List, with manifest pleasure. He insisted that he was "in favor of the reduction of the tariff wherever it can be done and still give a living measure of protection to those industries of the country that need it. But I insist that we have reached now a point . . . when everyone ought to realize that the tariff should not be changed and business disturbed except upon information which shall enable us to pass bills that will disturb it least. . . .

"The natural operation of the tariff . . . and American ingenuity is [*sic*] to continue to reduce the cost of production, and that in itself will secure . . . a reduction of the tariff rates from time to time; but to cut them now 'with blacksmith's tools,' is to invite . . . a revulsion of feeling and then a recurrence of higher rates and the old systems of high tariffs." [59]

When it was over, Taft could not make up his mind whether he had gained or lost politically. He was weary from work. The summer was fast drifting past and he had taken no vacation. "Sometimes I think I am going to be re-elected," he wrote, "but generally the conditions calmly considered are not very favorable. I am stronger than my party and I am not strong enough." He consoled himself over missing his vacation by reflecting that "next summer I'll have a longer vacation than I want [a delusion, ultimately to be blasted, that as president he could take small part in a national campaign] and then perhaps after that I'll be out for good." [60]

To his elder son, on the other hand, the President expressed optimism. He admitted that he was being attacked by Hearst and by the New York *World*. In the West, no doubt, there was a "general disposition to think that I am still in the hands of the reactionaries. . . .

"But, on the whole, I feel that at the end of the session we broke more than even with our Democratic and insurgent op-

[59] *Addresses,* Vol. XXII, pp. 122-123. [60] Taft to Helen H. Taft, July 28, Aug. 16, 1911.

ponents. Even our reactionary Republican friends agree that the extra session has done much to strengthen the party. It has enabled the country to know very clearly what the Democrats proposed to do, and it has given us fifteen to eighteen months to have the matter sink into the minds of the public. . . . It may be that the sinking in will only strengthen the feeling against us, but the expressions toward me personally have changed so much as to give . . . encouragement that we may have a 'gambler's chance' to win."

So he prepared to add to the chance by an extended tour which would carry him to the Pacific coast, back and forth through the broad valley of the Mississippi, into the insurgency-infested regions of the Northwest. The trip would be an ordeal. But, after all, he repeated, he would not be forced to campaign in the summer of 1912.[61] He had forgotten, momentarily, the machinations of Theodore Roosevelt.

[61] Taft to R. A. Taft, Aug. 27, 1911.

CHAPTER XXXII

MORE CREDITS

A S I LOOK back over the record of the administration," the President wrote when it was nearly over, "I feel very well satisfied that a great deal was accomplished which will be useful to the people in the future, and that, after all, is the only real satisfaction one gets out of any public service." [1]

"I have held the office of President once, and that is more than most men have," he confided to Mrs. Taft, "so I am content to retire from it with a consciousness that I have done the best I could, and have accomplished a good deal in one way or another. I have strengthened the Supreme Court, have given them [sic] a good deal of new and valuable legislation, have not interfered with business, have kept the peace, and on the whole have enabled people to pursue their various occupations without interruption. *It is a very humdrum, uninteresting administration, and it does not attract the attention or enthusiasm of anybody,* but after I am out I think that you and I can look back with some pleasure in having done something for the benefit of the public weal." [2]

If it was a humdrum and uninteresting administration, Taft had made it so by his inability to popularize or make exciting his accomplishments. Horace Taft, in some ways so much wiser than his older brother, had protested, late in 1910, against the interminable length of the annual message to Congress. The President's reply was stubbornly belligerent:

I am sorry you haven't time to read the message, but I am not writing a message for newspapers only. I am writing a message to cover the ground of government, and it is a pretty big ground to cover. . . . Your remarks about my message I take with due humility. I am conscious of the outrage I committed on the public . . . but there were so many subjects and my time was so short. [3]

[1] Taft to Bannard, Nov. 10, 1912. [2] Taft to Helen H. Taft, July 22, 1912. (Italics mine.) [3] Taft to Horace D. Taft, Dec. 12, 25, 1910.

So very little time remained for the things Taft wanted to do. He had so little chance of success. The House was Democratic. The Senate was nominally Republican, but the G.O.P. was badly split. As 1911 began, Roosevelt was momentarily quiet, but he would soon be on the warpath again. LaFollette would be opposing the President too. Even the business interests of the country, outraged by Attorney General Wickersham's attacks on the trusts, would be criticizing Taft. The President plodded along, however, while defeatism often overwhelmed him. Among other things he earned, although it was never accorded him, the right to be called "Father of the Federal Budget."

"Perhaps the most important question presented to this administration," the President informed Congress in December, 1909, "is that of economy in expenditures and sufficiency of revenue." [4] Six months earlier, at the close of the fiscal year, Taft had inherited a $59,000,000 deficit from Roosevelt. This had been partly due to the haphazard method by which federal funds had been appropriated. Estimates by department heads had gone directly to Congress. Unless that body, rarely a zealous advocate of economy, chose to do so, no check was made on whether the estimates were extravagant. The President, except through the drastic and almost impossible veto of an appropriation bill, had no supervision of government expenditures. It was difficult for him to have any detailed knowledge of the amounts being spent.

Taft, who was so careless about his personal finances, effected the first important revision of federal finances. By executive order he directed that all estimates must first come to him. He suggested where cuts might be made. He was able to report that estimates for the year ending June 30, 1911, were $42,818,000 lower than for the one which would terminate in June, 1910. But this, the President informed Congress, was not enough. If the cuts were to be permanent and if real efficiency in government was to be realized, a careful and detailed investigation of all departments and bureaus was needed. The Treasury Department had begun such an investigation in two or three branches. It should be extended, however, and several years given to the work. [5]

[4] *Addresses*, Vol. XVII, p. 28. [5] *Ibid.*, p. 29; *Saturday Evening Post*, Feb. 6, 1915.

In July, 1910, the President could point proudly to a surplus of $13,000,000 instead of the $40,000,000 deficit which had been anticipated. This was due in large measure to successful operation of the Payne-Aldrich act; economy, however, had also played its part.[6] In June, 1910— his party still controlled Congress— Taft obtained $100,000 for a detailed inquiry into expenditures, and this was started by the Treasury Department. In March, 1911, the President appointed a Commission on Efficiency and Economy to carry on the work. Frederick A. Cleveland, an expert in corporate management and finance, became chairman. The other members were: Frank J. Goodnow, an authority on administrative law and later president of Johns Hopkins University; William F. Willoughby, who had held administrative posts in Porto Rico and elsewhere; Walter W. Warwick, of General Goethals's staff at Panama; Merritt O. Chapman, formerly secretary to Secretary of War Root; Hervey S. Chase, a public accountant.

"No question was asked about politics," Taft revealed, "until about a year afterward when . . . I was amused to find that all except one held political views contrary to my own."

The duty of the commission, he subsequently explained, was "to find out exactly how the government of the United States was organized in each of its various branches." [7] The task was enormous. Until it was well under way, Chairman Cleveland pointed out, "not a living man knew what the government of the United States is; no one person knew how the government was organized; what it was doing; what methods were being employed in establishments that reached around the world." [8] The President gave all possible assistance to the commission's work by directing that department heads answer its inquiries for information.[9] On January 17, 1912, he informed Congress regarding the preliminary accomplishments of Cleveland and his associates. Archaic business methods still prevailed in many departments. Certain branches operated under laws passed a century ago. In the revenue cutter service, alone, $1,000,000 a year might be saved. The cost of handling outgoing mail varied from $5.94 per 1,000 letters in one department to $69.89 in another. Government employees, as a whole, spent $12,-

[6] Taft to Longworth, July 15, 1910. [7] *Saturday Evening Post*, Feb. 13, 1912. [8] Buffalo *News*, Sept. 29, 1912. [9] Taft to department heads, Jan. 14, 1912.

000,000 annually for traveling expenses, alone, and nobody knew why. No unified system governed purchases; in certain branches the cost was extreme. It was a "serious mistake," Taft said, for Congress to assume that the people had no interest in government expenditures which reached a gross of $1,000,000,000 a year:

The United States is the only great nation whose government is operated without a budget. This fact seems to be the more striking when it is considered that budgets and budget procedures are the outgrowth of democratic doctrines and have an important part in the development of modern constitutional rights. The American commonwealth has suffered much from irresponsibility on the part of its governing agencies. The constitutional purpose of a budget is to make government responsive to public opinion and responsible for its acts.

—2—

All this was general enough so that the members of Congress, whether approving or not, could take no specific exception. The message contained references to patronage and political appointments, however, which were quite different. The President remarked that the "removal of local officers from the realm of political patronage . . . would reduce the payroll of the field service." He continued:

At the present time the incumbents of many of these positions leave the actual performance of many of their duties to deputies and assistants. The government often pays two persons for doing work that could easily be done by one. What is the loss to the government cannot be stated, but that it is very large can not be denied.

Taft then asked for a total appropriation of $250,000 for the commission. Its recommendations already made, he said, would save the taxpayers $2,000,000 a year.[10] The gentlemen of Congress were highly alarmed, of course, by the heretical idea that local officers were to be named without benefit of their approval or that a single appointee, through competence, might be able to do the

[10] *Addresses*, Vol. XVI, pp. 187-213.

work of two. The Cleveland commission was immediately the object of extreme suspicion. A grant of $75,000 for its work was made, but the bill provided that not more than three of its members or employees could be paid more than $4,000 a year. The President vainly protested that this would cripple the work, that such a ruling would cut off six experts.[11] The stipulation stood, however, and the resignations began to come in.[12] A similar fate awaited the President's recommendation to Congress, on June 27, 1912, that a budget be adopted. On August 24, the legislative branch attempted to wreck the whole movement by specifying that estimates for appropriations should be submitted to Congress alone. Taft's protest was prompt and forceful; the limitation was unconstitutional:

> I could not for a moment entertain, as reasonable, such a construction. . . . Under the Constitution, the President is entrusted with the executive power, and is responsible for the acts of heads of departments . . . and he can use them to assist him in his constitutional duties, one of which is to recommend measures to Congress. . . . If Congress is permitted to assume exclusive jurisdiction over what the President may seek to learn about the business transacted by the departments; if Congress is to say that the President shall not find out what is the present manner of doing business, what results are being obtained, what it is that officers for which [sic] he is responsible propose to do, and what amounts are being asked for future expenditures; if heads of departments are to be considered purely as the ministerial agents of Congress in the preparation and submission of estimates, then as far as the business of the government is concerned, the President of the United States is shorn of his most important executive power and duty.[13]

So the President ordered his Cabinet members and their staff to submit data on their financial requirements. A detailed budget was drafted and transmitted to Congress for the fiscal year terminating on June 30, 1914. It was, of course, ignored. No further funds were supplied for the efficiency commission. Ex-President Taft, in a lecture at Columbia University in 1915, pointed out that the "dust is accumulating" on the commission's reports.[14] Dust lay thick, too,

---

[11] Taft to F. E. Warren, June 12, 1912. [12] Taft to H. E. Chase, Aug. 10, 1912. [13] Taft to MacVeagh, Sept. 19, 1912. [14] Taft, *Our Chief Magistrate and His Powers*, pp. 64-65.

on the budget, itself, although Taft hoped "it may sometime prove useful." [15] That day did not arrive until after 1920. And then, strangely enough, it was Harding of Ohio who injected new order into government spending.

—3—

Taft's interest in civil service reform evolved from his belief in the necessity for governmental economy. To an equal or even greater extent, it came from the disgust which overcame him when, on taking office, he learned that a major part of the President's time was consumed by the importunities of job seekers and by patronage problems. He rapidly reached a conclusion that not only the Chief Executive but the members of Congress as well would benefit greatly if all except the most important officers were placed under the merit system.

As presidents go, Taft was an honest and fairly effective friend of civil service. It may at least be said that he was a better one than Theodore Roosevelt, who had been a member of the United States Civil Service Commission from 1889 to 1895 and who was known, therefore, as an apostle of this reform as long as he lived. Like all presidents, Taft was inundated in March, 1909, with pleas of the spoilsmen. Certainly three-quarters of his early letters— it is, perhaps, no exaggeration to say that a quarter of all the letters he wrote while in the White House— dealt with appointments. His patience was often strained when men wrote that some post would be acceptable now that he was in the presidency.

"You are laboring under a wrong impression; that all you have to do is just to ask for an office and it will come to you," he snapped to one of these. ". . . offices are . . . made from a district because the man selected is supposed to be as good a man as can be gotten and to have a number of friends in the district who support him and believe that he is a representative man there." [16]

Taft's perplexities were the greater because, relatively speaking, he had so few places which he could fill. He could not turn out the faithful who had been installed by Roosevelt.

[15] *Saturday Evening Post,* Feb. 13, 1915. [16] Taft to G. B. Heidt, March 29, 1909.

"My coming into office," he complained, "was exactly as if Roosevelt had succeeded himself." [17]

The most troublesome factor was the presidential power to waive, in certain instances, the requirements of the civil service laws. Demands for such exemptions were incessant. In September, 1909, for example, Secretary of War Dickinson requested the appointment of some candidate on the ground that he had served in the army for three years. Taft refused. His policy would be to make no exceptions "save in the most extraordinary cases." [18]

"I have not lifted the civil service rules in any cases except those that I am willing to state the reason for in the order. . . ," he wrote. "Otherwise there would be no stopping the applications." [19]

Thus by the end of 1910, the President was yearning for an extension of the classified service. He said that he would strengthen the civil service as much as he could and did not care whether Republican defeat resulted or not.[20] He felt that he had done more than any previous president.[21]

"You will see that I have gone as far as any crank . . ." he told his brother. "I have adopted an ironclad rule that all local officers, i.e., postmasters, collectors, appraisers, etc., shall remain in office or be reappointed and that no congressman or senator can have them removed. This is going to cause some kicks, but it is going to save me a lot of trouble and it will make the service much more economical." [22]

This was a reference to that year's message to Congress. Taft had called for a law extending protection to the members of the consular and diplomatic services because "assurance of permanency of tenure and promotion on merit" would bring about "the entry of capable young men into the service." The President, informing Congress that he had put all assistant postmasters under civil service, also recommended that first-, second- and third-class postmasters be given similar protection. Most of the fourth-class group were already in the system. It would be necessary for Congress to approve

---

[17] Taft to H. H. Lurton, March 29, 1909. [18] Taft to Dickinson, Sept. 5, 1909. [19] Taft to Ansley Wilcox, Dec. 16, 1909. [20] Taft to G. H. Hamilton, Nov. 25, 1910. [21] Taft to Wilcox, Dec. 14, 1910. [22] Taft to Horace D. Taft, Dec. 25, 1910.

this sweeping change and take from the Senate its power to confirm these appointments. Taft continued:

I am aware that this is inviting from the Senate a concession in respect to its quasi-executive power that is considerable, but I believe it to be in the interest of good administration and efficiency of service. To make this change would take the postmasters out of politics; would relieve congressmen who now are burdened with the necessity of making recommendations of a responsibility that must be irksome and *can create nothing but trouble;* and it would result in . . . greater attention to business, greater fidelity, and consequently greater economy and efficiency.[23]

"If we have all these appointments regularly made under the civil service rules," the President told a group of postmasters in September, 1912, "you who are in the offices will sleep better and have more opportunity to work for the government, and those whose responsibility it is to fill the offices— and that is where I come in— will sleep better and have more opportunity to work for the government." [24]

The more he considered the matter the more convinced Taft became that patronage created "nothing but trouble," even for the politicians who were ready to defend it with their lives. All administrative officers should be continued in office as long as they did their work well, he said. Under the present system "the President and members of Congress devote to matters of patronage time which they should devote to questions of policy and administration." [25] Nothing was done, of course. Taft was aware that he could not convert Congress to the notion that patronage was a liability. ". . . perhaps public opinion can exert a good deal of influence," he said, "if we can arouse public opinion on the subject." [26] But William Howard Taft was always signally unsuccessful in his attempts to swing popular support behind his measures. His best utterance on the subject was not made until, again, he was enjoying the blessings of private life:

I do not mean to say that some congressmen and some senators do not make such patronage politically useful for themselves, but I

[23] *Addresses,* Vol. XX, pp. 16, 43-44. (Italics mine.) [24] *Ibid.,* Vol. XXX, p. 18. [25] *Ibid.,* Vol. XXVI, p. 196. [26] Taft to L. B. Swift, Oct. 11, 1910.

Photo by J. A. Ramsey

THE FIRST MOTORIZED PRESIDENT

AS PRESIDENTIAL NOMINEE, KANSAS CITY, OCTOBER, 1908

MOBILIZATION OF ATLANTIC FLEET IN HUDSON RIVER NOVEMBER 2, 1911.

ADMIRAL W.SIMPRÓN
SECRETARY OF THE NAVY MEYER.
PRESIDENT TAFT.
LIEUT. COMDR. PALMER.

THE COMMANDER IN CHIEF OF THE UNITED STATES NAVY

See page 526]

venture to think . . . that the having, and the use of, such patron-age more often injures than helps the user in securing his renomina-tion and re-election. It is a saying in Washington, justified by the fact, that an appointment of a first-, second-, third- or fourth-class postmaster not infrequently creates for the congressman who secures it one ingrate and ten enemies. . . .

I cannot exaggerate the waste of the President's time and the consumption of his nervous vitality involved in listening to con-gressmen's intercession as to local appointments. Why should the President have to have his time taken up in a discussion over . . . who shall be postmistress at the town of Devil's Lake in North Dakota? How should he be able to know . . . who is best fitted to fill such a place? [27]

It is, though, an ironical fact that Taft would almost surely have been defeated by Roosevelt for the 1912 nomination had it not been for the officeholders, transformed for the moment into dele-gates, who voted for him at the convention. They did so on com-mand of state and city bosses who also were officeholders. Without these postmasters and collectors and appraisers, the Bull Moose forces would have been victorious.

The President, himself, had relatively little to do with the machine victory at Chicago. Perhaps, deep in his heart, he did not really care enough about it. During the four years of his incumbency he vacillated, to a degree, in dealing with patronage. No other course was possible than to consult the members of Congress. Thus in June, 1909, he promised to confer with Senators William Lorimer and A. J. Hopkins of Illinois.[28] At the start of his administration he said that he would not oppose the organization of Boss William L. Ward in New York.[29] He bowed, on occasion, to Penrose of Pennsylvania [30] and to Bill Barnes of New York.[31] Pending his recommendations on civil service, Taft said, he would consult senators or congressmen on local appointments. In Demo-cratic communities, he would confer with the G.O.P. representa-tives. An exception would be made regarding judicial officers: ". . . while I listen with due regard to the recommendations of the senator," the President said, "I must exercise my own judgment." [32]

[27] Taft, op. cit., pp. 65-67. [28] Taft to Hopkins, June 4, 1909. [29] Taft to Ward, April 30, 1909. [30] Taft to Eugene Hale, Jan. 30, 1911. [31] Taft to Barnes, Jan. 26, 1911. [32] Taft to Burton, May 9, 1911.

A more astute president, no matter how repellent the system may have been to him, might have used his appointing power to force through Congress the laws he favored. Taft seems to have done so relatively little. He won adoption of certain tariff clauses in 1909 by other methods. But he did discriminate against the insurgent bloc in Congress. In January, 1910, rumors were current that the insurgents who sought, again, the defeat of Speaker Cannon would be denied their due of federal patronage. Representative George W. Norris of Nebraska asked whether the report was correct. It was not true, he said, that his colleagues had taken a "stand against the present administration." Were they being penalized because of their war on Cannonism? [33] Taft denied, with emphasis, that the recommendations of any congressmen would be ignored on account of his position in the Cannon fight. On the other hand, members who did not support administration measures might find their suggestions ignored.[34] Norris answered at once:

Speaking for myself . . . I am in favor of increasing the power of the Interstate Commerce Commission; of the government regulation and control of industrial and railroad corporations; the physical valuation of railroads; the publication of campaign expenses; the enactment of a reasonable postal savings bank law; the reasonable and fair conservation of natural resources; the regulation of injunctions as outlined in the Republican platform; the reform of federal court procedure as advocated by you, and a permanent nonpartisan tariff commission. As a matter of fact, it will be found that the speaker and his followers are at heart opposed to practically all of these reforms. And it is common knowledge . . . that the committees of the House have been by the speaker so constituted as to prevent the enactment of many, if not all, of these measures. . . .

I have noted carefully what you said in your letter in regard to the custom . . . to honor the recommendations of Republican congressmen for local appointments, and have likewise noted that . . . you state . . . that with respect to legislation which you have recommended requests for appointments will be held up from those congressmen who are not willing to follow your recommendations. . . . I desire most respectfully to call your attention to the fact that . . . there is grave danger that the charge might be made that you are guilty of using the executive power of the government to influ-

[33] Norris to Taft, Jan. 6, 1910. [34] Taft to Norris, Jan. 7, 1910.

ence and control the members of the legislative branch in the exercise of their constitutional functions.[35]

The President's answer was a degree specious. Mr. Norris's apprehension that he would "influence legislation by withholding patronage" was unfounded. However:

If I conclude to withhold the patronage from any person . . . it will not be for the purpose of compelling him to vote for the legislation . . . but it will be for the purpose of preventing his use of the patronage in the district which he represents to create opposition to the Republican administration and its policies, with the probable result of sending a Democrat back to Congress. . . . I have the most reliable information that in certain districts . . . the patronage which is to be dispensed by my hand is being tendered to fortify opponents of the administration and opponents of the declared policies of the Republican party.[36]

This was similar to President Roosevelt's denial, in February, 1908, that he was using his appointive power to obtain support for Taft's presidential candidacy. "I appointed no man *for the purpose* of creating Taft sentiment," he said, "but I have appointed men *in recognition* of the Taft sentiment already in existence." [37] Before 1910 was well under way, President Taft had abandoned even the pretense that he did not discriminate against the insurgents. He selected a postmaster for an Arkansas village because his sponsor "did not belong to the yellow dog class of which we seem to have quite a number in the House at present." [38] A few weeks later he ordered the postmaster general to investigate, with a view to removal, a Wisconsin postmaster who had been guilty of a "vicious partisan attack against the administration." [39]

The President neglected to make one appointment at about this time, however, which would have constituted a footnote, at least, in certain biographies of the future. His secretary, in October, 1910, received a communication from President David Starr Jordan of Stanford University:

[35] Norris to Taft, Jan. 10, 1910. [36] Taft to Norris, Jan. 11, 1910. [37] Pringle, H. F., *Theodore Roosevelt, a Biography,* p. 497. [38] Taft to Hitchcock, Jan. 18, 1910. [39] *Idem,* Feb. 26, 1910.

I would like to call to your notice a young man, available for executive service, and who possesses the greatest talent for work in that line.

Herbert Clark Hoover, now resident at "The Red House," Hornton Street, W., London, is a graduate in mining at Stanford University in 1895. He has risen to the front of his profession, having no superior in executive work, and having become a millionaire is now retiring at the age of 37 to return to America— probably to New York— with a view to entering public life.

He is a very presentable man, of quiet, frank manner, but carrying conviction whenever he speaks. He has lately declined the deanship of the Columbia School of Mines, which fact testifies to his professional standing. In executive matters, especially those involving a knowledge of finance, he shows rare ability. In short, should he enter public life in any capacity, he is a man who will make himself felt.

Secretary Norton acknowledged the letter of recommendation. He would "be glad to bear his name in mind in the event of a vacancy occurring where a man of Mr. Hoover's qualifications could be placed." But the President, apparently, was not shown Dr. Jordan's communication.[40] Mr. Hoover's entry into public life was delayed.

—4—

Another item of the final two years for which Taft never received credit was his part in the ousting of United States Senator Lorimer. Roosevelt would charge, during the approaching campaign, that Taft had befriended the Illinois senator. But it was an untrue charge. Roosevelt knew that it was untrue.

The unseating of Lorimer was a journalistic victory won by the Chicago *Tribune*. He had been elected by the Illinois legislature in May, 1909. Suspicion of fraud did not arise until the spring of 1910 and the President regarded him merely as one of the Republican members whose support for legislation was essential to his program. Lorimer was not among the senators upon whom Taft leaned heavily. He appears to have sent his photograph to the President in November, 1909, however.

[40] Jordan to Norton, Oct. 7, 1910; Norton to Jordan, Oct. 14, 1910.

"I doubt if Brother Lorimer ever smiles so that you can tell what his feelings are," Taft commented, when he saw it. "His face would be useful in the good old American game!" [41]

Some weeks later, Taft invited Lorimer to confer at the White House. He was anxious, he said, "to work in co-operation with both the senators from your state and not to do anything which is not the result of full and free consultation with both." [42] After the Chicago *Tribune* began publication of its evidence that bribery and corruption had attended the election of Lorimer, the President denied that he had "lent the weight of the administration" to his candidacy. He had never met Lorimer until after he came to Washington. At the most— during the balloting in the Illinois legislature— he had expressed a hope that a Republican would be named. [43]

In September, 1910, a Rooseveltian gesture called national attention to the Lorimer case. The ex-President was campaigning, ostensibly on behalf of the G.O.P. but also on behalf of T. R., and was tendered a banquet by the Hamilton Club of Chicago on the night of September 8. A committee from the club boarded his train as it drew near to Chicago and Roosevelt learned that Lorimer was to be a guest at the dinner.

"You may do as you wish," he said, "but I shall not attend if Senator Lorimer is there."

So the dinner committee had no course except to telegraph Lorimer that Roosevelt "positively declines to sit at the same table with you. Our invitation to you for this evening is therefore withdrawn." It was all done, of course, with appropriate publicity. The elated editors of the Chicago *Tribune,* thus fortified in their crusade against Lorimer, published a cartoon of a banquet table with a conspicuously vacant seat. "One Seat Lorimer Couldn't Buy" was the caption. [44]

Lorimer was not yet on trial by his peers of the Senate. The investigating committee convened at Chicago on September 20, 1910. But four members of the Illinois legislature had already confessed regarding the irregularities of his election. Criminal charges had

[41] Taft to Medill McCormick, Nov. 26, 1910. [42] Taft to Lorimer, Dec. 21, 1909. [43] Taft to O. Gresham, Sept. 8, Oct. 11, 1910. [44] New York *Tribune,* Sept. 9, 1910; Davis, O. K., *Released for Publication,* p. 222.

been brought against another participant in the plot.[45] At the White House, Taft read the accounts of the Roosevelt gesture and observed the emphatic public endorsement it had received. He complained to Archie Butt that it was unjust in Roosevelt to condemn Lorimer until he had been tried and convicted.

"And now," the President continued, "he goes to Cincinnati and meets at his own son-in-law's home Boss Cox, who, if no worse than Lorimer, is certainly no better. It is just one of those inconsistencies which you wish Roosevelt would not commit." [46]

Taft's judicial attitude toward Lorimer had vanished by the end of 1910. He was disgusted that the Senate investigating committee had voted to exonerate its colleague.

"There is, in my judgment, ample evidence to require the vacating of his seat," he told Horace Taft, "but he commands the support of the packers of Chicago, of the lumbering interests of the whole country, the oleomargarine people and the brewing interests. So Bailey [Senator J. W. Bailey of Texas] and all the Democrats except one on the committee have rallied to his support. When I think of their position in respect to Lorimer and contrast it in respect to Ballinger, the more I think of dogs. Of course this is peculiarly a Senate question and I have to be careful not to be public in my efforts, but I am doing everything I can to rouse some regulars to the attack. It is neither right nor politic that the insurgents should be left alone to uphold the cause of decency in this case." [47]

The President now worked actively and intelligently against Lorimer. Because it was "peculiarly a Senate question," he labored behind the scenes. A report reached him in January that Roosevelt, in his capacity as associate editor of the *Outlook,* was going to write an article attacking the Illinois senator. He advised Roosevelt not to do this:

I have been doing everything that I could legitimately to have the closest examination made into the . . . case. I have read as much of the evidence as I could get at and *am convinced that there was a mess and mass of corruption upon which his election was*

[45] New York *Tribune,* Sept. 11, 1910. [46] Butt, Archie, *Taft and Roosevelt,* Vol. II, p. 509. [47] Taft to Horace D. Taft, Dec. 25, 1910.

founded that ought to be stamped with the disapproval of the Senate. But I want the movement to oust him to succeed. I have urged different senators to read the record carefully, and after a talk with Root, Burton . . . and some others, I believe we are going to line up a good many of the regular Republicans on the side of what I consider decency and honesty in politics.

Caution was vital, however. Word had leaked out, Taft said, "that I have been taking some interest in the matter and it has not helped the situation . . . because of the strong feeling of clubdom in the Senate and that resentment against outside interference which nobody who is not intimately acquainted with the situation can understand the weight of." The President continued:

I saw Borah this morning. I have consulted a good deal with him on the subject, and he and I agree that it would be unwise for you or for me to come out now against Lorimer . . . that it would enable those who are determined to keep him in . . . to use an argument against outside interference that would hold a number of Democrats and would deprive us of the strength we should get by a quiet presentation of the full facts on the floor of the Senate, from the Senate itself. Root is going to make a speech. So is Burton, and I believe that Lodge will do the same thing. Now, nothing would have stronger weight than speeches from them. . . . I suggest, therefore, that if you have an article on this subject, you hold it until after the issues are more plainly made . . . on the floor of the body in which the contest is to be won. I want to win. So do you. That is my excuse for writing you.[48]

A few days later, the President reported to Roosevelt that Lodge was weakening in his intention of speaking against Lorimer. He hoped that his predecessor in the White House would "drop a line to Lodge to stiffen him." [49] Even Root, Taft soon learned, was momentarily inclined to back down. Vice-president Sherman, it appeared, had been using his wiles on the New York senator.

"I am always disappointed when Root leans to the wrong side," the President confided to Archie Butt. "Root is a lawyer, if you know what I mean by that. I can always tell when Sherman has had hold of him."

[48] Taft to Roosevelt, Jan. 6, 1911. (Italics mine.) [49] *Ibid.*, Jan. 10, 1911.

Another complication was the possibility that the fight on Lorimer might cost Taft the Irish vote. Father Francis C. Kelly of Chicago called at the White House on January 27, 1911, and warned him that such would be the result. Taft told Captain Butt about the warning.

"I think I made myself pretty plain to Father Kelly," he said. "I was very angry, but I controlled myself and said in my softest voice that if the entire Catholic Church stood before me I should not be moved in my attitude toward Lorimer." [50]

"I have your letter . . ." wrote the President to Father Kelly after the visit. "I must confess to you that I do not like its tone. There is a studied threat in its terms that I resent. I don't hesitate to say to you, as I said to you verbally when you were here, that the question of what I have done has been one of duty and such injury as you intimate I will suffer could not move me for a minute to change my position." [51]

To Taft's relief and pleasure, Senator Root spoke against Lorimer; it was one of the major speeches of his career and the President was fulsome in his praise.

"It was . . . one of the greatest things you have done, and I couldn't say more," he wrote. ". . . I know the cost and the reluctance with which one goes into a discussion like this, when taking the right position makes enemies and creates uncomfortable relations." [52]

It was July, 1912, however, before the Senate finally became convinced that Lorimer's election had been tainted by corruption. He was unseated on July 13 by 55 votes to 28. The President's satisfaction was clouded by the fact that the Chicago *Tribune,* so hostile to his own drive for re-election, would receive much of the credit.

"It will be a good thing to get Lorimer out of the Senate," Taft wrote. "He is a man of some taking qualities, but he is utterly despised in Illinois, *and while I think he has not been fairly treated,* his influence has never been particularly good. The Chicago *Tribune,* which is bitterly opposed to him, is an agency that is as vicious as any I know, and the only bad phase of the Lorimer ousting is that it is a victory for the *Tribune."* [53]

[50] Butt, Archie, *op. cit.,* Vol. II, pp. 584-585. [51] Taft to F. C. Kelly, Jan. 30, 1911. [52] Taft to Root, Feb. 4, 1911. [53] Taft to Helen H. Taft, July 13, 1912. (Italics mine.)

Precisely what Taft meant by his suggestion that Lorimer had been unfairly treated is nowhere explained. It was a reversal of his earlier belief. The only logical interpretation is that he believed the Chicago *Tribune,* so grossly unfair in the presidential campaign then in progress, could not possibly be just on any subject.

—5—

Through all the four years labor was a troublesome issue. The majority of the nation's organized workers were opposed to the President. To a degree, he deserved their hostility. It is not that he was consciously unfair. Taft's difficulty was that he had as yet— although he later learned a good deal— small knowledge of the problems of the factory worker, the miner or the railroad employee. He appears actually to have believed that the poor man enjoyed equality with the wealthy man before the law. His viewpoint was strictly legalistic. He rarely remembered that the poor man was powerless to engage competent counsel, that his chance of honest treatment was remote in many a court of the land.

"The laboring man and the trade-unionist, if I understand him, ask only equality before the law," was a sentiment Taft often repeated. "Class legislation and unequal privilege, though expressly in his favor, will in the end work no benefit to him or to society." [54]

The answer of the laboring man, of course, was that entrenched wealth had always enjoyed unequal privileges. His leaders attacked Taft and said that he was labor's foe. The President, in turn, was resentful and often bitter. He had changed little, if at all, since the days when he had been on the Superior Court of Ohio and on the Federal Circuit Court. He believed that labor had the right to strike (peacefully, obviously) and this right could not be abridged. But the boycott was illegal. The injunction in labor disputes, while its application was open to abuse and should be limited, was vitally necessary if the courts were to function.

Taft emphatically denied any prejudice. His denials were sincere. While his attitude toward labor had not changed materially since his years on the bench, he no longer was alarmed, as he had

[54] Taft to W. S. Carter, June 23, 1910.

620 THE LIFE AND TIMES OF WILLIAM HOWARD TAFT

been during the Pullman strike in 1894, over the possibility that civil war might result from its struggle for freedom.

". . . the labor people opposed me," he wrote in December, 1909, regarding the 1908 campaign, "and I opposed them, so that my relations with them are well understood and I feel quite free from embarrassment because of the fact that they have opposed me as bitterly as they could and have not succeeded. It does not make me *any more prejudiced against them.*" [55]

"I am very glad that you are attending to Brother Gompers's cuticle," he told a supporter who had been making derogatory speeches about the head of the American Federation of Labor.[56]

Yet Taft, according to his lights, strove to make life better and more full for the American workingman. The injunction plank he had drafted for the 1908 platform would have been effective; the compromise ultimately adopted had been dictated by such organizations as the National Association of Manufacturers and Taft bowed to their dictates only after Roosevelt had endorsed the plank. In his acceptance speech on July 28, 1908, in fact, Taft even admitted the necessity for amendment of the antitrust law so that it would not affect workers engaged in "a peaceable and lawful strike to secure better wages." He did not believe that the Supreme Court would hold such a strike in violation of the act. If it did, "general legislation amending the law is necessary." [57] But the President lost patience when labor pressed, instead, for a legalization of boycotts.

". . . the defiant attitude of labor organizations with respect to boycotts and the action of the courts is such," he admitted, "that they are not entitled to what I would otherwise be willing to grant them; so to phrase the antitrust law as not to include them." [58]

The President did, however, ask Congress to amend the injunction statute. He requested the second session of the Sixty-first Congress to remember the pledge of the 1908 platform.[59] No action had been taken by December, 1910, when Taft renewed his "urgent recommendation." The change was of "especial importance . . .

because . . . it will . . . take away all semblance of support for the extremely radical legislation that they [the labor leaders] propose, which will be most pernicious if adopted, will sap the foundations of judicial power, and legalize that cruel social instrument, the secondary boycott." [60]

Congress continued however, to be deaf to the President's pleas. The voice of the National Association of Manufacturers was still loud in its marble halls. Campaigning in 1912, Taft was unable to point to this reform as an administration accomplishment. He could cite other laws, though, of benefit to the workingman. The President paused at Fostoria, Ohio, in May, 1912, to answer the Roosevelt indictment that he had been faithless to his trust. The unhappy Chief Executive pleaded not guilty. He told of what he had done for labor:

We passed a mining bureau bill to discover the nature of those dreadful explosions and loss of life in mines. We passed safety appliance bills to reduce the loss of life and limbs to railroad employees. We passed an employers liability act to make easier recovery of damages by injured employees. We have just passed through the Senate a workman's compensation act . . . requiring the railroads to insure their employees against the accidents of a dangerous employment. We passed the children's bureau bill calculated to prevent children from being employed too early in factories. We passed the white phosphorus match bill to stamp out the making of white phosphorus matches which results in dreadful diseases to those engaged in their manufacture.[61]

All this was true although the measures were, of course, palliatives. They did not affect the fundamental issue in the war between capital and labor. They were the measures of a kindly man, a humane man, who was quite unable to perceive that a bitter war was raging. Thus the President was entirely willing, in the fall of 1909, for Labor Commissioner Charles P. Neill to investigate the barbaric working conditions in the steel industry. But he specified that there was to be no sensationalism as a result.

"I do not wish it advertised," he ordered. "I do not think that is the best way to carry on an investigation. After you have the

[60] *Ibid.,* Vol. XXIII, p. 116. [61] *Ibid.,* Vol. XXIX, p. 166.

matter investigated . . . what you have done can be given in the report, but I am not in favor of exploiting the business in advance. . . . We can stand the feeling of bitterness in the labor papers if we are doing what we ought to do . . . I am not in favor of a grandstand performance in advance." [62]

In short there were to be no Rooseveltian onslaughts such as the ones against filthy packing houses. Perhaps Taft regretted, as time went on and his power waned, that he had been thus restrained. He urged support of two Senate bills, in January, 1910, to promote safety on the railroads.

"They ought to pass," he wrote, "and it will help us politically to have them pass." [63]

At first, too, the President had been dubious about the wisdom of a federal bureau to deal with the problems of children in industry. He protested that interest "in the education of children and their development is one thing, but recourse to the national government for a bureau of this sort is another thing." He deprecated the "disposition to unload everything on the federal government that the states ought to look after." The tendency in this direction was increasing alarmingly.[64]

The President would be impotent, though, against one powerful influence which demanded a Children's Bureau. This was the personality of white-haired Aunt Delia, his mother's sister. She had often been at the White House, where she busily read newspapers and government documents and rocked in her chair as cheerfully as she had always rocked back in Millbury, Massachusetts. The clarity of Delia Torrey's mind was undimmed by all the years. She told her distinguished nephew that it was a good bill. So he affixed his signature to the official, engrossed copy.[65]

The records do not disclose, though, whether Aunt Delia persuaded the President to make an appointment which was decidedly novel, an even-radical departure. He announced on April 15, 1912, that he had appointed Julia Lathrop chief of the bureau at a salary of $5,000. She was the first woman in the history of the government, the President's statement said, to become a bureau

[62] Taft to C. P. Neill, Sept. 13, 1909. [63] Taft to S. B. Elkins, Jan. 12, 1910. [64] Taft to M. P. E. Groszman, April 12, 1910. [65] Taft to Delia Torrey, April 12, 1912.

chief. This important step in the slow march of feminism had been decided upon only after careful inquiry into its legality. Attorney General Wickersham assured the President that he was violating no statute.

"The word *male*," he pointed out, "does not occur anywhere in this bill." [66]

The President offended organized labor again, however, when he vetoed a bill which required the ability to read some language or dialect for admission to the United States. Congress approved the literacy test in the closing weeks of the Taft administration. It had been assumed that the President would approve it. But Secretary of Commerce and Labor Nagel advised against it. He was, himself, the son of an immigrant. He pointed out that such a provision, had it been in existence for the past ten or twenty years, would have barred many men who had risen to importance in their adopted country and had served their country well. The subject was discussed at a Cabinet meeting in February, 1913. At the President's request, Nagel prepared a memorandum in opposition. On February 14, Taft sent his veto message to the Senate. The bill was excellent in many respects, he said; the literacy test had been endorsed by Congress and recommended by an able investigating commission. None the less, literacy was not a sound test for admission. Regretfully, he returned the bill without his approval.[67]

—6—

Sometimes the President's nerves were close to the breaking point during his unhappy final years. Sometimes it seemed as though fate worked against him. In August, 1911, word reached the White House that Senator W. P. Frye of Maine was dead.

"The Lord seems to be against the Republican party," Taft wrote, "for that means another Democrat, and at once." [68]

A new touch of acidity crept into some of his letters. "I am glad to find one thing upon which you and I have common thoughts," he told Henry Lee Higginson when the banker pro-

[66] Wickersham to Taft, April 15, 1912. [67] Nagel to author, Feb. 18, 1935; Taft to Senate, Feb. 14, 1913. [68] Taft to Helen H. Taft, Aug. 9, 1911.

tested against rumors that the telegraph companies might be taken over by the government; the President said he had no intention of permitting this socialistic move.[69]

In June, 1912, a naval officer committed some offense. No useful purpose is served by mentioning his name. Regarding him, the President wrote to the secretary of the navy:

He is a drunken galoot. He is a very courageous fighting officer but . . . he has been a disgrace to the navy for years and years. . . . Now . . . satisfy my conscience which requires that —— shall sizzle at the end of Florida for his past sins.[70]

Yet it was still possible for Taft to be warm and gracious. Dr. S. Weir Mitchell of Philadelphia had called at the White House in the spring of that year and had for some reason been denied an audience. Taft wrote in haste that the "stupidity of an usher as to persons cannot be insured against."

I am constantly . . . protesting against the distances between the vestibule or outer office of the White House and the rooms where we live. Try again when you come to Washington and drop me a note that you'll be here so that I can shoot down in cold blood those who would keep you out.[71]

He told Mrs. Taft, in July, that he had attended the ceremony at which the daughter of Brigadier General E. A. Garlington had been married to a young army lieutenant. The bride, he said, was "very pretty." He wondered whether her officer-husband had any money. He supposed "they will get into a nest like birds and live on what they have. That is what army girls are used to, and I like to see army matches on that account." [72]

An inner conviction that defeat was probable in 1912 did not cause Taft to abandon, though, his fight for increased postal rates for newspapers and magazines. He continued to insist that the higher rates were not excessive, that the post office would still lose money in handling second-class mail.[73] His anger against the pub-

[69] Taft to H. L. Higginson, Jan. 18, 1912. [70] Taft to Meyer, June 11, 1912. [71] Taft to S. W. Mitchell, April 21, 1912. [72] Taft to Helen H. Taft, July 24, 1912. [73] Taft to J. A. Sleicher, Feb. 9, 1911.

lishers as they continued to fight was great. Never "in all my knowledge of lobbies and of organized efforts to influence legislation" had he seen "such bold, defiant attempts by payment of the heaviest advertising bills to arouse the press of the country against the proposed legislation," he declared in February, 1911. He continued:

The publishers profess to be the agents of heaven in establishing virtue, and therefore that they ought to receive some subsidy from the government. I can ask no stronger refutation to this claim . . . than the utterly unscrupulous methods pursued by them in seeking to influence Congress on this subject.[74]

The G.O.P. leaders became alarmed as it seemed probable that the fight would drag on into 1912. In response to their pleas, although he did not agree to the justice of further inquiry, the President appointed President Lowell of Harvard, Lawrence Maxwell and Associate Supreme Court Justice Hughes to constitute a commission of investigation.[75] Its findings upheld the President in large measure and the rates were increased. But Taft's wrath against "these hogs of magazine publishers, of whom Albert Shaw [editor of the *Review of Reviews*] is the leading one" did not diminish while he was still in the White House.[76]

After the campaign of 1912, however, he concluded that the fight had been among his fatal errors. "It was not necessary for me to run amuck among the magazines" he wrote.[77]

[74] Taft to F. P. Flint, Feb. 15, 1911. [75] Taft to Penrose, March 2, 1911; to A. L. Lowell, March 20, 1911. [76] Taft to Murray Crane, Aug. 3, 1912. [77] Taft to Bannard, Nov. 10, 1912.

CHAPTER XXXIII

ON THE OTHER HAND

O N THE other hand, there was Charles W. Morse. On the other hand, too, President Taft surrendered to the rapacity of the Grand Army veterans and permitted the payment of higher pensions. A third count on the debit side was his decision to scrap the Hay-Pauncefote treaty and exempt American coastwise vessels from Panama Canal tolls.

"There is no subject upon which I am more obdurate," the President wrote sternly in January, 1910, "than upon the necessity for wealthy criminals serving their sentence, and it must be a case of rare exception in which the executive clemency will be exercised under such conditions." [1]

Taft held forth on this theme quite frequently. When he had been in the White House for eighteen months he observed that he had "sought in every way to avoid interfering with the administration of justice by yielding to maudlin sentimentality." It was "discouraging" to learn that prominent people were all too willing to sign petitions for clemency. [2]

"You needn't be afraid," he promised Brother Horace, "that pardons will be granted too readily in this administration." [3]

The President reckoned, however, without knowing that a convict named Morse was, apparently, a consummate actor. He did not take into consideration the cunning of Harry M. Daugherty. He did not fully realize how easily misled the medical profession could be. In a lecture at Yale in 1914 the President looked back ruefully on this incident of the presidential years; he was describing the various powers of the President:

Another . . . is the power of pardons and reprieves. This is not to be determined by rules of law or, indeed, by absolute rules of

[1] Taft to T. E. Watson, Jan. 20, 1910. [2] Taft to Daniel Gibbons, Oct. 11, 1910. [3] Taft to Horace D. Taft, March 17, 1910.

any kind and must, therefore, be wielded skillfully lest it destroy the supremacy of law. *Sometimes one is deceived.* I was. Two men were brought before me, both of whom were represented as dying. When a convict is near his end, it has been the custom to send him home to die. So, after having all the surgeons in the War Department examine them to see that the statements made to me about them were correct, I exercised the pardoning power in their favor. Well, one of them kept his contract and died, but the other seems to be one of the healthiest men in the community today.[4]

The other was destined, indeed, to remain so healthy that he would survive Taft, himself, by almost three years. Charles W. Morse deserves a prominent place in the crowded gallery of American rogues. He was an unattractive individual, chunky in build and distinguished in appearance only because of his eyes, which were shrewd and masterful. He was in his early fifties when, at last, the law which he had long taken lightly dispatched him to the penitentiary. But he came of sound enough stock. He was born at Bath, Maine, and his father was prosperous. After the son was graduated from Bowdoin College in 1877 he organized a shipping company with his father.

Morse had talent in business. The opportunities in New England did not satisfy him and he went to New York in 1897. Tammany had just returned to power. Morse was quick to appreciate the profits which lay in the alliance between corrupt politics and corrupt business. He formed the Consolidated Ice Company and merged it, before long, with the American Ice Company at a generously watered capitalization of $60,000,000. On May 1, 1900, his company sharply increased the price of ice. This was a mistake; the resulting public outcry brought about an investigation which disclosed that Morse had obtained important docking privileges from Tammany Hall. It also revealed that Mayor Robert Van Wyck and Richard Croker, the boss of Tammany Hall, held American Ice Company stock. So Morse retired from the ice business, with estimated profits of $12,000,000.

He changed his title of "Ice King" for that of "Admiral of the Atlantic Coast"; that is, he went into shipping. Within six years he

[4] Taft, W. H., *Ethics in Service*, p. 60. (Italics mine.)

had a virtual monopoly of coastwise shipping from Bangor to Galveston. This was high finance. Morse also entered the banking field, in collaboration with F. Augustus Heinze who became president of the Mercantile National Bank. The two birds of prey got their talons on almost a dozen other New York banks. Their next step was to organize a copper pool which, like all such pools, was amazingly profitable until it broke and constituted a leading cause of the 1907 panic which so greatly alarmed President Roosevelt. J. P. Morgan & Company, with the consent of the President and Secretary of the Treasury George B. Cortelyou, took charge of the financial crisis. It was arranged that $25,000,000 in government funds would be deposited in the distressed banks. These were used, Mr. Cortelyou later testified, for the "relief of the community generally." He admitted he did not know how much had gone to equally distressed stock exchange houses.[5]

At the request of more conservative financiers, Morse and Heinze retired from banking during the panic. When it was over, Morse was, to an extent, the scapegoat. United States Attorney Stimson presented evidence against him to the Grand Jury. He was indicted for misappropriating funds of the Bank of North America, a Heinze-Morse institution. He was convicted and sentenced, on November 15, 1908, to fifteen years in federal prison. On January 2, 1910, he was taken to Atlanta.

Morse considered himself grievously wronged. The sentence was the "most brutal . . . ever pronounced against a citizen in a civilized country," he said. "There is no one in Wall Street," he added with possible truth, "who is not doing daily as I have done." [6] The others, he neglected to mention, had thus far evaded detection. But it is doubtful that had they, too, gone to jail, they would have been remotely as successful as Morse in cutting short the brutal sentence of the court.

—2—

Morse had been languishing in the federal penitentiary for a scant twelve months when the drive for his freedom began. Senator

[5] Pringle, H. F., *Theodore Roosevelt, a Biography*, pp. 437-440. [6] New York *Times*, Jan. 3, 1910.

Hale of Maine called at the White House to present an appeal from Mrs. Morse. Taft directed Attorney General Wickersham to see Hale and to learn the facts.[7] No action was taken by the President, however. He was to make it quite clear that he regarded the fifteen-year sentence fair.

The President knew Morse, if at all, very slightly. As secretary of war, in January, 1907, he had given him a letter of introduction to Chief Engineer Stevens of the Isthmian Canal Commission. Morse was planning to visit Panama in connection with an extension of his steamship lines and the secretary of war merely commended "Mr. Morse and his associates to your courteous attention."[8] By 1911, though, Morse's name was to be all too familiar. James M. Beck, the noted authority on conservative constitutional law, was among the many who recommended a pardon. Augustin Van Wyck, a brother of the Tammany Hall mayor who had profited from Morse ice stock, was another.[9] But the President was deaf to their pleas. In May, 1911, he denied a pardon, but said that the application could be renewed after January 1, 1913.[10]

Meanwhile forces of which Taft was innocently unaware were at work. Their manipulator was Daugherty of Ohio. He told Secretary Hilles on July 28, 1911— the date is important— that he wished to interview Morse regarding certain litigation he had undertaken on behalf of the prisoner. Wickersham appeared unwilling to allow this. Could the President's secretary, Daugherty asked, use his influence? The telegram said nothing at all about releasing Morse.[11] It later appeared that Daugherty, who was associated with T. B. Felder of Atlanta in the supposed litigation, desired to interview the convict without a guard being present. But Wickersham was adamant. This was against the rules. He saw no reason why permission should be granted.[12]

In effect, if not actually, Daugherty and Felder ignored the Department of Justice ruling. The first hint that the Ohio politician had any interest in Morse's release reached Washington at the end of August, 1911. He painted a harrowing picture of the prisoner's condition in a letter to Hilles. Morse, he said, would not live

[7] Taft to Wickersham, Dec. 13, 1910. [8] Taft to Stevens, Jan. 5, 1907. [9] J. M. Beck to Taft, March 14, 1911; A. Van Wyck to Taft, Feb. 6, 1911. [10] White House memorandum, May 24, 1911. [11] Daugherty to Hilles, July 28, 1911. [12] Department of Justice memorandum, July 29, 1911.

eighteen months in prison. His life was wasting away with increasing rapidity, day by day. Specifically, he suffered from Bright's disease. His right side was paralyzed and was "shriveling" at a fast rate. Daugherty repeated that it had not been his original intention to take up the "criminal side of Morse's case." His interest had been merely the settlement of important civil matters in which "high-class people" were involved and would lose fortunes unless action was prompt. But now, having been informed of Morse's illness, he wished to present the facts to the President.

"Please congratulate the President upon his speech and position and upon the general approval of the public," was an oily postscript to the letter.[13]

Daugherty continued to be very active on the criminal side of the situation. He saw Mr. Stimson, now secretary of war, and the other attorneys who had prosecuted Morse.[14] He presented a report by Dr. A. L. Fowler of Atlanta, "one of the most eminent physicians in this part of the country," testifying to Morse's acute illness.[15]

A crisis was approaching by the close of 1911. Among all the absurdities of the American system there have been few more profound than this case in which a president was forced to pass on the probable life span of a convicted felon. By now, Wickersham had fallen a victim to the plot. On November 22 he sent to Taft a report from the penitentiary physician who found, after consultation with Dr. Fowler, that Morse's pulse was abnormally high, that

... his lower eyelids are chronically swollen ... his urine is markedly hematuric bloody, and the quantity for the last twenty-four hours amounts to only twelve ounces and which normally should be fifty ounces; microscopic examination of his urine discloses red blood cells, granular casts and blood casts; diagnosis that of Bright's disease; patient is surely and rapidly losing ground and there can be no doubt but that his time is now drawing to a close and that liberation only will prolong his life and even that not for a long period.

"I think what these gentlemen say can be accepted as reliable," the attorney general pointed out.[16]

[13] Daugherty to Hilles, Aug. 29, 1911. [14] *Idem*, Oct. 27, 1911. [15] *Idem*, Aug. 29, 1911. [16] Wickersham to Taft, Nov. 22, 1911.

On the same day, Daugherty telegraphed Hilles that Morse might not live an additional twenty-four hours.[17] A president of the United States, it might be assumed, is too busy or too important an official to deal with the kidney excretions of even the most influential convict. But Taft had to take them under advisement. He ordered Morse removed to the post hospital at Fort McPherson, Georgia, for observation. A White House memorandum pointed out that he could be cared for as well there as anywhere. He could even engage private physicians, but he would, technically, remain in custody.[18] This, however, was by no means enough for Daugherty and his associate, Felder. This was not what they had contracted with Morse to accomplish. The details were not made public until a decade had passed.

Appeals to the White House continued during November and December, 1911. C. W. Barron of the *Wall Street Journal* told Taft he had talked with Stimson on the case, that Stimson agreed that the sentence had been too severe. Barron was confident that Morse had never been touched by moral turpitude. He hoped that the President would grant an interview at which further facts on behalf of leniency could be laid before him.[19] Daugherty kept appealing to Secretary Hilles. He hoped, he said, that the President did not suppose he had been employed on Morse's behalf because of their friendship. It had come through Felder.

"I do not now want to influence the President in the least," he insisted. "I want him to know that I am not in the case because I am known to be an acquaintance and friend of his. . . . I am satisfied that the President's purpose in the Morse matter is to do the humane thing. . . . He will never be well; he is liable to die any day, and yet he may live a short time if he were released. . . . I hope the President will pardon him soon in order that he may have a little while before he dies to work for others as well as himself." [20]

Such a letter could hardly fail to move a warmhearted and truly humane president. Taft instructed examination of Morse by army surgeons.[21] "Let me know as soon as it comes," he scrawled on the message which told him that their report would soon be

[17] Daugherty to Hilles, Nov. 22, 1911. [18] White House memorandum, Nov. 24, 1911. [19] C. W. Barron to Taft, Nov. 25, 1911. [20] Daugherty to Hilles, Dec. 8, 1911. [21] Leonard Wood to Wickersham, Dec. 21, 1911.

made.[22] This was a first examination. It resulted in a prediction that further imprisonment would probably shorten Morse's life and on this, alone, the President was not willing to act. He told the attorney general:

I do not find his condition such as to require the exercise of executive clemency. . . . The considerations that ought to govern the Executive in ordering the release of a prisoner . . . who is suffering from illness likely to result in death are difficult to state. Generally, the Executive is moved to avoid for any prisoner a death in custody in order that the last hours of his life may . . . have some pleasure in them. But there is no rule that requires the Executive to release one because he has an incurable disease, which, at some indefinite time, is likely to result in death, or which may be affected prejudicially by continued imprisonment . . . If it were to be certified to me that the prisoner here would certainly die in two weeks, I would release him.

So Morse, the President instructed, was to be detained at the army hospital and his condition reported to the White House from month to month.[23] Taft's position would have been stronger, in the end, had he held to this demand for certification that Morse could not live more than two weeks. The evidence is not clear— no mention of it is in his letters— but there are indications that he did not depend entirely on the opinion of the army medical men in his final decision to set Morse free. It is established, for instance, that John McLean, owner of the Cincinnati *Enquirer* and the Washington *Post,* used his friendship as the basis of an appeal to the President.[24] But there is, of course, no hint whatever of corruption on Taft's part.

The army reports were alarming enough. A special board examined the prisoner at Fort McPherson late in December and stated that his death could be expected unless he was pardoned; it mentioned no time limit, however, and denied any "immediate danger." [25] The most lurid predictions came from Major David Baker, the post surgeon at the fort. On January 2, 1912, he said that "further imprisonment will be injurious if not speedily fatal." Four

[22] J. A. Fowler to Taft, Dec. 21, 1911. [23] Taft to Wickersham, Dec. 27, 1911. [24] Sullivan, Mark, *Our Times,* Vol. VI, p. 21. [25] G. H. Torney to War Department, Dec. 30, 1911.

days later, Dr. Baker said that Morse's condition was "very grave." On January 11, he reported no improvement.[26]

Maudlin public sentiment was beginning to swing toward Morse. From the president of the Board of Trade at Bath, Maine, came an impertinent appeal for the home-town boy who had made good in New York:

The time seems to be rapidly approaching when death will end the confinement of Charles W. Morse, no other means appearing to be effective. Will you assure his relatives and townsmen that his remains will be delivered to them and not retained by the government upon the happening of that event? We respectfully request a reply . . . in order that the press may have it for publication with this message.[27]

The President did not reply, of course. He hesitated a week after even Wickersham had expressed concern that Morse would die.[28] The pardon was granted on January 18, with a public explanation that Morse's illness was "incurable and progressive." Taft said that Morse had suffered a heart attack three days earlier and that this was an "ominous occurrence."

"In my opinion," he concluded, "the prisoner's duration of life will in all probability be less than one month if kept in confinement, and in the event of his release . . . it is not probable that he will live as long as six months." [29]

That same day came a message of appreciation from the Bath Merchants Association which assured the President that his action had been enthusiastically received in "Morse's home town."[30] The New York *Commercial* also praised the pardon.[31] Before long, however, a disquieting flood of protests began to reach Washington. A typical one was from August Ganzenmüller of Sea Cliff, Long Island, who must otherwise remain unidentified. Mr. Ganzenmüller told Taft he had encouraged the "growth of . . . contempt of the law by your act." He demanded to know whether Morse, if "plain John Smith, unknown, of modest means, without power and in-

---

[26] David Baker to commanding officer, Fort McPherson, Jan. 2, 4, 1912; to warden, Federal Prison, Atlanta, Jan. 11, 1912. [27] N. G. Jackson to Taft, Dec. 28, 1911. [28] Wickersham to Taft, Nov. 12, 1911. [29] White House statement, Jan. 18, 1912. [30] F. E. Burns to Taft, Jan. 18, 1912. [31] New York *Commercial*, Jan. 19, 1912.

fluence" would not "have died, as he should have died, in prison, and as a convict." [32]

If Morse had not employed Harry Daugherty he would probably have remained in Atlanta, although it is doubtful that he would have died there. He went abroad immediately after his release. He returned in the early summer and by fall newspaper headlines told of a new $1,000,000 steamship company which he had formed and of the rugged health he appeared to be enjoying.[33] A year later, having retired from the White House, Taft remarked in a lecture that Morse was apparently "in excellent health and seeking to re-establish himself in the world in which he committed a penitentiary offense."

"This shakes one's faith in expert examinations," said the former President sadly.[34]

—3—

Taft did not yet know all the facts behind Morse's release. Some of them will never be known and the accuracy of others may be questioned. Few of them would have become public at all had it not been that Morse, very foolishly, refused to meet his obligations to Daugherty and Felder. Morse prospered, in his fashion, in the decade after his release. By 1915 he controlled a Hudson River steamship line and was sued for unfair competition. As American entry into the war drew near he entered the ship-construction field and obtained contracts for thirty-six vessels from the United States Shipping Company. In 1922 he was indicted for fraud and acquitted. In 1922, by one of those strange turns of fate, Harry Daugherty was attorney general of the United States and in charge of the prosecution of war frauds.[35]

Daugherty had his enemies and an effective one was Senator T. H. Caraway, a Democrat of Arkansas. Mr. Caraway thought that Daugherty was not a fit person to bring war profiteers to justice. On May 2, 1922, he declared in the Senate that his activities as an attorney had consisted of getting criminals out of jail. In obtain-

[32] August Ganzenmuller to Taft, Feb. 6, 1912. [33] Kansas City *Post*, Sept. 6, 1912. [34] New York *Times*, Nov. 16, 1913. [35] *Dictionary of American Biography*, Vol. XIII, pp. 239-242.

ing a release for Morse, for instance, he was paid $30,000. Senator James Watson of Indiana interrupted Caraway to deny that this was true. How did he know it? Why, it was a slanderous falsehood— from statements made to him by Attorney General Daugherty himself.[36]

Not quite three weeks later, Senator Caraway spoke again. This time he read into the record a contract between Morse and Felder, the Atlanta attorney. This engaged the services of Felder and Daugherty for "civil and criminal matters"; it was dated August 4, 1911, a few days after the time when Daugherty was asking for permission to see Morse without the embarrassing presence of a prison guard. A retainer of $5,000 was paid on execution of the document.

"We are to receive in the event that we secure an unconditional pardon or commutation for you," it continued, "the sum of $25,000."

The attorney general, seen by the correspondents that night, had nothing to say. T. B. Felder, interviewed in New York, could see nothing improper in the agreement.[37] Two days later, Caraway offered additional fascinating details. He read into the record a letter from Felder to Leon O. Bailey, a New York attorney. This was dated August 12, 1917, and it was a request that Bailey attempt to collect the $25,000 which Morse had promised but had not paid. Felder described at length the clever work done by Daugherty and himself. He told Bailey that Daugherty had been brought into the case because he "stood as close to the President as any other lawyer." The supposed intimacy had proved disappointing, however. The President would not release Morse, even for Daugherty, and the pair had carried their bad news to the ex-financier's cell. He then promised $100,000 for a pardon.

"Gentlemen," Morse promised, "I will make you both rich if you get me out of here."

Felder, in his letter to Bailey, then recalled noticing that Morse seemed in bad health. He consulted Dr. Fowler, who had been prison physician when Morse was admitted, and was gratified to learn that his charts disclosed "incipient Bright's disease." Felder said that "with this cue" he redoubled his activities with Daugherty

[36] New York *Times*, May 3, 1922. [37] *Ibid.*, May 21, 1922.

and the final result was the pardon on January 18, 1912. When they attempted to collect their fee, however, Morse told them he was penniless. He sailed for Europe.

Daugherty, said Felder in his account to Bailey, was greatly annoyed. He was annoyed, himself. But they had hesitated to bring suit against Morse because of the danger that the attorney general's office, now ruled by the Democratic party, might revoke the pardon.

"We were informed," he told Bailey, "that the department [Department of Justice] was in the possession of evidence going to show that after physicians were appointed to examine Morse and before they appeared on the scene, that soapsuds or chemicals or something would be taken by him to produce a hemorrhage of the kidneys, and as soon as the examination was over, the patient would recuperate rapidly."

Felder hastened to assure Bailey that neither he nor Daugherty had any knowledge of such deceit upon the medical men. But Senator Caraway, after reading it to his senatorial colleagues, pointed to a clause in the contract with Morse whereby the prisoner agreed to give "full control" of his case to the two lawyers and "accept implicitly" their "counsel and advice." Would such sweeping obedience have been promised, the senator asked, unless evil practices were being planned? He demanded the resignation of Daugherty as attorney general.[38]

Daugherty did not resign. Next day he issued a statement which said nothing about the soapsuds plot, nor did it deny the main counts in Caraway's indictment. He did, however, exhibit letters from Wickersham and Taft dated November 17, 1915. They constitute, perhaps, the most serious reflection on those two gentlemen. But politics was involved. In 1915 Daugherty was a candidate for senator from Ohio. Wickersham said that his conduct in the Morse case had been "perfectly straightforward. . . . I do not recall any special insistence on your part in the matter." Taft said that "in no way did you influence me in respect to the pardon. . . . My recollection is that you told me you were counsel for Morse, but that you had declined to present the matter to me." [39] The endorsements by Taft and Wickersham had been written in response to

[38] New York *Times*, May 23, 1922. [39] *Ibid.*, May 24, 1922.

appeals from Daugherty. "General Wickersham," he told Taft, "knows that I never deceived him about anything." [40]

All in all, it is a shabby story which reflects credit on no one. The weight of evidence indicates that the medical men were stupid rather than misled by a chemical diet on Morse's part. There is this, at least, to be said for the issue of the pardon. The Circuit Court of Appeals had reversed Morse's conviction on all but three of the fifteen counts and this, in pure justice, would have brought a sentence of only five years. No parole system then existed. Taft had no authority to reduce the sentence; Morse could receive freedom or nothing. Mr. Wickersham, looking back on the case in later years, said it was clear that they had trusted the army surgeons too completely. [41]

—4—

The exigencies of politics, not the scheming of a Harry Daugherty, would force the President to eat his first brave words regarding pensions for the G.A.R. He had been in the White House for about a year when it appeared that one of the innumerable bills granting additional millions to the Civil War heroes might pass.

"If I were to act on my present view," Taft said, "I should veto it. I think the time has come when a halt must be called to this indiscriminate pension giving." [42]

This had small effect, though, on the tendency of Congress to win votes by dipping into the national treasury. An occasional member protested against this method of obtaining re-election. In January, 1911, Representative William Hughes earned for himself a unique, if forgotten, place in history.

"I want to say this, here and now, though I realize the effect of my vote upon this question," he declared, "that $50,090,000 a year is too big a price for the country to pay to bring me back to Congress." [43]

To the majority of the forthright Hughes's fellows, however, $50,000,000, more or less, of the taxpayers' money was a wholly

---

[40] Daugherty to Taft, Nov. 17, 1915. [41] Wickersham to author, Jan. 23, 1935. [42] Taft to C. F. Adams, April 27, 1910. [43] *Congressional Record,* Jan. 10, 1911, p. 750.

638 THE LIFE AND TIMES OF WILLIAM HOWARD TAFT

reasonable expenditure for so laudable and essential a purpose. The President noted, in January, 1911, sadly, that there were "some courageous members . . . but they were few and far between." Representatives Payne, Longworth, Dalzell were among them. Senator Crane was also "doing most effective work. . . .

"The House passed the pension bill under the whip of Joe Cannon who found no distinction between insurgents and regulars in the cowardly haste with which they all sought to buy votes out of the burdened treasury of the United States," Taft added. ". . . I don't know whether the bill will pass the Senate or not. Crane thinks he can stop it, but I doubt it. By its present terms, it will cost the country $55,000,000 . . . and will probably run up to $70,000,-000. Crane was anxious to have me agree on a compromise at $16,000,000. . . . But I can't do it. It would only prove a weak palliative. . . . *Somebody has got to step into the breach and I am determined to do it, because, no matter how much it may affect my personal fortunes,* one such protest by an effective veto will give voice to a silent indignation that pervades all the responsible American citizenship except the immediate beneficiaries and their friends and dependents and the pension agents. *We have done all we ought to do for the pensioners.* If the list could be scrutinized and the frauds eliminated, I should be glad to increase amounts for deserving men, but in these wholesale increases, it is the unworthy and undeserving that form the majority of those who enjoy the nation's bounty. *If it is the last act of my life, I'll veto any pension bill, giving a general increase."* [44]

These fine phrases, ultimately to be swallowed by the President, were written in January, 1911. He might have held to this strong position had it not been for the political perplexities— among which Theodore Roosevelt was the worst— of the next eighteen months. He might have spurned the indigestible meal if the "responsible American citizenship," as he had wistfully hoped, had supported him in a stand against the itching palms of the veterans. The responsible Americans were to remain almost entirely silent, though, while their representatives in Washington were to hear, instead, only the clamor which said that no sums could reward sufficiently the incomparable heroism of Bull Run, Antietam and

[44] Taft to Aldrich, Jan. 29, 1911. (Italics mine.)

the march through the Wilderness. In any event, said the clamor, the heroes had the votes. Besides, the President was handicapped by the record of his party and the position on pensions publicly taken by the G.O.P. The Bloody Shirt, so effective when the "bullet-headed generals" roamed the land, was more frayed than ever now and even its crimson color had faded. It was no longer enough for campaign orators merely to claim that the Grand Old Party had saved the Union. Cash, not compliments, was what the veterans wanted.

So, during the 1908 campaign, the party had pledged itself to "generous provision for those who have fought the country's battles and for the widows and orphans of those who have fallen." It urged an increase in widows' pensions as well as a "liberal administration of all pension laws, to the end that the people's gratitude may grow deeper as the memories of heroic sacrifice grow more sacred with the years." [45] This nonsense, it may be assumed, had been approved by Theodore Roosevelt who was watching every detail of the campaign. Taft, himself, went almost as far. In his speech of acceptance at Cincinnati he confessed to humiliation that he was "lacking in one qualification of all Republican presidents since Lincoln, that of having been exposed to danger and death on the field of battle in defense of our country." Roosevelt, he meant, had been comparably heroic in the Spanish War.

"I hope," said the candidate, "that this lack will not make the veterans think I am any less deeply thrilled by the memory of . . . Grant, Hayes, Garfield, Harrison and McKinley, all sons of Ohio, who left records reflecting glory upon their state and nation, or that my sympathies with the valor and courage and patriotism of those who faced death . . . are any less earnest and sincere than they would be had I the right to wear a button of the Grand Army." [46]

In his December, 1910, annual message, he said that the nation's pension policy had "always been of the most liberal character." The debt to the veterans "has not been and should not be computed in a begrudging or parsimonious spirit." This time, however, Taft also warned against generosity to "absurd lengths" and he deprecated larger widows' pensions which might cause ambitious ladies to

[45] *Republican Campaign Textbook,* 1908, p. 466. [46] *Addresses,* Vol. XI, p. 94.

"obtain some legal relation with an old veteran now tottering on the brink of the grave." [47]

The pensions, if not already absurd, had certainly been generous. About $4,000,000,000 had been paid, up to the close of 1911, in pensions and other grants.[48] Like the American Legion of future decades, the Grand Army of the Republic had been founded with lofty ideals, to perpetuate the memories and glories of the war. At first it had no ulterior purposes. But by 1872, with the war hardly over, the G.A.R. was virtually defunct. A more practical group of leaders then assumed command. In 1874 the G.A.R. was demanding increased pensions. A decade later— this device, too would be adopted by the American Legion— it denied free speech to the posts which did not agree with the majority opinion. If certain of them were opposed to larger payments, they must keep silent. The G.A.R.'s first important victory came when President Harrison appointed "Corporal" James Tanner, as he called himself, to a strategically vital office, that of commissioner of pensions. This was in 1889; times had been fairly prosperous and the nation's books showed a surplus.[49]

"I will drive a six-mule team through the treasury," boasted Tanner as he assumed office. "God help the surplus!" [50]

In some ways Corporal Tanner was an admirable figure. He believed sincerely that the veterans were entitled to the largest possible payments. His heart was as large as it was warm. He was open and frank as he did what he could, in his official position, to increase benefits. Tanner was, moreover, a genuine soldier who had fought for his country. He had lost both his legs in battle. He was exceptional, among the majority of those who demanded money, in that his sufferings had been acute.

Few men in any walk of life dared to give a realistic picture of the veterans. Among the few, the most effective was Charles Francis Adams, the older brother of Henry Adams. He knew whereof he spoke. He had served in the Union armies for almost four years and had retired with the rank of brevet brigadier general. While the pension debates went on in the Taft administration he offered a

---

[47] *Addresses*, Vol. XI, p. 94. [48] Adams, Claude F., "The Civil War Pension Lack-of-System," Reprint from Dec., 1911-Feb., 1912 *World's Work*. [49] Powell, Talcott, *Tattered Banners*, pp. 160-166. [50] *Nation*, May 30, 1889.

blistering description of the heroes with whom he had fought. Those engaged in the war, he said, were "uniformly referred to . . . as 'veterans' and 'heroes'; as being 'battle-scarred,' and invariably as 'deserving and worthy'; men who 'enlisted at the call of duty with no thought of emoluments, pay or pension. . . .' Furthermore, they are uniformly described as 'old and infirm,' some blind, some crippled, some bed-ridden; most of them poor and many destitute." But these laudatory phrases, Mr. Adams said, came from the lips of politicians:

To those who themselves personally took part in the struggle, none of these statements or implications commend themselves. They are simply absurd in their exaggeration. Speaking coldly, and bearing witness as one personally acquainted with the facts in the case, the army of the Union, numbering more than two million, was a very miscellaneous body, composed of material of all sorts and conditions.

Vast numbers of the "heroes" now seeking larger payments, Mr. Adams said, were merely mercenaries drawn into the army by the bounties paid for enlistment. The bounty-bought men, said Mr. Adams, "constituted a large percentage of the whole Civil War levy." They were, for the most part, worthless as soldiers. A major problem of the war had been "preventing these 'patriots' and 'worthy soldiers' from deserting the moment they had handled their bounty money. . . . Then, far more battle-scared than battle-scarred, they are [now] indiscriminately pensioned as 'disinterested heroes!' " Finally, he asked, what of the deserters? Their number had officially been fixed at 508,494 and Congress, by special pension bills, was all too anxious to award these scoundrels pensions too. Mr. Adams marveled at the "amount of cant and fustian— nauseating twaddle, perhaps, would not be too extreme a term . . ." which had appeared in the *Congressional Record* concerning the veterans of the G.A.R. [51]

Mr. Adams sent his biting criticisms directly to the White House. Most of the recruits assigned to replenish his own command in the closing years of the war, he wrote, had been "deserters, bounty jumpers and outcasts." Before the bitter struggle had ended "any

[51] Adams, C. F., *op. cit.,* pp. 26-30.

man who could carry a musket or ride a horse,— imbecile, outcast
or even criminal— was eagerly accepted and munificently paid for."
Not one of the pension bills under discussion, he said, was tolerable.
They were all "in the direct line of a vicious system which has been
steadily pursued for over thirty years." The only remedy was complete revision of the pension rolls whereby none but the deserving
should be paid.[52] Occasionally, but all too rarely, the voice of a
veteran would also be raised in protest against the forthcoming
raids. C. W. Noyes, formerly of the 72nd Illinois Infantry, was
one; he wrote from Los Angeles saying he had never asked for a
pension and never would. Neither "prestige or votes," he said,
would be lost through a presidential veto. He added:

The amount now being paid is ample to make all the old
soldiers comfortable, both in health and sickness.
It is a sad comment to say that a large number will spend increase for liquor.
The number of designing women that live on pension money
paid them by old soldiers is surprising.[53]

Far more typical were the outraged protests when Secretary of
the Treasury MacVeagh dared to point to the increasing cost of the
veterans' doles and to say that the pension lists had never been
systematically compiled.[54] The Colonel D. W. Jones Post, No. 172,
of Tyrone, Pennsylvania, offered a resolution pointing out that the
secretary of the treasury drew a large federal salary and that this
was possible only because the "old soldiers, by their sacrifices at $13
a month" saved the Union.[55] A post in Philadelphia said that Mac-
Veagh must either apologize or resign.[56] From the west coast
arrived a resolution of the Morton Post, No. 10, of the Department
of Washington and Alaska, in which the members viewed "with
grief and indignation the wicked, evil and, as they hope and believe,
false and calumnious reports of the enemies of the 'Old Soldiers.' "
It requested the President to send a special message to Congress
favoring the passage of a pension bill and "showing that you have

[52] Adams to Norton, Feb. 1, 1911. [53] C. W. Noyes to Taft, Feb. 2, 1911. [54] MacVeagh
to Hilles, May 31, 1911. [55] Daniel Griston to Taft, April 22, 1911. [56] Edward Johnson to
Taft, April 19, 1911.

THE PRESIDENT AND HIS MILITARY AIDE

See page 538]

PRESIDENT TAFT INSPECTS THE PANAMA CANAL

THE PRESIDENT TURNS THE FIRST SHOVEL FOR THE PANAMA-PACIFIC EXPOSITION. SAN FRANCISCO, OCTOBER, 1911
[*See page* 580

Lincoln's sense of Justice and Love for the Old Soldier and Grant's feeling of Comradeship towards those who saved the Nation." [57]

The first general pension act— one giving blanket grants without relation to war casualties or need— awarded $6 to $12 a month for veterans who had served ninety days and were sixty years old. The trend had been gradually upward, particularly during periods when, as Corporal Tanner noted, there was a surplus waiting to be consumed. Under Roosevelt in 1907, the veterans put through increases. The following year their widows were favored. The total expenditures had jumped from $138,155,000 in 1907 to $153,093,000 in 1908. But this was far from enough. The 1909 encampment of the G.A.R. recommended more liberal bounties still for widows and thereby delighted many an avaricious hussy who had wondered whether it would be worth while to switch an intriguing petticoat at some befuddled old man, marry him and then live on Uncle Sam long after he had gone to a hero's grave. In 1910, at their annual meeting, the G.A.R. leaders told their followers that nothing had yet been obtained from the Taft administration because of the deficit. But the corporation tax, the new tariff and the economies effected by the President had resulted, at last, in a surplus.[58] God help William Howard Taft!

The G.A.R. committee worked faithfully during the winter of 1910-1911, but failed to get a bill through both houses of Congress because certain posts could not agree on the amount of loot which might be obtained. In April, 1911, Representative Isaac R. Sherwood, chairman of the Invalid Pension Committee and, himself, a hero, offered a measure which gave payments of from $15 to $30 a month for service ranging from ninety days to a year or more. His committee recommended the bill on August 19, 1911, but it did not pass.[59] This was partly, although not wholly, due to opposition from Taft who called it the "worst bill that has ever been proposed" and who estimated its cost at $75,000,000 annually within two years. He promised that he would "stop it at the White House." [60] Secretary of War Stimson, as energetically opposed as the President, suggested an "offensive-defensive method" of dealing with the pres-

---

[57] H. B. Fay to Taft, May 15, 1911. [58] Glasson, E. W., *Federal Military Pensions in the United States*, pp. 233, 251-252, 253-254. [59] *Ibid.*, pp. 256-257. [60] Taft to Stimson, Aug. 28, 1911.

sure. Why did the administration not publish the pension roll which, "replete as it is with fraudulent and unworthy pensions, has been successfully kept from public view . . .?" [61] But the President, it appears, was not ready for so drastic a step.

He was weakening. Veiled assurances went out from the White House that the President was no die-hard foe of veterans' relief and that any bill enacted by Congress would have "his very careful and full consideration." [62] To his credit, Taft declined to issue a statement pledging himself to sign a reasonable pension bill. His political advisers urged him to do so.

"The President *again* said he would *not* make such a statement," noted Rudolph Forster, the White House executive assistant, on the memorandum which presented the matter.[63] And to his brother, Horace, Taft repeated that "if I follow my present purpose I will veto any bill that comes to me." But he admitted that he might change his mind. This was in March, 1912.[64]

He was not alone in his retreat. When Congress met in December, 1911, Representative C. A. Sulloway of New Hampshire, who was a Republican, had offered a bill which would cost but $45,000,000 as compared with the estimated $75,000,000 of the Sherwood act, again under discussion. The latter bill passed the House almost immediately by 229 votes to 93. It was blocked in the Senate, though, and in conference between the two houses the general terms of the Sulloway bill were agreed upon. It increased pensions, but not so drastically. Their cost, including administration, would be $176,000,000 in 1913 as against $155,000,000 in 1912.[65]

Taft was in a quandary. Both Root and Lodge, he said, had been to him and "have advised me to sign this as the best thing to do" although both had urged a veto of the Sherwood bill. The President felt that it was "just about half as bad" as the other.[66] Appeals for his approval were legion. Senator Crane said that it must be signed immediately.[67] The President's apologia was dictated on May 10, 1912, as the measure was rushed through Congress. He wrote, of course, to his younger brother:

[61] Stimson to Taft, Aug. 31, 1911. [62] Carmi Thompson to J. T. Lamson, March 8, 1912. [63] White House memorandum, March 16, 1912. [64] Taft to Horace D. Taft, March 29, 1912. [65] Glasson, E. W., *op. cit.*, pp. 233, 256-259. [66] Taft to Horace D. Taft, April 8, 1912. [67] Crane to Taft, May 10, 1912.

Lodge and Root and all those who opposed the bill in the Senate tell me that it would pass over my veto . . . The question, therefore, is whether it is wise for me to utter *brutum fulmen* and lose. It would certainly lose the soldier vote in Ohio and elsewhere. . . . I hate to sign it, but I do not see any escape; and I hate to lose your respect; and if it concerned only the giving up of the office I hold or the subordination of my personal ambition, I would be entirely willing; but *I feel seriously that I represent the people's cause, that I represent the cause of constitutional government, that I represent the cause of liberty regulated by law.*[68]

In those final phrases lies the reason for Taft's action; possibly, too, they were the salve to his troubled conscience. For Theodore Roosevelt was abroad in the land. His hat was in the ring. He was seeking delegates, and winning them, for the convention which was now but a few weeks off. He was tearing down, in Taft's mind, the pillars of the temple of government. To Charles Francis Adams, whose protests against the treasury raid had been so vivid, the President dictated another sorrowful apology. It is significant, mainly, for a phrase which appears in a first draft and then is omitted:

". . . under these conditions, and facing as I do a crisis with Mr. Roosevelt . . . the question is whether I ought not to yield and sign the bill."

But he retained, in the letter, his assertion that "one of the chief grounds for further complaint against Mr. Roosevelt is the necessity that he has put me under of doing this." A veto would have meant the loss of Massachusetts as well as Ohio. The President prayed that Adams would sympathize, would understand the "agony of spirit that I suffer." [69]

The response of a New Englander, particularly a New Englander who was brother to Henry Adams, could not fail to be warm. The Adamses had known futility themselves:

Had you taken me into your counsel . . . I could not have advised you to any other course . . . and yet that course is as repugnant to me as your letter indicates it is to you. . . . I must say that Theodore Roosevelt has as respects you distinctly crossed the line

[68] Taft to Horace D. Taft, May 10, 1912. (Italics mine.) [69] Taft to C. F. Adams, May 10, 1912.

defining what is permissible among men in dealing one with another.[70]

—5—

The exigencies of politics may also be discerned in the third
item on these debit pages of Taft's ledger; the decision to hold
lightly the terms of the Hay-Pauncefote treaty with Great Britain.
It is strange that Taft, so often the most legalistic of men, should
have surrendered to the public insistence that words in a solemn
covenant did not mean what they said. The American public, to its
discredit, cared little about the treaty, however. The taxpayers had
spent $400,000,000 for the Panama Canal. Why, then, should their
own ships pay tolls? No longer was there proud talk of a canal
built, as Roosevelt had so often proclaimed in justifying his rape of
Colombia, in the "interests of the world at large." [71] Such idealism
was all very well when no canal existed. But toward the close of
Taft's term the ditch from sea to sea was actually being finished.
The interests of the world at large were subordinated to the possibility that free passage for American vessels might cut freight rates.
The high cost of living, in which transportation was a factor, would
be among the vital issues of the 1912 campaign.

And in that campaign Taft, Roosevelt and Wilson alike, would
stand for favoritism for American ships. "We have a perfect right
to permit our coastwise traffic . . . to pass through the canal on any
terms we choose, and I personally think that no toll should be
charged on such traffic," Roosevelt would declare, in August, 1912,
to the Progressive party in convention.[72] Far more cautiously— he
had not yet looked into the matter carefully and would ultimately
reverse himself— Wilson also recommended exemption.[73]

American public opinion was misinformed rather than maliciously anxious to break an agreement with England. The background of international negotiations which led to the construction
of the canal had been forgotten. No one remembered, any longer,
that a route through Nicaragua had first been the accepted one for

[70] Adams to Taft, May 11, 1912. [71] Roosevelt, Theodore, *Works*, National Edition,
Vol. XX, p. 513. [72] *Ibid.*, Vol. XVII, pp. 295-296. [73] Baker, Ray S., *Woodrow Wilson, Life
and Letters*, Vol. IV, pp. 396-397.

an isthmian canal. It was the discovery of California gold in 1848 which had first made a canal seem essential. The experts all recommended Nicaragua, but an obstacle in the path to construction by the United States was the fact that Great Britain held Greytown, the Atlantic terminus of that route. Besides, the English had a powerful navy and to build a canal without their co-operation seemed impossible. So the Clayton-Bulwer treaty was signed in 1850. This specified that the United States and Great Britain would have joint control, that the canal should be neutral and not fortified. Domination of Greytown was surrendered by the British. But it was cleverly specified by their diplomats that the agreement would apply to any route across Panama as well as through Nicaragua.[74]

The United States did not build a canal, however. The years passed. The transcontinental railroads crept across the nation on the makeshift roadbeds and flimsy bridges which were so greatly to alarm Rudyard Kipling on his American tour. American interest faded and in 1889, having squandered $260,000,000 in an enterprise fraught with corruption, Ferdinand de Lesseps was forced to admit that the French attempt was a failure. Slimy jungle vines covered the dredges and steam shovels of the French company, de Lesseps died in disgrace and greedy men wrangled over the carcass of that once brave enterprise. The United States was still uninterested. But then Hearst and Pulitzer drummed up a war with Spain. The U.S.S. *Oregon* steamed at forced draft around the Horn to join the fleet off Cuba. The foolish war ended, and the United States, in the peace treaty at Paris, became the owner of the Philippine Islands. Interest in a canal revived. But it was no longer conceivable that this could be done as a joint enterprise with Great Britain, that it could remain unfortified. The Clayton-Bulwer agreement had to be revised.[75]

No one had any doubt that the agreement was still valid. Secretary of State Richard Olney, of President Cleveland's Cabinet, had declared with emphasis that changed conditions might have made stipulations, "once deemed advantageous," inapplicable. The "true remedy," he said, "is not in ingenious attempts to deny the existence of the treaty or to explain away its provisions, but in a direct and

[74] Latané, John H., in *American Journal of International Law*, January, 1913, pp. 17-18. [75] Pringle, H. F., *op. cit.*, pp. 301-303.

straightforward application to Great Britain for a reconsideration of the whole matter." [76] The task fell on the shoulders of John Hay, whose first draft was rejected by the Senate because it still specified that the canal could not be fortified. Roosevelt, then governor of New York, opposed this but only on the ground of military and naval policy; he said nothing about tolls. [77] Secretary Hay continued the conversations with Lord Pauncefote, and a revised treaty was ratified by the Senate on December 16, 1901. The United States could build and exclusively control a canal under its terms. Article III, in view of the action to be taken by the Taft administration, was the most important. This set forth that the canal should be open to "vessels of war and commerce of *all nations* . . ."; to commerce which observed the rules of the Constantinople Convention of 1888 for the navigation of Suez. These provided that there should be "no discrimination against any such nation, or its citizens or its subjects, in respect of the *conditions or charges of traffic,* or otherwise. Such conditions and charges of traffic shall be equitable." It was clearly understood, however, that the United States had the right to build fortifications in the Canal Zone. The only limitation was with respect to tolls. But the advocates of exemption for American vessels were to insist that "all nations" meant "all other nations." [78]

President Taft discussed canal tolls in his December, 1910, Congressional message but he did not mention exemption for American vessels. [79] Privately, however, he expressed the thought that it might be wise to appropriate from public funds "money enough to pay the tolls on all public vessels and all merchant vessels of the United States passing through the Panama Canal." He added that he would favor a provision that this should not apply to coastwise vessels owned in whole or in part by the railroads. The dominating thought in Taft's mind, obviously, was the reduction of transcontinental freight charges. [80] A few weeks later, he insisted "that the clause in the treaty did not prevent our granting subsidies . . . which we had the right to do, and which is done in the Suez Canal by a good many countries." [81] Up to this point, it should be noted, the President was talking about subsidies which would be borne by all the tax-

[76] Latané, J. H., *op. cit.,* p. 18. [77] Bishop, J. B., *Theodore Roosevelt and His Time,* Vol. I, pp. 144-145. [78] Latané, J. H., *op. cit.,* pp. 18-21. (Italics mine.) [79] *Addresses,* Vol. XX, pp. 34-36. [80] Taft to W. P. Frye, Dec. 26, 1910. [81] Taft to E. F. Baldwin, Jan. 26, 1911.

payers. Toll exemptions, on the contrary, would be deductions from the total earnings of the canal and might be made the basis for a higher charge against foreign ships. The distinction is vital; Taft's position would have been stronger if he had held to his first idea.

Within six months, however, he was declaring, instead, that "when the treaties are properly construed, owning the canal and paying for it as we do, we have the right and power, if we choose, to discriminate in favor of our own ships." The policy of doing so, he added, was a "different thing." He inclined to the belief that the United States shall levy tolls at first, "experiment with them, and possibly give them up." [82] By the end of the year, Taft had been completely converted and informed Congress:

I am very confident that the United States has the power to relieve from the payment of tolls *any part of our shipping* that Congress deems wise. We own the canal. It was our money that built it. We have the right to charge tolls for its use. Those charges must be the same for everyone; but when we are dealing with our own ships, the practice of so many governments of subsidizing their own merchant vessels is so well established in general that a subsidy equal to the tolls, an equivalent remission of tolls, cannot be held to be a discrimination in the use of the canal.[83]

The protests from abroad were immediate. In England, this was held in violation of the Hay-Pauncefote treaty and one outraged editor branded it a "barefaced robbery" as well as "grand larceny." [84] This had no effect on Congress; if anything, it strengthened the determination of exemption advocates to show England that she should not interfere in American affairs. The House approved exemption for coastwise vessels toward the close of May, 1912, and there seemed to be no doubt that the Senate would follow. To statements that American honor was in danger, the President issued warm denials:

I do not differ with you in the slightest as to the necessity for preserving national honor. I claim to be as careful about that as anybody— but, on the other hand— I don't think it is essential for us to

---

[82] Taft to H. S. Drinker, July 27, 1911. [83] *Addresses,* Vol. XXVI, pp. 140-141. (Italics mine.) [84] Sullivan, Mark, *op. cit.,* Vol. IV, p. 587.

give away national rights and legitimate national advantage, growing out of our expenditure of $400,000,000 . . . without having bound ourselves to do so; and I am very clear in the construction of the treaty that there is no such obligation. . . . The history of the two treaties, and the history of the construction of the canal— the change from a plan by which two nations were to protect a private enterprise in the construction of the canal, to a situation in which one nation is to build the canal— makes the construction of the treaty entirely clear to me. There is no right to discriminate as between two customers of the canal, but the owner of the canal with reference to its own citizens . . . can do what it chooses.[85]

The Hay-Pauncefote treaty, however, had not admitted a changed status because of construction by the United States. The agreement, moreover, was clear in its specification that "no change of sovereignty" of the countries concerned affected the obligations of the United States or Great Britain.[86] As the Senate was about to take final action approving exemption for coastwise, not all American shipping, formal dissatisfaction was expressed on behalf of England by Sir Edward Grey at the Foreign Office in London. Ambassador Reid wrote that never before, while he had represented his country in England, had the United States "so bad a press."

"Sir Edward . . . made it plain," the ambassador wrote in recounting a conversation at the Foreign Office, "that he thought the Hay-Pauncefote treaty absolutely clear in pledging the United States against the policy . . . proposed in Congress." [87]

Taft, it is clear, began to have doubts of his own before the Senate acted. Ten days before he signed the bill on August 24, 1912, he insisted that he would not veto the measure.[88] Two days later he told Mrs. Taft that he was "not clear what ought to be done . . . it presents some difficult issues growing out of a very decided difference of opinion in respect to the construction of the treaty. . . .

"Knox and Stimson and Fisher [Secretary of the Interior Fisher] and Wickersham and I," he added, "are all clear in respect to the matter, and I consider these four, barring myself, excellent

[85] Taft to W. W. Keen, Aug. 13, 1912. [86] Latané, J. H., op. cit., pp. 24-25. [87] Reid to Taft, Sept. 6, 1912. [88] Taft to W. W. Keen, Aug. 13, 1912.

lawyers. Root and Burton are the other way, and of course the altruists all over the country are the other way." [89]

At the last moment, the President suggested an amendment which would enable foreign shippers to test the bill before the United States Supreme Court.[90] This was to silence demands that the subject be offered for arbitration, at The Hague or elsewhere. Taft was, in theory, a confirmed proponent of arbitration, but not in this case for the excellent reason that "we may lose"; a doctrine more truly Rooseveltian than any expressed by Taft in many a weary month. He added:

> The trouble we will have in getting into arbitration is that all Europe will be interested and all their representatives will be against us, whereas if we could make an arbitration for ourselves, by reference to the Supreme Court, we could get an unbiased decision which would stand us in good stead thereafter.[91]

Senator Root, said the President, had complained "that he found a very strong tendency among European nations to stand by each other in arbitrations. . . . I don't use this as a reason why we should not have arbitration, but I think it indicates that we have to train the nations of the world to have the same sense of absolute impartiality . . . that the English and American judges are trained to have. . . . The civilian judge, the judge of the Latin race, feels it entirely proper, in matters in which the government is interestd, to follow the governmental desire rather than to decide the case as if the government were a party and only entitled to the rights of a party." [92]

Congress would not accept the President's recommendation for a prearbitration ruling by the Supreme Court, so he signed the measure anyway. Great Britain asked for adjudication under the arbitration treaty of 1908. Meanwhile, by asking for too much, the English had weakened their position. Secretary of State Knox told the President that Great Britain insisted that there was no "difference in principle between charging tolls only to refund them and remitting tolls altogether." [93] This was an utterly untenable position. It meant,

[89] Taft to Helen H. Taft, Aug. 15, 1912. [90] Taft to W. C. Adamson, Aug. 16, 1912. [91] Taft to Hilles, Aug. 20, 1912. [92] Taft to Theodore Marburg, Aug. 21, 1912. [93] Knox to Taft, Aug. 15, 1912.

as the President pointed out, allowing "Great Britain and every other country to subsidize its vessels with a special subsidy consisting of the payment of the canal tolls, and the United States could not do so. . . . That is absurd. It is a well-known custom in the Suez Canal for countries to pay, as a subsidy to their vessels, the tolls of the canal." [94] Taft was wholly correct.

The bill he signed, however, provided for exemption, not an identical subsidy which would come from the national treasury. The British continued to press for arbitration.[95] The President assured Andrew Carnegie that he would not avoid it, that it was a proper subject for such settlement.[96] Although the act gave the Chief Executive power to discriminate in favor of vessels in international trade, he pledged that he would "never do so." Coastwise shipping was, in any event, an American monopoly.[97]

A minority in the land believed that American honor had been stained and said so. Robert Underwood Johnson, editor of the *Century Magazine,* had no doubt that a solemn pledge had been broken and pointed to the peril lest the United States become the "welsher of the nations." He hoped that Congress would promptly repeal the bill. Otherwise the "great cause of arbitration . . . will be set back for unreckonable years." The tragedy was the greater, Mr. Johnson wrote, because it was the "championship of arbitration, together with his farsighted . . . defense and extension of the merit system, which will give the President his highest claim to the respect of posterity." [98]

But Taft could be very stubborn. He could not see, at the close of January, 1913, "what ground either England or Root has to stand upon." [99] The matter was a degree academic, in any event, since the canal would not open for traffic for another year at least. Meanwhile, those who regarded the action of Congress with distaste were appealing to President-elect Wilson. To Professor John H. Latané of Johns Hopkins University must go some of the credit for the ultimate repeal of tolls exemption. Dr. Latané, whom Wilson knew intimately, wrote an article on "The Panama Canal Act and the British Protest" which was published in the January, 1913, issue of

[94] Taft to W. W. Keen, Aug. 13, 1912. [95] A. M. Innes to Knox, Aug. 27, 1912. [96] Taft to Carnegie, Nov. 20, 1912. [97] Taft to Theodore Marburg, Aug. 21, 1912. [98] *Century Magazine,* November, 1912. [99] Taft to Knox, Jan. 27, 1912.

the *American Journal of International Law.* This was a convincing argument that the Hay-Pauncefote treaty had been broken. On taking office, Wilson first gave his attention to other matters. But in March, 1914, he asked Congress to cancel the discrimination. After a stiff fight, he obtained repeal of toll exemptions in June of that year.[100]

[100] Baker, R. S., *op. cit.,* Vol. IV, pp. 397-398, 418.

CHAPTER XXXIV

BIG BUSINESS

WILLIAM HOWARD TAFT was never a servant of the trusts as Senator Aldrich was, or Foraker of Ohio, or Representative J. C. Sibley of Pennsylvania, who did the bidding of the Standard Oil Company. The fact is that he knew rather little about industry or finance and rarely regretted his ignorance. He was unique among the great lawyers of his day in that the brand of "corporation attorney" could never be placed upon him. Neither before he became president nor afterward did Taft often accept large retainers from the country's corporations. They were eager to hire Root, Knox, Wickersham and Hughes— all of whom were his contemporaries— and they would undoubtedly have capitalized Taft's prestige when he left the White House. But he had no taste for private practice. He took few cases. He continued to teach law until he became chief justice of the United States.

The accusation was made— it was one of many that were untrue— that President Taft did not diligently prosecute the monopolies and combinations which sought to throttle competition. The truth is that he attempted much more, if far less noisily, than Roosevelt. This was in harmony with his record. In the spring of 1892, when Taft mounted the Federal Circuit Court, the Sherman Antitrust Act was all but dead. The Supreme Court had limited its application so that virtually no prosecutions were brought. But in 1898 the Circuit Court of Appeals— with Taft, Harlan and Lurton sitting— ruled in the Addystone Pipe case that a combination to restrain trade was illegal when sales were made across a state line. Thus it fell within control of Congress. Thus the Sherman act applied to it. Taft, himself, wrote this decision. The law would be further revived in 1904 in the Northern Securities case, brought by President Roosevelt to halt the Harriman-Hill transportation monopoly in the Northwest. In 1905, the Supreme Court ruled against a conspiracy of meat packers, and the government's powers were augmented again.[1]

In December, 1907, when his nomination for the presidency was almost a certainty, Secretary of War Taft attacked the "use of accumulated wealth in illegal ways." The laws forbidding the illegalities, he added, had been "almost a dead letter" until Theodore Roosevelt came into power. Behind this view was the belief, held jointly with Roosevelt, that the capitalist system was better than any other devised by man. Unless the abuses under it were stopped, capitalism would be replaced by socialism or some other evil. Taft was aware, when he entered the White House, that much remained to be done. As president, Taft insisted that he would hear all sides before deciding upon a policy to be followed. He would consult with the representatives of the railroads, the industrial corporations, the banks and the public.[2] But his reverence for Wall Street was slight. In February, 1910, uncertainty and doubt again shook the leaders of that hysterical thoroughfare and reports were current that the President, in a New York speech, would give assurance that the government had no plan for further nefarious attacks. Instead, he did not mention the subject.

"As you say," he told his brother, "Wall Street, as an aggregation, is the biggest ass that I have ever run across."[3] Another time, referring to opposition to his program, he wondered "how far this reaches beyond the Wall Street and the general kid-gloved, swallow-tailed element."[4] Nor did Taft have the slightest patience when complaints reached him that the Sherman act was difficult to understand, that its terms were harsh, that business could not operate properly under such cruel limitations.

"I confess that I don't see where the uncertainty arises in respect to future business," he snapped. "The decisions of the Supreme Court are easily interpreted and anyone can follow them if he is only willing to understand that . . . combinations to . . . suppress competition, to control prices and to establish a monopoly are unlawful in so far as they affect interstate trade."[5]

In November, 1911, Charles F. Brooker, a prominent and pros-

---

[1] Taft, W. H., *The Anti-Trust Act and the Supreme Court*, pp. 70-82. [2] Taft to A. H. Walker, Jan. 24, 1910. [3] Taft to Henry Taft, Feb. 21, 1910. [4] Taft to C. P. Taft, Oct. 18, 1910. [5] Taft to H. L. Higginson, Sept. 8, 1911.

perous Republican of Connecticut, was under indictment for violation of the Sherman law. That a gentleman of culture, who also was
a loyal Republican, should be subjected to such indignity seemed an
outrage to other members of the party. To one appeal that something should be done on Brooker's behalf, the President's reply was
vehement:

He violated the law and he has had to pay the penalty for it.
That is all! There seems to be a sort of feeling on the part of businessmen who violate the law that their prosecution for doing this
calls for some explanation. I think the law is a good law that ought
to be enforced, and I propose to enforce it. I greatly regret that in
doing so I have to strain or break off relations with real friends.
That is my misfortune, but I cannot but feel from your attitude . . .
that in some way or other you are trying to find out some sort of
apology for me to make to Brooker for allowing an indictment to
be found against him because he violated the law.[6]

—2—

Taft's program of trust control was in direct charge of Attorney
General Wickersham, whom he had selected for this task. At the
end of 1911, the President granted an interview to Frances E. Leupp
which was ultimately published in the *Outlook*. Taft explained
and defended his administration. One criticism, he said, had been
the excessive number of lawyers whom he had inducted into his
Cabinet. The President's answer— it appears in the original draft
of the interview but was stricken from the published version— was
that he wanted the government to have "at least as good legal
services as any private corporation and . . . lawyers who thoroughly understood corporation methods could best advise me how
to compel them to obey the law." He continued:

Wall Street's dismay when it found that George Wickersham's
campaign against the monopoly was in earnest was amusing.
"Why!" gasped the Street, "he is going back on *us!*" Now, I know
something about professional ethics, and their first principle is that

[6] Taft to A. R. Kimball, Nov. 21, 1911.

a lawyer shall be loyal to his present client, regardless of whom he may have served in the past. Wickersham has the government for his client now, and the tirades aimed at him are the most eloquent of tributes to his good faith.[7]

It was characteristic for Taft to eliminate one of the most striking passages in the whole Leupp interview. And yet there is no doubt that his campaign against the trusts was clearly understood in the circles where it was felt the most. At about the same time the New York *Journal of Commerce* remarked editorially that "President Taft has very few friends in Wall Street." Even Theodore Roosevelt, continued this voice of big business, might be preferable to this president who insisted on enforcement of the law. The editorial said:

President Taft has not been as loud or spectacular in his attacks upon the "trusts" as was his predecessor in the White House, but he has been consistent, persistent and unwavering and results have been achieved or at any rate have culminated during his administration that have been distressing to Wall Street.[8]

When Taft became president in March, 1909, the Sherman act was a fairly practical statute under which corporate greed could be restrained. Lawyers knew what it meant. The government was aware of its power under it. A lucid opinion by Justice Holmes in the Meat Packers case had defined commerce. The contention of the government in the litigation had been that dealers in fresh meat had agreed not to bid against each other in the Chicago, Omaha, Kansas City and other markets. Thus they controlled prices paid to the cattlemen. But the dealers had answered that their offense, if one existed, was not related to interstate commerce because each sale, even if collusive, took place in one single market in a single state. Mr. Justice Holmes brushed this contention aside:

It is said that this charge does not set forth a case of commerce among the states. Commerce among the states is not a technical legal conception, but a practical one, drawn from the course of business.

[7] *Outlook*, Dec. 2, 1911; cf. unpublished manuscript, Library of Congress. [8] New York *World*, Nov. 19, 1911.

658 THE LIFE AND TIMES OF WILLIAM HOWARD TAFT

When cattle are sent for sale from a place in one state, with the expectation that they will end their transit, after purchase, in another, and when in effect they do so, with only the interruption necessary to find a purchaser at the stock-yards, and when this is a typical, constantly recurring course, the current thus existing is a current of commerce among the states, and the purchase of the cattle is a part and incident of such commerce. . . . Although the combination alleged embraces restraint and monopoly of trade within a single state, its effect upon commerce among the states is not accidental, secondary, remote or merely probable. It is a direct object, it is that for the sake of which the several specific acts and courses of conduct are done and accepted.[9]

Taft vacillated, to an extent, in his views on the efficacy of the Sherman act as interpreted by the Supreme Court. That tribunal's famous "rule of reason" had not yet been enunciated when he took office. It would be laid down in the Standard Oil opinion by Chief Justice White in May, 1911. In September, 1909, the President was leaning toward a conviction that the scope of the act might be narrowed somewhat. As it stood, he said, the law forbade all contracts in restraint of trade whether their intent was to suppress competition or not. This had been "seized upon by those who do not favor the law at all as a ground for ridiculing its provisions and as a means of demonstrating its absurdity." [10] The President's belief that a change, limiting the act, might be advisable was due to decisions by certain of the circuit judges in which "absurdly unimportant combinations and arrangements" had been enjoined.[11] He soon concluded, however, that "the act is too valuable, with its judicial interpretations to permit amendments." To allow the courts, he said, to distinguish between righteous and wicked trusts would be "to give them a power which it would be dangerous and impossible for them to exercise." [12]

Taft recommended to Congress, however, a law permitting federal incorporation of companies engaged in interstate commerce. This would inaugurate supervision from Washington of stocks issued and would require full reports of operations to the Department of Commerce and Labor. The companies would, save

[9] Taft, W. H., op. cit., pp. 80-81. [10] Addresses, Vol. XV, pp. 93-95. [11] Ibid., Vol. XVII, p. 86. [12] Taft to R. D. Silliman, Dec. 31, 1909.

in special cases, be barred from holding stock in other corporations. They would still be subject to all the provisions of the Sherman law. Nor did the President's suggestion mean any modification of the drive against monopolies. Taft was confident, he said, that the plan was constitutional under the power to regulate commerce. He saw little weight in the contention that it meant an undue extension of centralized government. In any event, "no other method can be suggested which offers federal protection on the one hand and close federal supervision on the other of these great organizations that are in fact federal because they are as wide as the country and are entirely unlimited in their business by state lines."

He had no doubt that the large industries would hasten to accept federal incorporation. They had no other logical course, owing to the "thorough and sweeping" injunctions being placed upon them through the Sherman law. If they did not accept, they would be forced to dissolve "into their component parts . . . with a consequent loss to themselves of capital and effective organization and to the country of concentrated energy and enterprise." If they attempted to continue as monopolies, in defiance of the law, they would "incur the penalties of contempt and bring on inevitable criminal prosecution." [13] But Taft did not press the issue. No bill was passed. In December, 1911, he supplemented the idea with a suggestion for a Federal Corporation Commission which would supervise companies holding national charters and also assist the courts "in the dissolution and re-creation of trusts within the law." [14] But this idea, too, died under Congressional nonaction.

—3—

The Supreme Court's two major decisions of the Taft administration were in litigations started during the Roosevelt years. John D. Rockefeller, the elder, regarded himself as a greatly maligned individual as blows rained upon him in 1907. In August the Standard Oil Company of Indiana had been fined $29,240,000 by Federal Judge Kenesaw Mountain Landis for accepting railroad

[13] *Addresses*, Vol. XVII, pp. 88-90. [14] *Ibid.*, Vol. XXVI, pp. 15-16.

rebates. "A great injustice has been done," lamented Mr. Rocke-feller, but he cannot have been greatly disturbed. His lawyers must have predicted the ultimate reversal of the penalty.[15] Even Taft, who had no use for the Standard Oil, seems to have viewed the fine with misgivings.

"I have no criticism to make of Judge Landis," he subsequently wrote, "except . . . that he is too much of an actor and too much occupied with how he appears to the public to be a good judge." [16]

A far more serious onslaught on the Standard Oil was the gov-ernment suit, instituted in the Federal Circuit Court of Missouri in September, 1907, charging that the Standard Oil Company of New Jersey, the parent concern, was a monopoly in the refining and shipment of oil. The allegations were based, in part, on an exhaustive investigation which had been conducted by the com-missioner of corporations. Frank B. Kellogg, who would one day be secretary of state, was designated the special prosecutor in the action.

Looking back on the "great and crucial Standard Oil case" in later years, Taft said that it had "applied the interstate commerce law to the greatest monopoly and combination in restraint of trade in the world." The oil trust, he wrote, had been a chief reason for the passage of the Sherman law in 1890. By then, it had been growing for two decades. When the government's suit was filed in 1907, nine distinct Standard Oil companies were in existence and sixty-two other corporations which ran oil wells, re-fineries, pipe lines and tank lines. The New Jersey company held stock in these concerns and controlled about eighty-five per cent of the nation's petroleum industry.

"It was indeed an octopus," ex-President Taft wrote, "that held the trade in its tentacles, and the few actual independent concerns that kept alive were allowed to exist by sufferance to maintain the appearance of competition." [17]

Kellogg spent most of 1908 assembling the intricate history of the Standard Oil and presenting it to the court. On November 20, 1909, a decision was handed down which upheld the government.

[15] Flynn, John T., *God's Gold, the Story of Rockefeller and His Times*, p. 426.
[16] Taft to Otto Gresham, Jan. 28, 1910. [17] Taft, W. H., *op. cit.*, pp. 85-86.

The Standard Oil of New Jersey was ordered to divest itself, within thirty days, of all its subsidiaries.

"I congratulate you," the President telegraphed to Kellogg, "on . . . the complete victory that you have won . . . much of which is due to the thorough preparation and presentation, on your part, of the government's case." [18]

An appeal to the highest tribunal at Washington was immediately taken, of course. Meanwhile John D. Rockefeller had finally surrendered to the advisers who implored him to woo good will through the machinations of publicity. Good will was sorely needed. The Landis fine and the dissolution decree had been augmented by the publication, in the campaign of 1908, of the letters from Standard Oil officials to Foraker and other politicians. It was no longer enough for Rockefeller to murmur privately that he was misunderstood.

"They will know me better when I am dead," he once said. "There has been nothing in my life that will not bear the utmost scrutiny. Is it not patent that I have been made into a sort of frightful ogre, to slay which has become a favorite resource of men seeking public favor?"

To end, if possible, this cruel distortion, J. I. C. Clarke, a veteran journalist, was engaged as press agent. He was successful, to a degree. Friendly little articles on Rockefeller began to appear. The *Woman's Home Companion,* for instance, delighted its readers with a nicely written account of how the "World's Richest Man" was accustomed to spending Christmas. Mr. Rockefeller blossomed out as an author, himself. His memoirs started in the October, 1908, issue of *World's Work.* Their content was strikingly different from Miss Ida Tarbell's history of the Standard Oil. It would be unjust to state dogmatically that magnificent donations made by Mr. Rockefeller during this period were also an attempt to win public favor. He undoubtedly believed in the causes to which he contributed. It may be noted, though, that one $32,000,000 gift was made shortly before the Landis fine in August, 1907. And in 1910, while the Supreme Court was debating the Standard Oil appeal from the dissolution decree, an even more stupendous largess seemed about to drop from the exhaustless Rockefeller cornucopia.

[18] Taft to Kellogg, Nov. 21, 1909.

The company attorneys filed their briefs with the Supreme Court on March 9, 1910. Five days earlier a bill to create the Rockefeller Foundation, as a national corporation, had been introduced in Congress. It would have $100,000,000 to devote to humanity. It would be a clearinghouse for nearly all the Rockefeller good works.[19]

It seemed like an excellent plan and it received prompt endorsement from various clergymen who, perhaps, yearned for a share of the income from $100,000,000. But there were protests too. The Springfield *Republican* warned that very careful thought should be given to the measure and Attorney General Wickersham was scandalized by it. He wrote to the President opposing it. Never, he supposed, had there been "submitted to Congress, or to any legislative body, such an indefinite scheme for perpetuating vast wealth as this; and personally I believe it to be entirely inconsistent with the public interest that any such bill should be passed." He continued:

> The power which, under such bill, would be vested in and exercised by a small body of men, in absolute control of the income of $100,000,000 or more, to be expended for the general indefinite objects described in the bill, might be in the highest degree corrupt in its influence. The medieval statutes against mortmain were enacted to prevent just such perpetuation of wealth in a few hands under the cloak of such a charitable purpose as this. . . . It was not without much reason that the English common law and English statutes required bequests for charitable purposes to be definite and specific in their terms. Such legislation was the result of experience with the indefinite charities which the monastic and other medieval institutions erected, and which were the occasion of so much scandal and corruption. It is true that the questions there were accentuated by exemptions from taxation; nevertheless the underlying evil was the centralization of wealth in a few hands under the guise of charity.

> The Rockefeller Foundation bill, the attorney general said, "proposes that this vast sum be placed in the hands of a small body of men for the indefinite objects of promoting the welfare and advancing the civilization of the people of the United States . . .

---

[19] Flynn, J. T., *op. cit.*, pp. 423, 442-444, 451-452.

'in the acquisition and dissemination of knowledge,' 'in the prevention and relief of suffering'; and in the 'promotion of any and all of the elements of human progress.'" Mr. Wickersham could not "imagine anything that might not be made to fall within one of these purposes." Besides, the Supreme Court was at that moment, February, 1911, considering evidence against the Standard Oil:

There is no doubt, indeed the evidence in the suit brought by the United States against the Standard Oil Company clearly demonstrates, that the vast wealth of Mr. Rockefeller was achieved largely by methods which the law has denounced, which the courts of the United States have condemned, and which the judgment of all thoughtful men . . . may be fairly said to agree were immoral, when measured by recognized ethical standards. Is it, then, appropriate that, at the moment when the United States through its courts is seeking in a measure to destroy the great combination of wealth which has been built up by Mr. Rockefeller . . . the Congress of the United States should assist in the enactment of a law to create and perpetuate in his name an institution to hold and administer a large portion of this vast wealth? [20]

"I agree," answered Taft, "with your . . . characterization of the proposed act to incorporate John D. Rockefeller." [21] So the Rockefeller Foundation bill was withdrawn and introduced again in 1912 with amendments limiting its powers. This failed to pass, however, and ultimately a charter was granted by New York State.[22]

The President waited impatiently for the Supreme Court's decision; so must presidents often worry and grow irritable as the oracle fails to speak. He was expecting a ruling in October, 1910; the delay was "very aggravating, because it prevents my using the present Congress to put through the National Incorporation act which I believe I could get through this Congress if I had the decision of the Supreme Court as a basis. God knows what we can do with the new Congress!" [23] The new Congress would have a Democratic House, and nothing, as it turned out, was to be done regarding national corporations.

[20] Wickersham to Taft, Feb. 7, 1911. [21] Taft to Wickersham, Feb. 9, 1911. [22] Flynn, J. T., op. cit., p. 453. [23] Taft to F. B. Kellogg, Oct. 12, 1910.

The court acted on May 15, 1911. Ponderously, because he was large in body, Chief Justice White mounted the bench with his colleagues. The spectators in the old Supreme Court chambers may have noted that Associate Justice Harlan, never wholly happy after the elevation of White instead of himself to the highest place on the court, seemed even more irascible than usual. For while he concurred in the illegality of the Standard Oil, he disagreed violently with the reasoning of the other eight jurists. His was to be the dissent from an otherwise unanimous decision. The Chief Justice read the 20,000-word opinion upholding the government and ordering the dissolution of the Standard Oil Company. He traced in detail the history of its growth and the methods it had used to expand. No "disinterested mind," he said, could "survey the period in question without being irresistibly driven to the conclusion that the very genius for commercial development and organization which . . . was manifested from the beginning soon begot an intent and purpose to exclude others which were frequently manifested by acts and dealings wholly inconsistent" with legal business development. The intent had been, he said, "to drive others from the field and to exclude them from their right to trade." The history of the Rockefeller companies and their methods "all lead the mind up to a conviction of purpose and intent which we think is so certain as practically to cause the subject not to be within the domain of *reasonable contention*." [24]

This, "reasonable contention," was one form of the legal conception of reasonableness over which such controversy would rage. The Chief Justice also said, referring to the Sherman act:

In view of the many new forms of contracts and combinations, which were being evolved from existing economic conditions, it was deemed essential by an all-embracing enumeration to make sure that no form of contract or combination by which an *undue restraint* of interstate or foreign commerce was brought about could save such restraint from condemnation.

The statute under this view evidenced the intent not to restrain the right to make and enforce contracts, whether resulting from combination or otherwise, which did not *unduly restrain* interstate

[24] Flynn, J. T., *op. cit.*, pp. 444-445. (Italics mine.)

and foreign commerce, but to protect that commerce from being restrained by such methods, whether old or new, which would constitute an interference that is *undue restraint*.[25]

What the Chief Justice was doing, of course, was to base his opinion on the common-law exemption of "reasonable" restraint of trade agreements from attack. It was this theory to which Taft had objected in 1910, although he would now reverse himself and agree with the court. Justice Harlan, however, could not tolerate this limitation of the antitrust law. The Court, he said, while he angrily pounded the bench in front of him, had put "words into the antitrust act which Congress did not put there." He pictured the confusion which, in his judgment, would surely result. He said that many a trust would crawl through this new hole in the law.[26]

But the President— perhaps he was already swinging toward the distaste for dissenting opinions which would mark his career as chief justice— said that this was a "good opinion— the Standard Oil Company will have to dissolve." True, the Court's reasoning "did not take exactly the line of distinction I have drawn, but it certainly approximates it." Taft regretted Harlan's action, which he called a "nasty, carping and demagogic opinion, directed at the Chief Justice and intended to furnish LaFollette and his crowd as much pabulum as possible." [27]

The Standard Oil decision demanded that the parent concern, the Standard Oil Company of New Jersey, divest itself of its thirty or more subsidiaries within thirty days. All the corporations and their officers were enjoined from conspiring to re-establish the monopoly.[28] Two weeks after the ruling, the court handed down its decision in the prosecution of the tobacco trust. This action, against the American Tobacco Company and twenty-eight other companies, had also been started under Roosevelt. The Chief Justice again wrote the opinion and it reiterated the doctrine that "reasonable" restraint was lawful. It was not true, he insisted, that the Sherman law was thereby weakened. On the contrary, no longer would there be any possibility of frustrating the act "by resorting to any disguise or subterfuge of form, since resort to reason rendered

[25] Taft, W. H., *op. cit.*, pp. 87-88. (Italics mine.) [26] Flynn, J. T., *op. cit.*, p. 445.
[27] Taft to Helen H. Taft, May 16, 1911. [28] *Addresses*, Vol. XXVI, p. 16.

it impossible to escape by any indirection the prohibitions of the statute." [29]

The President decided to uphold this interpretation. There was, he insisted, "no conflict between what I have said and what the court says." Instead, "there is a real resemblance between them that makes me proud."

"I was contending throughout for a reasonable construction of the act with a view to the evil aimed at," Taft claimed. "What I was criticizing in the use of the word reasonable was when it was proposed to be applied to a monopoly or a partial monopoly or a restraint of trade for the purpose of enhancing prices, and it was supposed to distinguish between restraints of this character and leave it to the court to say that those in which the profits exacted by such means were moderate were lawful, and those in which they were exorbitant were to be condemned." [30]

Taft insisted that the "rule of reason" did not permit the Supreme Court to distinguish between "good" and "bad" trusts and that the Standard Oil and Tobacco Trust cases had strengthened the law rather than the reverse.[31] These legalistic theories interested the public very little, however. The decisions undoubtedly supplied ammunition to Taft's enemies, in his own party and among the Democrats who sought victory in 1912. Meanwhile the Standard Oil Company of New Jersey's directors were struggling with the problem of delivering to its stockholders their due share of stock in the subsidiaries about to be cast out. At the end of the thirty days allowed, there were thirty-four companies with a board of directors for each instead of the New Jersey directors. It was all a good deal of a farce. The same men held the stock in the subsidiaries and could, in theory, control the directorates as they wished. Before very long, though, John D. Rockefeller abandoned active participation in the Standard Oil.[32] While he grew older and still older— while he evolved from a wicked ogre into a senile nonagenarian who distributed dimes and devoted every ounce of his being to the mere feat of keeping alive— new influences entered the petroleum industry. Oil gushed from new hillsides and

---

[29] Taft, W. H., *op. cit.*, pp. 88-89. [30] Taft to J. A. Shauck, June 10, 1911. [31] *Addresses*, Vol. XXVI, pp. 14-15; Taft, W. H., *op. cit.*, pp. 94-95. [32] Flynn, J. T., *op. cit.*, pp. 446-448.

new valleys in the Southwest, in California and in Central America. Competition bloomed again, but for this the Supreme Court could take no credit.

—4—

Meanwhile the Tobacco Trust was also being "dissolved." The President, in December, 1911, explained the process at length to Congress. The plan was to distribute the various branches of the industry, he said, "between two or more companies with a division of the prominent brands in the same tobacco products, so as to make competition not only possible, but necessary." Thus smoking and chewing tobacco had been split up; likewise cigars, cigarettes and snuff. The President denied the validity of a contention, current when the terms of the dissolution became public, that injustice had been done to struggling independents because some corporations with enormous resources were still in business. The Sherman act, he said, was not "intended . . . to prevent the accumulation of large capital in business enterprises in which such a combination can secure reduced cost of production, sale and distribution." It applied to such accumulation only "when its purpose is that of stifling competition." It was not, he added, a "purpose of the statute to confiscate the property and capital of the offending trusts. Methods of punishment by fine or imprisonment of the individual offenders, by fine of the corporation . . . are provided, but the *proceeding in equity* is a specific remedy to stop the operation of the trust by injunction and prevent the future use of the plant and capital in violation of the statute." [33]

But who would be on guard to see that corporations, almost as powerful after their dissolution as before and operated, generally speaking, by identical officers, did not again combine to stifle competition? Many a small businessman would drift from bankruptcy to despair while his appeals— not in the Taft administration alone— remained clogged in the files of the Department of Justice. It is astonishing that the nation's industrial leaders resented the Taft trust-control problem as much as they did. The President's consistent policy was to start, first, the equity proceedings whereby the facts

[33] *Addresses*, Vol. XXVI, pp. 18-19.

of law violation would be ascertained and not, as he expressed it, "resort to indictments and criminal proceedings until after the injunction has been sustained." [34] But which of the Standard Oil heads, declared guilty of criminal acts in the equity courts, ever went to jail? Who among the officials of the tobacco monopoly was indicted, fined or punished?

And doubt swept the country, too, that disbandment or dissolution was a valid cure for monopoly. As 1911 closed, Andrew Carnegie— who was an expert on the subject— drafted a letter to George W. Perkins of the International Harvester Company and sent a copy to the White House. The only cure, said the master of iron who was now retired and thus friendly to reform, was regulation of prices by the government. Mr. Carnegie added a postscript to his letter. He agreed, he said, that "Standard Oil and Tobacco are laughing at the government. Who isn't? 'Disbandment' is futile." [35]

None the less, an extreme degree of alarm was felt by certain of the nation's industrialists and their Washington spokesmen conveyed it to the White House. It was caused, in part, by an address delivered by Attorney General Wickersham before the Michigan State Bar Association on July 6, 1911. He analyzed the Sherman act and offered the subversive thought that the "only legitimate end and object of all government is the greatest good of the greatest number of the people." Wickersham said that the Standard Oil and Tobacco Trust decisions had narrowed the "area of uncertainty" in the antitrust law. In conclusion he quoted, strangely enough, a passage from the writings of Woodrow Wilson. When a Princeton professor, the New Jersey governor had analyzed the development of law among the members of the English race. Henceforth, Wickersham said, the Sherman act would "be used, to employ Dr. Wilson's language, as a part of the running machinery of our political system, adapted to the needs of our social condition." [36]

The industrialists' apprehension was heightened when the New York *World* quoted Wickersham as saying that probably one hun-

[34] Taft to MacVeagh, July 12, 1910. [35] Carnegie to G. W. Perkins (copy in Taft files), Nov. 29, 1911. [36] Wickersham, G. W., *Recent Interpretation of the Sherman Act*, 1911; Wickersham to author, Jan. 23, 1935.

dred additional corporations would be called to account under the Sherman act, that their guilty officials would go to jail, that the United States Steel Corporation was clearly among the unregenerate. The Springfield *Republican,* among other journals, noted with consternation that the attorney general confirmed the interview as "substantially" correct; he had not, however, supposed that he was talking for publication and he had said nothing about the steel corporation. The editor lamented that such indiscreet sentiments had been voiced "at a time when near-panic conditions prevailed in the stock market." [37] Wickersham telegraphed the President that the interview had been "somewhat inaccurate." On the other hand:

The *World* man stated that he had evidence that the big financial interests had served notice on the managers of the Republican party that no financial aid would be forthcoming unless the prosecutions of the packers in Chicago . . . were dropped and also all effort to dissolve the combination between the National City Bank and its subsidiary companies, to which I remarked that would be a fine issue on which to go to the country. I don't know that on the whole the interview is harmful, but I want you to know that I did not intentionally slop over.[38]

The President, himself, added to the discontent when he declared that "every trust of any size that violates the statute will, before the end of this administration in 1913, be brought into court to meet and acquiesce in a degree of disintegration by which competition between its parts shall be restored and preserved." [39]

"You have been thinking about it so much that you have become jaundiced on the subject," the President replied to one critic of his trust-control program, "and when you dream, you have Wickersham as a nightmare." [40]

There are indications, however, that even Taft occasionally felt that his attorney general was too energetic in his prosecutions. Was it necessary, he asked in January, 1912, for indictments in the Shoe Machinery case to be pressed? Could not the usual pro-

[37] Springfield *Republican*, Sept. 25, 26, 1911. [38] Wickersham to Taft, Sept. 23, 1911. [39] *Addresses*, Vol. XXII, p. 57. [40] Taft to Bannard, Jan. 26, 1912.

cedure be followed of civil action before criminal trial?[41] But Wickersham answered that the indictments had been found after prolonged investigation and he saw no reason to delay action on them.[42] Nor would the forthright Wickersham listen to pleas that the officers of the National Cash Register Company be spared the humiliation of prosecution.[43] So the industrialists grew even angrier.

"Isn't it possible," asked the President in pretended alarm, "I might be in danger of physical violence if I were to land on the lower end of Manhattan Island?"[44]

—5—

In his trust-control program, Taft was carrying out the injunctions of Theodore Roosevelt against the wealthy malefactors. Even approximate justice would have spared him criticism from Roosevelt on this. But this was not to be. The suit filed against the United States Steel Corporation offended Roosevelt mortally. Among the allegations of the government was one which struck deep in his Achilles heel, his ego. For it was charged in the bill that the steel trust's monopolistic strength had been augmented during the panic of 1907 when, by deceiving and misleading President Roosevelt, it had obtained permission to take over the Tennessee Coal, Iron and Railroad Company.

"Roosevelt Fooled," proclaimed newspaper headlines the next day.[45]

This specification was not placed in the petition by Taft. He did not know of its existence until it was too late. But ignorance is the weakest of defenses for a president of the United States. Nor did it matter that the specification was true. It was another of the strategical mistakes— perhaps the most serious of them all— which led to the ultimate downfall of William Howard Taft.

Although he had dined with H. C. Frick of the United States Steel Corporation, to the consternation of Archie Butt, Taft cer-

[41] Taft to Wickersham, Jan. 22, 1912. [42] Wickersham to Taft, Jan. 26, 1912. [43] Wickersham to Hilles, Feb. 13, 1912. [44] Taft to H. W. Taft, Oct. 29, 1911. [45] J. M. Dickinson to Taft, Sept. 21, 1925.

tainly had no reverence for the company itself. In June, 1910, he instructed the attorney general to transmit to a House committee all evidence in his files relating to possible violation of the Sherman act.[46] He co-operated with Secretary of Commerce and Labor Nagel during an inquiry into the barbaric labor conditions whereby it was shown that a quarter of some 90,000 workers in the iron and steel industry labored twelve hours daily for seven days a week. It was also brought out that almost half of these employees were paid less than eighteen cents an hour.[47] Taft was deaf to the pleas which followed the Standard Oil and Tobacco Trust decisions that a suit against the steel corporation would merely further disturb business. Wickersham reported "all sorts of pressure" upon him for "a statement . . . that the steel combine was not to be prosecuted." No such statement was made.[48]

The attorney general considered himself disqualified from taking charge because he had served as attorney for the corporation in the past. Because of this, the President instructed Solicitor General Bowers and, after his death, Solicitor General F. W. Lehman to act.[49] The final arrangement was the appointment of former Secretary of War Dickinson as a special assistant to prepare an action in equity against the United States Steel Corporation. In September, 1911, the attorney general told the President that this would be done "as speedily as possible," probably by the middle of October. Taft officially approved this course of action.[50]

The utmost secrecy was preserved to prevent possible speculation in steel securities. Fourteen years afterward Dickinson drafted a letter explaining exactly what had happened. He told Taft that he had never brought the bill to his attention. Wickersham, alone, had seen the draft. This, Dickinson said, had been written in Nashville, Tennessee, after two months of study:

When I studied the question and drew the allegations in regard to the acquirement of the Tennessee Coal, Iron and Railroad Company by the United States Steel Corporation, I felt then and I feel now that President Roosevelt in effect sanctioned what was unlawful. My relations with him had for many years been of the closest

[46] Taft to Wickersham, June 23, 1910. [47] Nagel to Taft, July 29, 1911. [48] Wickersham to Taft, Sept. 29, 1911. [49] Taft to F. W. Lehman, Jan. 22, 1911. [50] Wickersham to Taft, Sept. 7, 1911.

character. I was then his warm friend and admirer and have so continued up to the present time. I felt that he had been deceived and that if the whole facts had been placed before him, he would not have taken the course that he did. . . . There was nothing said about him that reflected upon his integrity, patriotism or judgment. What was said was based entirely upon his having been misled by a failure to put the whole matter before him.

Taft had gone west in September. "I feel confident that you never saw the bill nor these allegations about Colonel Roosevelt," Dickinson wrote. He recalled that the President had passed through Chicago on his way east after the litigation had started. Knowing that Taft would be anxious for details, Dickinson had called upon him there.

"Mac, what is this about the bill against the steel corporation, Colonel Roosevelt and the Tennessee Coal, Iron and Railroad Company?" he remembered that Taft had asked.

Thereupon, the special prosecutor had explained the case in detail.[51]

Thus Taft could plead ignorance to the suit which so greatly offended Roosevelt. Attorney General Wickersham, on the other hand, had no such excuse. He remembered that Dickinson had submitted a draft for approval. He remembered that it was drawn in the all-inclusive phraseology characteristic of Dickinson and nearly all other southern lawyers.

"I don't want you to put anything in that you cannot prove," the attorney general warned.

"I can prove everything there," Dickinson answered.[52]

So the bill was filed on October 26, 1911. Wickersham assured the President that Dickinson was confident it was a "matter of ready proof, either by records or by testimony easily obtained." [53] But no records or testimony could conceivably convince Roosevelt that he had erred in sanctioning the absorption of the Tennessee Company. He had already denied this allegation repeatedly. He had told the House committee which investigated the steel corporation that the results of the merger had been "beneficial from every standpoint. . . . I never had any doubt of the wisdom of

[51] Dickinson to Taft, Sept. 21, 1925.   [52] Wickersham to author, Jan. 23, 1935.
[53] Wickersham to Taft, Oct. 26, 1911.

my action— not for a moment." [54] His answer to Dickinson's bill of complaint was equally vehement. It was not true that he had been deceived by Gary and Frick.

"I reaffirm everything," was his final shot in an editorial in the *Outlook*.[55]

Until now, perhaps, a chance existed that the friction between Taft and Roosevelt would not last. There was an outside chance that harmony, of a sort, might be achieved again. But it was not possible after the steel suit. Toward the middle of January, 1912, Roosevelt's younger sister, Mrs. Douglas Robinson, was a guest at the home of Alice Longworth in Washington. Archie Butt was also present and took Mrs. Robinson in to lunch. He found "only a great sadness in her mind— no resentment, no bitterness, only a deep regret that things should have turned out as they have." But Mrs. Robinson said, wrote the military aide, that her brother would "never forgive the President for introducing or allowing his name to be introduced into the steel suit."

"Oh, Major Butt," she said. ". . . If it had not been for that steel suit! I was talking with Theodore only last week, and he said that he could never forgive."

"Of course you know that the President never saw that suit until it was filed?"

"Yes," said Mrs. Robinson, "and Theodore knows that, and that in his eyes is the worst feature of the case— that such a thing could have been done without his knowledge." [56]

An impartial examination of the evidence can lead to no conclusion except that Roosevelt had acted hastily and without due regard for the facts. After all, the incident had been one of those financial problems so baffling to a president who knew little about finance. The crisis in New York had been acute when the markets closed on Saturday, October 27, 1907. A reassurance by Archbishop Farley at a special mass the next morning— "I have confidence in the banks," said his Grace— was not convincing enough for J. P. Morgan.

One large factor in the distressed situation was the fact that some $5,000,000 in the stock of the Tennessee Coal and Iron Com-

---

[54] Pringle, H. F., *Theodore Roosevelt, a Biography*, p. 445. [55] *Outlook*, Nov. 18, 1911. [56] Butt, Archie, *Taft and Roosevelt*, Vol. II, p. 813.

pany was held as collateral by Moore & Schley, a brokerage house, and that this could not be moved. The firm might crash on Monday, which would drag down other Wall Street firms and banks. At a conference in Morgan's library on Sunday a plan was evolved; briefly, that the United States Steel Corporation should purchase the Tennessee Coal and Iron for $45,000,000, thereby rehabilitate its stock and thereby save Moore & Schley. But would Roosevelt, the trust buster, penalize this altruism with a suit charging that United States Steel was in violation of the Sherman act? A special train carried Messrs. Gary and Frick to Washington that night. Roosevelt interrupted his breakfast to see them before the market opened on Monday morning. Judge Gary explained that the steel corporation did not really want the Tennessee concern and that $45,000,000 was rather more than it was worth. He subsequently quoted the President as saying that he would not, under the circumstances, object to the purchase. Roosevelt's own explanation was that Gary and Frick told him a "certain business firm," the name of which they did not mention, would fail unless the deal went through. He was under the impression that a "big trust company" would also crash. So, while he could not specifically advise the action, he "felt it no public duty . . . to interpose any objections."

But the heads of Moore & Schley, the "business concern" in question, later testified that a mere loan of $5,000,000 would have relieved their embarrassment. By 1908, Judge Gary was testifying that $200,000,000, even two or three times that gigantic sum, was a fair enough valuation on the T. C. and I. In the passage of time it became increasingly clear that $45,000,000, the price actually paid, was an extraordinary bargain.[57] Frick, however, insisted for years that the steel corporation had acted with the highest motives. He had been opposed to buying the Tennessee company "at any price," he said, and had agreed only to "save the country from a very disastrous panic." Mr. Frick was deeply grieved when the Taft administration made the purchase a specification in its suit for dissolution. He felt that Taft had bowed to the clamor of mob will in permitting the suit to be brought.[58]

[57] Pringle, H. F., op. cit., pp. 440-45. [58] Harvey, George, Henry Clay Frick, the Man, pp. 310-311.

AUNT DELIA TORREY, TAFT'S AUNT, IN 1909

See page 622]

THE TAFT HOME IN MURRAY BAY—IN WINTER, AS THE TAFTS NEVER SAW IT

The suit was to drag on for years. The Supreme Court finally ruled, in March, 1920, that the United States Steel Corporation was not a monopoly within the meaning of the Sherman act. So nothing whatever was gained by citing the Tennessee company on October 26, 1911. It did nothing to aid the slow, hard struggle toward corporation control. It meant, merely, that a rapprochement with Theodore Roosevelt was impossible.

—6—

Further fuel was added to the fires of bitterness when action was brought in April, 1912, to dissolve the International Harvester Company. This would be among the issues of the 1912 campaign, for George W. Perkins, a director of the company, was one of Roosevelt's most active backers. The history of the International Harvester Company would be described by President Taft when, at last, he surrendered to desperate necessity and took the stump in his own defense. The charge would be made that Roosevelt, as president, had not been duly diligent in bringing the company to account. Not Taft but the Warrior of Armageddon— such would be the accusation— was the friend of big business.

The President and Attorney General Wickersham appear to have believed that the International Harvester Company would mend its ways after the Supreme Court had ruled in the Standard Oil and Tobacco cases. H. H. Kohlsaat, the politician-editor of Chicago, urged in the summer of 1911 that no suit be started until the company had been given an opportunity to work out a dissolution plan. The President thereupon instructed Wickersham to wait.[59] But Wickersham grew discouraged as the weeks passed. He reported in November that "practically nothing" had been done; his judgment was that "they will do nothing that we can possibly approve until we actually bring suit against them." [60] Taft's patience lasted, however, until the following spring. On April 24, 1912, he conferred with attorneys for the company and decided that no chance of valid voluntary reform existed. He instructed

[59] Kohlsaat to Taft, Aug. 3, 1911; Wickersham to Rudolph Forster, Sept. 15, 1911.
[60] Wickersham to Taft, Nov. 4, 1911.

the attorney general to file the bill against the company imme-diately.[61]

As Election Day of 1912 approached, the President reviewed his trust-control program and called it "firm, consistent and effective." In the seven and one-half years of Theodore Roosevelt's incum-bency, he pointed out, forty-four cases against monopolies had been started. In less than four years, his own administration had brought twenty-two civil suits while, in criminal actions, forty-five indict-ments had been found.

"Great corporations seeking to monopolize industry have been dissolved," the President said. ". . . It is not surprising that the powerful interests which hitherto have enjoyed immunity from prosecution should employ strenuous and devious methods to create the impression that these prosecutions are ineffective, on the one hand, and certain to destroy the prosperity of the nation on the other. . . . Time will demonstrate the source of the opposition to my enforcement of the antitrust law." [62]

President Taft declined, however, to follow a recommendation by his attorney general that the National City Bank of New York should be forbidden to operate the National City Company as its subsidiary. The National City Company had been organized in the summer of 1911 for the purpose, according to its circular, of making investments and transacting "other business which though often very profitable may not be within the express corporate powers of a national bank." Wickersham told Taft it was "perfectly obvious" that this was in violation of the national banking act.[63] Secretary of the Treasury MacVeagh, on the other hand, assured the President that the arrangement was legal. He said that Secretary of State Knox held the same view.[64] Late in August, the attorney general urged immediate action so that "this flagrant evasion of the statute" would be "brought to book." [65] Taft's answer was to request a detailed opinion from Wickersham and Solicitor General Lehman.[66]

Wickersham submitted Lehman's opinion on November 15, 1911, and concurred in all its details. This had cited, among

[61] Taft to Wickersham, April 24, 1912. [62] *Saturday Evening Post,* Oct. 18, 1912. [63] F. W. Lehman to Wickersham, Wickersham to Taft, Aug. 1, 1911. [64] MacVeagh to Taft, Aug. 23, 1911. [65] Wickersham to Hilles, Aug. 24, 1911. [66] Taft to Wickersham, Sept. 7, 1911.

other dangers, the possibility that the National City Company would acquire control of many banks.

"Examples are recent and significant," Lehman wrote, "of the peril to a bank, incident to the dual and diverse interests of its officers and directors. If many enterprises and many banks are brought and bound together in the nexus of a great holding corporation, the failure of one may involve all in a common disaster." [67]

The President, dissuaded by MacVeagh and Knox, concluded to take no action, however.[68] Had he followed Wickersham's lead and had the Supreme Court upheld the attorney general's contention, it is interesting to note, a banking crisis of twenty years later might have been less grave. For the banks could not, to the same degree, have been pouring their money into the stock market. And some of the crazy holding-company structures— which seemed to tower to the sky— might have been less flimsy and might not have crashed so disastrously.

[67] Lehman to Wickersham, Nov. 6, 1911; Wickersham to Taft, Nov. 15, 1911.
[68] Taft to Wickersham, Feb. 20, 1913; Wickersham to author, Jan. 23, 1935.

CHAPTER XXXV

DOLLAR DIPLOMACY

". . . it is pathetic," wrote Secretary of State Bryan to President Wilson in the summer of 1913, "to see Nicaragua struggling in the grip of an oppressive financial agreement . . . we see in these transactions a perfect picture of dollar diplomacy. The financiers charge excessive rates on the ground that they must be *paid* for the risk that they take and as soon as they collect their pay for the risk, they then proceed to demand of the respective governments that the *risk* shall be eliminated by governmental coercion. No wonder the people of these little republics are aroused to revolution by what they regard as a sacrifice of their interests."[1]

Mr. Bryan's description of the operations of "dollar diplomacy" was extremely accurate, and the fact that he was referring to Latin America does not detract from its application to other nations, principally China. But there was another side to the problem. President Taft, under whom this form of diplomacy was encouraged, spoke on the subject in May, 1910:

The theory that the field of diplomacy does not include in any degree commerce and the increase of trade relations is one to which Mr. Knox [the secretary of state] and this administration do not subscribe. We believe it to be of the utmost importance that while our foreign policy should not be turned a hair's breadth from the straight path of justice, it may be well made to include active intervention to secure for our merchandise and our capitalists opportunity for profitable investment which shall insure to the benefit of both countries concerned. There is nothing inconsistent in the promotion of peaceful relations, and the promotion of trade relations, and if the protection which the United States shall assure to her citizens in the assertion of just rights under investment made in foreign countries, shall promote the amount of such trade, it is a result to be commended. To call such diplomacy "dollar diplomacy" . . . is to

[1] Baker, R. S., *Woodrow Wilson, Life and Letters,* Vol. IV, pp. 437-438.

ignore entirely a most useful office to be performed by a government in its dealings with foreign governments.[2]

"If the American dollar can aid suffering humanity and lift the burden of financial difficulty from states with which we live on terms of intimate intercourse and earnest friendship . . ." said Secretary Knox in December, 1911, "all I can say is that it would be hard to find better employment." [3]

But who would decide whether the dollar would really work its wonders thus altruistically? The bankers, it may be assumed, were less interested in high motives than in profits. The United States government had no adequate way to determine whether loans to foreign countries, for these were the chief objective of dollar diplomacy, carried fair interest rates. The inevitable outcome, if obligations were not met, was a demand that the United States government collect the debt. The Taft years, however, were ones during which American capital was seeking foreign outlets. The evil effects of the 1907 panic had vanished and funds were available. It was, moreover, an era when American industrialists sought orders from abroad. Dollar diplomacy worked two ways; it provided a market for surplus capital and, through agreements that the loans would be used for American goods, it increased the business of manufacturers of steel and iron, railroad equipment, battleships and munitions.

"Every diplomat a salesman" might, to a degree, have been a slogan of the Taft years. Thus from Athens came word that the American minister to Greece, George H. Moses, had succeeded in obtaining for the Bethlehem Steel Company the contract for the guns and armor of a new Greek man-of-war. He had achieved this despite the united and vicious opposition of the European armor pool, Minister Moses told the President with pride, and although the pool had been aided to the utmost by its diplomatic representatives. The Bethlehem company, Mr. Moses reported, would receive between $500,000 and $600,000 more than under the original bid.[4]

In Peru, at about the same time, negotiations were in progress

[2] *Addresses*, Vol. XVIII, pp. 240-241. [3] Bemis, S. F., *The American Secretaries of State and Their Diplomacy*, Vol. IX, pp. 327-328.

for an American naval coaling station at Chimbote Bay. President Leguia of that somewhat rickety nation had informed H. Clay Howard, the American minister, of his country's willingness to cede enough land for the purpose. He had declared that it would strengthen his country to have so powerful a nation interested, to this extent, in Peru. He agreed that an actual defensive alliance was probably impossible. Minister Howard was also active as a salesman. He reported a conversation with Señor Leguia in which he had told his Excellency of knowledge in the United States that Peru had ordered two submarines and a warship from France. The proposition for a naval station, Minister Howard then said he had told Leguia, would receive more consideration "if I could first cable that a contract for American-made submarines had been executed, and one-third of the purchase money bonds delivered." Leguia saw the reason in this. He promised that it would be done immediately.[5]

The commercial proselyting was carried on even by the members of Taft's Cabinet. In February, 1912, Secretary of War Stimson addressed an official letter to Taft regarding a request by the Chilean government for the assignment of an American artillery officer to instruct its troops. Mr. Stimson urged that this be done. Guidance of South American armies had too long been in the hands of European officers, he said, and the presence of a United States officer would bring closer the two nations. Such was Stimson's official letter, to be placed in the regular presidential files. On the following day, February 29, the secretary of war sent another communication with the suggestion that its contents should not be made public or transmitted to Congress. There was another reason for the assignment of the American officers, he therein pointed out. Most of the South American countries were about to remodel their coast defenses. If their coast artillery stations were under American supervision it was very probable that an American type of seacoast defense material would be used. And this, he said, was no small matter to the manufacturers of the United States.[6]

After all, why not? The foreigners would receive the best quality of American manufactures. American industrialists would

[4] G. H. Moses to Taft, July 26, 1912. [5] Meyer to Taft, Nov. 11, 1911 [6] Stimson to Taft, Feb. 28, 29, 1911.

profit. Only occasionally was a voice raised in opposition. Among the few was that of *LaFollette's Weekly,* the personal organ of the Wisconsin senator. This charged that dollar diplomacy had "traded our navy's secrets" for contracts for the shipbuilding company of Charles M. Schwab; by that the weekly meant that our naval designers had co-operated in the construction of foreign war vessels. It said that the United States was interfering in Turkey to obtain railroad concessions for American financiers. It said that New York bankers had been encouraged to make loans in Manchuria.

"Is there anything," it asked, "which Mr. Knox and President Taft will not give to foreign nations in exchange for 'business' desired by their friends in Wall Street?" [7]

—2—

But this was a jaundiced view. The investment of American capital had, in China at least, its sincere proponents. It is not easy, for instance, to impugn the motives of Willard D. Straight.

He was among the most versatile of men. Although trained in architecture at Cornell University, he had gone to China after graduation in 1901 as an official for the Imperial Maritime Customs Service. Then he became a newspaper correspondent; his first major assignment was the Russo-Japanese War. By 1906, Straight had entered the American diplomatic service. He held various minor posts in China and Korea. He spent a brief period in Cuba. His most important post was as consul general at Mukden, Manchuria. In the five years since graduation from college, Straight had studied the Far Eastern question profoundly. He was now only twenty-five years old. He was to be the spokesman and leading proponent of the doctrine that China's territorial integrity might be preserved if American funds, in large quantities, were invested in its internal improvements. Straight would not admit that Japan, the war lord of the Eastern world, must be allowed to have its way in Manchuria as in Korea.

Mukden, in 1906, was a crossroad in the East. Railroad lines leading southwest to Peking formed a junction with the lines to

[7] *LaFollette's Weekly,* March 4, 1911.

Korea on the southeast. Directly south lay Port Arthur, awarded to Japan after the war. Northward across the Manchurian wastes lay incomprehensible Siberia and its great railway. So the consulate at Mukden was a post of vast importance. Chinese and Japanese officials paused there. European observers called. American army officers who had been detailed to the Japanese or Russian forces stopped to learn, if they could, about the latest imperial designs of Japan. They found an unusual host in Consul General Straight. He had surrounded himself with an able staff. Through the long years ahead its members recalled exciting days when the Manchurian dust storms filled the air. They also remembered glamorous nights. They remembered the nights most, perhaps; surely poignant memories of them came back on a day in December, 1918, when word came from Paris that Major Straight of the American Expeditionary Forces was dead from pneumonia.

Straight seems to have been endowed with more than his share of gifts. He was a financier and a diplomat. He was an extraordinary linguist. He was an artist of rare skill. He could sing, self-accompanied on the guitar, in a voice which was effortless and clear. It was thus that his friends remembered him— after dinner in the gardens of the consulate. A moon might hang in the sky, slightly tinged with red if the winds had been moving the dust that day. The air was soft with the fragrance of Oriental blossoms. And Straight would strum on his guitar and would offer old Cornell songs, the ballads of Kipling or Negro melodies. But what lay behind the beauty? Would Japan seize Manchuria as she had seized Korea? And when would her ambitions turn to the Philippine Islands? And what would be the outcome of discrimination on the Pacific coast against Japanese immigrants? [8]

Straight, like Taft and Knox, became a defender of dollar diplomacy. It was, he said, "the financial expression of John Hay's 'Open Door' policy . . . which makes of international finance a guaranty for the preservation, rather than the destruction of China's integrity. . . . 'Dollar diplomacy' is a logical manifestation of our national growth, and of the rightful assumption by the United States of a more important place at the council table of nations

[8] *Dictionary of American Biography,* Vol. XVIII, pp. 121-122; Croly, Herbert, *Willard Straight,* p. 219.

... a government desiring to secure a market for its nationals must, because of the pressure of its competitors, either acquire territory or insist on an equality of commercial opportunity. It must either stake out its own claim or induce other interested powers to preserve the 'Open Door.' . . . The people of the United States do not desire fresh territory over-seas. . . . A far-seeing administration has therefore inaugurated a new policy, the alliance of diplomacy, with industry, commerce and finance." [9]

All of which would have been far more effective— these laudable purposes might have come to fruition— had the record of the United States been more friendly to China. By the Burlingame treaty of 1868 the United States had guaranteed free passage of all citizens from one country to another. By 1894, however, Chinese were not admitted to the United States. Indignities, even murders, had been perpetrated against Chinese in San Francisco.[10] Nor was there basis for confidence in Taft's own activities, as the emissary of President Roosevelt, in the Far East. In July, 1905, it will be recalled, Secretary of War Taft was entirely complacent over the domination of Korea by Japan and was, in fact, the go-between whereby Roosevelt made virtually a secret treaty endorsing Japanese influence. On a second trip to the Far East, in the fall of 1907, Taft cabled the President regarding Japan's determination to control China. He expressed no disapproval of the policy. Willard Straight, who conferred with Taft at Vladivostok in November of that year, seems to have misunderstood the views of the secretary of war. He reported that Taft was a defender of Chinese rights— possibly he was misled by outer amiability— and said that if President Roosevelt took the advice of his Cabinet member he "will be inclined to regard Manchuria as a fair field and not one which must be approached with special regard for the susceptibilities of the Japanese." [11]

The Chinese, particularly the young patriots who had been educated in Harvard, Yale and Princeton and who were soon to overthrow their backward empire, would have been even more dismayed had they been privileged to read confidential letters

[9] Straight, W. D., *China's Loan Negotiations, An Address*, 1912. [10] Bland, J. O. P., *Recent Events and Present Policies in China*, p. 304. [11] Croly, Herbert, *op. cit.*, pp. 249-251.

which passed between President Taft and his predecessor three years later. The discussion related, specifically, to the Japanese immigration question on the Coast, but it also touched on Korea and Manchuria. Roosevelt told Taft in December, 1910, that the Japanese were very sensitive regarding their vital interests in Manchuria, where their powers and intentions must "if we are sensible, be judged on the actual facts of the case and not by any mere study of treaties." [12] Roosevelt repeated these forthright views in an interview with Knox, which the secretary of state reported to his chief. Roosevelt, it appeared, had conferred with Baron Takahira, formerly Japanese ambassador to the United States, while in Europe on his way back from Africa. Knox wrote:

What he told me he said to Takahira was this: that the American people would not tolerate Japanese laborers coming to this country in large numbers . . . that upon the other hand the United States should recognize Japan's paramount influence and interest in Korea and Manchuria; that the situation in the East should be dealt with as a fact and not on theories of interest based upon treaties; that the Japanese were an ambitious, proud and progressive people, greatly elated by their success in the war with Russia; that they were rapidly increasing in numbers and in their activities, and that they needed and must have room for expansion, and if they kept away from our shores, and we should insist that they must, that we should not interfere with their plans in Korea and Manchuria.

The colonel stated that the Chinese were weak, lacked cohesion, and were unreliable; that we could not depend upon them as allies and that we should not get into an attitude of supporting them against the Japanese in our efforts to prevent what the colonel conceived to be the inevitable movement of the Japanese in Manchuria with the necessary consequences of gradually increasing control over the Manchurian provinces.[13]

What Roosevelt was proposing, in effect, was a deal whereby California was to be permitted to bar Japanese immigrants while Japan worked her will in Manchuria; such were the views of the ex-President who would soon demand war with Germany for violation of the Belgian neutrality treaty. So strongly did Roosevelt

[12] Roosevelt to Taft, Dec. 8, 1910. [13] Knox to Taft, Dec. 19, 1910.

feel on the subject that he reiterated to Taft on December 22, 1910, the vital necessity for dealing softly with Japan. The fact was, he said, that a war with Japan over Manchuria would require a fleet as powerful as that of England and an army as large as Germany's. An alliance with China would be worse than useless. As for the open door, Roosevelt agreed that it was a good thing and might be effective in the future. But the policy was worthless as soon as any nation was willing to risk war rather than endure its limitations.[14]

Secretary Knox, however, had no stomach for such strong meat. He prepared a draft reply for the President to sign and send to Roosevelt. This denied any intention "to interfere with any legitimate purpose of Japan in Manchuria." The United States would not block the migrations of Japanese citizens in the Far East as long as its commercial rights were not infringed. Knox continued, on behalf of Taft:

Why the Japanese *need* Manchuria any more than does China who owns it now, or why it is more "vital" to them than it is to China is not apparent.

I admit that reference to the "Open Door" has been abused, often through misunderstanding of what was meant by the expression. What we mean by the "Open Door" in Manchuria is surely nothing more than fair play for our own commercial interests, which certainly are not insignificant, and for China, territorially and administratively.

That certainly is the meaning of our policy in China, as enunciated by Secretary Hay and continued and developed under your own administration. The aim of the present administration has been merely to reduce the theory to practice. . . .

There has been no serious thought of an alliance with China. . . . But your letter seems to imply that there is no alternative between silently renouncing our historic policy in China whenever it may cross the interest of another power and being prepared to go to war in the defense of that policy. . . . Whether the American people would ever go to war or not in defense of our interests in China I am not prepared to say. But in any case, it is certainly not for us to prejudice our case at the start by admitting to the world that we

[14] Roosevelt to Taft, Dec. 22, 1910.

would *not,* under any circumstances, go to war. We can at least allow others to draw their own conclusions. . . .

I still believe that the wisest and best way . . . is for us to stand firmly by our pronounced policy and let it be known . . . that we expect fair play all round. The Japanese government is certainly not indifferent to public opinion, and it is much better that we should continue to try to bring Japan's policy in China up to the level of ours, where we may differ, than to lower our policy to the levels of hers.[15]

But the President was unwilling to commit himself in such detail. He conferred with Knox and Senator Root, whose knowledge of the problem was detailed. He delayed his answer for a fortnight; it was a pallid version compared with the Knox draft:

I assume that in what you say about our treatment of Japan in Manchuria you mean that there shall be implied an understanding that, while we should not take any steps as regards Manchuria which will give the Japanese cause to feel that we are hostile to them or are menacing their interests, nevertheless we are not to abandon our rights to equal opportunities under the open-door principle. We have carefully refrained from going beyond the natural and proper steps to foster and promote our own competitive interests in that region. I suppose that we could not properly do less and I quite agree with you that we should not undertake to do more.[16]

This, however, was not in the least what Roosevelt had meant. It all must have been more than a little confusing to the Japanese. For Roosevelt, however careful to disavow his official standing, had given his views to Takahira. How could the far-off Japanese realize that an ex-president's views meant nothing, particularly when they were aware that this ex-president had elected the man who succeeded him in the White House?

In substance, the Taft-Knox Far Eastern policy was a forced and unhappy marriage between idealism and commercialism. The inherent weakness of the policy was due to the amateurish failure of the State Department to acquire accurate information on Asiatic-European affairs. In his memoirs, Roosevelt criticized Taft's management of the situation.[17] He meant, largely, that Taft had not

---

[15] Draft by Knox for Taft, no date, not mailed. [16] Taft to Roosevelt, Jan. 17, 1911.
[17] Roosevelt, Theodore, *Autobiography,* p. 380.

followed Roosevelt's program which was actually abandonment of the open door in return for Japan's friendship. Both administrations, in truth, labored under misapprehensions. Roosevelt's hope, when he aided in bringing the Russo-Japanese War to a close, had been that the two powers would check each other in the East and thereby preserve the interests of the United States. Taft was not aware— he gave, at least, no indication of it— that the Far Eastern tangle had changed sharply in the years between his 1905 interview with Katsura in Japan and 1910. He did not know, or did not fully appreciate, the alliance between Great Britain and Japan whereby England's interests in North China had been sacrificed in return for peace in Europe. He does not seem to have known, either, of the rapprochement between Japan and Russia. Through secret treaties with Russia, Japan had violated her pledge to protect the open door in Manchuria. This was known in all the chancelleries of Europe. The cynical eyes of their ministers saw China only as a means for peace in Europe. If "spheres of influence" would prevent war, they would be authorized. If partition would do it, partition would be decreed.[18] But President Taft and Secretary Knox plunged on in the belief, nurtured by Willard Straight, that the investment of American dollars would bring peace, too. They played a lone hand and they were destined to fail.

—3—

Philander C. Knox was an excellent lawyer. He was a shrewd politician too, and Taft leaned on him more, perhaps, than on any other member of the Cabinet. Knox had helped to form the Carnegie Steel Corporation in 1900. Roosevelt had selected him for attorney general in 1901, and he had instituted Roosevelt's celebrated antitrust suit against the Northern Securities Company. He left Roosevelt's Cabinet to become senator from Pennsylvania. But Knox, although demonstrably competent, was not really trained in the complicated mysteries of foreign affairs and his appointment as secretary of state was due to Taft's desire for as many lawyers as possible in his official family. Ambassador James Bryce, ever an

[18] Dennett, Tyler, *Roosevelt and the Russo-Japanese War*, p. 324.

objective student of American affairs and personalities, thought Knox "gave the impression of having cared little, known little or thought little of foreign politics until he became a minister."

The first project for a financial invasion of China was conceived by the extremely practical E. H. Harriman and was encouraged by the idealistic Willard Straight. Harriman had a grandiose plan for a round-the-world transportation system. He dreamed of a combination which would link his transcontinental lines to his Pacific steamship holdings. He would then use the South Manchurian Railway north to the Trans-Siberian Railway, where he expected to acquire trackage rights. The final stage would be by steamer, westward on the Atlantic. Harriman was in Yokohama in the summer and fall of 1905 where Count Katsura, the Japanese premier, and Marquis Ito, Japan's elder statesman, agreed tentatively that American capitalists might acquire a half interest in the South Manchurian line. This had been forfeited by Russia at Portsmouth. But other influences in Japan strenuously objected to the proposal and it was abandoned. Straight had discussed the plan with Harriman and had encouraged him to press it.[19]

This was the first failure. The next was a plan, apparently initiated by Straight, for a Manchurian bank with $20,000,000 in American capital. His Excellency Tang Shao-ki, a graduate of Yale who was governor of Fengtien in Manchuria, signed a memorandum agreeing to this. It would have supplied funds for railroad and other internal improvements in Manchuria. This time, however, the scheme was blocked by the depression in the United States. The plan reached New York at the moment when the important bankers were far more concerned with the panic of 1907 than with China.[20] Straight was not unduly discouraged, however. He returned to the United States in September, 1908, to urge Harriman and his bankers, Kuhn, Loeb & Company, to carry on with their project for railroad acquisitions. They were favorably inclined. China's suspicion of the United States had been somewhat allayed by President Roosevelt's recommendation that the United States remit a portion of the Boxer indemnity. Its leaders now proposed an international loan of $300,000,000, sponsored by the United States.

[19] Bland, J. O. P., op. cit., p. 309; Dennett, Tyler, op. cit., pp. 311-313. [20] Croly, Herbert, op. cit., pp. 240-242.

His Excellency Tang set out for the United States to urge it. But at this point the powerful Empress Dowager of China and the Emperor Kuang Hsu died. Again, the negotiations failed because the friendly premier, Yuan Shih-kai, was dismissed.[21]

All these negotiations, it should be noted, were prior to the inauguration of President Taft. ". . . the President and Mr. Knox," Straight recalled, "became keenly interested and the Department of State desired, as soon as an opportune moment should arise, to reopen the question of customs revision . . . as well as currency reform, in accordance with the stipulations of our Commercial Treaty with China of 1903. With a view to taking up the proposed loan at the proper time, the American bankers . . . closely followed the situation." [22] It soon became clear that China, at the instigation of England, France and Germany, was to violate the terms of that treaty. By now, Straight was no longer in the consular service. He was the agent of an American banking group: J. P. Morgan & Company, Kuhn, Loeb & Company, the National City Bank, the First National Bank and E. H. Harriman.

By the 1903 treaty, reiterated the following year, China had promised that American capital would be granted equal opportunity with that of England and the European countries. The Taft administration echoed the indignation of J. P. Morgan and his associates when this appeared unlikely. The United States minister at Peking, W. W. Rockhill, was ordered to give warning that China might forfeit the Boxer indemnity refund unless it reversed this policy. President Taft went to the unprecedented length of sending a cable directly to Prince Chun, who had become regent of China. It was a sharp message, which expressed official disturbance over the rumors that American capital might be discriminated against in a proposed loan for the Hukuang railways running westward and southward from Hankow. The President pointed to the fact that "the wishes of the United States are based not only on China's promises of 1903 and 1904, confirmed last month, but also upon broad national and personal principles of equity and good policy . . ." Taft explained that he had "resorted to this somewhat unusually direct communication to Your Im-

[21] *Ibid.*, pp. 269-278. [22] Straight, W. D., *op. cit.*, p. 9.

perial Highness because of the high importance that I attach to the successful result of our present negotiations." [23]

"No one could be more friendly to China than we are," Taft insisted in a private letter, "and it is as much in her interest as it is in ours that we insist on having the part of the loan which was stipulated . . . for the reason that we shall be in a position where we can exert our influence to save China and help her in her development whenever opportunity shall arise." [24]

China backed down in the face of these threats and warnings; the villainous British, French and German interests were thwarted in their hope for a monopoly. But months and years of wrangling were ahead. Meanwhile, Knox conceived still another plan. He proposed to the powers of Europe that the railways in Manchuria should be neutralized. Surely this would minimize the danger of partition in China and, at the least, hold ajar the open door. Knox's plan was for an international syndicate to purchase the railway holdings of Russia and Japan. The existing lines and any that might be built were then to be in control of this syndicate. But Knox failed, again, because he was not familiar with Europe's network of treaties. England and Russia were conspiring to isolate Germany. The United States policy, wrote J. O. P. Bland, who was on the scene, was one "of righteousness, tempered by enlightened self-interest, but it required the delicate handling of a Metternich to make it effective and to dominate the equally enlightened self-interest of the other powers." [25]

Secretary Knox, unschooled in statecraft, was far from being a Metternich. One possible path to success was open and he did not take it. He might have forced neutralization in Manchuria if he had first obtained consent of Russia. Japan might then have been forced to come in. Instead, Knox addressed a note to Great Britain on the subject in November, 1909. Sir Edward Grey replied on November 25 that his government approved "in principle," but added that no step should be taken which would offend Japan. Incredibly, Knox does not seem to have realized that the actual answer was flat disapproval; he did not know that England was standing by her ally. He blundered on, with identical notes to

[23] Croly, Herbert, op. cit., pp. 293-295; Taft to Chun, July 15, 1909. [24] Taft to G. W. Painter, Sept. 6, 1909. [25] Bland, J. O. P., op. cit., p. 319.

France, Germany, Russia and Japan. On January 31, 1910, Russia notified China that neutralization must not even be attempted without the consent of St. Petersburg. On February 2— so similar were the notes that consultation between the two countries must have preceded their drafting— Japan ordered China to do nothing without consulting Tokyo. A political prophet might have read into the answers then made to Knox's proposal an accurate alignment of the nations which would be at each other's throats by the summer of 1914. Germany, of course, approved of neutralization in Manchuria. France, the ally of Russia, did not. On July 4, 1910, Russia and Japan signed a treaty of amity. This was the end of the open door in Manchuria.[26]

—4—

One other plan remained, a loan whereby China's currency would be stabilized. If the young Chinese who would soon be struggling with the agonies of revolution had illusions before, they had none now. On December 5, 1910, Liang Tun-yen— who had been sent to the United States by his government— called on Secretary Knox regarding a possible loan of 50,000,000 taels. He told the secretary of state that Great Britain was no longer friendly to China, owing to the alliance with Japan. If only the United States, itself, would make the loan, China would willingly consent to the appointment of a financial adviser.[27] Naturally enough, Liang viewed with foreboding any participation by Russia and Japan in a currency loan; it would be a new mortgage on his troubled country.

Again, Straight was the active proponent of the currency loan; in April, 1911, an agreement was signed by the representatives of the various bankers which specified equal participation. But an obstacle, by now, was the growing strength of the Young China party whose leaders, as Straight described it, greatly resented the bankers' demand that their agents be placed in control of Chinese finances as soon as a loan was granted. Straight recognized the

[26] Croly, Herbert, *op. cit.*, pp. 309-313, 331; Bland, J. O. P., *op. cit.*, pp. 319-322.
[27] State Department memorandum, Dec. 5, 1910.

necessity of such control in so chaotic a country, but he saw, too, that the Young China leaders regarded it as "subversive of China's sovereign rights."[28] There were additional complications. Ambassador W. J. Calhoun, who had succeeded Rockhill at Peking, transmitted to the State Department authenticated reports of statements made in Paris by Isvolsky, the Russian ambassador to France:

> The local manager French bank here has shown me in strict confidence a letter from his Paris manager dated November 12, 1911, in which the latter said that Isvolsky . . . had sent for him and told him that Russia and Japan . . . had agreed that for the future in all Chinese loans negotiated for territory north of the Great Wall in Mongolia or Manchuria participation therein must be allowed Russia and Japan on the basis of sixty per cent for them and forty for the quadruple groups. . . .
>
> Isvolsky further said that Russia and Japan now have a thorough understanding on the subject; that their policy is one and the same and they will resist together to the utmost any proposed departure therefrom. He further said they would likewise resist any neutralization policy . . . by the United States in Manchuria; that both Russia and Japan had acquired their interests there by the sacrifice of much blood and treasure while the Americans had made no sacrifices.[29]

No language could have been more plain. The State Department now knew that Russia and Japan would "resist together to the utmost" any attempt to float loans without their consent, any attempt to make neutral the Manchurian railways. But President Taft, whose ignorance of actual conditions in China was at least equal to that of Knox, continued to express optimism and pointed with pride, in his December, 1911, message to Congress, to preliminary loan agreements signed and to their ultimate salutary effect on the open door. He did not realize that the door had finally been jammed shut by Russia and Japan. The loan negotiations were ended by the Chinese revolution. A year later, however, the President still spoke of his "policy of encouraging financial in-

[28] Straight, W. D., op. cit., p. 15. [29] Calhoun to Knox, Dec. 5, 1911.

vestment" in China which, he said, "has had the result of giving new life and practical application to the open-door policy." [30]

Willard Straight knew that success, if it came at all, lay in the distant future. He sent to the President a speech in which he had reviewed the situation. Mr. Taft, he said, had "been so much interested in the Far East, and especially in these loan negotiations, that I trust you may find the document amusing at any rate. Up to the present time the results have been largely confined to literature and oratory. I trust that some day we shall have something to show besides 'hot air' and hope." [31]

It was to be further delayed, however, by Woodrow Wilson's hostility toward dollar diplomacy. Straight wasted no time. He called on Secretary of State Bryan on March 9, 1913, and asked for the administration's policy. Bryan was cordial but evasive; he knew nothing at all about the Chinese loan. But after study he was emphatically opposed and this was the conclusion reached by President Wilson also. The President said publicly that the conditions of the loan "touch very nearly the administrative independence of China itself" and the responsibility placed upon the United States might even involve "forcible interference." The enterprise was "obnoxious to the principles upon which the government of our people rests." This was a complete reversal of the Taft-Knox policy. No longer could the bankers count on a friendly State Department, so Straight and his backers withdrew from the group still trying to obtain the loan.[32]

—5—

All this while the Taft administration was also encouraging the penetration of the American dollar into Central and South America. To a degree, penetration was accomplished although the result did not always bring lasting happiness to the purchasers of Latin-American bonds. On the one hand, the problem was simpler than in the Far East because it did not involve the war apprehensions of Europe. But it was replete with complications too; deep

[30] *Messages,* Dec. 7, 1911, pp. 13-14; Dec. 3, 1912, p. 9. [31] Straight to Taft, Dec. 26, 1912. [32] Baker, R. S., *Woodrow Wilson, Life and Letters,* Vol. IV, pp. 69-72.

distrust of the United States existed in the republics lying to the South. It was a distrust born of incident after incident in the relations between the United States and the Latin-American nations. The distrust had now reached a new depth because of Theodore Roosevelt's seizure of Panama, his frequently expressed low opinion of "these Dagos" who were their leaders and because of his rugged amplification of the Monroe Doctrine.

President Taft's devotion to the Monroe Doctrine was slowly acquired, like a taste for olives. A brief six years before he became president, it will be recalled, Taft had expressed distaste for the doctrine. But that was in those well-nigh forgotten days when the nightmare of the White House had not yet caused Taft's large frame to toss in the night. He had not yet even taken office as secretary of war. Taft had been president for hardly a few months, however, before his opinion of the Latin-American countries was almost as robust as Roosevelt's. Those nations, Roosevelt had said, would "be happy if only they will be good." If they were wicked, chastisement by the United States would swiftly follow.[33]

Taft expressed it, at first, more smoothly. The "relation of guardian and ward . . ." he said, "helps along the cause of international peace and indicates progress and civilization." [34] The President was an amiable man with more than the normal amount of good will. But even Taft was soon exasperated as complications arose with Nicaragua and Santo Domingo. He would soon find it necessary to risk the bones of the United States marines; bones by no means unaccustomed, by the way, to peril in Latin America. By the end of 1909, Taft had concluded that he could never be contented until he possessed "some formal right to compel the peace between those Central-American governments." He yearned, he told Secretary Knox, for the "right to knock their heads together until they should maintain peace between them." [35] These were private expressions of irritation, naturally. Outwardly, the Taft administration sounded the same old notes of good will and benign brotherhood to which Latin Americans had, with growing cynicism, been listening for years. The secretary of state, for example, declared that the Monroe Doctrine required the United States to

[33] Pringle, H. F., *Theodore Roosevelt, a Biography,* pp. 294-295. [34] Taft to Royal Melandy, April 28, 1909. [35] Taft to Knox, Dec. 22, 1909.

"respond to the needs still felt by some few of our Latin-American neighbors in their progress toward good government, by assisting them to meet their just obligations and to keep out of trouble." Such, he added, had been Roosevelt's purpose in Santo Domingo.[36]

Otherwise obscure Santo Domingo was responsible for Roosevelt's enlargement of the Monroe Doctrine as expressed in his Corollary of 1904. Santo Domingo had piled up some $18,000,000 in foreign debts without the slightest apparent intention of paying them. Roosevelt was afraid that some European country would attempt to collect its money and, in doing so, might acquire territory. So he told Congress that the United States, alone, would undertake interference in the internal affairs of Latin-American nations. Interference, in the case of, Santo Domingo, took the form of sending representatives who supervised customs receipts and government expenditures in general. Roosevelt was not disturbed by the Senate's refusal to ratify the agreement with Santo Domingo by which this was done. He saw justification, enough, in the fact that great progress toward financial security was made and the danger of European intervention lifted.[37] A disgruntled Senate finally approved the Dominican treaty in February, 1907. Administration of the small country's affairs by the United States continued. In theory, Taft should have had no trouble with Santo Domingo.

The American suzerainty in Santo Domingo was successful from 1905 until November, 1911. At that time, in the words of a State Department summary submitted to Taft, President Ramon Caceres was "unfortunately assassinated." The power, according to the inevitable Latin-American custom, was seized by Alfredo Victoria, who was the head of the army. The comandante persuaded, by means not specified, his countrymen to select his uncle, Eladio Victoria, as temporary president. In February, 1912, he brought about, again by means not specified, the election of Uncle Eladio for a regular term. But the new President could not establish order. Several other aspirants for power arose. Disorder spread through a number of provinces. A quarrel broke out with Haiti over the boundary line between the two nations.

The most serious factor so far as the United States was con-

[36] Bemis, S. F., *op. cit.*, Vol. IX, p. 335. [37] Pringle, H. F., *op. cit.*, pp. 295-296.

cerned was the financial turmoil. In less than a year, the Dominican government increased its indebtedness by $1,500,000. The employees of the receiver general of customs had been dismissed and replaced with incompetents, a step which was in violation, at the least, of the spirit of the treaty. Meanwhile President Victoria had grown excessively unpopular and revolution hung, like the threat of a hurricane, over the miniature republic.

"Unless this government," concluded the State Department summary, "is prepared practically to take over the management of the Dominican Republic (which would be productive, no doubt, of a hue and cry throughout Latin America of the 'Yankee Peril') the solution of the problem is difficult." [38]

So President Taft, as though he did not have enough worries with the 1912 campaign under way, was forced to take action in Santo Domingo in the fall of that year. On September 19, Undersecretary of State Huntington Wilson submitted a lengthy series of notes which, he urged, should be pressed upon the Dominican minister for foreign affairs. In the usual diplomatic verbiage, these warned that the treaty with the United States had been violated. Prior to the notes, Mr. Wilson suggested, a first-class war vessel with an adequate landing force should be dispatched to Santo Domingo City. The arrival of the ship, he said, should "synchronize the presentation" of the communications from Washington. And should the "solemn presentation of such a note fail to produce the desired results, this government would be face to face with a situation involving whether the United States should sit by and see its whole Dominican policy fail . . . or should transmute its recommendations into demands which, of course, would involve preparedness to enforce these demands by such measures short of war as could be justified." Among other things, diplomatic relations should be severed. Also, continued Mr. Wilson with that euphemistic touch so characteristic of diplomatic correspondence, the customhouse should be subjected to "forcible protection"; the American policy might even include the "withholding of the customs revenues pending the installation of a government responsive to its obligations." [39]

[38] State Department memorandum, Sept. 17, 1912. [39] Wilson to Taft, Sept. 19, 1912.

Taft followed this advice, in part. He dispatched Brigadier General Frank McIntyre and a Mr. Doyle of the State Department as special commissioners to bring harmony. To assist them the U.S.S. *Prairie* with 750 marines was ordered to Santo Domingo.[40] But the American mixture of force and moral suasion did not bring tranquillity either. A harassed president of the United States— Election Day was but a few days off— was informed on October 29, 1912, that the revolutionists were rapidly overpowering President Victoria, that the customhouse employees were in flight. Secretary of State Knox urged the immediate dispatch of additional war vessels.[41] These did not save Victoria, however. He abdicated and Archbishop Nouel became provisional president of the Dominican Republic, to serve until peace had come and another election could be held.[42] By February, 1913, the turmoil had quieted to a point where the National City Bank of New York made a loan of $1,500,000.[43]

"The efforts which have been made appear to have resulted in the restoration of normal conditions throughout the Republic," was President Taft's hopeful report to Congress.[44]

The Dominican problem was among the many discovered in the "unfinished business" file by Woodrow Wilson, however. Bitter resentment, probably encouraged by the rival Banco Nacional of Santo Domingo, followed the award of the $1,500,000 loan to the National City Bank. Disorder continued until almost the end of 1914.[45]

—6—

However laudable in its purpose, Taft's Latin-American policy was largely a failure in bringing peace to the chaotic nations which were supposed to benefit thereby. The President pointed out in May, 1910, that stability in Guatemala, Honduras, San Salvador, Nicaragua and Costa Rica had long been a primary objective of the State Department. It was more to be desired, even, than peace in South America because of their proximity to the Panama Canal.

[40] Wilson to American legation, Santo Domingo, Sept. 24, 1912. [41] Knox to Taft, Oct. 29, 1912. [42] *Idem*, Dec. 19, 1912. [43] Knox to S. M. Jarvis, Feb. 12, 1913. [44] Message, Dec. 3, 1912. [45] Baker, R. S., *op. cit.*, Vol. IV, pp. 441-451.

Taft pointed to José Santos Zelaya, the dictatorial President of Nicaragua from 1893 to 1910, as the particular villain of the drama. Zelaya, he said, was "tyrannical and unprincipled." His "brutal and cruel exactions" had brought civil war to his country. By playing the role of "marplot," he had blocked all attempts to establish peace in the five republics. American citizens had been killed in Nicaragua, resulting in the landing of American forces. Taft found satisfaction in the fact "that the attitude of the United States toward Zelaya so injured his prestige and brought him so clearly to the bar of the public opinion of the world as an international criminal that he was obliged to abdicate and leave his government to a better man." [46]

This was in December, 1909. The "better man," however, did not achieve peace either. The United States attempted to apply to Nicaragua its Santo Domingo plan for rehabilitation of the republic's finances. A treaty was signed on June 6, 1911, in which it was specified that a receiver general of customs would be appointed, subject to the approval of the President of the United States. The Nicaraguan government would uphold his acts and "the United States shall afford him such protection as it may deem requisite." Then the United States would attempt to persuade its bankers to grant loans, on equitable terms, which would enable Nicaragua to emerge from its chaos.[47] The United States Senate was, however, again growing restive under these treaty-making activities by the President. It declined to ratify the Nicaraguan convention. Only a small, temporary loan was issued by the American bankers. Late in 1911 another revolution broke out and again the United States marines were landed. In February, 1910, Secretary Knox was dispatched by the President on a good-will tour to Central and South America in the hope that "such a trip will be productive of good and will enable us to carry to a successful end the policy of friendship and assistance we have been pursuing in respect to those countries." [48] Knox paused in Nicaragua to assure its people that the United States was wholly altruistic, that it had no thirst for land.[49]

The secretary of state cabled Washington, also, a vigorous ap-

[46] *Addresses,* Vol. XVIII, p. 239. [47] Bemis, S. F., *op. cit.,* pp. 335-338. [48] Taft to Knox, Feb. 10, 1912. [49] Bemis, S. F., *op. cit.,* Vol. IX, pp. 339-340.

peal in which he said that the Nicaraguans were "anxiously and prayerfully hoping for prompt action by our Senate" on the treaty. The President transmitted his message to the leaders of the Senate and pointed out that New York bankers were ready to lend $15,000,000 as soon as the treaty had been confirmed.[50] But the Senate declined to do this, on the ground that the terms were too onerous. Nicaragua, too, was among the perplexities which faced President Wilson in March, 1913. He was to learn that dollar diplomacy might be a repugnant policy. But finding a better plan was very difficult.[51]

All in all, dollar diplomacy was less than an outstanding success during the Taft years. It failed in China. It was somewhat successful in Santo Domingo. It failed in Nicaragua. And attempts to negotiate a treaty with Honduras were blocked in Washington. But dollar diplomacy did enrich a few American shipyards, a few manufacturers of guns and munitions. The President called attention to the fact, in May, 1910, that the Argentine Republic had placed orders for two battleships costing $23,000,000.[52]

[50] Taft to J. W. Bailey, March 14, 1912. [51] Baker, R. S., *op. cit.*, Vol. IV, pp. 430-440. [52] *Addresses*, Vol. XVIII, p. 240.

CHAPTER XXXVI

MEXICO AND JAPAN

O N OCCASIONS in the years ahead William Howard Taft must have pondered that few problems were spared him during his four years in the White House. He did not escape tariff revision and its consequences. Fate decreed that he should be in office when his party was torn by insurgency. Unrest in Latin America disturbed him through most of his administration. Even the Mexican revolutionary caldron had to boil over.

". . . it is inevitable," the President had written to Mrs. Taft in October, 1909, "that in case of a revolution or internecine strife we should interfere, and I sincerely hope that the old man's [Porfirio Diaz] official life will extend beyond mine, for that trouble would present a problem of the utmost difficulty." [1]

It was to forestall this calamity that the President of the United States had, in the fall of 1909, exchanged visits with the President of Mexico at the border. The aging Diaz had hoped, as Taft described it, that knowledge in his country "of the friendship of the United States for him . . . will strengthen him with his own people, and tend to discourage revolutionists' efforts to establish a different government." So Taft and Diaz formally greeted each other, formally sipped champagne and formally parted. But the meeting did not dispel the clouds over Mexico. American lives would still be in danger. Some $2,000,000,000 in American investments would remain in jeopardy.

"My own impression has been," Taft wrote more than a year before the revolution broke out, "that Diaz has done more for the people of Mexico than any other Latin American has done for any of his people." [2]

This judgment, unfortunately, was not shared by the peons of Mexico. After all, they had benefited little from the capital Diaz had attracted to their country or by the material progress he had

[1] Taft to Helen H. Taft, Oct. 17, 1909. [2] Taft to Horace D. Taft, Jan. 19, 1911.

made. In November, 1910, while en route to the Canal Zone on the U.S.S. *Tennessee,* President Taft was informed by wireless that rioting had started in Mexico City. He remained confident, however, that the iron hand of Diaz had not lost its strength. He could not, he wrote, "conceive a situation" in which the Mexican ruler would not effectively defend American interests.[3]

The President's optimism was shaken, however, when Henry Lane Wilson, American ambassador to Mexico, journeyed to the United States on leave of absence and called at the White House early in 1911.

"He painted a most pessimistic picture of the conditions . . ." Taft wrote. "He said that the Mexican army was, on paper, 34,000, but was in reality not more than 14,000; that ninety per cent of the people are in sympathy with the insurrectionist movement; that the anti-American riots some three months ago and the little insurrections occurring all over Mexico were merely symptomatic of a volcano-like condition which, with any leadership at all, would be certain to result in an explosion, throwing President Diaz over and producing a chaos in which the 70,000 Americans now in Mexico and the $1,000,000,000 [*sic*] invested capital owned by Americans would be certain to suffer. He regarded the situation as most critical, and could not tell when a catastrophe might ensue."

Thereupon the President summoned War Secretary Dickinson, Chief of Staff Leonard Wood and their aides and ordered mobilization of 20,000 men on the Mexican border. The President acted with punctilious regard for Mexican sensibilities. He assured its government "that this massing of forces in Texas and California was not intended as an act hostile to the friendly Mexican government." His only purpose was better to police the border and prevent the organization of insurrectionary expeditions along it. Taft was forced to move cautiously. He could not make public the reason for his action, because that would have meant that Wilson could not return to his post in Mexico City. Taft disavowed any intention of permitting the troops to cross the border; before doing so, he said, he would ask for authority from Congress.[4] At the same time the President instructed General Wood to use every precaution against

[3] Taft to Knox, Nov. 10, 1911. [4] Taft to Roosevelt, March 22, 1911.

friction. The mobilization was to be pictured as a training maneuver for the American army.[5]

It was impossible, of course, to keep secret the movements of 20,000 troops and Taft lugubriously observed that he was being criticized for "yielding to Wall Street influence" demanding intervention. He denied receiving any "communication of any sort" from any individual or company holding property in Mexico.[6] But Theodore Roosevelt, at least, was delighted by the possibility, even if remote, of a first-class war. He supposed that there was "nothing in this war talk" and he expressed, to Taft, his earnest hope "that we will not have to intervene even to do temporary police duty in Mexico." Yet on the "one chance in a thousand of serious trouble such as would occur if Japan or some other big power were to back Mexico," Roosevelt wrote for permission to apply for the command of a division of cavalry. It would have to be a bona fide war, the former Rough Rider warned. He would not be interested in the "peculiarly irksome" duty of merely patrolling the border. A "serious war, a war in which Mexico was backed by Japan or some other big power" would be worth his while, however. In that event, said Roosevelt, he would wish to raise a division of three cavalry brigades.

"If given a free hand," he promised, "I could render it . . . as formidable a body of horse riflemen . . . as those of Sheridan, Forest [sic] and Stuart, as has ever been seen." [7]

"I have noted carefully your wish," Taft replied, "and if occasion offers— which Heaven forfend— I shall be glad to conform to your desires. It would be necessary, of course, to secure legislation to permit it, but I think that could be accomplished. As I write, however, I have not the slightest idea that there will be any war in which Japan will take a part." [8]

Such would prove to be the case. Roosevelt was denied this opportunity to gallop madly into shot and shell in the Civil War manner of Jeb Stuart and Phil Sheridan. When his chance came again, the coldly hostile Woodrow Wilson was commander in chief. A great deal had been learned about modern warfare in the three

[5] Taft to Wood, March 12, 1911. [6] Taft to Roosevelt, March 22, 1911. [7] Bishop, J. B., *Theodore Roosevelt and His Time*, Vol. II, pp. 311-312. [8] Taft to Roosevelt, March 22, 1911.

years of the European struggle. Among other changes, it was no longer a cinematic cavalry pageant.

—2—

The friction in Mexico heightened. It was too late for Diaz to make gestures toward liberalism now. For Francisco Madero, surely one of the strangest figures in the long struggle for liberty of man, was passing swiftly from village to village under the hot, white sun and exhorting his followers to strike. Madero was an idealist, with all the virtues and most of the faults of his kind. Victory would come to him and then the necessity for being practical. He could not be practical and so he would die. The doom of Diaz was not far off in March, 1911, but Taft continued to be optimistic and to think that the presence of the American troops across the Rio Grande would have a restraining effect.[9] The situation grew worse as the month ended. Anarchy flourished in Lower California.[10]

May 23, 1911, was the eve of disaster. Diaz had refused to hand his resignation to Congress on that day and the streets of Mexico City were filled with surging crowds carrying Madero banners. By four-thirty that afternoon they were massed in front of the President's residence, but toward dusk they cleared a path for the limousine which bore the ambassador from the United States. Mr. Wilson described the historic scene in a dispatch to the State Department. He found, he said, "a most pathetic and dramatic scene." The President's friends had gathered at his home earlier in the day and now they were huddled in the balcony above the patio. The women were weeping. The men knew that an era had ended, that the days when vast haciendas lay tranquil in the winelike air of Mexico were over. Never again, they knew, would it be possible to profit handsomely through contracts with foreign capitalists. But they had only contempt for the visionary Madero and the spokesmen for his democracy.

Ambassador Wilson did not see the President when he called.

[9] Taft to Admiral Wainwright, March 12, 1911. [10] Taft to Hemphill, March 25, 1911.

Mrs. Diaz said that he was prostrated with illness and anxiety. She brought from his bed a message of appreciation. She was gratified when the ambassador— who seems never to have looked beneath the surface and discerned the misery of the people— said that mob violence could never obliterate the thirty years of accomplishment under her husband. Then Wilson left. It was twilight now. The blankets over the shoulders of the men were somber in the fading light. The crowd was packed and jammed in the street and seemed more than a little threatening. But it made way, again, for Wilson's motor and no word of hostility reached the ambassador's ears. Instead, there were cheers for the United States. "Viva el Embajador Americano!" the crowd shouted when Wilson's car was blocked, because of it, for ten minutes or so.

In the rioting that night, however, between fifty and eighty people were killed. Diaz, even then, would not give in to the swine who dared to question his beneficent despotism. On May 24, additional lives were lost. At four o'clock the dictator bowed to the inevitable and sent his resignation to Congress. But the final chapter was less than heroic. To Wilson's surprise, Diaz fled toward Vera Cruz before he abdicated; the "undignified flight," the ambassador reported, had made an unpleasant impression on the foreign colony in Mexico City. The deposed dictator was leaving for Europe on the first boat.[11]

"I write to express my feeling of warm friendship and admiration for you as a man, a statesman, and as a patriot," wrote Taft, in his own hand, to Diaz. "After your long and faithful service to Mexico and the Mexican people, it arouses in me the profoundest feeling of sympathy and sorrow to see what you have done temporarily forgotten. . . . In your highly honorable retirement, I would send this message of appreciation and good will." [12]

"The revolution did not triumph by force of arms; I could have restored order; and it would not have been the first time . . ." answered Diaz from the safety of Paris— perhaps the memory of the firing squads he had ordered was in his mind— "but it would have been through a long and bloody war . . . and as it was said that my presence in the executive chair was the sole cause of the insur-

[11] Wilson to Knox, May 31, 1911. [12] Taft to Diaz, June 7, 1911.

rection, I made the last sacrifice for peace, that of my personal pride." [13]

He died four years later, a bitter old man of eighty-five. To his credit it may be said, at least, that he broke the normal custom of overthrown Latin-American dictators: he did not loot the Mexican treasury and he lived, to the end, on the charity of friends.[14] His "last sacrifice for peace, that of my personal pride" did not bring peace to Mexico. Francisco Leon de la Barrarra, a Maderist, became provisional president pending an election at which Madero would certainly be chosen. The leader for freedom entered Mexico City on June 7, 1911, while 100,000 of his followers cheered and drank tequila. Ambassador Wilson, watching the celebration, told his superiors in Washington, that "all danger of . . . anarchy in the City of Mexico passed away" upon Madero's arrival. But he was not so confident concerning conditions in the outlying parts of the republic.

"The attitude of the old aristocracy, which largely supported the government of General Diaz, toward the new government is contemptuous, cynical and hostile," he added significantly.[15]

Like the Kerensky who would one day hold in his hands the command of Russia, and allow it to slip away because he did not have strong fingers, Madero was a leader of causes but not a ruler of men. By July, Wilson was reporting a formidable opposition against the new government and it was due, he said, to "a growing conviction that the leader lacks that decision of character, uniformity of policy and close insight into situations which is . . . of especial need in Mexico." The army was dissatisfied and verging on rebellion. The Roman Catholic Church was criticizing Madero, who would be formally elected president in November. The remnants of the Diaz regime were desperately seeking any means, however detrimental to Mexico, to recover some part of their old power. Even the Maderists were beginning to look upon their leader "as a dreamer and false prophet." The ambassador added:

I have met Mr. Madero upon several occasions. . . . He is insignificant in appearance, of diffident manners and hesitating speech, and seems to be highly nervous and uncertain as to his course in

[13] Diaz to Taft, July 20, 1911. [14] Hammond, J. H., *The Autobiography of John Hays Hammond,* Vol. II, pp. 571-572. [15] Wilson to Knox, June 23, 1911.

regard to many important public questions. He has, however, one redeeming feature— a pair of excellent eyes, which indicate to me earnestness, truthfulness and loyalty, and, it may be, reserves of strength and force of character which time may more fully reveal.[16]

—3—

Six months or more passed without violent disturbances. In February, 1912, President Taft directed the secretary of war to "increase the guard along the border, as quietly as possible, to such strength as will amply ensure the protection of American citizens and their interests." [17] Madero could not stamp out the bandits— they called themselves revolutionists and patriots, of course— who started to roam Mexico, to rob and murder. On March 14, 1912, Congress by joint resolution prohibited the shipment of arms or ammunition to any nation on the two American continents where conditions of domestic violence were found to exist.[18] This was a blow at the revolutionists in Mexico, but they continued to undermine the Madero government. The embargo applied to all the accepted articles of war, such as guns, ammunition and supplies. In April a novel question arose. The revolutionists, it appeared, had purchased an airplane in France and it had been shipped to the border at El Paso. It was to be used to drop explosives on the federal troops and the Mexican consul had protested that it was, even if not specified in the congressional resolution, an article of war. But Secretary Stimson asked for a ruling from the attorney general.

Mr. Wickersham, in a solemn and lengthy opinion, ruled that the new contraption was "clearly within the intendment of the . . . articles absolutely contraband of war. . . . I have the honor to advise you . . . that the French aeroplane referred to in the telegram of the secretary of war should not be permitted exportation into Mexico." [19]

Murder and robbery continued to flourish in the spring of 1912. Secretary of the Navy Meyer asked Congress for permission to enlist an additional two thousand men for service in the event of

[16] Wilson to Knox, July 27, 1911. [17] Taft to Stimson, Feb. 4, 1912. [18] Wickersham to Taft, March 25, 1912. [19] *Idem*, April 1, 1912.

PANAMA CANAL

ISTHMIAN GAMES.

EVENT No. 1.—EXTENDING THE COLD ELBOW.

Reproduced by permission of the Proprietors of London "PUNCH ©"

See page 646]

A MERE MATTER OF HONOUR.

President Taft. "HERE, SWALLOW THIS!"

America. "THANKS, I'M AN EAGLE; I'M NOT A VULTURE."

Reproduced by permission of the Proprietors of London "PUNCH ©"

[See page 652

intervention.[20] A report from Mazatlán, in the state of Sinaloa on the west coast of Mexico, told of American suffering in the interior. The city was crowded with refugees. Guy L. Jones, whose hacienda had been seized and who had fled to Mazatlán, sent a poignant appeal to Washington:

There are so many Americans, and they so fill the Plaza Machado, where they gather on the benches to talk it over, that it has been dubbed the "American Club." Seven thousand persons have fled here. . . . Only one topic can for more than a moment hold attention. "Are you wounded, Henry?" asks one American, as he meets a compatriot who has just reached town. "No," says the other, "but I hiked it the last 30 kilometers. They even took the mules out of my buckboard." Were it not so expensive it would be ludicrous, for no two bands are fighting for the same thing, nor does anyone know exactly for what he is fighting. The government appears absolutely powerless, and the present state of affairs will keep on indefinitely.[21]

The people of El Paso were alarmed because of reports that Juarez, in the hands of the insurgents, was about to be attacked by federal forces, which meant that bullets would certainly fly across the border. The President instructed the secretary of state to acquaint the Madero government with this situation and to caution it against the possibility of injury to Americans.[22] Meanwhile, discouraging reports continued to flow from the pen of Ambassador Wilson in Mexico City. By August, he had lost all patience with Madero, who at one moment was harsh and severe toward the revolutionists and then mild and conciliatory. Whatever the federal policy, Wilson said, "the situation remains the same; growing crops are destroyed, homes are burned, women are ravished and wholesale murders take place." Wilson wondered whether Madero was, perhaps, insane:

. . . the President is one day a conservative, a reactionary, the stern avenger of society against brigandage, the tyrant who wants an eye for an eye and a tooth for a tooth, in a word, a Diaz come again; and the next an apostle of peace, the friend of the poor and down-

[20] Meyer to L. P. Paget, April 17, 1912. [21] G. L. Jones to Nagel, April 22, 1912. [22] Taft to Knox, June 19, 1912.

trodden, the apologist for important bandits and criminals, and the enemy of monopolies, landholders and privileged characters and classes.

"There is quite a widespread opinion," the ambassador added, "that the President is possessed of certain mental weaknesses which totally unfit him for the office which he occupies. . . . Peculiar stories are told of his irrelevancy, of his lack of memory, of his inaccurate information and of his unreasonable and petulant reception of such matters as are ordinarily presented to a chief executive."

As for the economic situation, Wilson was certain that it had not improved and it "will grow steadily worse." [23] The pressure on Taft to intervene or, failing that, to make the strongest representations to Mexico increased steadily. Undersecretary of State Huntington Wilson informed the President in September that Ambassador Calero of Mexico would call officially and suggested that the diplomat be given the "talking to of his life." [24] The meeting took place on September 4 and the undersecretary, who was present, described how "earnestly and energetically" the President portrayed the wrongs inflicted upon American citizens in Mexico and how "solemnly" he had outlined his duty, as chief executive, to see that they did not continue. Señor Calero, Wilson noted, "was evidently a good deal worried by the seriousness of the President's tone from the very beginning." The interview was terminated when Taft expressed the hope that the Mexican government did not mistake for weakness the extreme patience which the United States had shown.[25]

Two days later, Secretary Knox dispatched a lengthy rebuke in which murders of American citizens and other outrages were detailed, prejudice against American business interests described and warning given— in the carefully polite phrases of diplomatic usage, but solemn warning none the less— that the United States would act unless the Madero government exhibited some ability to rule. One course, the note intimated, might be to lift the arms embargo which would mean victory for the insurgents.[26]

[23] Wilson to Knox, Aug. 28, 1912. [24] Huntington Wilson to Taft, Sept. 4, 1912. [25] Memorandum by Huntington Wilson, Sept. 4, 1912. [26] Knox to H. L. Wilson, Sept. 6, 1912.

"I am not going to intervene . . . until no other course is possible, but I must protect our people in Mexico, as far as possible, and their property by having the government understand there is a God in Israel and he is on duty," wrote Taft privately.[27]

The Mexican government, however, was not afraid to retort to God in Israel when it received Knox's note. It denied that murderers remained unwhipped of justice. And even if they did, in some cases, asked Pedro Lascurain, minister for foreign affairs, was this not also true in the United States? He gave a list of Mexican citizens who had been slain in Texas and California. He told stories, too, of inhuman cruelties inflicted upon Mexicans in the land which boasted of its civilization. The perpetrators, he said, had never been punished.[28]

The President resisted, with fine courage and sanity, the widespread demands that war with Mexico was the only honorable course. On August 1, 1912, he accepted the Republican presidential nomination and, according to custom, summed up the problems and accomplishments of his years in the White House. Discussing Mexico, he said the administration had "been conscious that one hostile step in intervention and the passing of the border by one regiment of troops would mean war with Mexico, the expenditure of hundreds of millions of dollars, the loss of thousands of lives." No one "with a sense of responsibility," the President said, would involve the American people "in the almost unending burden and thankless task of enforcing peace upon these 15,000,000 of people fighting among themselves." America's experiences in the Philippines and in Cuba, alone, forbade it. Consequently, it was the "course of patriotism and of wisdom to subject ourselves and our citizens to some degree of suffering and inconvenience" rather than, too hastily, to plunge into so costly and futile a war.[29]

Ambassador Wilson continued to demand, however, a policy of severity toward Mexico. So pronounced were his views, in fact, that Secretary Knox protested to the President regarding Wilson's

[27] Taft to A. B. Farquhar, Sept. 11, 1912. [28] Lascurain to Montgomery Schuyler, Nov. 22, 1912. [29] Acceptance Speech, Aug. 1, 1912.

tendency "to force this government's hand in its dealings" with the situation.[30] The ambassador's dispatches were increasingly pessimistic in January and early February, 1913. Mexico City was soon the scene of street fighting. Wilson complained that his protests to Madero "against this barbarous warfare" were again ineffective.[31] Certainly Wilson was more than a little highhanded. On February 15, the Mexican embassy at Washington reported that he had inspired his fellow diplomats to call on Madero and persuade him to resign.

"The President," reported the embassy, "refused to recognize the right of the diplomatic representatives . . . to interfere in the domestic affairs of the nation and informed them that he was resolved to die at his post before permitting foreign interference." [32]

The ambassador admitted that he had called upon Madero for that purpose, but said that he had done so unofficially. He said he had called the diplomatic corps into conference at the American embassy on February 14 to discuss the grave predicament of the Madero regime. His colleagues had unanimously decided that "even without instructions" from their governments, they should ask Madero to quit. But the President of Mexico had abruptly rejected their advice.[33]

Madero was doomed, however. His supporters were divided. His army was disloyal. On February 18, 1913, General Victoriano Huerta, doubtless with satisfaction, dispatched a telegram to the President of the United States.

"I have the honor to inform you," he said, "that I have overthrown this government, the forces are with me and from now on peace and prosperity will reign." [34]

This was oratory rather than prophecy; it would be long years before either peace or prosperity reigned. Ambassador Wilson was almost as jubilant as Huerta, himself. There is evidence, but not proof, that he actively assisted in the overthrow of Madero. The cordiality of his relationship with Huerta is indicated by the fact that Mexico's new ruler consulted him on the fate of Madero.

"My advice as to whether it was best to send the ex-President out of the country or place him in a lunatic asylum was asked by

[30] Knox to Taft, Jan. 27, 1913. [31] Wilson to Knox, Feb. 12, 1913. [32] Knox to Wilson, Feb. 15, 1913. [33] Wilson to Knox, Feb. 15, 17, 1913. [34] Huerta to Taft, Feb. 18, 1913.

General Huerta," Wilson reported, "to which I replied that that which was *best for the peace of the country ought to be done by him.*" [35]

These were careless words, almost unbelievable words, for an American diplomat to utter. Three days later both Madero and Piño Suárez, the vice-president, were assassinated.

"I am disposed to accept the government's version of the affair and consider it a closed incident, in spite of all current rumors," telegraphed Wilson to Secretary Knox.[36]

The secretary of state was less callous. The newspapers of the United States, he told the ambassador, were unanimous in their horror and in their suspicion that Huerta might have been responsible. Knox instructed Wilson to be "carefully guided by the President's direction that, for the present, no formal recognition is to be accorded those *de facto* in control." Horror spread through Mexico too. The impractical Madero may have been a very bad president. He may have vacillated and been weak. He may even have been a lunatic. But what of that? He had swept through the vast stretches of Mexico with a dream of better days for the common man. He had vanquished the powerful and defiant Diaz. He had been the liberator of Mexico and now he was murdered. The death of Madero was to make idle Huerta's boast that prosperity and peace would dwell in the land. Still another problem was left for Woodrow Wilson, now president-elect, to solve.[37]

Taft, although he could not finish the task, had never bowed to the oil and other interests which demanded intervention in Mexico and used, as their chief argument, the dangers to which American citizens were subjected. These interests were soon in full cry after President Wilson, who proved to be just as stubborn.

"I have to pause and remind myself that I am President of the United States," said Wilson after he had wrestled with the situation for months, "and not of a small group of Americans with vested interests in Mexico." [38]

[35] Wilson to Knox, Feb. 19, 1913. (Italics mine.) [36] *Idem*, Feb. 24, 1913. [37] Baker, R. S., *Woodrow Wilson, Life and Letters*, Vol. IV, pp. 239-241. [38] Tumulty, J. P., *Woodrow Wilson as I Knew Him*, p. 146.

—5—

Meanwhile, the Japanese problem was a minor annoyance of the Taft years. The President, as we have noted already, rejected Theodore Roosevelt's forthright proposal to abandon the open door in the Far East if only Japan would not become too unpleasant over discrimination against its citizens in California and other American states. Taft was less nervous over the Yellow Peril than Roosevelt had been. For one thing, he was spared the excitement of inflammatory letters from the German Kaiser who, alarmed by the British-Japanese alliance, had frequently assured Roosevelt that Nippon had nefarious designs against the United States.[39] Taft's friendly attitude toward Japan and his reluctance to believe that danger lay in the Far East were due, in part, to the contacts and friendships he had made during visits to Yokohama and Tokyo.

"I am on excellent terms with all the Japanese authorities . . ." he explained. "The truth is that my closeness to the leading men of Japan has been a comfort to me in all these sensational attempts to create difficulties between the countries."[40]

As though to agree with Roosevelt's apprehensions, he told the former President that the "Japanese matter . . . concerns me much."[41] Taft was really not impressed, however, by dire predictions that the warriors of the island empire could defeat Uncle Sam if it came to a fight. He was cool to suggestions that the army and navy should be vastly augmented to repel the Japanese invador.

"I think we could do something while Japan was doing what is threatened . . ." he sanely observed, "and I think our navy could be made useful to the point of rendering it the most hazardous military expedition ever attempted to send the thousands of troops needed from Japan across the Pacific."[42]

The chief danger was further discriminatory legislation in California. With guile unusual in so honest and straightforward a character— and with a very sound knowledge of California psychology— the President supported with enthusiasm the proposition

[39] Pringle, H. F., *Theodore Roosevelt, a Biography*, pp. 406-409. [40] Taft to Martin Egan, Nov. 24, 1910. [41] Taft to Roosevelt, Dec. 2, 1910. [42] Taft to F. P. Flint, Dec. 9, 1909.

for a world's fair in San Francisco. New Orleans also was anxious to have an exposition and Taft pointed out that he had no personal preference save for a "very strong reason of state which induces me to make such effort as I can to induce Congress to give the choice to San Francisco." He recalled that Roosevelt had put down the anti-Japanese agitation in that city only with the greatest difficulty. But now California was relatively quiet.

"I have not the slightest doubt," said the President, "that if the fair goes to San Francisco we can count on tranquillity there. Indeed, San Francisco will thus be put under bonds to keep the peace. It is for this reason that I am very anxious to have the fair go there." [43]

This gentle strategy was successful to a degree. Governor Hiram Johnson of California was conciliatory. Taft told him that a new treaty, in the process of negotiation, would fully protect California rights.[44] And how embarrassing it would be, he noted, "to ask Eastern countries to come here to an exposition in California" should that state pass laws barring Orientals from the rights and privileges enjoyed by other foreigners.[45]

The 1894 Japanese-American treaty would have expired in July, 1912. Similar agreements with other powers, entered into by Japan at about the same time, ran out in 1911, however, and Taft was entirely willing to have a new document drafted at once. All the deliberations were predicated upon Japan's promise to continue voluntary limitation of emigration to the United States.[46] This had been successful. During the year which ended June 30, 1908, a total of 9,544 Japanese had been admitted. Next year, under the "gentlemen's agreement," only 2,432 had come in and these included all classes. Of the total, only 713 were laborers. Even fewer had emigrated to the United States in 1910. The immigration authorities at Washington were wholly satisfied with the plan.[47]

President Taft and Secretary Knox proved themselves sincere friends of Japan by agreeing, in the new treaty, to omit the clause of the 1894 pact which barred Japanese laborers. Knox explained this to Roosevelt during the conference at Oyster Bay when the

[43] Taft to A. R. Johnson, Jan. 28, 1911. [44] Taft to Hiram Johnson, Feb. 23, 1911. [45] Taft to Huntington Wilson, March 15, 1911. [46] Presidential Message, Dec. 7, 1911. [47] Taft to Roosevelt (draft by Knox, not mailed), Dec. 22, 1910.

entire subject of Far Eastern relations had been discussed. He told Roosevelt that the omission would be made on the understanding that the "existing diplomatic arrangement for restricted immigration should continue in force." It was specified, in addition, that the treaty might be terminated on six months' notice. Thus, if voluntary restriction ceased to work, the United States could pass any law that it liked. Roosevelt listened attentively, Knox reported to Taft, but with misgivings.[48] He expressed his misgivings, in a day or two, to the President. He was afraid, Roosevelt said, that such a treaty would cause the most extreme resentment in California. He did not believe that the United States should in any manner limit its right to exclude any body of people from its boundaries.[49]

Taft would not be deflected, however. The exclusion clause in the 1894 treaty, he told Roosevelt, was reasonably viewed as discriminatory by the Japanese because "we haven't the same clause in our treaties with the Western civilized powers. Japan feels this is a remnant of the old order of things under which she was treated as half civilized. . . . Of course it is not to be expected that any treaty could be ratified without the consent of the Pacific coast or that the coast would be satisfied unless the arrangement made is effective . . . for their protection." [50]

The treaty was drafted according to the Taft-Knox specifications and went into effect. But success was jeopardized for a time by rumors, in the spring of 1911, that a Japanese syndicate had purchased 400,000 acres in the Magdalena Bay region of Lower California and that this would be used for a coaling station. Denials were prompt. Baron Uchida, the Japanese ambassador, said that his country was not seeking territory in any part of Mexico. President Madero said there was no truth in the report.[51] Apprehension over the rumors continued for a year, however. It was nurtured, in the main, by Senator Cabot Lodge of Massachusetts, who offered a resolution opposing the deal.[52] The resolution passed the Senate, but Taft was not unduly disturbed.

"I don't regard the Lodge resolution as very important," he told President Jordan of Stanford University. "He has had this bee in

[48] Knox to Taft, Dec. 19, 1910. [49] Roosevelt to Taft, Dec. 22, 1910. [50] Taft to Roosevelt, Jan. 17, 1911. [51] Bemis, S. F., *The American Secretaries of State and Their Diplomacy*, Vol. IX, pp. 340-341; New York *Herald*, March 11, 1911; New York *Sun*, April 5, 1912. [52] Taft to Huntington Wilson, April 5, 1912.

his bonnet for some time, and he started in on Magdalena Bay, having been fooled by a lawyer who was hunting a defunct client. . . . The Senate cannot declare the policy of this government, at any rate, because it cannot make it. It is only part of the treaty-making power . . . I should not feel under any obligation to follow a resolution like this." [53]

Roosevelt, in his autobiography, said that Taft had followed a "most mistaken and ill-advised policy" in dealing with Japan in that the new treaty constituted a surrender of the right to exclude aliens. The criticism must have been born of Roosevelt's hostility toward Taft; it was written soon after the 1912 campaign. For the treaty did nothing of the sort. That right was inherent in any sovereign nation, as Knox had pointed out, and did not need the emphasis of a treaty. The situation was actually not complicated. California could pass any law applying to *all* aliens as long as it did not contravene a treaty or the Constitution of the United States. It could not enact legislation applying to Japanese and not to other aliens. Governor Johnson had conceded as much during the immigration controversy.[54] By May, 1913, however, California had passed the Alien Landholding bill which was a specific discrimination against the Japanese right to own land. But by May, 1913, Taft was happily aloof as an ex-president of the United States and President Wilson had to deal with the problem too. Roosevelt was as little pleased with Wilson's policy as he had been with Taft's.

". . . the attitude of the President and Mr. Bryan has been hopelessly weak," he said.[55]

[53] Taft to Jordan, Aug. 5, 1912. [54] Johnson to Huntington Wilson, March 24, 1911. [55] Nevins, Allan, *Henry White*, p. 317.

CHAPTER XXXVII

SO LITTLE TIME REMAINED

So LITTLE time remained after the Congressional elections of 1910 for the many things which Taft hoped to accomplish as president. Peace in Mexico, more amicable relations with Central and South America, added efficiency in the federal government, treaties which might make world peace a degree more likely, reduction of living costs; such were only some of the problems with which Taft wrestled in vain and finally passed on to Woodrow Wilson. The Taft administration would prove, if any proof were needed, the futility of being president for only one term.

Another major problem for which there was not enough time was revision of the banking system and the establishment of a more flexible currency. This was an ancient puzzle. The bankers, who might have effected necessary changes, were either corrupt or so narrow in their viewpoint that they rarely considered the interests of the public. The politicians were ignorant or partisan; that is, they bowed to the western debtors who demanded easy money or to the eastern creditors who wanted hard money. In consequence, the American banking system was chaotic and inefficient. The currency was too rigid. At regular intervals panics racked the nation.

In the summer of 1905, Dr. Butler of Columbia University had discussed, among other subjects, finance with Kaiser Wilhelm II. The All Highest asked who managed this complicated subject in the United States.

"God," answered President Butler.[1]

To Aldrich of Rhode Island, however, the matter rested in slightly less ecclesiastical, although entirely competent, hands. Six years later the senator was actively engaged in an attempt to improve the system. This was essential, he warned Professor Henry Fairfield

[1] Pringle, H. F., *Theodore Roosevelt, a Biography*, p. 432.

716

Osborn, the scientist, because ". . . we may not always have a Pierpont Morgan with us to meet the country's crisis." [2]

Theodore Roosevelt had recognized the necessity for a more stable banking structure, but his antipathy toward economics and finance disqualified him as a leader in the reform. He believed, with some justice, that panics were the fault of "our big financiers [who] are for the most part speculators." But Roosevelt, badly informed, was also easily frightened by these identical financiers when they warned him against tampering. He vaguely urged "better safeguards against commercial crises and financial panics" throughout his period in the White House. The 1907 panic intensified public demand that something be done. This was not, as in 1896, a cry that the poor should be protected at the expense of the rich. It was an intelligent plea which could not be denied; that the farmer, the merchant, the householder and the employee should not be forced to suffer because the master minds of the United States did not understand finance.[3]

A start, but not more than that, was made toward the close of Roosevelt's term. The Aldrich-Vreeland act of 1908 provided for additional currency, to be retired by taxation as soon as an emergency had passed. More important, it created a Monetary Commission which would really study the subject.[4] Everyone realized that the new currency was a palliative. Taft, in his acceptance address in July, 1908, called attention to the fact that emergency bank notes, based on commercial paper and high-grade bonds, could now be issued. But this was "expressly a temporary measure." The need, the nominee said, was for a currency which would meet the requirements of all classes, "in which every dollar shall be as good as gold, and which shall prevent rather than aid financial stringency in bringing on a panic." [5]

Only God, of course, could create so divinely perfect a system as that and the Deity, it would develop, was concerned with other matters. President Taft did hardly more than Roosevelt in leading the movement. His papers are singularly bare of references to currency revision. He delegated the subject to Senator Aldrich, who as chairman of the Monetary Commission labored zealously

[2] Stephenson, N. W., *Nelson W. Aldrich*, p. 384. [3] Pringle, H. F., *op. cit.*, pp. 432-433. [4] Stephenson, N. W., *op. cit.*, pp. 326-330. [5] *Addresses*, Vol. XI, pp. 42-43.

and with some intelligence. In the end, though, he surrendered to the bankers and was lost. So passed Taft's opportunity, duly to be seized by his successor, to write boldly on the scrolls of fame and create the federal reserve banking machinery. On the other hand, Woodrow Wilson benefited by the debates which raged in the Taft years. The public was educated, to an extent, away from the Jacksonian theory that any centralized control of banking was in violation of pure democracy.

—2—

The work of Aldrich's Monetary Commission began in the summer of 1908. He went abroad with three other members: Henry P. Davison of the House of Morgan, A. Piatt Andrew, Jr., of the Harvard faculty, and G. M. Reynolds, president of the American Bankers Association. While the campaign between Taft and Bryan raged at home they consulted the rather supercilious financiers of London, Paris and Berlin, who were quite certain that the representatives of the relatively new nation across the sea would accomplish nothing. They could not read the future or discern the abyss into which their own statesmen would soon plunge them. They did not know that after the nightmare of war, ruinous borrowing and inflation ahead, their governments would be sadly in debt to the brash nation which had become the financial center of the world. The British and European experts were friendly enough in 1908. They convinced Aldrich on two major points: that centralized banking was sound banking and that the commercial transactions of a nation, as represented by commercial paper held by the banks, constituted a very sound security on which to base currency.[6]

The contradictions of the financial mind are sometimes as remarkable as those of the political thinker. In the fall of 1909 the American Bankers Association's committee on federal legislation uttered solemn warning against the radical proposals of the Monetary Commission. It insisted on preservation of the individuality of the nation's banks. It opposed any central bank as yet

[6] Stephenson, N. W., op. cit., pp. 332-340.

suggested and it made itself thereby the heir of Jacksonian Democracy. But the proponents of centralized banking had their spokesmen too. The leading ones were Paul M. Warburg and Frank A. Vanderlip. They persuaded Aldrich, normally so aloof and so intolerant of public opinion, to fare forth into the heresy-riddled West, which also opposed a central bank, and expound his ideas. Aldrich did so, discovering to his probable astonishment that the masses were not so bad as he had supposed. In Aldrich's mind burned the dream that he might go down in history as the author of a new and wiser banking act. He was an old man, almost seventy, and this would be his final victory— if it came.[7]

No progress was made as far as Congress was concerned in 1909 or 1910. But Aldrich and his confreres were hard at work on the details of a program which would be known as the Aldrich Plan for Monetary Legislation. In the fall of 1910, Aldrich, Davison, Vanderlip and Warburg journeyed to Jekyl Island off the Georgia coast after elaborately announcing that they would merely shoot ducks. Instead, they argued finance for ten days. They evolved what they called a Reserve Association of America which would be, in substance, a bankers' bank. It would make liquid, through discounting a second time, the commercial paper already accepted by its member banks. Against this paper could be issued currency which would remain in circulation as long as the assets against which it was issued were in its hands. These, very roughly, were the highlights of the new system. There was, in the long run, a far more important angle. How would the Reserve Association of America be controlled? Aldrich said that the government would be represented and would have full knowledge of all of the association's affairs. But actual control, he insisted, must lie with the bankers and not with the proletariat publicists who ran the nation.[8]

If President Taft played any major part in these deliberations, it is not revealed in his correspondence. True, there was a White House conference in January, 1911, at which Alfred Ripley, the financier, and a few bankers were present.[9] During the previous summer the President had conferred with Aldrich at Beverly and he was kept informed, from time to time, of progress made.

"It seems to me that you have met the requirement . . ." he

---

[7] *Ibid.*, pp. 363-372. [8] *Ibid.*, pp. 373-379. [9] Taft to Ripley *et al*, Jan. 4, 1911.

told the Rhode Island senator in January, 1911, "that a central bank . . . must not be within the control of politics or Wall Street. I observe that the insurgent press, in order to show their animus toward you and to use the proposed measure as an issue for demagogic attack, point with glee to the fact that your reserve associations are mere substitutes for a central bank, and so are objectionable as a future financial and greedy tyrant, missing altogether the point that while it is true that they are to do in certain respects a banking business for profit . . . the provisions for their formation and their control avoid the only real objection to a central bank, that of concentrating enormous fiscal power in a political head or a few money kings. . . . I believe you have reached a most admirable plan."

The President agreed to support the plan as thus far drafted. As a Republican, however, he was not optimistic that the Democratic Congress would accept it. There was, he said, "something inconsistent and incongruous as between monetary sanity and the mind of the average Democratic and thus necessarily demagogic congressman." [10]

Aldrich was destined to suffer final defeat because he compromised. It was a curious ending to a career in which compromise had played so slight a part. His original plan provided that executive control of the Reserve Association of America would be in the hands of a governor and two deputy governors to be selected by the President of the United States from a list submitted by the association's board of directors, which consisted of bankers. But the bankers had no intention of permitting even this control by Washington. Aldrich at last agreed to the proposal of the American Bankers Association committee. It specified a governor, selected by the President from a similar list. But he could be removed by the Reserve Association of America. The deputies were all to be chosen by the association and removed by it.[11]

This was enough to bring failure even had Aldrich, discredited by the 1909 tariff act which bore his name, possessed the confidence of the electorate. When a bill was introduced it was provided, as a gesture toward those who believed politicians to be at least as able as bankers, that the secretaries of the treasury and commerce and also the comptroller of the currency were to be members of the

[10] Taft to Aldrich, Jan. 29, 1911. [11] Stephenson, N. W., op. cit., pp. 391-392.

association's directorate. It was not enough. The plan, as revised by the bankers, was made public in April, 1911. Professor Edwin W. Kemmerer, then of Cornell University, who had been an adviser to the Monetary Commission and who approved the purposes of the Aldrich plan, was among the critics of extreme banker-control. Wall Street, he remarked, dominated "either directly or indirectly a very substantial part of the country's principal banking institutions. The nauseous revelations we have been having repeatedly in high finance during the last decade have been calculated more to impress the public with the selfishness and the power of some of these great interests than with their sense of business honesty or their public spiritedness. . . .

"An institution so vitally connected with the public welfare and carrying such a large trusteeship," Kemmerer concluded, "should not be controlled so completely by any one business interest. At least six and probably more of these twelve directors should be appointed by the President of the United States independently of any nomination by the banking community." [12]

At first, Taft agreed that "the banks which would own the association should in the main manage it." This should be combined, he said, with "some form of government supervision and ultimate control"; he favored a "reasonable representation" on the executive board.[13] But 1912 was a year of turmoil. Governor Wilson of New Jersey declared that "the country will not brook any plan which concentrates control in the hands of the banks." At the Republican convention in June the relevant plank was written by Dr. Butler of Columbia and was an attempt, as he described it himself, to endorse "the principles of the Aldrich plan without mentioning his name and arousing unnecessary antagonism." [14] That fall came further revelations of the "nauseous" type mentioned by Kemmerer of Cornell. The House Committee on Banking and Currency began its investigation of the so-called "Money Trust." Morgan, George F. Baker and other eminent gentlemen squirmed under the searching examination of Samuel Untermyer, the committee's counsel. The findings of the Pujo committee, named after its chairman, Representative Arsène P. Pujo of Louisiana, further convinced the voting

[12] *South Atlantic Quarterly*, July, 1911. [13] Message, Dec. 21, 1911. [14] Stephenson, N. W., *op. cit.*, pp. 403, 410.

public that nearly all financiers were scoundrels.[15] In December, 1912, even the President— who addressed a last message to Congress on the subject— was convinced that the government "might very properly be given a greater voice" in the control of the new banking system.[16] By this time the Republican party was slipping into exile. The Aldrich plan, as such, was dead. The creation of an improved banking machine would soon fall into the hands of those Democrats who were, to Taft, so demagogic, so hostile to sound legislation of any variety and to sound monetary legislation in particular. They were, however, less dangerous than the retiring President supposed. Representative Carter Glass of Virginia had been studying the subject profoundly. William G. McAdoo was to be a stanch warrior in the struggle which should have ended, but did not, the theory that the Democratic party, by its devotion to Bryan in 1896, was forever disqualified from passing on financial or economic matters.

—3—

Another subject which worried President Taft in 1912, doubly grave because of the approaching election, was the rise in the cost of living. "I should like to have this report as soon as I can see it," he noted when Secretary of Commerce Nagel wrote, in November, 1911, that experts in his department were attempting to find out why prices for food and other necessities had gone up.[17] Secretary of Agriculture Wilson offered the explanation that the middleman was to blame, at least with respect to farm products.[18] Irving Fisher of Yale urged the appointment of an international commission to study world prices, and the President so recommended in a special message to Congress on February 2. A board of experts consisting of "unprejudiced and impartial persons," he thought, would shed "a great deal of very valuable light . . . upon the reasons for the high prices that have so distressed the people of the world." He requested that $20,000 be appropriated for a conference at Washington to which would be invited economists from all the important

[15] Pringle, H. F., *Big Frogs,* pp. 147-151. [16] Message, Dec. 6, 1912. [17] Nagel to Taft, Nov. 17, 1911. [18] Wilson to Taft, Nov. 18, 1911.

nations. Taft said that preliminary studies indicated that the price rise was world-wide.[19]

But presidents and the governments over which they preside always find it extremely difficult to control prices; it makes no difference, as Presidents Hoover and Roosevelt would appreciate in the years ahead, whether prices are too high or too low. They are forced to fall back, whether a boom or a depression is under way, on the excuse that the condition is world-wide and to admit that nothing much can be done. The Democrats said, quite naturally, that high prices were caused by the outrageous schedules of the Payne-Aldrich tariff and upbraided Taft because he would not permit downward revisions. The President offered evidence gathered by the State Department in reply. Food prices in all the important cities of Europe had been studied, he said, for the past twelve years. In England, France, Germany and Holland, for example, the cost of living had outstripped wage increases. A possible cure, Taft suggested, lay in the co-operative society plan which had been so popular in England. He described the methods of the co-operatives and remarked that only experiment could determine whether they were adaptable to the United States. The shopkeepers of Great Britain, he added, appeared to be less alarmed over competition by the co-operatives than when they had first been established.[20]

Taft undertook no movement for spreading the co-operative plan in the United States, however. It was probably just as well that he did not, for it would surely have aroused the most bitter opposition among the nation's merchants. The President contented himself with urging Congress to authorize the international conference on living costs. The Republican platform emphasized the world-wide nature of the problem and constituted, of course, a plea that the party could not be blamed.

"The fact that it is not due to the protective tariff system," it stated, "is evidenced by the existence of similar conditions in countries which have a tariff policy different from our own, as well as by the fact that the cost of living has increased while rates of duty have remained stationary or been reduced."

The party, promised this document of promises, would support

<hr/>

[19] Fisher to Taft, Jan. 2, 1912; *Addresses*, Vol. XXVII, p. 129. [20] Message, March 14, 1912.

a "prompt scientific inquiry into the causes which are operative." [21] But it did not do so. Neither did the Democratic leaders in Congress, who were apprehensive that any inquiry, scientific or otherwise, might invalidate their claims that only the tariff was at fault. No international conference was authorized.[22] The President, as the 1912 campaign progressed, was forced to rely on reiterations regarding high prices all over the world and to point out that "we are more prosperous than we have ever been." He said that the people received better wages, that railroad earnings were up, that the factories were working to capacity, that the year's agricultural harvest exceeded "in magnitude and money value the yield of any other year in our history." Surely, under such munificence, the voters would demand no change.[23] But an appreciable segment of the voters declined to credit these assurances.

—4—

As always, the cursed tariff remained to plague the President. It was still Taft's legacy of doom from the years when McKinley had done nothing about it, from the years when Roosevelt had listened to Uncle Joe Cannon and had evaded it. On taking office, Taft had forced the issue, perhaps with more honesty than skill. But he had not solved the insoluble. "I am a low-tariff man," he had insisted during the Payne-Aldrich debates in 1909. Except for his blundering Winona speech, he had admitted that the bill which was finally passed was less than perfect. The wool and woolen rates, which should have been slashed, remained virtually unchanged in the notorious Schedule K. This, said the President, was the "one important defect" in the Payne-Aldrich act. It was responsible, in a measure, for the Democratic capture of the House in the fall of 1910. It was behind the unending demands for further tariff revision in the last two years of Taft's administration.

The President's demand for trade reciprocity with Canada obscured, for a little while, the defects of the existing tariff bill. But that failed, too, after it had been approved by Congress, because the

[21] Republican Platform, 1912. [22] Fisher to Taft, Sept. 11, 1912. [23] Taft to W. W. Griest, Oct. 4, 1912.

Dominion government rejected the agreement. With reciprocity dead, Taft knew that the Democratic majority in the House would attempt to lower the Payne-Aldrich rates. He profoundly distrusted economic measures offered by the Democrats which would, as he felt, "play havoc" with industry. So he insisted that nothing should be done until after careful investigation by the Tariff Board. But an impatient Congress would not wait for the board's findings. The President was forced to veto reductions on wool, cotton, chemicals, metals and other products passed during the summer of 1911.

The board had been ordered to report on the wool and woolen rates by December, 1911. It did so, after arduous labor, in a document running to 1,200 pages. Taft sent this to Congress on December 11. His veto of the wool bill in August, he said, had been due to his knowledge that the Tariff Board would make its report in less than six months. He agreed that Schedule K should be revised downward. In August, however, he had not possessed adequate information on which to determine whether the proposed cuts were "in accord with my pledge to support a fair and reasonable protective policy." But now the Tariff Board was unanimous in its findings. On the basis of them, he recommended "that the Congress proceed to a consideration of this schedule with a view to its revision and a general reduction of its rates." This was an extremely technical subject and the President attempted to summarize it in a brief message to Congress. The rates in Schedule K, he pointed out, were based on unscoured wool with its grease content included. Where the grease content was high, thus leaving a small percentage of wool after cleaning, the rates were prohibitory as compared with Australian imports. A more equitable method would be assessment on scoured wool. As for woolen fabrics, also covered by Schedule K, the Tariff Board studies showed that the cost of turning wool into yarn in the United States was about double that of the leading competing country. The cost of weaving the yarn into cloth was also roughly double.

"Under the protective policy," Taft said, "a great industry, involving the welfare of hundreds of thousands of people, has been established despite these handicaps. In recommending revision and reduction I . . . urge that action be taken with these facts in mind, to the end that an important and established industry may not be jeopardized."

The President took occasion to praise the labors of the Tariff Board and to call its report a "monument to the thoroughness, industry, impartiality, and accuracy of the men engaged in its making." Its inquiry had extended to all parts of the world.[24]

That the Tariff Board had labored conscientiously is certain. But that its report failed to provide an adequate guide for wool and woolen tariffs is also clear. Dr. Taussig of Harvard analyzed the four-volume report in March, 1912, and emphasized the virtual impossibility of determining the cost of producing wool in the United States or anywhere else. And cost was the keynote of the Taft tariff theory. The rates on all products were, as closely as possible, to reconcile higher costs in the United States with lower costs abroad. Dr. Taussig quoted the Tariff Board's study which divided the sheep-producing areas of the United States into three sections: a general farming section extending from the Missouri River eastward, the range region of the Pacific coast and the southwest, and the Ohio region. The cost of raising wool varied from nothing at all in the farming section to 19 cents per pound in the Ohio districts. Dr. Taussig explained why this was so. The average farmer of the first section, he said, kept a few sheep for the sake of the mutton. Sale of the mutton met his costs, so such wool as he obtained was clear profit. The bulk of the wool produced in the United States came from the range regions where the climate was mild, where the rainfall was slight, where sheep were kept principally for their wool. The cost of production "is lower here than in any [other] part of the United States, and very likely as low as in competing foreign countries." So this section, under the Taft tariff doctrine, did not need protection, either. But the Ohio region, the smallest of all, was one, Dr. Taussig said, in which "sheep raising seems to be carried on with an approach to obstinacy." The district included eastern Ohio, near-by portions of Pennsylvania and West Virginia and certain parts of Michigan. The section was ill-adapted to sheep raising and yet the herds were maintained and the highest cost wool produced. In this, the smallest section, the need for protection was greatest.

[24] *Message,* Dec. 20, 1911.

"What light now," the Harvard economist asked, "do the results of the whole investigation throw on the expediency of maintaining the duty on wool, or on the rate of duty which should be levied, if one is to be maintained? I confess that the situation seems to be in no sensible degree cleared up for the legislator. So far as the general expediency of the duty on wool is concerned, he must still reach his conclusion upon general principles. . . . For myself, everything I read in the report strengthens the conviction which I have long held and declared, that there is no good ground for maintaining a duty on wool. . . . The strength of the wool duty lies not in economic reasoning, but in the inevitable wish of every industry in every part of the country to get its share of what seems to be the benefits of protection."

And even if the necessity for a tariff were admitted, Dr. Taussig continued, how were the rates to be determined? ". . . if you give a duty high enough to equalize cost of production for the producer having greatest expense," he said, "you give more than enough for the one who has less expense." Nor was the problem any easier when it came to woolen fabrics. He quoted, with apparent amusement, the president of the American Woolen Company, who had declared, in February, 1911, that Schedule K, if only properly understood, would be the "most appreciated of any schedule in the Payne-Aldrich act," that if all the schedules were comparably just and scientific the act "would be the most remarkable document, next to the Constitution of the United States, that the human mind has ever produced." Dr. Taussig did not share this enthusiasm. As far as fabrics were concerned, their cost of manufacture varied greatly in different parts of the country. The high-cost producer was demanding a tariff high enough to meet the penalties of his inefficiency. The study of the Tariff Board, concluded Dr. Taussig, gave indication, at least, that "efficiency is low and cost of production high in American mills." [25]

A reprint of Taussig's searching criticism of the Tariff Board's report was sent to the President and was filed with his papers. But it may be doubted that Taft read it, for Taussig, after all, was tainted with free-trade heresies. In any event, the President would tolerate no bill granting reductions in excess of those justified, as

[25] *American Economic Review*, June, 1912.

he saw it, by the Tariff Board report. The cuts proposed by Senator LaFollette, he said, "would close up the factories of New England." [26] The President would have been willing to sign either of the measures which first emerged from the House and the Senate. He rejected LaFollette's compromise measure.

"I shall veto it with a thump," he declared on August 5, 1912.[27] He did not care, he added, "what the public thinks. . . . If the people of the country want to go into the business of destroying the industries, why, they can do it through some other president than me." [28]

The second report of the Tariff Board related to cotton manufactures; again reductions were recommended. This time, LaFollette supported the administration measure and Taft tried to force such standpatters as Murray Crane into line.[29] The 1912 campaign was well under way by this time, however, and the bill died in Congress. Taft's faith in a protective tariff did not falter. The party platform on which he sought re-election contained all the old aphorisms about protection for the workingmen against competition by the wages of European countries. Taft's final word on this troublesome subject was in his December, 1912, message. He reiterated his conviction that protection was vital to American prosperity. But a new Congress had been elected "on a platform of a tariff for revenue only . . . and . . . it is needless for me to occupy the time of this Congress with arguments or recommendations in favor of a protective tariff." [30]

—5—

A minor annoyance of 1912 was the resignation of Harvey W. Wiley, the pure-food pioneer, as chief chemist for the Department of Agriculture. Taft was held responsible for this too, although there is nothing to indicate that he had anything whatever to do with it. At the time of his resignation, in fact, Wiley said he was "profoundly grateful" because the President had prevented "my forcible separation from the public service." [31] On the other

[26] Taft to Emery, July 26, 1912. [27] Taft to A. J. Pothier, Aug. 5, 1912. [28] Taft to J. J. Hill, Aug. 9, 1912. [29] Taft to Crane, Aug. 12, 1912. [30] *Addresses*, Vol. XXX, p. 264. [31] Wiley, H. W., *An Autobiography*, pp. 287-291.

hand, Taft probably did not adequately reassure Dr. Wiley that the enemies of pure-food legislation were the enemies of the White House too. It would have been difficult to do this. Even Theodore Roosevelt had found Dr. Wiley's fanatical zeal just a shade wearisome at times.[32] President Taft, like President Roosevelt, approved of Wiley's work, but doubted that his methods were always sound.

The necessary legislation had been passed in the Roosevelt years. Dr. Wiley's work had become largely administrative. "I mean to enforce the pure-food law as fully and fairly as possible," the President said when he took office, "and I expect to give Dr. Wiley the reasonable and just support that he is entitled to have. But when I feel that he has done an injustice I expect to differ with him even at the expense of having my motives questioned." [33]

No issue arose, whatever the President's inner doubts may have been. He formally upheld Dr. Wiley when charges were preferred against the chief chemist in the spring of 1911. The accusations were trivial. It was alleged that Wiley had employed certain pure-food experts in a manner not wholly in accordance with the law. Specifically, he had engaged Dr. H. H. Rusby, a distinguished pharmacologist, at a per diem rate of $20 when a Congressional act forbade compensation higher than $9. This had been done by allowing Dr. Rusby an annual salary and then limiting the number of days of work required. The President, reviewing the evidence, considered the accusation nonsensical. It was of doubtful wisdom, he added, that bureau chiefs should thus be hampered in the employment of needed experts.[34]

The President was distinctly annoyed that Secretary of Agriculture Wilson had allowed the charges to be brought and even considered getting rid of him because of the situation which "shows how poor a secretary he is."

"The Wiley business is a mess," he further confided to Mrs. Taft, "and I am inclined to think I may have to get a new secretary of agriculture. Uncle Jimmy is not strong enough to manage. But he stands well with the farmers and it might be difficult to get rid of him." [35]

[32] Pringle, H. F., *Theodore Roosevelt, a Biography*, p. 429. [33] Taft to H. D. Ward, March 24, 1919. [34] Taft to Wilson, Sept. 14, 1911. [35] Taft to Helen H. Taft, July 26, Aug. 19, 1911.

But the President did not, of course, dismiss the aged secretary. Nor did he— it would not have been characteristic— take a strong, public position in defense of Dr. Wiley. That the chief chemist's work was obstructed by political pressure is probable. Evidence was presented to the President that Wilson was an obstacle to adequate enforcement of the pure-food laws.[36] Taft, beyond upholding Wiley in the formal charges, took no sides and so was damned by each. In March, 1912, Wiley resigned. He realized, he said, "that conditions in the Department of Agriculture would be intolerable. Secretary Wilson, approaching his dotage, was alertly antagonistic." [37] His resignation became an issue in the approaching campaign. It was officially denied that the President had requested Wiley to resign,[38] but outraged protests filled the White House mail. The National Consumers' League's Food Committee declared it the "most serious blow that has fallen on pure-food legislation." [39]

Women were just becoming conscious of their political power. Few of them voted as yet, but they had mastered the devices of publicity. A committee of the New York State Federation of Women's Clubs demanded whether Taft, if elected, would reappoint Secretary Wilson to office.[40]

Even then, Taft did nothing. This, after all, was merely one detail in days which were brimming with trouble. The amiable Uncle Jimmy Wilson seems to have had no faint idea that he had added to the worries of his chief. At a Cabinet meeting he suggested that a Dr. Beale of Ohio would make an excellent successor to Wiley. He was well qualified. Besides, pointed out the secretary of agriculture, his appointment would please the Republicans of Ohio.[41] The President's energies must have been at a low ebb when this proposal to combine the pure-food cause with a G.O.P. victory in Ohio was made. His answer was pathetic. He said that he was willing to name Beale.

"I wish you would give out the fact that he is appointed on your recommendation," he told Secretary Wilson, "and not because he is an Ohio man." [42]

The ubiquitous Harry Daugherty also pleaded for Beale's ap-

[36] L. S. Dow to A. I. Vorys, Sept. 11, 1911. [37] Wiley, H. W., *op. cit.*, p. 291. [38] R. Forster to C. H. Davison, May 15, 1912. [39] Alice Lakey to Taft, May 21, 1912. [40] Mrs. C. A. Hirst to Taft, July 11, 1912. [41] Wilson to Taft, July 19, 1912. [42] Taft to Wilson, July 19, 1912.

pointment to aid the Ohio situation.[43] For some reason it was not made, however; perhaps the President's better nature came to his aid and prevented it. The matter was delayed until after Election Day, when Carl L. Alsberg, a biochemist of reputation and distinction, was selected. The President assured himself that Wiley's resignation had been no loss to the government. On the contrary, he wrote in the first draft of a private letter, his withdrawal had "removed a constant source of dissension and lack of harmony." He had been a "very earnest prosecutor of those whom he regarded as guilty of violating the Pure Food act, but it is doubtful whether he exercised the discretion and care in the selection of those whom he prosecuted which would have avoided unnecessary work and wasteful trouble in the department."

The paragraph fell under the watchful eye of Charles D. Hilles, who had returned to his post as presidential secretary after his faithful but futile efforts as chairman of the Republican National Committee. Wiley, meanwhile, had supported Woodrow Wilson in the campaign. Hilles scrawled a note opposite the offending lines:

"This would revive the Wiley controversy and be nuts for Wiley and probably turned to account in his Cabinet aspirations."

So the paragraph was stricken from a second draft of the letter.[44]

—6—

The Ballinger-Pinchot controversy echoed, too, through the last two years. The President had rejected the contention that his secretary of the interior had been less than vigilant in protecting the coal lands of Alaska. Pinchot, who had given credence and wide publicity to the charges against Ballinger, had been removed from his post as chief forester and was the martyred hero of the Republican insurgents. It was no secret, in early 1911, that he would support either LaFollette or Roosevelt for the 1912 nomination. Demands were incessant that the President bow before the political winds and request the resignation of his secretary of the interior. With that stubbornness which grew in him as his misfortunes increased, Taft brusquely declined to consider such action. He

[43] Daugherty to Taft, Aug. 12, 1912. [44] Taft to G. P. McQuade, Jan. 24, 1913.

resisted, even, that official's own desire to retire voluntarily. When the end had come, when in November, 1912, the President surveyed the wreckage and pondered on the causes behind it all, he did not deceive himself that the row over conservation had not been a principal cause.

"I might have let Ballinger go right away," he said, "but Ballinger's fate was the result of a deliberate conspiracy, and I can hardly hold myself responsible for the result of a malign combination.[45]

By January, 1911, the secretary of the interior was looking wistfully toward private life. He had discussed resigning at a Cabinet meeting and had been urged by Taft to delay it. In a poignant letter Ballinger expressed his gratitude for the President's expressions of confidence which "certainly compensate me in the largest measure for what I have suffered." But his health was bad, Ballinger added. He requested that his resignation be accepted at the earliest possible moment. Taft's reply was poignant too:

For reasons which have deeply impressed themselves in my heart and mind, I would never consent to consider your resignation on any ground that was based on the good of the service or of helping me personally or politically, for no such ground is tenable by me. Only on the score of your health or personal convenience or to prevent further pecuniary sacrifice on your part will I consider the possibility of accepting your resignation. But not even on the latter grounds will I consider it until after Congress adjourns, until after all unjust attacks are ended and . . . until we have reached the calm period which I hope will follow the present hurry and pressure.[46]

Yet it was futile to hope that any period without hurry and pressure would come until after March 4, 1913. Ballinger, whose heart was overburdened by all the criticism, renewed his pleas in March, 1911. His health and personal financial situation demanded relief, he said.[47] So the President consented to his resignation. In accepting it, he repeated his faith and confidence. He expressed again his conviction that Ballinger had been "the object of one

[45] Taft to O. T. Bannard, Nov. 10, 1912. [46] Ballinger to Taft, Jan. 19; Taft to Ballinger, Jan. 23, 1911. [47] Ballinger to Taft, March 6, 1911.

of the most unscrupulous conspiracies for the defamation of character that history can show."

With the hypocritical pretense that they did not accuse you of corruption in order to avoid the necessity, that even the worst criminal is entitled to . . . that of a definitely formulated charge of some misconduct, they showered you with suspicion and by the most pettifogging methods exploited to the public matters which had no relevancy to an issue of either corruption or efficiency in office, but which, paraded before an hysterical body of headline readers, served to blacken your character and to obscure the proper issue of your honesty and effectiveness as a public servant. The result has been a cruel tragedy. You and yours have lost health and have been burdened financially. The conspirators who have not hesitated . . . to resort to the meanest of methods . . . plume themselves, like the Pharisees of old, as the only pure members of society actuated by the spirit of self-sacrifice for their fellow men.

Every fiber of my nature rebels against such hypocrisy and nerves me to fight such a combination and such methods to the bitter end. . . . But personal consideration for you and yours makes me feel that I have no right to ask you for further sacrifice. . . .

As I say farewell to you, let me renew my expressions of affection and sincerest respect for you and of my profound gratitude for your hard work, your unvarying loyalty and your effective public service. I hope and pray that success may attend you in your profession and that real happiness will come to you and yours when you return to that community where you live and whose members know your worth as a man and a citizen and who will receive you again with open arms.[48]

Walter L. Fisher, a Chicago attorney long active in the conservation cause, was named successor to Ballinger in the Interior Department. He had been regarded as a Pinchot disciple and his appointment met with favor.

—7—

The farm problem, too, raised its head while Taft was president. Again, nothing concrete was done because the time was so short. The

[48] Taft to Ballinger, March 7, 1911.

problem was simple compared with the perplexities which would haunt other presidents before a decade had passed. The world of 1912 was relatively orderly. The markets of Europe still consumed part of any surplus in farm products. The people of Europe, in marked contrast to the postwar years, still could pay for what they bought. But the farmer of 1912, like the farmers of 1900 and 1936, felt that he was being discriminated against.

It was to this aspect of the farm problem that Taft gave attention. A Conference of Governors was scheduled to be held in Richmond, Virginia, in December, 1912. The President addressed a letter to the chief executives of all the states pointing to the need of "an adequate financial system as an aid to the farmers of this country." On their $6,000,000,000 of borrowed capital, he said, they paid an average of 8½ per cent interest, "considerably higher than that paid by our industrial corporations, railroads or municipalities." The President had instructed the Department of State to investigate loans to agriculture in France and Germany; the rates in those countries were 4½ to 3½ per cent. The disparity was due, he added, to the financial machinery at the command of the American industrialist and, as far as Germany and France were concerned, to assistance given by the governments of those countries.

Almost twenty-five years have passed since President Taft thus discussed a problem which would baffle all the presidents who followed him to the White House. A quarter century has made archaic one of his well-meant observations. He did not propose to subsidize the farmer, he said.

"Fortunately for this country," he observed, "he does not need it nor would he accept it."

The suggested plan was the establishment of credit unions under state and federal supervision. Such institutions would supply loans at lowered rates. They would, the President was confident, "secure to this country greater productivity, at less cost, from the farms that are now under cultivation, and, above all . . . give us more farms and more farmers." Obviously, Mr. Taft was disturbed by no visions of the years ahead when the farmers, denied a subsidy, would turn on the Republican party in vengeance, when the trouble with agriculture lay in too many farms, too many farmers, too much wheat and corn and little pigs.

President Taft urged that the Conference of Governors give due attention to the matter at the Richmond meeting.[49] This was done. Resolutions were adopted and committees appointed. The governors paused in Washington for a luncheon at the White House on December 11 and heard the President repeat his recommendation for cheap credit so that "the land now used shall produce double or treble what it has been accustomed to produce in the past." [50]

But Congress did not act on this vital matter, either. How could a defeated president enforce his will on its members? And Taft had, in all truth, been a defeated president from at least the start of 1912. Even in June, he had been embarrassed by the refusal of the legislative branch to appropriate the funds essential to the operation of the government and had been forced to appeal, by special message, so that the United States could continue to function.[51]

"I think Congress has dragged itself out to such a length that the people have become very impatient," the President observed as August ended. "The effort of Congress to put me in the hole, to pass bad legislation by saddling it as riders on appropriation bills, and the evident playing of politics, have not raised the opinion of the people as to the statesmanship of those who lead in the House of Representatives." [52]

All evils end at last, however. Congress finally grew weary. Its members hurried home to achieve re-election if possible. Only the short session, to convene in December, remained. Taft wrote two messages for its edification and instruction.

"I presume people will not be very much interested in what I have to say," he observed candidly, "because Congress will hear the messages read, or escape hearing them by going into the cloakrooms and then do nothing on the subject; as it is my valedictory, I have to say something." [53]

[49] Taft to Charles S. Dubeen et al. Oct. 11, 1912. [50] Stenographic transcript, White House conference, Dec. 7, 1912. [51] Taft to MacVeagh, June 25, 1912. [52] Taft to C. P. Taft, Aug. 25, 1912. [53] Idem, Dec. 2, 1912.

CHAPTER XXXVIII

A FINAL FUTILE DREAM

WAR CLOUDS, when they came, usually drifted up from the Caribbean and South America. Sometimes their dark mass took shape over Japan and China. Clouds were nearly always present, although these were not very menacing, above Mexico. But nobody worried greatly, for the myth of isolation persisted long after the close of the nineteenth century. Theodore Roosevelt, it is true, had occasionally been apprehensive that a war with Great Britain was a remote possibility and had, at times, regarded the German Kaiser with alarm. Generally speaking, though, conflict with a European power seemed as remote in the United States as war against another planet. For little was known of the dark labyrinths of European diplomacy. The year of cataclysm— 1914— might have been decades away.

William Howard Taft, in common with the vast majority of his fellow citizens, shared the belief that the chief danger lay southward. Yet he was to be, until he died, an ardent worker in behalf of international harmony. International altruism, to an extent, motivated his actions until the World War had arrived and the warring nations, once so comfortably far off, became alarmingly close. The possibility of war, Taft said soon after he became president, came "chiefly from irresponsibilities of governments . . . in those countries where the stability of internal control is lacking." Thus it was the duty of the United States to strengthen the nations— he referred, of course, to Central and South America— which still found self-government a difficult problem.

"The policy of the United States in avoiding war under all circumstances except those plainly inconsistent with honor . . ." the President wrote, "has been so clear to the whole world as hardly to need statement at my hands." [1]

It was true that the United States sought no new territory, nor

---

[1] Taft to Royal Melandy, April 28, 1909.

did it have other evil designs on any nation. Thus its presidents often shared the futile dream that the battle flags might ultimately be furled. Cleveland tried to hasten the day by negotiating an arbitration treaty with England. McKinley attempted to secure ratification of this agreement by the Senate. A National Arbitration Committee was formed in 1897 with John Bassett Moore, Charles W. Eliot of Harvard, Carl Schurz and Taft among its members.[2] Roosevelt, whose heart was less in the movement for peace, also attempted to negotiate arbitration agreements when he succeeded McKinley. He, too, ran headlong into the Senate's distaste.[3]

"A treaty entering the Senate," John Hay remarked sourly, "is like a bull going into the arena; no one can say just when or how the blow will fall— but one thing is certain— it will never leave the arena alive." [4]

So Cleveland had learned. So McKinley learned. Roosevelt and Taft had identical experiences. And Woodrow Wilson would die, bitter and brokenhearted, because his own dream of peace was shattered by the United States Senate. The attempts of President Taft to banish war with both Great Britain and France were, however, the first in which the arbitration treaties really meant anything. Questions affecting "vital interests" of the United States and other such all-inclusive and vague subjects as "national honor" and "independence" had been eliminated from the earlier agreements.[5] Pallid compacts were actually negotiated with England and other countries during Roosevelt's last years.

"We now have treaties of arbitration . . ." pointed out President Taft in October, 1911, "in which we agree to submit all questions that do not affect our national honor and do not affect our vital interest. Well, that seems to me to be an agreement to arbitrate everything that is highly unimportant. We leave out the questions which when they arise are likely to lead to war. If arbitration is worth anything it is an instrumentality for avoiding war. *But, it is asked, would you arbitrate a question of national honor? I am not afraid of that question. Of course I would."* [6]

He had been saying this, over and over, for eighteen months.

[2] Nevins, Allan, *Grover Cleveland, A Study in Courage,* pp. 719-720. [3] Dennett, Tyler, *John Hay,* pp. 410-411. [4] Thayer, W. R., *Life and Letters of John Hay,* Vol. II, p. 293. [5] Dennett, Tyler, *op. cit.,* pp. 435-436. [6] *Addresses,* Vol. XXIII, p. 299. (Italics mine.)

This was Taft's vital contribution to the cause of international peace. It was new. It was brave. True, it was visionary also, and was the lawyer's too-simple reliance upon law. Yet it is curious that Taft was ignored in the award of the Nobel Peace Prize although Roosevelt received it. He was a far better friend of peace than Roosevelt had ever been. For Roosevelt, having received the Nobel accolade for terminating the Russo-Japanese War, betrayed the cause by turning against Taft's arbitration agreements and by contributing materially to their defeat.

—2—

The peace movement of the Taft years was born on the night of February 6, 1910, when Theodore Marburg, a Baltimore publicist, gave a small dinner at which was organized the American Society for the Judicial Settlement of International Disputes. Letters of endorsement were read from Secretary of State Knox, Woodrow Wilson and President Taft.[7] The President, accepting the post of honorary president, believed that the organization might "have a very great influence on the development of public opinion on this important subject." It was only through an aroused public opinion in all the countries concerned with peace, he said, that the movement to end war could become effective.[8] Any president might with impunity have said as much as that, but Taft went further. He spoke in New York in March. He described the futility of war, even to the nation which emerged victorious. A permanent court of arbitration to which "all questions" would be referred would surely prove a deterrent to war. Then the President— this was his first public statement on the subject— boldly declared that questions of national honor must be included.

"I have noticed exceptions in our arbitration treaties," he said, "as to reference of questions of honor, of national honor, to courts of arbitration. Personally, I don't see any more reason why matters of national honor should not be referred to a court . . . any more than matters of property or matters of national proprietorship. I

[7] Hammond, J. H., *The Autobiography of John Hays Hammond*, Vol. II, pp. 612-613.
[8] Taft to Marburg, Jan. 31, 1910.

FOR AULD LANG SYNE.

UNCLE SAM (*philosophically watching the Taft-Roosevelt scrap*). "WAL! I GUESS OLD FRIENDS ARE THE BEST!"

HORACE TAFT, THE PRESIDENT AND THEIR AUNT, DELIA TORREY

Photo by The Wohlbruck Studio

know that is going further than most men are willing to go, but as among men, we have to submit differences even if they involve honor, now, if we obey the law, to the court, or let them go undecided. . . . I do not see why questions of honor may not be submitted to a tribunal supposed to be composed of men of honor who understand questions of national honor." [9]

He spoke again, in December, 1910; this time it was before Marburg's arbitration society. The issue was clear, the President said: ". . . if we do not have arbitration," he warned, "we shall have war."

"If we can now negotiate and put through an agreement with some great nation to abide the adjudication of an international arbitral court in every issue which cannot be settled by negotiation, no matter what it involves, whether honor, territory or money," Taft continued, "we shall have made a long step forward . . . the establishment of a general arbitral court for all nations is no longer the figment of the brain of a dreamy enthusiast." [10]

Applause echoed through the New Willard in Washington where the President had been speaking. As he sat down, Ambassador Jules Jusserand of France, seated at his right, plucked at the presidential sleeve.

"We will make such a treaty with you, if you will make it with us," he said.

"I'm your man," the President answered.[11]

Taft's hopes were high. No treaties had been drafted as yet. It was not yet apparent that the Senate would again guard jealously its prerogatives in the management of foreign affairs. Throughout the world, it seemed, men were desperately anxious that war might be prevented. Had not even Theodore Roosevelt, accepting the Nobel Prize at Christiania in May, asked for a League of Peace which would, "by force if necessary" establish peace among the nations of the earth? A careful reading of Roosevelt's address, it is true, might have brought foreboding to the friends of arbitration. It was, in Rooseveltian fashion, replete with references to "righteousness": ". . . the peace of righteousness and justice," the Rough Rider said, was "the only kind of peace worth having." Roosevelt,

---

[9] *Addresses,* Vol. XVIII, pp. 127-128. [10] *Ibid.,* Vol. XX, pp. 90-97. [11] *Ibid.,* Vol. XXIII, pp. 245-246.

as always, was a shade condescending toward peace; the goddess, after all, was an effeminate creature. Peace was a "very evil thing" if it became a "mask for cowardice and sloth." No nation "deserves to exist if it permits itself to lose the stern and virile virtues."

But even Roosevelt, "having freely admitted the limitations" to the peace movement, conceded the possibility of arbitration except with "states so backward" that any agreement would prove invalid. Only in "very rare cases" would questions arise concerning national honor, he said; such questions could not, of course, be arbitrated. Finally, there should be a League of Peace which would have the power to enforce its decrees.[12]

The public's endorsement of the peace movement was strong enough to impress Congress. Both houses, by joint resolution, called for the creation of a peace commission in June 1910. It would consist of five members appointed by the President. It would, in the words of the resolution, "consider the expediency of utilizing existing international agencies for the purpose of limiting the armaments of the nations of the world by international agreement, and of consti- tuting the combined navies of the world an international force for the preservation of universal peace, and to consider and report upon any other means to diminish the expenditures of governments for military purposes and to lessen the probabilities of war." [13]

". . . your proposition to have Mr. Roosevelt put at the head of the commission met my full concurrence," the President wrote to an adviser, "but he definitely declined to accept." [14]

The Congressional resolution, particularly in its suggestion for an international navy, was far too radical and nothing would come of it. The President's first step was to obtain the reaction of Euro- pean powers. On November 16, 1910, the State Department made inquiry of Austria-Hungary, Belgium, France, Germany, Great Britain, Italy, Japan, the Netherlands, Russia and Turkey. The replies, couched in the ambiguously friendly verbiage of diplomacy, were less than encouraging. From Austria-Hungary came word that the purpose behind the suggestion was laudable; but what was the attitude of the other nations? Little Belgium, in the words of its Foreign Office, found the joint resolution "too vague in its general

[12] Roosevelt, Theodore, Works, Homeward Bound Edition, Vol. VIII, pp. 2217-2223.
[13] Addresses, Vol. XX, p. 3. [14] Taft to Richard Bartholdt, July 3, 1910.

intent." Ambassador Bacon reported from Paris that France did not believe that the time was right for such action. Germany could not discern a "suitable basis" for discussion of the question. Great Britain would "most readily enter into a full and frank interchange of views with the United States government . . . and would lend their support to any well-considered and practical scheme." This was the best of all the replies, but it placed all responsibility and initiative on the United States. Italy, too, offered sweet words of endorsement. Russia could not "conceive that at the present time any practical measures for the attainment of those purposes could be agreed upon by all the powers." The State Department at Washington, analyzing the answers, thought that the powers "showed considerable hesitation for various reasons in participating in the movement." So the subject was quietly dropped.[15]

—3—

More important than these ineffective negotiations were the speeches which Taft had made in March and December, 1910; the speeches in which he had included national honor as among the subjects open to arbitration. Among others, Andrew Carnegie was delighted with them. The ironmaster had long been an ardent, if dreamy, peace disciple. Roosevelt, at his request and with Taft's approval, had agreed to discuss the subject with Kaiser Wilhelm II and with representatives of Great Britain during the course of his triumphant processional through Europe. But nothing resulted from these conversations, either.[16] Carnegie was not discouraged, though. His whiskers bristled with elation when he read the President's utterances on arbitration. On December 24, 1910, he gave $10,000,000 for the creation of a Carnegie Peace Fund. The revenue would be used to hasten the cause.

The shortest and easiest method by which peace could be achieved, Carnegie said, was to adopt the views of President Taft as expressed in his March, 1910, speech. Still faithful, to an extent, to

[15] State Department memorandum, June 2, 1911. [16] Hendrick, Burton J., *The Life of Andrew Carnegie*, Vol. II, pp. 302-318.

the simplified spelling which Roosevelt had briefly publicized and then abandoned, Mr. Carnegie wrote:

> When civilized nations enter into such treaties . . . and war is discarded as disgraceful to civilized man . . . the Trustees [of the Carnegie Peace Fund] will pleas then consider what is the next most degrading remaining evil or evils whose banishment . . . would most advance the progress, elevation and happiness of man, and so on from century to century without end, my trustees of each age shall determin how they can best aid man in his upward march to higher and higher stages of development unceasingly, for now we know that man was created, not with an instinct for his own degredation, but imbued with the desire and the power for improvement to which, perchance, there may be no limit short of perfection even here in this life upon erth.[17]

And to President Taft, in the same breath, the extraordinary and far too optimistic little Scot poured out his gratitude:

> You will note that your noble note of leadership among Rulers prompted me to create the fund. It is based upon your words. I saw clearly that peace was within our grasp because the other branch of our race (English speaking) was redy to follow you. You have only to put out your hand to secure this and, this secured, other nations will soon follow.[18]

But the Utopia whose gleaming pinnacles Carnegie had glimpsed against a peaceful sky was only a mirage, after all. A quarter of a century would pass and the world would be further still from its parliaments of arbitration. Before a brief five years had elapsed guns would be roaring on the western front and the Highland lads who tilled the soil around Carnegie's own dear Skibo Castle would parade to their doom on the skirl of bagpipes. Carnegie's fantastic march toward peace never began. For Theodore Roosevelt would soon be marching too, while in the Senate an earlier Battalion of Death, like the one which killed the League of Nations, was forming its platoons.

President Taft knew, by March of 1911, that Theodore would

[17] Carnegie to Carnegie Peace Fund trustees, Dec. 4, 1910. [18] Carnegie to Taft, Dec. 4, 1910.

be his foe in the fight for arbitration. Roosevelt, from his unsatisfactory sanctuary in the offices of the *Outlook,* had been expressing opposition to the proposal that all questions, even those affecting national honor, might be settled by peaceful methods.

"I am sorry that Theodore thought it necessary to come out in advance of a definite knowledge of what we are trying to do," the President told Carnegie, "but I venture to think that what he says is so much aside from the real point that both he and the public will see it, and that it will not interfere with the consummation of what you and I both desire." [19]

At first, the agreements were to be limited to Great Britain and France. Roosevelt's first public attack appeared in the *Outlook* in May, 1911. It was a confused journalistic effort which opened with the statement that a universal arbitration treaty between the United States and England was possible because "the two nations have achieved that point of civilization where each can be trusted not to do to the other any one of the offenses which ought to preclude any self-respecting nation from appealing to arbitration." Then followed an inaccurate comparison with the individual who would permit his wife's face to be slapped in his presence by another man. In relatively civilized countries, Roosevelt said, this could hardly happen and therefore "it is not necessary to say that a man reserves to himself the right to assault anyone who . . . slaps his wife's face." He added:

In just the same way, the United States ought never specifically to bind itself to arbitrate questions respecting its honor, independence, and integrity. Either it should be tacitly understood that the contracting powers no more agree to surrender their rights on such vital matters than a man in civil life agrees to surrender the right of self-defense; or else it should be explicitly stated that, because of the fact that it is now impossible for either party to take any action infringing the honor, independence, and integrity of the other, we are willing to arbitrate all questions.

". . . we should be very cautious of entering into a treaty with any nation, however closely knit to us, the form of which it would be impossible to follow in making treaties with other great civilized

[19] Taft to Carnegie, March 20, 1911.

and friendly nations," Roosevelt concluded.[20] What he meant, although he did not say so, was that an effective treaty, even with England, was inadvisable. Ten days later, however, his language was more clear. He repeated his earlier attacks on "mollycoddles" who did not like to fight. He expressed his contempt for "unrighteous peace." [21]

Taft may have been dismayed by Roosevelt's hostility, but Secretary of State Knox, by his order, proceeded with the work of negotiating agreements with Great Britain, France and possibly Germany. Germany hesitated and the President told Ambassador Bryce as July ended that he would not wait much longer.[22] Successful drafts with England and with France were obtained; Germany dropped out. The treaties were signed by the nations' representatives on August 3, 1911, and the President expressed hope that similar agreements with Germany, Russia, the Netherlands, Norway and Sweden might shortly be effected. Even Japan, he hoped, might be induced "to come in." [23] All this, of course, was subject to confirmation by the Senate.

Carnegie, watching with eager joy from Skibo Castle, was deliriously happy when word of the signing of the treaties reached him. "You have reached the summit of human glory," he cabled. "Countless ages are to honor and bless your name." [24]

The President was touched by the praise. "I am delighted that the arbitration treaties are signed," he replied. "The part that I have taken . . . will always be a great satisfaction to me and I thank you from the bottom of my heart not only for what you have been good enough to say in this cable, but for your constant and unvarying encouragement and support. . . . The treaties are now before the Senate and I am hopeful that they will be ratified there." [25]

—4—

Just what did the treaties provide and why did the Senate reject them? They covered, stated the first clause:

[20] *Outlook,* May 20, 1911. [21] New York *World,* May 31, 1911. [22] Taft to Bryce, July 26, 1911. [23] Taft to C. P. Taft, Aug. 3, 1911. [24] Carnegie to Taft, Aug. 4, 1911. [25] Taft to Carnegie, Aug. 5, 1911.

All differences . . . relating to international matters in which the high contracting parties are concerned by virtue of a claim of right made by one against the other under treaty or otherwise, and which are *justiciable* in their nature by reason of being susceptible of decision by the application of the principles of law or equity.

The important word in the clause is "justiciable." Taft's explanation of it— unfortunately, this particular definition was not offered until he had left the White House— was as clear as it was logical. As the agreements were being drafted, he explained, it had been "necessary to hit upon some term which would define, as a class, those causes of differences between nations that would constitute . . . an infringement of . . . legal rights analogous to rights remedial in municipal courts of justice between individuals." Secretary of State Knox had discovered the word "justiciable" in an opinion rendered by Chief Justice Fuller. Among other things, Taft pointed out, the inalienable right of a nation to self-preservation was not justiciable and could not be decided by arbitration.

All nations had domination over all matters in their own territories. They controlled, beyond question, "revenues, arts, agriculture and commerce." No nation could be forced "to observe the demands of comity, that is, of good neighborly feeling." Taft offered specific illustrations of justiciable questions. Great Britain, he said, might decline to take part in the Panama Exposition at San Francisco and this might cause bad feeling in California. No court of arbitration, however, could rule that England must participate. So it was, also, between individuals. You could not bring a man into court because he did not call on his neighbor.

". . . he may do a lot of unkind things . . . and show that he is a very mean man," Taft remarked. ". . . But these do not give any cause for a suit. In other words, there is a field into which the courts of justice cannot enter, whether they be municipal courts in a state, or arbitral courts between nations, and that distinction must be just as clear in an international court as in one of our domestic tribunals."

So justiciable differences, subject to arbitration, were "those causes of difference between nations that would constitute under the principles of international law, an infringement of the legal rights of another nation analogous to rights remedial in municipal courts of justice between nations." [26]

It is obvious, now, that Taft's plan, however noble, would not have worked. Sir Alfred Zimmern, historian of the League of Nations, pays tribute to his motives but questions his practicality.

"President Taft, in his whole approach to the problem of international politics, was beginning at the wrong end. His 'ideal,' closely examined, is not a world community living under the rule of law. It is a fraction of a system of world-government set up in a void. It is a judicature without a legislature, with only so much of an executive as is needed to enforce the decisions of the bench, and with no social consciousness to rest upon. The bench of Mr. Taft's imagination would have no law to administer. It would not even be *part* of a constitutional system. It would be an array of wigs and gowns vociferating in emptiness." [27]

—5—

The first clause of the treaties with England and France, which were almost identical, provided that "justiciable" differences should be submitted to the Permanent Court of Arbitration at The Hague or to some other tribunal agreed upon. Speaking in defense of the agreements on his western tour in October, 1911, President Taft explained this too:

This Joint High Commission shall consist of three Americans and three Englishmen [or Frenchmen]. Now the business of that Joint High Commission is first to take up all the differences that occur that have not been settled by negotiation, and they recommend to the two nations, after a year's delay, what settlement ought to be taken. *Their action is advisory.* They don't decide anything except one thing and that one thing is under the third clause.

By the terms of the third clause, the President said, the Joint High Commission would decide whether the question at issue was

[26] Taft, W. H., *The United States and Peace*, pp. 101-108. (Italics mine.) [27] Zimmern, Alfred, *The League of Nations and the Rule of Law*, pp. 124-125.

justiciable or not and whether it could be submitted for arbitration. It was this clause, however, to which the Senate took exception.

". . . it is the third clause," Taft pleaded, "that I am most interested to have go into the treaty, for the reason that that third clause makes this treaty mean something. If we are going to leave it to ourselves to decide, when a question arises, whether we think it is justiciable or not, then we will probably decide that it is justiciable and can be settled . . . when it is likely to come our way, and when it does not we will probably say that it is not justiciable. . . . To make a treaty that shall always work our way, to play the game of 'Heads I win, tails you lose,' is to accomplish nothing . . . in this world toward Christian civilization." [28]

It was specified that a vote of five to one by the High Commission would be necessary before an issue was declared valid and submitted to The Hague. Taft, as the treaties were being written, had wished to go further than "this . . . very mild provision." He had suggested to Knox that complaints might be submitted directly to The Hague, but the secretary of state had objected that so radical a proposal would be defeated by the Senate.[29] He was correct. That august tribunal would even reject the idea that two out of the three American members of the commission were competent to protect their country. The Senate, alone, was qualified to do so. A majority of the Foreign Relations Committee promptly decided against the treaties. The Senate ought not to surrender, to a High Commission or any other body, its power to rule when an issue should be arbitrated. But Taft was certain the people would disagree.

"I am going . . . to see," Taft said late in August, 1911, "if I cannot arouse the country. . . . Carnegie and all the peace cranks are interested in this, as well as the church, and I am hopeful that we may set a fire under the senators which may change their views." [30]

It is possible that he might have done so had not Roosevelt tossed water on the embers whenever they started to burn. Theodore Marburg, whose 1910 dinner in Baltimore had started the whole thing, told the President on August 13 that he had lunched with Roosevelt in New York:

[28] *Addresses*, Vol. XXIII, pp. 227-228. (Italics mine.) [29] Taft, W. H., *op. cit.*, pp. 110-111. [30] Taft to R. A. Taft, Aug. 27, 1911.

His talk was along the usual line, 'righteousness before peace.' The trouble about that doctrine is: who is to determine righteousness? Every nation thinks its cause is righteous. . . . Col. Roosevelt's attack on the arbitration treaties will not carry far. It is calling names rather than argument and people are beginning to realize that Col. Roosevelt is unfair. While abroad, I heard the opinion expressed that whereas when you took office they regarded you as Mr. Roosevelt's understudy, they now felt that you were decidedly the bigger man.[31]

Sweet words of encouragement, these, but they were less than accurate in their note of prophecy. For Marburg did not know, as Taft did not know himself, that the people nearly always listened to billingsgate, that argument and logic invariably fell on ears that would not hear.

The President deluded himself that the Rooseveltian opposition was unimportant. "The colonel's attacks on the treaties are a bit annoying," he admitted, "but I don't think they help him or hurt the cause much. He is so lacking in legal knowledge that his reasoning is just as deficient as Lodge's." [32] Taft's bitterness deepened as criticism of the treaties continued. He compared Roosevelt to those war-loving figures of Norse mythology, the berserkers:

The truth is he believes in war and wishes to be a Napoleon and to die on the battlefield. He has the spirit of the old berserkers. . . .

I shall continue . . . to discuss the treaties, and shall not notice the personal turn of his remarks. . . . It is curious how unfitted he is for courteous debate. I don't wonder he prefers the battle-ax.[33]

The colonel is obsessed with his love of war and the glory of it. That is the secret of his present attitude. . . . he would think it a real injury to mankind if we would not have war. . . . He can't quarrel with me, whatever he does, for it takes two to make a quarrel. He finds but little sympathy for his position and he rather accentuates and gives wide publicity to my views by attacking them. I shall go on and ignore his challenge of a personal color and attempt to meet his arguments when he really frames any.[34]

[31] Marburg to Taft, Aug. 13, 1911. [32] Taft to Mabel Boardman, Sept. 8, 1911. [33] Taft to Knox, Sept. 9, 1911. [34] Taft to Bannard, Sept. 10, 1911.

All this was actually part, of course, of the oncoming 1912 campaign. The President held stubbornly to his hope that it might not be necessary to strike back at the man who had been his friend but who now was assailing him. His resolution held through the threatening days of 1911. He was quiet until, at last, his patience snapped and he excoriated the "emotionalists or neurotics" who sought so basically to change the American form of government.[35] But the peace treaties already were doomed by then. It was February, 1912.

First, however, President Taft had appealed to the people. It is a little pathetic the way presidents of the United States, cherishing some project which is to benefit mankind, believe that the people will rout the opposition if only they can be made to understand. Woodrow Wilson would believe this when his League of Nations was being trampled upon by the Senate. Taft believed it as he set out on his western tour in the fall of 1911. His speeches were concise and forceful. He attempted to explain away the theory that the treaties would alter radically the conduct of foreign affairs by the President and the Senate. But he might as well have saved his breath. The people did not come to his rescue.

"We have had wars in this country— the War of Independence which gave us this great country and enabled us to be free," the President said at Marquette, Michigan, in September. "We had the war of 1812, in which our neighbor, England, asserted rights that she would not now think of pressing. *I think that war might have been settled without a fight and ought to have been. So with the Mexican War. So, I think, with the Spanish war."* [36]

These were courageous words and intelligent ones, although the reference to the war with Spain was probably ill-advised. That had been Theodore Roosevelt's personal embroilment and he must have been further annoyed with Taft when he saw the statement that it was an unnecessary one. The President did not mention Roosevelt in his speeches. He still hoped that a break might be averted. But his refutations of Roosevelt's views on war were specific enough. On October 7, 1911, he addressed the students and faculty at the University of Idaho. Was international peace impossible?

[35] Pringle, H. F., *Theodore Roosevelt, a Biography*, p. 556. [36] *Addresses*, Vol. XXII, p. 99. (Italics mine.)

Taft did not believe so. He recalled that dueling had long been the method of settling individual disputes.

"If a man insulted you and you were a gentleman, or thought you were," he said, "it was your business to send a friend to him and inform him that he had insulted you and unless he apologized nothing but blood would wipe out the stain. He sent back word that he had no apologies to make and would select his weapons— his pistols. And therefore, in order to wipe out the stain on your honor, you stood up at forty paces and let him make a target out of you with a pistol. That is the way you wiped out a stain on your honor. Of course, if you hit him, perhaps it was a satisfactory arrangement, but if he hit you and knocked you out, you would study a long time to see how that wiped out the stain on your honor."

War, Taft said, was no more rational than dueling. "If we go to battle and win," he said, "we come home and say the Lord is on our side, and that our honor has been avenged, but if our enemy happens to have a larger army and better guns, and a better navy, and we are driven off the field, we will have to reason a long time to understand how that satisfies our honor."

In a few years President Wilson would voice the conception that a nation might be too proud to fight, and earn anew the frenzied criticism of Theodore Roosevelt. Taft, in this speech amid the hills of Idaho, must have irritated the "berserker" almost as much.

"I don't think," he said, "that it indicates that a man lacks personal courage if he does not want to fight, but prefers to submit questions of national honor to a board of arbitration. . . . We are a great nation of 90,000,000 of people. We have power; we have wealth; we are afraid of no nation in the world so far as battle is concerned. We have no entangling alliances. The other nations who have entangling alliances and who cannot lead in this movement look to us to lead." [37]

On December 26, 1911, Roosevelt announced that he would not go to the New York Citizens' Peace Banquet to be held in New York City four days later. The President, as the principal speaker, was to argue for the arbitration agreements. It had been supposed

[37] *Addresses,* Vol. XXIII, pp. 226, 228.

that Roosevelt would attend. This was a deliberate blow at Taft. He was not going, said Roosevelt facetiously when the reporters swarmed to his office, "because I am not hungry." [38] But when the current issue of the *Outlook* appeared, the real reason was clear.

"These treaties, if ratified by the Senate unamended," Roosevelt wrote, "will explicitly promise, will explicitly pledge the honor and good faith of the American nation to arbitrate precisely such questions as that which at this very moment we announced that we will not . . . arbitrate in the case of Russia. Under these circumstances, to ratify the general arbitration treaties would put the American people in an attitude of peculiarly contemptible hypocrisy, and would rightly expose us to the derision of all thinking mankind; for we should put ourselves in the position of making sweeping and unnecessary promises, impossible of performance, at the very time when by our own actions we showed that we should certainly not keep such promises, nor translate them into action. . . . Hypocrisy is just as revolting in a nation as in a man; and in the long run I do not believe that it pays either man or nation." [39]

Roosevelt was either ignorant or mendacious when he cited the abrogation of the Russian treaty as proof of the Taft administration's hypocrisy. On the contrary, as the President explained at the New York peace dinner, the refusal to arbitrate this matter was proof that none but "justiciable" disputes would be submitted to The Hague and that the United States, Great Britain or France would not, through the arbitration agreements, sacrifice sovereignty over internal affairs. The Russian treaty had specified that naturalized Russians in the United State did not lose their allegiance to Russia. Russian aliens, moreover, could be punished for seeking American citizenship. This was contrary to the laws of the United States.

"I say that the inconsistency that is supposed to exist in our failure to invoke arbitration there does not exist," the President declared at the dinner and he was, of course, correct. [40]

The President was wounded, deeply wounded, by Roosevelt's article in the *Outlook*. "Nothing has hurt me more than T.R.'s lightly veiled attack," he told Carnegie. "It is temperamental, I sup-

[38] New York *Times*, Dec. 27, 28, 1911. [39] *Outlook*, Dec. 30, 1911. [40] *Addresses*, Vol. XXVI, pp. 184-185.

pose. Of course, such language as he uses hurts his cause and helps ours." [41]

It may be doubted, though that the arbitration treaties had been aided by the conflict. The dinner, itself, turned out to be a fearful fiasco and memory of it must have lingered, like the echo from a nightmare, in Taft's mind for years. Carnegie had warned the President that the function was of dubious standing and that it would be wiser not to go. Taft replied that he would go to any dinner where he might talk on peace, so Carnegie withdrew his objection. But Governor-elect John A. Dix of New York declined to attend and so did Governor Wilson of New Jersey. The diplomatic corps was sparsely represented. Bungling and mismanagement featured the affair. When the President, accompanied by Archie Butt, arrived at the Waldorf Hotel at six-thirty, the seating arrangements had not yet been made and they were forced to wait for almost an hour. Then the presidential temper broke.

"Oh, are you ready? Are matters adjusted?" he snapped when the committee escorted him to the dais. Butt heard reports that the hotel was filled with Roosevelt men and that a demonstration against the President might be staged. Police and secret-service operatives, dressed as guests, were scattered through the banquet hall to forestall it. [42] Nothing happened, though. Taft threw off his discouragement to make a plea against war which was forceful and convincing. [43] Roosevelt's accusations persisted in his mind, however. Taft knew now, if he did not know before, that never again could they really be friends.

"It is very hard to take all the slaps Roosevelt is handing me at this time, Archie," the President told his aide. "Everyone wants me to answer his last attack on the peace treaties in which he practically calls me a hypocrite. If it were anyone else I would know just what to do, but I can't get into a public row with him. He knows that, and he has me at a disadvantage. I don't understand Roosevelt. I don't know what he is driving at except to make my way more difficult. I could not ask his advice on all questions. I could not subordinate my administration to him and retain my self-respect,

[41] Taft to Carnegie, Jan. 2, 1912. [42] Butt, Archie, *Taft and Roosevelt,* Vol. II, pp. 796, 803-805; New York *Times,* Dec. 31, 1911. [43] *Addresses,* Vol. XXVI, pp. 172-187.

but it is hard, very hard, Archie, to see a devoted friendship going to pieces like a rope of sand." [44]

—6—

Taft still hoped, on the other hand, that ratification by the Senate might be obtained. He must have been encouraged by the opinion of the New York *World,* normally critical, that "no ruler in the world has made so noble an ending of the old year as the citizen President of the United States with his speech . . . in this city on international arbitration and peace. . . . The mission in which President Taft would make this nation a leader is the greatest ever presented in practical form for the betterment of the world." [45] The New York *Times* made note of the "ill-natured and ill-mannered loquacity from Mr. Roosevelt" and praised the arbitration proposal as a "just, wise and practical mode of dealing with international differences." The American people, "undisturbed by the snarling of any jealous critic," would surely support the President on this issue.[46] From Carnegie, meanwhile, came another message of praise; it was well that old Andrew, so soon to be bitterly disappointed and to blame Taft for the defeat of the treaties, could not read the future. He said on New Year's Day, 1912:

"Again long and happy life to the world's foremost citizen and all those near and dear to him, leader of the hosts of International Peace and marching sure to victory. He cannot fail." [47]

Failure was not far off. When the treaties "got to the Senate," Taft recalled in a speech in December, 1918, "that august body truncated them and amended them in such a way that their own father could not recognize them." [48] The first two amendments were on behalf of California, still nervous over the yellow peril. They provided that questions affecting the admission of aliens could not be arbitrated, nor could the admission of aliens to schools. The third reservation excluded any issue involving the "territorial integrity of the several states or of the United States." The fourth

---

[44] Butt, Archie, *op. cit.,* Vol. II, p. 804. [45] New York *World,* Jan. 1, 1912. [46] New York *Times,* Jan. 1, 1912. [47] Carnegie to Taft, Jan. 1, 1912. [48] Marburg, Theodore, and Flack, Horace E., *Taft Papers on the League of Nations,* p. 178.

ruled that questions relating to the debts of any state could not be decided at The Hague; this, obviously, was to reassure the southern states that debts incurred under the Confederacy or during reconstruction would not be made the subject of suits by foreign investors. The last amendment provided that issues arising under the Monroe Doctrine were exempt. Superimposed on these reservations was an even greater one. The Senate eliminated the provision whereby the Joint High Commission would decide, by a unanimous vote or by five to one, whether the issue at stake was justiciable. Instead, the President and the Senate would decide and thereby the commission became merely a debating society. To President Taft this was the most important feature of the agreements with Great Britain and France. The actual reason for such drastic changes, he ultimately wrote, "was an unwillingness to assent to the principle of arbitration without knowing something in advance of whether we were going to win or lose. That spirit is not one which will promote the cause of arbitration." [49]

Ambassadors Bryce and Jusserand, speaking for their countries, expressed dissatisfaction with the amended treaties.[50] The President was grievously disappointed when, in March, 1912, the Senate confirmed the amended versions by a vote of 76 to 3. He had not decided, he said, whether he would ask Great Britain and France to consider approval of the new treaties.[51]

"I recognize that this treaty . . . falls short of fulfilling the purpose of the treaty in the form originally agreed upon," he wrote to Bryce and Jusserand. But he added that the project for a genuine arbitration agreement must not be abandoned and he expressed the hope that negotiations might be continued.[52] M. Jusserand agreed that "what remains . . . is far distant from the ideal marked by you in your famous speech of December 17, 1910, as the goal towards which we should move. . . . Time has, however, a healing virtue, and . . . there is certainly no reason why we should not study whether we could not do something . . . when the moment comes." [53] The President told Carnegie that the campaign for arbitration would go on.[54] A start toward new negotiations with

[49] Taft, W. H., op. cit., pp. 111-126. [50] Taft to Carnegie, Dec. 29, 1911. [51] Taft to Huntington Wilson, March 11, 1912. [52] Taft to Bryce and Jusserand, March 15, 1912. [53] Jusserand to Taft, March 17, 1912. [54] Taft to Carnegie, March 28, 1912.

England and France was made.[55] But no one's heart was really in it. Before long, the burdens of the 1912 campaign, alone, were almost more than Taft could endure. William Jennings Bryan, who had frequently encouraged Taft in his fight for arbitration, took up the cause when he became secretary of state. He actually obtained agreements with thirty nations and obtained confirmation by the Senate. His debt to the Taft agreements was clear. For it was provided that all questions, including those relating to national honor, were to be submitted to an international commission. A year was to be given to investigation of the issue. War could not come until after that period. But Germany did not sign. Soon the Bryan treaties were wholly forgotten while the old and terrible arbitrament by cannon started.[56]

Andrew Carnegie was tragically disappointed, of course, by the action of the Senate in March, 1912. He reproached President Taft. He had failed, Carnegie wrote, because he had not taken the Senate into his confidence.

"Refer to Secretary Knox," scrawled Taft across this letter. "Isn't it pleasant to be told how it could be done?" [57]

He mentioned the treaties again during an address on the League of Nations in December, 1918, and described the extent to which the Senate had emasculated them. In their final form, he said, they did little to advance peace. At this point the Taft chuckle began to bubble.

"So I put them on the shelf," he said, "and let the dust accumulate on them in the hope that the senators might change their minds, or that the people might change the Senate; instead of which they changed me." [58]

[55] Taft to J. H. Choate, April 19, 1912. [56] Baker, R. S., *Woodrow Wilson, Life and Letters*, Vol. IV, pp. 84-92. [57] Carnegie to Taft, Dec. 15, 1912. [58] Marburg, T., and Flack, H. E., *op. cit.*, p. 179.

CHAPTER XXXIX

IT IS CHARGED THAT . . .

As 1911 ended, hope ended, too, that Roosevelt would support President Taft for the Republican nomination. As recently as the previous May the outlook had been different. Roosevelt, himself, had privately expressed the belief that he could not run again. It would be, he said, "not only a misfortune to me, but undesirable from the standpoint of the party and the people. . . . I expect every real friend and supporter . . . to do everything in his power to prevent . . . my nomination." [1]

He had changed his mind as 1911 closed. True, he still insisted that he was not a candidate. [2] He confided to Cabot Lodge, on the other hand, that he had declined to promise that he would not accept a bid if it came "in the form of a duty." [3] And in the middle of January, 1912, Jim Garfield, who had been Roosevelt's secretary of the interior and was very close to his beloved leader, dropped in at the American embassy in Mexico City. Henry Lane Wilson, the ambassador, promptly summarized the conversation and dispatched it to Washington:

He [Garfield] said that the situation had been growing steadily worse on account of the inability of the President and his friends to understand the impossibility of his re-election and that the situation would define itself within the next two months, within which time the President would either withdraw from the contest or new alignments would be made. . . . He said that the state of Ohio would send a delegation opposed to Taft to the next National Convention and that his nomination was becoming every day more doubtful. He said that the belief existed in many quarters that the President would eventually withdraw in favor of Justice Hughes. [4]

Taft, however, had no intention whatever of withdrawing or permitting the naming of a compromise candidate. He was heart-

[1] Victor Rosewater to C. D. Hilles, April 23, 1912. [2] Philadelphia *North American*, Nov. 26, 1911. [3] Lodge, H. C., Vol. II, p. 417. [4] H. L. Wilson to Taft, Jan. 18, 1912.

sick and unhappy. "If I am defeated," he wrote, "I hope that somebody, sometime, will recognize the agony of spirit that I have
undergone." [5] Yet Taft remained in the contest. He fought to the
limit of his too-tranquil nature because he envisioned the issue as
far more than a personal one. The "whole fate of constitutional
government," he said, was at stake.[6]

Where lay the genesis of this historic and bitter quarrel? On
the eve of Election Day, 1912, the President granted an interview to
Louis Seibold, the correspondent of the New York *World*, and then
forbade its publication. A stenographic transcript reposed in the
presidential files, however, and it throws some light.

"Was there," Seibold asked, "some period . . . that marked the
beginning of the creation of this new faction of dissent— not merely
fomented by Mr. Roosevelt?"

"No," Taft replied. "The party naturally divided itself. The
interests of the East, particularly the manufacturing portions, required a continuance of the tariff and a careful protection of the
tariff. The interests of the farming community, it was supposed, led
to a reduction of the tariff, and there were many, like Senator Cummins of Iowa and some others in the so-called insurgent states, who
were most insistent on the unfairness of the tariff in protecting the
East and offering no particular benefit to the West or to the farming
community."

"That is where the break began?" asked the correspondent.

"That is where the break began," answered the President.[7]

Taft was referring, obviously, to the disruption within the Republican party rather than to the personal break between Roosevelt
and himself. He was accurate enough in his analysis, although the
tariff was only one of the causes. Unfortunately for drama, one
searches in vain for any one occasion on which the two men met
and then separated on paths which grew further and further apart
and then led, in the end, to the same unsatisfactory destination—
defeat. The biographer can raise no curtain to show a stubborn,
angry Taft being berated, for his sins, by a volubly excited Roosevelt. For there was no such meeting. When they saw each other

[5] Taft to Horace D. Taft, May 10, 1912. [6] Taft to J. G. Schurman, Feb. 29, 1912.
[7] Seibold interview, Nov. 1, 1912, Taft papers, Library of Congress.

prior to the final parting, indeed, they forced smiles to their faces and conversed with nervously simulated amicability.

The clues to the beginning of the quarrel are elusive. It is necessary to look back across the years since Taft— so reluctantly and with misgivings— had bowed to the demands of Roosevelt and his own family and had agreed to run for the presidency. Roosevelt had been fervent in his praise of Taft. But during the campaign of 1908 the first suspicions dawned in his mind. This protégé, for all his talents, did not campaign lustily enough and was too judicial, Roosevelt feared. He brushed the suspicions away, of course, for they carried with them the impossible assumption that he had made a mistake in naming his successor.

No break occurred at the beginning nor was there any sign of one. It is necessary briefly to recall a few details. Roosevelt was not resentful over Taft's Cabinet selections. He did not advise an alliance with the House insurgents; indeed, he cautioned Taft against friction with powerful old Uncle Joe Cannon. The psychological factors which moved the Rough Rider are more difficult to set forth categorically. He was a young man and retirement from power, as he frankly admitted, had come too soon. His intentions were of the best. He did not want to interfere, and so he left the country. And Taft, who had leaned on Roosevelt for so long, sat by himself in the lonely house above the Potomac River.

Taft looked for support, because he did not know what else to do, to Aldrich of Rhode Island and the other Old Guard senators. With no talent at all for guiding public opinion, he allowed it to appear that he had turned his back on the liberals of his party and on the friends of Roosevelt. Word of this was soon carried to the too-receptive ears of the colonel. Then came the Payne-Aldrich tariff act. Then came the unfair charges against Ballinger. Then Taft was forced to dismiss Pinchot from his post as chief forester.

"We have a government of limited power under the Constitution," was Taft's philosophy, "and we have got to work out our problems on the basis of law."

In that gospel— not in the tariff or in conservation or in any other single issue— lay the seed of the inescapable conflict. The break was delayed. The hunter returned from his African hills in June, 1910. Each man knew that doubt and distrust clouded the mind of the other. But a Congressional campaign was approaching and the G.O.P. was in peril. Roosevelt was persuaded to campaign for the ticket. He was, however, constantly in conference with the insurgent groups, by now the open adversaries of the President, and Taft was grievously hurt. This was a strange campaign. Roosevelt, while urging a Republican House of Representatives, was also sounding the tenets of his New Nationalism. Taft was puzzled, dismayed and finally angry over the radical utterances of his former friend. He soon regarded Roosevelt as the enemy of the Constitution and the Supreme Court. He heard repeated rumors that Roosevelt would fight against his renomination.

Defeat in November, 1910, brought a lull during which Roosevelt swore that he was finished with politics forever and had become a country squire. The two men exchanged a cordial letter or two. Taft agreed to send Roosevelt to war, if only Japan would interfere in Mexico and bring about a first-rate emergency. They combined to oust Senator Lorimer of Illinois. The poison against Taft was ingrained in Roosevelt's soul, though. The wounds of the President still festered. In the fall of 1911 came the ultimate mistake; the suit to dissolve the United States Steel Corporation which set forth that Roosevelt had been misled in 1907.

—2—

Roosevelt's utterances in the 1910 campaign, in particular his celebrated speech at Osawatomie, Kansas, had sent through Taft's heart a chill foreboding that never again would they work in harmony. In October, pondering the innumerable perplexities while at Beverly, the President thought it probable that "Mr. Roosevelt expects to be called on to be the Republican candidate in 1912 and to yield to the call." Taft could not understand the hostility which now seemed so apparent. One report was that Roosevelt had been annoyed because, in the final months of his term, Taft had not defended him in his controversies with Congress.

"It is news to me that he had any such desire— if I had known it I would have been glad to do what I could," Taft explained. "All these are personal matters and quite beneath the consideration of a great statesman looking at government from the standpoint of measures and progress instead of personal feeling and prerogative. . . . With my knowledge of Theodore Roosevelt, I must think that these counts of the indictment he formulates against me with his friends are only . . . justifications which he uses to himself . . . the real reason is a mixture of inevitable circumstance and temperament." [8]

From judicially-minded bewilderment, the President's attitude shifted toward indignant condemnation of Roosevelt. Sometimes, in conversation with the members of his family or with intimates, he referred to his predecessor as though he were an unruly child.

"Theodore can't hear a dog bark without wanting to try conclusions with him," he once said to Horace Taft. [9]

"I don't know what I have done to offend Theodore," he protested late in 1911. "I can think of only two things and both of these are trivial. I have heard that he is offended because we did not do enough for Mrs. Roosevelt while he was in Africa. My other offense, I am told, was that I mentioned Charley in that letter in which I thanked Theodore for what he had done for me. What else could it have been? I offered to appoint anyone he named. But he didn't ask me to appoint anyone." [10]

The President would have been far happier if honor and his conscience had permitted him to withdraw from this repugnant contest. He would have been inexpressibly relieved had it been possible for him to retire to private life and his lawbooks, and in the summer, perhaps, to sit again on the porch at Murray Bay and watch the gulls dip and turn over the lovely St. Lawrence. But these things could not be. Instead, his depression deepened and with it his anger against Theodore Roosevelt. The day would come very soon when rumors that Theodore was insane or was drinking to excess reached his ears. Taft did not believe them. But he passed them on, while denying that they could be true, to his friends. They constituted, after all, one of the few explanations for conduct so irrational. But there was rarely malice in Taft. For the most part he was merely worried and unhappy.

"The truth is," he wrote in September, 1911, "that I am not very

[8] Taft to F. W. Carpenter, Oct. 10, 1910. [9] Horace D. Taft to author, July 12, 1933. [10] Henry W. Taft to author, Jan. 24, 1935.

happy in this renomination and re-election business. I have to set my teeth and go through with it as best I can. I am not going to squeal or run away. . . . But after it is all over I shall be glad to retire and let another take the burden. . . . There is so much demagoguery these days and the people seem to like it. It will not hurt them to have their noses rubbed in it. It seems to me that intelligent men have lost their heads and are leaning toward fool, radical views in a way I never thought possible. Perhaps we'll have to get worse before we get better. The day of the demagogue, the liar and the silly is on." [11]

Sometimes, on the other hand, Taft's resolution would stiffen and he would strike back at the repeated assertions, seldom accurate and often completely untrue, that everything in the administration had been fraught with failure.

"I am not conscious of having done anything which disentitles me to stand as a candidate for a second term or requires a departure from the time-honored and very safe tradition against the third term," he protested in January. "I am, of course, conscious of having made errors, but there are few presidents who do not, and, on the whole, I believe I can show as good a balance on the credit side of the ledgers as most administrations. Of course, my political judgment is not particularly valuable, but I feel certain that if Theodore Roosevelt were nominated he would be stronger the day of the convention than ever after and there would arise up against him in four months' discussion the real reasons why he should not be made more deserving than Washington, Jefferson, Jackson, Lincoln or Grant." [12]

Thus he insisted in the suppressed Seibold interview too. "Men that want to praise me begin frequently with the statement, 'He has made mistakes.' Sometimes I feel like saying, 'I would like to have you specify to me and give me a chance to answer what mistakes I have made.' Of course, every man knows that if he acted on his hindsight he could have done better than if he acted on his foresight, but there are a great many things assumed to be mistakes that I would like to be heard on before they are finally decided." [13]

The bludgeonings were often almost more than Taft could bear.

[11] Taft to C. P. Taft, Sept. 6, 1911. [12] Taft to Bannard, Jan. 22, 1912. [13] Seibold interview.

Seldom, these days, did the contagion of his chuckle spread laughter among those who felt it. Seldom did Taft's hearty boom of mirth crash from the executive offices into the corridors of the White House.

". . . the Colonel hangs over him like a big, black cloud and seems to be his nemesis," noted Archie Butt. "He frets under it, I can see." The military aide felt that the President was not without fault. He remarked that Taft had been careful to make no public criticism of Roosevelt, but he had "talked against the Colonel, speaking slightingly of him in private, and all these remarks have been repeated." [14]

—3—

So the amiable, sunny Taft vanished and in his place appeared an irritable man. It grew harder, as the first weeks of 1912 passed, for him to accept advice.

"He had," was the profound analysis of Secretary of Commerce and Labor Nagel, "the stubbornness of an uncertain man."

The meetings of the Taft Cabinet, once such cheerful sessions, became gloomy and futile. "We are drifting" had been the warning from Uncle Joe Cannon and this was repeated at the Cabinet sessions. Postmaster General Hitchcock, Secretary of the Treasury MacVeagh, Secretary Nagel and Secretary of the Navy Meyer all urged that he assume the offensive and launch an attack on Roosevelt. But Taft would not do this yet. He was as deaf to their urgings as he had been a year before. For even towards the end of 1910 his official family had warned him that Roosevelt was a candidate for the 1912 nomination.

"Theodore wouldn't do that," the President insisted, and the matter was dropped.[15]

Attorney General Wickersham, too, felt that all was lost unless the President exhibited qualities of leadership. But Taft, he remembered, years later, "was too judicially minded and indisposed to act swiftly, as an executive often must, without waiting to debate the pros and cons." [16]

[14] Butt, Archie, *Taft and Roosevelt*, Vol. II, pp. 794, 805. [15] Nagel to author, Oct. 25, 1934. [16] Wickersham to author, Jan. 23, 1935.

It may have been that the obesity against which he had struggled so long was too much of a burden when combined with these mental hazards. The artist, Zorn, was commissioned at this time to do a portrait of the President. There were several sittings, but Zorn could find no life or animation in the tired countenance before him.

"The President is so weary that it shows in his face," the artist said in an appeal to Secretary Nagel. "Can't you come over and talk to him so I can paint him as he really is?"

Nagel did so and attempted to liven up the sittings. But the stratagem was not very successful.[17] Word even reached the newspapers that the President had fallen asleep when another artist, Theodore Molkenboer, had attempted to do his portrait. A Mrs. Minnie H. Pilling, at whose home in Washington the artist was staying, had apparently been responsible for the report. A White House attaché inquired whether her name should be stricken from the official guest list.

"Don't notice it," was the notation, in Taft's hand, across the face of the memorandum.[18]

No wonder Taft was weary. Added to all the other perplexities was the question of loyalty among those who had been his friends, even among the men who had accepted office at his hands. Reports were incessant that Hitchcock, who had managed his campaign in 1908, was now actually in favor of Roosevelt. Archie Butt made no secret of his belief that this was so.[19] Taft did not credit the rumors. It would have been disastrous had they been true, for Hitchcock was an influential politician. As postmaster general he had dispensed patronage for the administration. He controlled many delegates. The President, although he did not believe the rumors, was none the less apprehensive. Hitchcock was not an easy man to understand. He exchanged few confidences. He was inclined to brood by himself. At last, apparently in January, Taft could withhold no longer the direct question which would dissolve the doubt. The President could be extremely impressive on the infrequent occasions when he was aroused; this time he stood up, at the end of the Cabinet table, and pointed his finger at the postmaster general.

[17] Nagel to author, Oct. 25, 1934. [18] Washington *Times,* March 29, 1912. White House memorandum, March 29, 1912. [19] Butt, Archie, *op. cit.,* Vol. II, p. 817.

"Frank!" he demanded. "Are you for me or against me?"

Hitchcock, his face crimson, also arose from his seat. "I am for you, Mr. President," he said.[20]

Taft gave confidential assurances to the correspondents on January 23 that Hitchcock was loyal.[21] On the same day he explained to a constituent that the rumors had been caused by the desertion of men trained by Hitchcock in the 1908 campaign and, since then, more or less closely associated with the postmaster general. Hitchcock "is strong for me and I haven't the slightest doubt as to his fidelity and earnestness," the President insisted.[22] To Hitchcock, on the same day, he transmitted one of the accounts of his supposed treason.

"This is a sample of the way you are being maligned," he wrote.[23]

No doubt remained, by early January of 1912, that Roosevelt was a candidate for the nomination. Taft knew this. He found comfort, though, in his growing conviction that he represented the cause of constitutionalism and orderly government while the colonel stood for revolution. And so he would fight.

"I am afraid I am in for a hard fight," he wrote, "without any knowledge of military strategy, and with very little material for organization, but I am going to stay in anyhow. . . . I believe I represent a safer and saner view of our government and its Constitution than does Theodore Roosevelt, and whether beaten or not I mean to continue to labor in the vineyard for those principles."[24]

Almost pathetically, the President clung to a belief that the campaign could be conducted on a high plane, that he would not have to attack the man who had been his friend, that the discussion could be limited to issues. He instructed his supporters not to denounce Roosevelt.

"Personal abuse is not likely to control ultimately in this campaign; and I certainly don't want to be responsible for it if it does," he wrote. "I believe the arguments pro and con will force themselves upon the electorate without the use of denunciation and personal attack."[25]

[20] Nagel to author, Oct. 25, Nov. 14, 1935. [21] Butt, Archie, op. cit., Vol. II, p. 819. [22] Taft to G. B. Lockwood, Jan. 23, 1912. [23] Taft to Hitchcock, Jan. 23, 1912. [24] Taft to Bannard, Jan. 22, 1912. [25] Taft to W. O. Bradley, Feb. 5, 1912.

The hope persisted even after Roosevelt, on February 21, sent his hat spinning into the ring and chilled the blood of the respectables with his "Charter of Democracy" address at Columbus, Ohio. A "dignified course of discussing only the real issues," Taft repeated, would win "the sympathy of the intelligent and business members of the community . . . and make us feel, when we win, that we have deserved to win." [26] It is strange that some of the Old Guard leaders, to whom Taft would shortly be clinging for support and who were wise in the mysteries of politics, did not tell him that the intelligent members of any community were in the decided minority.

Another factor influenced Taft in his decision not to cross swords in personal combat. The man who berated him now had been his friend and benefactor. Try as he might, the President could not forget the debt that he owed to Roosevelt. True, Roosevelt had betrayed him. True, Roosevelt was distorting the administration's policies and coming close to downright falsehood in his criticisms. But Taft would not "be dragged into a series of controversial . . . speeches, attempting to follow him and to show his perversion of my language and meaning. My relations to him forbid." [27] In March, William Allen White, who knew both men and loved them, called at the White House. He found a perplexed President and he reported the substance of their conversation to Roosevelt:

> He said that nothing would induce him to say— or allow anyone whom he could control to say— anything against you personally; that he had never ceased to avail himself of every opportunity to express his gratitude for all you have done for him; that you made him President (he said nothing about his brother Charles in that connection); and that he never can forget the old and happy relations of intimacy. . . . He said that he could not help hoping that when all this turmoil of politics had passed, you and he would get together again and be as of old.[28]

A few weeks later the President still insisted that he would not "descend into the game of crimination and recrimination. . . . In

[26] Taft to W. B. McKinley, March 12, 1912. [27] Taft to F. W. Cram, March 25, 1912. [28] Pringle, H. F., *Theodore Roosevelt, a Biography*, p. 556.

the few speeches I shall make between now and the convention, I shall find material enough in the pernicious cause he represents— that is, the destruction of an independent judiciary and representative government— to discuss it and show why it ought not to prevail without any personal reference to him." [29]

Taft meant all this, although the day was not far distant when he could no longer keep from mentioning Roosevelt by name. The ordeal would be so great that he could not hold back the tears after it was over. And yet, even in February, the President said things which were so directly applicable to Roosevelt and his followers that the effect was the same. He spoke on Lincoln's Birthday before the Republican Club in New York and the address began, calmly enough, with a tribute to the martyred President. But the judicial note soon faded. He did not mention Roosevelt. No one in the room misinterpreted, however, the President's reference to "political emotionalists or neurotics." He said:

There are those who look upon the present situation as one full of evil and corruption and as a tyranny of concentrated wealth, and who in apparent despair at any ordinary remedy are seeking to pull down those things which have been regarded as the pillars of the temple of freedom and representative government, and to reconstruct our whole society on some new principle, not definitely formulated, and with no intelligent or intelligible forecast of the exact constitutional or statutory results to be attained.

With the effort to make the selection of candidates, the enactment of legislation, and the decision of the courts to depend on the momentary passions of a people necessarily indifferently informed as to the issues presented, and without the opportunity for time and study and that deliberation which gives security and common sense to the government of the people, such extremists would hurry us into a condition which could find no parallel except in the French revolution, or in that bubbling anarchy that once characterized the South American Republics. *Such extremists are not progressives— they are political emotionalists or neurotics—* who have lost that sense of proportion, that clear and candid consideration of their own weaknesses as a whole, and that clear perception of the necessity for checks upon hasty popular action which made our people, who

[29] Taft to J. T. Adams, April 5, 1912.

fought the Revolution and drafted the Constitution, the greatest self-governing people that the world ever knew.[30]

—4—

On his other flank, all this time, Taft was subjected to onslaughts of the LaFollette supporters. The President had even less use for LaFollette, if that was possible, than for Roosevelt. The presidential chances of the Wisconsin senator had been diminishing since the close of 1911. LaFollette would soon know, and a conviction that Roosevelt had betrayed him would become an obsession in his mind, that the nomination would be denied him. Actually, there was no betrayal. Roosevelt never specifically pledged himself to the LaFollette boom, although he gave it encouragement and so did his disciples. Gifford Pinchot and Medill McCormick of Chicago both contributed to LaFollette's campaign prior to the end of 1911. After January, 1912, they began to switch their financial and moral support to Roosevelt. Infinitely chagrined, LaFollette's nerves gave way. His health had not been good, in addition. On February 2, 1912, at Philadelphia he made that speech which remains among the most tragic in the history of politics. He kept repeating himself, endlessly and angrily, until the hour grew late and restless diners left the banquet hall or cried, without pity, "Sit down!" while the flow of words went on.[31]

So Roosevelt decided that the people— the liberals, at least, among the people— were calling him. He would heed their call. First, however, it was necessary to devise the mechanics of the theoretically spontaneous demand that he stand for the nomination. Certain midwestern governors were delegated to be the voices of destiny. It was arranged that they should sign a letter asking Roosevelt to run. While they were doing this, the colonel prepared his answer.[32] The plea of the governors was made public on February 10.[33] It was already known that funds would be supplied by Frank A. Munsey, the publisher, George W. Perkins, a partner of J. P. Morgan, and Medill McCormick.[34] The issues were

[30] *Addresses*, Vol. XXVII, p. 145. (Italics mine.) [31] Pringle, H. F., *op. cit.*, p. 553. [32] Howland, Harold, *Theodore Roosevelt*, pp. 204-208. [33] New York *Times*, Feb. 11, 1912. [34] *Ibid.*, Jan. 30, Feb. 6, 1912.

becoming a degree confused. All these men had great wealth. None was a radical. Not one of them failed, I suspect, to squirm a little when Roosevelt, speaking at Columbus ten days later, declared that "wealth should be the servant, not the master of the people." Mr. Munsey, Mr. Perkins and Mr. McCormick must have had faint, faint misgivings when he added that "the wealthy man . . . holds his wealth subject to the general right of the community to regulate its business use as the public welfare requires." [35]

Pausing at Cleveland, en route to Columbus, Roosevelt voiced his famous battle-cry: "My hat is in the ring." [36] But it was the speech, itself, which so greatly alarmed President Taft and solidi-fied his intention to go down fighting. For Roosevelt struck at his cherished law and at his revered courts. ". . . legalistic justice is a dead thing," the colonel cried; ". . . never forget that the judge is as much a servant of the people as any other official." It was "nonsense," Roosevelt added, to suppose that impeachment was a practical remedy for a bad judiciary. A "quicker . . . more summary" method was needed. The recall of judges should be applied with caution, he admitted. But "when a judge decides a constitutional question, when he decides what the people as a whole can or cannot do, the people should have the right to recall that decision if they think it wrong." Roosevelt was re-ferring, of course, to judges in the several states. He called, too, for the initiative and referendum on state laws and for the recall of elective state and municipal officials.

"Our aim," he concluded in characteristic vein, "must be the moralization of the individual, of the government, of the people as a whole." [37]

"I will accept the nomination for President if it is tendered to me," he told the seven petitioning governors three days later, "and I will adhere to this decision until the convention has ex-pressed its preference." [38]

As yet, it will be noted, Roosevelt made no threat to bolt or to organize a party of his own. There is no evidence that any such intention had yet taken shape in his mind. Naturally enough, Presi-

[35] Roosevelt, Theodore, *Works,* National Edition, Vol. XVII, pp. 120, 130-131. [36] New York *Times,* Feb. 23, 1912. [37] Roosevelt, Theodore, *op. cit.,* Vol. XVII, pp. 137-139, 134-135, 147-148. [38] *Ibid.,* Vol. XVII, p. 149.

dent Taft was greatly cast down when the dispatches from Columbus reached him. He went walking, that day, with Major Butt and told of his "strong presentiment that the colonel is going to beat me in the convention. It is almost a conviction with me. I shall continue to fight to the last moment, but when you see me claiming a victory or my friends claiming a victory for me, remember that I feel I am losing a battle and that I am not blind myself, no matter what my friends may put out."

Rarely, during the trying months ahead, did this defeatist mood lift. When he had vanquished Roosevelt in the convention, Taft was certain that he would lose in the three-cornered fight for the election. Publicly, of course, he expressed confidence and exhorted his adherents, to the extent of his ability, to follow in his van to victory. But his words carried no conviction. His spirits remained low. And yet his sense of humor did not wholly desert him at any time. Mrs. Taft's discouragement was great when word reached the White House that the colonel had decided to run.

"I told you so four years ago and you would not believe me," she pointed out.

For a final time in months to come, the Taft chuckle rose. "I know you did, my dear," he said, "and I think you are perfectly happy now. You would have preferred the colonel to come out against me than to have been wrong yourself." [39]

The President was momentarily cheered by certain reactions to the Columbus speech. Cabot Lodge, as might have been expected, pointed out that "the Colonel and I have long since agreed to disagree on a number of points." More surprisingly, Borah of Idaho said that the "recall of judicial decisions is bosh." [40] Reading these reports, Taft decided that Roosevelt had "stirred up a veritable hornet's nest of disapproval among the press and the people generally, and my mail is burdened with reassuring messages. . . . However, I am none the less unhappy." [41] At the same time, his

[39] Butt, Archie, *op. cit.,* Vol. II, pp. 846, 850. [40] New York *Times,* Feb. 23, 1912. [41] Taft to C. P. Taft, Feb. 28, 1912.

anger increased. One of the Cincinnati familiars wrote to express loyalty, and he answered:

I am glad that Roosevelt's conduct makes you angry, because it necessarily has the same effect on other people. . . . He is manifesting a side of his character that is not lovely and does not commend him to those who like fair play. He has claimed to be a good sportsman, but he does not disclose that characteristic in these conditions. I am very sorry. It is pathetic to think of his great position and to see how he has stepped down from it and is now wallowing in the mire and moat of the politician of the hustings who has lost all his sense of responsibility. Every New York paper and every other paper that I have seen has an editorial on the subject.[42]

Roosevelt, too, was a degree alarmed over the effect of his Columbus address. On March 20, in New York, he pointed out that he did not "advocate the recall of judges in all states and in all communities." He asked that his position be clearly understood. He did *not* refer to the Supreme Court or the federal Constitution or to ordinary litigation, civil or criminal, between individuals. He was merely suggesting "that in a certain class of cases involving police power, when a state court has set aside as unconstitutional a law passed by the legislature for the general welfare," the people should, by vote, have the final determination.

"I am not speaking of the recall of judges," Roosevelt said, and this was, unquestionably, a recession from his earlier statements.[43]

In his letter to the seven governors, Roosevelt had urged the establishment of direct primaries, whereby the people could express their preference whenever possible.[44] Soon the charge was made, and its truth cannot be doubted, that the Taft supporters were blocking primary legislation in certain states— Massachusetts and Michigan were among them— where its establishment was pending.[45] For the Taft fight would be made on the lines followed by every president seeking a second term; through patronage and through officeholders who also would be delegates.

After victory of a sort in North Dakota, where LaFollette

[42] Taft to Jennie H. Anderson, March 28, 1912. [43] Roosevelt, Theodore, *op. cit.*, Vol. XVII, p. 156. [44] *Ibid.*, Vol. XVII, p. 150. [45] New York *Times*, March 11, 1912.

TAKING CANDY FROM A BABY.

Cartoon by C. R Macauley, June 13, 1912, Courtesy New York World

See page 799]

HORACE D. TAFT, YOUNGER BROTHER OF WILLIAM HOWARD TAFT

carried the state and Taft won but a few scattering districts,[46] the tide of battle began to turn against Roosevelt and he became increasingly shrill. Taft was leading in Indiana.[47] On March 26, New York held its primaries and the result was 83 delegates for the administration and only 7 for Roosevelt. That corruption marked the balloting is fairly certain. That Taft would have won even had the primary been run wholly honestly is equally obvious. For the party workers and the officeholders went to the polls while the average citizen-at-large did not bother to do so. The direct primary, apparently, was not working too well. But Roosevelt was outraged and he hinted, for the first time, that he might break with his party.

"They are stealing the primary elections from us," he said. "Never has there been anything more scandalous than the conduct of the Republican New York County machine in this fight. . . . All I ask is a square deal. If the contest goes against us in a square fight . . . I have no complaint to make. But I cannot and will not stand quietly by while the opinion of the people is being suppressed and their will thwarted. I am fighting for the people and not for myself." [48]

President Taft wondered, as he listened, whether Theodore was not "temperamentally irresponsible." [49] "He has become so violent," he added, "that some people fear he is losing his reason, others say he is drinking but I do not think so." Taft agreed, though, that Roosevelt was "beside himself with rage." [50] "The conduct of the colonel is certainly that of a desperate man who stops at nothing. . . ." [51]

—6—

Taft, in due time, was gratified by the race for delegates. By the end of March, he had lined up 274 although only 540 were needed for a choice in the convention.[52] Then the tide shifted again. Roosevelt carried Illinois and Taft looked to Pennsylvania to stand steady.

[46] *Ibid.*, March 20, 1912. [47] *Ibid.*, March 25, 1912. [48] *Ibid.*, March 27, 1912. [49] Taft to Mrs. M. A. Hanna, March 31, 1912. [50] Taft to C. P. Taft, April 1, 1912. [51] Taft to J. D. Brannan, April 10, 1912. [52] Taft to F. W. Carpenter, March 29, 1912.

"Pennsylvania and Massachusetts," he said, "will be a sufficient answer to the cry that I cannot win by the vote of the people." [53]

The answer did not come from Pennsylvania, which gave Roosevelt 56 out of 76 delegates.[54] Cabot Lodge would hold Massachusetts. But even more disastrous blows were imminent. Ohio would reject its one-time cherished son. Maryland and California returned majorities for Roosevelt. And the President, of course, was again cast into gloom. It began with the Pennsylvania debacle.

"One of the burdens that a man leading a cause has to carry," he told Horace Taft, "is the disappointment that his friends and sympathizers feel at every recurring disaster. For instance, when I read this morning that Roosevelt had carried Pennsylvania . . . I felt more sorrow at Nellie's disappointment and yours, and that of all who have become absorbed in the fight, than I did myself. Of course, such a defeat is very significant in the hold which Roosevelt still has over the plain people and no explanation of the result is sufficient which does not make this the chief element. . . . We had hoped by May 1 to have votes enough to nominate, but now we may have to depend on the May states. I shall not withdraw under any condition. I represent a cause that would make it cowardly for me to withdraw now. It seems to me that I am the only hope against radicalism and demagogy, and that even if I go down to defeat, it is my duty to secure the nomination if I can, under the rules that the Republican party convention has established, in spite of all the threats to bolt or to establish a third party." [55]

Taft resented the gross unfairness of Roosevelt's accusations. There was, for instance, the charge that the President was being supported by the party bosses. Roosevelt had named some of the sinister figures on the party bandwagon. Among others, there were Penrose of Pennsylvania, Ballinger of Washington, Barnes and Samuel S. Koenig of New York, Aldrich of Rhode Island and Cox of Ohio.[56] Self-hypnosis was controlling Roosevelt again as he made these assertions. They were true enough. But he had, himself, accepted the support of all of them in the past. The

[53] Taft to J. D. Brannan, April 10, 1912. [54] New York *Times,* April 14, 1912. [55] Taft to Horace D. Taft, April 14, 1912. [56] New York *Times,* March 28, 1912.

colonel was ignoring the realities of politics in berating Taft for countenancing machine support. Who, precisely, were his own manipulators in the primary contests going on? For every boss, in every community, there is a rival boss who seeks power by effecting a revolt. Many of them had joined their destinies with Roosevelt's. If he won the nomination, the old boss would fall and in their own receptive hands would lie the patronage and the other emoluments of political power. Taft saw, very clearly, the forces at play.

"It is true that I have had the bosses with me . . . ," he said. "Lorimer professed to support me, not at my request but because he hated Roosevelt more. In Pennsylvania I had Penrose's support. . . . I cannot complain. I have no doubt that the election was fair. But the expenditure of money on Roosevelt's behalf has been extraordinary. In Pennsylvania, William Flinn, one of the most notorious of political bosses and contractors, who made a shameless political contract with Quay which found the light of publicity, put up a very large fund and expects to be one of the beneficiaries of Roosevelt's success. . . . Association with them when it is by and for Roosevelt has nothing of evil in it. It is only when they support me that bosses are wicked. Considering the use which Roosevelt has made of bosses in the past, one would think the hypocrisy of such attacks would be seen, but not in the case of a popular idol." [57]

This was expressed in private. A fortnight later, able to keep silent no longer, the President said the same thing to an audience in Boston. Walter Brown, he said, "the only boss in full commission in the state," was behind Roosevelt in Ohio. So was William Ward, the Westchester County leader in New York State.

"The truth with respect to me is the same as it is with respect to Mr. Roosevelt," said Taft, with honesty rarely heard in a political campaign. "When I am running for the presidency I gratefully accept such support as comes to me. Mr. Roosevelt has done so in the past; he is doing so now. . . . I do not hesitate to say that it involves the most audacious effrontery on his part to attack me because men he characterizes as bosses are now supporting me. This is peculiarly unfair on his part in view of his well-known

[57] Taft to Horace D. Taft, April 14, 1912.

political history, and is another instance of his departing from the rule of the square deal." [58]

The decision to speak out was one of the hardest ever faced by Taft. Even in the middle of April, when Roosevelt had been accusing his adversaries of corruption and had been deliberately distorting the evidence, the President continued to insist that he would not answer "although . . . his lies and unblushing misrepresentations are such that I cannot expect those in charge of the campaign to refrain from pointing out his mendacity." [59] Taft changed his mind in a few days, however, and wondered "whether I ought to come out in a speech . . . quoting some letters I have, to show his knowledge of facts he is misrepresenting." [60]

"I agree with you," he told his friend, Mabel Boardman, "that the time has come when it is necessary for me to speak out in my own defense. I shall do so sorrowfully. I dislike to speak with directness about Theodore Roosevelt, but I cannot longer refrain from refuting his false accusations." [61]

Heavy of heart, the President entrained for New England.

[58] *Addresses,* Vol. XXVIII, pp. 184-185. [59] Taft to Horace D. Taft, April 14, 1912. [60] Taft to Bannard, April 17, 1912. [61] Taft to Mabel Boardman, April 23, 1912.

CHAPTER XL

PLEA OF NOT GUILTY

BY THE end of April, 1912, spring had come to the valley of the Connecticut River. The presidential special ran between meadows which were faintly green with the beginning crops. Here and there a precocious fruit tree bloomed, like foam on a rolling breaker, against the dark green of the woods.

But there was no spring in the heart of William Howard Taft, for he had come into Massachusetts to attack his one-time friend, leader and benefactor. This was the Gethsemane of all his crowded years in public life. Boston was the scene of his main address, and Taft had prepared it with great care. His train paused at Springfield and again at the little town of Palmer as it turned east toward Boston. There were other stops where the President defended his record. The crowds listened to his defense with respect and a few among them doubtless remembered the details. Most of the thousands, though, must have carried for years a mental picture of the troubled, earnest man who was President of the United States.

"This wrenches my soul," he kept saying as the people gathered at the rear of his train or in some hall. "I am here to reply to an old and true friend of mine, Theodore Roosevelt, who has made many charges against me. I deny those charges. I deny all of them. I do not want to fight Theodore Roosevelt, but sometimes a man in a corner fights. I am going to fight.

"Neither in thought, nor word nor action have I been disloyal to the friendship I owe Theodore Roosevelt. When the time came for this campaign to begin I let the people know I would like to have my administration approved by their giving me another term. At that time Theodore Roosevelt said that he was not a candidate and that it would be a calamity if he were nominated. Since then he has changed his mind." [1]

[1] New York *Times*, April 26, 1912.

The President spoke repeatedly on this sorrowful April 25 before, at last, he could return to his private car in the Boston railroad yards and, his nerves shattered by the ordeal, begin the journey back to Washington.

"One of the things that Mr. Roosevelt has not learned in all his long and useful and honorable life," the President said at one of the towns where his train halted, "is to be a good loser." [2] That night in Boston he added:

Mr. Roosevelt prides himself on being a true sportsman, and he likes to take from the rules and language of sport, maxims to be applied to life in general. The maxim which he has exalted above all others, to which he has given currency the country over, and which he . . . wishes to have it thought he exemplifies, is that every man is entitled to a square deal. I propose to examine the charges he makes against me, and to ask you whether in making them he is giving me a square deal.[3]

The President was able to prove far more than lack of sportsmanship in Roosevelt. He showed that evidence had been falsified. He showed that his predecessor in the White House had reversed himself on major policies. He showed that Roosevelt's accusations were, in large measure, untrue. The train moved eastward from Springfield through Palmer to Worcester and then to Boston. "I propose to begin all my speeches on this trip," Taft said, "by acknowledging in full my debt of gratitude to Theodore Roosevelt." [4] He reiterated that he would have kept silent had the issue been merely personal and he insisted that criticism, alone, did not bother him "because the presidency thickens your skin a little bit and makes it a hide." [5]

The address in the Arena at Boston was interminably long, as the messages and speeches of Taft nearly always were. He took up every charge made against him by Roosevelt and offered refutation. He included so many letters exchanged with the colonel, to prove his points, that the time grew short and he had to omit some of them from his speech. In summary, he said, Roosevelt's indictment was:

[2] *Addresses,* Vol. XXVIII, p. 207. [3] *Ibid.,* Vol. XVIII, pp. 182-183. [4] *Ibid.,* Vol. XXVIII, p. 221. [5] *Ibid.,* Vol. XXVIII, p. 214.

By excerpts from my speeches he has sought to show and has charged that I am one who has publicly announced that I am in favor of an aristocracy of political bosses, and that I am linked with political bosses in seeking my renomination. He charges that the patronage of the government is being shamelessly used to secure my renomination, and that in the conventions and primaries which have been held, fraud and violence have been systematically used to defeat the will of the people and to secure delegates for me. He says that I am not a progressive, but a reactionary; that I was nominated by progressives, and after election joined the ranks of those who opposed me for nomination; and he intimates that I have not the spirit of the progressive, or the imagination or the clearheaded purpose essential to the make-up of such a person. In short, he intimates pretty broadly that I am puzzle-witted. . . . He minimizes and flouts the importance of the laws enacted and the executive action taken during my administration.

Soberly and convincingly, but without great brilliance, the President proceeded to deny all the counts in the indictment. As to the first: at Carnegie Hall Roosevelt had quoted a speech made by Taft at Toledo and had garbled the quotation. The President had been describing the government of the United States as one in which less than one-fourth of all the people voted; he said that it was a government by a representative part of the people.

"Does Mr. Roosevelt deny this fact?" he asked. "Can he or any fair man maintain that in stating such a palpable truth . . . I was advocating a government by an oligarchy? . . . Was it honest, was it fair in Theodore Roosevelt to seize one sentence from a speech, to garble it and then to give it a meaning which he knew from the context it could not bear? Do the just people of Massachusetts approve such methods of warfare? Do they think that in carrying it on Mr. Roosevelt is giving to his successor a square deal?"

Taft then discussed, in detail, the support being given to the Roosevelt preconvention drive by Flinn of Pennsylvania and other bosses. He next turned to Senator Lorimer of Illinois.[6] It had been grossly unfair for Roosevelt, campaigning in Illinois, to "give the impression to his auditors that a vote for me was a vote for Mr.

[6] *Ibid.*, Vol. XXVIII, pp. 181-185.

Lorimer. I have not seen Mr. Lorimer for two years, and have had no communication with, or from him." The President recounted the part he had played in the attempt to oust Lorimer from the Senate on charges which were still pending. He read to his Boston audience a letter he had written Roosevelt in January, 1911, in which he had expressed his belief that Lorimer's election had been accompanied by "a mess and mass of corruption." He told of using his influence with members of the Senate against Lorimer. Was it honest, then, he pleaded, for Roosevelt now falsely to declare that Taft had changed his mind and was in combination with the Illinois senator? [7]

Third, there was the matter of reciprocity with Canada; that plan for tearing down the Canadian-American tariff walls in which Taft had so profoundly believed and which had been rejected by the people of the Dominion after approval by the American Congress. Roosevelt had approved the reciprocity agreement too. He now explained, however, that this had been due only to his desire to support the President. He had "supposed"— the quotations are Taft's— that the agreement was one he could approve, but having "looked into it carefully . . . under no circumstances . . . will I ever sanction the reintroduction of such an agreement." [8] The President declared that Roosevelt had shifted because of the reaction of the farmers against reciprocity. He recalled that he had conferred with him ten days before the agreement had been made and had explained all its details. He exhibited their correspondence on the subject.

"It seems to me that what you propose to do with Canada is admirable from every standpoint," Roosevelt had written. "I firmly believe in free trade with Canada for both economic and political reasons. . . . It may damage the Republican party for a while, but it will surely benefit the party in the end."

Yet now, "in the exigency of his contest for the nomination," the President said, "and with the purpose of accentuating the supposed feeling of the farmers against me, he recants his approval. . . . I submit that Mr. Roosevelt's course on reciprocity is not in accord with the square deal."

Fourth, there were Roosevelt's loud cries that the G.O.P. ma-

[7] *Addresses*, Vol. XXVIII, pp. 185-187. [8] New York *Times*, April 9, 1912.

chine, by corrupt methods, was stealing delegates for Taft. He had said that Taft was "receiving stolen goods" and profiting by "the use of dirty instruments." Even this grave indictment— surely no more serious one could be made by one man against another— received calm, sober attention as Taft continued speaking. He did not make sweeping denials, as Roosevelt would have done, or consign his accuser to an Ananias Club. He said, realistically, that he could not be familiar with the facts in all the primary contests and conventions in all the states. He could not swear that no instances of fraud had occurred. But why did not Roosevelt go to the courts if he had evidence of illegalities? Was it fair, the President asked, "to run away from the opportunity provided by law to establish fraud and injustice and only claim it in the newspapers and in charges against one's opponent?" He continued:

In Indianapolis, I am informed, the complaint of the Roosevelt committee that fraud had been committed in the primaries appeared in an afternoon paper sold on the streets before the primaries were opened. The truth is that it has been perfectly plain from the first that the deliberate plan . . . has been to claim everything exultingly and with the utmost confidence and to meet the reports of the election of adverse delegates by directing in advance the bringing of trumped-up contests.

Fifth, there was the Roosevelt contention that "never before has patronage been so shamelessly used in politics as . . . to secure my nomination." Again, Taft's reply was realistic. He did not deny that under the existing political system federal officeholders took part in such a contest. On the contrary, he admitted that they will "support those to whose appointment they attribute their preferment." He pointed out, though, that at least seventy per cent of the men holding federal jobs had been appointed by Roosevelt, not himself; a large number of them were therefore favoring Roosevelt and not Taft. But "not a single man" had been removed from office for doing so.

—2—

Having disposed of these specific charges, the President then defended his administration and his record as a progressive. He repeated the warning voiced by Roosevelt against a break with Uncle Joe Cannon. He described the effect of the Payne-Aldrich act. He listed such accomplishments as the drive for governmental economy, the passage of the postal savings law, the conservation bill, the amended railroad-regulation act and various laws for the protection of labor.

"This was all progressive legislation. But I am not to have any credit for it because it was accomplished through regular Republicans," Taft observed accurately. "In all Mr. Roosevelt's history he never failed to use as instruments for his purpose those whom he found in power. Indeed, throughout his life he has defended that course as the only sensible course to pursue. I have merely followed his example, and I do not hesitate to point with satisfaction to the legislation which has been enacted in my three years. For him now to deny credit for this, after he gave it to me in his speech in the New York Convention [in 1910], is another instance of his failure to meet his standard of a square deal."

Concluding this Boston speech, the President defended his trust-control program and criticized Roosevelt's proposal to differentiate between "good" and "bad" trusts by some form of executive tribunal. He declared, and this was the weakest part of the speech, that Roosevelt's nomination would alarm the business community and would cause a depression. Thereby Taft aligned himself, even while he denied it, with the financial and industrial interests. But the final phrases of the address were effective and moving. He was now discharging, he said, "one of the most painful duties of my life" for still another reason. This was that Roosevelt had already been in the White House for seven and one-half years and had specifically promised, after the 1904 campaign, that never again would he be a candidate. Here, said Taft, was a fundamental issue:

Mr. Roosevelt would accept a nomination for a third term on what ground? Not because he wishes it for himself. He has disclaimed any such desire. He is convinced that the American people think that he is the only one to do the job (as he terms it), and for this he is ready to sacrifice his personal comfort. He does not define exactly what "the job" is which he is to do, but if we may infer from his Columbus platform it is to bring about a change of the social institutions of this country by legislation and other means

which he may be able to secure as President. . . . I need hardly
say that such an ambitious plan could not be carried out in one short
four years. . . . We are left to infer, therefore, that "the job" which
Mr. Roosevelt is to perform is one that may take a long time, perhaps the rest of his natural life. There is not the slightest reason
why, if he secures a third term, and the limitation of the Washington, Jefferson and Jackson tradition is broken down, he should not
have as many terms as his natural life will permit. If he is necessary
now to the government, why not later?

One who so lightly regards constitutional principles, and especially the independence of the judiciary, one who is so naturally
impatient of legal restraints, and of due legal procedure, and who
has so misunderstood what liberty regulated by law is, could not
safely be intrusted with successive presidential terms. I say this sorrowfully, but I say it with the full conviction of truth.[9]

An overflow meeting was held at Symphony Hall at which
the President congratulated the crowd "that you were not able to
get into the Arena. What I did to that audience I am not going
to tell you, and I am not going to do to you what I did to it."
He summarized, briefly, the longer address and hoped that "my
speech will be reported in the morning, and you will be able to
look it all through and see if I have not made out a case to indicate that . . . Mr. Roosevelt does not understand the rule of
fair dealing." [10]

The day ended, at last. The President had spoken to thousands. Hundreds of thousands had thronged to see him. He had
cause for exhilaration, perhaps, in the cheers that had greeted him.
But Taft was exhausted. He had strained his voice until it had
become almost a whisper. Weariness and depression were the only
sensations he felt as he was driven toward the waiting train. It
was remarked, as he boarded his car, that he seemed very much
shaken. Seibold of the *World* had been traveling with the official
party and on boarding the special he went back to the President's
car to ask some question. Taft was seated in one of the lounges,
slumped over, with his head between his hands. As the journalist
entered he looked up.

[9] *Addresses*, Vol. XXVIII, pp. 187-199. [10] *Ibid.*, Vol. XXVIII, pp. 232-236.

"Roosevelt was my closest friend," he said brokenly. Then he could restrain himself no longer, and he began to weep.[11]

This, however, was only the beginning of an ordeal which would be unbroken until, at last, Election Day arrived and Taft could retire, quite without regret, into the relatively obscure status of a defeated president. Roosevelt answered his Massachusetts speeches, of course, and his high-pitched voice became even more shrill as he did so. It was, he said, "the grossest and most astounding hypocrisy" for Taft to say that he had been loyal. It was "untrue," Roosevelt incredibly asserted, that he had changed front on reciprocity. The colonel was outraged that Taft had published his letter on this subject for "one of the unpardonable sins on the part of any man calling himself a gentleman is to publish confidential correspondence without permission." He attempted, too, to reply to Taft's declaration that he had advised harmony with Speaker Cannon.

"I advised him to meet everyone," Roosevelt said vaguely.[12]

"I do not wish this to be a campaign of personalities," he said on the following night.[13]

It could, of course, be nothing else although Taft, far more than Roosevelt, attempted to discuss the issues. The President again went into Massachusetts on the eve of the April 30 primary. "He's a liar," came hurtling down from the galleries of the hall at Lowell as he described Roosevelt's accusation in the Lorimer case. The President held up his hand.

"No," he said slowly, "that isn't in my vocabulary. My experience on the bench has taught me the value of words. One of the most unsafe things to do is to go further than to show the facts."

The bench had not taught Taft the political peril that lurked in words, however. Otherwise he would never, in that campaign speech in 1908, have referred to General Grant's weakness for liquor. Otherwise, he would never have hastily called the Payne-Aldrich tariff the best in history. He was just as careless now.

"Condemn me if you will," he said in this same address, "but condemn me by other witnesses than Theodore Roosevelt. I was

[11] Seibold to author, Dec. 13, 1934. [12] New York *Times,* April 27, 1912. [13] *Ibid.,* April 28, 1912.

a man of straw, but I have been a man of straw long enough. Every man who has blood in his body, and who has been misrepresented as I have been is forced to fight." [14]

The President of the United States, thus protesting, seemed to admit that he was, in fact, a man of straw and that only desperation could force him to combat. ". . . my dear friends," he repeated, "when you are backed up against a wall, and a man is hitting you in each eye and punishing you in every way, both above and below the belt, by George, if you have any manhood in you, you have got to fight!" [15] And at Hyattsville, Maryland, the following week, came the most disastrous phrase of all.

"I am a man of peace," pleaded Taft, "and I don't want to fight. But when I do fight I want to hit hard. *Even a rat in a corner will fight.*" [16] Those eight, final, tragic words do not appear in the stenographic transcript of this speech. Perhaps a discreet stenographer did not take them down. Perhaps they were later stricken out. Perhaps Taft never said them. But it did not matter. They were carried by the newspapers. Their effect was just the same.

—3—

Meanwhile, would Theodore Roosevelt bolt the convention if he failed to win the nomination in June? This was what William Jennings Bryan wanted to know; his influence in the Democratic party was waning but his power was still great. Champ Clark, the probable nominee, wanted to know too. So did Woodrow Wilson. So did all the Democrats who had been hungry through all the famine years since 1897. And so, of course, did Taft.

"Do you intend to support the Republican nominee, whoever he may be?" the correspondents had asked Roosevelt as February ended.

"Of course I shall," he answered.[17] But he was far less emphatic after the Taft forces had come out ahead in the New York primaries. He raised the issue of honesty. The only honest primary, it would seem, was a contest in which Roosevelt won.

---

[14] *Ibid.*, April 30, 1912. [15] *Addresses*, Vol. XXVIII, p. 267. [16] New York *Times*, May 5, 1912. (Italics mine.) [17] *Ibid.*, Feb. 27, 1912.

"I don't know whether the colonel will bolt the convention or not," the President observed. "I think not. A man with a bolt is a man who gets very little sympathy anywhere." [18]

By June, however, Taft had changed his mind and was certain that Roosevelt would not abide by the vote of the delegates.[19] There was ample reason for his pessimism. Only "by deliberate cheating in the national convention," Roosevelt had already declared, could the administration forces hope to win.

"I want our opponents to understand this; if the people are against me I have nothing to say," the colonel warned. "But if the people decide for me and the discredited bosses and politicians try to offset their judgment and decide against me, I will have a great deal to say, and I won't stand it for a moment." [20]

The campaign in Ohio began on May 12 and lasted for eight days. As he left, the President wrote a lengthy letter to Horace Taft:

I don't expect to be successful. I think the American people are not quite alive to the dangers of Roosevelt's success and that there is too short a time to teach them in the preliminaries of a primary. However, from a sense of duty I am going through this fight, distasteful and undignified as it is. "Ich kann nicht anders." . . . The trend is toward Roosevelt. I have thought he would be certain to be defeated if nominated, but I am not sure now, though I still think so. He can't keep up a campaign of bluff and pretense for four months. . . . It is all very discouraging for the time, but in the end I have abiding faith in the American people and they can not be always fooled by such a fraud, dangerous as he is.[21]

Taft drove himself to exhaustion in Ohio. He made fifty-five speeches. He repeated over and over his denial of the charges brought by Roosevelt. He defended his administration until he must have been utterly sick of it all. There had been a time when Taft's heart had been warmed by campaigning in his native state. Through all his life he had been familiar with the cities of Ohio. The stout and able young lawyer of the eighties had visited them and had extolled the virtues of the Republican party. The stout young lawyer had visited, too, the small, white towns which rested

[18] Taft to Delia Torrey, March 27, 1912. [19] Taft to Bannard, June 8, 1912. [20] New York *Times*, May 26, 1912. [21] Taft to Horace D. Taft, May 12, 1912.

on the banks of the winding rivers. This was his own land. These
were his own people. They had loved him always: when he had
been a judge, when he had returned in glory from the Philippines, when he had been secretary of war, when he had crusaded
for Theodore Roosevelt, when he had been a candidate for president. In almost all the small, white towns and in all the smoky
cities there had been intimates who called him "Will" and at whose
homes he could go for a spot of gossip as the day was ending.

But now all was changed. The crowds still flocked to hear his
speeches, of course, for he was President of the United States. But
among them, always, there were many who had just been listening
to Theodore Roosevelt. Stolidity, instead of friendship, lay on the
faces of some of those in front of him. And he felt so much
alone. For even Elihu Root— the cherished Elihu— had found it
inexpedient to aid him in the Ohio primary campaign.

"One of the interesting results of such a crisis as this," the
President told Horace, "is the new light it gives one of one's supporters. Old Knox has shown his courage and his ability in his
speech at Los Angeles. Root has failed me. He is bitterly against
Roosevelt, he tells me, but he will not come out to Ohio to help
me. Fisher and Stimson hang back. They are afraid of T.R. and
so are many of the congressmen and senators, though they know
his character and sympathize with me. But seats in the bandwagon
are popular and I shall expect to see many more turn to him when
it becomes apparent, as it may and probably will become after
Ohio and California, that I cannot win." [22]

Taft deplored rather than criticized the decision of Root, his
old and dear friend. Root had explained his position and had
pledged all possible assistance as senator from New York. But
he could not bring himself to speak on "questions as between the
two administrations, and questions of Theodore's personal right
or wrong conduct . . . and comparisons between his course and
yours."

. . . the fact cannot be ignored that I was a member of his
administration, bearing the most high confidential relations, cog-
nizant of his acts and the reasons for them, consulted about them,

[22] *Idem.*

and with a knowledge of them derived from him under the highest obligations of confidence and loyalty. I could not enter upon a discussion of the matters to which I bore such a relation, in an adverse attitude towards him, without being subject, and I think justly subject, to the charge of betraying confidence and disloyalty. Nor could I discuss him personally nor contrast you with him in public discussion without involving the knowledge which I obtained in this way and using against him the qualifications for the discussion which I obtained through his trust in me.

I have no question that you are justified in attacking him in your own defense, because he attacked you, but he has not attacked me. He has never said a word as far as I know, certainly in public, regarding me which was not kindly and laudatory. There has been nothing to releive [*sic*] me from my obligation, and I feel that if I were to take part in a public attack . . . I should be subject to universal condemnation in which I should be forced myself to join. . . . I hope you will pull through. I believe you will. I think it would be a great misfortune if you should not.

Besides, added Mr. Root, he was "too old and running too close to the edge of that line which separates health from a complete breakdown to be of any real service in such a campaign as this." He was sixty-seven years old. "My fighting days are over," said Mr. Root in this premature obituary, "and as I look about upon the political conditions of our country I feel that the time cannot come too soon for me to step aside and let a younger generation work out in their own way the new ideas which seem inseparable from turmoil and strife. I cannot tell you, old friend, how deeply I sympathize with you or how strongly I desire and hope for you success." [23]

Such are the perplexities of civil war. Root remained, "faithfully and affectionately" the friend of Taft. But there are no neutrals in war. In a few weeks Root would be presiding at the Republican convention and would be earning the bitter and lasting hatred of Theodore Roosevelt for his rulings in favor of the G.O.P. machine.

[23] Root to Taft, May 15, 1912.

—4—

The tide continued, now, to run against the President. There can be no reasonable doubt that Roosevelt, not Taft, was the popular choice for the Republican nomination. Ohio was a grievous blow. Then came an arduous campaign in New Jersey and another defeat. ". . . there appears to be nothing saved," Taft said when the returns came in.[24]

"I do not think you need be overcome with mortification," he assured a supporter. "You had a pretty heavy candidate to carry. . . . We are fighting on." [25]

But California, too, had already slipped into the Roosevelt column. The influence of Hiram Johnson, who would be the candidate for vice-president on the Bull Moose ticket, had prevailed in the primaries.

"One of these days," the President said, "the people of California are going to wake up to the bunco game which has been practiced on them by the pseudo reformers, and those men are going to receive their reward in an oblivion that in a decade will have covered them over. They are not made of stuff to last!" [26]

Actually, Taft was deeply discouraged by the repeated disasters. His resentment toward Roosevelt heightened. He no longer believed, as he had believed earlier in the year, that the quarrel would one day be forgotten and that the sweet, warm friendship of the past would be restored. To his aunt Delia, a very old lady now but still keenly interested in the fortunes of her nephew, he poured out the sorrow in his heart:

I have a sense of wrong in the attitude of Theodore Roosevelt toward me which I doubt if I can ever get over. The fact is that I do not think I ought ever to get over it. But I have an abiding confidence, my dear Aunt Delia, in the eventual justice of the American people, and I am quite sure that in the end the hypocrisy, the insincerity, the selfishness, the monumental egotism, and almost the insanity of megalomania that possess Theodore Roosevelt will make themselves known to the American people, in such a way that his place in history will be accurately defined.

[24] Taft to William Worthington, May 29, 1912. [25] Taft to F. O. Briggs, May 30, 1912. [26] Taft to C. C. Moore, June 6, 1912.

He did a great deal in leading the crusade against the dangers of concentrated wealth. He has done very little in the way of constructive statesmanship, and whenever he has attempted it it has been really a farce. That is the case with his present recall of judicial decisions.[27]

There were curious contradictions in the preconvention campaign. Taft, who would be denounced as the candidate of wealth and conservatism, found it difficult to obtain donations for the expenses of his campaign. The Republican National Committee deluded itself, at first, that Charles P. Taft would take care of all the costs. He contributed heavily, but he was irritated by the assumption.

"I am not made of money," he had protested in December, 1911, when the purpose of the National Committee became clear to him. "The committee has got no money, and it can't raise any, and it will be the same thing after the convention. . . . My only complaint is that they expect me to do it all." Mr. Taft recalled the lamentations of a millionaire friend on the cost of installing, through the marriage of his daughter, a European prince in his family.

"He ought to have tried getting a president into one," Mr. Taft observed.[28]

As always, though, Brother Charles was liberal. He promised to give $50,000 and sent half of it at once.[29] The Roosevelt forces of righteousness were well-heeled. Only Albert Beveridge, it would seem, worried in the least over the sources from which the money came. Lucius Littauer, the glove manufacturer whose plea for special treatment in the Payne-Aldrich act had been indignantly rejected by Taft, was among the contributors.

"If we're not careful," Beveridge warned, "we'll be labeled as a Wall Street promotion." [30]

There is ground for suspicion, at the least, that the trust-control program so vigorously prosecuted by Attorney General Wickersham under Taft's direction had alienated certain of the traditional backers of the Republican party. Perkins, Munsey and Alexander S.

[27] Taft to Delia Torrey, May 12, 1912. [28] Butt, Archie, *Taft and Roosevelt*, Vol. II, pp. 790-791. [29] Hilles to C. P. Taft, Jan. 29, Feb. 6, 1912. [30] Bowers, Claude, *Beveridge and the Progressive Era*, p. 435.

Cochran, the carpet king, gave $15,000 each for Roosevelt's New York primary contest. The total was $59,200 and all of it was spent within the limits of Manhattan where only 15,000 Roosevelt votes were polled.

"The fact that the Roosevelt committee has filed a certified statement . . . admitting the expenditure of $4 for each Roosevelt voter in New York City, at the recent primary," Taft noted, "shows the length to which our adversaries will go. Men conspicuous in the Steel Corporation and the Steel Pool are furnishing the money and the organizing ability." [31]

That a great deal of money was spent on behalf of Roosevelt is certain. A senatorial committee looked into the subject of campaign expenses later in the year; its purpose, of course, was to embarrass Roosevelt. This disclosed a probable total of $338,000 spent before the convention assembled in Chicago. Not all of it was handled by Senator Joseph Dixon of Montana, who commanded the Roosevelt forces. William Flinn testified that he had spent $99,384.18 in Allegheny County, Pennsylvania. Another witness said that $30,000 had been used in Pittsburgh. Thomas W. Lawson, the sensational financier, testified that he had paid out $100,000 personally, not through any of the committees, for Roosevelt. Walter Brown, the Ohio boss, reported that about $50,000 had been used in the primary fight in his state.[32]

The President convinced himself, in due time, that the United States Steel Corporation and Roosevelt were virtually synonymous; ". . . letting the people rule . . ." he said, "is letting the Steel Trust rule." [33] He could not comprehend why, as they appeared to be doing, the nation's industrialists should even consider supporting Roosevelt:

The businessmen are fools, like some of the voters. For a time they don't see their real interest; they don't have the power of discrimination. That man, T. Coleman du Pont, is one such man. I have no use for him whatever. They don't see beyond their noses. They only think of their particular interest and don't take a broader view. They are in favor of special privilege in the sense of having

[31] Taft to J. C. Hemphill, April 19, 1912. [32] Clapp Committee, Vol. I, pp. 286, 311, 353-355, 730, 741, 1042. [33] Taft to G. B. Edwards, April 22, 1912.

themselves favored and everybody else prosecuted. That is the attitude of Gary and Perkins and du Pont and others.[34]

—5—

Thus indignant, Taft naturally made an issue of the fact that
Roosevelt, as president, had refrained from prosecuting the International Harvester Company under the Sherman act. Pressure had
been applied on Taft, too, as we have seen, to permit the company
voluntarily to abandon certain monopolistic practices, and Attorney
General Wickersham had been instructed to delay bringing a dissolution suit. But when nothing was done, the action was filed
at the close of April, 1912, just as the president, able to keep silent
no longer, was openly attacking Theodore Roosevelt. Taft was reluctant to declare in public that his predecessor had befriended one
of the large corporations. First mention of the matter was made
by Representative Augustus P. Gardner of Massachusetts, the son-
in-law of Cabot Lodge. Gardner challenged Roosevelt to debate.
He said that the Morgan interests had been favored by the Roosevelt administration. He said that certain papers, proving this, had
been suppressed. Immediately, of course, Roosevelt said that the
son-in-law of his closest friend was a liar.[35] Taft then yielded to
the demands of his supporters that the papers in the case be made
public. This was done by the expedient of a Senate resolution, on
April 24, 1912, requesting the President to furnish all papers and
letters relating to prosecution of the International Harvester Company in the summer of 1907.[36]

The evidence was damaging to Roosevelt's claim of trust buster,
but it proved no corruption. On August 22, 1907, when president,
he had informed Attorney General Bonaparte of a visit from
George W. Perkins in which the financier had emphasized the
good intentions of his company. Herbert Knox Smith, commissioner of corporations, was conducting an investigation, Mr. Perkins
had pointed out. A suit under the antitrust law, he said, would
expose the company to expense and damage. He asked that the

[34] Taft to C. P. Taft, June 2, 1912. [35] New York *Times*, April 22, 24, 1912. [36] *Ibid.*,
April 25, 1912.

litigation be postponed until the Smith inquiry had been completed.

"Will you see Mr. Perkins and Commissioner Smith, go over the matter in full and report to me thereon?" President Roosevelt requested his attorney general. "Please do not file the suit until I hear from you."

Commissioner Smith reported back to Roosevelt on September 21, 1907, and his letter contained phrases which would surely have been eliminated had ultimate publication been remotely considered. He said he had seen Mr. Perkins and had been assured that the harvester company's only wish was to obey the law. Perkins had pointed out that the company employed 25,000 men and did $100,-000,000 a year in business. Smith added:

He concluded with great emphasis with the remark that if, after all the endeavors of this company and the other Morgan interests to uphold the policy of the administration and to adopt their methods of modern publicity, this company was now to be attacked in a purely technical case, the interests he represented were "going to fight."

Commissioner Smith said he knew of no "moral grounds for attacks" on the International Harvester Company. A suit under the Sherman act, he felt, would be unjust. The situation raised the distinction between "good and bad trusts." Then came an indiscreet sentence. Smith wrote:

While the administration has never hesitated to grapple with any financial interest, no matter how great, when it is believed that a substantial wrong is being committed, nevertheless, it is *a very practical question whether it is well to throw away now the great influence of the so-called Morgan interests,* which up to this time have supported the advanced policy of the administration.[37]

In the background, of course, lay the financial disturbances which would culminate in the 1907 panic in a few weeks and would so greatly alarm Roosevelt. The President's enthusiasm for trust prosecutions cooled as the economic situation grew acute. The

[37] United States Senate, 62nd Congress, 2nd Session, Sen. Doc. 694.

International Harvester Company, like most of the other Sherman act prosecutions, was left for Taft to handle. Again, there were delays; three years passed before the suit was brought. In March, 1913, Luther Conant, Jr., who had succeeded Smith as commissioner of corporations, submitted a lengthy report on the harvester company. Its position in the industry, Mr. Conant thought, "is chiefly attributable to a monopolistic combination in the harvesting-machine business, certain unfair competitive methods, and superior command of capital." [38]

President Taft, referring in 1912 to the International Harvester Company matter, was careful not to draw the conclusion that Perkins, in contributing to Roosevelt's cause, was making payment for illicit services rendered in 1907.

"I don't charge that there is any corruption there," he said, "but I ask you to look at and consider the courageous audacity of a man who comes and impeaches me with belonging to the interests when there is that evidence on the record. . . . I ask you with your knowledge of the method by which Theodore Roosevelt has brought charges against me, what he would say if the case were reversed and George Perkins were supporting me, and I had not sued the Steel Trust and the Harvester Trust." [39]

In one major detail of his answer to Taft's harvester company exposé Roosevelt trifled with the truth. He said that Taft, in his Cabinet at the time, had fully approved the decision to delay the antitrust prosecution.[40] This is not possible. Secretary of War Taft left Washington on August 18, 1907, to begin his journey to the Philippines and thence around the world. Perkins, according to Roosevelt's own letter, did not confer at the White House until August 24. Mr. Taft was on the Pacific Ocean when Commissioner Smith wrote his ill-advised letter concerning the importance of the Morgan interests. He knew nothing whatever about the International Harvester Company nor was he consulted regarding the suit. This was pointed out to Roosevelt by Charles D. Hilles, and the colonel then shifted his ground. He said that Taft had given his approval in January, 1908, after returning to the United

[38] Report, commissioner of corporations on the International Harvester Company, 1913.
[39] *Addresses*, Vol. XXVIII, p. 283. [40] New York *Times*, April 24, 1912.

States. But this is equally hard to believe. The matter was a dead issue by then.[41]

—6—

Sometimes the President was encouraged as the convention drew near. He had, on May 29, enough delegates to ensure the nomination. Taft did not feel that the contests— the Roosevelt forces had announced their intention of protesting the eligibility of many of the Taft delegates— "are really at all serious" although there were "some . . . of course, which Roosevelt ought to win." [42] As for the nomination itself, "We do not propose to be defrauded or bulldozed out of it," he said.[43]

More often, Taft was discouraged. Root, among others, was apprehensive that the Taft delegates would not stand firm under pressure from Roosevelt. Among the southern delegations, in particular, defections had already taken place.[44] The President brooded, meanwhile, over criticism that he had damaged the prestige of his high office by taking an active part in the preconvention campaign.

"I have been through, in the Massachusetts, Ohio and New Jersey campaigns," he said, "an experience which I do not care to repeat. . . . Public critics are always the same. In the first place, they criticize you for not doing a thing which they would like to see done; their sympathies being aroused in this case against Roosevelt, they urged that some answer be made to his false accusations. Then, just as soon as I came out . . . and now that I have . . . gone into the fight, they make but little distinction between him and me as to who is to blame for the unprecedented spectacle." [45]

But there was another side to it. The President outlined this in his letter of May 12 to his brother:

Still, my dear old boy, I have had so much good fortune. I have had so much opportunity . . . to help along the cause of good gov-

[41] Statement by Hilles, April 25, 1912. [42] Taft to William Worthington, May 29, 1912. [43] Taft to Clarence Kelsey, May 22, 1912. [44] Root to D. T. Flynn, May 24, 1912. [45] Taft to Worthington, May 29, 1912.

ernment. Why should I mourn, or become a misanthrope or a pessimist because I may go down in a preliminary skirmish? Do you remember those lines of Matthew Arnold which run something like this:

> "And when the Forts of Folly fall
> May find my body near the wall."

I shall be only fifty-five when I lay down my office and shall still have some opportunity to strike a blow for decent government and the better things and I mean to do it. But this letter is nearly as egotistical as Roosevelt.[46]

As he left to attend the convention in Chicago, Root called at the White House to ask what the President would do, if defeated, as to a third candidate.

"I said that I had no great desire to run again," Taft wrote, describing the conversation, "provided I could get somebody who does not represent what Theodore Roosevelt represents; but that I would not withdraw in favor of LaFollette, Cummins or Roosevelt; and that if he [Root] or Hughes or a man of like conservative standing were to be seriously suggested he would find no difficulty with me. I don't know that this amounts to anything." [47]

Four years would pass, though, before Hughes could be beguiled from his haven on the Supreme Court, and Root reiterated that he was "out of the question as a Dark Horse, if for no other reason, because I shall be sixty-eight years old at the time of the next inauguration, and no man of that age is fit to be president." [48]

Peril lurked in any public admission by Taft that he was meditating a withdrawal. It would almost certainly have meant a weakening in his lines and a desertion of delegates to Roosevelt. So the President told Hilles, his commander in chief at Chicago, to state unequivocally that he was in the battle to stay.[49] Only privately did Taft continue to say how happy he would be if only Hughes or some other could be chosen in his place.

"If I could nominate . . . Hughes by a withdrawal it would give me great pleasure to bring it about. My chief purpose in staying in is to defeat Mr. Roosevelt, whose nomination . . . would be a great danger and menace to the country," he said. "His con-

[46] Taft to Horace D. Taft, May 12, 1912. [47] Taft to Hilles, June 12, 1912. [48] Root to Flynn, May 25, 1912. [49] Taft to Hilles, June 14, 1912.

stitutional views are of such character, and his mendacity, his un-scrupulousness displayed in deceiving the public and arousing one class against the other, all alike make him a man to be avoided if possible as a candidate. Were I now to withdraw I am very sure that of the delegates pledged to me a number would go at once to Mr. Roosevelt, and that I cannot permit. Personally, I have no desire to continue as a candidate. I had no desire to do so when I went on the stump, but the fear of Mr. Roosevelt's success made it necessary." [50]

That, at least, Taft would be able to prevent. Even so amiable and gentle a man, in whose heart vengeance seldom lingered for long, must have found satisfaction in the years ahead that he had blocked the ambitions of the man who had injured him so greatly and whose theories of government, as Taft more and more believed, augured ruin for the American system. Roosevelt, too, had no desire for a compromise as all trains disgorged their delegates at Chicago.

"I'll name the compromise candidate," he had boasted. "He'll be me. I'll name the compromise platform. It will be our platform." [51]

The President would wait, irritable and despondent, at the White House to hear the returns. Roosevelt, ever the dramatist, would go in person to Chicago. There was something dismally prophetic in Taft's choice of a speaker to place in nomination his name when the convention assembled. He chose a hack politician from Ohio who had just been elected a delegate at large through the power of the Old Guard machine.

"I know you can do it weil," the President wrote in tendering the invitation, "and I should be delighted to . . . have it done by a man who represents the state so worthily as you do." [52]

So Warren Gamaliel Harding offered Taft's name to a party convention where hostility reigned and disaster was in the air.

[50] *Idem*, June 18, 1912. [51] New York *Times*, May 21, 1912. [52] Taft to Harding, June 5, 1912.

CHAPTER XLI

THE INESCAPABLE CONFLICT

IT WAS widely assumed that Theodore Roosevelt would take personal command of his forces at the Chicago convention. Early in June, when the elaborate political circus was still a fortnight away, some horsemen were training their livery stable mounts in Chicago's parks. They were not particularly dashing equestrians, but they were to serve as synthetic Rough Riders when the Roosevelt delegations paraded through the city. Their uniforms were being manufactured. They were a detail in the ballyhoo which accompanies the selection of presidential candidates.[1] Roosevelt, meanwhile, kept both his friends and his foes in suspense. "Fake, pure fake," he had said when reports were current that he would attend the convention. "I may alter my plans," he added, through characteristically clenched teeth and spacing his words to give emphasis. "If— circumstances— demand, of— course— I'll— go!"[2] The sessions of the convention would open on June 18. But everything would have been settled before that day.

The President's anger toward Roosevelt mounted. "I am counting on your presence in Chicago to call the bluff and bluster of the Roosevelt people," he told one leader. "There is a suggestion of physical force in their attitude that it will gratify me to have met in a proper spirit."[3]

Taft had been forced into a position which must have vexed him sorely. It was an incongruous position, false to the honesty of his character and the purity of his motives. He would be presented to the convention and then to the voters as the candidate of the Old Guard. The evil Penrose and the equally evil Barnes of New York were among his champions. So was Jim Watson of Indiana. So was Harry Daugherty. Daugherty and Warren Harding would exchange drinks jovially at the Chicago bars in June of

---

[1] New York *Times,* June 2, 1912. [2] Sullivan, Mark, *Our Times,* Vol. IV, p. 497.
[3] Taft to D. T. Flynn, June 2, 1912.

1912. And before a decade had passed they would march, arm in arm, on Washington and the Republican party would sink into a mire of corruption. Taft had nothing in common with such men. But he needed them and used them, as all presidents must, when seeking a renomination.

Corrupt leaders, as we have seen, were behind Roosevelt too. They were relatively inconspicuous, though, because the colonel had, beyond serious question, the support of the rank and file of the Republican party. He had been victorious in every state primary except two, and in these LaFollette had won. He carried Illinois by 139,436 votes; New Jersey by 17,213; Pennsylvania by 105,899; California by 69,218; Ohio by 47,447. In Nebraska, Roosevelt polled 16,769 more votes than Taft and LaFollette combined. A total of 388 delegates had been selected in the presidential primaries and of these Roosevelt won 281, Taft 71, and LaFollette 36.

It had been far different in the states where the delegates had been selected by the traditional convention method. The President had triumphed in those states. The delegates pledged to him, as the curtain was about to rise in Chicago, exceeded those instructed for his rival.[4] But were the Taft delegates honestly chosen or, as Roosevelt hotly charged, had they been fraudulently selected? This was the first issue in the 1912 battle. It would be settled, according to the law and the custom of the party, by the members of the Republican National Committee who had taken office at the close of the 1908 convention. There were fifty-three members of the committee and they were, in the main, adherents of Taft. They had been selected at the convention dominated by Roosevelt, strangely enough, and under the party rules approved by him. A national committeeman is a disciplined party leader, however. His loyalty remains with the titular head of the party, and Taft was now that head.

—2—

Roosevelt's only real hope was to alter the party rules and have his charges of fraud decided by the newly elected national committeemen, many of whom were friendly to his cause. By im-

[4] Sullivan, Mark, op. cit., Vol. IV, p. 494.

memorial rule of the party, however, these men would not take office until after the convention. Roosevelt determined to change this, if he could. On May 29, in Chicago, National Committeeman Harry S. New expressed scandalized astonishment over the idea. He had heard that R. B. Howell, of Nebraska, who had defeated Victor Rosewater, the incumbent, in the primaries, would shortly arrive and demand his seat. Pounding the table, Colonel New called this preposterous. A national committeeman, he said, held office for four years, like the President of the United States. It would have been just as absurd for President-elect Taft to have demanded an inauguration in November, 1908. The leaders of the party were "full-grown men who are not going to get scared over any threats" by Roosevelt to alter the party machinery.[5]

It may be assumed that a proportion of the Taft delegates had been illegally chosen. The delegates to a national convention are selected under state election laws, many of them lax and many badly enforced. In certain parts of the country, fraud is the custom, rather than the exception, in the naming of delegates. But it may be stated as a fact that Roosevelt, asserting that 238 of the Taft delegates were not entitled to their seats, was motivated by grim political necessity rather than by a thirst for honesty or the truth. He was doomed unless some of the Taft delegates were barred.

So he contested as many of the elections as he could, and some of his evidence was so weak that it was rejected by even his own supporters. Some light on the Roosevelt preconvention strategy was thrown by an injudicious dispatch written by Judson C. Welliver for the Washington *Times*. This was a newspaper owned by Frank Munsey, an ardent Rooseveltian; its friendly attitude toward the colonel was obvious. On June 9, while the hearings on the contests were under way, Welliver pointed out that Taft had been far in the lead early in the campaign. He continued:

. . . there was no chance to develop the real Roosevelt strength in the great northern states until later. For psychological effect, as a move in practical politics, it was necessary for the Roosevelt people to start contests on these early Taft selections in order that a tabula-

[5] New York *Times*, May 30, 1912.

tion of delegate strength could be put out that would show Roosevelt holding a good hand. In the game a table showing Taft 150, Roosevelt 18, contested none, would not be very much calculated to inspire confidence, whereas one showing Taft 23, Roosevelt 19, contested 127, looked very different. That is the whole story of the larger number of southern contests that were started early in the game. It was never expected that they would be taken very seriously. They served a useful purpose, and now the National Committee is deciding them in favor of Taft in most cases without real division.[6]

The sessions of the committee were to begin on June 7 at Chicago. On May 31, the President suggested that the meetings should be open to representatives of the press associations, a proposal which Roosevelt promptly endorsed. Taft ordered that the contests should be impartially judged.

"I do not want any contest decided in my favor merely for the purpose of giving me the majority," he said.[7]

That the majority of the contests were, as Taft phrased it, "flimsy" in nature and due to the "bluff and bluster of the general Roosevelt campaign"[8] was quickly demonstrated when the hearings began. The Rough Rider was not without friends on the committee. Among them were Borah of Idaho, T. Coleman du Pont, Frank B. Kellogg of Minnesota, Cecil Lyon of Texas and Bill Ward of New York. The first meeting considered twenty-four delegates from Alabama and seated all of the Taft men. On June 8, the President was awarded forty-eight more, and Borah, a Roosevelt supporter, said that "the 9th Alabama district and the 5th Arkansas were the only contests heard thus far which in my opinion had any merit." On June 10, with the consent of every Roosevelt committeeman, twelve Indiana contests were decided for Taft.

"There have been many frauds at the primaries," Borah said; "I don't say there were not. But there was no evidence of that fact presented. . . . Under the circumstances, I could not vote to sustain the Roosevelt delegates."

On the following day, however, Borah was joined by Governor

[6] *Statement Relating to the Contests over Seats in the Republican National Convention,* July 29, 1912, p. 5. [7] Taft to Victor Rosewater, May 31, 1912. [8] Taft to S. J. Elder, June 15, 1912.

Herbert S. Hadley of Missouri in a vigorous struggle over the Kentucky contest. It ended with seventeen delegates for Taft and one for Roosevelt.[9] The colonel, meanwhile, was berating the committee with all the invective at his command. All this, he screamed, was "political brigandage . . . frank and cynical defiance of the emphatic action of the people." [10] The National Committee was guilty of conduct "dangerously near being treason to the whole spirit of our institutions; to the whole spirit of free democratic government." [11]

"There is no form of rascality which the Taft men have not resorted to," said Roosevelt on June 12, and prepared to leave for the front.[12]

In contrast, the President took no part in the charges and countercharges. A telephone wire to Chicago was open for several hours each day, and Taft received detailed reports.[13]

"The report that I am in any way considering the possibility of a compromise candidate is wholly unfounded and you are authorized emphatically to deny the report," he told Hilles in a message for circulation among his supporters. "With confidence, I abide the judgment of the convention." [14]

Roosevelt would abide no judgment save his own. The morning papers of June 14 carried to Oyster Bay dire tidings from the battlefield. It was said that Taft would surely win, that he already had enough delegates. Roosevelt motored into town as usual that morning and swept into the offices of the *Outlook* an hour or so later. Fire was in his eye. He was wearing a large, black, felt hat which was apparently new. Undeniably, it was a Rough Rider hat and it was an outward symbol of Roosevelt the Warrior. Ever since the glorious days of the Spanish War a similar wide-brimmed felt hat had marked Theodore's moments of high emotion. He wore one during his campaign for governor of New York when he told epic tales of the valor of which he had been part. He wore one, again, at the Republican National Convention of 1900 when he had been chosen, protesting loudly but not loudly enough, for the vice-presidency.

The colonel left New York on the afternoon of June 14 and the excitement in Chicago mounted toward hysteria as his train clicked off the westward miles. Vast crowds were at the station and at the Congress Hotel where he would stay. They howled for a speech until he appeared on a balcony while a band played songs nostalgic of Cuba— "There'll Be a Hot Time in the Old Town Tonight" was the favorite. Roosevelt looked down, and ground his teeth again.

"It is a fight against theft," he shouted, "and the thieves will not win!"

At this moment somebody in the crowd raised a banner declaring that California's twenty-six votes belonged to Roosevelt. "They are mine and shall be counted for me!" he called. ". . . The people have spoken and the politicians will be made to understand that they are the servants and not the masters of the . . . plain citizens of the Republican party."

The mob responded to his wrath. "Soak 'em, Teddy," its members called back as he returned to his rooms. Then the newspaper correspondents crowded in. How did he feel? Was he ready for the fray?

"I'm feeling like a Bull Moose!" he snapped, and inspired, thereby, the emblem which would stand for the principles and the hopes of the Progressive party.[15]

—3—

Roosevelt still denied, however, that he would bolt. The rumors were "all nonsense." The decisions of the National Committee on the delegates would be challenged in the Credentials Committee and on the floor of the convention, he said. But Root, reaching Chicago on June 16, was pessimistic in the extreme. The party was in grave peril, he said, for Roosevelt would certainly shatter it.[16]

So Chicago seethed and the Roosevelt forces, by now aroused to religious fervor, sang "Onward, Christian Soldiers" and 20,000 people flocked to the Auditorium where their messiah was to speak

[15] New York *Times,* June 15, 16, 1912; Sullivan, Mark, *op. cit.,* Vol. IV, pp. 505-506. [16] New York *Times,* June 17, 1912.

on the eve of the convention. Barely a quarter of them could get into the hall, and they heard one of the greatest speeches of Roosevelt's career.

"As far as Mr. Taft and I are personally concerned," he began, "it little matters what the fate of either may be." He then began a detailed, bitter and far from accurate attack on the President. Taft was the child of the party bosses, he said, and these bosses were stealing the nomination. The convention, itself, was the only proper judge of the qualifications of its members. Roosevelt said he had personally examined the evidence and there was "no element of doubt" that his own contestants, not Taft's delegates, "were honorably and lawfully chosen by the people." The colonel ended with a magnificent burst of oratory in which were blended high emotion, defiance and sacrifice. He said:

Our cause is the cause of justice for all in the interest of all. The present contest is but a phase of the larger struggle. Assuredly the fight will go on whether we win or lose; but it will be a sore disaster to lose. What happens to me is not of the slightest consequence; I am to be used, as in a doubtful battle any man is used, to his hurt or not, so long as he is useful, and is then cast aside or left to die. I wish you to feel this. I mean it; and I shall need no sympathy when you are through with me, for this fight is far too great to permit us to concern ourselves about any one man's welfare. If we are true to ourselves by putting far above our own interests the triumph of the high cause for which we battle we shall not lose. It would be far better to fail honorably for the cause we champion than it would be to win by foul methods the foul victory for which our opponents hope. But the victory shall be ours, and it shall be won as we have already won so many victories, by clean and honest fighting for the loftiest of causes. We fight in honorable fashion for the good of mankind; fearless of the future; unheeding of our individual fates; with unflinching hearts and undimmed eyes; we stand at Armageddon, and we battle for the Lord.[17]

It was magnificent. It was epic, even if nobody knew where Armageddon was, exactly, and why the Lord had suddenly become an opponent of William Howard Taft. Roosevelt probably

[17] Roosevelt, Theodore, *Works*, National Edition, Vol. XVII, pp. 204-231.

TAFT AT YALE—FORMAL AND INFORMAL

See page 856]

Cartoon by Harold Heaton, Courtesy Chicago Inter Ocean

believed, as he spoke, that he was telling the truth. But the weight of the evidence is against him. He had forgotten that precisely the same methods had been used to achieve his own nomination in 1904 and that he had used them for Taft in 1908. He did not know that by 1916 he would be back in the ranks of the G.O.P. and would be working with the very bosses whom he now condemned. Roosevelt was the child of the moment. When, as he rarely did, he looked back across the years he remembered things as he wished to remember rather than as they were. He seldom looked into the future at all.

But what could poor Taft do against such showmanship? Happily, he did not have to do anything. Wisely, he held his tongue. Privately, he thought it probable, on the day of Roosevelt's speech, that his lines would hold firm. He had 557 delegates, or seventeen more than were needed for the nomination. Roosevelt lacked about eighty votes.

"It is possible that by bulldozing, bribery and other dishonorable means, he may reduce my vote to slightly less than enough to nominate," the President observed, "but I very much doubt that he can nominate himself as long as I stay in the field— and I shall stay as long as my remaining will interfere with his success. . . . However, though it will be a disappointment if I cannot by my nomination defeat Roosevelt's purpose, the struggle will doubtless not end there. All the people are not as crazy or as blind as those lost in admiration of him and his methods, and sometime they will say so with emphasis." [18]

—4—

The convention assembled in the Chicago Coliseum on June 18. Despite the fervor of the Roosevelt followers, gloom hung in the air. The regulars were apprehensive that the party would be badly demoralized, whoever won the nomination, and that the Democrats would win in the fall. It was a belief shared, but with elation, by William Jennings Bryan, who was covering the gathering for a news syndicate. Victor Rosewater, chairman of the National Com-

[18] Taft to Archbishop Ireland, June 17, 1912.

mittee, opened the meeting and there was the usual mumbled prayer to which no one listened. The first order of business was the election of a temporary chairman. Job E. Hedges placed the name of Elihu Root in nomination and astutely quoted Roosevelt's remarks of a few years before that he was "the ablest man that has appeared in the public life of any country in any position in my time." The Bull Moose selection was Governor Francis E. Mc-Govern of Wisconsin. He had been chosen in the hope that the LaFollette forces would support their native son.

Roosevelt's strategists did not take into due account, however, the brooding bitterness of LaFollette over his own vanished hopes for the presidency. The twenty-six Wisconsin delegates split their vote. This was the end of Roosevelt's chance to win the nomination within the party. Root was elected temporary chairman by 558 to 502 votes. The regular organization was in control of the party. A Credentials Committee sympathetic to Taft would hear the evidence on contested delegations. Bill Barnes of New York had been floor leader for Taft. Bill Flinn of Pittsburgh had been offici-ating for Roosevelt. They were a pretty pair, alike in their political morality.

Root, weariness marked deeply in his face, began his keynote address amid hisses and catcalls. But soon the angry voices died down. Small in stature and with a voice by no means powerful, he nevertheless dominated the scene. And yet it was not a great speech; keynote addresses seldom are. Root recounted the accomplishments of the Taft administration. His only really significant passages were in defense of the Constitution and the courts. The Republican party, he said, would uphold their integrity. In this, the speech was a curious one, for it was directed against Theodore Roosevelt instead of the Democratic candidate, to be chosen very soon.[19]

"My office is empty. My usual callers are in Chicago and all is quiet on the Potomac," Taft wrote as word of the first victory reached him. "Root's election as temporary chairman was satis-factory in several aspects. First, it showed that I have enough votes to nominate me if they will stick. . . . Second, it established and organized a convention with a fixed membership, which makes a standard of regularity and puts Roosevelt and his faction

[19] New York *Times*, June 19, 1912; Sullivan, Mark, *op. cit.,* Vol. IV, pp. 514-523.

in the attitude of bolters if they leave the convention or attempt action under anything but the present organization. . . . They in their proposals come as near being revolutionary as they can, but they have not yet taken the physical course, which will make them rebels. . . . One of the very funny phases of the situation is the anxiety of LaFollette not to help Roosevelt. Some of his followers would desert . . . for Roosevelt but for the fear of LaFollette's anger in Wisconsin. So the delegation is broken up and the delegates are calling each other names." [20]

—5—

The Roosevelt bolt was not quite due, however. Warring emotions surged within the colonel. The heritage of all his years warned him that it was futile to seek a political objective without the benefit of an established organization. Thus he had declined to leave his party in 1884 although he had grave doubts regarding Blaine's integrity. Thus in 1900 he had written: "At times a man must cut loose from his associates and stand alone for a great cause; but the necessity for such action is almost as rare as the necessity for revolution." [21] Perhaps, though, the hour for revolution had come at last. Roosevelt could not quite decide. Beveridge called on him after the first session and they talked merely about Taft's grievous faults.[22] But a newspaper correspondent, cornering the Rough Rider at about the same time, asked why he remained in Chicago when the election of Root as temporary chairman proved the impossibility of defeating the President.

"I intend to see," Roosevelt answered, "that Mr. Taft is nominated." [23]

This was interpreted to mean that no compromise candidate would be tolerated. Taft, too, was insisting on a fight to the end, although he would be glad, he repeated to his intimates, "to yield to a third candidate who stands for my principles, like Hughes or Root." He would tolerate no man tainted with Rooseveltism.[24]

[20] Taft to Horace D. Taft, June 18, 1912. [21] Pringle, H. F., *Theodore Roosevelt, a Biography*, p. 556. [22] Bowers, Claude, *Beveridge and the Progressive Era*, p. 420. [23] Arthur Krock to author, July 19, 1930. [24] Taft to H. C. Coe, June 20, 1912.

The Old Guard Credentials Committee went into session on the afternoon of the second day to endorse the action of the Republican National Committee in barring Roosevelt's delegates. While it deliberated, turmoil shook the convention hall. Never before, perhaps, had violence been so imminent at the gathering of a great political party, and white-faced patrolmen, pacing the aisles, gripped their night sticks and prayed to their Catholic saints that nothing would happen. Even the masterful Root could not control this frenzied mob. The issue was now whether seventy-two Roosevelt men— the number had dwindled to this from the original 238 in dispute— should not be awarded the seats held by Taft delegates. Governor Hadley of Missouri took the floor to move that this be done. The Taft delegates were "burglars and pirates," he said, elected by "naked theft." He then made a telling point. The seventy-two seated Taft delegates, he said, must not vote on the qualifications of any of their number. But Root denied this and quoted the rules of the House of Representatives in support. A delegate could not vote on the question of his own right to a seat. But he could pass on the validity of the other seventy-one contests. So Hadley's motion to seat the seventy-two Roosevelt delegates would be lost too.

How accurate were Roosevelt's charges of theft, brigandage and near treason? It is possible, now, to present evidence which proves that even the Rough Rider had no facts, or few, which indicated that seventy-two delegates had been illegally seated. He trifled with the truth in his Armageddon speech when he boasted of examining the evidence personally, of being convinced that fraud had been perpetrated.

In April, 1913, President Butler of Columbia University was traveling to Boston and saw that Governor Hadley of Missouri was in his car. They chatted for a few minutes.

"Governor, there is one point I should like very much to ask you," Dr. Butler then said. "The whole thing is past and gone now and it makes little practical difference who was right and who was wrong; but I have always been anxious to know how you arrived at the precise number . . . in the list of delegates whose right to seats you protested."

Dr. Butler, reporting the conversation to Taft, said that Governor Hadley laughed as he replied: "I will tell you how that came about. After the National Committee adjourned some of us . . . made up our minds that there were twenty-eight seats which should have gone to Roosevelt delegates." He added that Borah and Frank Kellogg had been among the Progressive leaders who concurred in this decision. Hadley was delegated to present the list to Roosevelt as soon as the candidate reached Chicago. This was done, and the colonel's wrath was great.

"Twenty-eight?" he exclaimed. "Twenty-eight! Why, if you got the whole lot, it wouldn't change the result or give you control of the convention. You must make it at least a hundred. Contest at least a hundred seats!"

Governor Hadley laughed again as he concluded his story.[25] It had not been possible to find a hundred dubious Taft delegates, however, and so the compromise of seventy-two contests had been reached.

—6—

Excitement at the convention heightened as the Roosevelt forces were being routed. "Teddy, Teddy, we want Teddy!" his adherents chanted. Then appeared the traditional attractive young woman. There is often, at national conventions, a pretty girl who becomes, for a brief moment, the focal point of all the insanity and then fades back into obscurity. This time it was a Mrs. W. A. Davis, the wife of a lumber dealer, who leaned out from the gallery and unfurled a large campaign portrait of T.R. Her voice, clear and feminine, rose above the rumbling males beneath her. "A cheer for Teddy!" she called, and a demonstration started. Men jumped on their seats and fist fights broke out through the hall. They dragged the woman from her gallery seat and paraded her to the platform. Root watched, his face a mask, while this lasted for almost an hour. Then he called for a vote on the motion to unseat the Taft delegates.

No stampede resulted; nor could it, for the Taft lines held firm. Two explosions were not far off, however; the first of them took place that same night. At ten-thirty the Roosevelt men broke

[25] Butler to Taft, Nov. 12, 1915.

from the room where the Credentials Committee was meeting. At two o'clock that morning, June 20, they convened in the Florentine Room of the Congress Hotel and were joined by a horde of sympathetic rebels. Roosevelt spoke to them.[26]

"So far as I am concerned," he said, "I am through. If you are voted down I hope you, the real and lawful majority of the convention, will organize as such. . . . I hope you will refuse any longer to recognize a majority thus composed as having any title in law or morals to be called a Republican Convention."

Thereupon Hiram Johnson of California jumped to a table and announced that a new political party would be born later that day. Plans were tentatively made for a rump convention to be held in Orchestra Hall. Roosevelt, though, was far less certain. These were the Hotspurs among his followers. What of Bill Flinn and the rest? What of Borah and Beveridge? They had been willing to battle for the Lord at a vague Armageddon, but a heavenly war which led to a Democratic victory in November was less to their liking.[27] Taft, watching from Washington, discerned the dilemma of his foe.

"Chaos is still a proper term for conditions at Chicago so far as the Roosevelt forces are concerned," he wrote. "The question Roosevelt has to settle is whether to break now or to wait and vote some more. He wishes to do so now. Many of his lieutenants are against his doing so. My lines are reported firm, but no one can tell when the break may come. There are men on both sides, seeking a third candidate, but who shall it be? . . . Roosevelt is struggling to secure as many of his followers as possible to join him in a bolt, and it is their reluctance or refusal that makes the situation doubtful. He has given specific notice of his intention to bolt. If he does not do it at once, it will look like so many of his bluffs. They have bought delegates right and left. They have poured out money like water. If I win the nomination and Roosevelt bolts, it means a long, hard fight with probable defeat. But I can stand defeat if we retain the regular Republican party as a nucleus for future conservative action."[28]

This much was certain: the time had passed when Roosevelt

[26] New York *Times,* June 20, 1912; Sullivan, Mark, *op. cit.,* Vol. IV, pp. 524-525.
[27] New York *Times,* June 21, 1912. [28] Taft to M. T. Herrick, June 20, 1912.

would even consider the nomination of someone else, no matter how progressive his views. The fight was more personal than ever now, and he rejected suggestions that Hadley of Missouri be named. Roosevelt said he would not recognize the convention at all until the seventy-two Taft thieves had been cast out.[29]

So everything awaited the second explosion. Bill Barnes said that the nomination of Taft was certain. Roosevelt replied that he would remain in the fight "even if I do not get a single electoral vote." [30] He was uncertain about the financing of a new party, however. Then Perkins and Munsey, meeting in his room in the Chicago hotel, gave pledges that they would see him through.[31] The publisher announced that a new political organization would be created.[32]

Sonorously, late on Saturday, June 22, Warren Harding of Ohio began the speech which placed Taft's name in nomination. Root had become permanent as well as temporary chairman. The Roosevelt men sat sullenly in their seats. For a brief moment, only, had the gloom been broken by laughter that day. Clark Grier, a Rooseveltian from Georgia, had shouted for recognition on a point of order while Chairman Root had been steadily ruling down the insurgent motions.

"I make the point that the steam roller is exceeding the speed limit!" he called. A flicker of amusement swept Root's face, but he did not pull in the throttle.

The President received 561 votes. The rest were split as follows: Roosevelt, 107; LaFollette, 41; Cummins, 17; Hughes, 2. Significantly, however, 344 delegates refused to vote at all. Then Vice-president Sherman was renominated, only to die before election day. Weary and disillusioned, the Taft delegates prepared to leave Chicago.

"The only question now," said Chauncey M. Depew, "is which corpse gets the most flowers." [33]

The corpse of Taft would be far less popular, of course. But Roosevelt had his desertions too. Among them was Borah, who

---

[29] Davis, O. K., *Released for Publication*, pp. 303-305; New York *Times*, June 21, 1912. [30] *Ibid.*, June 21, 1912. [31] Stoddard, H. L., *As I Knew Them*, pp. 305-306. [32] New York *Times*, June 23, 1912. [33] Sullivan, Mark, *op. cit.*, Vol. IV, p. 531.

was seeking re-election that year. He went to Roosevelt's hotel suite after Taft had been chosen.

"I have come to tell you good-bye," he said. "I guess I have done all I can. The thing is over."

"I had a man out hunting for you," Roosevelt answered. "I do not know how you feel about it by this time, but . . . I should like to have you join my friends in this meeting at the theater tonight."

Borah said he had no taste for third parties. He would not join it. If Roosevelt went to Orchestra Hall he would be irrevocably committed to a third party.

"What would you have me do?" the colonel answered, irritated. "These men are in earnest. If they do not nominate me, they will nominate LaFollette."

"Colonel," insisted Borah, "those men will do just as you tell them. . . . Call in some of the leaders and tell them that you do not want any such action and they will not take any such action."

Roosevelt was deaf to these pleas. He would break the Solid South, he swore. He would run. Just then the door of the room swung in and excited Rooseveltians appear with stacks of telegrams. "The country is on fire; you must lead us!" they cried. So Borah edged out of the room.[34]

Beveridge, too, was doubtful that the meeting was wise. He declined Roosevelt's invitation to serve as chairman of the Notification Committee. Beveridge insisted that a rump convention was a strategical mistake.

"You may be right," Roosevelt said, "but it is too late to change things now."[35]

The meeting was held. "Thou Shalt Not Steal," began Roosevelt in the speech in which he agreed to run as a third candidate. A convention of the new party would be held, in due course, to which delegates would be elected.[36]

[34] Johnson, Claudius O., *Borah of Idaho*, pp. 137-140. [35] Bowers, Claude, *op. cit.*, p. 420. [36] New York *Times*, June 23, 1912.

—7—

The convention over, the White House was deluged with congratulatory messages. The President answered them patiently and simulated the attitude of a man who had cause for cheer. "It is really a great victory to remove the danger of Roosevelt's accession to the presidency. . . . The victory was a great one in the sense that it makes Roosevelt harmless as a presidential quantity," he kept repeating.

"He will now do his best to beat me," Taft added, "but the country can much better stand such a result than Roosevelt's success and the consequences. November is a full four months away, and much may happen in that time." [37]

Such expressions were harmless enough. But the scars had been burned very deep into Taft's soul and their evil lay in the fact that he was convinced anew that his trust in the Old Guard had not been misplaced. He thanked Harry Daugherty for the part he had played in Chicago.[38] He told Senator Hemenway of Indiana that "I owe my nomination to such veterans as you and Jim Watson, Penrose, McKinley, Root, Olmsted and Hilles, and a number of others who understood what real politics were and met the fury and foam of the Rooseveltian attack with cold steel." [39] Worst of all, he dictated a fulsome message to Barnes of New York:

I cannot allow this letter to go without expressing my deep gratitude to you as a citizen for what you did in Chicago. I know you were moved to it by the soundest and highest principle and not by personal relation to me, and yet such a result and such co-operation necessarily produce in one's mind a feeling of personal gratitude that needs expression. . . . I do not mean to say that you alone brought about what was brought about in Chicago; but I do mean to say that but for your presence and your staying qualities and your attachment to principle . . . the party would have had the burden of Rooseveltism fastened on it in such a way that it might have been fastened upon the country in November, and in any event in such a way that the party would have ceased to be the exponent of

[37] Taft to May Patten, to Caroline E. Bates, June 23, 1912. [38] Taft to Daugherty, June 26, 1912. [39] Taft to Hemenway, June 26, 1912.

Republican doctrine and of liberty regulated by law, as you and I understand it.[40]

Had he been thinking with half his normal clarity, Taft would never have attributed the "highest principle" to Barnes nor would he have supposed, for an instant, that the New York boss had the remotest interest in "liberty regulated by law." But the President was not thinking too clearly. Added to his other worries was the charge, now renewed, that his aides had stolen the nomination by refusing to seat the duly elected Roosevelt delegates. No more loathsome accusation could have faced a man who had been a lawyer and then a judge, who had the blackest contempt for evasions of his beloved law. He hastened to refute the charge. Dr. Butler urged an immediate educational campaign on this point,[41] but the President needed no persuasion. He directed Thomas H. Devine, chairman of the Credentials Committee, to forward at once the final reports.[42] Completely convinced that no dishonesty had marked the proceedings, Taft said that the whole record, "with the arguments, *pro* and *con,*" should be published at the earliest moment, "so that the public may judge, themselves, from the evidence." [43] Only a microscopic fraction of the voters would study the record, however. Far more of them read, and many believed Roosevelt's accusations in the *Outlook.* "Seriously and literally," he wrote, "President Taft's renomination was stolen for him from the American people." The Republican National Committee had transformed "the minority of a national convention into a majority." [44]

The President, himself, studied all the evidence in the case and dictated a lengthy statement which was thereupon published by National Chairman Hilles. Running across the document fifteen years later, Chief Justice Taft directed that it be filed, with his other papers, in the Library of Congress.[45] Roosevelt's indictment, Taft had written toward the close of July, 1912, was "grossly and maliciously untrue." He then analyzed the complicated process by which the contested delegates had been chosen. He pointed out, again, that in certain cases the Roosevelt supporters on the National Committee

⁴⁰ Taft to Barnes, June 29, 1912. ⁴¹ Butler to Taft, June 24, 1912. ⁴² Taft to Devine, July 2, 1912. ⁴³ Taft to J. H. Hammond, June 26, 1912. ⁴⁴ Roosevelt, Theodore, *Works,* National Edition, Vol. XVII, p. 232. ⁴⁵ Taft memorandum, Dec. 31, 1927.

and the Credentials Committee had ruled against their own candidate.[46]

Roosevelt, writing in the *Outlook,* forgot completely the conversation with Hadley in which he had demanded at least a hundred contests. He said there was "practically no room for dispute as to the facts" in the cases of California, Arizona, Washington and Texas.[47] It is significant that he was basing his case largely on thirty delegates from four states. Thus, even in the accusations made, had Roosevelt's case dwindled. In the early stages of the campaign he had insisted that 238 Taft delegates were frauds. Then he had cut the number to seventy-two. Finally, the figure was cut again. What is the baffled biographer to decide? The day has long passed when it would be possible to study the exact conditions under which the primaries or state conventions, at which the delegates were chosen, were held. Most of the thieves, if thieves there were, have moldered in their graves for years. Most of the honest men, if honest men there were, rest forever in virtue.

A major implication of Roosevelt's accusation may be settled, however. He pointed out that Taft received 561 votes in the convention, only twenty-one more than he needed. The votes of California, Arizona, Washington and Texas were more than enough to have defeated the President.[48] On the other hand, could Roosevelt have possibly been nominated? This is where his case falls down. He got 107 votes. It may be assumed that the 344 rebels, who did not vote, were on his side. Thus Roosevelt's maximum strength was 451 votes. Six delegates were absent. Seven of the Iowa delegates, bound by the unit rule for Cummins, favored Roosevelt. Hughes got two votes. If this block of fifteen is added, Roosevelt had a maximum strength of 466. So he needed, to be nominated, seventy-four additional delegates. Where would he have obtained them? Surely LaFollette would have surrendered none of his forty-one votes.

But whether thirty votes were stolen or seventy-two or none has no real bearing on the outcome in Chicago during those humid days of June, 1912. The Republican party was in the hands of the forces which favored Taft's renomination. That is the essen-

[46] New York *Times,* July 29, 1912. [47] Roosevelt, Theodore, *op. cit.,* Vol. XVII, p. 233. [48] *Ibid.*

tial point. Those forces, facing defeat, would have disqualified Roosevelt delegates to the extent that was necessary.

". . . our campaign," said the President when the convention ended, "has got to be one of conciliation instead of alienation. We must educate rather than excoriate." [49]

Roosevelt, unfortunately, would limit himself to excoriation.

[49] Taft to C. A. Ricks, June 26, 1912.

CHAPTER XLII

UTAH AND VERMONT

PRECISELY four years before, in June of 1908, President Theodore Roosevelt had received with elation the news that Taft had been nominated at Chicago.

"I do not believe there can be found in the whole country," he said, "a man so well fitted to be president."

No wonder it was virtually impossible for President Taft to believe, in the summer of 1912, that the man who now reviled him had once been so ardently friendly. He poured out, in a letter to Mrs. Taft, the anger in his heart:

> As the campaign goes on and the unscrupulousness of Roosevelt develops, it is hard to realize that we are talking about the same man whom we knew in the presidency. It is true he gave evidences in his humorous and cynical way of indifference to moral restraint, but I always assumed that it was humorous. I knew, of course, that his memory was defective about the things he did not want to remember, that he was so intense in his pugnaciousness and in making his enemy beware of him that he could think almost as he wished to think, but it is impossible to conceive of him as the fakir, the juggler, the green goods man, the gold brick man that he has come to be.
>
> He is to be classed with the leaders of religious cults who promote things over their followers by any sort of physical [sic] manipulation and deception. He is seeking to make his followers "Holy Rollers," and I hope that the country is beginning to see this. . . . I have not any feeling of enmity against Roosevelt or any feeling of hatred. I look upon him as an historical character of a most peculiar type in whom are embodied elements of real greatness, together with certain traits that have now shown themselves in unfitting him for any trust or confidence by the people. I look upon him as I look upon a freak, almost, in the zoological garden, a kind of animal not often found. So far as personal relations with him are concerned, they don't exist— I do not have any feeling one way or the other.[1]

[1] Taft to Helen H. Taft, Aug. 26, 1912.

No feeling, more accurately, save the hatred which he denied. Gradually Taft sublimated his detestation into a conviction that the Bull Moose candidate was a grave menace to the nation. Throughout the campaign he reiterated that the election of Woodrow Wilson, even if he was a low-tariff man and a Democrat and, therefore, unsound, was preferable to the election of Roosevelt. All in all, he had a low opinion of Wilson in 1912. He distrusted the "general radicalism" of the New Jersey governor's views.

"I know that Wilson is a very agreeable speaker," he admitted, "and that people will doubtless flock to hear him, but he is academic rather than soul-stirring, and what he says, though given in graceful form and pleasant to the ear, has not a great deal of substantial sediment that remains with those who hear him. They are conscious of a pleasurable sensation, but they don't carry away much." [2] The President hoped "that the real character of Wilson may be so disclosed to the people in four months as to render his election improbable." [3] Further: "I have very little confidence in the judgment of Wilson. He has changed his views so often that he seems an utter opportunist." [4] After Wilson had been nominated at Baltimore, Taft studied the Democratic nominee's acceptance speech. He found it "purring and ladylike . . . he says very little of anything." [5]

Clearly, Taft was undergoing another lapse from judicial impartiality. The "real difficulty" with the Democrats, he confided to Horace D. Taft, was that "they are incapable; they do not know how to run a government . . . they have never had the training of governmental responsibility. . . .

"The consequence is," he concluded, "that they are all at odds when it comes to agreeing to anything affirmative, and it is not very far from the truth that with the know-it-all methods of Woodrow Wilson, his dictatorial manner and his inconsiderateness, he will leave the situation in Washington such that no two Democrats will speak together with cordiality. That is what Job Hedges says, and Job comes from Princeton and knows." [6]

Taft's prophecy was not entirely wrong, although it would be 1918— and a war would have shaken the world— before the Demo-

---

[2] Taft to J. D. Long, July 5, 1912. [3] Taft to Archbishop Ireland, July 9, 1912. [4] Taft to Colston, July 14, 1912. [5] Taft to Mabel Boardman, Aug. 9, 1912. [6] Taft to Horace D. Taft (undated).

crats snarled at each other with quite the predicted virulence. Wilson, of course, was watching the quarrel among his Republican adversaries with delight.

"Nothing new is happening in politics, except Mr. Roosevelt, who is always new, being bound by nothing in the heavens above or in the earth below," he had written in March, 1912. "He is now rampant and very diligently employed in splitting the party wide open— so that we may get in!" [7]

The New Jersey governor's reaction to Roosevelt was similar to Taft's. "God save us of another four years of him *now* in his present insane distemper of egotism," he prayed late in May.[8]

Wilson's nomination was far from assured as the Democratic party prepared to assemble. He campaigned vigorously, but Champ Clark of Missouri had the better organization. If it had not been for the two-thirds rule, Clark would have won the nomination. He was known and respected by the politicians. He was safe. Wilson was too independent. He was regarded, also, as too radical. But he had powerful support. The progressives of the party were behind him. He had the crusading, effective backing of the New York *World*. Finally, and most important of all, Bryan turned from Champ Clark and cast the votes of Nebraska for Wilson.[9] The campaign began with Wilson regarding Roosevelt, not Taft, as his more dangerous adversary.

"I feel that Roosevelt's strength is altogether incalculable," he wrote. "The contest is between him and me, not between Taft and me. I think Taft will run third— at any rate in the popular, if not in the electoral, vote. But just what will happen, as between Roosevelt and me, with party lines utterly confused and broken, is all guesswork . . . I am by no means confident." [10]

And Taft, of course, was far from confident too. "Sometimes," he wrote in July, "I think I might as well give up so far as being a candidate is concerned. There are so many people in the country who don't like me. Without knowing much about me, they don't like me— apparently on the Dr. Fell principle . . . they don't exactly know the reason, but it is on the principle:

[7] Baker, R. S., *Woodrow Wilson, Life and Letters*, Vol. III, p. 278. [8] *Ibid.*, Vol. III, p. 316. [9] *Ibid.*, Vol. III, pp. 320-363. [10] *Ibid.*, Vol. III, p. 390.

'I don't like you, Dr. Fell,
The reason why I can not tell,
But this I know and know full well,
I don't like you, Dr. Fell.' " [11]

In any event, the President insisted, he would make no speeches except for his acceptance address.[12] He was irritated when his advisers protested that Wilson and Roosevelt were getting columns of publicity "and there is no news from me except that I played golf. I seem to have heard that before. It always makes me impatient, as if I were running a P. T. Barnum show, with two or three shows across the street, and as if I ought to have as much advertising as the rest. . . . I decline to take any responsibility." [13]

But the 1912 campaign was, in fact, a Barnum show and Taft, if he hoped to win, had to compete against the performances of Wilson and Roosevelt. He did not do so, and in due time only Utah and Vermont would cast their electoral votes for him. Besides, Taft had so few important men to help him. Again, Root was hanging back and pleading that he was physically unable to play a leading part. He would make one address, he promised, but not yet.[14]

"He is very timid in certain ways, and sometimes makes you feel that he is afraid to get out into the open in his controversy with Roosevelt," Taft observed sadly. "He has gone so far now that I would think he would cut his bridges behind him and go as far as he can for the cause which he really believes in." [15]

Many people besides Taft were unhappy during these weeks. Representative Longworth, the son-in-law of Roosevelt, found himself in a devilish predicament. He was running for re-election and needed the Ohio Republican organization. His political views were distinctly more conservative than those of his father-in-law. But he was damned by both the Taft supporters and the Rooseveltians as, for some weeks, he remained silent.[16] The President received reports, from time to time, regarding Nick's loyalty.

"Will Herron told me yesterday that he had a long talk with

[11] Taft to Helen H. Taft, July 22, 1912. [12] Idem, July 16, 1912. [13] Idem, July 22, 1912. [14] Root to Taft, Sept. 4, 1912. [15] Taft to Helen H. Taft, July 16, 1912. [16] Chambrun, C. L. de, The Making of Nicholas Longworth, p. 204.

Nick Longworth," he told Mrs. Taft, "and that Nick had told him that his whole sympathies were with me, but that the question which he had to meet was one of family feeling, and therefore he had to be quiet and unhappy about it." [17]

"I don't know what poor Nick Longworth is going to do," the President commented in August.[18] In the end Longworth remained loyal to the G.O.P., and was defeated in November.

—2—

During the weeks which followed the Republican convention and Roosevelt's bolt, the newly born Bull Moose came close to losing himself in the forests of political confusion. Munsey and Perkins might guarantee to supply the funds, but they could not prevent nervous politicians from flocking back to the haven of the regular Republican organization. Bill Ward of Westchester County, among others, deserted Roosevelt late in June.[19] Borah, of course, had already assumed his traditional occupation of fence-straddling. Norris of Nebraska expressed doubt that a third party could succeed.[20] Governor Hadley of Missouri was supposed to be wavering.

Taft did what he could to beguile these independents back into his own fold. He told Hadley and Borah that he would be delighted to confer with them at the White House.[21] The President, naturally enough, was pleased that inner turmoil was not limited to his own party.

"The papers may be misleading," he noted, "but the general impression they are giving now is that the colonel is having a hard time getting support for his Bull Moose ticket. He is at odds with some of his chief lieutenants who are anxious about their local tickets." [22]

Then Borah dined at the White House, to the President's further encouragement:

I have been helping Borah with some legislation of his and he is rather disposed . . . to be friendly. At any rate, it appears that

[17] Taft to Helen H. Taft, July 29, 1912. [18] Idem, Aug. 11, 1912. [19] New York Times, June 29, 1912. [20] New York World, July 1, 1912. [21] Taft to Borah, to Hadley, July 16, 1912. [22] Taft to Helen H. Taft, July 21, 1912.

LaFollette has weaned away from Roosevelt all but two or three insurgent senators. Borah told me . . . that Cummins told him that he would rather have me in the White House than Roosevelt. He is very bitter against Roosevelt because he thinks that Roosevelt might have nominated him instead of me, and I think that Borah, although he does not admit it, has much the same feeling with respect to himself. The truth is they have found Roosevelt to be intensely selfish and completely self-absorbed. They say they are not going to join him in the third party movement. While I did not think it wise to say anything directly, we discussed the Chicago convention and the funny phases of it, of which Borah had a number to tell. . . . He said that the whole business would collapse in October . . . that it could not hold out. I don't know whether he is oversanguine in this regard, because Roosevelt will hang on until death.[23]

The emotional Beveridge stood fast with Roosevelt, however. He was promised that the new party would adopt a truly vital platform. He deceived himself that this would be the basis, whatever the fate of the Bull Moose, for a liberal movement in the future. So he agreed to be chairman of the convention and to deliver the keynote address.[24] A call for the gathering had been issued on July 7, by the somewhat nebulous authority of the Roosevelt rump convention at Chicago. Its sessions would begin in the same city on August 5 and part of the cost would be met by the sale of seats at $10. The price was too high, though, and tickets had dropped to $3 and lower by the opening day.[25] Enthusiasm mounted, on the other hand, with the arrival of Roosevelt on the morning of August 5. At least 10,000 people were in the convention hall. Hiram Johnson marched in with his California cohorts who sang, "I want to be a Bull Moose, and with the Bull Moose stand!" Oscar S. Straus, the Jewish philanthropist, was at the head of the New York delegation which fervently sang "Onward, Christian Soldiers." [26]

The battle for the Lord was scheduled to begin at noon on August 5 and Beveridge, who so dearly loved to indulge in oratory, considered it one of the great moments of his life. His keynote speech was replete with splendid phrases. "We stand for a nobler

[23] Taft to Helen H. Taft, July 29, 1912. [24] Bowers, Claude, *Beveridge and the Progressive Era*, p. 423. [25] New York *World*, Aug. 5, 1912. [26] Bowers, Claude, *op. cit.*, p. 425.

America," he began and then painted an alluring picture of a nation in which political bosses— he did not mention Bill Flinn of Pittsburgh who had remained loyal to Roosevelt— would be cast into the darkness into which Lucifer plunged. Beveridge declared his enmity for both the established parties. He was against the interests. He was against invisible government. He was against abuse of the laboring man. He spoke for the underfed child, for the underpaid workingman.

"Hunger should never walk," he cried, "in these thinly peopled gardens of plenty."

But Beveridge was practical too. Let no one fear, he said, that the Bull Moose might, in his wrath, trample the vineyards of Big Business. The Progressive party would "try to make little business big, and all business honest, instead of striving to make Big Business little, and yet letting it remain dishonest." Nor was the Bull Moose in favor of doing away with the tariff— at this point the Bull Moose antlers began to fade a little. His body became thicker. His nose lengthened and he started to look not a little like the G.O.P. elephant. The Progressive party, Beveridge said, endorsed a tariff high enough to ensure the American market to American producers "when they make honest goods and sell them at honest prices." Yet Beveridge did call, as he closed, for social security for the aged. He demanded a Constitution which was "a living thing, growing with the people's growth . . . aiding the people in their struggles for life, liberty, and the pursuit of happiness." [27]

—3—

Roosevelt addressed the convention on the following day and called his speech "A Confession of Faith." Actually, his speech was 20,000 words in length, but the candidate wisely cut it by half in reading it. Like Beveridge, he expressed his contempt for the existing political parties. The Progressives, however, would be forthright and honest. The platform would be "a contract with the people . . . and . . . we shall hold ourselves under honorable obligations to

[27] *Ibid.,* pp. 426-429.

fulfill every promise it contains as loyally as if it were actually enforceable under penalties of the law." [28]

President Taft, studying the proceedings, understood only partially what was going on. He thought that the convention had been "in a certain sense . . . a success. They have had . . . 15,000 people to listen to Roosevelt." As for their nature:

> From all I can see of what has been done, every crank, every academic enthusiast, every wild theorist with any proposition for the solution of any social problem, has been gathered there by invitation. That has made up a curious collection of informed but not intelligent people who are looking for the impossible— woman's suffrage enthusiasts, ex-officeholders who wish to resume office, and the discontented who have failed to get office. It has been a conglomeration of elements as varied, as impossible of mixture and as impossible of accomplishment as the platform which he enunciates in his "Confession of Faith."

Thus far the President, if somewhat harsh in his description of the Bull Moose adherents, was fairly accurate. He was thinking less clearly when he declared that Roosevelt had been "radical to the last degree in state socialism" and continued:

> He has not advocated the appropriation of rich men's property to distribute among the poor, but that is only another step and perhaps is one involved in the really successful accomplishment of those steps which he proposes. My own judgment is that his appeals will reach quite as far into those who might otherwise support Wilson as into our own ranks. The truth is that much of what he he has done and said will have a tendency to drive back into regularity a good many who have followed him thus far.[29]

It was far from accurate to say that Roosevelt was radical. His speech at the convention was distinctly to the right, as compared with his position in 1910 and earlier in 1912. In believing that his adversary was dangerously radical, Taft allowed himself to be pushed further and further to the right and therein, again, lay one of the causes for his defeat.

[28] Pringle, H. F., *Theodore Roosevelt, a Biography*, pp. 566-567. [29] Taft to Hilles, Aug. 7, 1912.

"I have no part to play but that of a conservative," he insisted, "and that I am going to play." [30]

What nonsense to say that Roosevelt was a radical! What nonsense to say that Wilson was a radical! Each of them believed, and so did Bryan and LaFollette, that a full and free life for the average man could be achieved by gradual amendment of the existing system. Henry George might dream of a new taxation which would lift that burden from the average man. But Roosevelt and Wilson had no use for it. Altgeld of Illinois might dream of a better day when troops, the mercenaries of the established order, did not march against men who were striking for a living wage— for the mere right to exist. But Roosevelt considered Altgeld an anarchist and Wilson's scholastic idealism could never quite include direct action of any kind. The gentle Debs might speak out for the average man and deny that America had been founded merely so that the shrewd men, the hard men and the dishonest men should thrive in disproportion to their worth. But Debs was an anarchist too, said these radicals of 1912— and Wilson allowed him to rot behind penitentiary bars. Roosevelt, Wilson, LaFollete and Bryan were liberals, not radicals. America in 1912, and for almost twenty-five years thereafter, was controlled by its chambers of commerce and its merchants associations and its associations of manufacturers. James A. Emery of the National Association of Manufacturers continued to be powerful whether Wilson or Coolidge or Harding or Hoover chanced to be president of the United States.

The New Nationalism of Theodore Roosevelt was poisoned by practical politics. So was the New Freedom of Woodrow Wilson. It was Taft's tragedy that he was misled, partly by alarm, into misinterpreting both these gospels. Let us glance, for a moment, at the platforms of Taft, Roosevelt and Wilson and see whether, among all the myriad planks they contained, there were many on which even a liberal could stand.

—4—

The Republican platform opened with the usual repetitious tribute to Lincoln. The party had been responsible for the "greatest

[30] Taft to Delia Torrey, Aug. 1, 1912.

national advances" in the history of the United States. It believed—
this was a dig at Roosevelt— in "a government of laws, not of men."
It was the stanch defender of constitutional government and it was
"as always, a party of advanced and constructive statesmanship,"
sworn— another dig at Roosevelt— "to uphold at all times the
authority and integrity of the courts, both state and federal." The
G.O.P. regarded "the recall of judges as unnecessary and unwise."
At this point, though, the platform carpenters had paused. The
recall of judges was a nefarious Roosevelt doctrine, yet "we favor
such action as may be necessary to simplify the process by which
any judge who is found to be derelict in his duty may be removed
from office."

The Republican party was "opposed to special privilege and
monopoly." Had it not passed the Sherman Antitrust Act years ago?
And now it favored supplementary legislation to strengthen that
law which would "define as criminal offenses those specific acts
that uniformly mark attempts to restrain and monopolize trade, to
the end that those who honestly intend to obey the law may have
a guide for their action and that those who aim to violate the law
may the more surely be punished." The platform favored a protective
tariff which, as President Taft had so often urged, would not be
unreasonably high. It disavowed any responsibility for increased
costs of living. It reaffirmed the Republican belief in a sound, if
more elastic, monetary system. The party stood for the merit system,
for publicity of campaign contributions, for conservation of natural
resources: in short, for all the shopworn policies which G.O.P.
orators had been expounding for years.

The document did not mention women suffrage, however.
"Our friends being deluged with requests for planks favoring
woman suffrage. Will be glad to learn your wishes," Hilles had
telegraphed to the President during the Chicago convention sessions.
"I will not make a declaration in the face of the convention on the
woman suffrage business any more than I have already done,"
Taft answered.[31]

"I cannot change my view . . . just to suit the exigencies of
the campaign, and if it is going to hurt me I think it will have to
hurt me," he insisted some weeks later. ". . . It is really a matter for

[31] Hilles to Taft, Taft to Hilles, June 14, 1912.

state action and I would have no right to commit the party to anything beyond the fact that it is a state question." [32]

But over a million women would vote, for the first time, in
this election. Roosevelt, who was far from a feminist and whose
belief in the superiority of the male was profound, had surrendered
to the equal rights proponents in June.[33] Advocacy of woman
suffrage, therefore, was included in the Progressive party platform.
Then came planks on nearly every conceivable subject. Had he
been asking for a twenty-year term in the White House, Roosevelt
would still have found it impossible to carry out, as he had promised
the convention, all these proposals. The Bull Moose party stood for
campaign fund publicity; the registration of lobbyists; restriction
of labor injunctions; conservation of human resources through adequate workmen's compensation, safety, wages and limitation of
hours of work statutes; physical valuation of railroad properties; revision of the currency; conservation of natural resources; good roads;
reduction of the cost of living; cutting down of illiteracy; a more
adequate patent law; the extension of foreign commerce; flood
control; the development of Alaska; repeal of the American offer
for tariff reciprocity with Canada; federal inheritance and income
taxes; fair pensions for Civil War veterans; parcels post; protection
against fraudulent investments; reorganization of the federal departments.

These, in the main, were laudable objectives and in urging
them Roosevelt advanced the day when some of them became law.
Most of them, particularly the planks relating to social welfare and
security, were so visionary that they did not unduly alarm the conservative interests.[34] The tariff was Roosevelt's first surrender to
conservatism. His second surrender was on control of trusts. Mystery
still surrounds the "Missing Plank," as Woodrow Wilson effectively
branded it in the campaign, which related to trusts. The draft which
left the Bull Moose Resolutions Committee was forthright and
honest. It was released for publication by the Associated Press and
would beyond any question have been adopted by the convention.
Before it was printed in the newspapers, however, it met the eye of
George Perkins, the angel of the campaign. He went into imme-

[32] Taft to Hilles, Aug. 14, 1912. [33] New York *Times,* June 13, 1912. [34] Progressive
party National Convention, *Proceedings,* pp. 243-268.

diate conference with Roosevelt. The plank was recalled and re-
drafted to meet Perkins's instructions. The new version was mild
in comparison with the original.[35] It did not call for an end of the
monopolies which had been crushing the spirit of competition. It
was another expression of Roosevelt's ancient theory that a line could
be drawn between good and bad trusts.

On the recall of judges, Roosevelt was evasive too. But this was
to be expected, inasmuch as he had been steadily backing away
from the bold assertions he had made in 1910 and in his "Charter of
Democracy" speech. The Progressive party said merely that ref-
erenda on judicial decisions which invalidated the police powers
of the states by the state courts should be authorized. Further, the
invalidation of state laws by the highest state tribunals on the
ground that they violated the federal Constitution should be subject to review by the United States Supreme Court.[36]

Of the Democratic platform it may be said, at least, that it
was more liberal than Roosevelt's or Taft's. The tariff was to be
for revenue only. Trusts were to be prosecuted in the criminal and
civil courts and stock watering was to be forbidden. The banking
laws were to be revised. An income tax was to be passed. Presidential primaries were to be established and senators elected by
popular vote. Railway, express, telephone and telegraph companies
were to be subjected to federal supervision. The Democratic platform had innumerable weak spots, of course. It was vague on
monetary reform. It recommended a single term for president,
without specifying the length of the term. It called for encouragement of the merchant marine, but said nothing as to how this would
be accomplished. It advocated exemption from tolls for American
coastwise ships passing through the Panama Canal, a point on
which Wilson, to his credit, would overrule his party.[37]

[35] Hapgood, Norman, *The Changing Years, Reminiscences of Norman Hapgood*, pp.
220-221. [36] Progressive party National Convention, *Proceedings*, pp. 251-268. [37] New York
World, July 5, 1912.

—5—

Meanwhile, however dark the outlook for Taft, there was work to be done. A chairman had to be found for the National Committee. Money had to be raised for the campaign. The President and Hilles dined alone at the White House on the night of July 13 and discussed the possible reactions of Mrs. Taft toward impending defeat. Hilles, aware of the part that the President's wife had played in persuading him to run in 1908, asked whether the disappointment might be cruel.

"I told him," Taft reported to her, "the contrary was the case, that you had for a long time not expected me to be re-elected, and that you were most gratified, as we all were, in the accomplishment of the more important purpose of defeating Roosevelt at Chicago. I hope that I stated your views with exactness." [38]

The most pressing problem was the selection of the party chairman; he would be the executive officer in the campaign and would, in large measure, he responsible for success or failure. With extraordinary arrogance, considering his notorious reputation, Bill Barnes of New York wanted the post. No men are so blind as the members of a political Old Guard: Penrose of Pennsylvania, Uncle Joe Cannon and Representative McKinley all urged the President to select Barnes. But Taft had more intelligence and was "opposed to it from the first because it would . . . emphasize Roosevelt's charge that we are in the hands of the bosses." Another candidate was Daugherty of Ohio, who had worked valiantly in the preconvention crisis and whose honor was, as yet, only faintly tarnished. A. I. Vorys, Taft's old Cincinnati friend and supporter, had journeyed to Washington with Daugherty to back his claim for the job.

Taft had heard rumors that Daugherty was "a lobbyist and that there might be some weaknesses in his record"; he does not appear to have remembered or resented, however, the activities of the Ohio politician in obtaining that presidential pardon for Morse, the swindler. Taft rejected Daugherty's candidacy for the chairmanship on the ground that he was not well enough known.[39]

[38] Taft to Helen H. Taft, July 14, 1912. [39] *Idem.*, July 9, 1912.

"I am very sorry indeed that your feelings were hurt," he apologized a week later. "I was inclined to favor your appointment. . . . I feel very grateful . . . for the work which you have done for me, and personally I should have been entirely willing to have you chairman, had it met with the views of those with whom I had to consult in making the selection." [40]

Taft's endorsement of Daugherty was even more fervent in October; he was, the President said, "entitled to every support that the party can give him. I consider him a warm personal friend of mine." [41] And Daugherty remained trusted and loved, until a puzzled Chief Justice of the United States could no longer close his ears to the proof that an attorney general and his gang from Ohio had achieved a new low mark in governmental corruption.

Taft brought about the selection of Hilles— "the best politician I know" [42]— because he was the only man on whom all the party factions could agree. Hilles was reductant to accept, and with reason.[43] He would probably have refused to serve if he had foreseen the complications which awaited him. For the financiers and the industrialists and the other hardheaded businessmen of the United States were to prove extremely reductant, in this campaign, to give their usual support to the Grand Old Party. The party had saved them from the menace of Bryan in 1896, and they had reached feverishly for their checkbooks when Mark Hanna had so commanded. They had contributed gladly, and for the same reason, four years later. In 1904, it is true, they had been less certain and a proportion among them had secretly hoped that conservative Judge Parker, the Democratic nominee, might be elected instead of Roosevelt. In 1908, of course, it had been quite simple, because Bryan was making his third and final race. This three-cornered contest, however, was very puzzling. Was it not vital, whatever else might happen, to crush Roosevelt? Was not Taft the weakest of the three candidates? Was it not wiser, then, to place bets on Woodrow Wilson who, alone, could save the land from socialism and worse?

Thus they reasoned and Hilles, beginning his work, found proof of their misgivings in his inability to obtain a treasurer for the National Committee. It was a humiliating spectacle. The Re-

---

[40] Taft to Daugherty, July 17, 1912. [41] Taft to Myron T. Herrick, Oct. 25, 1912. [42] Taft to H. C. Hemphill, Nov. 16, 1911. [43] Taft to Helen H. Taft, July 9, 1912.

publican party, which had ruled the nation since the Civil War save for Cleveland's two terms, searched in vain among the men who were qualified to manage its finances. The new national chairman described his exasperation after George R. Sheldon, treasurer in 1908, said he would not continue in office. Charles G. Dawes, John Wanamaker, E. T. Stotesbury, Otto T. Bannard, and A. Barton Hepburn had all been tendered the post and had declined. Now Hilles was in pursuit of Cornelius W. Bliss, Jr., whose father had collected something over $2,000,000, three-quarters of it from corporations, for Roosevelt in 1904. Discouraged, Hilles said he would make the best fight that he could. He reported that the New York financiers would vote for Wilson if this seemed the only way to defeat Roosevelt. They preferred Taft to either Wilson or Roosevelt, but they were apprehensive that he could not win. It would be their policy, then, to delay any campaign contributions until the outcome was more certain.[44]

Bliss declined the treasurership and the search went on in August. The ever-faithful William Nelson Cromwell was helping with assistance and advice, but his career and exploits made him, unfortunately, ineligible for the post himself. Hilles told the President that a financial officer must be found at once or the G.O.P. forces would be demoralized. ". . . you have my great sympathy," Taft answered.[45] At last, Sheldon heard the call of duty and withdrew his refusal to serve again.[46]

—6—

Congress was still in session, although this was mid-August, and Taft watched, with mingled appreciation and apprehension, a Machiavellian scheme to embarrass Roosevelt by investigating the source of the Progressive party's funds. Behind the plan were LaFollette and Penrose, who detested the Bull Moose nominee with equal vigor but for utterly different reasons.

"It is rather interesting and amusing to watch them now working together, Penrose calling LaFollette 'Bob' and lunching with

[44] Hilles to H. W. Taft, Aug. 1, 1912. [45] Hilles to Taft, Aug. 4, 10, 1912; Taft to Hilles, Aug. 12, 1912. [46] Taft to Helen H. Taft, Aug. 15, 1912.

him and associating with him in every way," commented the President.[47] Taft had no objection to any investigation which might impugn Roosevelt's contention that he was, without reproach, the champion of the plain people. The President had "no doubt that he had a campaign fund of $2,000,000 or $3,000,000, and if the truth were known, it would be most interesting reading and most significant to the American people as to his associations and relations." It was not probable, however, that the investigators would get at the truth, Taft added, for Roosevelt "is utterly lacking in veracity, and those who are about him are equally so." Even worse, "the agitation about contributions makes everybody who is willing to give sensitive . . . lest his name may be dragged out in a public way." [48]

A committee was appointed, none the less, with Senator Clapp at its head, with wide powers to investigate previous elections. Its revelations concerning the 1904 campaign were of the greatest interest. At the close of that contest the New York *World,* on behalf of Judge Parker, had accused the Republican National Committee of receiving vast corporation donations and had drawn a blistering denial from Roosevelt. At about the same time Roosevelt had publicly rejected a gift of $100,000 from the Standard Oil.[49] But now, after eight years, it became known that most of the large corporations poured funds into the Roosevelt coffers, that J. P. Morgan and James Stillman and James Hazen Hyde had given substantial sums. It was disclosed, too, that Roosevelt's 1904 order to return the Standard Oil contribution had been coolly ignored by Treasurer Bliss. Taft reported all this, not without satisfaction, to his wife. He also told of a conversation he had just had with Secretary of State Knox:

> Knox said he came into the office of Roosevelt one day in October, 1904, and heard him dictating a letter directing the return of $100,000 to the Standard Oil Company. He said to him, "Why, Mr. President, the money has been spent. They cannot pay it back— they haven't got it." "Well," said the President, "the letter will look well on the record, anyhow," and so he let it go.

[47] Taft to Helen H. Taft, Aug. 26, 1912. [48] Taft to C. P. Taft, Aug. 25, 1912. [49] Pringle, H. F., *op. cit.,* p. 356.

"He is referring to this letter now as an evidence that he never approved the receipt of the money," Taft pointed out.[50]

The traditional cartoonist's symbol for the Republican party— an overstuffed gentleman wearing a silk hat, morning coat and spats— was sadly inappropriate for this campaign. A more accurate presentation would have been a bedraggled old reprobate with patches on his clothes. The gleaming watch chain had vanished from across his ample middle; it had been hocked, no doubt, to satisfy one or two of the demands. Money is vital to a presidential campaign, for purposes legitimate as well as illicit. Special trains must be hired. There are all the burdens of speakers, banners, red fire, bands and rallies. These are the publicly admitted costs. More important, even, are grants from the National Committee to state and other local committees. These appropriations are to be used, in part, to bring out the vote on Election Day. There are committeemen to be satisfied and minor bosses to be greased. A national committee is bombarded, as a campaign closes, for funds for these lofty and essential purposes. The Republican National Committee of 1912 did not have the money, though, and so, again, the President was doomed.

The Republican County Committee of Phoenix, Arizona, for example, wanted $1,000, and Hilles had to refuse. The Colorado Republican State Committee wanted $25,000. But the National Committee was in no position to contribute $25,000 to Colorado, reported the chairman. The leaders in Utah asked for $10,000, with the same result.[51] Again, the President sympathized with Hilles in "the dreadful effort to collect money." Ohio, too, had been clamoring for assistance and Taft sent a personal check for $2,500. At the same time he dispatched $7,500 to Hilles.[52] The national chairman, with reason, became profoundly discouraged. He told the President about an Indiana Republican, worth $400,000, who had contributed only $1,000. He pointed out that Vice-president Sherman had given nothing at all. But Andrew Carnegie, who contributed $25,000 when the drive opened, had been appealed to and had written a check for $10,000 more.[53] On the eve of Election Day, the President told Horace D. Taft that

[50] Taft to Helen H. Taft, Aug. 22, 1912. [51] Hilles to J. E. Wilson, J. F. McDonald, Henry Gardner, Oct. 15, 1912. [52] Taft to Hilles, Oct. 7, 1912. [53] Hilles to Taft, no date.

Hilles "had to run the campaign on less than a million dollars whereas campaigns heretofore have usually reached the two-million and sometimes the three-million dollar mark. In addition to that, he had to raise the money for the preconvention campaign which was a burden that other managers have not had to bear. This was due to the intervention of the Bull Moose, with all the purifying effect that a savior of mankind like Roosevelt brings into politics." Hilles had done an extraordinary job, Taft was sure. He had shown "wonderful control of the situation, considering the lack of means, the necessary lack of organization. . . . Without speakers, he had introduced other and new measures of publicity to reach the voters." [54]

—7—

The notification ceremonies had been held at Washington on August 1 and the occasion had not been an inspiring one. Root made the notification speech. The President's reply was not among his better utterances. He began, naturally enough, by attacking Roosevelt "whose recently avowed political views would have committed the party to radical proposals involving dangerous changes in our present constitutional form of representative government and our independent judiciary."

The President reiterated, of course, the ancient and untrue claim that "substantially all" the advancement and progress of the past fifty years in the United States had been due to the G.O.P. The paramount issue, Taft said, was preservation of a constitutional form of government. But he was not quite so conservative, in developing this theme, as might be supposed. The day had passed, he said, when it was clearly obvious that the least government was the best government. The duty of government to protect the weaker classes by "positive law" was now recognized.

"It has been suggested that under our Constitution, such tendency to so-called paternalism was impossible. Nothing is further from the fact," the President added. ". . . The Republican party stands for the Constitution as it is, *with such amendments adopted*

54 Taft to Horace D. Taft, Nov. 1, 1912.

according to its provisions as new conditions thoroughly understood may require." [55]

The President's acerbity increased as the weeks dragged by; he had so many worries. The loyalty of Frank Hitchcock, his postmaster general, was questioned again in the late summer and fall. "What under heaven is the matter with your people in Ohio?" Taft demanded of Hitchcock after receiving a protest from Daugherty that the postal workers were not sufficiently steadfast. "They are engaged in working against me at every hand. Now, can you not give some attention to this, and see to it that the men who are there are at least neutral?" [56] Taft continued to insist that Hitchcock was "anxious to do all he can." [57] His conduct, from a political viewpoint, was strange at the best, though. His disciplinary methods had been so severe as to alienate, in particular, the railway mail clerks.[58]

"I'll be damned if I don't propose to resign this job if Hitchcock's conduct in putting things over is not stopped," raged Daugherty in September. "I spend half my time listening to the stories of the damage being done by employees of the Post Office Department." [59]

The estimable Daugherty's protests may be discounted. In late October, however, the postmaster general made a needlessly harsh ruling. The mail clerks held passes on the railroads, for their work. They had always used these passes, on Election Day, to reach their homes. It was now decreed that they must pay the usual fares if they wished to vote.

Another irritation was the charge, grossly unfair and quite untrue, that Taft had pandered to the Catholic Church. He was challenged to an absurd degree on this question. In 1908 he had been berated as an Antichrist because he was a Unitarian. The 1912 accusation, equally foolish, seems to have been an echo of Taft's activities, as governor general of the Philippines, in going to Rome on the Vatican lands problem. The whisperers added to this the nonsensical charge that the late Major Butt, abroad on the fateful vacation journey which ended when the *Titanic* went down, had

[55] Acceptance Speech, Aug. 1, 1912. Government Printing Office. (Italics mine.) [56] Taft to Hitchcock, Sept. 13, 1912. [57] Taft to Daugherty, Sept. 27, 1912. [58] Taft to Helen H. Taft, July 12, 1912. [59] Daugherty to Carmi Thompson, Sept. 11, 1912.

been on a secret mission from the White House to the Pope. This was based on nothing save a formal letter of introduction which Taft had written. The President, writhing with indignation, issued a formal denial prior to the Republican convention.[60] After that he said nothing for publication.

"I deny utterly," he wrote privately, "that I have ever cultivated the Catholic Church for political purposes. I believe the Catholic Church to be one of the bulwarks against socialism and anarchy in this country, and I welcome its presence here, but I decide every question that comes up on the merits as I understand them, and that whether it is for or against the church. But it is useless to persuade a man with the anti-Catholic virus to look with patience at any treatment of the Catholic Church that does not involve . . . hostility." [61]

—8—

Roosevelt would, of course, take the offensive in the campaign. Taft declared that, for his part, dignity would rule. "I have been told that I ought to do this, ought to do that . . . that I do not keep myself in the headlines," the President told the newspaper correspondents. "I know it, but I can't do it. I couldn't if I would, and I wouldn't if I could." [62] Thus he would make almost no speeches after his acceptance address on August 1. He would lean on Root, Lodge, the members of his Cabinet and the other heavy guns of the party. Dignity had no place in the Roosevelt crusade, and Taft again viewed the whole movement as "a religious cult with a fakir at the head of it." [63] The colonel of the Rough Riders rode into New England in the middle of August and lambasted Murray Crane, Penrose and the other Old Guard leaders. In September he started a transcontinental tour, attacking Wilson as well as Taft. He had the extraordinary gall, in view of the Congressional revelations on the 1904 campaign funds, to say that the Standard Oil Company and the political bosses were rallying to the Democratic nominee. Turning eastward, he grew increasingly harsh, increasingly unfair.

"I have noticed several Taft badges in your town," he shouted

[60] White House memorandum, May 12, 1912. [61] Taft to G. H. Grosvenor, July 22, 1912. [62] New York *Times,* Aug. 13, 1912. [63] Taft to Horace D. Taft, Aug. 26, 1912.

PEACE AGAIN. PROFESSOR TAFT OF YALE

See page 866]

ONE STING SUFFICIENT.

Cartoon by C. K. Berryman, Courtesy Washington Star

[*See page 883*

at Springfield, Missouri, "and they are the appropriate color of yellow." [64]

The best campaign, by far, was made by Wilson. He found exhilaration in his contacts with the crowd. He was gayer and more spontaneous than at any other period of his career. Tariff reduction was the main theme of his speeches, a shrewd choice because it was Taft's weakest point and because Roosevelt, as always, was ignorant of this economic problem. He talked about trust control too, and said he would not compromise in the fight to restore the competitive system. He called the Progressive platform a collection of impossible pledges.

"I do not want to promise heaven unless I can bring it to you," Wilson told one audience. "I can only see a little way up the road." He was fair too. The third party, he said, deserved careful consideration because "some of the sober and finer forces of the country are now dedicated to the promotion of this new movement and party." [65]

Taft whistled, from time to time, in the political darkness. A three-cornered contest in Vermont resulted in a narrow victory for the organization Republican candidate. The President seized upon this as proof that Roosevelt could not get any electoral votes in New England. [66] The September balloting in Maine, he said, refuted the rumors of a heavy Democratic drift. All in all, it appeared that Roosevelt was "on the toboggan and will run a poor third in the election." This would be true, in any event, if "every lover of sane, constitutional government would take off his coat and work, refusing to be misled by the cajolings of Mr. Wilson or by Mr. Roosevelt's assertion that he is 'battling for the Lord.' " [67] The President did not really believe all this. His whistling echoed, most of the time, among the tombstones of hopes long since buried. He faced, he confessed to Henry Taft, "unprecedented difficulties and a most unscrupulous enemy. I believe I am already reconciled to defeat, although if it actually comes, I would doubtless find that uncertainty was pleasanter than certainty in that respect." [68]

The mercurial Roosevelt, too, was having his period of de-

---

[64] New York *World*, Aug. 18, Sept. 18, 24, 1912. [65] Baker, R. S., *op. cit.*, Vol. III, pp. 377-390. [66] Taft to Bannard, Sept. 7, 1912. [67] Taft to Samuel Mather, Sept. 29, 1912. [68] Taft to H. W. Taft, Sept. 18, 1912.

pression. Friction had developed among the soldiers of the Lord. Vice-presidential nominee Johnson sulked in his tent, occasionally, because he felt that his talents were not being properly used. A more serious danger lay in the probability that the strain of the campaign was proving too much for Roosevelt. His voice was bothering him seriously. Reports reached the Bull Moose headquarters that he was losing his grip, that he was repeating himself disastrously.[69] He was forced to cancel two addresses scheduled for the Middle West because of his throat. The disability was bad enough to raise the possibility that he could speak no more. The destiny which had always been Roosevelt's benefactor was kind again, if a shade rash, at this crisis. The colonel insisted on speaking in Milwaukee on the night of October 14. On the way to the hall he was shot by John Shrank, a lunatic. Roosevelt had never in his life missed an opportunity to make a dramatic gesture. He did not falter now, but completed the scheduled address before physicians were allowed to determine the gravity of his wound. It was not serious and wild enthusiasm again surged through Bull Moose breasts.[70]

Taft's first reaction was to recoil with horror. He sent an immediate message, warm with sympathy.[71] His concern cooled rapidly, however. "Just what effect Roosevelt's shooting is going to have I don't know," he remarked. "His supporters, and I have no doubt he is willing to profit by it, are making as much of it as they can." [72] "Of course," he added, "sentiment plays a large part in elections." [73] In any event, Roosevelt had a fortnight's rest in the hospital. He was ruddy and cheerful, and in fine voice, when he spoke again on the night of October 30.

In contrast, fate seemed to be working against the Republicans. Vice-president Sherman had been seriously ill and died on October 30. Sherman had added no particular strength to the ticket, but it is possible that the hurried substitution of President Butler of Columbia University further puzzled the voters. Taft felt so.

". . . on the eve of the election," he wrote, "when the Republican party has suffered from an unjust minimizing of strength by

[69] Davis, O. K., *Released for Publication*, pp. 349-358. [70] Pringle, H. F., *op. cit.*, pp. 568-570. [71] White House memorandum, Oct. 15, 1912. [72] Taft to Nagel, Oct. 16, 1912. [73] Taft to Mrs. R. H. Taylor, Oct. 17, 1912.

the press, and by the public at large, confusion has been sent among the voters by the death of one of the Republican candidates. If we survive these blows, we shall indeed show a strength that savors well for the future." [74]

—9—

Election Day was November 5. On Thursday, October 31, Louis Seibold of the New York *World* called at the White House and pleaded with the President to discuss frankly the issues of the campaign and to tell in detail the story of his relationship with Roosevelt. The political writer expressed the fear that the Bull Moose nominee might poll more votes than Taft. A forthright statement of the Republican side, if published on Saturday morning, might be very important. The President agreed. He invited Seibold to come back, with the questions he desired to ask, on the following morning. The correspondent found Taft in excellent spirits. W. W. Mischler, his confidential secretary, was present. The interview was given. Seibold left with a promise that the transcript would be ready that evening. He would not limit publication to the *World,* he said. The interview would be released to the Associated Press and the other news agencies and would be printed throughout the nation.

Later that day, however, Seibold was notified that the President wished to make some minor corrections. He was leaving Washington at five o'clock to attend the funeral of Vice-president Sherman in Utica. If Seibold would accompany the presidential party as far as New York, he would be handed the revised version en route. The writer had dinner with the President on the special train and stressed again the importance of haste. Space was being saved in every newspaper, he pointed out. Taft agreed, and retired to his stateroom. An hour passed while the train roared on to New York and while Seibold grew increasingly nervous. Then Captain Cary Grayson emerged from the President's room.

"I think the old man is slipping on that interview," he said.

This proved to be the case. Taft told Seibold that he was apprehensive over some of the statements he had made. He had decided

[74] Taft to Horace D. Taft, Nov. 1, 1912.

to consult Root, Wickersham and Barnes at the Manhattan Hotel between trains. He could not have the interview ready until Saturday morning.

"It can't be printed until Sunday then," Seibold said. "I'm afraid that's too late."

"But Roosevelt was my closest friend," answered Taft.

Harry Dunlap, another *World* reporter, accompanied the party to the funeral at Utica and begged the President to permit publication. But Taft, although his advisers joined in the urging, was adamant. The interview never appeared. A month later, Seibold asked for a copy as a historical document.

"There is no copy; I have ordered it destroyed," the President told him.

"Why can't I have one made from Mischler's notes?"

"I told him to burn his book," said Taft.[75]

The President's instructions regarding the transcript were not fully obeyed. One copy was filed with his private papers. The statements it contains are certainly pallid enough, in view of Taft's vacillation and apparent belief that he had voiced a too-vigorous attack. He hurled no epithets at Roosevelt. He did not even disclose how grossly unfair Roosevelt had been. The corrections made on the special train— they appear in his own hand on the copy which survived— are of phraseology only. And yet the interview might have attracted some support. It revealed the process whereby he had abandoned his desire to return to the bench and had agreed to stand for the presidency in 1908. He described the widening breach between the liberal and conservative wings of the party.

". . . beyond the personal ambition of Mr. Roosevelt," Seibold asked, "what do you think chiefly actuated him in precipitating himself into this contest, in which there was really no demand for him?"

"I don't think I had better discuss that," the President answered, "because I have had personalities enough."

The correspondent persisted, though, and Taft finally said:

Mr. Roosevelt is so constituted that it is impossible for him to go into controversy without becoming personal. What I mean is

[75] Seibold to author, Dec. 13, 1934.

this: Mr. Roosevelt is not a logician, and he never argues. His power of concentrated statement is that of a genius. His power of making a statement in such phrases as to give them currency is equal to that of any man I know. He never makes a sustained argument that appeals to you. He is not looking for an argument. Each blow he strikes is a hard one, because it calls attention to some defect in his enemy's armor, or some great claim to right on his part, but he does not establish a conclusion by one step and then another and another. He has not either patience or power to do that. He once said to me, "When I fight I like to get close up to a man." Well, by that he meant— he could not mean otherwise— that he fought not only the man's argument but the man himself. He could not ascribe to the man, differing from him radically, any other than an improper motive. He could not differ from a man in memory without imputing something more than a mistake of memory to him.

"Mr. President," Seibold said, "do you believe that if he could have foreseen . . . the wrecking of the Republican party, he would have gone into the contest?"

"Well, I cannot tell. I do not know. I know that as he went on, step by step, his desire for destruction grew stronger and stronger. I don't think he went deliberately into it that way. I don't think Mr. Roosevelt is a planner ahead so far as that question of yours indicates. I think he acts from day to day, and acting from day to day is led on by these peculiarities of temperament of his."

Then came a lengthy analysis of his administration, with its problems and disappointments. Taft turned, at its conclusion, to the disappointments of the campaign now ending.

"I am in a philosophical state," he said. "I have had to be. The experience I have had in the presidency has made me so, and what I am very hopeful is that whatever happens the country will go on to ultimate happiness. It may lose some in prosperity. Indeed, my judgment is that it will lose a good deal. The fact is that we have been treading on air, and we need to get down to the ground again." [76]

And so the futile, repugnant struggle closed. Taft went to Cincinnati to vote. The result was fairly clear within a few hours after the balloting ended. Wilson claimed victory at 10:45 P.M. and

[76] Seibold interview, Nov. 1, 1912.

Roosevelt admitted defeat an hour later.[77] Wilson received 6,286,214 popular votes; Roosevelt, 4,126,020; Taft, 3,483,922. It was the electoral vote which showed more clearly the magnitude of the Taft debacle, the worst ever suffered by a president. He received only the eight pathetic votes of Vermont and Utah. Wilson had 435 electoral votes and Roosevelt 88. The President, too, admitted Wilson's election at an early hour on Tuesday night and bitterness marked his first statement.

"This means," he said, "an early change in the economic policy of the government in reference to the tariff. If the change can be made without halting prosperity, I sincerely hope that it may." Clearly, the President did not believe that it could. He then gave warning that the votes polled by Roosevelt and by Debs, the Socialist nominee, were proof that the propaganda for fundamental change in the American form of government "has formidable support." [78] Although his hopes had never been high, Taft had not believed that defeat, if it came, would be so sweeping. He later wrote:

I am becoming convinced . . . that the number of Republicans who voted for Wilson, in order to escape the danger of Roosevelt, reaches into the hundreds of thousands, and I must think, therefore, that Roosevelt drew a great many Democratic votes from Wilson of the labor, socialistic, discontented, ragtag and bobtail variety. Roosevelt had in addition the votes of the faddists, the radical progressives, the people with isms, the emotional clergymen and women, in states where women voted, and all the factional sore-heads in the Republican party. . . . What I got was the irreducible minimum of the Republican party that was left after Roosevelt got through with it and after Wilson drew from it the votes of those Republicans who feared Roosevelt. Roosevelt polled a much larger vote than I thought was possible.[79]

A conviction grew in Taft that preservation of the Constitution rested upon preservation of the Republican party. He repeated that Wilson was not a serious menace. He hoped that the President-elect might show, "now that he has power, greater conservative tend-

[77] New York *Times*, Nov. 6, 1912. [78] White House memorandum, Nov. 5, 1912. [79] Taft to Bannard, Nov. 10, 1912.

encies than his preliminary campaign indicated. Whether he does or not, the country will tire of him and his party after one or two terms, and in that time I do not think he or the party will attempt greatly to change our fundamental law. . . . I may do the party wrong . . . but I cannot help feeling that . . . the incapacity of the Democratic party and of their leader will make itself known to the country in a way unmistakable." [80]

Roosevelt was far, far different. Who could know better than Taft how able he was in swinging misguided American voters away from sound governmental doctrine and into the radical forests of judicial recall, the referendum, war on big business? Roosevelt, said the vanquished President, was "the most dangerous man that we have had in this country since its origin, and . . . by preventing his election to a third term we are entitled to the gratitude of all patriots." The enemy had been thrown back, but was he wholly vanquished? Taft said it was essential "that we organize in some way so as to continue to prevent his success and that of the pernicious principles he advocates." The best plan, Taft concluded, was "the organization of a Constitutional Club with a view to spreading constitutional principles throughout the country." [81] Such an organization should have "money enough to circulate literature and also to employ lecturers and send them over the country, especially into our colleges and universities, to bring the youth and the professors down to earth, instead of allowing them to soar in the blue skies with their heads in the clouds." [82]

The serious aspect of the 1912 campaign may well have been, then, that it heightened in Taft the conservatism he had shaken off under the influence of Roosevelt. This would not have been important had he merely retired to private life and become another somewhat futile former president of the United States. In a few brief years, however, he would be the highest judicial officer in the world. Yet the essential sweetness of Taft's nature did not change. He remained, all in all, a reasonable man. He refused to believe that anything was basically wrong with the majority of the American people. His friends, offering sympathy in his dark hour, sug-

[80] Taft to C. H. Kelsey, Nov. 8, 1912. [81] Idem. [82] Taft to Herbert Parsons, Nov. 8, 1912.

gested that the people were ungrateful, hysterical, unsound. He answered:

I do not share this feeling of resentment toward the people at all. The situation was most peculiar. . . . I have no word of criticism for the people at large. I think a great many of them were misled by the misrepresentations contained in the muckraking press and in the magazines, and I must wait for years if I would be vindicated by the people. . . . I am content to wait.[83]

Among the bitter letters addressed to the President was one from Mrs. Wallingford of Cincinnati, whom Taft had known all his life. He hastened to comfort her:

. . . my dear Nannie, I am afraid that your nerves are over-wrought and that you have allowed yourself to become too greatly excited. . . . I would not have your peace of mind disturbed— it is not necessary. The people of the United States did not owe me another election. I hope I am properly grateful for the one term of the presidency which they gave me, and the fact that they withheld the second is no occasion for my resentment or feeling a sense of injustice. . . .

The press generally has been very kindly in its treatment of me and my fate, and I beg you to believe, my dear Nannie, that I am as free from disappointment and as full of happiness as you would have me and as I would have you. . . .

As I look out of my study window I see Lucy's [Lucy Laughlin, his sister-in-law] two boys and the fraulein running up and down the lawn, while the Washington Monument looks down upon them with benignity and encouragement. It exercises the same office with me. This is the only country we have, my dear Nannie, and we have to make the best of it; and such popular manifestations as we had the other day are not to be taken as an evidence of governmental incapacity. . . . There was nothing done which cannot be recalled and which will not be recalled promptly when the time comes, and in the end we shall see that popular government is the most enduring and the most just and the most effective.[84]

[83] Taft to J. W. Hill, Nov. 10, 1912. [84] Taft to Mrs. B. A. Wallingford, Jr., Nov. 9, 1912.

CHAPTER XLIII

A DISSOLVING VIEW

THE NEARER I get to the inauguration of my successor," the President wrote, "the greater the relief I feel." [1] True, he sometimes wondered whether tranquillity might not bore him. "Doubtless later on I shall have a restlessness . . . growing out of the absence of the excitement of a strenuous political life," he admitted. [2] This seemed, though, a remote possibility as his administration was ending. Taft was gay again, instead of morose. His even temper returned. The moments of irritability were few. And the charm of his personality— it was often almost radiance and so men loved him— returned too.

He had promised, before the election, to speak at the annual banquet of the Lotos Club in New York on November 16, 1912, and he prepared to keep the engagement. The address which he dictated is perhaps the best of his whole career.

"The legend of the lotos eaters," he began, "was that if they partook of the fruit of the lotos tree they forgot what had happened in their country and were left in a state of philosophic calm in which they had no desire to return to it. I do not know what was in the mind of your distinguished committee when I was asked to attend this banquet. They came to me before the election. At first I hesitated to accept lest when the dinner came, by the election, I should be shorn of interest as a guest and be changed from an active and virile participant in the day's doings of the nation to merely a dissolving view." [3]

It was precisely the right note for a defeated president of the United States to strike. The response of the audience was tumultuous. Taft went on to say that the normal desire of diners on such occasions was "to have a guest whose society should bring them more closely into contact with the great present and future and not

[1] Taft to H. C. Ide, Dec. 16, 1912. [2] Taft to E. S. Dana, Jan. 27, 1913. [3] *Lotos Club Address*, p. 3.

be merely a reminder of what has been. But, after further consideration, I saw in the name of your club the possibility that you were not merely cold, selfish seekers after pleasures of your own, and that perhaps you were organized to furnish consolation to those who mourn, oblivion to those who would forget, a swan song for those about to disappear." He had not been without suspicion, the President added, that November 5 might be a day of storms, and "I concluded that it was just as well to cast an anchor to windward and accept as much real condolence as I could gather in such a hospitable presence as this, and therefore, my friends, I . . . am here."

Mr. Taft then became serious. The title of his address was "The President," so he would discuss the powers and obligations of the presidency. It had been called the most powerful office in the world, but those who held it were more often conscious of the limitations which blocked the execution of a program.

"Of course," he added slyly, and no one failed to appreciate the reference to Roosevelt, "there are happy individuals who are able entirely to ignore these limitations both in mind and practice, and as to them the result may be different."

Roosevelt was in Taft's mind, again, when he said that in an era "of progress, reform, uplift and improvement a man does not show himself abreast of the age unless he has some changes to suggest. It is the recommended change that marks his being up to date." Taft's own proposed changes in the presidency were mildly constructive. Merely to show "that though I am a conservative, I am not a reactionary or a trilobite, I venture the suggestion that it would aid the efficiency of the Executive . . . if he were made ineligible after serving one term of six years." A second recommendation was that members of the cabinet should have seats in the House and the Senate so that they could inform Congress regarding the activities of the executive branch. This might alleviate some of the criticism so often leveled at the President by the legislators.

"One of the results of my observation in the presidency," he said, "is that the position is not a place to be enjoyed by a sensitive man. . . . I don't know that this evil has been any greater in this administration. . . . All I know is that it was my first experience and that it seemed to me as if I had been more greatly tried than most presidents by such methods. The result in some respects is unfortunate in that after one or two efforts to meet the unfounded accusations, despair in the matter leads to indifference and perhaps to an indifference toward both just and unjust criticism. This condition helps the comfort of the patient, but I doubt that it makes him a better president. Of course, the reassuring formula that history will right one and will give one his just meed of praise is consolatory, but it is not altogether satisfactory, because . . . the time for remedying the injustice may be postponed until one is gathered to his fathers . . . when he is not particularly interested in earthly history."

Having thus opened his heart and having explained, to a degree greater than he knew, perhaps, the failures of the past four years, the President said that he left office, "despite the emphatic verdict," with only the deepest gratitude to the people. His outstanding regret was that the arbitration treaties with France and Great Britain had been rejected by the Senate.

"I do not despair of ultimate success. We must hope and work on," Taft declared.

—2—

These serious moments merely heightened the humor which ran through this Lotos Club valedictory. "What are we to do with our ex-presidents?" Taft asked:

I am not sure Dr. Osler's method of dealing with elderly men would not usefully apply to the treatment of ex-presidents. The proper and scientific administration of a dose of chloroform or of the fruit of the lotos tree, and the reduction of the flesh of the thus quietly departed to ashes in a funeral pyre to satisfy the wishes of his friends and the families, might make a fitting end to the life of one who has held the highest office, and at the same time would secure the country from the troublesome fear that the occupant could ever come back. His record would have been made by one term and his demise in the honorable ceremony . . . would relieve the country from the burden of thinking how he is to support himself and his family, would fix his place in history, and enable the public to pass on to new men and new measures. I commend this method for consideration.

Another method had been advanced for dealing with rejected presidents; that they should be given a seat in the Senate, without a vote. Its sponsor was William Jennings Bryan and a chuckle began in the Taft abdominal regions as he discussed it:

Mr. Bryan has not exactly had the experience of being a president. He has been a "near president" three times, and possibly that qualified him as an expert. . . . He proposes that ex-presidents should be confined to the business of sitting in the Senate and listening to the discussions in that body. . . . Why Mr. Bryan should think it necessary to add to the discussion in the Senate the lucubrations of ex-presidents, I am at a loss to say. I cannot conceive of any reform in the Senate which does not lead to a limit to their debate. For many reasons I object to Mr. Bryan's disposition of ex-presidents. If I must go and disappear into oblivion, I prefer to go by the chloroform or lotos method. It's pleasanter and it's less drawn out.

The valedictory was nearly over. At its close, Mr. Taft grew serious again. The presidency was still in his keeping, he said. His mind was dwelling on the man on whom its awful burdens so soon would fall.

"I wish to express deep gratitude . . ." said the President of the United States earnestly. "I close with a sentiment and a toast to which I most sincerely and cordially ask your unanimous acclaim—

"Health and success to the able, distinguished, and patriotic gentleman who is to be

"The next President of the United States!" [4]

The public reaction to the Lotos Club speech was extraordinary. Even before he made it, the people had been praising Taft. This was partly the normal American reaction to a good loser, to a man whose sportsmanship was as genuine as it was appealing. Only Utah and Vermont may have wanted him for president, again, but a large proportion of the people who had voted against him now called him a fine old boy. Taft, of course, was greatly pleased. "I had a great time in New York and a very delightful experience at

[4] *Lotos Club Address*, pp. 3-13.

the Lotos Club where they were most cordial in the reception of my speech," he wrote.[5] It was left for the cynical Root to ponder the vacillations of the voter.

"The way your speech has been received by the dear public is really delightful," he observed. It was the only sour note.[6]

—3—

The President decided, immediately after the election, that he would return to Cincinnati and practice law. He knew he would be criticized if he used his prestige to attract large retainers from all varieties of client and consented to argue their cases in court. Taft was not blind to the proprieties, and he had no intention of doing this. "I hope I may be able to secure enough cases in which I can act as counsel," he said, "with a few arguments possibly in the higher courts . . . so that I may keep the wolf from the door without any undue accumulation of funds. . . . My profession is my means of livelihood, and unless the country manifests its opposition to such a course by furnishing a pension to its ex-presidents, I don't see that there is anything left for me to do." [7]

An opportunity arose for Taft to live in luxury and idleness. Andrew Carnegie offered a pension of $25,000 a year to former presidents and to their widows. "I can't take the pension for obvious reasons," the President told his younger brother, "but I think the old man wanted to do the right thing." He was entertained by the violent criticism which the proposal aroused: ". . . some of our cheapest statesmen whom, if such an offer were made, you could not see for the dust they would make in hurrying to the paymaster are in conniption fits over the insult the old man has offered to the nation and the impudence that prompted his action." [8] Taft knew that Carnegie's offer, however well meant, could not be accepted. He pointed out that it would be impossible to escape, "if you were an ex-president, the feeling of embarrassment every time you met old Carnegie . . . it is not probable that he would ever meet you without referring in a genial way to the comfortable posi-

[5] Taft to C. P. Taft, Nov. 20, 1912. [6] Root to Taft, Nov. 23, 1912. [7] Taft to Bannard, Nov. 10, 1912. [8] Taft to Horace D. Taft, Nov. 24, 1912.

tion in which the pension he had arranged had placed you." The question had a far more important aspect, however:

Suppose Carnegie were to say that, instead of giving us a pension, he thought that our salaries were not large enough to enable us to make proper provision for the future, and, therefore, he proposed to add to the $75,000 a year allowed us by the government, $225,000 a year during the term, making $300,000 a year, all told. Now it is easy, I think, for anyone to see that that would induce a divided allegiance, and a motive at least for a sense of allegiance to the private donor, greater even than the allegiance to the government, and it would be contrary to public policy to allow such an addition to the salary received from the proper authorities representing the whole people. Now when you come to examine the matter closely, you will find that as to a president who has not yet become an ex-president, and I have not even become an ex-president, it is impossible to regard the pension proposed as being anything other than an addition to the salary that he is to receive for his four years.[9]

Actually, Taft did not need the Carnegie pension or any other. ". . . after leaving the presidency," he said, "I shall change my social status from that of the automobile to that of the pedestrian class." [10] But he revealed in a delightfully frank letter to Woodrow Wilson that no truth lay in the idea that being president was a drain on private resources. On the contrary, it was an exceedingly well-paid job. Taft, who had very slight acumen in financial matters and no taste for economy, had put aside $100,000 in his four-year term. He reassured the President-elect:

You will find . . . that Congress is very generous to the President. You have all your transportation paid for, and all servants in the White House except such valet and maid as you and Mrs. Wilson choose to employ. Your flowers for entertainments and otherwise are furnished from the conservatory, and if they are not sufficient there is an appropriation from which they add to the supply. Music for all your entertainments, by the Marine Band or some other band, is always at hand. Provision is made by which when you leave in the summer you may at government expense take such of

[9] Taft to J. D. Brannan, Nov. 25, 1912. [10] Taft to Mrs. William Hooper, Feb. 3, 1913.

the household as you need to your summer home, and the expense of their traveling and living is met under the appropriation. Your laundry is looked after in the White House, both when you are here and when you are away. Altogether, you can calculate that your expenses are only those of furnishing food to a large boardinghouse of servants and to your family, and your own personal expenses of clothing, etc. This, of course, makes the salary of $75,000 with $25,000 for traveling expenses, very much more than is generally supposed.

I have been able to save from my four years about $100,000. I give you these personal details because I am afraid I shall not have an opportunity, in view of your engagements, to meet you under conditions that will enable me to have a long talk with you, and I feel as if I would have liked the same kind of information when I came in.[11]

Mr. Wilson answered the letter at once, and expressed his gratitude for such valuable information which was, he said, precisely what he needed.[12]

Taft, after decades in public life, was not wealthy. Indeed, he was decidedly poor in comparison with Root or other lawyers who had engaged in private practice and won lucrative corporation fees. But he had saved enough to bring a small income:

Nellie and I can assemble in mortgage notes and $6,250 of stock, $150,000 which pays us $8,000 annually. In addition to that I hope to save $10,000 out of the four months' pay yet to come. . . . In addition we have a lot in Washington worth from $13,000 to $15,-000. . . . So you see we have saved something out of the United States. . . . I omitted to say that I have some life insurance that would bring Nellie $60,000 if I were to depart this life.

He was in the happy position of a husband and father who was not "troubled about Nellie's future and that of Helen, for there will be enough for them to live upon, and the boys can very well hustle for themselves, with an education and a profession." [13]

It is a safe assumption that Taft did not look forward too cheerfully to the law, in Cincinnati or elsewhere. He had not prac-

[11] Taft to Wilson, Jan. 6, 1913. [12] Wilson to Taft, Jan. 8, 1913. [13] Taft to Horace D. Taft, Nov. 24, 1912.

ticed since he was a very young man. Then, he had been less than a meteor in the legal sky. For success at the bar requires a competitive quality which had never been a marked characteristic of William Howard Taft. The President must have been greatly relieved, the middle of November, when an escape suddenly appeared. He attended a meeting of the Yale Corporation at New Haven. President Hadley cornered him before it began and explained that a professorship of law was vacant; that the university authorities would be gratified if he would accept the post. As always, Taft consulted his brothers:

The duties are more than nominal, but they are very much what the professor wishes to make them. They involve a course of lectures to the senior class in the academic department on constitutional and governmental law, and such courses as he sees fit to give at the Law School. . . . They are quite disposed to let me do about as I please if I accept. . . . I suppose it is the advertisement or association of my name with the institution that they would like to cultivate. . . .

This would take me away from Cincinnati, of course, and perhaps make me a resident of Connecticut in which I am about as much a political factor as I am in Ohio, which is very small. The proposition has some very attractive features about it. I do not retire to the practice of the law; I retire to the academic shades of Yale to teach it, and this very act takes me out of the maelstrom of politics. It is a dignified retirement, one which Cleveland had at Princeton, and one which would approve itself to the general sense of propriety of the country. The practice such as I would get would be incidental and it would attract less criticism. I submitted the matter to the Cabinet yesterday and they all thought it was an admirable suggestion and one that fitted itself remarkably well into the situation. . . . The only thing I do not like about it is that it takes me away from Cincinnati. . . . I forgot to say that the salary is $5,000 a year, which is the largest salary they pay. This would be enough for us to live on in New Haven with the income we have, and perhaps I could be reasonably certain to earn enough more to keep the wolf from the door, especially in view of the fact that I do not expect to eat so much after leaving the White House.[14]

---

[14] Taft to C. P. Taft, to Horace D. Taft, Nov. 20, 1912.

Taft was pleased when everyone endorsed the plan.[15] There was another aspect to a professorship at Yale which attracted him greatly. It would enable him "to proclaim the evangel of constitutionalism and international peace— the two subjects that I have been anxious to use [sic] the rest of my life so that someday we shall secure that advantage which we lost during my administration." [16] Peace, although ever close to Taft's heart, was at the moment secondary to combating the poison of Roosevelt's radicalism. The President pointed out that he would be permitted to influence the young men in the academic department of Yale, not merely the budding lawyers.

"I feel as if there has been a good deal of erroneous doctrine taught in our universities," he said, "and that young men go out without having the proper sense of proportion as to the actualities of life, and especially that their political and economic concepts need revision. If I can do anything to help this along, it will be full satisfaction to me, for there is nothing in life quite equal to the thought of being useful." [17] His enthusiasm mounted. He would, if possible, "keep the heterodox and wild notions that are prompted by some professors of political economy" out of the heads of the men of Yale and thereby "I think I shall be doing God's service." [18] It was a vastly different service than the one to which Taft had dedicated himself hardly five years before. Then, he had made himself the spokesman for the doctrines of Theodore Roosevelt and had proclaimed himself a progressive to the core of his being. Roosevelt had changed in the five years. Taft had changed too. The change, in part, was due to the fact that he was an older man who had suffered great disappointment.

Taft learned, immediately upon the convening of Congress in December, that a defeated president is a figure of relatively small importance to the House and Senate. He sent his usual annual message and several additional ones. But when Representative William M. Calder of New York asked for another communication recommending some bill he said that it was futile.

[15] Taft to Horace D. Taft, Nov. 24, 1912. [16] Taft to Root, Nov. 20, 1912. [17] Taft to A. P. Stokes, Dec. 14, 1912. [18] Taft to J. D. Brannan, Feb. 14, 1913.

"I'll sign the bill," he promised, "but I don't think my sending a message will do any good." [19]

The President was not, it may be assumed, greatly interested in the deliberations on Capitol Hill. He went to Panama on a final, hurried trip of inspection in late December.[20] His friendly interest in the problems of President-elect and Mrs. Wilson continued. Soon after the election it was suggested that they should be invited to stay at the White House. Taft considered the idea and was, at first, inclined to favor it. Mrs. Taft, however, vetoed the plan. She remembered all too well the night of March 3, 1909, when President Roosevelt was retiring and when the Tafts had been guests at the Executive Mansion. It had not been a cheerful occasion.[21]

But the President responded promptly when Dr. Wilson asked for his candid opinion of the White House housekeeper, Mrs. Jaffray. The President-elect craved pardon for inquiring about so domestic a subject, but added that he saw no escape from doing so.[22] Taft's recommendation of Mrs. Jaffray was warm. He added that Arthur Brooks, "without exception the most trustworthy colored man in the District of Columbia," had served as his major-domo and might also well be retained.[23]

"... we are all looking forward to the fourth of March with feelings of contentment and satisfaction, when we shall go to Augusta and spend a month of rest and golf," the President wrote late in February. "I doubt not that after that there will come over us a yearning for the greatness of the past and for the responsibilities and opportunities for usefulness in great matters." [24]

Taft never permitted himself to be deluded, as other vanquished presidents have done, into a belief that the people would repent of their error and recall him from private life at the next election.

"I do not share with you the view that there is any probability

[19] White House memorandum, Feb. 19, 1913. [20] Taft to Max Pam, Jan. 2, 1913. [21] Taft to Mabel Boardman, Nov. 10, 1912. [22] Wilson to Taft, Jan. 2, 1913. [23] Taft to Ellen A. Wilson, Jan. 3, 1913. [24] Taft to Howard Hollister, Feb. 20, 1913.

of my being selected as a candidate for the Republicans at the end of four years," he told Dr. John Wesley Hill. "I have proven to be a burdensome leader and not one that aroused the multitude, not one that was calculated to lead on to victory in a close contest. I am entirely content to serve in the ranks. . . . I harbor no ill will against anybody, even Beveridge— could I put it more strongly?" [25]

Serenity continued to mark the final days. Behind it was a happy man, never convinced that he had been qualified for the presidency and relieved that his period in the White House was ending. The final days were busy, of course. Many routine matters had to be concluded. The President put them aside on the night of March 1, however, to appear at a farewell function of the National Press Club. As in his address to the Lotos Club, he was frank, humorous and charming. Why, he asked, should he feel bitter? Taft recalled that he had held public office ever since he was twenty-two; a slight exaggeration since he was actually twenty-four years old when appointed assistant prosecutor of Hamilton County, Ohio, in 1881.

"Now, gentlemen," he asked, "after that record, still in health, do you suppose that I regret anything; that I have an occasion for kicking or squealing? What kind of a man would I be if I did? Now I am looking to see if I can't repay the country and fortune for the good things given me."

The President's mind shifted, at this point, to his own failings as chief executive. He exaggerated them, perhaps. "My sin," he said, "is an indisposition to labor as hard as I might, a disposition to procrastinate and a disposition to enjoy the fellowship of other men more than I should." [26]

—5—

President-elect Wilson arrived in Washington on the afternoon of Monday, March 3, and went at once to the Shoreham Hotel. At six o'clock, with Mrs. Wilson, he called at the White House. Immediately afterward, President and Mrs. Taft returned the call. Taft had been very busy this last day. He had received the newspaper correspondents, however, and had discussed with them the triumphs and the failures of his administration. Above all other things, the President said, he was proudest of the fact that six of the nine members of the Supreme Court, including the Chief Justice, bore his commission.

"And I have said to them," Taft chuckled, " 'Damn you, if any of you die, I'll disown you.' "

That night, the President worked late at his desk. His final task was to sign his name again and again, to satisfy the thousands of requests for his autograph. He did this for hours, until midnight came and the muscles of his hand were weary. Then he went to bed, only to worry and toss because so many autographs remained to be scribbled. So he arose at two-thirty and worked for another hour and a half.[27]

March 4 was a warm, fine day— in marked contrast to the winds and the sleet of four years before when Taft had been sworn in. It was, of course, Woodrow Wilson's day. The President-elect was escorted to the White House and was then driven, with the President, to the Capitol. At 1:10 P.M. he took the oath of office and William Howard Taft passed into private life. Then came the return trip to the White House, with the two men again in the same carriage. It must have been heartening, to the man who had become a dissolving view, to hear greetings and cheers that were almost as loud as the ones for the new President.

"I wish you a successful administration," Taft had declared warmly when Wilson had finished his inaugural address, "and the carrying out of your aims. We will all be behind you." [28]

It is necessary, at this point, to refute a malicious account of these final hours in which Ike Hoover, chief usher at the White House for many years, described what he termed a "faux pas" by Taft. Hoover related how Wilson and Taft, "both plainly embarrassed," reached the White House from the Capitol soon after two o'clock. Meanwhile, guests had been gathering for a buffet luncheon being given by the new President and Mrs. Wilson. Hoover's account is as follows:

[27] New York *Times*, March 4, 1913. [28] *Ibid.*, March 5, 1913.

Presently one of the ushers approached and informed Mr. Wilson that the luncheon party had already assembled in the dining room. The new President, taking the hint, gallantly turned to Mr. Taft *and invited him to join him at lunch. . . . I have no doubt that Mr. Wilson expected Mr. Taft to decline his invitation for he looked ready to say good-bye.* On the contrary . . . Mr. Taft was determined to have that lunch. . . . It was really sad to observe Mr. Taft. No one seemed to pay any attention to him. It was now necessary for him to do a little hustling for himself, but he managed somehow to get hold of a bit of salad and a sandwich. Word finally came that Mrs. Taft would not wait for him any longer, but would continue on to the station. . . . This had the desired effect and he was practically dragged from the scene of his former achievements.[29]

The account is as inaccurate as it is unfair. The facts are that Mrs. Taft, busy with the last-minute details of departure, had declined a formal invitation to the luncheon. Taft had been asked to attend at least a week before March 4, and had accepted.

"I am very glad that the President can be with us on Tuesday at luncheon," Mrs. Wilson had written to Mrs. Taft, "and very sorry that you cannot: but I understand perfectly the difficulties due to your early departure."[30]

Former President and Mrs. Taft boarded the 3:10 train for Augusta after a hurried automobile ride during which, again, the people who saw them bowed and cheered. They would arrive in Georgia early the following morning. Perhaps Mr. Taft read, as his train chugged south, an editorial published in the New York *Times* that day. It was a friendly editorial and a discerning one. It reviewed the difficulties of the four years just over.

"President Taft," it began, "has been the victim of too much Roosevelt."[31]

[29] Hoover, Irwin Hood (Ike), *Forty-Two Years in the White House*, pp. 56-57. (Italics mine.) [30] Ellen A. Wilson to Helen H. Taft, Feb. 26, 1913. [31] New York *Times*, March 5, 1913.

CHAPTER XLIV

THE ELMS AGAIN

RETIREMENT to Yale was not to mean idleness. "Being a dead politician, I have become a statesman, as Tom Reed defined the change," Taft observed. "I am on the tower of St. Simeon Stylites, or up a tree, to use a more homely expression, where I witness the passing show with continued sympathy, with freedom from the sense of responsibility that I have had to have for nearly twenty-five years, and with a sense of freedom that I have never had before." [1]

But this was partly pretense. Taft was not, really, the lazy man he had proclaimed himself to the Washington newspapermen as he was leaving the presidency. That is, he would work at a fierce pace on problems which interested him deeply. He did not spare himself when the welfare of his family was concerned. He procrastinated only when the task at hand seemed beyond his ability. He had been baffled, not lazy, in the White House.

The eight years during which the former President was, technically, a professor at Yale were to be very busy ones indeed. If anything, Taft drove himself beyond the limits of common sense. He was away from New Haven as much as he was there. It became apparent, by the spring of 1913, that an ex-president of the United States was in great demand as a lecturer and speaker. Before long the faithful Mischler, his private secretary, had organized a one-man lecture bureau and was accepting engagements from civic organizations, ladies' clubs, conventions, lyceums and Chautauqua agencies. Mischler attended to all the details. He made it clear that his principal would appear gratis only under exceptional circumstances, for this was a chief source of income. Taft's fees, invariably called "honoraria" by Mischler, ranged from $150 to as high as $1,000— with $400 as a probable average. In addition, Taft wrote numerous articles for the *Saturday Evening Post,* the *Ladies'*

---

[1] Taft to Mrs. S. G. Rhett, Dec. 1, 1913.

Home Journal and other magazines and received, very often, $1,000 for each. All in all, he added considerably to his savings between 1913 and 1921 when he became chief justice of the United States.

If he could maintain these earnings for three or four more years, he noted in 1915, he would have enough capital to ensure an income of $10,000 a year "without work at all," and would, with his life insurance, leave an estate of $250,000.[2] This was not bad at all for a man whose years had been spent in public life.

The twenty-five days at Augusta, where Taft rested with Mrs. Taft in March, 1913, were "of almost unalloyed sweetness." He had been having trouble with his prostate gland and this had been relieved by treatment. He congratulated himself that no longer would life be an almost incessant round of banquets, that he could again reduce his weight. Mrs. Taft, too, was very much better.[3] In twelve months her husband was able to report happily that she was feeling as she had not felt since before the attack in the White House.[4]

His vacation over, Taft went directly to New Haven after vetoing plans for an escort of the Connecticut National Guard. He was a private citizen, Taft said, and such a demonstration "would be out of keeping with the character . . . I should like to maintain in your dear old city."[5] Until Commencement at Yale, the Tafts took quarters at the Hotel Taft, erected by his brother. Then they settled in a house at 367 Prospect Street; by themselves, because the three children were away. Offices were maintained at the hotel, about a mile distant.

Taft was a happy man and no small part of his joy, naturally, lay in the quality of his children. Robert, the oldest son, had been praised by Dean Thayer of the Harvard Law School as the most remarkable young man he had known at the school. Charles P. Taft, II, was being educated by Uncle Horace and was making astonishingly high grades.[6] Helen had returned to Bryn Mawr to work for the degree which had been interrupted when her mother fell ill and she had been called to the White House to be official

[2] Taft to Horace D. Taft, Oct. 8, 1915. [3] Taft to Dr. Frederick Forschheimer, April 2, 1913. [4] Taft to Mrs. Eugene Stafford, July 9, 1914. [5] Taft to Major G. F. Hewlett, Feb. 3, 1913. [6] Taft to Delia Torrey, June 29, 1913.

hostess. In due course, Robert Taft was married. In the summer of 1915, William Howard Taft became a grandfather.

"His face," the grandfather wrote of the infant, "is like the faces of all babies, having no expression and no resemblance to any member of the family that I could see, but he has a fine head, and while he was small when born . . . he has shown a family trait in increasing his weight quite rapidly." [7]

—2—

The resolution to arouse the nation to the perils confronting the Constitution was not forgotten by Taft. In July, 1913, he was still "strongly convinced that the country is passing through a very dangerous crisis"; the "evil genius of the situation" was, of course, Theodore Roosevelt. Roosevelt was a Socialist, whatever his denials of that label. He was "probably the most dangerous demagogue in history." Taft congratulated himself, again, that he had helped to thwart Roosevelt's ambition to be in the White House, and decided that this danger was over forever. On the other hand, the colonel would "have force enough to interfere with the success of the Republican party. . . .

"The intervention of Mr. Wilson and his Democratic administration has been a great boon, in that it kept Roosevelt out," Taft concluded, "and we must be content to submit to great inconveniences that arise from Democratic mistakes in this supreme advantage." [8]

As always, Taft was intrigued by Roosevelt and watched his activities with keen interest. At about this time Roosevelt began a libel action against an obscure Michigan editor who had charged him, without basis, with being a heavy drinker. Taft called the action "amusing," but added honestly:

I have no doubt that Roosevelt will be vindicated, because I think the charge against him is unfounded. I think the intoxication was altogether with his own verbosity. . . . I would make an excellent witness in his defense. [9]

[7] Taft to G. H. Grosvenor, Oct. 9, 1915.   [8] Taft to C. S. Shepard, July 6, 1913.   [9] Taft to C. P. Taft, May 27, 1913.

The wounds of the 1912 campaign were still fresh. They never entirely healed. Roosevelt and Taft met again, for the first time since the fall of 1910, in April, 1915. The occasion, appropriately enough, was a funeral. On April 11, Professor Taft was invited to serve as honorary pallbearer at the services for Professor Thomas A. Lounsbury of Yale. He was informed at the same time that the widow had invited Roosevelt, an intimate friend of Lounsbury's, to act in the same capacity. Taft was, at first, inclined to avoid the embarrassing meeting. He had an engagement of long standing in Boston; this would serve as an excuse. Or would it? "I bethought myself that my staying away might be misunderstood," Taft feared, and so he decided to go. He was most thoughtful of Roosevelt's own reaction when informed that the colonel did not know their meeting was to take place. Word that Taft, too, was a pallbearer, was sent to Oyster Bay.[10] Anson Phelps Stokes, secretary of Yale, handled the delicate situation by wire and Roosevelt answered that it was quite satisfactory to have Taft present at the funeral. It would all be made as easy as possible, Dr. Stokes promised. They would ride to the grave in separate carriages.[11]

"I don't know how he will conduct himself, but I shall try to be pleasant," Taft said on the night before. ". . . It is the man who has done the wrong who finds it difficult to forgive the man whom he has treated badly. He has been so very anxious to get back into the Republican party and his effusive greeting of Aldrich may indicate that he has concluded it is just as wise to strike a truce . . . so far as personal nonintercourse is concerned. Well, I am very content. I don't like to be on such bad terms with anybody that I may be embarrassed in meeting him."[12]

Roosevelt, too, was well aware of the amenities. The meeting at the funeral may have made an obscure corpse out of poor Professor Lounsbury, but it was otherwise quite colorless. Roosevelt inquired about Mrs. Taft. And was Mrs. Roosevelt well? returned Taft.

"It was pleasant enough, but it was not cordial or intimate," Taft wrote. "I am glad to have . . . the status between us fixed—

---

[10] Taft to Mabel Boardman, April 12, 1913. [11] Stokes to Taft, April 12, 1913. [12] Taft to Mabel Boardman, April 12, 1913.

that of an armed neutrality. . . . It was a bit stiff but it was all right. . . . He is not looking especially well . . . his face seems fatter and flabbier. . . . I should think he looked a bit coarser, but perhaps that is because I haven't seen him recently." [13]

All in all, little progress toward a reconciliation was made. No campaign was in progress in April, 1915. The healing influences of practical politics were not yet called into play.

—3—

Nothing much came of Taft's plan, following his defeat in November, for organizing a Constitutional Club which would disseminate sound, non-Rooseveltian governmental principles throughout the nation. He wrote and talked a great deal about preserving the Constitution, though, and was even alarmed by the published views of Roscoe Pound of the Harvard Law School. [14] Taft was scandalized by Dr. Charles A. Beard of Columbia whom he lumped with "all the fools I have run across . . . the professors of political economy and of philosophy." Beard had just published his *Economic Interpretation of the Constitution of the United States* and this annoyed Taft, partly because the Columbia economist had investigated the personal financial status of the founding fathers. Would Beard, he demanded, have been better satisfied if the immortal instrument had been drafted by "dead bodies, out-at-the-elbows demagogues, cranks who never had any money, and representatives of the purlieus [*sic*] of the population?" [15]

In November, 1913, the former President gave an address, "The Signs of the Times," before the Electrical Manufacturers' Club at Hot Springs, Virginia, which became very much of a favorite with chambers of commerce and similar organizations of industrialists and capitalists. Mischler put it at the head of a printed list of lectures which Taft could deliver, and he repeated it many times. The views in the lecture were those of an essentially reasonable, if conservative, man looking for the causes behind "our present somewhat confused and chaotic conditions, political and social." The

[13] Taft to Karger, April 14, 1915. [14] Taft to J. D. Brannan, April 4, 1913. [15] Taft to Root, May 5, 1913.

address presented nothing new. It was a hodgepodge of all the presidential speeches in the campaign of 1912. Taft admitted the evils of the past— the greed of the corporate interests, the need for social welfare legislation, the plight of the laborer who struggled, unaided by unionism, against a powerful employer. He appeared to believe, however, that all these evils had now been ended. The signs of the times, he said, pointed to the danger that the people did not realize their blessings and would ask more and more of government until socialism had been reached.[16]

Taft, in the White House, had been fairly tolerant toward amendments to the Constitution. He was now growing opposed to any changes in the fundamental law. Logically, he said, in May, 1918, the federal government should regulate marriage and divorce. But he favored postponement of the question "until the time when the amendment or annulment or abolition of the Constitution . . . may have ceased to be a serious political issue." [17]

Partly for this reason and partly because he had always believed that centralized control of the liquor question was unsound, Taft allied himself with the opponents of national prohibition. The arid age was fast approaching, even in 1913. The militant leaders of the dry hosts were encouraged by the decision of Secretary of State Bryan to serve no intoxicants at official dinners. Taft was amused by the violent discussion this provoked. He supposed "they will have to provide late entertainments at the Metropolitan Club for dejected diplomats. However, it does not lose a vote and it gains a great many." [18]

The former President was correct in judging that prohibition was a popular cause. Both the major parties would soon surrender to the drys. The question seemed very simple: if you made liquor illegal, nobody would drink. Taft knew better than that. He had opposed prohibition in the campaign of 1908 on the ground that sumptuary laws could not be enforced in localities where the people disagreed with their wisdom. By 1914, as the prohibitionists prepared to force passage in Congress of a resolution for an amendment, Taft was even more emphatic.

"I concede," he said, "the evil that comes from overindulgence.

[16] *Addresses*, Vol. XXXI, pp. 186-225. [17] Taft to H. W. Rose, May 18, 1913. [18] Taft to Clara de Chambrun, April 28, 1913.

862   THE LIFE AND TIMES OF WILLIAM HOWARD TAFT

... My impression is that there is less drinking among the intelligent people than ever before. . . . That in small units . . . by the system of local option, proximity to liquor may be reduced . . . but that either state prohibition or national prohibition would do any good seems to me to have been clearly demonstrated in the negative by experiments in the states." [19]

The resolution was defeated in December, 1914, and Taft was gratified.[20] The cause had become a holy one, though, and legislators were growing increasingly panicky over the danger of offending the drys. Taft gave warning after warning in vain. The amendment would call "for a horde of federal officials . . . and would give to an unscrupulous manipulator in national politics . . . a power that would be dangerous to the Republic," he said. Besides, no amendment was needed. Washington had ample power to bar liquor from interstate commerce and thereby protect the dry states.[21]

Lawlessness, Taft declared as he had declared in 1908, would follow prohibition. "It would . . . introduce into politics in our large cities an element which, bad as the present intervention of saloonkeepers in politics is, would be far more pernicious." [22] Besides, Taft could not believe that alcohol was so fearful a menace. It was wiser for people to leave it alone, as Taft himself did, "but I don't know that I would say that one who partakes moderately of wine, or other beverage, is deliberately disqualifying himself for advancement. That is too strong . . ." [23]

The lawmakers did not listen to Taft. They did not listen to Woodrow Wilson. Congress passed the resolution and the amendment went to the states. Prohibition became law and the bootleggers started to organize their evil syndicates. Taft never became a spokesman for repeal; as chief justice, naturally, he was silenced. When the amendment had been passed he called for enactment of the laws needed to enforce it. He regarded as absurd the claim that the Eighteenth Amendment had not been legally passed.[24]

[19] Taft to C. N. Prouty, April 2, 1914. [20] Taft to Horace D. Taft, Dec. 27, 1914. [21] Taft to E. H. Tilton, Jan. 3, 1915. [22] Taft to Cooper Lyon, May 17, 1915. [23] Taft to R. S. Mack, March 13, 1916. [24] Mischler to H. B. Knapp, Jan. 21, 1919.

—4—

From the quiet of New Haven, Taft watched the political scene with absorbed interest. He did not suppose for an instant that he would re-enter the arena. He would make speeches for his party in future national elections; a retired president could not escape doing so. Taft declined, however, to accept membership on the Republican National Committee. He declared himself unfitted for the post and "I have too much to do." [25]

Sometimes the whole thing seemed a farce. Taft was disgusted with politics when he glanced toward Ohio, his home state. "Fads and frauds and hypocrisies seem to catch our people out there with more success than almost anywhere else in the country," he wrote. "Reform under Walter Brown and Dan Hanna is such a howling farce that sensible people, I should think, would become disgusted with it. They will in the end, but, O Lord, when?" [26]

Yet the former President kept an eye on the activities of the new man in the White House. Taft's sources of information were only fairly good. He received regular letters from Gus J. Karger, Washington correspondent for Charles P. Taft's Cincinnati paper, and scattering reports from Senator Root and others. Most of the men who wrote him were ardent Republicans. Taft was well aware that he, himself, was prejudiced.

". . . the minister who is removed from the pulpit and put in a pew never thinks much of the sermons of his successor," he observed.[27]

On the other hand, he was quite without envy: "I wish to keep as far in the background as I can. I have grown fully used to reading the papers without my name in them, and it is not an unpleasant change." [28] He adhered rigidly to one policy from the start. He would make no suggestions to the new administration unless invited and would ask for no favors.[29]

Wilson's Cabinet, with the exception of Bryan, seemed to Taft "about as good" as the President could find. True, Secretary of

[25] Taft to Frank B. Brandegee, Nov. 27, 1913. [26] Taft to R. D. Cole, April 29, 1913. [27] Taft to Mrs. William Hooper, Nov. 13, 1913. [28] Taft to Mabel Boardman, April 16, 1913. [29] Taft to R. L. Bourgois, March 28, 1913.

the Treasury McAdoo was close to Wall Street. Secretary of War
Garrison was an excellent lawyer "and that is what is needed in the
War Department with its present functions." Taft had little to say
regarding Secretary of Labor Wilson or Secretary of Commerce
Redfield. He thought that Josephus Daniels had no qualifications
for the Navy Department. He felt that Postmaster General Burleson, being a politician, would be useful to Wilson.

The appointment of James Clark McReynolds as attorney general was among the most satisfactory of Wilson's selections. Taft
called him "an able lawyer, an active one, a fierce prosecutor, a
little inclined to be too fierce and unbending." The future associate
justice, with whom Taft would sit on the Supreme Court and then
dislike exceedingly, would succeed if he would "only moderate his
disposition to be too stiff-necked and too rambunctious." He would,
in any event, enforce the law. Bryan, however, seemed merely a
joke. He was "utterly unfitted to be secretary of state." [30]

Taft, in common with many of his fellow citizens, was not
without malice in poking fun at Bryan. He criticized him for going
on lecture tours; this was a shade unfortunate for Taft, too, would
soon be barnstorming.[31] "Bryan is achieving greater sublimity as
an ass than I had thought possible," he wrote in September, 1913.[32]
Naturally appreciative of good stories, Taft found particular pleasure in the innumerable ones which told of the blunders, actual
or imagined, of the secretary of state. Bryan, for example, had
addressed a delegation from San Salvador, the Central American
republic. He concluded his remarks by expressing disappointment
that he had never visited their lovely island. He had, of course,
confused the republic with the small island in the West Indies, of
the same name, discovered by Columbus. Taft repeated the story
with glee and told another.

Henry Morgenthau, an ardent Wilson supporter, and a Jew,
had been offered the post of ambassador to Turkey and had hesitated in the hope of a more important assignment. Bryan was attempting to persuade him to accept and was painting an alluring
picture of Turkey.

[30] Taft to Horace D. Taft, March 8, 1913; to H. H. Lurton, March 20, 1913. [31] Taft
to R. A. Taft, July 19, 1913. [32] Taft to Karger, Sept. 17, 1913.

"And, Mr. Morgenthau, consider your opportunity," Taft quoted Bryan as saying.

"What opportunity?"

"Why," answered Bryan, "the greatest opportunity that any of our ambassadors has . . . the bringing of Christian influences to bear on the Turks."

Taft thought the story demonstrated the "tact that Bryan is showing in the duties of his position." [33]

His low opinion of Bryan was also based on important mistakes which, Taft felt, the Wilson administration was committing. The President's foreign policy had "gone to ducks and drakes" by the summer of 1913. The Democrats were doing nothing to encourage expansion of American capital in the Far East. They had wrecked American prestige in Mexico by declining recognition of Huerta.[34] Taft was astonishingly calloused in his views of the proper course in Mexico. What if Huerta had climbed to power by the murder of Madero?

"Huerta may be a murderer in fact as Diaz doubtless was, before he became president," Taft calmly observed. "They are not Sunday-school superintendents down there, and we cannot make the qualifications of Sunday-school superintendents square with the necessities of the situation where anarchy prevails." [35]

Taft hoped that there would be no war with Mexico. He was equally hard-boiled, however, in his recommended treatment of that nation if it came. A new and more scientific frontier should be drawn after victory, he confided to Root. By this the United States should seize part of northern Mexico and portions of Lower California.

"You will say that I am betraying the spirit of the buccaneer," he wrote. "Not at all. But what I feel is that we ought not to embarrass ourselves, if we go into war, with any self-denying civilization." [36]

Taft was shocked, not merely critical, when it appeared that the Democrats would abandon the policies which, as civil governor and secretary of war, he had established for the Philippine Islands.

[33] Taft to R. A. Taft, Nov. 20, 1913. [34] *Idem,* July 19, 1913. [35] Taft to Karger, July 22, 1913. [36] Taft to Root, Nov. 9, 1913.

". . . from the time that McKinley sent me out there until now," Taft said, "no politics have played any part . . . and it remains for Wilson to bring them in." [37] At the same time he predicted disaster if independence were granted to the islands.[38]

—5—

As a professor at Yale, Taft maintained, more or less, the associations which had marked his final two years in the White House. They were conservative, even reactionary, influences. It is well, in view of the fact that Taft was to be chief justice by 1921, that precisely opposing philosophies were to surround him for a time— when he served with the War Labor Board in Washington and listened, with a really open mind, to Frank P. Walsh and others.

In October, 1913, he conferred with Nelson P. Aldrich, Murray Crane, former Secretary of State Knox and H. P. Davison, the Morgan partner, regarding President Wilson's proposal to revise the banking and currency system. Taft was afraid, he wrote, that the meeting might get into the newspapers and that "it would be assumed we had come together for reactionary political purposes." Mr. Davison had given assurance, though, "that the matter will not be public." [39] The conference was held on the Aldrich yacht during a sail from New York to the former senator's country place in Rhode Island. Aldrich was to write an article on the currency situation and they discussed this on the trip. Taft was duly impressed by the magnificence of the estate on Narragansett Bay. He was invited to plant an elm tree, which he did. Aldrich pointed out to Taft another elm, planted by Roosevelt in the days when Big Business was inclined to regard him with favor.

"Aldrich told me that Morgan told him that he would like . . . an opportunity to cut that down with an ax."

The excursion and other influences convinced Taft that the President could not possibly succeed in his fight for a Federal Reserve System. He would "injure business and for a poor banking system give us a worse one. . . . In every measure he shows

[37] Taft to J. R. Mann, July 22, 1913. [38] Taft to H. A. Wolfe, Aug. 27, 1913. [39] Taft to Mabel Boardman, Oct. 8, 1913.

SINCERE SOLICITUDE.

Cartoon by C. K. Berryman, Courtesy Washington Star

See page 888]

Taft: "The little darling—he doesn't mean it."

Cartoon by Marcus, Courtesy New York Times

[See page 949

that schoolmaster's disposition of knowing it all and of avoiding any information from sources that he regards in the slightest degree antagonistic to him or prejudiced." [40]

Similarly, the tariff; for a man who had boasted during the Payne-Aldrich debates that he stood for reduction, Taft was showing himself very rigidly a protectionist as the administration sought to cut the rates. Prosperity would be halted, he warned. But there was a bright side to it. The disaster certain to follow would throw the Democrats out of power and bring back salutary Republican rule. [41]

Taft viewed Wilson with combined disapproval and envy. The President was "as much of an opportunist as anybody we have had in the White House." [42] The President "plays politics every minute, quite as much as our friend D'Artagnan [Roosevelt] did." But Taft paid frank tribute to Wilsonian qualities he never, himself, possessed.

"The use of the Washington correspondents by this administration has been masterly and . . . moves me to say that Theodore is not the only pebble on the beach in the use of the press. It shows a keenness of the use of political instruments and an ability in this direction that rouses my very great admiration, however much it may break the ideal that so many people have formed of Woodrow's character." [43]

By the end of 1913, Taft admitted that Wilson was "on the top of the wave . . . having secured the passage of the currency bill and the tariff bill, and he must be enjoying a Merry Christmas. I don't grudge it. . . . I cannot say that my opinion of him as a man has improved, though my opinion of him as a shrewd politician has grown greatly." [44] Wilson had erred, of course, and greatly: he had injured the civil service and the standing of the diplomatic corps. His Mexican policy had been wholly bad. But Taft would "very much prefer to have him continue and be reelected, than to incur any danger at all of Roosevelt's success." [45]

His personal relations with the President, although most infrequent, were cordial. Wilson had asked Taft to serve as chairman

[40] Taft to R. A. Taft, Nov. 20, 1913. [41] Taft to Marshall Bullitt, April 6, 1913; to H. C. Lodge, April 24, 1913. [42] Taft to Horace Taft, April 18, 1913. [43] Taft to Root, Nov. 8, 1913. [44] Taft to Mabel Boardman, Dec. 27, 1913. [45] Taft to W. L. Fisher, Jan. 3, 1914.

of the Lincoln Memorial Commission, charged with the duty of erecting the lovely shrine which now graces Washington. He went to the capital from time to time in connection with this project. In March, 1914, he had lunch at the White House and decided he had never seen the President "looking stronger and better." Root was there. They had discussed various matters of state. Wilson had been "very pleasant, as Root was, and I quite enjoyed the luncheon." [46]

[46] Taft to Karger, March 3, 1914.

CHAPTER XLV

GUNS FROM AFAR

BY FEBRUARY, 1915, the World War had been raging for more than half a year. Belgium had been occupied. The dull, bloody monotony of trench fighting had started and nobody believed any longer that it would be a short war and a gay one. To Taft, who had dreamed of world peace in the White House but had seen his arbitration treaties wrecked by the Senate, the European conflict was a sickening and disheartening shock. To Woodrow Wilson, whose own dream of peace was still unborn, the war meant the end of his domestic program and the death of his New Freedom.

On February 25 the President's secretary, Joseph P. Tumulty, showed Mr. Wilson a clipping from the New York *World*. It was an account of an address made by Taft at Morristown, New Jersey.

"We must abide," he had said, "by the judgment of those to whom we have intrusted the authority, and when the President shall act, we must stand by him to the end. . . . All will forget their differences in self-sacrificing loyalty to our common flag and our common country." [1]

Wilson was already aware that the differences would not be forgotten and that Theodore Roosevelt, among others, would be vindictively critical of everything he did. He glanced at the newspaper account of his predecessor's pledge of loyalty.

"This is certainly fine and generous," he wrote at the bottom of Tumulty's memorandum which accompanied it.

Correspondent Karger of the Cincinnati *Times-Star* dropped in on the President's secretary that day and was shown the note. He was presented with the document and prepared to send it to Taft. First, however, he let Senator Lodge see it. Lodge read the President's memorandum.

"Yes, too damned fine and generous," was his sour comment.

[1] New York *World*, Feb. 23, 1915.

But Counselor Robert Lansing of the State Department, one day to be secretary of state, disagreed with Lodge. Taft's position, he said, had "created an American policy. It has made the administration's policy an American policy." [2]

In the chancelleries of Europe there had been warnings enough in 1914 that a war might break out. But the United States was almost totally unaware of the danger. And so was Woodrow Wilson. As recently as July 24, 1914, he had sent to the Senate an additional score of the Bryan peace treaties. The President had been encouraged, too, by increasing stability in Mexico. On August 2, when the barrage of ultimatums had crashed across Europe, Wilson still called it "this incredible European catastrophe." [3] Soon it was all too credible. On August 4 formal tenders of good offices went from Washington to the belligerents and were acknowledged with sardonic expressions of appreciation. Two days later, Wilson called for neutrality and amplified this, a fortnight later, with a plea that the United States "must be neutral in fact as well as in name." [4]

With all of this, Taft prayerfully agreed. The jovial former President was not without influence upon his countrymen. The people had discovered that Taft was no mere deceased politician. He was, instead, a very vocal guide, an amiable and often wise counselor at large. He talked a lot, but he made sense. The New York *World* contrasted him with Roosevelt whom Taft had "succeeded . . . in the public ear and eye" as he had "succeeded the Colonel in Washington." The editor continued:

From the lips of this genial tourist, counsel flows golden and widely diversified. The nation is told how long it must keep the Philippines. Schoolgirls are warned to acquire the means of self support and not to rush blindly into handicapping marriage. The state is informed of the perils of initiative, referendum and recall. College boys hear of the high purpose of higher education. Local option is commended over and above prohibition. . . .

We are glad that Mr. Taft takes so readily and without mischievousness to the task of showing that there really is no such question as that of what to do with our ex-Presidents. His way is quite

[2] Karger to Taft, Feb. 25, 1915. [3] Baker, R. S., *Woodrow Wilson, Life and Letters*, Vol. IV, pp. 460-461. [4] Sullivan, Mark, *Our Times*, Vol. V, pp. 40-44.

opposite to that of the colonel, who raised torrentially for a time the query as to what he might do with us.

The professor from New Haven is a friendly and generally optimistic counselor. Whether we take his advice or not, we are always inclined to take him kindly. In the public esteem, as in avoirdupois, he bulks large.[5]

—2—

Taft was resting at Murray Bay when the first reports of war came. On July 28 Austria-Hungary declared war on Serbia; it was certain that Germany would march against Russia. To Taft, as to Wilson, it was all incredible. It was doubly so at distant, remote and peaceful Murray Bay. It was deplorable, Taft said when the newspapers asked him for a statement, that war should occur "when all good people have been hoping that the sentiment in favor of peace was growing. . . . All we can do now is to hope that those responsible for the foreign policy of Russia and Germany will . . . localize the trouble, so that we shall not have a general European war . . . its actual coming is unthinkable." [6]

Taft's horror increased as the days passed and the armies of the world went into action. "Nothing like it has occurred since the great Napoleonic Wars . . . nothing has occurred like it since the world began," he wrote. "It is a cataclysm. It is a retrograde step in Christian civilization." At first the gentle jurist could discern no possible good in the conflict. Later, in common with the rest of those who sympathized with the Allies, he would regard it as a struggle against autocracy. As it began, he could see only that the commerce of all the nations, including the United States, would be destroyed. True, a few American industries might be expanded into "feverish activity . . . but on the whole we shall suffer with the rest of the world, except that we shall not be destroying our existing wealth or sacrificing the lives of our best young men."

From the shelter of Murray Bay, Taft looked out with prophetic vision. The "loss to the conqueror," he thought, would be "only less, if indeed it be less, than the loss to the conquered. With a high patriotic spirit, people enter upon war with confidence and with

[5] New York *World*, Jan. 25, 1915. [6] Statement by Taft, July 29, 1914.

the thought of martial glory and success. The sacrifices they have to make . . . are generally such that if victory does not rest upon their banners, they seek a scapegoat . . . in the head of the state, and the King or Emperor who begins a war . . . puts at stake . . . the stability and integrity of his dynasty." [7]

On August 6, 1914, word reached Murray Bay that Mrs. Wilson, long ill, had died. Taft had sent a message of heartfelt condolence.[8] For he knew, better than any other man, the depth of the President's loss and grief. He, too, when Mrs. Taft had been stricken in the White House, had faced the possibility of the loss of his consort.

"I know . . . something of the strain and responsibility of office with private anxiety and sorrow," Taft told Mabel Boardman. "Mrs. Wilson was a very sweet woman and offered an antidote to his [Wilson's] somewhat angular disregard of other people's feelings. . . . The White House will seem very solitary to him without her, for . . . there is a splendid isolation about it that makes sorrow keener." [9]

Taft pored over his newspapers and obtained what information he could from the vague, inaccurate dispatches on the war. As August ended, he had swung to the conclusion that "Germany will be beaten and that militarism will receive a blow." Austria might have "initiated the war on the surface" but "I think William was behind it all the time." [10]

Roosevelt, meanwhile, was watching the war with the delight and appreciation of a professional soldier. He would soon be insisting that President Wilson had been supine in failing to go to the rescue of Belgium. As the war opened, though, he defended Germany's course.

"When giants are engaged in a death struggle," he wrote, "as they reel to and fro they are certain to trample on whomever gets in the way." [11]

In contrast, Taft was publicly silent. "I have some very definite views," he wrote. But it was "our business to maintain neutrality as far as we possibly can." [12] In contrast, too, he saw no justification

[7] Taft to Hamilton Holt, Aug. 2, 1914. [8] Taft to Wilson, Aug. 6, 7, 1914. [9] Taft to Mabel Boardman, Aug. 10, 1914. [10] Taft to E. W. White, Aug. 25, 1914; to Karger, Sept. 11, 1914. [11] Pringle, H. F., *Theodore Roosevelt, a Biography*, p. 579. [12] Taft to C. W. Baker, Sept. 19, 1914.

for the invasion of Belgium. It would forever be a stain on "the escutcheon of Germany." [13] Yet he was fair too. "It does seem," he concluded, "as if Belgium suffered from both her friends and her enemies . . . I would think that England might very well waive the danger of the use of food supplies going into Germany by Belgium in order to help the people of that ill-fated state." [14]

The President of the United States had learned, meanwhile, that the gods of war, like nature, abhor a vacuum. The vacuum of neutrality, Mr. Wilson found, was almost impossible to preserve. Great Britain greatly expanded the definition of war contraband. She became suspicious, not without grounds, of numerous American export houses and assumed they were doing business with Germany. That England was violating accepted international law was obvious. American vessels were illegally searched, illegally seized. Then Germany, in January, 1915, declared the waters surrounding the British Isles to be a war zone and the submarine menace arose.

Taft's chief interest, during these trying months, was the preservation of American neutrality and the avoidance of entanglement. The more theoretical peace advocates suggested a ban on the shipment of arms to all belligerents. But Taft saw that this would benefit Germany and vitally wound England; it was not an act of neutrality.[15]

Unlike Roosevelt and Cabot Lodge, who were rapidly assuming leadership of the American war party, Taft continued to pray for peace. He could not conceive that Germany desired friction with the United States, although he granted that "we cannot afford to have Germany violate international law and acquiesce in it."

"I am quite sure," he wrote, "that neither Bryan nor Wilson desires war, and therefore I am sure that they will do what they can to avoid it. . . . I think the communications that have been sent are dignified and forcible." [16]

"Lodge and Roosevelt," he concluded, "would get us into war if they could." [17]

[13] Taft to George Washburn, Oct. 12, 1914. [14] Taft to Marburg, Dec. 22, 1914. [15] Taft to Edmund von Mach, Jan. 26, 1915. [16] Taft to Mabel Boardman, Feb. 16, 1915. [17] Taft to Karger, Feb. 28, 1915.

874 THE LIFE AND TIMES OF WILLIAM HOWARD TAFT

—3—

Roosevelt's anger was soon at white heat. He told Sir Cecil Spring Rice, by now British ambassador to the United States, that he was "bitterly humiliated at what this administration has done. I am not merely humiliated but profoundly angered by the attitude of the professional German-Americans. . . . We are not an alert people. We do not understand foreign affairs and, when a President misleads us, as Wilson has done, some very good people tend to follow him; but I believe . . . that down at the bottom this people is sound." [18]

Down at the bottom, as the campaign of 1916 would prove, the American people did not want war. Wilson and Taft, the future would prove, were closer to the convictions of the American people than Theodore Roosevelt. Spring Rice, too, agreed that the vast majority were determined not to be drawn in. On a visit to New York, he reported, Wilson had been received with acclaim greater than that accorded to any president in years.[19]

Even the sinking of the *Lusitania,* while it outraged public sentiment and greatly increased the strength of the war party, was not enough to bring a demand for war with Germany. The German embassy at Washington had published warnings on May 1 that ships carrying the flag of Great Britain, or of any of her allies, were liable to destruction. But this did not keep over 1,200 passengers from embarking on the *Lusitania.* The liner was off the coast of Ireland on the Morning of Friday, May 7. Just after two o'clock that afternoon she was hit by a torpedo and sank swiftly. Only 726 of the 1,924 men and women aboard were saved and among the lost were 63 pitiful babies and children. The Americans killed numbered 114.[20]

Taft, of course, was appalled when he heard the news. " 'Whom the Gods wish to destroy, they first make mad,' " he quoted in a note of condolence to Melville Stone of the Associated Press whose son was among the victims. "The ruthless spirit of inhumanity

18 Gwynn, Stephen, *The Letters and Friendships of Sir Cecil Spring Rice,* Vol. II, p. 251. 19 Gwynn, Stephen, *op. cit.,* Vol. II, p. 268. 20 Sullivan, Mark, *op. cit.,* Vol. V, pp. 109-114.

which led to the tragedy, I need not comment on . . . and the punishment which Germany will have to suffer for this eventually will be commensurate." [21]

However awful the crime, Taft felt, it still did not justify war against Germany. Roosevelt called it "murder on the high seas," demanded seizure of all German ships in American waters and a ban on commerce with the guilty nation.[22] Once again, the contrast between Roosevelt and Taft may be noted. The former was utterly certain that he, among all men, was best fitted to be president and best qualified to act wisely in this or any other crisis. Taft continued to watch with sympathy and understanding the torment of the man who had succeeded him.

"I sincerely hope that President Wilson will save us from war," he wrote. "It seems to me that Wickersham and Roosevelt made asses of themselves and were most boyish in yielding to the passionate expressions that they uttered. I have been president, and I know what an awful responsibility a man has to carry in such a crisis and how trying such blatherskiting is when a man is trying to find the right way." [23]

The right way, to Woodrow Wilson, was not war with Germany. But Colonel Edward M. House, the President's closest adviser, who was in London when the *Lusitania* was destroyed, could see no other solution ". . . unless Germany promises to cease her policy of making war upon noncombatants."

"If you do not call her to account over the loss of American lives caused by the sinking of the *Lusitania,*" he told the President, "her next act will probably be the sinking of an American liner." House received no word as to Wilson's policy until the case was six days old. He was repelled when he heard that the President had offered the doctrine that a nation might be too proud to fight.[24]

The historic phrase was in a speech made in Philadelphia on May 10. Wilson did not mention the tragedy off the Irish coast.

"The example of America," he said as he closed, "must be the example not merely of peace because it will not fight, but of peace because peace is the healing and elevating influence of the world

---

[21] Taft to Melville Stone, May 11, 1915. [22] Pringle, H. F., *op. cit.,* p. 583. [23] Taft to Mabel Boardman, May 10, 1915; to C. H. Kelsey, May 15, 1915. [24] Seymour, Charles, *The Intimate Papers of Colonel House,* Vol. I, pp. 433-438.

and strife is not. There is such a thing as a nation being so right that it doesn't need to convince others by force that it is right. . . . There is such a thing as a man being too proud to fight." [25]

All this Taft watched— and approved in almost every detail. On May 10, 1915, as Wilson prepared to make his Philadelphia speech, the former President had dictated a letter to his successor. He was led to do so, he told Wilson, by the "heavy weight of responsibility that has fallen on you, in view of the *Lusitania* disaster." He was anxious "to express, in a deeply sympathetic way, my appreciation of the difficult situation which you face." Taft continued:

> It seems to me that it is the duty of every thoughtful, patriotic citizen to avoid embarrassing you in your judgment and not to yield to the impulse of deep indignation which the circumstances naturally arouse, and demand at once a resort to extreme measures which mean war. It may be that the attitude of Germany will ultimately require us . . . to join the Allies. . . .
>
> But have we reached that point yet? War is a dreadful thing. It would involve such enormous cost of life and treasure for us that if it can now be avoided, in a manner consistent with the dignity and honor of our country, we should make every effort to this end.

Was there no alternative, Taft asked, between a mere protest to Germany and the summoning of Congress to declare war? He granted that Germany's "bold assertion to the . . . unheard-of rights of a belligerent in the use of mines, torpedoes and submarines" caused a protest to "seem to be hardly more than an acquiescence." With all respect, then, Taft offered a plan:

> Could you not . . . on the ground that you wish to sever diplomatic relations with a power conducting war in a manner so utterly inhumane, withdraw our ambassador from Berlin and give would certainly give force to your protest. But it would not necessarily involve us in war. Such a severing of relations has precedents to the German ambassador in Washington his passports? That in which war did not result. Germany in her madness might insist on making this a *casus belli*. I doubt if she would. Of course if

[25] Sullivan, Mark, *op. cit.*, Vol. V, p. 125.

she did, war could not be avoided. . . . You might then await the meeting of Congress in December and submit the situation . . . for its action. The country meantime would have a chance to recover its calm and consider the *pros* and *cons* before Congress meets. Of course I am not in a position to measure the disadvantage we would sustain by thus cutting off diplomatic relations. But I can not think it would be very burdensome.

A special session of Congress, Taft believed, would probably mean war; the plan he had suggested might bring delay, and time was "a great solvent of many of these troubles." He concluded the communication to Wilson:

You have able counselors about you, and these suggestions of mine of course are made without the study which they have been able to give. Perhaps reasons will occur to you for rejecting at once what I have suggested, but, even so, I am glad to have the opportunity for expressing to you my confidence that you will take the wise and patriotic course and that you will avoid war, if it is possible. If you see no other course open than now to summon Congress and declare war, of course the whole people will be with you without regard to party.

With earnest prayer that you may good deliverance make, believe me, my dear Mr. President.

The President was warm and grateful in his reply, written three days later. The whole nation admired as he did, Wilson said, Taft's generous spirit in submerging party differences and coming to the administration's support. As for the proposed plan to sever diplomatic relations— here Wilson was less direct. It would receive his most serious thought. All the light he could get was welcome, as it would have been to Taft under similar circumstances. He hoped and prayed for a successful solution.

Wilson was far from ready for the role of war lord. ". . . impartial mediation is the most cherished ambition of the President, who rightly thinks that he would thereby do an imperishable service to humanity," observed Ambassador Spring Rice.[26]

The President did not send von Bernstoff packing. He did not recall Gerard from Berlin. Instead, he began the series of notes

[26] Gwynn, Stephen, *op. cit.*, Vol. II, p. 247.

which were exchanged with the German government for twelve long months. It was not until April, 1916, that anything approaching an ultimatum was drafted by Wilson; meanwhile American citizens continued to die on torpedoed ships. In May, Germany promised, with certain reservations, that merchant vessels offering no resistance would not be sunk without warning. For nine months, the pledge was observed.[27]

Taft had no pride of authorship in the plan he had offered Wilson. Until the 1916 presidential campaign had warped his impartiality he continued to pledge support. The first of Wilson's notes was dispatched to Berlin on May 13, 1915, and Taft said it was "admirable in tone . . . it may well call for our earnest concurrence and confirmation." [28]

Two days earlier, but following the "too proud to fight" phrase, Taft addressed the Union League Club of Philadelphia. He had prepared the speech on the train. He was "a little uncertain whether I ought to deliver it or not, but . . . I concluded to let it go. It is a great deal more important in cases like this to allay public excitement than to give passionate expression to a sense of wrong." [29] So Taft's words were conciliatory. Both the principal belligerents, he said, had "announced policies with respect to the trade and rights of neutrals that are contrary to heretofore accepted principles of international law." True, Germany was the worst offender. Her conduct was inhumane, "but in the heat of even just indignation is not the best time to act."

It was the President of the United States, Taft said, upon whom rested, under the Constitution, the burden of foreign affairs and often of war. And so, "every president with respect for his oath, and the rule of the people, will in moments of popular excitement and just indignation pointing to war, act as a brake— will caution against haste, will hunt for some escape. . . .

"A demand for war that cannot survive the passion of the first days of public indignation and will not endure the test of delay . . . is one that should not be yielded to. Look back on our history and answer me if the resistance of presidents to the demands of the extremists for war has not earned for them, in historical re-

[27] Sullivan, Mark, op. cit., Vol. V, pp. 126-132. [28] Seymour, Charles, op. cit., Vol. I, p. 439. [29] Taft to Karger, May 15, 1915.

view, the gratitude of their country. Is it remembered now to the discredit of Washington that he kept us out of war with England, or of Grant, that he kept us out of war with Spain in the Virginius affair, or of McKinley that he struggled so hard against just such warlike expressions as we hear now, to keep us out of the war with Spain?" [30]

Taft's mind did not often dwell on the parallels of history. Was he thinking, as he spoke, that Theodore Roosevelt had been among the most strident voices calling for war with Spain? A few weeks later, on June 4, 1915, at Bryn Mawr College, Taft would say: "If we had a jingo in the White House this country would now be at war with Germany. Instead, our Chief Executive is a man who appreciates his responsibility." [31]

Did Taft remember, as he finished his Union League Club speech, the night of November 16, 1912, when he had found it possible to accept defeat and had offered a graceful valedictory to the Lotos Club of New York? Then he had asked for a toast to President-elect Wilson; he had been thinking, that night, of the burdens so soon to be carried by his successor. The burdens were now greater, infinitely greater, than had seemed possible. Taft's mind was on the White House as he concluded his talk in Philadelphia.

"The task of the President is a heavy one," he said. "He is our President. He is acting for the whole country. He is anxious to find a way out of the present difficulty without war. Before party, before ourselves, we . . . are for our country. That is what he is working for. Shall we not stand by in this work?"

Even the Republicans of Philadelphia's Union League Club were moved and the applause was heavy. "We shall!" called a voice in answer to Taft's rhetorical question.

"Let us stand by him in this juncture," repeated Taft earnestly. "Our honor is safe with him. I give you the toast, 'The President of the United States.' " [32]

[30] *Addresses,* Vol. XXXIV, pp. 327-330.   [31] New York *Times,* June 5, 1915.
[32] *Addresses,* Vol. XXXIV, pp. 330-331.

—4—

Before very long, as Wilson's protests to Germany became more emphatic, Secretary of State Bryan resigned in protest and went forth, a somewhat lugubrious prince of peace, to warn his countrymen against approaching war. Bryan was laughed at, as always. Cartoonists and editorial writers jeered at him. "Bryan as usual is an ass, but he is an ass with a good deal of opportunity for mischief," declared Taft.[33] But in the light of history the position Bryan took in June, 1915, is something less than idiotic. It is no longer certain that the Allies were the holy guardians of Right in the World War and the Central Powers the wicked proponents of Wrong. War guilt, the scholars have shown, is at least debatable. Bryan urged an edict against Americans on belligerent vessels. All export of munitions from the United States should be forbidden, he said. These were suggestions to be advanced by President Franklin D. Roosevelt after more than two decades had passed and another war threatened.

By the spring of 1916, Taft was less open in his endorsements of the Wilson war program. He regarded the administration as a colossal failure, on the whole. Its domestic program was far too radical. Wilson, he was sure, had surrendered to labor. He had bungled the Mexican situation too. With the bad sportsmanship which is characteristic of the political mind, the Democrats were using Taft's pleas to stand behind Wilson on the World War to embarrass him and his fellow Republicans.[34] So Taft declared that the administration's preparedness program was inadequate. He urged compulsory universal military training.[35] He agreed to write an article for the October issue of the *Yale Review* in which he reviewed all phases of Wilson's years at Washington. This time Taft forgot his earlier admission that the President, surrounded by able counselors, was in the best position to decide what should be done in the European crisis. Wilson, he wrote, had been dila-

[33] Taft to C. P. Taft, June 12, 1915. [34] *What Taft Thinks of Wilson*, political pamphlet, 1916 campaign. [35] Taft to P. J. Roosevelt, May 15, 1916; to W. H. Cowles, June 6, 1916.

tory following the sinking of the *Lusitania* and had "exposed this country to the charge of weakness and vacillation. . . .

"It was the duty of the President to withhold action until a reasonable time was given for a clear perception of the issue. . . . His allowing the discussion to drag along for a year, however, subjected the nation to additional humiliation in the sinking of other ships and the drowning of other Americans. If within one month . . . avowal or disavowal had been exacted from Germany, as it was later, by a threat of severance of diplomatic relations in case of an avowal, we should have been in a much better position than we are today. The proneness of the administration to write a note well and appropriately phrased, and to deem the incident closed, has exposed the nation to ridicule. The administration cannot say that it has thus kept us out of war, for it has itself demonstrated by the result of the ultimate demand that it might earlier have secured the same result without the loss of prestige and the actual loss of lives which the delay has entailed. . . .

"In the last three years, I have squared my conduct to my conviction that . . . we should forget party and support the President in a critical juncture. . . . But it is absurd to say that when the question is whether we shall continue the President as the guide of our international policies, we may not properly discuss and criticize in all its details his conduct of our foreign relations." [36]

[36] *Addresses,* Vol. XXXVII, pp. 162-163.

CHAPTER XLVI

DANGER OF RESURRECTION

THE FORMER President of the United States must have been amused, in February of 1914, when he read a letter from a friend in Seattle:

Last year when Lincoln's birthday came around, the superintendent of the grade schools in San Francisco was in one of the schools in the Italian quarter and said, "I want you all to write what you know about our martyred President. Of course you all know who he is." When the essays came in the principal was surprised to find that nearly all of them began "Our martyred President, William Howard Taft." [1]

Taft had no real desire for political resurrection. Yet he was never permitted to lie wholly quietly in the pleasant, comfortable grave which the 1912 campaign had provided him. The votes had hardly been counted when he started to discount reports that he might be a candidate in 1916.[2] Yet Taft was sometimes momentarily tempted to re-enter politics. He gave serious consideration to a suggestion that he stand for Congress from the New Haven district of Connecticut: ". . . the only possible motive I might have," he explained, "was in promoting the cause of judicial procedure. . . . If I could get on the Judiciary Committee in the House, I believe I might make a fuss on the subject."

The Congressional boom, which was brief, started in jest. It was June, 1914. Max Pam, a fairly close friend of Taft's, and Hilles chanced to be in New Haven and they discussed the approaching Congressional campaign. Colonel Isaac Ullman, a corset manufacturer and also the Republican political boss of New Haven, wanted to know whether Taft could suggest a good man to make the race for that district.

[1] Erastus Brainerd to Taft, Feb. 14, 1914. [2] Taft to J. W. Hill, Nov. 10, 1912.

"In a jocular way," Taft reported, "I suggested to them the wisdom of my coming to Congress. They both turned it down with a thump, which quite met my view. . . . What was my surprise . . . to have a telephone call from Max Pam to say that he and Hilles . . . had had a conference and had concluded that the suggestion . . . was a most pregnant one." [3]

Behind the plan to transform former President Taft into Representative Taft of Connecticut was a notion that thereby he would remain in the public eye and be increasingly eligible for the presidential nomination two years away. Taft reacted against this with the honest clarity so characteristic of his normal mind:

A man never goes through four years in the presidency, such as I did, without confidence that if he were given another opportunity, he could avoid certain mistakes and could render greater service, after his experience, than he did the first time; and naturally, therefore, if he could get over the awful agony of a campaign, or of two campaigns, he might enjoy trying a practiced hand in bringing relief to what I must call a "harried" country, by insisting upon a respite from experimental, restrictive legislation, and a campaign of hostility against the sources of comfort and happiness and of real progress. But when I consider it from a personal standpoint, and count over the circumstances that make it an impossibility, I think I succeed in putting away any such dream from me and in avoiding unhappiness by either thoughts or efforts.

Taft looked at both sides of the question. He was confident that a reaction against Wilson had begun. An element among the voters was open-minded toward a second term, he felt, because it believed he had been unjustly treated by Roosevelt, "because they think I have proved to be a good loser and have conducted myself sensibly since the election." There was a dearth of suitable candidates; these factors led to the possibility that "the Republicans may turn to me as the only possible solution." But there was another side. The masses still were poisoned by the attacks of Roosevelt, Bryan, the Progressives and such newspapers as the Chicago *Tribune* and the Kansas City *Star*. As a presidential candidate, moreover, he would be opposed by the prohibitionists, the bigoted

[3] Taft to Mabel Boardman, June 27, 1914.

Protestants, who accused him of Catholic leanings, and by the old-line bosses. So if he went to Congress, Taft concluded, it would be with no belief whatever that greater things lay beyond. He would, as always, consult his brothers.[4]

By mid-August he had decided that he would not run. "You will acquit me," he said, "of any false pride which would prevent my accepting an office like that of representative when I have already been president. That does not play the slightest part with me." But his candidacy would be principally interpreted as a bid to get back into politics. He was happy at Yale. He hoped and thought that he was doing some good.

"I think I have been in the public eye long enough," he wrote, "and whatever I think on this subject, a great many people think so."

A final reason was a major one: Mrs. Taft was happy in New Haven and had been greatly benefited by the quiet life. A campaign might "disturb the even flow and happiness of her existence."[5]

—2—

How could Wilsonism with all its evils be defeated in 1916? Where was the standard-bearer who could lead to victory? Taft's choice, from the start, appears to have been Associate Justice Hughes. But, he feared, "the Hughes talk is absurd, because Hughes would not permit himself to accept a nomination."[6] The outlook was not too hopeful for 1916. "I am bound to say," Taft lamented, "that the material for the presidency available to the Republicans is not of a reassuring kind. Borah and Cummins and LaFollette don't commend themselves to me for anything. If Hughes could be taken, he would . . . be elected . . . but Hughes's . . . desire to regard his accession to the bench as the taking of a vow against a personal political future is so worthy of approval and encouragement that I should think him out of the question. But the Lord works these things out better than we poor mortals."[7]

In the end the Lord, ably assisted by delegates to the Republican National Convention, would overcome Hughes's scruples and he

[4] Taft to Hilles, July 20, 1914. [5] Taft to Pam and Egan, Aug. 15, 1914. [6] Taft to Hilles, Aug. 23, 1913. [7] Taft to W. L. Fisher, Jan. 3, 1914.

would run. Meanwhile, who else? There was, of course, the astonishing Root whose capabilities for the office were beyond question. "Root would delight me," Taft said. Yet Root would be "seventy-two or seventy-three when the nomination came to be made, and he would be far too old to stand the strain of the campaign and the office. More than that, however, unjustly, Root's professional relations would be used against him to injure him." [8] As always, Root would have none of it. Taft had written to congratulate him on the award of the Nobel Peace Prize and the senator expressed appreciation for this.

"Also for the presidential boom which you and Carnegie and other millionaires swing at me," he added in a postscript. "I have avoided being knocked off the boat by ducking." [9]

As time passed, Taft grew more hopeful that Hughes might make the race. It is not clear whether he originated the strategy by which this result ultimately was achieved. Taft probably conferred with the G.O.P. leaders about it. The best plan, he thought, was "to let all these little fellows scheme for the nomination. When I say 'little fellows' I mean fellows like Whitman in New York, Willis in Ohio, and Borah in Idaho, and Cummins in Iowa and Hadley in Missouri, and after this day of small things has impressed itself on the assembled convention, there will be a yearning for a big man . . . and we can then secure a unanimous nomination from the convention for Hughes. I think he can hardly resist that call."

Taft had, in fact, called on Chief Justice White for a hint as to the attitude of Justice Hughes: ". . . he told me he thought that Hughes would yield," Taft reported. He thought that the reason "he did not yield in 1912 was that he did not think that the party could elect a candidate. I like to think also that he was moved to some degree by his loyalty to me. I would have been glad to turn the nomination over to him if I could have delivered it. . . . I think we can control this matter. We cannot consult Hughes, because he would decline in advance, probably, and we must make it apparent that it will become a duty on his part to unite a party whose existence and victory are necessary to the good of the country. It

[8] Taft to Felix Agnus, Dec. 17, 1913; to Knox, Dec. 18, 1913. [9] Root to Taft, Dec. 18, 1913.

would flatten out Rooseveltism, would bring in all the Progressives because they could so easily regard Hughes as a Progressive."

Taft admitted that Hughes entertained a few "Progressive notions," but the associate justice was not fatally poisoned by that virus. He was "sound on the courts, and he would not injure the governmental structure in any way. He is a good administrator, and a very able man." [10]

The talk about Hughes did not entirely end the talk about Taft. Continuing to disparage it, he still did not close and seal the door. The thought persisted that "I could do better a second time." If the prize came to him without effort on his part or that of his friends, "I would not decline. . . . If it does come, it must be because the convention can find no one else." [11]

But eight months later, in October, 1915, Taft did not even dream of it longer.

"My candidacy is resting in the tomb where it ought to be," he said and no regret whatever is discernible in his realization of that fact.[12]

—3—

Wilson's first major political hurdle was the Congressional election of 1914 and Taft, watching eagerly, prayed that it would constitute a setback for Democracy. He had small use, if any, for the President's domestic program and increasingly less for his character and personality. His analysis of Wilson, as the Congressional campaign got under way, was exceedingly harsh. To Karger of the Cincinnati *Times-Star,* he wrote:

I think Wilson must be a remarkable man in being able to tell you correspondents things that you know not to be true and still retain an influence over you. He had not the slightest hesitation in saying that white is black . . . he out-Teddys Teddy. He never argues with you— he just tells you. He is a peculiar man. He really seems to think that by the most emphatic assertion, with unction and elaboration, he can make prosperity out of hard times . . . can make leading business men think they are being helped by legisla-

[10] Taft to Mabel Boardman, Nov. 9, 1914. [11] Taft to Felix Agnus, Feb. 9, 1915. [12] Taft to Hemphill, Oct. 9, 1915.

tion directed against their legitimate freedom, can make the people believe that he is more to be pitied than the seventeen or eighteen marines who were shot at Vera Cruz, and is suffering greater torment than their relatives, can convince people who are paying higher prices for meat and all the necessities of life, that the "New Freedom" has been successful and many other absurdities that would seem to be so palpable that children could recognize them.[13]

During his first year of private life Taft had tried valiantly to be fair and had, to a large degree, succeeded. By the fall of 1914 he was— save only on the vital issue of peace— partisanship personified. The administration was "surrendering everything to Gompers. . . . I don't know that we have a right to complain, because the Democratic party has boldly avowed its desire to make labor unions a favored class, and we are getting a dose of what a Democratic victory logically means." [14]

The truth was that Wilson's accomplishments in two years had been very real. He had put through the Federal Reserve System. The Federal Trade Commission had been established. The farmers had been benefited by a Farm Loan act. The Sherman act had been strengthened by the Clayton act. Labor would soon be provided with an eight-hour day on the railroads and already enjoyed, on the sea, the provisions of the LaFollette act. The tariff, of course, had been slashed. Wilson could go to the people, for the 1914 elections, with a record of vital legislation effected.[15]

But only two things apparently mattered to Taft: a setback for Democracy and further proof that Roosevelt's strength was waning. "Party solidarity is necessary in this country," he kept reiterating, "and especially to maintain principle in legislation and policy in government." Taft balked at very little in advancing this cause, which was almost holy to him. So he argued, during that fall of 1914 on behalf of Boies Penrose:

. . . not only would I vote for Penrose, but I am sincerely hopeful of his election. I don't think any Republican in Pennsylvania who is a real Republican, and in favor of Republican principles, can vote any other way. Penrose is an able man. He is a machine

[13] Taft to Karger, July 20, 1914. [14] Taft to Root, Sept. 16, 1914. [15] Sullivan, Mark, *Our Times*, Vol. V, pp. 35-37.

man and has acted as a boss. But so have other men and there are other bosses, and if you exclude them from the list of men for whom you will vote, you will not vote for your principle at all.[16]

So, too, with Warren Harding, who was running for the Senate in Ohio. He was, Taft declared, "a man of marked ability, of sanity, of much legislative experience, and he is a regular Republican of principle, and not a 'trimmer.' " The election over, and Harding the victor, Taft's congratulations were warm. "You will have a great future before you," he prophesied.[17]

Most anxiously of all, Taft watched the gyrations of Roosevelt as that leader pondered whether the hosts of Armageddon might march again or were merely the phantom troops of a cause that was lost. Roosevelt had no desire to be the commander of a ghostly army. Beveridge and the rest listened in vain for a battle cry. Now, if ever, the Indianian cried in September, 1913, was the time for the clarion call "that will sound from ocean to ocean and which will reassure those who have rallied to his colors." But only silence echoed. Roosevelt sailed for South America where, symbolically, he discovered the River of Doubt.[18]

Taft heard rumors and reveled in them, that Roosevelt's power was waning still more. Dr. Butler of Columbia said that his name was no longer an influence in New York politics. Karger reported this, too, from Washington. To the newspaper correspondent it was pathetic to watch the suppliant Progressives at the feet of their faltering leader and to know that he was debating the best method of deserting them. Karger had no doubt that Roosevelt wanted to be president again. He would run on the Republican ticket if only he could get rid of the Bull Moose whose coat, once so fine and glowing, was now bedraggled.[19] The suppliants should have known that their leader led no longer. The 1912 campaign had just ended when a friend traveled to Oyster Bay and talked of another crusade in 1916.

"The fight is over," Roosevelt said. "We are beaten. There is only one thing to do and that is to go back to the Republican party.

[16] Taft to Hemphill, Oct. 20, 1914. [17] Statement, Oct. 20, 1914; Taft papers, Library of Congress; Taft to Harding, Nov. 10, 1914. [18] Bowers, Claude, *Beveridge and the Progressive Era*, pp. 448-449. [19] Karger to Taft, May 28, 1914.

You can't hold a party like the Progressive party together . . . there are no loaves and fishes." [20]

The campaign of 1914 would be the end. Gifford Pinchot was fighting still, against Penrose for the Senate in Pennsylvania. Senator Clapp of Minnesota was loyal. So were Jim Garfield in Ohio and Hiram Johnson in California. Beveridge, nominated by the Progressives for the Senate, went on the stump to plead against an alliance with the G.O.P. But that was about all. Borah, of course, was with the party; he had never abandoned it and never would.[21] The result of the election was a defection from Democracy in the House of Representatives and in the Senate, but Beveridge was defeated.

Taft was delighted. The election, he said, "seems to relegate the Progressive party and its leaders to innocuous desuetude. I am reconciled to this result." He had listened to the returns in New Haven and "it was a sensation that I had not had for six years to hear anything favorable from an election. I consider that on the whole we could not have had a better result. I don't think it would have been a good thing for the Republicans to have acquired control of the House. It would have relieved Mr. Wilson and his party of responsibility for government." [22]

Taft's elation was greatest when he gazed down on the vanquished Roosevelt who had, in fact, been running for no office at all but whose cohorts had met with sharp reverses. "We have squeezed Roosevelt out, and we can attend to the Democrats in two years," Taft said. "He is a gone-gosling." [23]

Four months later, Taft heard of a visit Roosevelt had made to the Century Club in New York and a description of the Rough Rider as "the loneliest man in the country" who was "struggling to get back somewhere."

"It is very evident," Taft concluded, "that T.R. is taking a running jump back into the party." [24]

When the leap had been negotiated Taft would stretch out, in public, a hand of welcome.

[20] Pringle, H. F., *Theodore Roosevelt, a Biography*, p. 571. [21] Bowers, Claude, *op. cit.*, pp. 449, 453. [22] Statement, Nov. 3, 1914; Taft to Mabel Boardman, Nov. 9, 1914. [23] Taft to M. M. Shoemaker, Nov. 8, 1914. [24] Taft to Helen H. Taft, April 10, 1915.

—4—

"I am very much interested in what you say about Hughes," wrote Taft to Karger in the spring of 1915. "If it is true that he is listening a little more to the buzzing of the bee, I think we can secure his nomination." [25]

This was in answer to Karger's report that Hughes, at a conference with newspapermen, had extravagantly praised the Jews of America. A deduction was drawn from this that political yearnings had finally penetrated the cloister of the Supreme Court.[26] In a fortnight, though, Taft's hopes that Hughes would accept were dashed again. The associate justice declared himself unavailable. Taft concluded that he meant it.[27] "I am quite sure that Justice Hughes will not be a candidate," he concluded in November. "He is not a man who says a thing without meaning it." [28]

Whatever happened, a "regular Republican" who would appeal to the conservative interests of the nation must be selected, Taft insisted. Borah continued to be "impossible. He is as unstable as water. He cannot be trusted to maintain the same opinion between morning and night." [29] The Republican party, as of old, was the fount of all blessings. A correspondent asked Taft to state what the country required to bring back prosperity.

"It needs a return of the Republican party to power," he replied. "That will restore full confidence, and will lead to a return to a proper economic policy, and the two will produce permanent prosperity." [30]

"The hope of the Republican party," Taft concluded as the year turned, "is in the conservative element of the country, and by this I mean the business men." [31]

Taft announced that he would not go to the convention. He declined, after one expression in favor of Root, to make public his preference although, actually, it was still for Hughes. Senator Theodore E. Burton of Ohio, an active contender, was wholly acceptable and there was, Taft said, "not sufficient difference in

[25] Taft to Karger, April 30, 1915. [26] Karger to Taft, April 28, 1915. [27] Taft to Karger, May 10, 1915. [28] Taft to G. V. Howard, Nov. 28, 1915. [29] Taft to M. E. Hay, Aug. 30, 1915. [30] Taft to T. F. Logan, Oct. 5, 1915. [31] Taft to Karger, Jan. 3, 1916.

the capabilities" of Root, Hughes or Burton "to outweigh the consideration of availability." Availability was paramount if Wilsonism was to be defeated.[32]

Roosevelt, in any event, had no chance, Taft decided. He was not ready, as yet, to extend a political olive branch to his adversary of 1912. But Roosevelt was more than willing to forget and forgive; Karger reported, in May, 1916, a conference with the colonel.

"I don't want you gentlemen to print anything about it now," he quoted Roosevelt, "but I hope to get a letter from Will Taft showing that he appreciates the necessities of this occasion. Will Taft is like myself— a man who does not hold animosities."

"I am very much interested and amused," Taft told Karger. "I don't know who is going to get the letter, or what basis there was for Roosevelt's hope that such a letter would come. I never had the slightest idea of writing it. There was a feeler put out to Hilles by a Roosevelt man to see if I would meet the colonel at lunch and, without consulting me, Hilles felt justified, as he was, in pricking that bubble. I did not think the colonel was quite such a rainbow chaser . . . as this conversation seems to indicate."

"I am loath to have it known publicly that I am for Hughes," Taft said at this time.[33] Privately, he was doing everything possible to advance the candidacy of the associate justice. Memory of Hughes as governor of New York was still bitter in the minds of many faithful Republicans. He had been an austere individual with horrid notions of efficiency in government, notions which ruthlessly disregarded necessary rewards for party workers. Taft was confident, in 1916, that these faults no longer marked him.

"I think he has learned a great deal since he was governor . . . and . . . will have more sense and a greater breadth of view," he wrote.[34]

Taft's analysis of Hughes was correct, at least in so far as it related to a greater geniality than during his governorship. After the nomination had been effected in June, he amplified his character sketch of Hughes. Taft was not "entirely sure of his judgment of men, but he has been taught by life at Washington and his experience in Albany the wisdom of keeping on good terms with

[32] Taft to A. B. Hall, May 8, 1916. [33] Karger to Taft, May 10, 1916; Taft to Karger, May 15, 1916. [34] Taft to David Baid, March 6, 1916.

Congress when he needs its co-operation to carry out his policies. . . ."

He is of Welsh blood and the Welsh are as cunning as the Scotch. He is rigid and sounds metallic in matters in which perhaps wiser men would yield a bit, but he is genial, a good fellow, will sit up late into the night drinking Scotch whisky and soda, has a keen sense of humor and is the best campaigner for votes I have ever met. His speeches are fair, without epithet or denunciation. . . . He is not an academic stylist like Wilson, but he is a much harder hitter.[35]

Beveridge and a few others had been hoping against hope that the Progressive party might still survive. By June, 1915, even Beveridge was thoroughly disillusioned. It would, he wrote, have "been a noble thing" if the purpose of the Progressives had been "to establish a great national liberal party. . . . But, as it turned out, the movement was not a genuine one . . . but a mere political maneuver."

And such— Merely a Political Maneuver— must be the epitaph on the tombstone of the once powerful Bull Moose. The conventions of the Progressive party and the Republican party met concurrently in Chicago and the former was a farce. A few among the Progressive delegates still imagined that the Old Guard gathering might, after all, accept Roosevelt. They were curtly informed by Senator Smoot of Utah, representing the Republican convention, that he was the one impossible candidate. So they telegraphed Roosevelt to ask whether a compromise nomination could be made. Consternation swept the convention when Roosevelt suggested, of all people, Henry Cabot Lodge. Lodge! He was cold, unfriendly, conservative to the core. He had remained in the Republican party in 1912. The suggestion of his name was the final insult and, sardonically, the Progressives nominated Roosevelt. His declination was prompt. So ended the battle for the Lord.[36] Roosevelt had sent Lodge's name to the Republican convention as well. There, too, no heed was paid.

Taft was torn between satisfaction that Roosevelt was through and pity for the cruel nature of his political demise.

[35] Taft to Gordon McCabe, June 19, 1916. [36] Bowers, Claude, *op. cit.,* pp. 487-489.

"No vengeful person," he commented, "could be so cruel as to wish any greater humiliation to Roosevelt than that which came to him as the result of his dickering with the two conventions. His suggestion of Lodge's name, so late that he was rejected with scant courtesy by the Republican convention and with ridicule by the Progressive convention, is a circumstance reflecting on the desperate condition of mind in which he was. . . . His suggestion of Lodge at the eleventh hour showed . . . that he was groggy. He is not a good loser. He is a squealer, with all his boasted sportsmanship." [37]

—5—

Naturally, Taft was delighted with the nomination of Hughes and saw in it certainty that "we are going to rally to victory and oust this administration of pretense, opportunism and incompetency." [38] To Hughes he promised active support and begged to be commanded. It was to be a hard fight, but "I cannot doubt the result." [39]

Taft could not, at first, decide whether it would benefit or injure the nominee to have Roosevelt's support. Hughes, he knew, was anxious for it. But a candidate, Taft observed wisely, "is more or less like a woman about to bear a child. He loses, somewhat, his sense of proportion. He may find Roosevelt something of a danger in the campaign if he becomes vociferous. . . . Still, an opposition candidate is not nearly so much embarrassed by a lack of consistency in the reasons that move his supporters as the man in office supposes." [40]

A bridge was being prepared, although Taft was doubtless unaware of it, for the partial reconciliation which marked the closing years between Roosevelt and himself. Taft's position had changed. He was no longer the bewildered, newly elected President who looked in vain for his vanished guide and benefactor. He was no longer the resentful target of Roosevelt's unfair criticisms. He was strong, now, and secure and he could afford to be magnanimous. His mind kept dwelling, during these weeks, on the sad predicament of his fallen foe:

[37] Taft to Karger, June 20, 1916. [38] Taft to R. S. Taylor, June 12, 1916. [39] Taft to Hughes, June 12, 1916. [40] Taft to Gordon McCabe, June 19, 1916.

No one with any pity will wish him the agony of spirit that has been his for the last week, and that will disappear temporarily when he persuades himself that he can lead Hughes's campaign and his administration, only to meet another disappointment when issues come on for settlement after Hughes is presented with the responsibility for action. Ultimately he must cease to occupy the front pages of the newspapers. Then his cup will be full of the bitter draught.

He is the most interesting character in his generation. He has many lovable qualities. I greatly regret that circumstances have made me aware in a trying way of his qualities that are unlovely, but I feel and hope that I can look over the interval of our separation and enjoy the retrospect of a delightful association with so powerful and fascinating a personality. But for the ego that has dimmed his sight, his usefulness to his country, which has been great, could have been greatly expanded; and he would not have been led to some of the evil he has caused by his irresponsible attacks upon the courts and his wild suggestions as to the recall of judicial decisions and of judges.

He is not a real democrat. He has not the spirit that makes him bow to the will of the people. His advocacy of the referendum, recall, general primary and woman suffrage was all the result of a personal relation to politics. He was vigorously opposed to them when I was in his confidence. He is for the people when they follow him and contemptuous of them when they do not. This is part of the Napoleonic phase of his character. The greatest instance of unconscious humor in his marvelous career is his reiterated conviction that he resembles Lincoln. Lincoln is the prototype of much, almost everything, that Roosevelt is not.[41]

The issues of the campaign were made to appear involved. There was a vast amount of talk, on both sides, about prosperity, the Philippines, labor, Mexico, currency and the tariff. Actually, the danger of war was the only major issue and preparedness was the only subsidiary one. President Wilson was shrewd. He put Hughes on the defensive almost from the start. This was a strange predicament for the opposition party, which should have been able to berate and attack.

"... if the Republican party is put into power ..." the Presi-

41 Taft to Gordon McCabe, June 19, 1916.

dent said, "our foreign policy will be radically changed. They say all our present policy is wrong. If it is wrong and they are men of conscience, they must change it; and if they are going to change it, in what direction are they going to change it? There is only one choice against peace and that is war." [42]

Impossibilities faced Hughes on every hand. When he declared for peace, he played into the hands of the Democrats who called him a mere echo. When he called for war he alienated the German-Americans and the other believers in peace. He had to reconcile the two wings of a party torn, a brief four years before, by civil war. On the one hand, he had Roosevelt—who was discredited—working for him. On the other, he had Taft, so overwhelmingly defeated in 1912. If he was friendly to labor he aroused the scorn of the G.O.P. conservatives. If he criticized Wilson's liberal labor policies he reaped the hatred of the unions.

Taft, perhaps more than any other prominent Republican, was aware of these perplexities. "I would rather not make any speeches at all in this campaign," he said, "because I don't know that I can help. I differ in my view from Roosevelt, from Root and from Lodge, as to the way of fighting the campaign. I think we can overdo the jingo part." [43] But he would make speeches, Taft promised, if the leaders so desired although there were some elements, "notably among the labor leaders, who would seek to make capital against Mr. Hughes because of my support of him." [44]

He was restless and worried as the drive went on. He was "not entirely certain that Hughes's speeches are all that they could be." He was wholly certain that the campaign was not well managed. William R. Willcox, whom Hughes had selected for chairman of the National Committee, was a man without great experience in politics. Indeed, to Taft, Willcox was a "blunderhead." [45] The national chairman appeared to lack decision. The bothered former President hoped that Hughes, when he returned from the West, would "put a burr under the tail" of his campaign manager. [46]

Yet Taft concurred in the most costly decision of the Republican High Command, the decision which was— more than anything

[42] Sullivan, Mark, op. cit., Vol. V, p. 238. [43] Taft to Karger, July 16, 1916. [44] Taft to W. R. Willcox, Aug. 16, 1916. [45] Taft to Karger, Aug. 15, 1916. [46] Taft to Murray Crane, Sept. 3, 1916.

else— to cost Hughes the presidency. "I quite agree with you in the necessity of having Mr. Hughes go to the Pacific coast," he said in late June.[47] California should have been safely Republican. But the party, then, was having a factional quarrel. Governor Hiram Johnson, still loyal to the Bull Moose, was running in the primaries for the senatorial nomination. William H. Crocker, national committeeman and Old Guard leader, was Johnson's bitter foe.

". . . with local differences I have no concern," Hughes said on arriving in California on August 18. This was impossible. He allowed himself to be surrounded to too great a degree, perhaps, by Crocker and the other standpatters. But Hughes had no intention whatever of alienating the Progressive wing and the legends that he deliberately snubbed Hiram Johnson are without foundation.

The Progressives were feeling their oats. Their emissary told Hughes, on a train to Los Angeles soon after he reached California, that he must declare himself for Johnson or lose the state. This, of course, the nominee could not do nor was it essential. In all probability he could have carried the state anyway. Johnson had promised, before the national convention, to support the regular ticket. Then occurred one of those mishaps which mark the history of both major parties. Hughes reached Los Angeles on August 20 and was taken in hand by the boosters of that booming city. At noon some similar enthusiasts from neighboring Long Beach took him over. They showed him the beauteous Pacific and held a reception at the hotel. Hughes then returned to Los Angeles and prepared for dinner. He was dressing when a campaign manager came to his room.

"Did you know that Hiram Johnson was at that hotel in Long Beach?" he was asked.

"Why, that's astonishing," said Hughes. "I wanted to see him. I wanted him to preside at our Sacramento meeting this week. You go back to Long Beach at once, explain the situation, and invite the governor to preside."

The messenger did so. He returned, however, with a declination and word from Johnson that Hughes had "surrounded himself with my enemies."

It is impossible, obviously, to state categorically that thereby

[47] Taft to Erastus Brainerd, June 20, 1916.

Hughes lost California and the presidency. Johnson did make a speech or two for the nominee. The final outcome, though, was defeat by a mere 3,800 votes, and the chances are overwhelming that this slight lead of Wilson's could have been overcome had it not been for the resentment of the Progressives.[48] Taft missed, completely, the significance of what had occurred.

"I think Johnson is on such a decline . . . that he is making a desperate struggle to regain his hold and is seeking to use Hughes for his purpose," he said when reports of the incident reached Murray Bay.[49]

So far was he from being in a decline that Johnson was elected to the Senate by 296,815 votes.

—6—

It was vital, the campaign leaders felt, for Taft and Roosevelt to stage a touching reconciliation scene. Taft was willing enough, now that Roosevelt had been defeated at the convention.

"Why shouldn't we work together to a common end?" he asked.[50]

He added that it might be a good idea for them to meet because there was "a very considerable part of the low-minded press that had given the impression that if Roosevelt and I met, he would curse me and I would curse him, and each would kick the other in the stomach.[51]

The arrangements were made by Root. A reception was being held for Nominee Hughes at the Union League Club in New York on October 3, he told Taft. Roosevelt would probably attend and he urged that Taft be present too.

"The example will be vastly beneficial throughout the country," Root said. ". . . In the nature of things you must both be significant and active figures in the public life of the country for many years to come. You are not going to avoid each other, and the sooner the press understands it need not look for a private brawl when you meet, the better." [52]

[48] *New Yorker,* July 6, 1935; Sullivan, Mark, *op. cit.,* Vol. V, pp. 241-243. [49] Taft to Karger, Aug. 21, 1916. [50] Taft to J. W. Hamilton, July 8, 1916. [51] Taft to Horace D. Taft, Sept. 19, 1916. [52] Root to Taft, Sept. 12, 1916.

Taft replied that he was "not hunting contact" with Roosevelt, but that he would come to the reception if the date could be shifted to October 4.[53] So the meeting was held, and Taft described it to his wife. With his escort, he said, he had been taken to the club's library.

Pretty soon Cameron Forbes came in and after him Roosevelt. We shook hands with a Howdy Do and that was all. Then we stood up in line. Depew was between Roosevelt and me. . . . The club was crowded. After the handshaking we went into the meeting room where Root made a good speech and Hughes responded in an excellent and forcible reply. Then they called for Roosevelt and he promptly responded. He talked well and ill. But he talked long. He spoke six minutes longer than Hughes. When R. had finished they called me out and really the reception they gave me was most flattering. Root and Hughes shook hands. When I had finished, we all entered the elevator together. They all made some reference to my last remark about the ex-Presidents' club to which Roosevelt and I were going to elect Wilson. Roosevelt said "Yes, we'll not blackball him for that." I waited until he went out and followed him.[54]

The public show of love may have won a few votes for Hughes but it did not alter Taft's feeling toward his enemy. He noted, a few days later, that Roosevelt was going to campaign in Arizona.

"I am glad of it," he said. "The further he goes away the better."[55]

Taft's detestation for Wilson rivaled, as the campaign progressed, his hatred for Roosevelt four years before; this was "the most critical election we have had in a half century."[56] What grieved him most was "to see a lot of intelligent men voting for Wilson when they don't seem to realize the catastrophe that will come to this country in having the Supreme Court reorganized by him." Had not Wilson already undermined the court by nominating Brandeis, Taft's assailant in the Ballinger controversy? The President would have the appointment of four additional justices and he was

---

[53] Taft to Root, Sept. 16, 1916. [54] Taft to Helen H. Taft, Oct. 5, 1916. [55] Taft to Horace D. Taft, Oct. 11, 1916. [56] Taft to Wickersham, Oct. 15, 1916.

EN ROUTE TO THE SUPREME COURT. CHIEF JUSTICE TAFT IN 1924

See page 964]

THE CHIEF JUSTICE AND HIS ASSOCIATES. 1921 TERM OF COURT

Front row, left to right: Associate Justices William R. Day, Joseph McKenna; Chief Justice William H. Taft; Associate Justices Oliver Wendell Holmes and Willis Van Devanter. *Back row, left to right*: Associate Justices Louis D. Brandeis, Mahlon Pitney, James Clark McReynolds and John H. Clarke

See page 968]

"seeking to break down the guaranties of the Constitution by select-ing men who are radical in their views." [57]

On the eve of the election Taft was depressed. He had "an uneasy feeling that we may be facing a landslide for Wilson on the labor and 'he kept us out of war' issues. . . . It will be very hard for me to bear another administration of Wilson. I despise him so be-cause of his hypocrisy. He will go far toward wrecking our system of government. He is perfectly ruthless and unscrupulous, but many people regard him as a saint. . . . May the bitter cup be turned from our lips." [58]

The cup had to be drained. For a time there seemed to be hope. Then the returns from California trickled in. "The fate of the nation is trembling in the balance this morning," Taft wrote as he waited.[59] His final disappointment seems to have been far more keen than when he listened in 1912 and found comfort, then, in the defeat of Roosevelt. The result was "due to the emotional votes of the women, to the extreme speeches of Roosevelt, and to the besotted comfort of the western farmers." [60] Most of all, it was due to Roosevelt, who had been an asset at the start of the drive, but a liability at the close.[61] The specter of Roosevelt as a presidential candidate simply would not down. Taft observed that he was "planning again for 1920. . . . He is like an old man of the sea on the back of the Republican party." [62] But death, which respects no parties at all, would remove the incubus.

Taft expressed his bitterness to Mrs. Taft. "You and I have had defeat before and we can stand it after we grow used to it," he wrote. "We must buckle down. . . . Poor Hughes is lifted out of the Supreme Court and he must begin again in the practice. How-ever, he'll soon be earning more than his judicial salary. Still, it must be a great disappointment when he was so near to the great prize." [63]

Hughes, however, bore his disappointment graciously. "I have been sitting up with the mourners and there has been no opportunity to answer your kind letter," he replied to consolations from Taft. "You must not chide yourself for urging me to make the fight. I

[57] Taft to Robert Windsow, to James Markham, Oct. 21, 1916. [58] Taft to Helen H. Taft, Oct. 31, 1916. [59] Taft to Karger, Nov. 8, 1916. [60] Taft to H. C. Coe, Nov. 14, 1916. [61] Taft to C. H. Kelsey, Nov. 18, 1916. [62] Taft to W. A. Peters, Nov. 19, 1916. [63] Taft to Helen H. Taft, Nov. 10, 1916.

had no honorable alternative in view of the action of the convention, and I do not think that anyone of common sense has entertained the idea that my acceptance hurt the dignity of the court. I did not wish to leave the bench, but it was a high privilege to be chosen to lead in the endeavor to establish sounder national policies and to make the Republican party once more an effective instrument of national service. So far as I am personally concerned, I have no complaints and no regrets."

Indeed, there were "some grounds for gratification." Wilson's appeal to labor, Hughes thought, had succeeded only partially. Too, the vote had not divided along the lines of sympathy with the warring nations. "On the other hand, it is mortifying that the cry of 'Peace and Prosperity' was so potent. . . .

"The bitterness of the factional struggle in California passes belief," Hughes continued, "and I presume that it accounts for the result. Of course, I did not snub Johnson. I had no idea that he was in the Long Beach Hotel when I was there. . . . All the facts doubtless will appear in due time. . . . I have been waiting for the official count in California— the vote was so close, I could not do otherwise— to close this chapter, and on January 1 I shall return to the practice of the law in New York with a feeling of eagerness for the varied activities it permits." [64]

[64] Hughes to Taft, Nov. 20, 1916.

CHAPTER XLVII

AMERICA GOES IN

ALL THE dreams of peace were futile dreams. The ambitious dream of President Wilson that he might end the war from his high pinnacle of neutrality vanished as that pinnacle trembled and then crashed into the abyss of war. The wholly selfless dream of William Howard Taft that the best minds of the world would form an effective parliament for peace died too, although stubbornly. One moment, even as war came, his hopes would be bright and he would believe that a League for Peace, backed by force, would really materialize. Then would come bitter disappointment, chagrin and discouragement. For the nations of the world— the United States among them— were poisoned by nationalism, distrust and suspicion. The war to end wars would not actually end at all on that delirious November day in 1918. The horsemen changed their garb, but they still rode furiously and have been riding, now, for an additional twenty years. Sometimes they have been dictators of the right or the left. Sometimes they have been the couriers of depression. Whatever their uniforms, the horsemen have continued to ride: across Europe, in the Balkans, in Russia, in the far-off East.

A day would come when Taft would hold that Woodrow Wilson and Henry Cabot Lodge were, through narrow-minded recalcitrance, equally to blame for the defeat of the treaty which created the League of Nations. But he worked for a league throughout the war. He supported Wilson privately and publicly. When the final Senate battle came he used what influence he had. Then, sick at heart, he again bowed to partisan politics and supported Harding for the presidency in 1920.

The election banners and posters, flaunted so proudly in a presidential campaign, grow smeared with rain and dingy with soot when the contest is over, for nobody bothers to take them down. In many a city and village, after November, 1916, the posters and banners flapped loosely in the wind. And the Democratic slogan "He Kept Us out of War" was already fading by December. The smudged and flyspecked posters were symbolic. Even before the election, carefully coded cables had ticked into Washington giving warning that Germany would resume unrestricted submarine warfare. Ambassador von Bernstorff, from Washington, warned his government that this would mean war with the United States. But the military and naval chieftains had cemented their grip on Germany. By submarine ruthlessness, they said, the war could quickly be ended with victory for the Central Powers.

Wilson determined to write another note, and succeeded chiefly in enraging the Allies by doing so. While he was drafting it a communication from Berlin held out a desire for a peace conference. There was no prospect, however, that anything save a peace with victory would be considered.[1] To Taft, still praying for peace, public comment was impossible. Privately, he said that Germany's proposals seemed "utterly inadequate . . . they are not made with the idea that the Allies will accept, and I don't think this is going to change the situation except that it will enable Germany to say to her people and to the world that she tried to make peace." [2]

British Ambassador Spring Rice, increasingly at odds with the Wilson administration and always pessimistic regarding war action by America, could not see that the people would "take any other part than that of sympathetic spectators. Germany will be the villain of the piece, but they will do no injury to the actor." Springy was puzzled by Wilson:

The President rarely sees anybody. He practically never sees Ambassadors, and when he does, exchanges no ideas with them. Mr. Lansing is treated as a clerk who receives orders which he has to obey at once and without question . . . the real business of foreign politics is transacted by the President alone.[3]

The truth, of course, was that Wilson, whatever he might say in order to bring a united front when war came, had no illusions that it was a struggle between unsullied righteousness on one side

[1] Seymour, Charles, *The Intimate Papers of Colonel House*, Vol. II, pp. 387-408.
[2] Taft to Hamilton Holt, Dec. 13, 1916. [3] Gwynn, Stephen, *The Letters and Friendships of Sir Cecil Spring Rice*, Vol. II, p. 360.

and blackhearted evil on the other. To Taft, whose mind was simpler, it would soon be obvious that the Allies must win. Even the faithful House grew apprehensive as the President continued to hope that war might still be avoided. "I have promised to go to Washington next week," he noted in his diary on December 23, "but I have no stomach for it." A declaration by Germany of the submarine blockade was certain in January. Wilson, pondering the misty future and looking past the fateful Treaty of Versailles, was formulating his conception of a just peace. He offered this to the Senate on January 22. Peace depended on freedom for all nations, he said. Freedom for all nations depended on a "peace without victory." But the world was not ready for that, nor was it when the delegates assembled in Paris.

On January 31, Count von Bernstorff informed the State Department that the blockade would start in less than twenty-four hours. One American vessel a week, marked as the German government commanded and following specific lanes, would be permitted to sail in each direction.[4] On February 3 the President took the only possible course. It was, curiously, a course suggested by Taft when the *Lusitania* had been torpedoed in May, 1915. Wilson, like Taft, clung to the hope that even severance of diplomatic relations might not result in war. But now it was too late. Von Bernstorff and his staff were handed their passports.

"We are now ourselves in the war— at least I don't see any escape, if Germany pursues her course as she evidently intends to do," noted Taft. "While I deplore the fact, it is a satisfaction to know that we shall be ranged on the side of those who are fighting for the rights of civilization and to subdue an evil, the virus of which shows itself every day." [5]

—2—

Taft supported the President. The responsibilities of the Chief Executive and Congress, he said, were crushing. "They should know and do know that the American people will back them to the end in their decision. May God give them good deliverance." [6] On the

---

[4] Seymour, Charles, *op. cit.,* Vol. II, pp. 413, 417-418, 437. [5] Taft to G. M. Wrong, Feb. 5, 1917. [6] *Addresses,* Vol. XXXVII, p. 221.

other hand, he worried over the probability that "we are going to muddle through this German war just as we always have before." [7]

Even before war was declared, Taft favored compulsory military service and did all he could to hasten through Congress the administration's conscription measure.

"What I fear," he told Secretary of War Baker, "is that we shall have such a mushroom growth of volunteer regiments as we had in the Spanish War, at great expense." [8]

He grew impatient as Congress delayed. "Why are a lot of them such fools that they want to commit the blunders of previous wars in regard to the volunteer system and insist on going down through the slough of mistakes that England has just been through? . . . I don't think the representatives in Congress know what the popular feeling is on this subject. I have been through the South, North, East and the West, and those people who are favoring the volunteer system on the theory that the people wish it, are riding with their backs to the engine, or are affected by a small knot of pacifists." [9]

Taft watched with amused hostility the vehement demand of Theodore Roosevelt that he be sent to France at the head of a volunteer division. This, Taft knew, was delaying the Conscription bill. "Roosevelt, with all his professed desire to facilitate war, is really the stumbling block," he observed in May.[10] Such was the fact. As far back as 1915, the colonel had been rehearsing a heroic military role for the day when the United States should enter the war. He compiled a list of officers to serve as his divisional aides. Roosevelt seems to have had no conception at all that war had changed since the absurd little skirmish with Spain. On February 2 he told Secretary of War Baker that his volunteer division would consist of cavalry and mounted infantry. Pathetically, a short time later, he cited the fact that he had, as president, been commander in chief, and boasted of his services as a Rough Rider— to prove his fitness for command. He was fully aware, of course, of the President's enmity toward him, an enmity which he had fully earned. He suppressed, for the moment, his outbreaks against the administration.

[7] Taft to Horace D. Taft, Feb. 6, 1917. [8] Taft to Baker, Feb. 6, 1917. [9] Taft to Julius Kahn, April 14, 1917. [10] Taft to R. A. Taft, May 15, 1917.

"I say nothing in public about Wilson now," he confided to Senator Lodge.

From Baker came a cold rejection of Roosevelt's offer. Even a personal appeal to the President was unavailing. Roosevelt used political weapons too. He asked Lodge to force provision for his division in any plan for volunteer forces. The debates on this delayed conscription.

Apart from the fact that Wilson undoubtedly took pleasure in doing so, the rejection of Roosevelt was the only possible course. A volunteer body would have drained the nation of its best men. The officers Roosevelt demanded were absolutely essential for the training of troops. Besides, Pershing, as commander of the A.E.F., had no taste for so troublesome a junior officer.[11]

Taft saw all this. "I should doubt his capacity to command a division, though Wilson may think it wise to unite public opinion by giving him the opportunity he seeks," he said when Roosevelt's petitions started.[12] He was pleased when the White House showed no disposition to surrender:

> I see Theodore is humble and only wishes to be a major general subordinate to some other "crank" major general, presumably Wood. That Presbyterian hater in the White House will have to see more clearly than he does now before yielding and giving to Theodore the stage of the world for the building of another presidential campaign. As between these two gentlemen, I am indifferent . . . but I should think . . . it would involve great risk to entrust 25,000 men to a commander so lacking in real military experience and so utterly insubordinate in his nature.[13]
>
> It may be that Wilson will give him an opportunity . . . to strut up and down as a major general, but not unless [he] has changed his Presbyterian Calvinistic nature and his Indian memory. To think that the four Roosevelt boys will have to accept commissions in a compulsory service and not under the "King," their father, is dreadful. I don't think that the colonel can do anything but go over and solicit a commission from the French government and, in a French uniform, parade up and down shrinking from the public gaze. Seriously, of course, Baker was right.[14]

[11] Pringle, H. F., *Theodore Roosevelt, a Biography*, pp. 590-598. [12] Taft to Bryce, Feb. 8, 1917. [13] *Idem*, Feb. 8, 1917. [14] *Idem*, April 9, 1917.

—3—

Taft's personal stake in the struggle in France was soon vital.
Both his sons offered themselves. Robert, the older, was rejected
because of bad eyesight and served, instead, with the Hoover Commission. On May 21, Charles P. Taft, II, left Yale to enlist with a
regular army field artillery unit. Charlie was only nineteen. A few
weeks later he became engaged to Eleanor Chase, whom he had
known at school, and his father was pleased because "an association
of that sort strengthens a boy against temptations which crowd
on him in the army." On January 10, 1918, having been promoted
to sergeant major from the lowly rank of private, Charlie sailed for
France.[15]

The father was proud as his son prepared to go. But anguish
lay in his heart. Taft was a man of scrupulous personal morals. He
had complete confidence in his son. And yet . . .

Demoralization exists as never before in France and you will
almost be raped unless you brace yourself. It is such a comfort
to know that you have your sweet, loving wife, Eleanor, to whom
you have plighted your faith and whose appealing fond glances
will always rise before you when you are confronted by sinful love.
It is hard, my darling boy, to let you go. You are the apple of our
eye. But we would not have it different. . . . And now, Charlie
my loving son, good-bye till we meet again. You are knight *sans
peur et sans reproche*. God bless you and keep you.[16]

So the headlines, now, had new and terrible significance. Dread
never faded of a telegram from the War Department beginning
"We regret to announce . . ." On a morning late in March the
newspapers carried reports of a new German offensive and of English reverses.

"I wish Charlie were not over there," Mrs. Taft said.

The father wrote to his son and quoted the remark; he was
sure she had not really meant it:

Whatever happens, we know that you will do your duty and
face death with a pure heart and a clear conscience and a spirit

    [15] Taft to C. P. Taft, May 22, 1917; to C. H. Kelsey, July 14, 1917; Mischler to
Taft, Jan. 11, 1918. [16] Taft to C. P. Taft, II, Dec. 19, 1917.

that either in you or in others will win the war for the right. . . .
It is a solemn and sacrificial moment, and I am glad you are
there, much as it presses my heart to think of the possibilities. We
are all proud of you.[17]

The former President was inclined, at first, to believe that very
real progress was being made in prosecuting the war. "Roosevelt's
attacks upon our past preparations and on our present lack of
material don't help a bit, in my judgment," he said. "They only
serve to discourage the feeling of the people that should be high
and enthusiastic. They misrepresent conditions." [18]

He threw himself into war work; speaking for the Liberty
Loans and touring the cantonments, where he explained to "the
soldiers of the draft in a rational way the reasons why we had to
enter the war, and the reason why we have to continue it through
to the end. Washington had received disquieting reports . . . as to
the attitude of the men who had been drafted, their wish to leave
the camps if they could, their asserted ignorance of why we are
in the war." [19] He would give unsparingly of his time, also, to
preserving a measure of industrial peace and would take up residence in Washington to serve as joint chairman of the War Labor
Board.

Taft soon became caustically critical of the President, however.
"I shall not be content unless we dictate a just peace in Berlin,"
he said. And Wilson, of course, still held stubbornly to his more
lofty conception of a peace which would leave Germany uncrushed,
able to rise again. Taft forgot, in his irritation, that he had, himself,
once believed that materials and not men would be America's
contribution. He forgot that the transports were moving steadily
to France. He expressed to Lord Bryce his grave doubts regarding
Wilson, whom he branded "one of the enigmas of the war, and
one of the obstacles we shall have to overcome in winning it."

I have been accumulating evidence that his idea was never
to send troops abroad, but only to furnish the Allies with food and
material and money. Such a pusillanimous course it is difficult to
think he could support, but the truth is, Lord Bryce, our President

[17] *Idem,* March 24, 1918. [18] Taft to G. Dixon, Oct. 9, 1918. [19] Taft to Mrs. William
Hooper, Jan. 8, 1918.

is a pacifist at heart, and he is surrounded by men with a similar weakness. He has a passion for . . . men of the highest ideals in point of triumphant, graceful and charming phrasing. . . . Brandeis, Barney Baruch, Walter Lipman [*sic*] and [Felix] Frankfurter all are close to him at one time or another and not one in his heart believes in fighting the war through. He and they have some absurd notion that the war can be won and international agreements secured through a show of force and a joint debate. Don't misunderstand me as foreshadowing an inconclusive peace as the result of conditions here. Events and public opinion force the President along.[20]

Soon from the commander in chief of the A.E.F. came word that all was not well. General Pershing wrote that England and France had reached the virtual limit of their fighting powers. The morale of their people, Pershing thought, was not high; confidence that they could cope with the enemy was waning. The American troops, on the other hand, were aggressive and determined to win. The sole desire of the men, Pershing said, was to engage with the enemy. They would soon be the best fighters in Europe. But it was vital to bend every effort to send men and supplies as rapidly as possible— while the enthusiasm was at its height.[21]

Taft talked with Major General Enoch H. Crowder and then quoted the general, who was in charge of the draft, as saying it was "the damnedest, most leisurely war" in his experience. The administration, Taft was certain, was even falling down in drafting an army. The first class would be exhausted by September and a new law, enlarging the number of eligible men, should be passed immediately.[22]

There had been basis enough for discouragement during the twelve months just ending. One Italian army had collapsed in the fall of 1917 and had become a retreating mob. In Russia the Czar had fallen; the Kerensky regime, which might have carried on the war, proved ineffective. In 1918 came the humiliating Russo-German treaty of Brest-Litovsk which meant that Russia would no longer be a factor. This brought the release of German divisions for the western front.

[20] Taft to Bryce, March 24, 1918. [21] Pershing to Taft, June 27, 1918. [22] Taft to C. H. Kelsey, Aug. 4, 1918.

A mutual hatred for Wilson was drawing Roosevelt and Taft closer during these months. The two men agreed that the only possible policy was intervention in Russia. Roosevelt wrote that the United States should join with Japan and support the White Russians. Indeed, he would back either Trotsky or Lenin, he said, if only it meant ending German influence in Russia.[23]

"The force which will be sent must be followed by larger forces," was Taft's view, "and no matter how the administration tries to masquerade it, it is action against the Bolsheviki, and the Bolsheviki are the power which Germany will back, and which Germany will have to back. . . . All this gush about not using Russia to wage war against Russia is utterly without substance. . . . She is loaded with Germany, and we have got to kick Germany out. The only way we can kick her out is by the use of military force."[24] The trouble, he added, was that Wilson "has really been in sympathy with the Bolsheviki." Taft was alarmed by the tendency of Americans to sympathize with the Russian experiment. Alas, even estimable people did so. Alas, even his own daughter had been tainted by such organs of radical thought as the *New Republic*. Taft's lamentation was poignant:

There is a yellow layer in our social and political community, which includes Wilson and Brandeis and the editors of the *New Republic* . . . and the ultraprogressives of Roosevelt, who have no limitation or restriction in respect to law and order when the presumed rights of the downtrodden are trumpeted by avowed exponents of pure democracy. . . . They did not want to intervene in Russia, lest they might alienate this gang of robbers and cutthroats; and now they find that the Bolsheviki have just surrendered to Germany, and public opinion and circumstances have forced them in. . . .

I made a speech at an alumni dinner at Yale in June, advocating intervention in Russia, and Anson Stokes— and indeed Helen, who seems to be influenced by the opinions of the *New Republic*— shook their heads at my advocacy of any such policy. . . . Now we are sending 25,000 men, including Japanese, Canadians and Americans to Vladivostok where we really need 100,000 . . . all on the theory that we can send a small force and not be responsible for military

[23] Roosevelt to Taft, June 5, 1918. [24] Taft to Karger, Aug. 10, 1918.

intervention as if we sent a large force. . . . Our weak little puling policy in this regard reminds me of the plea of the girl who had an illegitimate baby, who sought an excuse of her offense by saying that it was such a little one.[25]

By the summer of 1918, at last, the jealous and quarreling Allies had agreed on a unified command and under the leadership of Foch the German offensive was broken. Then came the Allied thrust, in which the forces of America played their part. Among the awful tragedies of war is the fact that neither adversary really knows the strength of his opponent. Germany was close to collapse on October 1. If the Allies had only known this, five weeks of blood and death might have been avoided. On October 5, 1918, Germany sued for peace and suggested an armistice. American public opinion agreed that this was merely a trick whereby the enemy sought time to rebuild its shattered strength. Abysmally ignorant members of the Senate, such as Cabot Lodge, proclaimed, as if they had knowledge of the facts, that an armistice was equivalent to losing the war. Wilson was perplexed. The President's anxiety was due to the possibility that the military position of the Allies might be weakened if he dealt with Germany without proper guaranties. But he was quite unwilling to close the door. His ultimate answer was that the United States would consider the bid for peace if the Central Powers would accept the Fourteen Points and other doctrines advanced by America. This was wise, astute; it made it necessary for Germany to carry on the negotiations.[26]

Taft, as we have already seen, had abandoned his earlier, reasonable position that Wilson knew the facts better than any outsider, even a predecessor in the same high office. His reaction to Wilson's reply was bitter. It was outrageous that the President had not "consulted the Allies before he wrote the note . . . he would never do that— that is just the kind of man he is. He recognizes no obligations of partnership or of decent courtesy. He thinks he is running the whole show himself. I do not know whether Lloyd George and Clemenceau now have the courage to tell him what is what, but if they do he will turn tail." [27]

[25] Taft to C. P. Taft, II, Aug. 19, 1918. [26] Seymour, Charles, op. cit., Vol. IV, pp. 1, 73-74, 76-80. [27] Taft to C. D. Norton, Oct. 14, 1918.

"The German peace offensive was most ingeniously baited," Taft added. "It appealed to his vanity, and successfully, because it sought to use his indefinite literary phrases in his Fourteen Points as the basis of peace. It was to be his peace and nobody else's peace. Sometimes I feel like bursting, but as Theodore does the bursting, perhaps I can pursue some other function." [28]

But when the Armistice finally came Taft was enormously gratified, of course. His judicial calm returned, in part. He prepared to support Woodrow Wilson's fight for an effective League of Nations.

—4—

First, however, came the Congressional campaign of 1918. This, at last, terminated the Roosevelt-Taft schism. Both agreed that a Republican Congress must be returned so that Wilson would be prodded into more rapid prosecution of the war. They met, conferred and approved each other's attacks on the miscreant in the White House. But it would not be accurate to say that the old relationship was really resumed. That had been based on love and trust and admiration. This was an alliance born of hatred. Their letters were cordial enough, but the warmth was gone.

"We have strongly agreed as to the President," Taft said, "and that I think is the chief bond between us. I presume that a great many people will regard this of political importance but I don't. Life is too short to preserve these personal attitudes of enmity, and I am glad to have the normal status resumed." [29]

In contemplating the campaign, Taft struggled with his natural tendency to be fair-minded. The administration was entitled to credit for the Conscription act. Taft felt, too, that the construction of cantonments had been efficiently handled. But War Secretary Baker had erred in not deciding promptly on the type of rifles and machine guns to be used; this had delayed the preparation of troops by three months. As for the President:

The restraint of the Republicans up to this time has been wonderful considering the porcupine attitude of Wilson. How a man

[28] Taft to Glenn Frank, Oct. 16, 1918. [29] Taft to C. P. Taft, May 31, 1918.

loaded down with the responsibility he has for this war can absolutely exclude from his councils the members of Congress and of the Senate, both of his own party and of the party that is standing so loyally behind him, I cannot understand except by attributing to him a peanut soul and a gross self-absorption that exceeds anything we have had in our political history. When he sends for the senators he never confers with them at all —he just tells them what he wants. He doesn't know the meaning of conference or counsel. He has a conception that he is the arbiter of the universe and that he knows everything by intuition.[30]

The Roosevelt-Taft rapprochement was engineered by the astute Will Hays who had been elevated from Indiana politics to the chairmanship of the Republican National Committee in February, 1918. He urged that the two men meet. Taft answered that he had no objection at all; already, he pointed out, he had sent a message of sympathy when Roosevelt had been ill and this had been graciously acknowledged.[31] Now, Roosevelt was to speak in the Maine campaign. A letter was once more addressed to "My dear Theodore." In it, Taft gave approval of a speech which Roosevelt would make and suggested, merely, a somewhat lighter touch in the criticisms of Wilson's preparedness program.[32] Their meeting in Chicago in May was not prearranged. Taft learned, on reaching the Blackstone Hotel, that Roosevelt was alone in the dining room.

"I went up . . . and shook hands with him," Taft reported. "He was really very much pleased and very cordial. He is looking very well. . . . one thing that I observed in him is that he does not hear and he listens with an intenseness in order to hear. We talked about the President and agreed about him." [33]

The colonel was not well. He was blind in one eye and the hearing was gone from one ear. An infection picked up in South America still poisoned his blood. He was, that summer of 1918, close to the end of his stormy trail. Then in July came the awful blow of Quentin Roosevelt's death; the loss of the youngest son who had chosen to fly for his country left his father crushed. Taft's

[30] Taft to Louis Howland, March 3, 1918. [31] Taft to C. P. Taft, II, March 4, 1918. [32] Taft to Roosevelt, March 11, 1918. [33] Taft to Karger, May 31, 1918.

condolences were prompt and warm. He hoped against hope, he said, that Quentin might be a prisoner in Germany and still alive.[34]

Wilson's appeal to the nation for a Democratic Congress seemed, to Taft, an incredible blunder. "If he does not show the spirit of that German autocracy which he claims to be fighting, I cannot read English," Taft said.[35] It was an error "that was not expected from the master of politics that the President has shown himself to be. . . . It was one of those surprises in the career of a uniformly successful man which comes from his losing his bearings because of his political success. The adulation . . turned his head." [36]

And the Republican victory on Election Day was, of course, glorious. "The news is too good to be true," Taft exulted. ". . . The President can thank himself and his crass egotism." [37]

The reconciliation between Taft and Roosevelt was spared the strain of the colonel as a contender for the 1920 presidential nomination. For Roosevelt died at four o'clock on the morning of January 5, 1919. "I am shocked to hear the sad news. My heart goes out to you and yours in your great sorrow," Taft telegraphed to Mrs. Roosevelt. "The country can ill afford in this critical period of history to lose one who has done and could in the next decade have done so much for it and humanity. We have lost . . . the most commanding personality in our public life since Lincoln." [38] As time passed, Taft would somewhat forget the hurt and anger of the 1912 betrayal. He would forget, even, the outrageous policies which Roosevelt had advocated and which had made him, or so it had seemed, one of the most dangerous influences in American life.

"I want to say to you," he assured Mrs. Cowles, Roosevelt's sister, in 1921, "how glad I am that Theodore and I came together after that long painful interval. Had he died in a hostile state of mind toward me, I would have mourned the fact all my life. I loved him always and cherish his memory." [39]

[34] Taft to Roosevelt, July 19, 1918. [35] Taft to Horace D. Taft, Oct. 26, 1918. [36] Taft to Bryce, Dec. 5, 1918. [37] Taft to Horace D. Taft, Nov. 9, 1918. [38] Taft to Mrs. Roosevelt, Jan. 6, 1919. [39] Taft to Mrs. William Cowles, July 26, 1921.

It may be suspected, though, that Taft's grief was not unbearable when word reached him of Theodore's death. It was innate in him to do the gracious thing. He went to New York on January 8 for the funeral. The final irony was that the arrangements for receiving him at the services were bungled. He was placed, at first, in the pew with the family servants:

I met Alec Lambert, Roosevelt's physician. . . . He pushed me through the crowd to where the ushers were standing in the aisle. Loeb [William Loeb, who had been Roosevelt's secretary] took me up behind the ribbon and put me in a pew behind the family in the same seat with the family servants. Then Archie [Roosevelt] came up and said, "You're a dear personal friend and you must come up further." He took me up and put me in behind the Vicepresident who was representing the President and just in front of the Senate committee with Lodge at its head and the House with the Speaker, Uncle Joe Cannon. . . .

Taft accompanied the party to the grave. He watched the coffin of his friend and enemy make that final, sickening descent into the grave which gashed a light covering of snow. Undoubtedly he was greatly moved.

That night, however, he attended a theater party.[40]

40 Taft to Helen H. Taft, Jan. 9, 1919.

CHAPTER XLVIII

EDUCATIONAL INTERIM

O N APRIL 8, 1918, Taft became, by presidential appointment, a joint chairman of the National War Labor Board created to eliminate or reduce the employer-employee disputes which were endangering production in vital war industries. In theory, at least, the National War Labor Board was an impartial body. Taft and Frank P. Walsh, the other joint chairman, were classified by President Wilson as "representatives of the general public." The employers and the employees were represented equally by five members each.[1]

It was, at first glance, faintly absurd for Taft to be regarded as impartial in labor disputes. Organized labor had long viewed him as hostile to its interests. His appointment to the National War Labor Board had, in fact, been made on behalf of the employers. But if those capitalist gentlemen expected bias in their favor, they reckoned without due knowledge of Taft's judicial mind.

"The employers' side," Taft noted, not without amusement, the following August, "complains that the board is constituted of five employers, five trade-unionists, one advocate of the trade-unionists [Walsh] and one judge, and possibly it is not without truth, but I am hoping . . . both sides may acquire some judicial spirit and poise." [2]

Taft's period of service with the board, about fourteen months in all, was an educational experience for him of the first importance. Through all his years— as judge, as Cabinet member, as president, and as law professor at Yale— he had lived fairly remote from actual contact with the problems of the workingman. But now he came into a firsthand relationship with such issues as the minimum wage, the right to organize and the eight-hour day. A number of prejudices, based on inadequate knowledge, were removed during the fourteen months.

[1] Presidential proclamation, April 8, 1918. [2] Taft to J. E. King, Aug. 7, 1918.

915

As the work of the National War Labor Board started, in April, Taft was anxious to acquire as much practical information as possible. He agreed, for that reason, personally to preside at various hearings on disputes in the munitions and textile mills of the South. An extended trip was essential. Before leaving he conferred with W. Jett Lauck, who had been appointed secretary of the board. Lauck, a statistician and economist of liberal leanings, had long been identified with labor. He attempted to tell Taft something about the conditions he would find in the southern mills. But Taft, with complete good nature, stopped him.

"Don't fill me with labor propaganda," he said. "I know you're a Socialist."

"I'm not. I'm a conservative," Lauck protested. "I'm trying to give you the facts."

Late in May, in Chicago, they conferred again. Lauck noticed that Taft seemed tired and discouraged. He had been engaged in almost constant hearings in the South.

"Why didn't you tell me about the conditions down there?" he asked Lauck.

"I tried to."

"You didn't tell me anything. Why, I had no idea! How can people live on such wages!"

By Taft's order, approved by the board, the wages in question were doubled and tripled. From that time on Lauck and Walsh, wholly delighted, insisted that Taft was the most radical member of the National War Labor Board.[3]

—2—

It had been apparent by the fall of 1917 that prosecution of the war would suffer if strikes and lockouts continued. The cost of living was increasing. Certain employers refused to meet the rise with augmented wages. In this crisis the Council of National Defense suggested a conference among employers and labor leaders to find out, as Taft phrased it, "whether we can arrange a truce between labor and capital in this country." A preliminary body, the

[3] W. Jett Lauck to author, Oct. 5, 1937.

War Labor Conference Board, was created by Secretary of Labor William B. Wilson. As in the case of the succeeding National War Labor Board, Taft and Walsh were joint chairmen. The five employer members were picked by the National Industrial Conference Board and the five labor representatives by the American Federation of Labor.

The principal duty of the preliminary body was to draw up the specifications whereby, it was hoped, labor friction in war industries might be minimized. Taft began his task with misgivings, largely because he believed Frank Walsh to be radical and unsound.[4] It was not long, though, before he had changed his mind regarding Walsh, labor leaders and the wisdom of the American industrialist.

"With Walsh helping me," he reported, "we finally got the agreement drafted and signed. It was a great preliminary success. . . . I had to read the riot act to my people once or twice. . . . I came into curiously agreeable relations with the labor men." [5]

Several months later he amplified his opinion of Walsh:

Walsh is a curious man. . . . He has cultivated the use of emotion, of an hysterical character, to secure a flow of words. He weeps and he brings into requisition all the arts of the jury lawyer. . . . However, in dealing with me, behind closed doors, I have found him amenable. He is an Irishman, with all the camaraderie of an Irishman.[6]

It is not remarkable, in view of the principles adopted by the War Labor Conference Board, that Taft had found it necessary to "read the riot act" to the employer representatives. They were liberal principles. One of them, holding that "yellow-dog" contracts were not to be allowed during the war, was probably in contravention of a decision of the Supreme Court. The principles on which labor disputes were to be settled, together with a recommendation for the creation of a National War Labor Board, were promulgated on March 29, 1918. Taft, Walsh and all the other members signed them. They were:

[4] Taft to R. A. Taft, March 4, 1918. [5] Taft to Helen H. Taft, March 30, 1918. [6] Taft to C. P. Taft, II, Aug. 4, 1918.

The right to unionize and bargain collectively is recognized and affirmed and may not be "denied, abridged or interfered with by the employers in any manner whatsoever."

The right of employers to form associations or groups to bargain collectively is also recognized and shall not be interfered with by the workers.

Employers must not discharge workers for union membership nor "for legitimate trade-union activities."

The workers shall not coerce their fellows to join unions.

Where the union shop already exists it shall continue.

Shops with both union and nonunion workers are permitted, but this does not bar the organization of a closed shop.

Established health and safety regulations are not to be relaxed.

Women doing men's work receive the same wages as do men.

The basic eight-hour day continues where specified by law. In other cases the working day is to be determined by war needs and the health of the workers.

Maximum production in all war industries is to be maintained.

Wages and hours are to be fixed with due regard to conditions in the locality affected.

All workers, including common laborers, are entitled to a living wage. The minimum wage is to "insure the subsistence of the worker and his family in health and reasonable comfort." [7]

The last of these, setting up a living wage as the basis for the schedules to be fixed, was more or less revolutionary. It was greatly to accelerate the struggle of organized labor to obtain adequate pay. Walsh and Lauck were influential in persuading Taft to stand behind the living wage. Having given his word, he never faltered. Certain among his employer associates on the board were shocked and scandalized, however, when they discovered what had happened. Their protests were loud and long.[8]

The membership of the National War Labor Board was identical with that of the preliminary War Labor Conference Board. It was promptly swamped with complaints and petitions. It soon became clear that very few industries remained untouched by the war. Thus a total of 1,245 cases were heard during the life of the

[7] Presidential proclamation, April 8, 1918. [8] Lauck to author, Oct. 5, 1917.

board. Only fifty complaints were dismissed for lack of jurisdiction.[9]

Taft prepared to move to Washington and looked forward to
the work, although it would mean a cut of $6,000 in his income for
the year. His compensation was to be $25 for each day that he
gave to the board.[10] No member was more conscientious. Taft
read every document, every brief. He knew every detail about every
involved case.[11] All in all, it was pleasant being back in Washington.

"We have now become settled as far as I can be," he pointed
out that fall, "for I am a rotatory, gyratory individual. . . . we are
very comfortable." [12]

—3—

"The truth was," Taft wrote in May, "that the employers
thought that in the principles announced for our guidance they
could maintain a *status quo* of . . . the closed non-union shop,
namely a shop in which an employer refuses to have any union
men and makes them agree not to join the union, and discharges
them if they do. They did not wish, however, to make this prominent and so, as one of the employers' commissioners said, they
'pussyfooted' about it and they got left." [13]

It was specified, on the other hand, that the workers must waive
their right to strike. The board declined to hear any complaint
unless the men returned to work.[14]

The first major clash of the board was with the Western Union
Telegraph Company. Coincident with the ban on strikes was, of
course, an edict against lockouts. The Commercial Telegraphers'
Union had, in December, 1917, started secretly to organize the
Western Union employees. Between January and May, 1918, the
company discharged some 450 men. They promptly petitioned the
War Labor Board that this violated the principles set up by the
board and approved by President Wilson.

[9] Gregg, R. B., in *Harvard Law Review*, Nov. 1919. [10] Taft to Horace D. Taft, April
7, 1918; to C. P. Taft, II, May 19, 1918. [11] Lauck to author, Oct. 5, 1937. [12] Taft to
F. D. Cram, Nov. 21, 1918. [13] Taft to C. P. Taft, II, May 19, 1918. [14] Bureau of Labor
Statistics, *The National War Labor Board*, Bulletin 287, p. 52.

Newcomb Carlton, president of the company, agreed to arbitrate wages and hours. He declined to reinstate the dismissed men or to recognize the union unless, by vote, a majority of the workers desired to join it. But this was contrary to the rulings of the board "for the reason," as Taft explained, "that it denied to the minority of some 10,000 workers the right to join such union as they chose." [15] In opposing the position of Carlton, Taft gave the first indication that the War Labor Board would take a stand against the hated yellow-dog contracts whereby workers— usually on pain of failing to get jobs— agreed not to unionize. But the Supreme Court, in a recent decision, had encouraged the enforcement of just such agreements.[16]

"I think the making of such contracts after the proclamation of the President is not in accordance with our principles . . . though the making of them would be legal," Taft told Carlton. "I think the plan upon which our board acts contemplates a waiver by employers of such a right, just as it contemplates a waiver by employees of the legal right to strike." [17]

Joint Chairman Frank Walsh wrote the decree which provided that the dismissed men should be restored on condition they pledged themselves against a strike.

"You're just a conservative," Taft teased when he read the draft.[18]

It was, however, far too radical for the Western Union and the upshot was authorization by Congress for President Wilson to take over the telegraph and telephone lines.[19] The nation's industrialists were beginning to learn that, in war time at least, the long-established doctrines of free economy were no longer valid. Taft was learning too. He frequently remarked to Frank Walsh, as they toiled on some decision during a hot Washington night, that he was being forced to abandon the time-honored dicta of Adam Smith.[20]

"My experience on the National War Labor Board," admitted Taft as the work was terminating, "satisfies me that there ought to be a board upon which labor and capital shall both be represented

---

[15] Taft to Philadelphia *Public Ledger*, July 15, 1918. [16] *Hitchman Coal and Coke Co.* v. *Mitchell*, 245 U.S. 229. [17] Taft to Carlton, May 27, 1918. [18] Walsh to author, Sept. 29, 1937. [19] *Harvard Law Review*, November, 1919. [20] Walsh to author, Sept. 29, 1937.

to continue a refuge for both sides, *after they have tried economic powers,* as they call it, and reached no result." [21]

—4—

The members of the board were permitted to name alternates during periods when it was inconvenient for them to be in Washington. Anxious to have a breathing spell at Murray Bay, Taft requested Frederick N. Judson, a leader of the St. Louis bar, to serve in his place for part of the summer of 1918. Mr. Judson was functioning when the board, at last, found it necessary to take a final, emphatic stand against yellow-dog agreements. The employees of the Smith & Wesson Arms Company of Springfield, Massachusetts, complained to the board that such contracts had been required before they were given jobs. Taft, hearing the evidence before going on his vacation, agreed that they must be abolished for the war period. Joint Chairman Walsh then wrote the decree which said that "even if lawful when made" the yellow-dog contracts were contrary to the policies of the board. Mr. Judson was gravely disturbed, though, when requested to sign it in Taft's place.

"I'm an older man," he warned. "The Supreme Court has declared such contracts legal. How can you overrule the Supreme Court?"

Walsh assured him that Taft was in favor of the decree. In the end Mr. Judson signed. He drafted a memorandum citing the Supreme Court decision but pointing out that the "morality" of the situation required the new edict. The Smith & Wesson Company rejected the ruling. In short order its plant was commandeered by the government.[22]

Toward the end of July, 1918, Taft returned to Washington after protracted hearings at Schenectady, New York, into complaints filed by the employees of the General Electric Company. The night of July 30 was very hot. Joint Chairmen Taft and Walsh worked for hours at the offices of the board drafting details of the wage increases which were to be granted. Their two memoranda were

[21] Taft to W. D. Disston, Dec. 10, 1918. (Italics mine.) [22] Lauck to author, Oct. 5, 1937; Bureau of Labor Statistics, *op. cit.,* p. 260.

later to be incorporated into the official decree. At ten or eleven o'clock Taft wandered into Walsh's office. He was in his shirt sleeves and was soaked with perspiration. Lauck, secretary of the board, was with Walsh.

"What about those scrubwomen up there?" Taft asked.

"We haven't any jurisdiction," said Walsh. "They filed no complaint. We didn't hear their case."

"Well, their pay should be increased just the same."

"It's all right with me," Lauck said. "You've been the one who has insisted on jurisdiction."

"Well, let's put in an increase for the scrubwomen, anyway," Taft said.

It was so officially decreed. The women received a minimum wage of $10.50 a week. The General Electric Company made no protest. A tendency toward illegality was growing in Taft.[23]

The board's policy of awarding a living wage to all workers brought before it innumerable petitions from street railway employees. Taft presided at the majority of the hearings. He would not listen to the plea of the companies, nearly always made, that the increases were impossible unless higher fares were granted. Taft did not shrink, even, from the possibility that bankruptcies would result.

"In a hearing between the street car companies of Cleveland and Detroit and their men," he said, describing one case, "the companies pleaded that they should not be required to raise wages, because they had no income out of which to pay the increase. . . . The Joint Chairmen of the board, arbitrators in these cases, held that the financial condition of the company could not affect the issue which they must decide.

"It is impossible to escape this conclusion. Suppose the arbitration had been over the price of coal or steel rails furnished the companies, could anybody contend that the company could be heard to say that the coal dealer or rail maker must abate the reasonable market price because the companies were in financial straits? . . .

"To increase wages and throw the companies into bankruptcy, it was said, would obstruct efficiency. . . . But the evidence showed that the companies were having great difficulty in holding the

[23] Bureau of Labor Statistics, *op. cit.;* Walsh to author, Sept. 29, 1937.

men individually at the present wage rate. They were drifting into other, better paid employment." [24]

On the other hand, Taft was indignant because Wilson would take no action to add to the earnings of the traction companies. The Labor Board, with Walsh concurring, had suggested a tribunal to pass on higher rates, but the President said it was a matter for the local authorities.

"He seems utterly oblivious to the necessity for being just and square to capital in this exigency," Taft said.[25]

—5—

The National War Labor Board, although it had no legal authority to enforce its rulings, actually had vast powers. The nation's existence was at stake. War production, the public insisted, was not to be jeopardized by either capital or labor. All the emergency powers of the President were behind the decrees of the board. The workers, no less than the employers, were called sharply to account when they disobeyed its edicts. Late in August the munitions workers of Bridgeport, Connecticut, were given wage increases, a basic eight-hour day and most of the other concessions they had demanded. Dissatisfied, they went on strike none the less. From President Wilson then came a sharp rebuke and a threat to bar them from all war industry employment.

"Your strike . . ." the President wrote, "is a breach of faith calculated to reflect on the sincerity of organized labor in proclaiming its acceptance of the principles and machinery of the National War Labor Board. . . . to strike against the award is disloyalty and dishonor.

"The Smith & Wesson Company of Springfield, Massachusetts, engaged in government work, has refused to accept the mediation of the . . . board and has flaunted its rules of decision approved by Presidential proclamation. With my consent the War Department has taken over the plant and business of the company to secure continuity in production and to prevent industrial disturbance.

[24] Taft to Philadelphia *Public Ledger*, July 7, 1918. [25] Taft to Roosevelt, July 27, 1918.

". . . Having exercised a drastic remedy with recalcitrant employers, it is my duty to use means equally well adapted to the end with lawless and faithless employees.

"Therefore I desire that you return to work and abide by the award. If you refuse, each of you will be barred from employment in any war industry in the community in which the strike occurs for a period of one year. During that time the United States Employment Service will decline to obtain employment for you in any war industry elsewhere in the United States, as well as under the War and Navy departments, the Shipping Board, the Railroad Administration and all other government agencies, and the draft boards will be instructed to reject any claim of exemption based on your alleged usefulness on war production."

This was serious. It meant an abrupt end of gaudy silk shirts, new automobiles and relative luxury. Worse, it threatened service in the trenches. The men scrambled to return to work.

—6—

The accomplishments of the board were very real. Its awards and findings affected 1,100 establishments with 711,500 employees. Countless others were benefited, since awards made in a particular company were frequently adopted by the entire industry. A total of 138 strikes, some of them potentially disastrous, were averted. But the greatest importance of the board, in so far as the long struggle of labor against capital was concerned, was its influence toward the adoption of wage standards and maximum hours of employment.[26] Adam Smith, as Taft had noted, had finally been deposed as the ultimate authority on the economics of labor. Too, the War Labor Board constituted a precedent for the tribunal which would one day pass on railway labor disputes and for the National Labor Relations Board of the New Deal.

The pendulum would soon swing back. The majority of the employers who agreed to higher wages were, after all, operating under cost-plus contracts whereby the additional costs could be passed on to the government. After the Armistice, with sudden

[26] Bureau of Labor Statistics, *op. cit.*, pp. 198-208, 36, 19-20.

liquidation facing them, the employers were far less willing to accept the board's rulings. Secretary of Labor Wilson suggested on November 21, 1918, that the board continue to function until the peace treaties had been signed. The board agreed, but with the specification that all new cases should first be submitted to the Labor Department. Only after failure by that branch of the government would the National War Labor Board assume jurisdiction.[27]

For all practical purposes, however, the work of the board had ended. By the last week of June, 1919, it resolved to disband.[28] Taft's interest had been diverted elsewhere— to the fight for a League of Nations.

[27] W. B. Wilson to Taft and Walsh, Nov. 21, 1918; Taft *et al.* to National War Labor Board, Dec. 4, 1918. [28] Lauck to Secretary of Labor Wilson, June 25, 1919.

CHAPTER XLIX

A FEDERATION OF THE WORLD

B Y THE fall of 1919 the fight was nearly lost. The isolationists
had been riding high. The bitter-enders in the Senate were
loading the League of Nations with such reservations that
it would not be accepted abroad— nor by Woodrow Wilson.
Chagrin and disappointment overcame the American friends of the
league, but a few continued to fight. Among them was Taft.

As October opened he went, again, to Washington to bring
what pressure he could on the foes of the league. He found, Taft
reported, Senator Kellogg of Minnesota "in a state of great nervous-
ness," convinced of impending defeat:

> Kellogg then broke out into a damning of the President and
> of the treaty. . . . He said he wished the treaty was in Hell. I asked
> him whether he was for the treaty, and he said he was. I asked him,
> therefore, whether it was not his duty as a senator . . . to fight for
> what he believed was right, rather than to give way to feelings of
> hatred toward Wilson and to mere nervous weariness of the whole
> subject. Kellogg . . . made me very impatient, and I lost my
> temper.

The nerves of friends and foes alike were close to snapping after
the interminable Senate debate. The treaty reservations advanced
by Hiram Johnson of California were the most galling to Taft. At
this same meeting in Washington he berated Kellogg for helping
Johnson.

"Don't you know that you and these other conservatives are
giving Johnson great help in his campaign for the presidency?"
he demanded.

"I know we are," answered the senator. "Johnson is going to be
nominated and elected president of the United States."

"Do you wish him to be president?"

"No, of course not."

"You are just willing to make yourself a tail to his kite," Taft persisted.

"We cannot help it," was Kellogg's hopeless answer.

"Well," Taft exploded, "then you haven't any guts to stand up and make the fight."

Kellogg retorted that he would not take such a remark from anybody and left the room. Taft realized that he was accomplishing nothing by losing his temper and wrote a note of apology. He continued to hope during his stay in Washington that an adequate treaty might be approved, but he found slight basis for his hope. He was informed that Root, so often his trusted friend, "had been acting like a Machiavelli in all this business." Returning to New York, he met Secretary of the Treasury McAdoo on the train.

"McAdoo says the President is in a state of collapse— that his mind is clear but that he is so weak that his doctors would not permit him to discuss or think about any of these matters." Taft reported. "He says that he would like to help, but he is in a delicate situation, being the son-in-law of the President." [1]

Five years had passed, by now, since the war started. Five years earlier Taft had been dreaming that the United States might preserve neutrality. Even the invasion of Belgium, he had said, did not justify any policy save "to hold our tongues and to assume, as far as possible, the judicial silence in order that our usefulness as a mediator may be preserved." [2] In this, of course, he was behind President Wilson.

Taft had demonstrated, as president, his ardent belief in the judicial settlement of international disputes. His arbitration treaties, rejected by the Senate, had gone further than any previous ones. Those treaties were undoubtedly impracticable and set up no adequate machinery, but Taft's advocacy of them had done much to arouse public opinion for peace. He was still relying, even in early 1915, on the "force of public opinion" to enforce the rulings of this mythical international court. An international police force might not be necessary.

"I don't object to an international police force if it is needed to give security to the plan," he said, "but I think it is much more important that we should agree upon a court and establish that,

[1] Taft to A. L. Lowell, Oct. 5, 1919. [2] Taft to George Washburn, Oct. 12, 1914.

because the other will follow. . . . Let us get the court before we insist on the sheriff." [3]

So he was apathetic, at first, to another movement taking shape for an international peace drive. W. H. Short of the New York Peace Society had asked for a conference at New Haven. Taft said he had not wished to waste his time, but he saw Short and his associates briefly in New York. The former President was not precisely consistent. He expressed himself as "utterly out of sympathy with the movement, because it means so much wind and very little substantial good." Nor was he much more friendly toward still another drive, sponsored by Theodore Marburg and John Hays Hammond.

"All these propositions," Taft said, "have an element in them of the entirely impractical, that makes me quite impatient." [4]

In a very short time, however, Taft would be at the head of the Marburg movement and would be giving unsparingly of his time to it.

—2—

The League to Enforce Peace was conceived at the Century Club in New York on January 25, 1915, at a dinner attended by Hamilton Holt of the *Independent,* William B. Howland of the *Outlook,* and Marburg. At a second meeting a week later the original conception was enlarged and a doctrine added which would have vital importance in all the forthcoming discussions and debates over ending war. This, according to the phrasing of the Century Club confreres, was that international disputes must be settled without resort to arms *"under penalty of the employment against the offending nation of the united forces of the League."* Here was the international police force, the sheriff, which Taft had regarded as a step secondary to the establishment of a court.[5]

"The American plan," notes Zimmern, "took the form that might have been expected from its chief sponsor, whose mind was still moving in its pre-war groove. It may be described as the Taft treaties with a penalty clause attached. All 'justiciable' questions

---

[3] Taft to Ulric King, Jan. 17, 1915. [4] Taft to Mabel Boardman, Feb. 1, 1915.
[5] Latané, J. H., *Development of the League of Nations Idea,* Vol. I, p. vii. (Italics mine.)

were to go to a judicial tribunal 'for hearing and judgment.' The court thus set up would be empowered to decide whether a given case was justiciable or not. Thus the five-to-one majority of 1911 was swept away and a bare majority substituted. Moreover, entrance to the hall of judgment was no longer to be controlled by a body of laymen— the Joint High Commission of the 1911 treaties— but by the bench itself."

Disputes of a nonjusticiable nature were to be referred to a Council of Conciliation which would offer recommendations. The idea that force would be used— if nations rejected this machinery— was incorporated into the final draft of the League to Enforce Peace. In due time Woodrow Wilson would include this conception in his own project for a League of Nations.[6] The clause was:

"The signatory powers shall jointly use forthwith both their economic and military forces against any one of their number that goes to war, or commits acts of hostility, against another of the signatories."[7]

This was the first mention of economic force as a means of enforcing peace.[8]

It was all too simple. Innumerable questions were left unanswered. Innumerable problems were unsolved. But Taft, attending a Century Club dinner on April 9, 1915, abandoned his earlier belief that the project was impracticable.

". . . the important men they got," he wrote, describing the function, "were President Lowell of Harvard, James M. Beck, Kingsley of the New York Life and Pritchett [Henry S. Pritchett, president of the Carnegie Foundation]. . . . We got down to business, although I did not expect that we would, and we found ourselves able to agree in certain views. . . . One was that we favored an international arbitral court. The other was that we favored a league of the great powers of Europe with the United States, in which we agreed that any power that began war without submitting the issue upon which the war arose, if it were a justiciable question, to the court would be met by a remainder of the powers in war. If the questions were not justiciable, the matter would be submitted to a Commission of Conciliation, and that if war was begun

[6] Zimmern, Alfred, *The League of Nations and the Rule of Law*, pp. 163-164.
[7] Latané, J. H., *op. cit.*, Vol. I, p. viii.   [8] Zimmern, Alfred, *op. cit.*, p. 164.

without such submission for a stated period, the same result would follow. I don't know how this will strike Mr. Bryce and some others across the water, and it may turn out to be impracticable, but it contains some snap. Theodore Marburg was presiding officer, and he made a very good one. Shaw, of the *Review of Reviews* was there, and talked, but he did not talk to much purpose. Lowell was the most effective man." [9]

The project was launched on the sea of American public opinion in Philadelphia on June 17, 1915.

". . . my associates and I have not been unaware," began Taft, "that we might be likened to the Tailors of Tooley Street who mistook themselves for the People of England. We wish first to say that we represent nobody but ourselves."

He then sought to quiet apprehensions, expressed in the Allied countries, that the purpose of the League to Enforce Peace was to halt the raging war. He dwelt on the necessity of including the doctrine of force in any plan to end future wars.

"We are not peace-at-any-price men," he said, "because we do not think we have reached the time when a plan based on the complete abolition of war is practicable. As long as nations partake of the frailties of men who compose them war is a possibility. . . . We believe it is still necessary to use a threat of overwhelming force of a great league with a willingness to make the threat good in order to frighten nations into a use of rational and peaceful means."

Taft explained that compliance with the rulings of the court or recommendations of the Conciliation Commission would not be compelled by force. War would be declared jointly only against a nation which refused to submit its dispute.

". . . we believe," he pointed out, "that the forced submission and the truce taken to investigate the judicial decision or the conciliatory compromise recommended will form a material inducement to peace. It will cool the heat of passion and will give the men of peace in each nation time to still the jingoes." [10]

Taft accepted the presidency of the league. Its work got under way. A year later it had raised $350,000 for propaganda purposes.[11]

[9] Taft to Mabel Boardman, April 12, 1915. [10] *Addresses,* Vol. XXXIV, pp. 417-421. [11] Taft to W. A. Obenchain, May 28, 1916.

Photo by Central Press, London

TAFT AND AMBASSADOR HARVEY, LONDON, 1922

See page 1001]

THE CHIEF JUSTICE AND HELEN MANNING, HIS GRANDDAUGHTER

—3—

Support and opposition followed hard upon publication by the League to Enforce Peace of its proposed association of nations. As might have been expected, Roosevelt was prompt in his disapproval. The colonel had, in 1911, fought Taft's arbitration agreements and had caused the President great bitterness. Roosevelt, he had then written, "is obsessed with his love of war and the glory of it." In 1915 Taft was more amused than angry. "I don't think that Roosevelt's attack on the League of Peace will hurt," he wrote, "and I would not dignify it by answering it." [12]

"The fact that I am at the head of the league," he noted about a year later, "is like a red flag to a bull to Theodore." [13]

He was greatly entertained, in February, 1917, when he saw the current issue of the *Metropolitan Magazine* and, in particular, a typographical error on the cover. He described it:

One of the funniest incidents connected with the whole thing is the mistake which was made on the outside, illuminated page of the *Metropolitan,* in which Roosevelt published his bitter article on the league. He attacked the league, but he also sought to deprive us of any claim for original work in it by saying that he himself had invented it in a speech made for the Nobel Prize Committee in Sweden. . . . But then having claimed the invention, he repudiated it because of the motives of the present promoters. This gave peculiar point to the mistake which occurred on the illuminated title page giving notice of the article within. The words were:—

"The League to Enforce Peace a Mischievous Sham Unless—

By Theodore Roosevelt." [14]

In time, Roosevelt and Taft effected a partial reconciliation even on the subject of international peace, although the Rough Rider's conception of a League of Nations would remain, until he died, wholly different from that of Wilson or of the sponsors of the League to Enforce Peace.

"I am quite sure we can come together on this League to

[12] Taft to W. H. Short, Dec. 6, 1915. [13] Taft to Horace D. Taft, Jan. 8, 1917. [14] Taft to Mabel Boardman, Feb. 6, 1917.

Enforce Peace," wrote Taft to Roosevelt in August, 1918. He added that the peace movement did not contemplate disarmament. Roosevelt's answer was somewhat evasive. He was heartily for universal military training on the Swiss or Australian pattern, he said. A League of Nations might be an addition to, not a substitute for, this training for defense.[15] Taft, meanwhile, was forced by his dislike for President Wilson into a belief that Roosevelt's plan for a league was more to his liking than was the President's.[16] This was not actually true; Roosevelt wanted an alliance among the Allies. On the night he died, in a final editorial for the Kansas City *Star,* he urged a League of Allies which would hand out stern justice to the vanquished foe. In due time, as non-Allied nations qualified, the privileges of the league might be extended to them.[17]

A degree of encouragement came from abroad. Lord Bryce, who had been British ambassador at Washington during the Taft years, was leading a League of Nations Society in England and was in constant touch with officials of the American League to Enforce Peace. Marburg conferred with Sir Edward Grey, England's foreign secretary, in March, 1916, and received, at the least, encouragement. Sir Edward "goes the whole length with us," Marburg reported to Taft, "and expressed the opinion that if some such provision had been in existence when the present war threatened, Germany would have been forced to consent to a hearing and there would have been no war." [18]

". . . of course," explained Sir Edward Grey in a subsequent letter to Bryce, "I did not commit myself to the details of the program." [19]

Of course not; nor did the representatives of any nation. There was little, as yet, which constituted a basis for commitment.

Meanwhile, there was the President of the United States. Taft and his colleagues were never to know precisely where they stood with Wilson or to what degree he really believed in their League to Enforce Peace. Taft was fairly confident in May, 1916, that the President approved of the league. Had not he so signified in public? [20] But Taft might have reminded himself that even Cabot

[15] Taft to Roosevelt, Aug. 20, 1918; Roosevelt to Taft, Aug. 26, 1918. [16] Taft to T. W. Beckett, Oct. 30, 1918. [17] Pringle, H. F., *Theodore Roosevelt, a Biography,* p. 603. [18] Marburg to Taft, March 23, 1916. [19] Grey to Bryce (copy to Taft), Nov. 15, 1916. [20] Taft to W. A. Obenchain, May 28, 1916.

Lodge had indicated approval. A desire to shape the peace of the world, to mold it on lines of justice and good will, was the very keynote of Wilson's existence after the outbreak of the World War. But it was a safe assumption that any tribunal would, if possible, be dominated by Wilsonian doctrines of international equity. The principal of these was that political independence and territorial integrity were to be guaranteed for all the nations of the world.

Colonel House had warned Wilson that the program "of the League to Enforce Peace" was "impracticable at this time." A wiser first step, he believed, was to persuade the world to agree upon the broad principles of freedom of the seas, political independence and territorial inviolability. To this end there should be an association of nations. The President accepted House's advice, but agreed to address a dinner of the League to Enforce Peace on May 27, 1916. It was at this function, with former President Taft presiding, that Wilson set forth his views.[21] They were still general rather than specific. For Wilson was not willing, as Taft was willing, to believe that the Allies as a whole, or even England alone, fought wholly on the side of right. The United States must still hold aloof.

"It does not appear that he [Wilson] studied seriously the program of the League to Enforce Peace," wrote the editor of Colonel House's papers, "nor the plans of Elihu Root . . . although without the educational accomplishments of such advocates of the league idea, it is unlikely that even the later leadership of Wilson himself would have greatly availed. It is true that he was destined to incorporate many of their ideas in his own plan, but he did not ask for nor did he accept their co-operation. He was determined to keep the control of the movement in his own hands." [22]

It was all extremely annoying. A more egocentric man than Taft would probably have abandoned the whole thing, for graciousness was not a marked characteristic in Wilson. The President was taking no chance whatever that his dream of eternal peace might be shattered by bungling. Only by controlling the situation absolutely, Wilson appears to have felt, could this disaster be guarded against. And so rebuffs, couched in politeness, came from the White House. It was suggested in July, 1916, that Taft should go to Eu-

[21] Seymour, Charles, *The Intimate Papers of Colonel House,* Vol. II, pp. 296-298, 337. [22] *Ibid.,* Vol. IV, pp. 4-5.

934 THE LIFE AND TIMES OF WILLIAM HOWARD TAFT

rope and discuss with leading statesmen the League to Enforce
Peace. Taft, himself, was dubious regarding the wisdom of this. He
would not go unless assured that the President desired it. And such
a visit was just what Wilson did not want.[23]

At the beginning of 1917 it was still not clear whether the President would support the essential principle of the League to Enforce
Peace: that force would be used against nations which went to war
without consultation. Taft discounted reports that Wilson was
weakening. "He has committed himself too fully . . . to withdraw," he noted.[24] Reassurances and suggestions came from Colonel
House, who conferred with Hamilton Holt and W. H. Short, secretary of the league, on January 13. There was no truth, said
House, that Wilson had turned his back on force. Indeed, he was
not only behind the league but ready to go further. House thought
that the Democratic senators could be held in line for the league
but urged that pressure be brought upon members of both houses
and both parties. It was vital to convert Bryan, he added.

"The colonel urges," reported Short to Taft, "that this is no
time for nourishing and urging individual opinions, and that we
make this plain to men like Bryan and to others who have schemes
of their own for organizing permanent peace." [25]

The President's "Peace Without Victory" message to the Senate
on January 22, 1917, on the eve of American entry into the war,
included endorsement of the League to Enforce Peace. Taft was
a degree puzzled; "Wilson," he wrote, "never does a thing just as
he ought to do it. . . .

"The President has come out for the league . . . but . . in
such a way as to embarrass me, because I don't agree with much
of what he says in respect to the kind of peace that ought to be
achieved. . . . I am in favor of a just peace, but I don't think a
just peace can be attained without the victory of the Allies. . . .
However, it is an agitation for the league and that is a good
thing." [26]

Throughout 1917 Taft gave a large measure of his time to the
league. Toward the end of the year it was again suggested by Dr.

[23] Latané, J. H., *op. cit.*, Vol. I, pp. 133, 209, 226; Taft to H. A. Garfield, Nov. 30,
1916. [24] Taft to F. K. Carey, Jan. 7, 1917. [25] W. H. Short to Taft, Jan. 15, 1917. [26] Taft to
W. Murray Crane, Jan. 23, 1917.

Wallace Buttrick of the General Education Board that he should go abroad. The purpose, this time, was to explain to the English the war aims and purposes of the United States. On December 12, 1917, Taft was called to the White House to discuss the trip with the President. He was willing to go, he said, only on condition that an official invitation came from Great Britain and with reassurances that Wilson believed it wise. Taft preserved a memorandum of their conversation.

The President, again, was opposed. Again, Mr. Wilson disclosed the keynote of his war policy. It was not desirable, the President said, for England and the United States to be drawn too closely together. The two nations had divergent aims; it must not be indicated that the United States was involved in British policy. Mr. Wilson cited to Taft, in support of this, the obnoxious treaty between England and Italy. The motives of the United States were unselfish; those of Great Britain were less worthy and the treaty proved it. Indeed, said the President, too many Englishmen had already come to America to explain their country's war aims and he had asked Colonel House to say to them informally that they might well leave. There were additional reasons, the President continued, why such visits by Taft and other distinguished Americans to England would be harmful. The Irish in the United States and other anti-British elements would be alienated, he suggested. Besides, a visit by so distinguished an American as Taft would cause jealous resentment in France.

Taft listened patiently and then observed that Walter Hines Page, American ambassador to Great Britain, had suggested the journey.

"Page is really an Englishman," said Wilson, "and I have to discount whatever he says about the situation in Great Britain. I think you ought not to go and the same applies to the other members of the party. I would like you to make my attitude clear on this point." [27]

The President, it now appears, was devoting only passing attention to the question of peace during 1917; he was giving all of

[27] Memorandum, Dec. 14, 1917, Taft papers, Library of Congress, The memorandum offers further proof that Wilson had at least partial knowledge of the so-called "Secret Treaties," a knowledge he disavowed before the Senate Foreign Relations Committee in August, 1919.

his time to prosecuting the war. In September he assigned to the faithful House the task of collating all the material which related to peace and dismissed the matter, to a large degree, from his mind. But in January, 1918, he offered his Fourteen Points to the world and spoke again of a "general association of nations" which would be "formed under specific covenants for the purpose of affording mutual guaranties of political independence and territorial integrity to great and small states alike." [28] He was quick to act, too, when it appeared in March, 1918, that the League to Enforce Peace might endanger his own plans for international amity.

—4—

If details of a league were to be drafted, Wilson would draft them. But details, Wilson continued to insist, were still unwise. He told Marburg that the time had not come to discuss the formal constitution of a tribunal for peace.

"The principle is easy to adhere to," the President warned, "but the moment questions of organization are taken up all sorts of jealousies come to the front which ought not now to be added to other matters of delicacy. I am sure you will appreciate the force of these considerations."

This vetoed a suggestion that the League to Enforce Peace should work with the British League of Nations Society.[29] The Taft organization went ahead, however, with plans for a convention in Philadelphia in May, 1918. It was announced in early March.

On March 14, Bainbridge Colby, a "Wilson darling" according to Taft, was quietly at work as a member of the Shipping Board when he was surprised to receive a personal visit from the President.[30] It appeared that Wilson was alarmed over the Philadelphia gathering at which a league would be discussed. He so expressed himself to Colby. The future secretary of state immediately asked Taft, who was due in Washington, for a conference. It was held on the following day.

[28] Seymour, Charles, op. cit., Vol. IV, pp. 4-6. [29] Latané, J. H., op. cit., Vol. I, pp. 415, 418. [30] Taft to Helen H. Taft, March 16, 1918.

"He said the President said he was afraid that at the convention," dictated Taft in a long memorandum, "details of the proposed league would be discussed by men of prominence, and that it would embarrass him in such communications as he might wish to make for peace when the time arrived. I told Mr. Colby that the object of the convention was not to discuss the details of the league— that those we had been considering in a confidential way in a study committee. I told him the great purpose in holding the convention was to support the government in carrying through the war, to the defeat of Germany, on the ground that no League to Enforce Peace could be useful until we had defeated Germany."

It was concluded that an interview with the President was necessary and this was arranged for March 28. President Lowell of Harvard accompanied Taft.[31]

"The sum of the interview was that he did not object to the convention in view of the fact that it was a Win the War convention," Taft reported.[32]

A lengthy discussion preceded this presidential decision, though. Wilson reiterated that discussion at such a convention might make later negotiations difficult.

"The President," Taft wrote, "then took up the subject of what could be done by the nations after the war. He said he thought the nations might guarantee to one another their integrity and territory, and that if any violations of these were threatened or occurred special conferences might be called to consider the question. He said he knew this would be slow, but that the common law was built up that way. . . . He gave it as his opinion that the Senate . . . would be unwilling to enter into an agreement by which a majority of the other nations could tell the United States when they must go to war."

Taft and Lowell must have been greatly disheartened by these words; it looked as if Wilson, again, was turning against the use of force. President Lowell then asked whether the work of organizing a league might not be accelerated if, first, a definite and detailed program was adopted. Wilson's answer was not direct; he referred to the necessity of protecting the smaller nations. He added

[31] Memorandum by Taft, March 28, 1918, Taft papers, Library of Congress. [32] Taft to Helen H. Taft, March 29, 1918.

that it would be very difficult to obtain agreement among the various nations. The Taft memorandum continues:

He [the President] instanced the fact that there had been much difficulty in securing united action by the military forces of the Allies. He said he had pressed its necessity upon the Allies and had secured the military joint council, but that Haig [Sir Douglas Haig] had made a great fuss because report of its action had not been transmitted through him to the English government and had been sent direct. How he [the President] felt greatly pleased to hear that a commander in chief of the Allied forces had been agreed upon. President Lowell asked who it was. President Wilson answered that it was a Frenchman, as it ought to be, because the fighting was on French soil. He said the officer chosen was one whose name he had not heard before and it had escaped his memory.

After this indication of Wilson's lofty and isolated view of the war (and of Foch's obscurity in America), the conversation shifted back to peace. The President told Taft and Lowell "that, as we doubtless understood, his messages defining our attitude were intended to call the bluff of Germany and Austria in professing a desire to negotiate a peace and he had succeeded in showing it was a bluff, and that instead of announcing specific terms, their answers were vague and unintelligible":

He said he greatly deprecated Lloyd George's declaration that we must fight this war to a knockout of Germany. He said he did not think it possible and he thought such a statement, showing a desire to punish the German people, would keep them solidly behind the Kaiser and in sympathy with the military party, whereas he thought it was important to separate them from such influence and control and have them believe that we were ready to make a reasonable and just peace, as he was. He said they knew that the Austrian situation was a desperate one.

I said I did not think we could trust the present military dynasty of Germany to make a peace that would bind Germany to anything. He said he thought the German people would be near a break if this drive failed. . . . He said the peoples of the Allies were war weary. He did not believe that either the British people or our own would insist on fighting the war merely to restore Alsace-Lorraine to France and if that was all that stood between peace and continued war, Germany would be allowed to retain them.[33]

It was a discouraging session, all in all. Taft felt that Wilson's attitude, as expressed, had been "to take back and give up everything," he had said about the League to Enforce Peace "since he first referred to it." [34] A gesture or two toward Taft and the league were made. It would be "most wise and should be most helpful," the President told Colonel House, for a luncheon conference to be arranged with Taft, Lowell and Root and this was held in April. At it, Wilson's view that the Senate would never consent to force, by direction of a majority of nations, was repeated. Nobody at the conference, House noted in his diary, "altogether agreed with the President. They thought he did not go far enough." [35] But Wilson, it would soon develop, knew more about the Senate than did Taft.

"Wilson is in one of his moods where he has now become opposed to the plan of the league . . ." Taft concluded. "This does not discourage me, because he is nothing but a weathercock, and when he finds out . . . the solidity of the demand of the American people for . . . an organized force of the nations, he will come again to our view." [36]

The Armistice was finally signed and Taft, quite naturally, watched with eager anxiety the plans for the peace conference. He could not decide whether Wilson was wise in going abroad, himself. At first he regarded it as a mistake, "but he is spectacular and likes to do the unexpected and rare thing." [37] Later, Taft decided that "the trip is a good thing." It would bring the President "into close personal touch with the situation. I think it may bring home to him the demand of the common people of England, France and Italy that we have a League of Nations." [38] Not without malice, he thought that Wilson would "learn a lot of things that he does not know now, and he perhaps may be made more reasonable. . . .

[33] Memorandum, March 28, 1918. [34] Taft to Helen H. Taft, March 29, 1918. [35] Seymour, Charles, *op. cit.,* Vol. IV, pp. 12-16. [36] Taft to H. S. Canby, May 20, 1918. [37] Taft to H. W. Taft, Nov. 19, 1918. [38] Taft to Bryce, Dec. 5, 1918.

"Lloyd George and Clemenceau are not children, and he will find that he cannot handle them as if he were a schoolmaster. He will find himself at a disadvantage when he comes to make arguments with men who know more than he does. The trouble with him is that he is ignorant." [39] A few years later Taft heard from Lloyd George, himself, how cleverly Wilson had been handled.

For the Peace Commission selected by the President, Taft had only contempt and he gave way, again, to exasperated disapproval. There is no evidence at all that this was personal or based in any degree on disappointment that he had not been named. Yet save for Root, no man in the United States was better qualified for the task. He was an excellent conciliator. His great interest in a League of Nations had made him familiar with many of the problems. Most important, perhaps, Taft enjoyed the full confidence of the American public. Colonel House had recommended the appointment of Taft or Root or both, but Wilson had shown no inclination to name either. Attorney General T. W. Gregory, another close adviser, also suggested these two distinguished jurists.

"I could see," commented Gregory, recalling the interview at the White House, "that he drew back a little from the suggestion." [40]

"Mention of my name for the commission of peace was not infrequent," confided Taft to Lord Bryce, "and it was made more so by the statement of Creel and Burleson and others that had I not gone into the last campaign and signed a joint statement with Theodore, I certainly would have been selected. I wrote to Theodore that evil association with him, it was reported from the White House, had kept me out of the commission. I said to him that this was one of a number of misstatements coming from the White House, but the most remote from the truth; that under no conditions would I have been selected save one, and that one was that the choice should be by law limited to the two ex-presidents. Then I thought I might be preferred to him."

Taft's analysis was undoubtedly accurate. Wilson wanted men he could control. For the Republican member he chose Henry White, who was amiable rather than forceful. The other commis-

[39] Taft to Mrs. Lucien Wilson, Dec. 7, 1918. [40] Seymour, Charles, *op. cit.,* Vol. IV, pp. 221, 224.

sioners were House, Major General Tasker H. Bliss, and Secretary of State Lansing. Taft had little use for any of them. House was "a very pleasant gentleman, but quite superficial, a politician, a listener, a good reporter to the President." As for White, whom he had never liked: "He is of the type of your life-trained, hidebound, traditional English Continental diplomatist. . . . He is more of an Englishman than he is an American." Taft paid Lansing and Bliss the dubious compliment of saying nothing at all about them.[41] As a whole, the commission was "a cheap lot of skates. I could swear if it would do any good." [42]

Meanwhile, what chance was there that an effective League of Nations would result from the deliberations abroad? Taft dismissed with asperity the contention that a league was unconstitutional. This was "a mere bogey. It does not take away from Congress the power to declare war— it only creates an obligation to enter a war, which Congress may perform or not in its discretion. Every time we guarantee the integrity of another country, as we have of Panama, we enter into a contract to make war." [43]

Taft was not too sanguine over the prospects for success. The President had no plan; nobody knew what the Wilson league was, he said.[44] But in this he was not fully informed, for Wilson had prepared a draft of the covenant. From Robert A. Taft, who was in Paris with Hoover, arrived discouraging reports. Economic jealousies were already flaring, Taft's older son said. He was afraid "the President and the League of Nations are steadily losing ground. . . . The nebulous character of his League of Nations does not gain it any advocates." [45]

Former Attorney General Wickersham, a law partner of Henry Taft, had agreed to go abroad to observe the conference for the New York *Tribune*. Taft and President Lowell of Harvard, as leaders of the League to Enforce Peace, summarized for him the views, as they saw them, of the American people toward a league. They hoped he would transmit these to the delegates at Versailles.

"We feel," wrote Taft and Lowell, "that the people of the United States, with the issue of the league acutely before them,

---

[41] Taft to Bryce, Dec. 5, 1918. [42] Taft to C. P. Taft, Dec. 23, 1918. [43] Taft to S. T. Miller, Dec. 24, 1918. [44] Taft to V. P. Squires, Dec. 31, 1918. [45] R. A. Taft to Taft, Dec. 4, 1918.

942   THE LIFE AND TIMES OF WILLIAM HOWARD TAFT

will certainly approve its adoption. Organized labor has already passed a resolution . . . approving it. . . . The idea of the league met with the concurrence of every American audience before whom it was explained. . . . Up to this time, the League of Nations has not become a party question. . . . We do not understand that the adoption of a league includes compulsory disarmament." [46]

Not all the reports from the Peace Conference were gloomy. Taft was cheered as Wilson, whom he had believed to be faltering, pressed with vigor for a league. Moreover, it would apparently be an effective tribunal "with provisions to secure the enforcement and maintenance of the treaty provisions and the maintenance of peace." [47]

The League of Nations Committee of the Peace Conference met in Paris on February 3, 1919, and the complex task of compromising conflicting points of view began. Wilson had, by this time, made four drafts of the covenant.[48] Taft was convinced that it would be a real league, close enough to the principles of his own League to Enforce Peace to merit energetic support. He began preparations for a tour which would carry him through fifteen states. From President Wilson, still in Paris, came expressions of warm appreciation for the nonpartisan spirit Taft was showing.[49] He needed that support desperately. Astute representatives of the Allies were nullifying the Fourteen Points on which the Armistice had been based. At home, rumblings of dissent among the members of the new Senate, meeting on March 4, were ominous warnings that Wilson's league, any league that was not a sham, was facing strong opposition. The President, Taft soundly observed, was partly responsible "by his brutal ignoring of the Senate" in selecting his peace commissioners and by "his determination to hog all the credit of negotiating the treaty." But these were trivialities, however annoying, compared with the hope that the war had not been fought in vain, that the President might bring back "a treaty worth having, a league with [a] 'bite' in it."

Taft's journeyings for the league took him into Nevada and he pondered, as he traveled through that arid state, "over the narrow partisanship of the brute willingness of those little Americans

[46] Taft and Lowell to Wickersham, Dec. 11, 1918. [47] Taft to O. S. Straus, Jan. 19, 1919. [48] Zimmern, Alfred, op. cit., pp. 237-239. [49] Marie Mischler to Taft, Feb. 15, 1919.

in the Senate" who fought this dream of peace. He had been gratified to find the women of the hinterland enthusiastically behind the league and he wondered, after all, whether they should not be given the vote:

As I write, I look out upon the desert of Nevada, and it suggests the waste that war makes; and when I think of the vicious narrowness of Reed [Senator James A. Reed of Missouri], the explosive ignorance of Poindexter [Senator Miles Poindexter of Washington], the ponderous Websterian language and lack of stamina of Borah, the vanity of Lodge as an old diplomatic hand on the Foreign Relations Committee, the selfishness, laziness and narrow, lawyerlike acuteness of Knox, the emptiness and sly partisanship of Hale [Senator Fred Hale of Maine], with the utter nothingness of Fall [Senator Albert D. Fall of New Mexico], in the face of this great world's crisis, I confess I don't see where we have any advantage over the women— at least in this juncture.

I beg of you to believe I am not drunk or wild, but am only roused to the critical situation in world affairs that those who gather around the council board in Paris know, and that these barking critics do not seem to realize. It is their American selfishness, their American littleness, blinding them to the real interests of this nation as well as of the world, that arouses me. I can see that little head of Hays [Will Hays, chairman of the Republican National Committee] wagging over the errors I have made from a political standpoint. I can hear the discussions in the cloakrooms and the damning of me. I can hear the wiseacres say, "That shows what defeated the party in 1912, and here's a repetition of it. Weren't the Progressives justified in breaking off? Taft's loyalty to the party was always weak. Now, thank God, he is out of it." To have incurred this condemnation by so noble a body as the Republicans of the Senate, and such a shining leader as Fess [Senator Simeon D. Fess of Ohio], is certainly a sad fate, but I must bear it.[50]

His ire was further aroused by the Senate "round robin" which rejected a league and called, instead, for a mere treaty of peace. He applauded Wilson's stratagem by which the league was made part of the treaty itself.

"The treaty which will come back here for ratification by the Senate will contain a League of Nations in its web and woof," he

[50] Taft to Karger, Feb. 22, 1919.

told one critic. "The question will then be whether we shall continue a state of war by trying to amend the treaty and sending it back for another conference, or whether we shall accept the treaty and begin reconstruction. . . . Where will the businessmen be on that issue? Where will the *Wall Street Journal* be on that issue? The truth is there is a depth of misconception in respect to the situation that makes one marvel at the ignorance of you businessmen. You accept statements from senators stung with hatred of Wilson, as the businessmen of the country are, and who imagine that Wilson is merely postponing reconstruction to gratify a fad of his. That is not true in any degree. I don't like Wilson any better than you do, but I think I can rise above my personal attitude . . . in order to help along the world and the country. I don't care who gets the credit for the League of Nations, if it goes through." [51]

President Wilson returned to America with his league and Taft said that he would "vote for the covenant as it is, without hesitation, because I don't think it contains any of the dangers which are pointed out in the Senate. The Republicans and the Democrats who have signed the round robin have gotten themselves in such a situation that they may be rendered desperate and defeat the treaty with the league in it, unless they are given a ladder to climb out of the hole in which they have precipitated themselves . . . the plenary council of the commission has determined that the League of Nations must be a part of the treaty of peace, and Wilson, realizing the advantage which that gives him . . . will insist upon it." [52]

Taft had no objection to clarifying amendments, ones which did not vitiate the provision that the combined force of the covenanting nations should be used against violators. From Borah, in mid-February, came a plea that the Monroe Doctrine must be recognized specifically in the draft.[53] Taft agreed that this was wise and communicated directly with Wilson:

I venture to write you about the situation on this side in respect to the League of Nations. The senatorial opponents are speaking all over the country and are seeking to justify their attitude. Most

[51] Taft to J. G. Butler, March 17, 1919. [52] Taft to R. A. Taft, March 17, 1919. [53] Borah to Taft, Feb. 19, 1919.

of them aver their support of a League of Nations but criticize this one. If you bring back the treaty with the League of Nations in it, and make more specific reservation of the Monroe Doctrine, require expressly unanimity of action in the Executive Council and Body of Delegates . . . and add to Article XV a provision that where the Executive Council or the Body of Delegates finds the difference to grow out of an exclusively domestic policy, it shall recommend no settlement, the ground will be completely cut from under the opponents of the league in the Senate.[54]

These appeals followed Wilson's return to Paris. They were acknowledged, through Private Secretary Tumulty, with appreciation by the President.[55] Certainly Wilson should have been grateful. The league had no better friend in the United States than Taft. On March 4, the former President had spoken at the Metropolitan Opera House in New York at a vast League of Nations gathering at which Wilson had also defended his covenant.

"I dealt with the League and he with generalities," Taft observed, a degree complacently.[56]

Taft's approval of the revised covenant was due, in part, to the degree to which President Wilson had accepted his suggested changes in the first draft. Three of his recommendations were incorporated in almost the exact language in which he had submitted them: that a nation might withdraw on two years' notice, that purely domestic questions were not to be considered by the league, that plans for the limitation of armaments were to be revised every decade (Taft suggested five years). His recommendation for specific reference to the Monroe Doctrine was also adopted by Wilson, but in simplified form.[57]

—6—

As he had done so often in the past, Taft again misjudged both public opinion and the probable actions of politically minded men. Wilson, back at the Peace Conference, was giving ground, little by little, on his Fourteen Points. The President's all-in-all was the

[54] Taft to Wilson, March 12, 1919. [55] Taft to H. W. Taft, March 20, 1919. [56] Taft to R. A. Taft, March 17, 1919. [57] New York *World*, July 18, 1919.

league and so he sacrificed his principles on the Shantung and Fiume issues. It would be difficult, in the months ahead, for the American people to discern anything very idealistic about a League of Nations obtained at such cost. Taft, like Wilson, could see only that the revised league, incorporated in the final Treaty of Versailles, was an excellent and forceful safeguard against future wars.

"I think that the conference has much improved the covenant," he wrote in May, 1919, "and while I regret that its original form had deficiencies that could not be supplied, I am convinced that it will be a long step forward and that we ought to do everything we can to secure its ratification.

"The Republicans have been making fools of themselves, in my judgment, by allowing their bitter personal opposition to Wilson to control their good sense. The people of this country are in favor of the league. It looks now as if there would be a majority in the Senate to vote down amendments in that body. This majority is likely to be composed of forty-four or forty-five Democrats and half a dozen Republicans. . . . Lowell and I . . . with others, are going out on another tour to advocate the ratification of the amended covenant. We shall hold state conventions in about fifteen cities." [58]

Taft was able to enlist, even if but temporarily, the support of National Chairman Hays. They had a conference by telephone on May 20.

"He said," Taft dictated after the call, "he thought it was necessary to ratify the treaty in such a way that it would not have to go back to a conference. . . . I said that if the impression got abroad that the senators, merely because they hate Mr. Wilson, were willing to defeat the treaty and postpone the coming of resumption of business, it would furnish Mr. Wilson with an argument that might embarrass the Republican party. He said he agreed with me fully." [59]

The revised league with which President Wilson embarked for the United States as June ended was superior, Taft felt, because the original covenant "gave evidence . . . of hasty preparation. . . . Different terms meaning the same thing were used . . . suggesting

[58] Taft to Bryce, May 5, 1919. [59] Memorandum by Taft, May 20, 1919, Taft papers, Library of Congress.

a difference of opinion where none was intended." The specification that any nation might withdraw upon two years' notice was reasonable, he thought. The machinery of the tribunal had been improved. Taft could find no basis, in this draft, for alarm over Article X whereby the council of the league was empowered to take action against any nation making war for territory or conquest.

"With a constant representative on the council and a required unanimity in the method it advises," he pointed out, "the United States can be sure that the burden of maintaining its obligation will be reasonably distributed . . . and that the council will not advise that the United States send armies to countries in which it has but a remote interest. . . .

"The natural result of this necessity for agreement between [sic] the great nations . . . will be that the burden of maintaining Article X inviolate in the Western Hemisphere will fall upon the United States and the South American countries able to perform the obligation— an arrangement which is fair and which nobody can object to." In addition to all this, the Monroe Doctrine was specifically recognized in Article XXI. Taft made clear, too, his position with regard to reservations by the Senate.

"If the reservation is not an amendment to the league, such that it will have to go back and receive the concurrence of the other Allied powers, as well as that of Germany," he said, "then, of course, I have no objection. . . . That would be a mere announcement to the other countries that this was the attitude that the United States intended to take . . . with reference to the meaning of the treaty." [60]

The reservations offered in the Senate were, however, to be far more than mere statements of a national attitude; they undermined the league itself. President Wilson returned to the United States with deluded certainty that he could impose his will on the upper house. He announced a national tour on which he would carry his case to the people. On this, it was reported, he would calmly discuss the provisions of the league. When Secretary Tumulty urged refutation of the charge that a superstate had been created, Mr. Wilson refused.

"Taft has answered that completely," he said.[61]

[60] Taft to A. H. Vandenburg, June 4, 1919. [61] Karger to Taft, July 9, 1919.

Nobody had effectively answered it. Yet it was made the chief argument of the league's foes who said that America could be plunged into a war without her consent, who told a war-weary nation that the league would breed further hostilities. In September, 1919, the President began the tour which was to end in physical and virtual mental collapse and in defeat for his cherished hopes. He had not remembered to discuss the league dispassionately. Against its enemies, and his, he hurled such terms as "irreconcilables" and "bitter-enders"; they were, he swore, a "battalion of death."[62] But they were, too, the men on whom he depended for ratification of the treaty.

Taft grew discouraged as the President toured. "Wilson is playing into their hands by his speeches in the West," he wrote. ". . . It is impossible for him, schoolmaster that he is, to make speeches on the subject and explain the league without framing contemptuous phrases to characterize his opponents. . . . The President's attitude in not consenting to any reservations at all is an impossible one, and grows out of a persistent determination to be blind to facts that he does not like."[63] And there was small sympathy in Taft's heart when word came that the President had cracked under the strain of his trip: "The truth is, he has [so] insisted on hogging all the authority . . . trusting no one, that he has broken himself down."[64]

Will Hays, by now, was bowing to the bitter-enders; he endorsed the majority report of the Senate Foreign Relations Committee. "This is not only not right, but it is the poorest kind of politics," Taft rebuked, "and I wonder why you have allowed yourself to be drawn into it."[65] As for the reservations offered by the committee: "I don't like any . . . because of their offensive tone."[66] But in time Taft felt that a treaty thus amended was better than none at all. He discarded, although reluctantly, the Article X which had been so basic a principle of the League to Enforce Peace.[67]

"Oh, I beg of you, senator, to consider the consequences if you defeat the treaty," he pleaded with Senator Gilbert M. Hitch-

[62] Sullivan, Mark, *Our Times,* Vol. IV, pp. 553-555. [63] Taft to E. E. Whiting, Sept. 12, 1919; to Talcott Williams, Sept. 28, 1919. [64] Taft to W. A. Edwards, Oct. 27, 1919. [65] Taft to Hays, Sept. 10, 1919. [66] Taft to A. L. Lowell, Sept. 10, 1919. [67] Taft to Frank Cobb, Nov. 10, 1919.

cock of Nebraska. "The treaty, even with the reservations, represents enormous progress toward better conditions as to peace and war in the world. The barking dogs of opposition will cease their noise and the real conscience of the United States will assert itself in its actual participation in the doings of the league. We are in sight of the promised land. Don't, don't prevent our reaching there." [68]

Taft could hardly believe the news when word came from Washington in late October that the battle was being lost. He called it a "stunning blow." [69] He clung desperately to a hope "that the defeat of the treaty is not final, and that after the senators go home . . . they will come back with a willingness to put it through." [70] But from this he turned to rage against Wilson and Cabot Lodge who continued "to exalt their personal prestige and the saving of their ugly faces above the welfare of the country and the world." [71]

The hatred for Wilson became an obsession; Taft searched his vocabulary for terms with which to describe "that mulish enigma, that mountain of egotism and selfishness who lives in the White House." [72] Hatred led Taft to a conviction that Senator Harding, nominated for the presidency, was a better friend of peace than Wilson had been. True, the Republican League of Nations plank was weak. But he concluded to support Harding who was, besides, a Republican. [73] At times Taft was doubtful that he had been wise in backing the Ohio senator who was "certainly talking too much . . . and allowing himself to say things about the league that are embarrassing." [74] But when a clergyman in Missouri charged him with being a turncoat he replied at length and with spirit. He recited his long and zealous advocacy of peace by negotiation. He told how he had stood behind Wilson until it became apparent that Article X could not be accepted by the Senate. The President had refused to compromise, and the election of James M. Cox, the Democratic nominee, would merely prolong the deadlock. Taft said he had "a sincere hope that we may secure a very useful league through Mr. Harding. I am convinced that we can make no prog-

[68] Taft to Hitchcock, Nov. 15, 1919. [69] Taft to J. S. Williams, Oct. 24, 1919. [70] Taft to Robert McDougal, Nov. 24, 1919. [71] Taft to Mrs. Strong, Dec. 17, 1919. [72] Taft to G. M. Wrong, March 3, 1920. [73] Taft to J. J. Spurgeon, June 14, 1920. [74] Taft to W. Murray Crane, Aug. 14, 1920.

ress with Mr. Cox's election." Then Taft denied, with vehemence, that he had abandoned his sacred cause:

I have written this statement of my position not because the language and tone of your letter deserve it. I would have thrust your letter into the wastebasket without answer at all but for the fact that you are a minister of the gospel and are, I believe, sincere and enthusiastic in support of a good cause, and I dislike to be condemned by such a person as you have condemned me, without a word in justification of my course. You call me a "turncoat." You charge me with having forsaken principle and betrayed my conviction. You say I have paid a big price in the support of Senator Harding. You ask me if I take the American people for fools or for dupes. You ask me about Mr. Harding's stand. You say you would rather be dead than occupy the place that I now fill in the minds of the American people, that I am an actor in this drama who will have shrunk up terribly in size, and that I am a farcical actor whose part in the League of Nations fight beats all that was ever staged in the world's history and that you are one of millions disappointed and disgusted with my conduct. These expressions are hardly judicial. They prompt the question whether you have ever read my speeches and articles explaining my support of Mr. Harding and my opposition to Mr. Cox. I have no other knowledge of you, sir, except that you are a clergyman, and by reason of your cloth trained to deal justly and in a spirit of righteous kindliness with all. I ask you whether you don't think it is not only in accord with your religion but also with the rule of manly virtue to attribute to others as deep sincerity of conviction as you have yourself, unless the proof of such motives as those attributed to me is clear and unmistakable.[75]

Taft's mail was crowded, during the 1920 campaign, with other rebukes from disappointed League of Nations supporters. It appears that he actually read many of them. That he did so with sorrow is indicated by a note, scrawled in his own hand, across the face of a typical, chiding communication:

Misch:
    It would do no good to answer this man, but keep and file this letter. Some day he'll regret having written it.
                                        W. H. T.[76]

[75] Taft to W. H. Hargrave, Nov. 1, 1920. [76] F. H. Decker to Taft, Nov. 8, 1920.

CHAPTER L

AT LAST

URING his years at New Haven, Taft continued to gaze, wistfully more than with hope, toward, as he described it, the "sacred shrine" [1] that was the Supreme Court of the United States. Suggestions were often made by his friends— and even crept into print from time to time— that President Wilson might select Taft if Chief Justice White retired or died. This was still the highest desire of his heart. He would rather be chief justice than president, he often said. But he had no reason to suppose that Wilson, a Democrat, would select a Republican. Taft, of course, had appointed White, who was a Democrat. But that was a different matter.

"I am pleased . . . to have you suggest my competency to fill the chief justiceship, but it will never come," Taft told one friend who had written on the subject.[2]

Quite naturally, Taft watched with a coldly critical eye the Supreme Court appointments made by Wilson. Associate Justice Lurton died in the summer of 1914 and it seemed probable, at once, that the President would promote Attorney General McReynolds. This, Taft said, would be to "put a weak man on the bench," [3] a reversal of his praise when McReynolds had been put in Wilson's Cabinet. Subsequently, when Harding was elected and the chief justiceship became a possibility, Taft concluded that he would decline any save this most exalted office. In 1916, though, he admitted that he might take the post of associate justice. Another vacancy occurred in January of that year. "I am wicked enough to enjoy the assault upon Wilson to force him to offer me an appointment. Of course it will fail, but he does not like it." [4] Yet should it come, "I wouldn't say that I wouldn't accept." [5]

[1] Taft to Karger, March 20, 1916. [2] Taft to J. M. Dickinson, Jan. 18, 1914. [3] Taft to Mabel Boardman, July 15, 1914. [4] Taft to C. D. Norton, Jan. 16, 1916. [5] Taft to Karger, Jan. 16, 1916.

Instead, the President appointed Louis D. Brandeis. This was a fearful shock to Taft. In the years ahead, associating daily with Brandeis and learning the jurist's true greatness, Chief Justice Taft was fair enough and big enough to amend radically his opinion of Brandeis. In 1916 the memory of the Ballinger controversy was too vivid. Taft had no doubt that Brandeis, as counsel for Glavis, had been unfair if not unethical. He was, besides, a radical. Taft's condemnation, as he prepared to oppose confirmation by the Senate, equaled any he had heaped upon Theodore Roosevelt:

> . . . it is one of the deepest wounds that I have had as an American and a lover of the Constitution and a believer in progressive conservatism that such a man as Brandeis could be put in the court. . . . He is a muckraker, an emotionalist for his own purposes, a Socialist . . . a man who has certain high ideals in his imagination . . . of great tenacity of purpose and, in my judgment, of much power for evil. . . .
>
> The intelligent Jews of this country are as much opposed to Brandeis's nomination as I am, but there are politics in the Jewish community. . . . Wilson has projected a fight, which with master art he will give the color of a contest, on one side of which will be ranged the opposition of corporate wealth and racial prejudice, and on the other side the downtrodden, the oppressed, the uplifters, the labor unions and all the elements which are supposed to have votes in the election. This will lead to the confirmation because of the white-livered senators that we have. . . .
>
> But as so often happens in such a well-devised Machiavellian scheme, the ultimate result is not going to be to Wilson's advantage, if we nominate any man whose conservatism appeals to the businessmen. . . . This appointment will be remembered long after the excitement of the confirmation has passed away. . . . It is too ingenious and too unscrupulous. . . . When you consider Brandeis's appointment, and think that men were pressing me for the place, *es ist zum lachen*. . . . The thoughts of the judges [*sic*] of the Supreme Court, if they could be interpreted, would form interesting language.[6]

"I hope White will not end his judicial career with an apoplectic fit caused by the nomination," Taft wrote that same day.[7] Such

[6] Taft to Karger, Jan. 3, 1916, [7] Taft to H. W. Taft, Jan. 31, 1916.

an appointment, if often repeated, "would break down the Supreme Court as a bulwark of the guaranties of civil liberty." [8]

So Root, president of the American Bar Association, signed a petition of protest which was sent to the Senate Judiciary Committee. Taft and five other past presidents of the association joined in declaring that Brandeis was unfit.[9] None the less, Brandeis was confirmed and took his seat. Taft became convinced, again, that the 1916 election was "the most critical during my career." The next president would have four Supreme Court justices to name. By selecting Brandeis, Wilson had already "disgraced" the court.[10]

—2—

Taft's life was full and busy. He spent less time, perhaps, in New Haven than lecturing in all parts of the country. In the late summer of 1919 a personal problem confronted him. Andrew Carnegie was dead. His will, filed for probate, provided an income of $10,000 during Taft's life and the same sum for Mrs. Taft should she survive him. This was an echo of the $25,000 pension which Carnegie, still alive, had proposed for ex-presidents and which Taft had rejected. He was inclined to refuse the $10,000 annuity as well. For one thing, he did not need the money. His estate, including insurance, totaled about $300,000.

"I expect to go on earning what I can by reasonable work until I am too old," he said.[11]

On urging from Elihu Root and others, however, Taft changed his mind and decided to take the money. "Mrs. Taft wishes me to do it," he said, "and she is an interested party." [12]

He had never been too enthusiastic, in the campaign of 1920, about the qualities of Nominee Harding. He watched with some doubt as the President-elect prepared to pick a Cabinet.

"One thing I marvel at is that Harding seems to deal so much with Hays," he observed. "Hays is such an infernal lightweight. . . . Hays's appointment as postmaster general . . . will not strengthen the Cabinet." [13]

[8] Taft to T. G. Palmer, Jan. 31, 1916. [9] Taft to L. A. Coolidge, March 6, 1916. [10] Taft to James Markham, Oct. 21, 1916. [11] Taft to Karger, Aug. 30, 1916. [12] *Idem,* Jan. 1, 1920. [13] Taft to Hilles, Dec. 15, 1920.

Taft was even more apprehensive when he heard rumors that Albert D. Fall— he had never liked Fall— might be in the official family. Harding was considering Fall for secretary of state, it appeared, and this seemed preposterous in view of his jingo tendencies and his "Hearst view of Mexican politics. . . . It is possible that I do Fall injustice . . . [but] he has been a speculator and jack-leg kind of lawyer along the border."

It was all more than a little discouraging. Perhaps Taft remembered, as he worried, the rebukes which had been heaped on his head by League of Nations enthusiasts during the campaign. He did not look forward, in December, 1920, to an impending conference with the President-elect. "I really don't know how to deal with Harding when I see him," he said, "because I haven't known him personally very well, and I don't know whether entire frankness will be useful." Taft was a far better prophet than he realized as he contemplated the incoming administration. Mediocrities in the Cabinet, he said, would "launch his administration into a sea of certain failures."

Taft was able to envision, too, the possible social complications which would mark the turbulent Harding era. He was surprised that the Hardings were growing so close to the McLeans and their extravagant life in Washington.

"Of course," he added, "it is easy to see why the McLeans coddle the Hardings, because it will give them an even greater social importance than their wealth and means of entertainment in Washington would give, but it is a very dangerous relation for a president to have, and I fear that it is an evidence of the lack of conventional society experience of the Hardings."

Taft went to Marion, Ohio, for a breakfast appointment with the President-elect on December 24 and reported in detail, as always, to Mrs. Taft: "They were very cordial. . . . They had waffles and creamed chipped beef . . . with coffee and toast. They offered me eggs, but as I saw this was extra, I declined. . . . We had quite a long conversation over the social question. The senator was disposed to 'chuck' ceremony, to use his own term. Mrs. Harding took a different view, and I stood by her and insisted that it was essential. . . . When the senator left us for a while, I talked more with her and commented on the necessity of insisting that all his friends, except the family, should call him Mr. President instead of Warren as they do now. . . . I had not realized . . . how little they had known of the White House. . . . She is a nice woman, who will, I think, be all right. She is a little disposed to be anxious not to be backward, but she will readily adapt herself. She is four or five years older than Harding, and I think she tries him sometimes, but he is very considerate. She is not at all bad looking. Her newspaper pictures don't do her justice."

After breakfast Harding escorted Taft to his study where a discussion of the Cabinet was started at once. What the President-elect disclosed was encouraging; he had offered Hughes, Charles G. Dawes and Hoover places. They were good men, all. Taft was less certain about Harry Daugherty, destined to be attorney general.

"He [Harding] said he could see through Harry when Harry did not suspect it, but he said Harry was loyal and a good lawyer. I said yes, that he, Harding, was entitled to have such a friend in the Cabinet."

Then came the most astonishing part of the conversation:

"By the way," said Harding, "I want to ask you, would you accept a position on the Supreme Bench because if you would, I'll put you on that court."

I said it was and always had been the ambition of my life. I had declined it twice for reasons I explained, but I was obliged to say that now under circumstances of having been president, and having appointed three of the present bench and three others and having protested against Brandeis, I could not accept any place but the chief justiceship. He said nothing more about it and I could not make out whether he concluded that was satisfactory or whether he did not further wish to commit himself. . . .

In a note I sent him yesterday, I rather assumed the latter and said that if he concluded to take someone else as chief justice, as he well might, I should still be very grateful for the honor he had done in making the offer. *I told him in the note that many times in the past the Chief Justice had said he was holding the office for me and that he would give it back to a Republican administration.* . . .

I was nonplussed at the way in which he took me into his confidence and was nearly struck dumb when he asked me if I would go on the Supreme Court.[14]

[14] Taft to Helen H. Taft, Dec. 26, 1920. (Italics mine.)

Harding remained, for the moment, noncommittal on the dazzling suggestion. The Tafts went to Bermuda for a brief vacation. While there, Taft received an encouraging message from Gus Karger:

"I saw Harry Daugherty today. He told me of what a deep and lasting and agreeable impression you made on Senator and Mrs. Harding. . . . And he also told me . . . that Senator Harding had told him that he didn't care what anybody else would say about it or who Senator Knox's candidate might be, that he would appoint you chief justice of the United States. I had an impulse to kiss Harry when he told me so, but I fought it down. I pray to Heaven that Senator Harding will be quite as positive and firm when the time for action in the matter shall arrive." [15]

In due time Harding would waver. Taft saw the President again in late March, however, and was again assured that the appointment would be his when the vacancy occurred.

—3—

Unfortunately, the Chief Justice continued to be an obstacle in the path of Taft's appointment. Would he actually deliver the center chair on this "sacred shrine," as he had so often intimated, to the former President who had elevated him? After visiting Harding on March 26, Taft also called on the Chief Justice. The most kindly of men, Taft's anxious appraisal of the jurist's health was a degree ghoulish.

"He said nothing about retiring," he observed sadly, describing the interview. "He spoke of his illness. He said he could still read, though he had a cataract, and he complained of the burden of work that he had . . . and he bemoaned the critical nature of that work and the dangers that might arise from wrong decisions." [16]

The most ancient bromide was proving accurate again: the old men of the court seldom died and never retired. Taft grew discouraged.

"It has been reported that the Chief Justice was going to re-

[15] Karger to Taft, Jan. 14, 1921. [16] Taft to Karger, March 26, 1921.

tire . . ." he wrote. "But as a man comes to the actual retirement, after he is seventy years of age, he seems to regard it as an admission of weakness, a singing of the *Nunc Dimittis,* and he satisfies himself with many reasons why the time has not come. I am getting on myself— shall be sixty-four my next birthday, and it is not wise to appoint a man to that bench at such an age that he has to serve long after seventy to make up the ten years after which he can retire. . . . If the position, which I would rather have than any other in the world, is not to come to me, I have no right to complain, for the Lord has been very good to me." [17]

On May 19, 1921, Taft's hopes soared, for word reached him that the Chief Justice was dead. He composed a tribute for publication in the Philadelphia *Public-Ledger.*

"The unexpected has happened . . ." he wrote to Karger on the same day. "And now the question is, 'What is to be done?' I observe, in the Associated Press dispatches, opposition to me based on my age, and chiefly on the fact that I laid down the rule that I would appoint no man to the Supreme Court, or to any court, who was more than sixty years of age. Of course it is true that I sought to get men under sixty, but it isn't true that I did not appoint men over sixty."

Among them, he cited, had been Associate Justice Lurton. White, himself, had been sixty-six when Taft had promoted him.

Taft would be kept in suspense for forty days because a new complication had arisen. The President, he learned, had promised to elevate Senator George Sutherland of Utah to the Supreme Court at the first opportunity. Harding now desired to delay Taft's appointment until he could send both names to the Senate at once.

". . . in view . . . of this attack on me because of my age," Taft said, "it would seem to be better to make the appointment while I am sixty-three than to delay it until I am sixty-four."

Gus Karger became a personal lobbyist for Taft's ambition. He received fairly detailed instructions from his principal. Among other things, Taft wanted to know "how the Democrats stand. It would be the grossest ingratitude . . . if they were to oppose me, in view of the fact that I gave them three Democrats out of six appointments to that bench." Would Gus, however, sound out the

[17] Taft to C. S. Shepard, April 11, 1921.

important southern senators and report their reactions? Taft feared "a fight in the Senate, with Borah and Norris of the Judiciary Committee leading it, and with Reed of Missouri helping them."

Somewhat pathetically, Taft added a postscript. White and Lurton, he suggested, might have been considered eligible for the Supreme Court, despite their age, because of their long judicial experience:

"But I have had federal judicial experience, too. 1. Three years on the state bench. 2. Two years solicitor general, U.S. 3. Eight years presiding judge, U. S. Circuit. 4. Four years Court of Appeals, Sixth Circuit. 5. Four years secretary of war. 6. Four years president. 7. Eight years Kent professor, Yale University, five hours a week Federal Constitutional Law except one year Chairman National War Labor Board and one year arbitrator in case between Canadian government and Grand Trunk Railway. That would seem to indicate pretty continuous service in the line of judicial and other duties preparing one for service on the Supreme Court."[18]

Karger went to work. He cornered Senator Lodge and asked whether there would be any difficulty about Taft's confirmation, if named.

"None," answered the Massachusetts senator.

On May 25, Karger had a moment alone with Harding and his summary of the conversation brought both encouragement and disappointment. The President, he said, did not regard Taft's age as an argument against his selection; on the other hand, he was still determined to appoint Sutherland at the same time; a delay until fall was probable. A new and disturbing possibility had arisen: this was that Associate Justice Day was to be named chief justice with an understanding that he would resign in six months in favor of Taft.[19] To this proposal, Taft reacted with scorn.

"I sincerely hope that the President will not carry it out," he said. "No one should go into office like that under an obligation to lay it down at a particular time. The office is too exalted. . . . More than that, I venture to think that Day's memory of the understanding will grow as dim as the Chief Justice's frequent state-

[18] Taft to Karger, May 19, 1921.   [19] Karger to Taft, May 24, 25, 1921.

ment to me that he wished to retire as soon as I could be appointed." [20]

And so, as weeks passed, Taft lost heart. "I don't expect to be appointed," he concluded just a month before his name was sent to the Senate.[21]

Harry Daugherty, of all people, was the influence which persuaded Harding to accelerate the appointment which may remain the outstanding, single act of an otherwise shabby administration.

"Tell him not to worry," the attorney general instructed Karger on June 3. He added that he had talked with Harding, that the proposal to promote Associate Justice Day had been abandoned. Additional good news reached Taft on June 14; Karger had again interviewed Harding.

". . . say to the Big Chief that there has been a wonderfully fine expression with regard to him," said the amiable President.

The best news of all came a week later. Karger went to the White House on some journalistic errand.

"Tell the Big Chief," said Harding, "that I'm going to put that over about the first of July. Somewhere between the first and the fifteenth."

The importunings of Daugherty hastened the appointment even more. On June 30, 1921, Harding called in the correspondents. The attorney general, he said, had pointed out that the courts were congested. Additional judges were needed on the federal circuits. Daugherty had informed Harding that he needed the advice and guidance of Taft, as chief justice of the United States, to work out a solution. Concluding, Harding turned to Karger.

"I hope you approve of the appointment," he said.[22]

The nomination was confirmed, without reference to committee, although not unanimously, that same day.[23] A few weeks later, Taft was a guest at the home of George Wickersham. Mrs. Wickersham remarked that she was still unable to regard him, after all these years, as chief justice.

"I can't think of myself in that position," Taft said.[24]

[20] Taft to F. B. Brandegee, May 30, 1921; to Karger, May 30, 1921. [21] Taft to Pierce Butler, May 26, 1921. [22] Karger to Taft, June 3, 14, 21, 30, 1921. [23] F. B. Brandegee to Taft, June 30, 1921. [24] Wickersham to author, Jan. 23, 1935.

CHAPTER LI

THE CHIEF

HE WAS, quite naturally, a happy man. During the summer of 1921 he looked forward to living again in Washington for it would be "a return home. . . . We have been wanderers on the face of the earth and it will be good to be anchored in a city we like and where we have so many friends." [1]

There was a more important reason for Taft's high spirits. The *Nation* may have declared his elevation "a mistaken appointment," but that was to be expected. Opposition by Borah of Idaho was inevitable too.[2] These critical voices hardly reached the ears of the new Chief Justice. He heard, instead, a swelling chorus of praise and he concluded that retribution was at last being made for the wrongs he had suffered in the presidency and in the campaign of 1912. Before half a decade had passed, the unhappiness of his years in the White House was wholly forgotten.

"The truth is," he wrote in December, 1925, "that in my present life I don't remember that I ever was president." [3]

In the summer of 1921, as congratulatory messages poured in, Taft saw evidence "that in one sense or another I have come back from the status in which the campaign of 1912 left me . . . as if the American people were conscious that . . . my attitude toward public affairs had been misconstrued and injustice had been done me.

"One can afford to wait to have such a situation remedied by time, as it usually is," he added.[4]

The work ahead, Taft knew, involved "incessant labor and great responsibility." He admitted that he might "stumble at first." [5] But the doubts and lack of confidence which had so often marked the assumption of a new office or the start of a new un-

[1] Taft to Mrs. Mischler, July 31, 1921. [2] *Nation*, July 13, 1921. [3] Taft to W. K. Hutchinson, Dec. 29, 1925. [4] Taft to H. H. Kohlsaat, July 19, 1921. [5] Taft to Mrs. William Cowles, July 26, 1921.

dertaking seem quite absent. There would be no time for speeches or lectures and small social life, the Chief Justice knew.

"The Chief Justice," he explained, "goes into a monastery and confines himself to his judicial work." [6]

It was all true. The duties ahead were arduous in the extreme. Far back in 1790 Edmund Randolph, attorney general under Washington, described the qualities of mind which even an associate justice of the Supreme Court should have:

Those who pronounce the law of the land without appeal ought to be pre-eminent in most endowments of the mind. Survey the functions of a judge of the Supreme Court. He must be a master of the common law in all its divisions, a chancellor, a civilian, a federal jurist, and skilled in the laws of all the states. . . . But what leisure remains from their itinerant dispensation of justice? Sum up all the fragments of their time, hold their fatigue at naught, and let them bid adieu to all domestic concerns.[7]

Charles Evans Hughes, who had observed one chief justice from the intimate post of associate justice and who would succeed Taft as the head of the court, has pointed out that the Chief Justice is "the most important judicial officer in the world." True, he has merely one vote in the decisions— no more than each of his eight associates. The actual influence of the Chief Justice, Hughes said, depended "upon the strength of his character and the demonstration of his ability in the intimate relations of the judges." Yet the Chief Justice has "special opportunity for leadership" because of the method by which the court works. At the weekly, private conferences the Chief Justice normally gives his verbal opinion last. Further, he has the right to assign the writing of the decision to any associate justice after a conclusion has been reached. Any associate, that is, who agrees with the majority. If the Chief Justice, himself, is with the minority, the senior associate justice does the assigning. Finally, the Chief Justice may retain for himself any and all cases he likes.[8]

Preparing for his new duties, Taft drafted a schedule for his

[6] Taft to W. J. Moore, July 30, 1921. [7] Frankfurter, Felix, and Landis, James M., *The Business of the Supreme Court*, p. 15. [8] Hughes, C. E., *The Supreme Court of the United States*, pp. 56-59.

daily life. He rose at 5:15, began work at 6 o'clock and continued until breakfast was ready two hours later. After breakfast came another hour and three-quarters of work. Then, for his health and to reduce his weight, the Chief Justice walked to the Capitol. The court was in session from noon until half past four with a half-hour recess for lunch. Taft then was driven home, worked from five to seven, took an hour off for dinner and labored again until ten o'clock. This would be his hour to retire.

"If I can maintain this," he told Horace Taft, "I think I shall have time enough to do the work. You see it gives me, in addition to my court work of four hours, eight hours for work outside the court, two hours for meals, and seven hours for sleep, one hour for exercise and one hour for dressing. This makes twenty-three hours. Just where the other hour goes you can figure out for yourself— I haven't time." [9]

The Chief Justice, a check of the schedule discloses, had neglected to count in the half hour needed for the drive home after court and had miscalculated his periods of work and sleep. Never again would he be accused, fairly or unfairly, of laziness or lethargy. No one could say that he postponed the tasks before him or that he did other than labor long and efficiently. The truth is that Taft worked far too zealously as chief justice and he paid the inevitable penalty of impaired health. By 1926 he was forced to go more slowly.

". . . bear with me if I am a little light on myself in the distribution of cases," he pleaded. "Up to date I have written more cases than any of them during the five years of my service, and with the other work I have more than pulled my weight in the boat. They are all most considerate, and I am quite sure they will understand if I let up a bit." [10]

A year later the Chief Justice graphically described the burdens of his fellow jurists and himself. It was on the eve of the summer recess. "It seems a long vacation," he admitted, "but the work we have to do during the nine months that we are continually together deprives one of normal time for normal things." Then he went on:

[9] Taft to Horace Taft, Oct. 6, 1921. [10] Taft to J. M. Dickinson, Aug. 21, 1926.

I am never free from the burden of feeling that whenever I attempt to do anything else I am taking time from my judicial work. The exhausting character of it everyone testifies to. I was talking with my brother Brandeis yesterday, and he spoke of the comment that Judge Hughes made on the matter. He had been through a presidential campaign, and he has had as active a practice at the bar as anybody possible since he left the bench. He had been governor, but he said that he never found anything that took the "gimp" out of him as service on the Supreme bench.[11]

—2—

The last event of the Murray Bay season was, as usual, Taft's birthday party. Seventy-five neighbors came to his house to congratulate him on attaining the age of sixty-four. The celebration was doubly important this year because he was now chief justice. A few days later, on September 19, the family left for Washington. A house had already been purchased on Wyoming Avenue at Twenty-third Street for $75,000. It was spacious and comfortable, with three pleasant guest rooms. In due course extensive improvements would be made, including an elevator to Taft's study on the top floor. For his health was to fail more or less steadily and extreme exertion had to be avoided.[12]

He guarded himself carefully and went out to dine, that first winter, only twice a week. "To sit between two agreeable women, to eat a good dinner without eating too much and avoiding dangerous viands," he explained to his daughter, "is not a physical strain but in some sense is a rest." [13] The three-mile walk from Wyoming Avenue down through the city to the Capitol was the most important part of his health program. And the Chief Justice became, in due time, a beloved, respected figure and men would raise their hats to him as he trudged along.

Sometimes he would walk again after court. Then his route usually included the bridge which carried Connecticut Avenue traffic across the Rock Creek Park ravine— now known as the

[11] Taft to Moses Strauss, June 5, 1927. [12] Taft to Horace Taft, Sept. 13, 1921; to Brandeis, Aug. 19, 1921; to Maria Herron, Nov. 14, 1921; to R. A. Taft, Feb. 13, 1921. [13] Taft to Helen Manning, Dec. 4, 1921.

Taft Bridge. One day during the administration of President Coolidge, the Chief Justice happened to drop his cane just as a small boy of about seven came by. The boy picked up the cane and handed it politely to Taft, who thanked him with the radiant warmth which was so characteristic.

"I met the nicest old gentleman on the bridge today," said the youngster to his mother when he reached home. "He dropped his cane and I picked it up. He was very, very fat!"

The mother recognized Taft in the description. "That was a very famous man," she told her son. "He used to be president of the United States."

A day or two later they met again.

"I know who you are!" said the boy. "You used to be President Coolidge!"

Unfortunately— for a truthful biographer— the incident never took place, although the story became a Washington legend. It never occurred because Taft never mentioned it. And it is quite inconceivable that he would not have told again and again the story of an encounter which would have brought forth far more than a chuckle.

The Chief Justice greatly relished stories at his own expense. A favorite was about a visit to New England when president. The presidential party attended a wedding during the trip and Major Butt, wrapped in gold braid, was conspicuously ornamental. In due course the President heard from a member of the family about a conversation between the Irish gardener and his mistress after the ceremony.

"Ah, it was a foine occasion," he said.

"Yes, and it was pleasant to have the President of the United States," she answered.

"Yis, madame, yis, it was. He's a foine-looking man; and what a beautiful uniform he had! But who the divil was the fat old man that was following him around?"

The Irish dialect, it might be noted, was by the Chief Justice of the United States.[14]

Taft must have found infinite amusement, too, in the widespread notion, which followed his appointment, that he was per-

[14] Taft to L. B. Estopinal, March 26, 1923.

sonal attorney to anybody who took the trouble to write to him. Secretary Mischler answered these petitioners for legal advice, but the voice, very often, was the voice of Taft.

"The Chief Justice directs me to . . . say that he has nothing to do, and the court has nothing to do, with the methods taken to bring about tick eradication. . . . He says you should write to the Department of Agriculture," was typical.[15]

From Ohio arrived a penny postcard on which one Greel Falknor complained that he had "written you several times inquiring if a county has a right to appoint a guardian over Liberty Land [sic] bonds. If you don't answer this I will write the President you're not attending to business."

"The Chief Justice regrets," replied Mischler, "that you should feel it necessary to take such action, but he ventures to think that possibly the President will forgive him." [16]

A lady in Kansas, who is better unidentified, wrote:

Two years ago this fall I met a man in Texas and we became engaged. We were to be married about Christmas. His home was in another town, so he came to see me the first of December and told me he was married and didn't have a divorce but would get one soon. I have a baby fourteen months old. He has never offered to help support him or pay my doctor bill. . . . I want to know if there can be anything done with him.

Would like to hear from you soon.

All that Mischler could answer was that the Chief Justice, "in view of his judicial position," was unable to give advice.[17]

—3—

The oath for chief justice of the United States was given by Associate Justice McKenna on October 3. "The clerk was . . . considerably more rattled than I was, and forgot to furnish the copy of the oath which the Justice was to administer," Taft wrote, "and he sent up the Bible instead, so that the Justice trusted to his mem-

[15] Mischler to J. O. Tompkins, March 21, 1927. [16] Greel Falknor to Taft, Oct. 17, 1923; Mischler to Falknor, Oct. 20, 1923. [17] Miss ——— to Taft, Nov. 7, 1921; Mischler to Miss ———, Nov. 12, 1921.

ory, and it was remarkable. It necessitated a little halt . . . but we got through. It was considerably better than what happened when Chief Justice Fuller swore me in as president. He missed the oath and had me execute the Constitution instead of supporting and defending it. Of course, one could construe that properly or improperly." [18]

So began the long grind which was to be the final chapter of his life. It was to be a momentous decade during which men cried out for "normalcy," after the war, and found themselves surrounded by abnormalities of governmental corruption, stock speculation, unsound banking, and a prosperity which seemed real in the cities and increasingly unreal on the farms. Great changes would take place before Taft died in March, 1930.

"We want," said President Harding, "a period in America with less government in business and more business in government."

It was an excellent phrase and highly applauded by the National Association of Manufacturers. But this was not, actually, what the country's industrialists and financiers wanted. What they wanted was government in business— but they also wanted power to control the government. To a degree, at least, they achieved it. But there were problems which neither they nor the politicians could solve. The major one was stripping the government of some of the powers it had assumed during the emergency or of adjusting them to peace conditions. Railroads, taxation, prohibition, war claims, the war debts, the comparative powers of the states and the federal government in regulating commerce, monopolies, the national debt, the rights of labor— all these were vital questions which loomed on a troubled national horizon in the fall of 1921.[19]

And where did the Chief Justice of the United States stand on the issues of the day? Examination of the private viewpoint of a jurist is valid, but with this reservation: the really conscientious jurist will divorce himself of his private opinions in so far as he can and decide cases on the law. That Taft had changed in many respects since he became a federal circuit judge in 1892 cannot be doubted. The times had changed too. Behind Taft, among other

---

[18] Taft to Horace Taft, Oct. 6, 1921. [19] Morison, S. E., and Commager, H. S., *The Growth of the American Republic*. See Vol. II, Chap. XXII.

educational influences, was his period of service on the War Labor Board. But that the new Chief Justice was conservative, if not reactionary, in his political and social views is not open to question.

In October, 1921, as the Supreme Court term got under way, he acknowledged a volume, *Popular Government,* by Arnold B. Hall of the University of Wisconsin. ". . . it looked to me like interesting reading, and also orthodox . . . which is more important," said the Chief Justice.[20]

"The only class which is distinctly arrayed against the court is a class that does not like the courts at any rate, and that is organized labor," he told Horace Taft. "That faction we have to hit every little while, because they are continually violating the law and depending on threats and violence to accomplish their purpose."[21]

"It seems to me that on the whole Harding has done remarkably well," the Chief Justice said in February, 1923. "I think Mellon's presence at the head of the Treasury has done a great deal to steady the finances of the country. He has shown himself a very long-headed financier and a man with the courage to tell the truth."[22]

A tendency toward conservatism grew, perhaps, as the years passed. Old age does that even to men who have been left-wing in their younger years. Toward the end of his span, Taft worried over possible radical appointments to the Supreme Court:

I am older and slower and less acute and more confused. However, as long as things continue as they are, and I am able to answer in my place, I must stay on the court in order to prevent the Bolsheviki from getting control. . . .[23]

. . . the only hope we have of keeping a consistent declaration of constitutional law is for us to live as long as we can. . . . The truth is that Hoover is a Progressive just as Stone [Associate Justice Harlan Stone] is, and just as Brandeis is and just as Holmes is.[24]

To Taft, clearly, the difference between conservatism and radicalism was the difference between right and wrong, between the known and the unknown, between the sound and the unsound.

[20] Taft to A. B. Hall, Oct. 24, 1921. [21] Taft to Horace Taft, May 7, 1922. [22] Taft to Hilles, Feb. 5, 1927. [23] Taft to Horace Taft, Nov. 14, 1929. [24] *Idem,* Dec. 1, 1929.

The forces of conservatism had triumphed again in the 1924 presidential campaign— although the issue, seen not too clearly by Taft, was more than a little clouded.

"It was a famous victory and one most useful in the lessons to be drawn from it, one of which is that this country is no country for radicalism. *I think it is really the most conservative country in the world.* Whenever the people get the clear idea that the issue is as between radicalism and conservatism, as between maintaining the government we now have and going to something we know not of, the answer will always be the same." [25]

—4—

What kind of court was this over which Taft would preside for nearly a decade? For one thing, it was badly divided. For another, it was far behind in its calendar. Chief Justice Taft was to use all the influence he possessed to bring added harmony among the members and to cut down the number of dissents, but discord was still ruling when he resigned in 1930. He was to bring greatly increased efficiency to the court, however, by his successful advocacy of the Judiciary act of February 13, 1925. This gave the Supreme Court far more discretion over which cases it would admit for thorough consideration; it had time, after the passage of the act, to give prompt attention to questions involving constitutionality and other important matters.

Preparing to take his seat as chief justice, Taft naturally pondered the merits and faults of his associates on the high bench. The senior member was Joseph McKenna who had been appointed far back in the McKinley administration and was seventy-eight years old. McKenna was already failing by 1921 and the Chief Justice was soon close to despair over the justice's inability to do his work. "I don't know what course to take with respect to him, or what cases to assign to him," Taft confided to Brother Horace in April, 1922. ". . . I had to take back a case from him last Saturday because he would not write it in accordance with the vote of the court . . . and have taken it over to myself." [26]

[25] Taft to I. M. Ullman, Nov. 12, 1924. (Italics mine.) [26] Taft to Horace Taft, April 17, 1922.

"He is an Irishman, and he retains the old pugnacity . . . and he makes up his mind now on the impressionistic principle," the Chief Justice added fourteen months later. "He is a Cubist on the bench and Cubists are not safe on the bench. Holmes, though his senior by more than two years, has not lost his mental acumen so far as I can see, and his power of rapid work is still marvelous." [27]

Taft's relationship with Mr. Justice Holmes was to be a source of unending pleasure, and this despite their disagreement on many subjects and on the law. Almost daily, they went to court together— until 1926 on foot and after that by motor. The Chief Justice had momentary qualms regarding Holmes's fitness: ". . . both Holmes and McKenna ought to retire," he said in April, 1922.[28] As far as Holmes was concerned, this was doubtless due to that jurist's illness at the time. In any event, Taft soon changed his mind. "Association with Justice Holmes is a delight," he wrote. "He is feebler physically, but I cannot see that the acuteness of his mind has been affected at all. . . . In many ways he is the life of the court, and it is a great comfort to have such a well of pure common law undefiled immediately next one so that one can drink and be sure one is getting the pure article." [29]

The sweetness and intimacy of their relationship were never dimmed. Yet Chief Justice Taft was often critical of the legal and social views of Holmes. "I think perhaps his age makes him a little more subordinate or yielding to Brandeis, who is his constant companion, than he would have been in his prime," Taft noted in June, 1923.[30] "Justice Holmes is about to celebrate his eighty-fifth birthday," wrote the Chief Justice in March, 1926. ". . . He is, in my judgment, a very poor constitutional lawyer . . . he lacks the experience of affairs in government that would keep him straight on constitutional questions." [31] Taft's belief that Holmes was charming but unsound increased as the years passed and the dissents continued.

"I am very fond of the old gentleman, but he is so completely under the control of Brother Brandeis that it gives to Brandeis two votes instead of one. He has more interest in, and gives more

[27] Taft to Helen Manning, June 11, 1923. [28] Taft to Horace Taft, April 17, 1922. [29] Taft to Learned Hand, March 3, 1923. [30] Taft to Helen Manning, June 11, 1923. [31] Taft to C. P. Taft, II, March 7, 1926.

attention to, his dissents than he does to the opinions he writes for the court, which are very short and not very helpful," was the faintly despairing observation of the Chief Justice in May, 1928.[32]

When Mrs. Holmes died, Taft was deeply moved, for he knew how desolate his fellow jurist would be. He hurried to the house, although his own health was none too good, and took entire charge of the funeral. Mrs. Holmes, like himself, had been a Unitarian.

"One thing I do know how to do is run a Unitarian funeral," the Chief Justice observed.[33]

The most difficult personal problem which confronted Taft when he became chief justice was Associate Justice Brandeis. Deep resentment lingered in his heart. He could not forget the Ballinger case. But it was different when, in the summer of 1921, association with Brandeis on the revered tribunal was an accomplished fact. Taft was never lacking in graciousness. He was realist enough to know that rancor must vanish before the necessity of working in peace with his brothers on the court. Brandeis, no less than the Chief Justice, greatly desired this. In July, 1921, while Taft was still in Murray Bay, he wrote to express his support of the proposal to readjust the machinery of the federal courts so as to accelerate disposition of cases.

"I look forward with pleasure to joint consideration and co-operation with you in this and all other matters of the court," Taft answered.[34] ". . . I . . . am looking forward with pleasure to meeting you in Washington." [35]

Taft could not fail to be won over by the luminous mind and great learning of Justice Brandeis. After two sessions had passed, he said, "I have come to like Brandeis very much indeed." True, they differed in the field of "social economics . . . but withal he is a very hard worker," concluded the Chief Justice. "He thinks much of the court and is anxious to have it consistent and strong, and he pulls his weight in the boat." [36]

The doubts that persisted were political, social and legal. Late in 1924, Brandeis had indicated that he would vote with the Chief

[32] Taft to H. L. Stimson, May 18, 1928. [33] Helen Manning to author, July 11, 1939. [34] Taft to Brandeis, July 24, 1921. [35] Idem, Aug. 19, 1921. [36] Taft to Helen Manning, June 11, 1923.

Justice on an important prohibition opinion. But then, Taft complained, "he went up to Cambridge and must have communed with Frankfurter [Professor Felix Frankfurter of Harvard, now associate justice of the Supreme Court] and that crowd, and he came back with a notice to me that he was going to change his vote. Brandeis tries as hard as he can to be a good fellow, and in many respects he is." [37]

A "good fellow," in the mind of Chief Justice Taft, was an associate who did not come forward with embarrassing dissenting views, who added to the unanimity of the court and who was, all in all, a fairly strict constructionist on matters pertaining to the Constitution of the United States.

Associate Justice William Rufus Day, third in seniority on the court, had been appointed by Roosevelt in 1903. Taft dismissed him as among "the weak members of the court" along with Justices Mahlon Pitney and Joseph McKenna.[38] The Chief Justice's greatest severity was reserved for Justice McReynolds. Taft thought him selfish, prejudiced, "and one who seems to delight in making others uncomfortable. . . . He has a continual grouch, and is always offended because the court is doing something that he regards as undignified." In contrast, Justice Willis Van Devanter, whom Taft had elevated in 1910, was an unending joy and comfort.

"My mainstay in the court is Van Devanter," wrote Taft after he had presided for two years.[39]

In December, 1926, Taft suggested that Van Devanter be awarded an honorary degree by Yale. In praising his candidate, he wrote:

The value of a judge in conference, especially in such a court as ours, never becomes known except to the members of the court. Now I don't hesitate to say that Mr. Justice Van Devanter is far and away the most valuable man in our court in all these qualities. We have other learned and valuable members, with special knowledge in particular subjects, but Van Devanter has knowledge in every subject that comes before us. . . . Van Devanter exercises more influence, a good deal, than any other member of the court, just because the members of the court know his qualities.[40]

[37] Taft to Horace Taft, Dec. 26, 1924. [38] *Idem,* April 17, 1922. [39] Taft to Helen Manning, June 11, 1923. [40] Taft to James R. Angell, Dec. 2, 1926.

Regarding Justice John H. Clarke, appointed by Wilson in 1916, the Chief Justice expressed no opinion at all. He was due to retire in the fall of 1922. So would Day. And Pitney, too, would resign before the end of that year. McKenna hung on the longest. It was January of 1925 before he could be replaced. Taft's disapprobation of certain of his colleagues, even his dislike for certain of them, was a minor irritation in a happy life. The years that remained were enormously busy, enormously satisfactory.

". . . the court . . . next to my wife and children, is the nearest thing to my heart in life," he wrote in the spring of 1923.[41]

[41] Taft to H. S. Pritchett, April 25, 1923.

CHAPTER LII

THE DELUGE

THE SUPREME COURT OF THE UNITED STATES convened for its fall term of 1921 with the certain knowledge that month by month it would fall further behind in disposing of the cases already on the docket and the new ones which would be filed. The Chief Justice described the situation to the New York County Lawyers' Association on February 18, 1922.

"When the Court adjourned in June, last, the cases remaining undisposed of were 343," he said. "Those cases have increased to 764 at noon yesterday. Of those 764, 248 have been disposed of, and there are now on the docket 516 cases undisposed of. At this time last year, there were 447 cases undisposed of, showing that the cases are creeping up on us." [1]

They were, indeed, creeping up. Despite Taft's best efforts to accelerate the work of the court, the undisposed-of cases would climb to 438 by the October term in 1924 and to 533 in 1925. [2] And the deluge was, in part, the result of the war. It would be June, 1930, before the assistant attorney general in charge could note that the "war transaction cases . . . are gradually coming to an end." [3] Meanwhile claims and disputes in which billions of dollars were at stake had been passed upon.

It would have been bad enough even without the war. The Supreme Court, instead of being a high tribunal of final appeal, was saddled with many of the functions of a police court. Any case from any state court, in which a point of federal law could be raised, could go to a federal court as a matter of right and possibly reach the Supreme Court. It was widely believed that no lawyer had done his full duty, especially in criminal cases, until he had somehow battled his way to Washington and forced, if he could, nine weary and overworked jurists to hear his plea.

[1] Manuscript address, Feb. 18, 1922, Taft papers, Library of Congress. [2] *Attorney General's Report*, 1926, p. 11. [3] *Ibid.*, p. 69.

Ratification of the income tax amendment had brought one deluge of cases. War claims began, of course, prior to America's entrance, since disputes between foreign governments and contractors were frequent. These two groups may illustrate, perhaps, the bewilderment of the layman as he contemplates our judicial system and the Supreme Court. For these were not really legal problems at all— they were administrative in nature. How could the income tax be made to work? What rules should apply to purchases of munitions and other war supplies? Then came the Prohibition amendment on which the White court was forced to pass. Chief Justice White's strength was ebbing. The legality of prohibition was an issue on which members of the court differed violently. All in all, the burdens were too heavy. The White court was functioning badly in its final years.

The layman, if he thinks about the Supreme Court at all, does so through such well-remembered and famous cases as the Dred Scott and the Danbury Hatters and assumes, quite wrongly, that its work is limited to passing on profound constitutional issues. In fact, the court could keep extremely busy without deciding major cases at all. Certain matters come before it as a matter of right. During a single term these might include, and probably would, an issue involving a foreign nation or its representatives. The minister from Nicaragua might drive his car too fast or otherwise run afoul of the law; he could, then, go to the Supreme Court. Disputes between the states, on boundaries or rivers or other matters, might reach the nine justices. So might the activities of Indian wards; should a chief in Arkansas have received larger royalties from his oil lands? Questions arising in the dependencies— the Philippines, Porto Rico or the Virgin Islands— must often be decided. Federal and state taxation, such administrative tribunals as the Federal Trade Commission, government contracts, admiralty questions and employers' liability enactments all add to the heavy calendars of the federal courts. The function of the Supreme Court, then, is only partly legal interpretation. It is also a referee, an umpire.

The predicament of the Taft court, in 1921, was even worse because the World War had to be liquidated, and no previous struggle had brought even remotely so much litigation. "Get it done and worry about the details later" had been the policy of countless government departments, agencies and boards as well as of the army and navy. Cost-plus contracts for cantonments, ships, munitions and supplies were hastily drafted. The frenzy of war prosecution resulted, in due time, in inevitable wrangles and disagreements. All these had to be worked out when the war had ended and the Supreme Court of the United States did much of the working out. A few of the cases began in 1918 and some reached the White court for argument. The majority even of these were handed on to the Taft court for settlement. Added to all this was final disposition of alien property seized by the government. Again, billions were involved. Among the types of war cases were: war supplies for the army and navy; suits brought, usually by the railroads, for transportation of troops or property; libels filed against government vessels as a result of collisions or other accidents; claims by men and officers of the army and navy regarding their pay; war taxes; emergency war legislation; sedition acts.

A lesson for contractors in future wars may be found in the disposition of certain of these cases. On February 19, 1923, for instance, Chief Justice Taft delivered the opinion regarding a lumber concern which had supplied millions of feet of Douglas fir to the Puget Sound Navy Yard where submarine chasers were being built. The navy supply officers had estimated that a specific amount of lumber, 1,675,000 feet, would be needed but the agreement provided that any amount ordered by the navy must be delivered. The price of Douglas fir went up. The contractor, under protest, finally shipped over 3,500,000 feet and subsequently filed suit in the Court of Claims for some $20,000 added compensation. The Court of Claims ruled that he had no case and dismissed the action. Chief Justice Taft upheld the decision and wrote the opinion for a unanimous court.

"It may be, as counsel suggests," he noted, "that the plaintiff's course was influenced by a patriotic wish to help the government when it was engaged in war. If so, it was to be commended. But this cannot change the legal effect of its . . . failure to put the government on notice that it intended to claim a recovery . . . when it was delivering the extra 2,000,000 feet of lumber and

976   THE LIFE AND TIMES OF WILLIAM HOWARD TAFT

receiving the payments therefor from the government at the prices named in the bid." [4]

That the profits of wartime contractors were large can hardly be debated. But that the supposedly conservative Supreme Court of 1921 to 1929 stood behind either the big corporations or their profits is disproved by many of these war claims actions. In January, 1926, the Interocean Oil Company appeared before the court. This concern produced oil for army transports, at its plants in Carteret, New Jersey. It also had a refinery in Baltimore, where the oil was to be delivered, but had not built adequate storage facilities. A Major Ross of the Quartermaster's Department gave notice to officers of the Interocean Oil Company that its New Jersey tanks must be moved to Baltimore. This would be done forthwith by the government unless the company did so, the major threatened, but in the latter event full compensation for the cost of moving and for the loss of business in New York would be paid.

Major Ross's superior at the time was a Colonel Kimball whose signature was needed on the orders. The Interocean Oil Company started to move its tanks to Baltimore, but the written authorization was never received. Colonel Kimball left the service because of ill-health and died. Work on the tanks was not completed before the Armistice, after which they were not needed by the government. No payment was made, so the Interocean brought action for damages in the Court of Claims. Its plea was rejected by the Court of Claims. The Chief Justice agreed.

"All the statements of the petition united together," he wrote for a unanimous decision upholding the government, "are no more than to say that the company relied on the promise of Major Ross that Colonel Kimball would confirm the contract which Ross proposed to make and said that he had authority, subject to Kimball's confirmation, to make. But Kimball never confirmed it. The Court of Claims was right . . . the judgment is affirmed." [5]

Nor could "due process of law" under the Fifth and Fourteenth Amendments be relied upon by contractors or others who sought unfair profits from war conditions. Mr. Justice Butler pointed out on April 8, 1929, that the sanctity of contracts was a liberty which "may not be lightly impaired." But it was also, he added, well

[4] 261 U.S. 16. [5] 270 U.S. 65.

established by the decisions of the Supreme Court "that such liberty is not absolute or universal, and that Congress may regulate the making and performance of such contracts whenever reasonably necessary to effect any of the great purposes for which the national government was created." Justice Butler, in this case, spoke for a unanimous court against a coal dealer who had levied prices greater than a reasonable profit required and in excess of the rates fixed by President Wilson under the Lever act.[6]

"Valuable time," Chief Justice Taft complained regarding the postwar litigation in the spring of 1926, was being consumed "in hearing these cases." He was gratified that the Judiciary act of February 13, 1925, would soon take effect. For after that the judgments of "the Court of Claims . . . can only be reviewed here after a showing of merits." [7]

—2—

As president, it will be recalled, Taft had favored a federal amendment providing for an income tax. A resolution to that end was ratified by the required number of states in 1913. Thenceforth Congress had power "to lay and collect taxes on incomes, from whatever source derived."

Thereupon a gateway for a flood of federal taxes was opened and the Supreme Court was forced to rule on the validity of virtually every paragraph of every Congressional enactment. Congress had passed an income tax measure in 1894. This, cried the great lawyer, Joseph Choate, in opposing it, was based on "principles as communistic, Socialistic— what shall I call them?— populistic as ever have been addressed to any political assembly in the world." The Supreme Court, in its famous if not notorious five-to-four ruling, threw out the tax.

"The present assault upon capital is but the beginning," said Justice S. J. Field. "It will be but the stepping stone to others, larger and more sweeping, till our political contests will become a war of the poor against the rich; a war constantly growing in intensity and bitterness." [8]

[6] 279 U.S. 253. [7] 270 U.S. 124. [8] Corwin, E. S., *The Twilight of the Supreme Court*, pp. 92-93.

Mr. Justice Field, although lacking in liberalism, was not a bad prophet. The gigantic costs of the war, combined with revenue losses caused by the Eighteenth Amendment, made additional taxes vital if the federal government was to carry on its expanding functions. So many of the so-called war emergency taxes were continued. Taxes were levied on the excess profits of corporations. Inheritance and gift assessments were made. Nobody was particularly pleased except those lawyers who speedily became experts in tax litigation. They moved in phalanxes upon the inferior federal courts and then upon the Supreme Court itself. But the highest tribunal resisted, in the main, their attacks on the new taxes. While Taft presided as chief justice, and was often accused of conservatism, there occurred a steady redistribution of the wealth of the United States.

The members of the Supreme Court did not, on the other hand, consent to distribute that fraction of the national wealth which came to them in the form of their judicial salaries. Taft was faintly amused, soon after taking office, at the ruling already made by the majority of his brethren. The Chief Justice agreed with this decision of 1920— although other constitutional authorities did not— which said that to tax the salary of a federal judge already holding office was contrary to the provision that his compensation could not be reduced during his incumbency.[9] It was a decision, said Professor Edward S. Corwin of Princeton four years later, which "illustrates what curious results the judicial mind can sometimes achieve when it chooses to let itself go." [10] Chief Justice Taft, unfortunately, had been appointed after the passage of the income tax law.

"The situation in respect to the salaries of the Supreme Court and the President is very curious," he told Brother Horace in November, 1921. "Under the Constitution, the law provides that the salaries of federal judges shall not be diminished during their term. It provides that the salary of the President shall not be increased or diminished during his term. The Supreme Court has held that that exempts the officers concerned from the payment of an income tax, by a vote of seven to two, Holmes and Brandeis dissenting. The ruling, of course, does not aply to me, because the income tax was in force when I became chief justice, and therefore I must pay my income tax at any rate. The judges, however, will refuse to pay their taxes, and I suppose that the Executive will not insist on collecting it. At any rate, if there is an insistence, then there will be a fight in court and the court will come out ahead. . . . It leaves me, the Chief Justice, with a salary the net benefit from which will be about $1,500 or $2,000 less than that of my colleagues." [11]

But the nation's federal judges were not satisfied with the 1920 decision. The case of Judge Samuel J. Graham of the Court of Claims reached the Supreme Court in the spring of 1925. Judge Graham had mounted the bench in September, 1919, when the income tax law was in effect. He contended, however, that he was exempt from the provision that his judicial salary must be included in his gross income. Associate Justice McReynolds—this time only Brandeis dissented— wrote the opinion of the court which pointed out that inclusion of the salary in "gross income" for tax purposes would be to tax one federal judge differently from another. For gross income was subject to other earnings and to deductions. A specific tax on his salary alone would have been legal.[12]

The Chief Justice was a degree embarrassed. "The question came before us, and we could not avoid it. . . . I would have been glad not to sit," he said, "but the court had established the precedent that it was the duty of the judges to sit. Holmes and Brandeis . . . insisted on it. And so we held that Congress might reduce the salaries of the federal judges to apply to any that were subsequently appointed, but that the reduction had to be uniform and that it could not be done by a tax law which varied in its operation upon the individual judges."

In November Taft received a refund of $8,798.04 as a result of the decision. He had no doubt, he said, "that when these refunds— and mine particularly— are disclosed, as they will be in reports to Congress, there will be another yell against the courts. And what I am afraid of is that it will be made an excuse to stir up opposition to a pretty strong movement to increase the salaries of the federal judges . . . where an increase is most needed, and indeed vitally needed, in the salary of the district and circuit judges." [13]

The operations of the judicial mind are often, to one not a

[11] Taft to Horace Taft, Nov. 23, 1921. [12] 268 U.S. 501. [13] Taft to Horace Taft, Nov. 28, 1925.

lawyer, difficult to fathom. The Supreme Court had decided in 1918 that stock dividends were not taxable because they constituted, merely, a rearrangement of capital. That is to say, the stockholder already owned everything that came to him by means of such a dividend.[14] This opinion was confirmed, with Justice Brandeis dissenting, in 1920.[15] Immediate results were a sharp drop in income tax returns, an era of speculation in which stocks were split and juicy melons cut.[16] In October, 1921— Taft's first year as chief justice— the court modified this ruling in connection with the reorganization of the E. I. du Pont de Nemours Company. The new company thereby created had been incorporated in another state. Associate Justice Pitney, for the majority, said that an income tax could be levied on stock dividends paid as a result of the reorganization.[17]

Of greater importance was *Walter L. Marr* v. *United States* decided by a five-to-four vote in June, 1925. Justices Van Devanter, McReynolds, Sutherland and Butler dissented from the decision which put new teeth in the income tax law. Technically, it said that a tax must be paid on dividends unless, in corporate reorganizations, the exact identity of the first corporation was preserved. Justice Brandeis wrote the opinion and Chief Justice Taft, by his vote, created the majority which upheld the government.[18]

The states, as well as Washington, were seeking new revenues in the postwar years and the dockets of the Supreme Court were heavily burdened with cases growing out of state tax measures. These included inheritance and gift taxes, levies on "foreign corporations" and income taxes. The Supreme Court never impugned the right of the states to pass income, inheritance or gift taxes. In effect, if not actually, it encouraged them to do so. Congress ruled in 1926 that state inheritance taxes might be credited against federal levies. Florida objected on the ground that this was virtually to force all states to enact inheritance taxes; otherwise, the federal assessment would be correspondingly larger. Florida could not pass a state levy of this type, however, because its constitution forbade inheritance taxes. Justice Sutherland, for a unanimous court, said that the

---

[14] *Selected Essays*, Vol. I, Book V, p. 750. [15] 252 U.S. 189. [16] Drumond, Dwight, *Roosevelt to Roosevelt*, p. 311. [17] 257 U.S. 156. [18] 268 U.S. 536.

constitutional powers of a state must yield to those of the federal government if the two powers came into conflict.[19]

—3—

A wholly novel source of litigation before the Supreme Court was the Eighteenth Amendment, with its legislative supplement, the Volstead act. Taft's views on prohibition were well known. He had consistently and publicly opposed federal regulation of the liquor traffic on the ground that temperance by national law would be difficult or impossible to enforce.[20] But now federal prohibition was the law of the land, and Taft, as chief justice of the United States, was more than ever a passionate zealot for enforcement of all laws.

The Supreme Court had already ruled, when Taft became chief justice, that the Eighteenth Amendment was in harmony with the Constitution and, thereby, that the Volstead act was legal. In March, 1920, Elihu Root had argued in vain.

"If your Honors," he had said dramatically, "shall find a way to uphold the validity of this amendment, the government of the United States, as we have known it, will have ceased to exist. . . . Your Honors will have found a legislative authority hitherto unknown to the Constitution and untrammeled by any of its limitations. . . . In that case, your Honors, John Marshall need never have sat upon your bench." [21]

Root's argument that the amendment was in violation of the Constitution itself because the legislatures of the states, not the people, had endorsed it was doubtful law. Chief Justice Taft had no illusions regarding the status of the Prohibition act. He did not deceive himself, however, that successful enforcement would be easily accomplished.

"I am discouraged about the liquor situation," he admitted in November, 1922, "but perhaps we have no right to hope too much at this stage." [22]

[19] 273 U.S. 12. [20] See p. 375. [21] Jessup, P. C., *Elihu Root,* Vol. II, p. 480. [22] Taft to Horace Taft, Nov. 29, 1922.

As the months and the years passed, the Chief Justice abandoned, for virtual advocacy of temperance by law, his belief that prohibition was unenforceable. Those who opposed it did not, in his judgment, reflect accurately the viewpoint of the country. They were urban types and therefore prejudiced. They gravely damaged enforcement of all laws. Thus he looked askance at Governor Alfred E. Smith of New York, who was urging repeal of his state's enforcement act. He scolded his old friend, Clarence Kelsey, a New York resident:

"You live in a congested center of opposition to the Volstead law where one is likely to gather a rather false idea of public opinion in the country as a whole in respect to its enforcement. I suppose that Governor Smith . . . will receive the plaudits of the wets who predominate in New York City . . . but I venture to think that it will not only be embarrassing to Smith but that it will embarrass more the party of which he is a member. . . . The question of er *orcement of existing law is so fundamental that I think its discussion is not likely to make for the side that is innately in favor of violating the law and I don't think our friend Nicholas Murray Butler adds to his reputation by his attitude in respect to it." [23]

Dr. Butler had dared to question prohibition and was thus rebuked.

"It used to be that all the nuts were drys," Taft remarked later. "But now it seems all the nuts are wets." [24]

His wrath would soon descend on all advocates of repeal. That repeal might come even in the remote future seemed, to the Chief Justice, and to most other people, impossible.

"What's the practical situation with respect to it?" he demanded at a gathering of alumni at New Haven in June, 1923. "It is that there isn't the slightest chance that the constitutional amendment will be repealed. You know that and I know it."

He went on to condemn the wets. Such people, he said, "are the first to complain of mob law, lawless violence of laborites and other disturbances of the peace, but when it comes to a violation of the Eighteenth Amendment and the Volstead law they seem to

---

[23] Taft to C. H. Kelsey, May 18, 1923.   [24] Helen Manning to author, July 11, 1939.

feel no obligation to protest . . . they are justifying the principle of anarchy." [25]

Again, as in the White House, Taft was none too skilled in judging how public opinion would change; the Eighteenth Amendment would be repealed before ten years had passed. The Chief Justice became more rigid, and even more unhappy about the situation. By the end of 1923 he was harsh even toward those who called for modification to permit the sale of light wine and beer.

"The truth is," he said, "that what these people are trying to do is to nullify the amendment. They say they are opposed to saloons, but that they want a moderate limitation. What they really want is an opportunity to drink and to entertain others with drink, and all these suggestions are their conscious or unconscious outgrowth of that desire."

No other issue of the Supreme Court years, not even the scandals of the Harding administration, caused Taft anxiety comparable to his worry over prohibition. He savagely criticized those who believed that "all laws should be enforced except those which affect their comfort and convenience and tastes" and he added, sadly, that some of these "are members of my own family." [26]

Indeed were they members of his family. Mrs. Taft, herself, was an ardent although publicly silent wet. That the marriage between William Howard Taft and Helen Herron was as ideal as a marriage can be must now be clear. Taft cherished and loved his wife. She had brought him infinite happiness and also, as he often believed, the will to succeed. Rarely, in his most private letters, is there a breath of criticism of the consort who had graced his years and then, inevitably, it is softened by affection and amusement. But he was deeply hurt that she would not support the Eighteenth Amendment. He was so deeply hurt that he actually wrote, in a letter to Horace, condemning her views.

"The truth is that Nellie and I differ on prohibition," he said. "We might as well face that, because I am utterly out of sympathy with her and she with me." [27]

[25] Manuscript address, June 20, 1923, Taft papers, Library of Congress. [26] Taft to Gertrude Ely, Dec. 22, 1923. [27] Taft to Horace Taft, Oct. 3, 1929.

—4—

It is understandable, then, that Taft would influence the court, in so far as he could, toward strict enforcement and would worry when an erring judicial brother did not see eye to eye to him.

"I note what you say about Brother Butler," he told Justice Van Devanter regarding one prohibition case, "and shall try to steer [him] away from the suggestion that we are introducing any new law and new principle of constitutional construction, but are only adapting old principles and applying them to new conditions created by the change in the national policy which the Eighteenth Amendment requires." [28]

The first important prohibition case of the Taft court was argued in December, 1921, and decided on January 30, 1922. Three unfortunate citizens, it appeared, had purchased whisky prior to the adoption of the amendment and had stored it in government warehouses. Attempting to remove it for their own use, they had been blocked by the federal authorities. They had sued on the ground that their whisky had been taken without due process of law and the cases, on appeal, had come to the Supreme Court. Their attorneys called attention to the fact that a similar, although not identical, case had been decided in 1920 by the White court. In that case, the citizen had been given his liquor.

But the two cases, said Mr. Justice McKenna in the majority opinion, were not at all the same. The Volstead act, he observed, permitted the possession of legally acquired liquor for the use of the owner and his private guests. In the earlier case the owner had stored some $3,000 worth of wine and liquor in a private warehouse.

"The storage room," said Justice McKenna, "was obviously the use of a convenience very commonly employed and *contributory to* his dwelling."

That is, the room he had leased in the warehouse was, in effect, part of his home and therefore the liquor was *in* his home all the time. But there was no intention, said the learned judge, "to make all bonded warehouses of the country outbuildings of its dwellings." So the three appellants, having used a *government* warehouse, could

[28] Taft to Van Devanter, Dec. 23, 1924.

not have their whisky. The Chief Justice concurred in this curious opinion.

Justice McReynolds did not. The earlier case, he thought, had been bad law "but it has been adopted and . . . should be adhered to or frankly overruled. The effort to distinguish the present case from the earlier one is but toying with the immaterial." [29]

Justice Holmes attempted to strengthen this decision in April, 1922, by pointing out that to move liquors from a private warehouse to a dwelling "was no more transportation in the sense of the statute than to take them from the cellar to the dining room." The dispute, this time, was whether liquor could be shipped in bond across the United States from Canada to Mexico and other countries. A treaty with Great Britain permitted such shipments, so the court had to choose between the treaty and the Eighteenth Amendment. In a six-to-three decision, the Chief Justice with the majority, the court held for the amendment.

"It is obvious," wrote Holmes, "that those whose wishes and opinions were embodied in the amendment meant to stop the whole business. They did not want intoxicating liquor in the United States, and reasonably may have thought that if they let it in some of it was likely to stay."

This time Justice McKenna wrote a dissenting opinion in which Justices Day and Clarke concurred.[30] But McKenna, Day and Clarke would shortly leave the Supreme Court and the prohibition majority would be stronger than ever.

Double jeopardy was the next important question to be passed upon. Four gentlemen of the state of Washington— Vito Lanza, Dick Barto, Premo Mazzoncini and Eugini Mazzoncini respectively— had been indicted in April, 1920, for violating the Volstead act. They had also been charged under a Washington statute with manufacturing, transporting and having in possession the same liquor, and each had been fined $750. This was prior to ratification of the Eighteenth Amendment and before passage of the Volstead act. Indicted by the federal courts, the four defendants cited the Fifth Amendment to the Constitution— "nor shall any person be subject for the same offense to be twice put in jeopardy of life or limb"— and were upheld in the district federal court. The Chief

[29] 257 U.S. 491. (Italics mine.) [30] 257 U.S. 80.

Justice wrote the opinion, for a unanimous court, which reversed this ruling. No violation of the Fifth Amendment had taken place, he said:

> We have here two sovereignties, deriving power from different sources, capable of dealing with the same subject matter within the same territory. Each may, without interference by the other, enact laws to secure prohibition. . . . Each government, in determining what shall be an offense against its own peace and dignity, is exercising its own sovereignty, not that of the other.
>
> It follows that an act denounced as a crime by both national and state sovereignties is an offense against the peace and dignity of both, and may be punished by each. The Fifth Amendment, like all the other guaranties in the first eight amendments, applies only to proceedings by the federal government.

Taft added that this view was "supported by a long line of decisions by this court" and cited certain of them. If Congress saw fit to bar prosecutions by the federal government for acts also within the jurisdiction of the states it had power to do so, he added. No such action had been taken, however.

". . . it is not for us to discuss the wisdom of legislation," the Chief Justice concluded.[31]

The decision has been criticized as bad law and worse justice. "The opinion . . . treated the question as if it were a settled one," wrote Professor J. A. C. Grant of Stanford University. "The fact remains, however, that the Lanza case was the first in which the Supreme Court, faced with an actual instance of double prosecution, failed to find some remedy, consistent with the law, to avoid it. . . . Shall we allow federal government, our greatest contribution to political science, to undermine the rights of the individual and thus destroy its very *raison d'être?* Shall we fritter away our liberties upon a metaphysical subtlety, two sovereignties?"[32]

The Chief Justice appears to have had no inner doubts regarding the justice of the decision. Nor was he disturbed by editorial and other criticism. When another unregenerate Herron, Mrs. Charles Anderson, his sister-in-law, protested, he replied with complete good humor:

[31] 260 U.S. 377. [32] *Selected Essays, op. cit.,* Vol. II, pp. 1377, 1398.

I understand you are outraged because if you make or sell or transport liquor of intoxicating strength you may be punished in both the state and federal courts, the imprisonment of the one sentence to begin after the other has been served. This is the law, my dear sister, and you must beware. You say that this is different and more rigorous than in the case of heinous offenses like murder. But in this respect you are not fully advised. If you were to kill a mail agent in seeking to steal from the mail, you could be punished for murder by both the federal and state governments. Of course, if you were executed by one government, you could not be hung by the other, because you would not be here to be hung. But if the penalty were imprisonment, you could be punished by both governments.

I fear your feelings have been wrought up by seeing an editorial from the New York *World,* but you should not yield your emotions under the influence of that paper's editorials, on matters of constitutional or other law, for the writer of them is ludicrously ill-informed. So brace up, my dear Jennie, give up your bootlegging and join the saints. It is safer. Recognize that prohibition is with us and that it only gives your face a pain to make faces at it.[33]

Taft's old foreboding that prohibition would mean disruption and chaos was to be borne out in his own beloved court as well as in other agencies of the federal government. Dissents were to become increasingly frequent and heated disputes arose in the Saturday conferences.

"It would seem as if more feeling could be engendered over the Prohibition act than almost any other subject we have in the court," he complained in December, 1924.[34]

—5—

The bootlegging industry was, by now, growing stronger and more efficient. Enforcement was increasingly difficult for the reason, too, that public opinion was perceptibly turning against prohibition. The federal enforcement agencies were baffled by clever lawyers who blocked detection and prosecution by every possible method.

[33] Taft to Mrs. Charles Anderson, Dec. 29, 1922. [34] Taft to C. P. Taft, Dec. 28, 1924.

The automobile was, naturally, an important aid in running liquor and in escaping arrest. So the Supreme Court was asked to rule on whether an automobile, presumably used to transport liquor, could be searched without a warrant. This was in *Carroll* v. *United States,* argued toward the close of 1923. The Chief Justice wrote the opinion, that no constitutional protection barred such a search. McKenna and Sutherland dissented.

The defendants, George Carroll and John Kiro, had been convicted in the Michigan Federal District Court for transporting, as the Chief Justice cautiously observed, "so-called bonded whisky and gin." Evidence against them at the trial included one bottle of whisky and one of gin which had been taken from their automobile, stopped on the highway between Detroit and Grand Rapids. Their lawyers appealed on the ground that this evidence, seized without a warrant, was in violation of the Fourth Amendment. The prohibition agents making the arrest and the search, it appeared, had no actual knowledge that liquor was in the car. Taft observed, however, that they had excellent reason for suspecting it and sound basis for regarding the two men as bootleggers. The Fourth Amendment protected merely against unreasonable search and seizure, and this was not unreasonable. It would, he agreed, be "intolerable" if any prohibition agent were allowed to halt every car on the highway without "probable cause." In this case no doubt existed that the agents had "probable cause." [35]

"I don't know whether you have observed an opinion which I got through the Supreme Court after a great fight, with reference to the right to seize automobiles when there is reasonable ground for believing that they contain liquor," Taft wrote to Brother Henry. "It has made a great howl, but it is good law and I hope it will be a useful means of rendering the prosecution of crime through automobiles more possible." [36]

The Chief Justice took on his own shoulders the writing— and to a degree, therefore, the opprobrium— of the prohibition decisions. That same day, March 2, 1925, he upheld a Georgia law which made mere possession of liquor, acquired prior to enactment and intended for personal use alone, illegal.

"The ultimate legislative object of prohibition," Taft said, "is

[35] 267 U.S. 132. [36] Taft to H. W. Taft, April 3, 1925.

to prevent the drinking of intoxicating liquor by anyone. . . . The state has the power to subject those members of society who might indulge . . . without injury to themselves to a deprivation . . . in order to remove temptation from those whom its use would demoralize."

Mr. Justice Butler could not agree. The owner of the liquor in question was "a man of temperate habits, long accustomed to use alcoholic liquor as a beverage. He never sold or in any way illegally dealt with intoxicating liquors, and has never been accused of so doing. . . . the law is oppressive and arbitrary." [37]

In November, 1926, Taft cast the deciding vote in a five-to-four decision upholding the Volstead act's limitation on the quantity of liquor to be prescribed by a physician for legitimate medicinal use.[38] It sometimes seemed as though there were no lengths to which the Chief Justice would not go, and along which he would not attempt to lead the court, in his determination to uphold prohibition enforcement. He would even endorse wire tapping, which Mr. Justice Holmes would properly brand "such dirty business," by federal agents. But when danger arose that his beloved, revered judiciary might be smeared with the corruption which enforcement engendered, Taft promptly voted on the side of the wets.

The case, *Ed Tumey* v. *State of Ohio,* came up from Hamilton County where Taft had been born, where his career as a judge had started, whence he had gone forth to achieve renown in that outside world which had looked so grim and forbidding. His sons lived there now; Charlie Taft, in fact, was prosecutor of Hamilton County and was having his troubles attempting to convict the notorious bootlegger, George Remus, for murdering his wife, whom he charged with associating with a former "Ace of the Prohibition Department." An Ohio enforcement law permitted magistrates in courts of lowest jurisdiction to share in fines paid by prohibition violators. So the mayor of the village of North College Hill in Hamilton County, sitting as a magistrate, had presided at the trial of one Ed Tumey, charged with possessing liquor. Tumey was convicted and fined $100, out of which the mayor-judge received $12. During seven months he had made about $100 monthly in addition to his salary from such fines. Chief Justice Taft, for a unanimous

[37] 267 U.S. 188. [38] 272 U.S. 581.

court, halted this racket. Any man accused of a crime had the right to a fair, impartial trial and a judge who profited financially from a conviction might not be an impartial judge.[39]

This was in March, 1927. Some fourteen months later he voted for strict law enforcement in *Olmstead* v. *United States,* the wire-tapping case which subjected the Supreme Court to bitter criticism—criticism as bitter by the dissenting minority of four as by the press or the public. Taft, again, took on the burden of writing the opinion, but he worried perceptibly as he drafted it. He knew that Brandeis would dissent and he presumed that Butler would do the same. A hopeful note was that Sutherland had agreed to go along with the Chief Justice.[40] The dissenters were Brandeis, Holmes, Butler and Stone.

Roy Olmstead was head of a bootlegging ring which operated in and about Seattle, Washington, and sold $2,000,000 annually of liquor smuggled from British Columbia. The headquarters of the ring was in a Seattle office building to which orders for liquor were telephoned. Four federal agents intercepted telephone calls to the headquarters over a period of months, the result being convictions for conspiracy to violate the National Prohibition act. No tapping of wires had been done on the actual premises of the accused men.

Taft, as he so delighted to do, went back to common law to show that the admissibility of evidence was not affected by illegality in obtaining it. The Chief Justice drew a line between search of the mails and tapping telephone wires. The language of the Fourth Amendment, he said, "cannot be extended and expanded to include telephone wires reaching to the whole world from the defendant's house or office. . . . Congress may, of course, protect the secrecy of telephone messages . . . and thus depart from the common law of evidence. But the courts may not adopt such a policy by attributing an enlarged and unusual meaning to the Fourth Amendment."

"Whenever a telephone line is tapped," objected Justice Brandeis, "the privacy of the persons at both ends of the line is invaded and all conversations between them on any subject, and although proper, confidential and privileged may be overheard. . . . As a means of espionage, writs of assistance and general warrants are but puny instruments of tyranny and oppression when compared with

[39] 273 U.S. 510. [40] Taft to McReynolds, May 25, 1928.

wire tapping. . . . Decency, security and liberty alike demand that government officials shall be subjected to the same rules of conduct that are commands to the citizen. . . . Our government is the potent, the omnipresent teacher. For good or for ill, it teaches the whole people by its example. Crime is contagious. If the government becomes a lawbreaker it . . . invites anarchy."

To Justice Holmes, wire tapping was "such dirty business" that no agent of the government should have a hand in it. In his dissent appeared, also, his classic phrase: "We have to choose, and for my part I think it a less evil that some criminals should escape than that the government should play an ignoble part." [41]

The Chief Justice, although deploring another five-to-four decision, had no misgivings, however.

"You may have seen the severe criticisms of our judgment in the wire-tapping case," he wrote to Justice Sutherland that summer, "but I think the more the case is read and understood, the less effective will be the eloquence and denunciation of Brandeis and Holmes. I feel quite sure that we are right, and that this will be ultimately realized." [42]

[41] 277 U.S. 438. [42] Taft to Sutherland, July 25, 1928.

CHAPTER LIII

A MORE EFFICIENT COURT

THE PRIMARY interest, perhaps, of Chief Justice Taft as his incumbency began was making more efficient and more swift the machinery of the federal courts in general and the Supreme Court in particular. Behind this desire lay some pronounced convictions on the duties, functions and obligations of the courts. If more jurists had shared Taft's views and had acted accordingly, the respect of the average man for the judicial process would have been greatly heightened.

"The unconscious point of view of some judges in the conduct of business in the court," he wrote in December, 1922, "is that the people are made for the courts. Every judge should have constantly before him that the reason for the existence of the courts is to promote the happiness of all the people by speedy and careful administration of justice, and every judge should exert himself to the uttermost to see that in his rulings and in his conduct of business he is, so far as his action can accomplish it, making his court useful to the litigants and to the community." [1]

The Chief Justice had no patience with judges who did not do their work properly. He had no use for the ones who permitted undue delay. For delay, he pointed out, made justice so costly that justice was denied to the poor and reserved for the rich alone:

I am greatly interested in the problem of facilitating the dispatch of business in our courts and ridding them of the burden of complex procedure and delays.

In maintaining the equality between the rich and the poor in the court, the greatest difficulty is the delay. A rich man can stand the delay and profits by it, but the poor man always suffers.[2]

The Chief Justice had as little respect for harsh or dictatorial judges as he had for lazy ones. Ever considerate, himself, toward

[1] Taft to C. A. Boston, Dec. 1, 1922. [2] Taft to C. F. Ruggles, Nov. 4, 1924.

attorneys and witnesses, he realized that it was the duty of a judge to protect the rights of all. And so he would voice, from time to time, warnings against the arbitrary use of the court's power to punish for contempt. As presiding officer of the Supreme Court, and thereby the most influential jurist in the land, he said:

> The power of contempt . . . is most important and indispensable. But its exercise is a delicate one, and care is needed to avoid arbitrary or oppressive conclusions. This rule of caution is more mandatory where the contempt charged has in it the element of personal criticism or attack upon the judge. The judge must banish the slightest personal impulse to reprisal, but he should not bend backward and injure the authority of the court by too great leniency. The substitution of another judge would avoid either tendency, but it is not always possible.[3]

—2—

Chief Justice Taft was not ignorant— after all, he had been a judge for many years— of the reasons behind the snaillike movement of justice. One cause was that nobody was responsible. "A judicial force . . . ought to be under the executive direction of somebody, so that the number of judges needed to meet the arrears of business at a particular place should be under the control of one who knows what the need is," he urged. A second reason was that reform of the judicial process was a dull subject which aroused small public interest and few votes.

"Legislators," wrote Taft, "will not give their attention even though they may be properly-minded toward such legislation." [4]

When he was president of the United States, Taft had been "to a unique degree . . . interested in the effective working of the judicial machinery and conversant with the details of judicial administration." He was interested, but only partially successful. True, he forced the creation of the United States Commerce Court in June, 1910, but it was abolished by Congress less than three years later. Immersed in other problems and greatly baffled by politics, President

[3] 267 U.S. 539. [4] Taft to C. F. Ruggles, Nov. 4, 1924.

Taft—however interested—could give little attention to judicial reform. Members of the bar had long urged the creation of a Patent Court but the President, while approving the project, did not press it.[5]

As president, Taft had often failed dismally in persuading the politicians to do his will or the public to support him. As chief justice, however, he was to be successful in the two major objectives of his judicial reform program. The first of these was the creation of a Conference of Senior Circuit Court Judges, with the Chief Justice at its head. This brought co-ordination, for the first time, into the federal judicial system. The second was the act of February 13, 1925, known as the Judges' bill, which meant an end of unfinished dockets. The Supreme Court, after the reform, kept up with its work. Nor did Taft hesitate to use political methods to help his cherished shrine of justice. He appeared, himself, before Congressional committees. He persuaded his associates to do the same. He addressed appeals to members of both houses and urged them to support the legislation.[6]

The first problem to be attacked was the congestion and lack of organization in the district and circuit courts. Chaos in the administration of justice was an ancient evil, but inertia had blocked suggested remedies; inertia and resistance by southern Democrats to any extension of federal power. In 1906, agitation for reform started. Teaching constitutional law at Yale after leaving the White House in 1913, Taft was, naturally, keenly aware of the problem. His voice and his influence were powerful factors in the changes at last brought about in 1922. An address before the Cincinnati Law School in 1914 pointed the way. The English judicial system, he said, had already been modified to fit the times.

. . . the two great features of it are the simplicity of its procedure and the elasticity with which that procedure and the use of the judicial force provided by Parliament can be adapted to the disposition of business. The success of the system rests on the executive control vested in a council of judges to direct business and economize judicial force.

[5] Frankfurter, Felix, and Landis, James M., *The Business of the Supreme Court*, pp. 156, 173, 177-182. [6] Taft to G. W. Pepper, Nov. 19, 1924.

Some such mobility was necessary in the United States, the former President added. But the World War postponed the remedy. When it ended, the disruption and the load of litigation were even greater. Something had to be done.[7]

"I am glad to hear that you are interested in readjusting the machinery of the federal courts to better the dispatch of business," Taft wrote to Brandeis soon after he became chief justice. ". . . The statutory increase in the jurisdiction and business of the inferior federal courts has swamped them and something must be done to remove the 'hump' and enable them to keep up with their dockets."

The mere increase of courts or judges will not suffice. We must have machinery of a quasi-executive character to mass our judicial force at the place where the congestion is, or is likely to be. We must have teamwork and judges must be under some sort of disciplinary obligation to go where they are most needed. In this way, we shall get more effective work out of each judge and he will be made conscious of observation by someone in authority of the work he is doing. . . .

It seems to me that through a committee of the Chief Justice and the senior circuit judges, a survey of the state of business in the federal courts could be made each year and plans adopted to send district judges from one district to another in the same circuit and from one circuit to another, so as to take up the slack and utilize it where needed. . . . I don't know whether these suggestions if embodied in a bill would find sufficient legislative support to pass it; but now would seem to be the time to try it when the arrears caused by the Volstead prosecutions are impressive, and when Congress is seeking methods to secure a better enforcement of the law.[8]

Bills were introduced when Congress convened in December, 1921, which provided for twenty-four new district judges and for a Conference of Senior Circuit Judges. It was also provided that judges could be shifted to courts swamped with work. Congress approved highly of new judges. Their appointments constituted valuable patronage. But criticism was directed against what Senator John Sharp Williams of Mississippi called "a perambulatory judiciary." It was charged, too, that the conference of judges might

[7] Frankfurter, F. and Landis, J. M., op. cit., pp. 220-231. [8] Taft to Brandeis, July 24, 1921.

make a czar out of the Chief Justice, who would preside. Under this pressure, it was agreed that Taft and his successors might not move jurists at will. A certificate of need would have to be obtained first from the senior circuit judge in the new locality as well as one from the home circuit testifying that he could be spared.[9]

"There is not the slightest possibility of the abuse of this power . . ." Chief Justice Taft told Senator Lodge, and asked that the bill be passed.[10]

It became law on September 14, 1922, and the Chief Justice called the first annual conference for December 27, 1922. This was to have a profound influence on the operation of the federal courts. A body consisting of the Chief Justice and the nine senior circuit judges carried, naturally, great weight in suggesting reforms. These were to be many and diverse as the years went on. Had not the Chief Justice urged the change, it might have been postponed for years.[11]

—3—

Congestion in the Supreme Court antedated by decades the Taft court. Between 1850 and 1870, the pending cases increased from 253 to 636 and they had jumped to 1,816 two decades later. Frankfurter and Landis have cogently presented the reasons for that early deluge:

This swelling of the dockets was due to the growth of the country's business, the assumption of authority over cases heretofore left to state courts, the extension of the field of federal activity. The great commercial development brings its share of litigation . . . booms and panics alike furnish grist. . . . The vigorous stimulation of invention causes many and complicated patent controversies. The new seaborne traffic also carries a heavy load of admiralty business.

Added litigation in the lower courts meant, inevitably, added litigation before the nation's highest tribunal. The founding fathers had originally intended that the lower federal courts should serve two main functions: the adjudication of admiralty cases and the

---

[9] Frankfurter, F., and Landis, J. M., op. cit., pp. 237-239. [10] Taft to Lodge, Feb. 17, 1922. [11] Frankfurter, F., and Landis, J. M., op. cit., pp. 241-254.

protection of citizens who brought actions outside their home communities and faced, thereby, the possible hostility of unfriendly courts. But in 1875 Congress provided, in substance, that any case involving a constitutional claim could be initiated in the federal courts or transferred from the state courts. The Supreme Court added to its own burdens in 1885 by deciding that any suit against a corporation chartered by the federal government was within federal jurisdiction. Soon even negligence actions against railroads were appearing on the dockets.

Congress provided a degree of relief in 1891 when it created nine circuit courts of appeals. New business dropped from 623 cases in 1890 to 275 cases in 1892. The relief, though, was of short duration. Theodore Roosevelt's onslaughts against the wicked industrialists and the even more important reforms of Woodrow Wilson resulted in greatly increased powers for the federal government. Among the laws passed were the Safety Appliance act, the Hours of Service law, the Food and Drugs act, the Meat Inspection act, the Anti-Narcotic and Mann acts, the Packers and Stockyards and the Grain Futures acts, the Elkins act. But this was not all. In New York, Wisconsin and other states the legislatures were also taking action against the abuses of the railroads and other corporations, and appeals from their edicts would also reach Washington.

The problem of the Supreme Court's docket lay in the increase of all federal litigation and not in any desire of Congress to add to the burdens of the highest court. Only once, in 1914, did Congress directly expand the jurisdiction. Otherwise the tendency was steadily to keep the business of the Supreme Court within the ability of nine justices to handle it.[12] The theory of Congress, and it was wholly proper, was that a litigant suing in the federal courts, or being sued, had a right of appeal from the lower or trial court to the appellate circuit court. It was only on questions involving constitutionality, and thus of far greater importance and significance, that an appeal was to lie to the Supreme Court. On the other hand, nobody suggested for a moment that such an appeal should be denied. Chief Justice Taft explained the proposed reform in December, 1921. It was vital, he said in opening his drive for the Judges' bill, that cases before the court be reduced without limiting

[12] *Ibid.*, pp. 60-61, 69, 97-102, 105-107, 187.

the function of pronouncing "the last word on every important issue under the Constitution and the statutes of the United States." A Supreme Court, on the other hand, should not be a tribunal obligated to weigh justice among contesting parties.

"They have had all they have a right to claim," Taft said, "when they have had two courts in which to have adjudicated their controversy." [13]

A good deal might already have been accomplished toward this end had it not been for the belief of Chief Justice White that his colleagues should take no part in advocating judicial reform legislation. Chief Justice Taft did not share this belief. The initial request for assistance came from Senator Cummins, chairman of the Senate Judiciary Committee. Thereupon Taft named a committee consisting of Associate Justices Day, Van Devanter and McReynolds. Justice Sutherland, upon his appointment, aided in the work but was not a committee member. Taft, at the committee's request, also served. All this was in violation of Supreme Court tradition, but Taft violated tradition willingly when the welfare of his beloved court was at stake.[14]

The remedy for the congestion was to be increased resort to writs of *certiorari,* which the Supreme Court could decline to grant, and the practical abolition of writs of error. The Chief Justice explained this, too, to the members of the Chicago bar.

"Litigants . . . cannot complain," he said, "where they have had their two chances that there should be reserved to the discretion of the Supreme Court to say whether the issue between them is of sufficient importance to justify a hearing of it in the Supreme Court. The Supreme Court already has wide jurisdiction by *certiorari*. That court considers carefully the character of each case in which a *certiorari* is applied for. The examination of records for this purpose is part of the hard work of the court. . . .

"The new bill proposes to enlarge the field in which *certiorari* is to take the place of obligatory jurisdiction. . . . As it is now, the important governmental, constitutional questions that we have to advance and set down for immediate hearing postpone the regular docket and are likely to increase our arrears. . . . The Supreme

[13] Manuscript address, Dec. 27, 1911, Taft papers, Library of Congress. [14] Van Devanter to Taft, May 11, 1927.

Court will remain the supreme revisory tribunal, but it will be given sufficient control of the number and character of the cases which come before it to enable it to remain the one Supreme Court and to keep up with its work." [15]

Taft reiterated these views before the New York County Lawyers' Association on February 18, 1922, the day after the bill was introduced in both houses of Congress. He reassured the lawyers regarding the granting of *certiorari* writs allowing them to bring their cases before the Supreme Court.

"The impression has been given, but without real foundation, that the granting of *certiorari* by our court is a matter of guess and favor rather than one of careful consideration," he said. "I am glad to have an opportunity in this presence to assure the members of the bar that every case presented . . . has a thorough examination by each member of the court, and that a vote is taken after a thorough discussion of the character of the case, derived from a reading of the briefs, opinions in the lower courts and such examination of the records as may be necessary to verify the briefs. The disposition of cases on *certiorari* has come to be one of the very heavy tasks of the court, but the court is entirely willing to discharge that task if thereby it can keep the number within possible limits."

Taft then summarized the appeals or writs of error which came "as of right" to the Supreme Court. The Judges' bill, he said, limited these to actions from state supreme courts in which the constitutional validity of a state statute had been questioned or sustained.

"This is one appellate proceeding which is obligatory," the Chief Justice said.

"All the cases which come from the Circuit Courts of Appeals, all the cases which come from the Court of Appeals of the District of Columbia, all the cases which come from the Court of Claims, and a majority of the cases from the state supreme courts," he added, "must get into the Supreme Court on *certiorari,* if they get in at all."

Finally, the Chief Justice pointed out, the new bill would simplify and bring into one statute all the law on procedure which it was necessary for any attorney to know.[16]

---

[15] Address, Dec. 27, 1921. [16] Address, Dec. 11, 1927.

Congress debated the measure for almost three years and the Chief Justice reacted with irritation when it was criticized. He was scandalized, naturally, when a passing suggestion was made that the number of Supreme Court justices should be increased.

"The court are all of them very much opposed . . ." he wrote. "It would greatly inconvenience us. . . . I hope nothing will be done to give us a town meeting. . . . Consider the danger of setting a precedent to a demagogue Democratic administration." [17]

Taft and some of his brother justices lobbied vigorously and openly for the bill. "Van Devanter, McReynolds and I spent two full days at the Capitol, and Van and I one full day more to get the bill through," the Chief Justice reported in February, 1925, when, at last, it became law.[18] He was greatly elated. By December, 1926, he was able to show that the Judges' bill had accelerated the work of the court.[19] It was, in truth, a splendid achievement. In the words of Justice Frankfurter and Mr. Landis, the reform wrote into law the "aim of the Supreme Court to be allowed to confine its adjudications to issues of constitutionality and other matters of essentially national importance." [20]

—4—

In the summer of 1922, having launched his Judges' bill, the Chief Justice went to England to receive a degree from Oxford and also to study "the much simpler procedure of the English courts with a view of securing legislation of this kind in our federal system." [21] He received not merely one, but three, honorary degrees and had a magnificent time meeting the King and Queen, innumerable dukes, earls and knights, and also all the important barristers and judges of England. He returned convinced anew that "the English administration of justice is the best in the world." On the other hand, he found that "a great deal of what they do [is] entirely impracticable with us." [22]

Mrs. Taft went on the journey, of course; travel and association

[17] Taft to H. W. Taft, April 6, 1922. [18] Taft to R. A. Taft, Feb. 8, 1925. [19] Taft to Senator Norris, Dec. 15, 1926. [20] Frankfurter, F., and Landis, J. M., *op. cit.*, p. 280. [21] Taft to Clarence Kelsey, Jan. 18, 1922. [22] Taft to R. A. Taft, July 29, 1922.

with the great always delighted her. On returning to Murray Bay in July, the Chief Justice dictated an extraordinary and charmingly indiscreet account, a lengthy one of 30,000 words which he sent to his children. The Tafts stayed with Ambassador and Mrs. George Harvey, "who live on the fat of the land," and were plunged at once into a dazzling world. The first function was the Pilgrims Dinner on June 19, the day after arrival. Five to six hundred men and women, the elite of England, were there and the Chief Justice spoke pleasantly, but not profoundly, on Anglo-American relations and the role of the United States in international affairs. On the following day they were received at Buckingham Palace.

"The King is a very free talker and expresses himself with entire frankness," Taft wrote. "The Queen is a gracious person and comely in appearance. She is queenly in bearing . . . not stiff . . . or in any way offensive and so far as I could see very well dressed. . . . The conversation turned on Mr. Wilson's visit to Buckingham Palace. He stayed with them . . . and I inferred, not from anything they said directly, but from implications, that they did not like him or his manner of doing things when he was their guest."

The visit was formal and brief. On the following day they attended a court where Taft wore his judicial robes over his white tie and tails. Again, they had a private audience with the King and Queen and the Chief Justice was invited to sit down during the long ceremony— the only man save the King thus privileged. Otherwise, he explained, it would have "been a very great strain . . . because my knee is rheumatic." When the affair was over they "returned to the embassy, and your mother and the ambassador took some bottles of beer, and Mrs. Harvey and I confined ourselves to crackers and cheese and fruit."

On June 24, the Harveys gave a palatial banquet attended by the King and Queen, a fine selection of dukes, other nobles and titled personages.

"Of course," Taft wrote, "it is a great feather in the cap of the ambassador to have the King and Queen as guests. The King and Queen occasionally go out, but they don't go to every embassy."

The King escorted Mrs. Harvey to the table; the Queen went in on the arm of Harvey. Taft took in Lady Astor and Mrs. Taft was with the Earl of Balfour. It was all very satisfactory because

Mrs. Taft was seated next to the King while the Chief Justice was next to the Queen. Taft's description was detailed:

> It was the first time I had ever met Lady Astor. She was very lively, and apparently was anxious to show she was not overcome by the presence of their Majesties. She said things to the King and stood discussing matters with him, delaying the procession to the dining room. She sat next to me at the table and seemed determined to help me out with the Queen.
>
> I got along very well with the Queen. I found her quite willing to talk, and interested in quite a number of things. She discussed prohibition during the war in England, mentioned the fact that they had voluntarily banished everything of that sort from the table, but the doctor of the King advised him he was suffering from a want of some stimulant, to which he had been accustomed, and therefore, after a year or more urged that he take it up again. She suggested my not opening the subject with my neighbor, Lady Astor, who was very extreme on the subject as a prohibitionist. . . .
>
> Lady Astor was punching me in the leg, because she thought I was not getting along with the Queen comfortably, in which she was quite mistaken. Then she whispered to me, "isn't it awful?" supposing that I was suffering in silence. I had been a good deal prejudiced against Lady Astor by what I had seen in the newspapers and by what I had heard of her, and thought that she was using the immunity that pretty American women, especially in the South, enjoy to be rather impudent, though bright, in her conversations. But she is so charming and so direct and so sympathetic in a way that I changed my mind in respect to her. I was amused, however, to have her say that she thought Alice Roosevelt abused her privileges by mixing insolence with brightness. . . .

The King of England and the Chief Justice of the United States discovered, in a conversation after the dinner, that they had certain prejudices in common. His Majesty expressed sharp criticism of his country's labor unions and their demands for high wages. Business could not go on, he told Taft, unless they were cut.

"But I am a constitutional king," he then observed, "and I cannot say anything that my ministers don't allow me to say, but these are things I think."

Throughout his life, Taft had not been above a weakness for

gossip; he relished and repeated the tidbits he heard during the visit about the great of England. He learned that "Lady Astor and Margot Asquith don't like each other and make fun of each other." And:

When Margot was in this country, Mrs. Charles Dana Gibson entertained her. Margot wrote her a note to thank her for her kindness, but put in a postcript, "Nancy Astor is really making a fool of herself in London. Can't you do something about it?" This was calculated to make Mrs. Gibson happy and, of course, to put Nancy in a friendly condition of mind toward Margot because we can be certain that Mrs. Gibson at once communicated it to Lady Astor.

The Harveys told me that Lady Astor could imitate Margot to perfection, and when we were leaving Lady Astor's and something was said to her about our going to lunch with Mrs. Asquith, she gave us several exhibitions of Margot's method of speech which were very true to life, as I subsequently discovered, and which were excruciatingly funny.

The Chief Justice and Mrs. Taft hobnobbed with royalty again on June 28 at a fancy dress ball given under the auspices of Princess Mary. Taft was not greatly impressed by some of the costumes, in particular that of "one woman in a yellow and black check suit consisting of a waist and trousers or pants and stockings, with large hips." The Queen again summoned them and "I put my foot in it, I suppose, by inquiring of the Queen whether Princess Mary was there." Her absence seemed strange inasmuch as she was the affair's royal patron, and "the Queen's reply indicated that I had touched a sensitive spot, for she spoke up with a good deal of feeling."

"No, she is not here," Taft quoted her. "Lascelles [the Viscount Lascelles, her husband] has got some horses at Newmarket and of course she had to go down to be with him and his horses."

Soon afterward the Prince of Wales arrived. "I remember very well your presiding at the dinner the societies gave me in New York," the future King told Taft. "By the way, haven't they made you something since? Haven't you been made a secretary or put in the Cabinet or something?"

Taft, although amused, was in no way ruffled by Wales's ignorance and said it merely showed "that something may happen to you, which you deem to be of great importance . . . [and] may escape the attention of other people."

Clearly, the royal family, the statesmen and the jurists of England liked Taft for his own sake. They appreciated his legal learning. They enjoyed his charm. But they would not have been Englishmen had they refrained from trying to make practical use of his visit. They knew that he had the ear of President Harding and of some of the members of Congress. So they assured him, whenever an opportunity offered, that the British debt should be scaled down. King George began it, at the Harvey dinner. Taft remembered the substance of the conversation:

He said that if we insisted on collecting the debt from Great Britain, Great Britain would have to collect her debt from France, and that it would be very hard. He was evidently hoping that we would give up the debt. I told him that the debt was being relied upon now by men who were pressing for a bonus for service in the war, and that it would be quite unpopular to propose such a waiver.

The subject was brought up again by Lloyd George at a luncheon at 10 Downing street on July 5. The Chief Justice, at a previous meeting, had found the Prime Minister "a very fascinating man . . . direct, gracious and apparently open and straightforward and anxious to be agreeable, but not unpleasantly so." Lloyd George, it might be added, was also cunning. It may be assumed that he was not unaware that Taft held a low opinion of former President Wilson. So the Prime Minister, before mentioning debts or reparations, took pains to criticize Wilson's conduct at the Peace Conference:

He said that he made a great mistake in not sending somebody to represent him; that when as the head of the state he came down to negotiations, he put himself on the plane with Prime Ministers and did not have that reserve of background, that strength which he would have had at home in directing the course of agents abroad.

He said, "We had to treat him on our level and when we got him over here, then he was at our mercy. We could teach him a few things." I said . . . that I wondered how he got on with them, because his previous political course had been one of never answering arguments. . . . Lloyd George replied that they had him where they could make him answer.

The debt question arose after the Prime Minister had painted a black picture of conditions in Germany. He said that financial collapse and bolshevism loomed and that both England and the United States would be affected:

Then Lloyd George appealed to me— I think with the hope that something might filter through to Harding and to Hughes— in favor of the United States coming into a conference to help her in restraining France from her extreme severity toward Germany, and her unwillingness to give Germany a chance.

The Chief Justice learned that Ambassador Harvey, who was present at the luncheon, had already discussed the debt situation with Lloyd George and other members of the British Cabinet. He had told them that cancellation was impossible, but had offered a suggestion whereby the interest charges could be reduced radically. This was for the United States and Great Britain to issue bonds together for which they would be jointly responsible. Thus backed, an interest rate of only three per cent could be obtained, a cut of half. In due time the same thing might be done for the French debt, and in this way England and the United States would control the finances of the other nations and thereby preserve order and peace. The British Prime Minister, Taft wrote, did not seem fully to understand Harvey's plan. Personally, he added, it appeared to be "one that would work out admirably." [23]

On returning to Murray Bay, the Chief Justice endorsed Harvey's proposal, in a general way, to President Harding.

"I venture to predict that something will come of it," he told the President.[24]

Nothing did, of course. And the results, had such bonds been issued, must remain a subject for speculation only. The United States might have found itself responsible for both the interest and the principal of the loans which had been made to the Allied nations. On the other hand, stabilization might have been achieved.

[23] Taft to R. A. Taft, July 29, 1922. [24] Taft to Harding, July 21, 1922.

The Chief Justice promptly lost interest in the subject. The summer of 1922— like most of his summers and all his winters now— was busy in the extreme. In August he left the cool of the St. Lawrence River again; this time for the Bar Association meeting in San Francisco.

"I grudge the time," he said.[25]

[25] Taft to H. W. Taft, July 30, 1922.

CHAPTER LIV

HOW FAR MAY CONGRESS GO?

AMONG the issues which wrecked the Republican party in 1912 had been the relative powers of the federal government and the states. Issues are defined too glibly in a political campaign. Roosevelt had been labeled the proponent of greatly increased centralization. Taft had been damned on the ground that he held too rigidly to the constitutional doctrine that the states retained all rights not specifically granted to Washington. But it was more complicated than that. In his post as chief justice of the United States, Taft would affirm decision after decision which expanded the scope of the federal government. After he died, when President Franklin D. Roosevelt demanded a Supreme Court more closely geared to modern problems, there would be additional rulings augmenting the powers of Congress.

The work of the Supreme Court had not merely grown more burdensome. It had become far more involved. No longer, as former Assistant Attorney General John Dickinson has observed— he referred to due process cases but the thought is generally applicable—does "the Court simply draw chalk lines, as on a map, between mutually exclusive compartments of power. Rather, it traces filigree outlines along the facts of particular cases and leaves the line to be defined with greater or less accuracy by the perspective of the [law] profession." [1] Behind these determinations by the legal mind lay, according to its critics, a basic conservatism and a tendency to interpret the Constitution in the light of those earlier decisions which invalidated national or state laws.[2] Yet progress would be made, if slowly. The Supreme Court, like all agencies of government in a democracy, would not be wholly irresponsive to the popular will.

"Judges are apt to be naïve, simple-minded men, and they need

[1] *Selected Essays,* Vol. III, p. 3. [2] Corwin, E. S., *The Twilight of the Supreme Court,* p. xxiii.

something of Mephistopheles," Associate Justice Holmes had sagely remarked. "We too need education in the obvious— to learn to transcend our convictions and to leave room for much that we hold dear to be done away with short of revolution by the orderly change of law." [3]

It would be an exaggeration, however, to intimate that Chief Justice Taft used Mephistophelian methods. When the full story of Chief Justice Hughes is told, a faint touch of sulphur may, perhaps, be discerned. In any event, Chief Justice Hughes saved his court from the machinations of the White House and preserved the respect in which it was popularly held. Taft, it is safe to say, would not have enjoyed the task of doing so.

The question of how far Congress may go, under the Constitution, in remedial, regulatory or other legislation will never finally be settled. Numerous aspects of the problem reached the Taft court and a major one was the extent of federal power in the regulation of interstate commerce. In 1824 Chief Justice Marshall had said that commerce was more than merely traffic; it was intercourse. And the power of Congress to regulate this commercial intercourse was "sovereign," "complete," "plenary" and "absolute." [4] Ninety-four years later, in a five-to-four child labor decision, the Supreme Court would, in effect, nullify Chief Justice Marshall. This, in 1918, was the first child labor case and it forbade interstate transportation of goods which had been manufactured with the aid of child labor. The method of the court in shifting from the Marshall decision to the 1918 ruling was, in the words of Professor Corwin, "to be compared to that of those Chinese rivers which occasionally abandon the courses they have followed for decades and proceed to plow a new channel to the sea, at sharp angles to the first." [5]

—2—

When he was president, Taft had worked sincerely, if not too skillfully, for stricter federal regulation of the railroads and had even embraced so progressive a doctrine as valuation as a basis for

[3] Corwin, E. S., *The Twilight of the Supreme Court*, p. xxvi. [4] Corwin, E. S., *The Commerce Power Versus States Rights*, pp. 4-12. [5] *Ibid.*, pp. 17-18.

rate making. The war had brought chaos to the nation's transportation lines. After government operation they had been returned to private ownership; to solve some of their problems Congress passed the Transportation Act of 1920. This authorized the Interstate Commerce Commission to fix the fares and freight tariffs of all interstate lines and to provide, thereby, a fair return on their properties. Among other increases in passenger fares decreed was one for the railroads which crossed Wisconsin. A state commission agreed with the federal board regarding freight rates, but ruled that passenger fares could not be increased within the state because of a law which fixed these at two cents a mile. The Chicago, Burlington & Quincy Railroad Company thereupon sought an injunction against the Wisconsin Railroad Commission's attempt to suspend the higher rates fixed by the I.C.C. The case was first heard by the White court, but was argued again in December, 1921. Chief Justice Taft wrote the opinion which upheld the I.C.C., and all his associates agreed with it.

An absurd situation had been created in Wisconsin. A passenger traveling within the state could sit in a seat next to one bound for Minnesota or Michigan or elsewhere and pay two cents a mile as contrasted with three and six-tenths charged the interstate traveler. The railroads of Wisconsin would lose about $6,000,000 a year if the Wisconsin Railroad Commission's edict against the passenger fare increase was valid. The Chief Justice said that two questions had to be decided: did the intrastate fares "work undue prejudice against persons in interstate commerce, such as to justify a horizontal increase of them all?"; were "these intrastate fares an undue discrimination against interstate commerce as a whole which it is the duty of the commission to remove?"

Yes, would be the answer of the Supreme Court to both questions, and the power of Congress with regard to commerce within a state as well as its control of interstate commerce would be increased.

". . . under the Constitution," wrote the Chief Justice, "interstate and intrastate commerce are ordinarily subject to regulation by different sovereignties, yet when they are so mingled together that the supreme authority, the nation, cannot exercise complete, effective control over interstate commerce without incidental regulation of intrastate commerce, such incidental regulation is not an invasion of state authority."

By inference, at least, Taft approved all the provisions of the Transportation Act of 1920, including the one that a return of six per cent was to be the maximum allowed any railroad. Half of the earnings above this were to be turned over to a revolving fund from which aid could be given to the weaker roads. Upon the I.C.C., the Chief Justice said, had been "imposed an affirmative duty . . . to fix rates and to take other important steps to maintain an adequate railway service for the people of the United States." Taft reiterated the doctrine that the power of Congress in the control or development of interstate commerce was dominant.

"In such development," he said, "it can impose any reasonable condition on a state's use of interstate carriers for intrastate commerce it deems necessary or desirable. This is because of the supremacy of the national power in this field." [6]

This decision did not, specifically, pass on the constitutionality of the provision that earnings in excess of six per cent could be diverted to other railroads. The Supreme Court would so rule, however, in January, 1924. Spokesman for the "socialistic" viewpoint, as some critics called it, was, again, Chief Justice Taft.

The Dayton-Goose Creek Railway Company of Texas, a small but prosperous line, had earned some $33,000 above the six per cent limitation in 1921. The I.C.C. instructed it to place half of this in a reserve fund and to remit the other half, under the terms of the 1920 act. The company went into the lower federal courts for an injunction. The Chief Justice, again for a unanimous court, pointed out that the 1920 law went much further than previous regulatory acts. It sought "affirmatively to build up a system of railways prepared to handle promptly all the interstate traffic of the country. It aims to give the owners of the railways an opportunity to earn enough to maintain their properties and equipment in such a state of efficiency that they can carry well this burden."

It was an outstanding case and an outstanding decision. Most of the large railroads of the nation filed briefs supporting the little Texas line. The Chief Justice drew a sharp distinction between profits from investment in an ordinary private business and one

[6] 257 U.S. 563.

"dedicated to the public service." In the latter, the investor "cannot expect either high or speculative dividends, but . . . only fair or reasonable profit." Nor, Taft insisted, was Congress in passing this law limited by the Fifth or the Tenth Amendment. Here was no violation of state control over intrastate traffic, the court said, because Congress was dealing with a situation "in which state and interstate operations are inextricably commingled." [7]

The decision would open the door, in due time, for regulation of other industries. It is one which illustrates the peril which lies in any attempt to classify as liberal or conservative a member of the Supreme Court. Much of the legislation of the Roosevelt New Deal, as we shall see, could be upheld on the basis of Chief Justice Taft's doctrine that Congress was almost unrestricted in the regulation of interstate commerce; it had to be demonstrated in a given issue, naturally, that the commerce *was* interstate. This proved, the powers of Washington were as great as though no states existed.

Chief Justice Taft must have been somewhat dismayed early in 1924, however, if he heard that the *New Republic,* that unsound and radical organ, had hailed his opinion in the Dayton-Goose Creek case as an important contribution to "economic liberalism." The *New Republic* pointed to the Chief Justice's phrase that the railroads were "dedicated to the public service" and asked whether Congress might not shortly declare coal mining or the manufacture of public necessities similarly dedicated. And then might not Congress also declare that six or seven or eight per cent was an adequate return? The court was not ready for that, however.[8]

—3—

Nor would the Supreme Court permit Congress to effect all manner of reforms, however laudable, with either its power to regulate commerce or its power to tax. Through certain of the court's rulings the layman wanders as in a jungle of confusion. Far back in 1904 the court had upheld— in an opinion by Associate Justice White— a tax on oleomargarine when colored to resemble butter. Fostered by the dairy industry, the act made the tax so heavy as

[7] 263 U.S. 456. [8] Ragan, A. E., *Chief Justice Taft*, p. 49.

to prohibit the sale of the substitute for butter. But Mr. Justice White said that the power of Congress to tax was unrestrained "except as limited by the Constitution," and that the oleomargarine levy was not so barred. For the courts to invalidate legislation merely because, to the judicial mind, it might seem "unwise or unjust" would be "a mere act of judicial usurpation." [9]

Did this echo, perhaps, the voice of Theodore Roosevelt who was demanding, from the White House, reform and more reform and also a new morality in business, finance and government? But the decision of 1904 would be undermined by the first child labor decision in 1918. Congress had barred the products of child labor from interstate commerce. Associate Justice Day, for his majority of five which included Chief Justice White, said that the products were, in themselves, harmless whereas under the acts declared constitutional they had been harmful; he was not referring, specifically, to oleomargarine. Among these laws, of course, was the Mann act which sought to end the white slave trade and became, instead, a fruitful source of blackmail conspiracies.[10] In 1919 the Harrison Narcotic act— this time Chief Justice White dissented!— was affirmed.[11] In that same year the court approved an amendment to the postal laws forbidding the shipment of alcoholic beverages into states where their sale or manufacture was illegal.[12]

On May 15, 1922, in the second child labor case, Chief Justice Taft had the unpleasant duty of overruling, at last, the White opinion of 1904 which had interpreted so broadly the taxing powers of Congress and which had caused, all in all, some involved legal thinking at subsequent sessions of the court. It was characteristic for Taft to take the burden on his own shoulders. It was also typical of him to work zealously to persuade his associates to vote with him. He was successful in converting even Brandeis and Holmes to his views; Associate Justice Clarke, alone, disagreed.

This time Congress had attempted to use its taxing instead of its commerce power to crush the exploitation of children. Ten per cent of the profits per year was to be levied against companies or individuals who knowingly employed children younger than the limit prescribed by the act. Thus about $6,300 had been assessed

[9] 195 U.S. 27. [10] Corwin, E. S., *The Twilight of the Supreme Court*, pp. 26-34; 227 U.S. 308. [11] 249 U.S. 86. [12] 248 U.S. 420.

against the Drexel Furniture Company of North Carolina because, during 1919, a boy under fourteen had been at work in its factory. The Chief Justice asked whether this tax had "only that incidental restraint and regulation which a tax must inevitably involve"? Clearly, he said, this was not the case. A court "must be blind not to see that the so-called tax is imposed to stop the employment of children. . . . Its prohibitory and regulatory effect and purpose are palpable. All others can see and understand this. How can we properly shut our minds to it?

The good sought in unconstitutional legislation is an insidious feature because it leads citizens and legislators of good purpose to promote it without thought of the serious breach it will make in the ark of our covenant, or the harm which will come from breaking down recognized standards. . . .

Out of a proper respect for the acts of a co-ordinate branch of the government, this Court has gone far to sustain taxing acts as such, even though there has been ground for suspecting, from the weight of the tax, it was intended to destroy its subject. But in the act before us, the presumption of validity cannot prevail, because the proof of the contrary is found on the very face of its provisions. . . . To give such magic to the word "tax" would be to break down all constitutional limitation of the powers of Congress and completely wipe out the sovereignty of the states.[13]

The Chief Justice was confident, once more, that the decision was good law. Nor did Solicitor General Beck, whose duty it had been, on behalf of the government, to argue for its constitutionality, disagree. The solicitor general told Taft, after the ruling, that to have upheld the views of White would have grievously changed the American conception of government.

"I had an impression your soul was not wrapped up in the child labor cases," the Chief Justice answered, "although you certainly made as strong a case as could be." [14]

Yet so humane a man as Taft found it repugnant to be regarded as a foe of child labor control. The act just overthrown, he wrote, was "a mere effort of good people, who wish children pro-

[13] 259 U.S. 20. [14] J. M. Beck to Taft, May 16, 1922; Taft to Beck, May 17, 1922.

tected through the country, to compel certain states to conduct their police powers in accord with the views of the good people. . . . Unfortunately we cannot strain the Constitution of the United States to meet the wishes of good people." The Chief Justice was caustic in his comment that President-Emeritus Eliot of Harvard, "without the slightest knowledge of the situation," had condemned the court. He pointed out that Eliot's "favorite, Brandeis," had concurred.[15]

"It was very necessary," the Chief Justice added, "to notify Congress that their encroachment on state jurisdiction through the use of the taxing power was not unlimited." [16]

On the same day, May 15, 1922, the court unanimously rejected the so-called Future Trading act whereby illegal grain trades on the Chicago Board of Trade were to be controlled. Again, Congress had used its taxing power; a levy was imposed on all contracts except those made under specifications of the secretary of agriculture. The Chief Justice said that this, too, was an unwarranted use of the tax power. But he raised the question of whether Congress could not, under the commerce clause, accomplish the same purpose and proceeded to show the legislative branch how it could be done:

Can these regulations of boards of trade by Congress be sustained under the commerce clause of the Constitution? Such regulations are held to be within the police powers of the state. . . . There is not a word in the act from which it can be gathered that it is confined in its operation to interstate commerce. . . . A reading of the act makes it quite clear that Congress sought to use the taxing power to give validity to the act. It did not have the exercise of its power under the commerce clause in mind, and so did not introduce into the act the limitations which would accompany and mark an exercise of the power under the latter clause.[17]

He had so indicated in a private letter. "I am inclined to think," Taft wrote, "that they can probably draft a law which will stick with respect to the Chicago Board of Trade, but I don't think they can ever do it with respect to child labor." [18]

[15] Taft to Horace Taft, May 15, 1922. [16] Taft to J. R. Long, Dec. 12, 1922. [17] 259 U.S. 44. [18] Taft to Horace Taft, May 15, 1922.

Congress accepted the suggestion. On April 16, 1923, the new law, which had the identical purpose of regulating futures but did so under the commerce clause, was affirmed. The Board of Trade in Chicago, Taft wrote, was "affected with a public interest and is, therefore, subject to reasonable regulation in the public interest." The transactions on the board were clearly interstate commerce. The Supreme Court had already so decided in upholding the Stock Yards act of 1921. This had provided for regulation of the nation's stockyards and had prohibited unfair practices or attempts to create a monopoly. In that case, *Stafford* v. *Wallace,* decided in May, 1922, Taft had painted a graphic picture of the interstate nature of the packing industry:

> The stock yards are not a place of rest or final destination. . . . The stock yards are but a throat through which the current flows, and the transactions which occur therein are only incident to this current from the West to the East, and from one state to another. . . . The stock yards and the sales are necessary factors in the middle of this current of commerce.[19]

The Chief Justice stood squarely behind the broadest interpretation of federal power in the regulation of interstate commerce.

"The power of Congress in this respect," he said in a private letter in August, 1928, "is . . . exactly what it would be in a government without states."

He quoted Chief Justice Marshall in support of that sweeping viewpoint.[20] But Taft was never unreasonable, as a jurist or as a man. In the fall of 1922 the Champlain Realty Company, a lumber concern, prayed for relief from $484.50 assessed against certain of its logs by the town of Brattleboro, Vermont. The logs had been held in the West River in that town because high water and swift currents made it unsafe to send them on their journey to Hinsdale, New Hampshire, where the company's mills were located. The Supreme Court of Vermont held they were taxable since their interstate passage had been halted.

Few issues are new in the Supreme Court of the United States. Chief Justice Taft turned back through the law reports to the

[19] 262 U.S. 1; 258 U.S. 495; Ragan, A. E., *op. cit.,* pp. 53-55. [20] Taft to Justice Stone, Aug. 31, 1928.

leading case which covered this point, *Coe* v. *Errol,* in 1886. There, too, a town had attempted to tax some logs in transit. But in that case the logs had been held for an entire winter, not just because of dangerous water, and shipment to another state had been merely an intention in the mind of the owner. So the tax had been legal. In the case now before the court, Taft continued, there was an actual, continuous journey with a halt of part of the shipment only to save it from destruction. Thus the Champlain Realty Company was entitled to a refund. The real significance of the decision lay, however, in Taft's clear definition of the relation of interstate commerce to local taxation:

The interstate commerce clause of the Constitution does not give immunity to movable property from local taxation unless it is in actual, continuous transit in interstate commerce. When it is shipped by a common carrier from one state to another, in the course of such an uninterrupted journey it is clearly immune. The doubt arises when there are interruptions in the journey, and when the property, in its transportation, is under the complete control of the owner during the passage. If the interruptions are only to promote the safe or convenient transit, then the continuity of the interstate trip is not broken.[21]

Taft and his associate jurists applied, in the main, their own rule of reason to the puzzling subject of when goods in transit might be taxed, and their judgments were based on a factual recognition of the problems of modern commerce. Louisiana, thereby, was not permitted to tax the oil in storage tanks when it was merely waiting to be loaded on steamers; such a tax would have meant that the shipper, forced to use tank cars for storage, would have paid heavy demurrage charges to the railroad.[22] On the other hand, Texas was allowed to tax the sales of a New York oil dealer. The oil was sold in the tanks or cans in which it had been shipped.

"Is this a regulation of, or a burden upon, interstate commerce?" the Chief Justice asked. "We think it is neither. The oil had come to a state of rest in the warehouse. . . . The interstate transportation was at an end." [23]

[21] 260 U.S. 366. [22] Ragan, A. E., *op. cit.,* p. 60. [23] 262 U.S. 506.

The Supreme Court decided, too, that the commerce clause did not keep a state from making regulations regarding the trucks which, in increasing numbers, were thundering over the roads of the nation. In the absence of national legislation on the subject, Taft said, the state had power to act. The case in question was that of an Oregon trucking company which had been operating 22,000-pound trucks and had been ordered, because of damage to the state's highways, to reduce the load to 15,000 pounds. The company pleaded that it could not profitably compete with the railroads on that basis but this, said the court, did not mean that the regulation was "either discriminatory or unreasonable." [24]

—4—

To limit an account of Taft as chief justice to the law and to legal decisions would be to give an incomplete picture of the Supreme Court years. For the court, however absorbing and demanding, was less cloistered a monastery than Taft had pictured it at the start. Reports from the outside world penetrated its walls— among them reports from the busy world of politics. Taft, quite naturally, listened to them. He had, after all, been a part of that world most of his life. A good many of the reports were tragic. At first, to Taft, they seemed incredible, untrue. In the end, though, their veracity was apparent. William Howard Taft, the soul of integrity, watched fellow politicians and, far worse, fellow Republicans wallowing in a black swamp of corruption, thievery and bribery.

The small telegraph office at Murray Bay where the Chief Justice was resting in the summer of 1923, closed early, as always, on the night of August 2. It was not until the next morning that word reached Taft of the tragedy which had occurred at the Palace Hotel in San Francisco. On the morning of August 3— it must have been as soon as the office opened— a telegram marked "very urgent" arrived from Secretary of State Hughes:

"I have received the following telegram from Attorney General

[24] 274 U.S. 135.

Daugherty, 'The President died at 7:20 p.m. from a stroke of cerebral apoplexy. The end came peacefully and without warning.' " [25]

It was the second such message which Taft had received. Long, long before, in the sultry Philippines, he had been informed that McKinley was dead and that his impetuous friend, Roosevelt, was president of the United States. A far different man would succeed Warren Harding. Vice-president Coolidge was at his father's farmhouse in Plymouth, Vermont, and had retired according to his New England custom at 9 o'clock. Because of the difference in time, because there were inevitable delays on the Pacific Coast, Coolidge did not get the news until 2:30. [26]

Chief Justice Taft could not know that Harding was fortunate to have died when he did, that in the sanctity of the grave he would escape a measure of the disgrace which lay ahead. The Chief Justice appears to have known nothing at all, not even by rumor, of the sordid "House on H Street" to which "the boys," who really were shrewd-faced, scheming men, would slip away for poker and to drink liquor. [27] There, sometimes, they were joined by a president who was neither shrewd nor scheming, but whose political ethics did not require that he ask too many questions. Taft's reaction to Harding's death was one of pain and shock. His statement bore the usual phrases. The first sentences were true enough. The loss "was a deep, personal sorrow to me," he said. But the rest of the message was tragically, if innocently, false.

"The loss to the people of the United States," the Chief Justice wrote, "cannot be overestimated. He had impressed the whole country with his nobility of character, the sweetness of his nature, his wonderful patience, breadth of vision, high patriotism and his love of mankind. His death at this juncture in the affairs of the country and the world is a great calamity." [28]

Taft's fellow citizens reacted the same way. If anybody had suspicions that all was not well, it was a quiet, hard-working senator from Montana who for a year, more or less, had been attempting to unravel certain oil leases and who would hold his first public hearing three months later. Thomas J. Walsh said nothing, how-

[25] Hughes to Taft, Aug. 3, 1923. [26] Sullivan, Mark, *Our Times,* Vol. VI, p. 265.
[27] Allen, Frederick L., *Only Yesterday,* p. 128. [28] Statement, Aug. 3, 1923.

ever, and Harding was buried as a martyred president. The Chief Justice attended the funeral in Washington on August 10, of course. He walked in the final procession with the new President of the United States.[29] Apparently Coolidge, whom he had known but slightly, made a favorable impression.

". . . my feeling of deep regret is somewhat mitigated," he wrote in expressing, again, his sorrow, "by the confidence I have in the wisdom, conservatism and courage of his successor. Of course, he lacks the prestige and experience, but he is deeply imbued with a sense of obligation to follow Mr. Harding's policies, especially Mr. Harding's purpose to defend the institutions of the country against wild radicals." [30]

In short, Coolidge was a safe and sane Republican and all was not lost. Taft noted with satisfaction that his training had been partly at the hands of Murray Crane of Massachusetts.[31] By the close of September, the Chief Justice was able to report several conversations with the President and to record his further reassurance:

> . . . he is very self-contained, very simple, very direct and very shrewd in his observations. He is letting these gentlemen from the West who are troubled about the wheat farmers expound at great length methods by which the price of bread can be put up and the Treasury opened so as to support people who continue to plant the wheat, because it is a lazy man's method of farming, even though the land is hopeless as a source of profitable agriculture. Meantime I think the general business of farming has proved to be profitable this year, and the President thinks that prosperity is here now.

The President, Taft continued, "asked me what there was for him to do now"; and the answer proved to be the very basis of Coolidge's policy.

"I told him to do nothing," the Chief Justice reported. "I told him that I thought the public were glad to have him in the White House doing nothing— that . . . in the returning prosperity people were glad to have a rest from watching Washington, and that I thought his wisest course was to be quiet." [32]

[29] Sullivan, Mark, *op. cit.*, Vol. VI, pp. 262-264. [30] Taft to St. G. R. Fitzhugh, Aug. 14, 1923. [31] Taft to Clarence Kelsey, Sept. 29, 1923. [32] Taft to Horace Taft, Sept. 29, 1923.

The Chief Justice would in due time criticize the President for making politics the basis of his judicial and other appointments. For the moment, though, his enthusiasm was extravagant. He discovered that they shared a distaste for members of the Senate.

". . . he said to me confidentially," Taft told his brother, " 'the Republican senators are a lot of damned cowards.' " [33]

The story of corruption in the Harding administration began to unfold as 1923 closed but there was, as yet, no proof. Taft shared the astonishingly widespread belief that honest men were being traduced by Democratic politicians seeking campaign material. Senator Burton K. Wheeler of Montana, investigating Harry Daugherty's Department of Justice, and Walsh, going further and further into the Teapot Dome and Elk Hills oil leases, were called "Montana scandalmongers" by the New York *Tribune*. The New York *Times* said they were "assassins of character." [34] The Chief Justice echoed these views and lamented that "Congress may investigate everything that attracts any public attention, and that any cheap congressman or senator can draw attention to himself by attacking somebody else." [35]

He was not to remain thus complacent for long. In October, Secretary of the Interior Fall had arrogantly denied any improper motive in leasing the vast naval oil reserves to Edward L. Doheny and Harry F. Sinclair. Doheny had insisted that the lease was made "in the interest of the United States government." Sinclair declared that Fall had received no direct or indirect profit from the transaction. But soon reports reached Senator Walsh that Fall had been revealing sudden and inexplicable wealth on his New Mexico ranch; he had spent about $175,000 for improvements and additional land when, by common knowledge, he had been known to be on the edge of bankruptcy. Then Fall said that he had borrowed $100,000 from Edward B. McLean, the Washington publisher. Unwillingly, after frantic efforts to escape the witness stand, McLean denied that he had given any cash at all to the Cabinet officer.[36]

"They have discovered some real pay dirt apparently in the

[33] Taft to Horace Taft, Feb. 16, 1924. [34] Allen, F. L., *op. cit.*, p. 154. [35] Taft to A. I. Vorys, Jan. 3, 1924. [36] Sullivan, Mark, *op. cit.*, pp. 291-313.

'Teapot Dome' lease. Fall has lied. . . . The Democrats are going
to try to embarrass Coolidge with this, but I think it is rather far-
fetched. I have always had a poor opinion of Fall, but I did not
think he was so coarse as this. Perhaps he may be able to explain it." [37]

There would, however, be no explanation from Fall. It was
made by Doheny, the beneficiary of the Elk Hills lease, who said
he had lent $100,000 to the secretary of the interior. From Fall
came, merely, a refusal to give testimony before the Senate committee on the ground that it might incriminate and degrade him.
In July, 1931, he went to the penitentiary.[38] Taft's private comments
on the mess were few. He noted that Assistant Secretary of the
Navy Theodore Roosevelt, Jr., had personally, although innocently,
been involved in the transfer of the Teapot Dome reserve from the
Navy Department to Fall. He thought that the youthful colonel's
"political ambitions are for the time certainly ended." [39]

It was far more difficult— almost impossible— for Taft to
believe that Daugherty was personally dishonest. It is not inconceivable that he was right, in so far as actual receipt of money
is concerned. Indicted for conspiring to defraud the government,
Daugherty was acquitted after a lengthy jury deliberation. That
the office of the attorney general was pregnant with fraud and
corruption is unquestioned. But that Daugherty, himself, was taking
money remains unproved. Many others were. The most notorious
case involved John T. King, a Republican politician and business
manipulator. A corporation called the American Metal Company
had been seized by the alien property custodian during the war
and sold for $6,000,000. In 1921 the owners demanded the return
of this sum, with interest, on the ground that it never had been
a German company, but Swiss. One Richard Merton represented
the owners and engaged King, who knew his way around Washington, to accelerate action.

The money was returned. Merton paid King $441,000 and left
the country. It ultimately became known that $50,000 went to
Thomas W. Miller, the alien property custodian, and probably
$200,000 to Jess Smith who was the attorney general's closest per-

[37] Taft to F. B. Kellogg, Jan. 23, 1924. [38] Sullivan, Mark, *op. cit.*, pp. 313-349.
[39] Taft to Horace Taft, Feb. 21, 1924.

sonal aide. The shots fell even closer. Daugherty's brother, Mal, was the head of a bank in Washington Court House, Ohio. Some $50,000, at least, of Smith's $200,000 was deposited in the bank. Smith killed himself, or was murdered, in an apartment which he shared with Harry Daugherty. But this was not all. There had been outrageous grafting in the Veterans' Bureau. Daugherty, under senatorial investigation, was branded unfit for his high office.[40]

All of which Taft heard and watched with dismay and disbelief. Daugherty, he wrote, was "one of the finest fellows I know. He is loyal, hard-working, disinterested, honest and courageous." [41] The Chief Justice agreed, as the attacks on the attorney general continued, that Daugherty had outlived his usefulness in the Cabinet but he continued to believe that the senatorial committee would not "be able to show anything against him." Wheeler, in charge, was "a Socialist and one of that class of men in the Senate, of whom there are one too many, who use . . . immunity of speech . . . to defame men." [42] The plight of his friend and virtual benefactor— for without Daugherty's advocacy Taft might not have become chief justice— distressed him sorely. The attorney general had been instrumental in blocking partisan judicial appointments, he insisted.[43] Back of all the trouble, he thought, was Daugherty's ambition. He had not really been qualified for the post of attorney general.[44]

Almost two years passed. At the end of March, 1926, the former attorney general, having resigned under pressure, declined to testify in connection with the American Metal Company case. In an extraordinary statement he pointed out that he had been Harding's personal attorney and that the relationship was extremely confidential. The implication was clear, and was repeated at his trial, that he was shielding a president of the United States.[45]

Taft thought this possible, that "his statement that he did not intend to tesify . . . was made rather to save Harding's memory than to save himself." He granted, though, that Daugherty had been "very ill-advised as to what he has done." [46] As the trial

[40] Sullivan, Mark, op. cit., pp. 350-353; Allen, F. L., op. cit., pp. 150-153. [41] Taft to Vorys, June 10, 1923. [42] Taft to Horace Taft, Feb. 21, 1924. [43] Taft to R. A. Taft, Feb. 24, 1924. [44] Taft to Mrs. W. A. Edwards, Feb. 21, 1924. [45] Sullivan, Mark, op. cit., pp. 354-355. [46] Taft to G. D. Seymour, May 14, 1926.

progressed, the Chief Justice believed that Daugherty would be convicted. Testimony that he had destroyed evidence was damning.

"I am still of the opinion that Daugherty is honest personally . . ." wrote Taft doggedly. "It was probably done for the purpose of concealing scandals connected with the Harding administration, for which he will have to suffer. I am very, very sorry." [47]

Meanwhile a suit by the government to set aside the Elk Hills oil lease to Sinclair on the ground of fraud was moving through the federal courts. On October 10, 1927, the Supreme Court held that the "lease and supplemental agreement were fraudulently made to circumvent the law and to defeat public policy." [48] The opinion was written by Associate Justice Butler, and was highly praised by Taft.

"The case presents one of the most outrageous instances of a conspiracy of silence that I know of . . ." was the Chief Justice's final comment.[49]

—5—

The Supreme Court, although an imperfect refuge from all this, must have been a welcome one. His associates may sometimes have seemed unsound or too liberal or occasionally irascible. But they were honest men. They were scholarly men. They were as different from the avaricious, scheming politicians of the Harding regime as a country minister from a cardsharper at the county fair. Besides, there was the incessant work of the court. There was so much to do that Taft could not waste time in worrying about the Ohio gang.

No other case absorbed the Chief Justice more than *Myers* v. *United States,* decided in October, 1926, in which a divided court upheld the removal powers of the President. The Chief Justice wrote the opinion, which was very long, and he was extremely proud of it. No other case required so much work or aroused in him comparable bitterness when it became clear that all his brothers would not follow him.

[47] Taft to Horace Taft, Sept. 30, 1926. [48] 275 U.S. 13. [49] Taft to R. A. Taft, Oct. 9, 1927.

"It was a very hard case . . ." he observed in November, 1926, when, at last, the court had ruled. "I have really worked on it for a full year or longer." [50]

The Chief Justice's first draft had been completed in the fall of 1925— after concentrated labor at Murray Bay, which included research into the history of the American government. Brandeis, alas, announced that he would dissent and Taft felt confident that Holmes would do so too. He did not know where McReynolds stood.

"I think he is inclined to go with us," Taft told Horace Taft, "but he objects to long opinions, and he is cantankerous at any rate. . . . Brandeis puts himself where he naturally belongs. He is in favor evidently of the group system. He is opposed to a strong Executive. He loves the veto of the group upon effective legislation or effective administration. He loves the kicker, and is therefore in sympathy with the power of the Senate to prevent the Executive from removing obnoxious persons, because he always sympathizes with the obnoxious person. . . . I suppose we ought not to be impatient with some of our colleagues who do not agree with us." [51]

Part of this irritation toward Brandeis and Holmes was that of a thwarted author and historian who had worked long and hard and now found his brain child criticized. The Chief Justice made extensive revisions of his first draft. By January, 1926, it was evident that the decision could not be reached until spring and Taft's annoyance increased.

"Brandeis's dissenting opinion is here," he told his older son. "McReynolds is always inconsiderate. There is no reason why he should not have written his opinion before. . . . But I am old enough to know that the best way to get along with people is to restrain your impatience and consider that, doubtless, you have your own peculiarities that try other people." [52]

Expressions of annoyance, then, were probably limited to Taft's private correspondence. The Myers case had to go over to the October, 1926, term. Having delivered the opinion on October 25, the Chief Justice boiled over again:

[50] Taft to W. M. Bullitt, Nov. 4, 1926. [51] Taft to Horace Taft, Nov. 28, 1925. [52] Taft to R. A. Taft, Jan. 10, 1926.

McReynolds and Brandeis belong to a class of people that have no loyalty to the court and sacrifice almost everything to the gratification of their own publicity and wish to stir up dissatisfaction with the decision of the court, if they don't happen to agree with it.[53]

These were harsh words and unfair, particularly with respect to Associate Justice Brandeis, and Taft must have regretted them if he ever glanced back through the copies of his letters. They were particularly unfair aspersions in view of the disagreement of legal authorities, in the years which have followed, on the accuracy of the Chief Justice's historical references and on the validity of his legal thinking. He was able to swing Justices Van Devanter, Sutherland, Butler, Sanford and Stone to his side, however, and the Myers opinion stood until it was modified, to a degree, by the court in 1935.

"I never wrote an opinion that I felt to be so important in its effect," the Chief Justice said after the six-to-three decision had been handed down in October, 1926.[54]

The implications of the Myers case were far-reaching. In judging them, the fact cannot be ignored that Taft, now chief justice, had been president of the United States and knew full well how important to a chief executive was control of presidential appointments and removals. Frank S. Myers, who died before the decision, had been appointed postmaster of Portland, Oregon, in 1917 and had been dismissed by order of President Wilson in 1920. This, Myers contended, was contrary to a law passed by Congress in 1876 which provided that postmasters of the first, second, and third classes were to be appointed by, and also might be removed by, the President "by and with the advice and consent of the Senate, and shall hold their office for four years unless sooner removed or suspended according to law." Myers had not served his four years when dismissed.

The issue presented in the Myers case was not whether senatorial consent was necessary for the appointment of such a postmaster. This was admitted. The question was whether the 1876 law, which appeared to require senatorial agreement for dismissal

---

[53] Taft to Horace Taft, Oct. 27, 1926. [54] Taft to W. M. Bullitt, Nov. 4, 1926.

by the President, was constitutional. The Chief Justice said that it was not. He went back to the debates in the spring of 1789, in the First Congress, to prove that it was the intention of those wise and good members to give to the President full power to remove his appointees. But the first weakness in Taft's case lies in the fact that the debate related to Cabinet officers, the immediate subordinates and sometimes the actual spokesmen for the President, and not to a mere postmaster.

"The debates in the Constitutional Convention," Taft observed in his lengthy opinion, "indicated an intention to create a strong executive . . . so as to avoid the humiliating weakness of the Congress during the Revolution and under the articles of Confederation. . . . The vesting of the executive power in the President was essentially a grant of the power to execute the laws. But the President, alone and unaided, could not execute the laws. He must execute them by the assistance of subordinates. . . . The further implication must be, in absence of an express limitation respecting removals, that as his selection of administrative officers is essential to the execution of the laws by him, so must be his power of removing those for whom he cannot continue to be responsible."

The history of the senatorial check upon appointments, Taft continued, demonstrated that it had not been prompted by a desire to limit removals. He then quoted, again, from the debates in the First Congress. The Chief Justice could see no danger in giving to the President full power to dismiss federal officeholders. He pointed out that the Senate, prior to confirmation, had ample opportunity to examine any candidate's fitness for the office. But after the appointment, he said, the President was clearly more competent than the Senate to determine whether the appointee was competent and should continue in his post.

Justice Holmes could not agree. Ever polite, he nevertheless said that the arguments of his chief "seem to me spiders' webs inadequate to control the dominant facts." The office held by Myers, he said, was one "that owes its existence to Congress and that Congress may abolish tomorrow." He had no doubt that Congress had power to specify its tenure. Justice McReynolds's dissenting opinion was almost as long as the affirmative one of the Chief Justice. He, too, searched historical sources, but he came out with the conclusion that nowhere in the Constitution was there authority for the President to remove duly appointed officers nor was there any limitation on the right of Congress to restrict the removal power of the President with respect to inferior officers appointed by him. Justice Brandeis also dissented at length, but separately. He, too, could not agree with Taft's historical analysis or with his legal conclusions. The Constitutional Convention had rejected, he said, every proposal to confer on the President unlimited powers of removal. Protection of the individual, "even if he be an official, from the arbitrary or capricious exercise of power was then believed to be an essential of free government." [55]

Other critics have since agreed with the dissenting jurists in *Myers* v. *the United States*. Professor Corwin, retracing Taft's historical journey, has observed that "a mere fraction of a fraction, a minority of a minority" of the members of the First Congress had sponsored such broad removal powers for the President. The majority opinion in the Myers case, Corwin has insisted, was a menace to the administrative organization evolved over many years. Further, it was "a positive instigation to strife between the President and Congress." [56]

The Myers decision stood until President Franklin D. Roosevelt attempted to remove a member of the Federal Trade Commission. The Supreme Court held in 1935 that Congress could impose reasonable restrictions on the President when the function of the office was quasi-judicial and quasi-legislative. But the power of the President with respect to purely executive officeholders remained unlimited.[57]

—6—

A major function of the Supreme Court is and always must be to act as umpire in disputes between the states. These controversies were varied. They related to boundary lines, to water rights, to irrigation projects. When states in the Far West were involved, the cases were usually handled by Justice Sutherland, who came from Utah and had a profound knowledge of this complicated and technical body of law. Chief Justice Taft took relatively few

[55] 272 U.S. 52, 58. [56] *Selected Essays*, Vol. IV, pp. 1476, 1516. [57] 295 U.S. 602.

of them. He did, however, spend most of his summer in 1928 on Chicago's Sanitary District case, possibly because it was of great importance and because vital constitutional questions were involved.

The litigation concerned Chicago's efforts to dispose of her sewage. It was an ancient problem. Back in 1865 the Chicago River, at that time flowing toward Lake Michigan, had become a foul and loathsome stream because of the sewage deposited there by the growing city. An early remedy had been the diverting of water from the lake to dilute the sewage. This proved inadequate and it was then suggested that a canal be dug which would give Chicago a water connection with the Mississippi, that the flow of the Chicago River be reversed and that the necessary water be diverted from the lake. For this vast project the Chicago Sanitary District was created in 1889 and in due course over $100,000,000 was spent. Huge quantities of water, 4,167 cubic feet per second, were flowing from the lake into the canal and river by 1907. At that time Secretary of War Taft rejected a plea to raise the amount to 10,000 feet per second. For the diversion was lowering the level of Lake Michigan, was damaging shipping, was causing heavy financial loss to citizens of adjoining states.

The action which reached the Supreme Court and on which Taft read the opinion on January 14, 1929, was a demand of Wisconsin, Minnesota, Michigan and other states for an injunction preventing the Sanitary District from diverting 8,500 cubic feet per second. Former Supreme Court Justice Hughes had been appointed a special master by the court, so technical was the problem, to hear evidence. He reported that there was no doubt of the damage caused by the lowering of Lake Michigan and that all the other great lakes, except Lake Superior, had been affected. But the health of the people of Chicago and its environs might be gravely endangered if the diversion was stopped.

The complaining states said that Congress, under the commerce clause, could not transfer the navigable capacity of the Great Lakes to the Mississippi basin, that their citizens were being deprived of their property without due process of law, that the port of one state was being benefited at the expense of another state and that this, too, was contrary to the Constitution.

. "If one of these issues is decided in favor of the complaining states," observed the Chief Justice, "it ends the case in their favor and the diversion must be enjoined."

The situation was, however, more complicated. Taft upheld the actions of the various secretaries of war, including himself, in permitting limited diversion of Lake Michigan water. Leaning heavily on the report of Mr. Hughes, he concluded, however, that the present demand for 8,500 cubic feet per second was principally for sewage disposal and not for navigation purposes. It was, therefore, illegal. Taft berated "the inexcusable delays" of the federal court in Chicago in a suit brought by the United States to limit withdrawals in excess of 4,167 feet; a result of the court's tardiness had been continued withdrawal of 8,500 cubic feet per second. Yet the court could not ignore the health implications of the whole matter. It ordered that Chicago take immediate steps to build adequate sewage disposal plants. Thereby would result "gradual restoration" of the rights of the injured states. The case was referred back to Special Master Hughes with virtual instructions to work out the details of the final decree.

"The Court expresses its obligation to the master for his useful, fair and comprehensive report," said the Chief Justice.[58]

[58] 278 U.S. 367; Taft to Justice Butler, Jan. 7, 1929.

CHAPTER LV

THE LABOR PROBLEM AGAIN

THE APPREHENSIONS of organized labor, when Taft became chief justice, were not unfounded. But labor's attacks on him because of the opinions which he wrote or in which he concurred were not entirely fair. Through all his years— as a judge in Ohio, as president of the United States and as chief justice— two major premises stood behind Taft's thinking on the labor problem. He never fell from consistency.

The first premise was that labor had a perfect right to organize, to bargain collectively, to stop work and to strike. What one worker could do legally, many could combine to do. The second premise was that labor should enjoy no special privileges or immunities under law. It had no more right to resort to violence or intimidation than a banker, a railroad magnate or the average citizen. What Taft never could realize— either as an Ohio judge, or as president or as chief justice— was that the banker and the industrialist were far more powerful than labor, and that through the decades they had resorted to intimidation, violence and worse.

The Chief Justice of the United States— approaching sixty-five— was more restrained in the expression of his private views on labor than had been Circuit Judge Taft— approaching thirty-seven— back in 1894. He had been horrified, then, by the Pullman strike and by the activities of Eugene Debs, and had reacted with approval when news came from Chicago that thirty strikers had been killed by federal troops in the railroad riots.

". . . everybody hopes that it is true," Circuit Judge Taft had written.[1]

To Taft, Debs was still a villain in 1922. The Socialist leader had been imprisoned for obstructing the conduct of the war in 1918, had been nominated for the presidency while in the Atlanta penitentiary and had been released by order of President Harding

[1] See p. 128.

just before Christmas, 1921. The officials of the prison and the inmates had, alike, respected and loved him. But Debs had no use at all for the members of the Supreme Court. They had, after all, affirmed his conviction and when they did he called them "begowned, bewhiskered old fossils." [2]

Taft had not been on the court at that time. If he heard the remark, it must have fanned the fires of his resentment. In July, 1922, having returned from his excursion to England, the Chief Justice reported to Ambassador Harvey on the state of the nation:

> The situation in the United States now is . . . quite critical in respect to the coal strike and the railway strike. I doubt . . . if the brotherhoods are anxious to go into the fight. The latest dispatches yesterday indicate that the maintenance of way men are not going to join the shopmen in their controversy. If so, it is likely that the railroads can fight it out with the shopmen, especially if the President, as he seems likely to do, shall give the railroad authorities full protection in working nonunion men in their shops.
>
> The war and general lawlessness everywhere stimulate bloody, murderous violence on the part of the strikers and their sympathizers, but that is not so much a dangerous symptom as it is a symptom of the times. Debs has now rushed in with a general declaration of war, while Gompers continues his vaporings, but I don't think they help the labor people. They rather tend to solidify conservative public opinion.[3]

The times were, indeed, out of joint. The Chief Justice did not understand with any real clarity the reasons for the unrest. The basic cause was the war. The men of the A.E.F. returned from France, having made the world safe for democracy, to find that democracy had done little to make safe their jobs. The fervor of wartime patriotism had ended and so had the willingness of the employer, enjoying cost-plus contracts, to pay almost any wages demanded. Prices of food and other commodities were high.

It had been pleasant to wear silk shirts. It had been pleasant to bank vast war profits. The workingman found silk shirts too costly after the war and the employer sorely missed his extra dividends. On one point, emotionally if not intellectually, the employer

[2] Sullivan, Mark, *Our Times*, Vol. VI, pp. 218-219, 170. [3] Taft to Harvey, July 21, 1922.

and the employee agreed. The war had brought to both a belief in direct action, an intolerance toward delay and a rejection of reason. So the employer now sought to reduce his costs by cutting wages ruthlessly. The employee resisted, and strikes broke out in a violent rash. The harbor workers, the dress and waist makers, the building trades and the railroad shopmen walked out. The transit employees in Boston walked out. So did the printers and New York's actors and so did the bituminous coal miners. Even the police of Boston went on strike and elevated, thereby, a small New England politician to glory. In the summer of 1919 came a violent upheaval in the steel mills.

But the fortress of steel was still impregnable and many another industrial fortress was also stormed in vain. The strikers were branded Reds and Bolsheviki and public opinion turned against them. Soon there were rumors of vast Socialist and Communist conspiracies against the government itself and a Red Hunt of magnificent proportions was under way. This was the world, a nervous and nasty world, which Chief Justice Taft could not clearly see from the sanctuary of the Supreme Court.[4]

—2—

That fraction of the nation's workingmen who kept posted on litigation which affected their status must have marveled in December, 1921, when the Supreme Court at last ruled in *American Steel Foundries* v. *Tri-City Central Trades Council*. Taft had just mounted the bench as chief justice when it was reargued in October. It concerned a strike of seven years before and it first reached the Supreme Court in January, 1919. Dust had long since settled on the petitions, briefs and on pages and pages of testimony. Nobody, save by referring to the files, could have recalled in detail the dispute which had taken place in the spring of 1914 in Granite City, Illinois, where the American Steel Foundries operated a steel mill. A war had come and gone and many an employee in the Granite City plant had donned a uniform and then

[4] Allen, Frederick L., *Only Yesterday*, pp. 20, 45; Sullivan, Mark, *op. cit.*, Vol. VI, pp. 154-168.

had shed it. But all the while *American Steel Foundries* v. *Tri-City Central Trades Council* had been grinding through the courts.

Some sixteen hundred men had been employed by the company in Granite City prior to the previous November when the plant shut down. Opening in April, 1914, the American Steel Foundries took back three hundred men at sharply cut wages and with the provision that the plant would be an open shop. The Tri-City Central Trades Council called a strike, but succeeded in persuading only two men to leave their jobs. For three or four weeks the council picketed the factory. Sporadic outbreaks of violence occurred and on May 18 the Federal District Court of Southern Illinois issued a sweeping injunction which forbade the strikers or their union allies to interfere, even through "persuasion," with men who desired to work at the plant. Under its terms, effective prosecution of the strike was impossible. Meanwhile organized labor, so often blocked in the courts, had taken its fight to Congress. In October, 1914, the Clayton act became law and purported to prohibit injunctions in labor disputes except to prevent irreparable property damage or where violence was used. So the Circuit Court of Appeals eliminated the word "persuasion" from the lower court's order and substituted a ban against picketing "in a threatening or intimidating manner." This modification was stricken out by the Supreme Court on the ground that it left "compliance largely to the discretion of the pickets."

The Chief Justice wrote the opinion. He held that the Clayton act, although passed after the original injunction, applied to the case, but said that it merely affirmed what had always been the best practice of the courts. Reviewing the facts, Taft said it was clear from the evidence that violence had been used by the pickets in Granite City. Thereupon the Chief Justice took upon himself the task of saying just what pickets might do and still remain within the law. In going to and from work, he said, men had a right to a free passage. But the pickets could "in an inoffensive way" accost them and point out why they should not enter the plant.

"If, however, the offer is declined, as it may rightfully be," he wrote, "then persistence, importunity, following and dogging, be-

come unjustifiable annoyance and obstruction, which is likely soon
to savor of intimidation."

Taft observed that the council members had picketed in groups
of three and four; sometimes as many as twelve men had accosted
the workers. It was, he said, "idle to talk of peaceful communication
in such a place and under such conditions." What, then, must be
the numerical limitation? The Chief Justice thought that one
strikers' "representative for each point of ingress and egress in
the plant" was proper. But he added that this "is not laid down
as a rigid rule" and might be varied in other cases. He then affirmed, in language which echoed his earlier days on the bench,
the right of men to strike. The final part of the opinion was actually pro-labor in its connotations, although few realized it at the
time.

It had been contended that the Tri-City Central Trades Council had no right to interfere in the strike and that the strike, itself,
was therefore illegal. The Chief Justice did not agree. To render a
combination of workmen effective, he said, "employees must make
their combination extend beyond the shop. It is helpful to have
as many as may be in the same trade in the same community
united, because . . . they are bound to be affected by the standard
of wages of their trade in the neighborhood. . . ." [5]

The authorization, it should be noted, did not permit extending
strikes to other neighborhoods, communities or cities. Yet there
were two grounds on which Chief Justice Taft's opinion was a
real and definite step toward freeing labor from the domination
of the employing class. Under the Court's decision in *Hitchman
Coal and Coak Co.* v. *Mitchell et al.* in 1917, the unions had virtually
been stripped of all power. Picketing in any form, however peaceful, had been barred.[6] True, the employing class had not sought
to enforce these drastic limitations during the boom days of the
war. The need for doing so was slight, all in all, in view of the
enormous profits in war-time contracts. But there is sound reason
for believing that the Hitchman ruling would have been invoked
when peace came had not Taft, in this Tri-City case, invalidated it.

The second pro-labor feature of the Chief Justice's opinion
was his specification that the rule thereby adopted for picketing

[5] 257 U.S. 184. [6] 245 U.S. 229.

should not be regarded as a standard for labor disputes of the future. But both grounds were ignored as organized labor pondered the restrictions which Taft had imposed. They appeared to imply that the members of a picket line could dissuade workers or win recruits only by speaking in low and cultivated voices.

The resentment of organized labor over the rulings of the Supreme Court, particularly with respect to picketing and the use of the injunction, was partly justifiable. It availed little to be told that strikes were legal and then to be warned that any effective prosecution of the strike was against the law. And the leaders of labor knew well indeed how cleverly the delays and specious devices of clever corporation lawyers could be used against them and their followers. An injunction could be granted by a single federal judge, and no reversal was possible until long after a strike had been lost.

". . . It is to be remembered," as Professor Thomas Reed Powell has observed, "that it is contempt to disobey a temporary injunction even though in later appellate proceedings the injunctive decree is set aside. . . . The advantage to employers of the injunctive process as compared with civil actions or prosecutions for crime is not confined to the superiority of prevention over recompense or punishment. It is easier to get an order from one man than a verdict from twelve. . . ." [7]

—3—

Another labor case was being heard concurrently with that of the Tri-City Council in the fall of 1921 and it was decided two weeks later. This was to be criticized much more vigorously. In contrast to the unanimous decision in the former case, *Truax* v. *Corrigan* was one of those five-to-four rulings which so greatly annoyed the Chief Justice.

The facts which pass in review before the Supreme Court of the United States are as assorted as the headlines in a newspaper. No steel mill, this time, but a restaurant called the English Kitchen in far-off Bisbee, Arizona, was the center of the labor disturbance. Again, it was an old dispute and one which also illustrated how handicapped was labor in the whole injunction issue. The waiters

[7] *Selected Essays*, Vol. II, pp. 740-741, 760.

and other employees of the English Kitchen had struck in April, 1916, and William Truax, one of the proprietors, had sought to enjoin Michael Corrigan and his fellow members of the Restaurant Workers' Union from carrying on what he declared to be illegal attacks on his reputation and that of his restaurant. He also charged libelous statements by the strikers regarding his character. The workers had declared, among other things, that he assaulted ladies and chased his help down Bisbee's streets with a butcher knife.

Of all this, and more, Chief Justice Taft took judicial note and concluded that violence, intimidation and illegality had been rife. The important aspect of the case, though, lay in the fact that Arizona had passed a law almost identical with the Clayton act.[8] It provided, like the federal law, that no Arizona court could enjoin a strike unless irreparable injury, for which no other adequate remedy existed, was being done. The Supreme Court of Arizona had upheld this law. Taft thereupon invalidated it as contrary to the Fourteenth Amendment.

The opinion must have caused him almost as much work and worry as that in the Myers case, although there is no mention of it in his letters. He knew that Holmes and Brandeis would dissent. Even Pitney and Clarke would this time refuse to go along with him. So the opinion is very long; Taft felt that he must answer the arguments of his mistaken, but cogent, associates. He described in detail the acts of intimidation of the strikers, the threats they had uttered and their conduct near the restaurant. Business at the English Kitchen, he said, had dropped by three-quarters.

"Violence could not have been more effective," said the Chief Justice. "It was moral coercion by illegal annoyance and obstruction, and it was thus plainly a conspiracy."

Again, there is reason to believe that he was searching for a legality under which violence or its equivalent in labor disputes could be summarily halted. The restaurant proprietor of Bisbee, he said, had been denied equal protection for his property as guaranteed by the Fourteenth Amendment. The property, in this case, was his business.

Justice Holmes could not agree that business was property as

[8] *Selected Essays*, Vol. II, p. 754.

defined by his chief. Business, he said, was "a course of conduct; and, like other conduct, is subject to substantial modification according to time and circumstances." There was nothing, he added, that he deprecated more "than the use of the Fourteenth Amendment beyond the absolute compulsion of its words to prevent the making of social experiments that an important part of the community desires, in the insulated chambers afforded by the several states, even though the experiments may seem futile or even noxious to me and to those whose judgment I most respect."

On the contrary, said the Chief Justice anticipating this plea, the "Constitution was intended— its very purpose was— to prevent experimentation with the fundamental rights of the individual."

The dissent of Justice Pitney implied no endorsement of the Arizona anti-injunction law either, but he had no doubt of its legality. Associate Justice Brandeis, in another separate dissenting opinion, went back into English law to show that Arizona was within her rights. The states, he said, were as free now as before passage of the Fourteenth Amendment to expand or contract the equity jurisdiction of their courts. The degree to which Brandeis differed from Taft is clearly brought out by a concluding paragraph of his opinion:

The denial of the more adequate equitable remedy [the injunction] for private wrongs is, in essence, an exercise of the police power, by which, in the interest of the public, and in order to preserve the liberty and the property of the great majority of the citizens of a state, rights of property and the liberty of the individual must be remolded, from time to time, to meet the changing needs of society.[9]

From time to time the Chief Justice would reiterate his conviction that the labor unions were not contented with what he fondly imagined equal justice under the law. Regarding labor legislation pending in 1925, he said that "Brother Frey [John P. Frey of the metal trades and the A. F. of L.] is trying to . . . establish the members of the labor unions as privileged characters before the law." [10] The dicta of the Chief Justice and his associates doubt-

[9] 257 U.S. 312; Ragan, A. E., *Chief Justice Taft*, p. 29. [10] Taft to R. A. Taft, Feb. 23, 1925.

less influenced public opinion greatly, for it was a decade when only the labor leaders and one or two liberal statesmen cared anything at all about the problems of the workingman. The Stock Market and Coolidge Prosperity dominated the public mind.

Beneath the surface, though, the ranks of labor were being unified by their losses before the law. Another setback— or, in any event labor so regarded it— came as the Supreme Court prepared to recess for the summer in June, 1922, and a unanimous decision in *United Mine Workers of America et al.* v. *Coronado Coal Company et al.* was handed down. Chief Justice Taft observed that unincorporated associations were, at common law, not liable as a whole. Then he added— and the doctrine struck terror into the hearts of labor's organizers:

> But the growth and necessities of these great labor organizations have brought affirmative legal recognition of their existence and usefulness and provisions for their protection, which their members have found necessary. . . .
>
> In this state of federal legislation we think that such organizations are suable in the federal courts for their acts, and that funds accumulated to be expended in conducting strikes are subject to execution in suits for torts committed by such unions in strikes.

The Coronado case was another legacy from the White court, another product of judicial delay and lethargy which dated back to 1914. This time the injunction was not involved. The issues were whether an unincorporated union could be sued for the damage it caused, whether in this case the national organization was responsible for the wrongs committed by district unions and whether a union could be restrained for violation of the interstate commerce provisions of the Sherman act. They were questions of far-reaching significance. Had, in this case, all these questions been answered affirmatively, the American labor movement might have ceased to exist.

It was a long way from the twilight decorum of the Supreme Court chamber at the Capitol to the hills of Arkansas, defaced by coal mines, where the case originated. A world of education and manners stood between Charles E. Hughes, who returned to the dim chamber to argue on behalf of the United Mine Workers and the men who had been locked out, whose wages had been cut and who had struck back with violence in the Arkansas coal fields. Nor was there much similarity in outlook between John W. Davis, who would be a Democratic candidate for president of the United States in two years, and Franklin Bache, who had managed all the mines involved and whose counsel he was.

Nine coal companies, all in receivership, were operating in Arkansas in March, 1914, under a contract with the miners' union which did not expire until July. Bache decided to run on an open-shop basis in April, purchased ammunition and rifles and called in men from the Burns agency for protection. He was fully aware that he was in for a bitter fight and it came promptly. Company property was destroyed. At least two company employees were killed and others hurt. For the Arkansas coal fields had long been union territory and this was war. Taft, in reviewing the facts, leaves no reasonable doubt that most of the attacks were initiated by the district union.

The nine mining companies operated by Receiver Bache filed suit in September under the Sherman act against the United Mine Workers of America and its officers and against the district local and its officers. They charged a conspiracy to restrain interstate commerce and demanded treble damages. The District Court ruled for the miners, but was reversed by the Circuit Court of Appeals. The case was then tried again and damages of $745,000 assessed. This was more serious than the ruling in the Danbury Hatters' case of 1908 where, too, damages had been assessed. There, collection had to be from the members of the union. The United Mine Workers of America, with its 400,000 members, had large funds in its treasury although probably not so much as $745,000. Certain of these funds were attached after the Circuit Court ruling.

The case came to Washington on writ of error. The Chief Justice's first main point was suability of the national organization of the miners and on this, to the consternation of labor, he said Yes. But the actual result was not so serious, for he next held that the United Mine Workers and their officers had not been responsible for the illegalities of the local organization and that the lower court should have directed a verdict for them. So the funds of the United Mine Workers of America were, for the moment, safe. Nor could the Chief Justice find that there had been a conspiracy to violate the Sherman law.

"Coal mining is not interstate commerce," he said, "and the power of Congress does not extend to its regulation as such."

The output of the mines involved, he said, were but 5,000 tons a week as compared with a national output of 10,000,000 to 15,-000,000 tons. On such a basis, no appreciable effect on the price of coal was possible. Chief Justice Taft indicated clearly, as he closed, that neither litigant was entitled to much respect. On the one hand, he expressed regret that the damages assessed against the union could not be upheld. On the other, he deprecated the "hugger-mugger of . . . numerous corporations" whereby Bache had evaded his contract with the union. The case was sent back to the District Court in Arkansas a second time for still another trial.[11]

A protest followed the Chief Justice's use of "hugger-mugger." The Supreme Court reporter, Ernest Knaebel, wrote that Counselor Davis had objected on behalf of Receiver Bache that it had an "unpleasant connotation." Could some "less dubious word," perhaps, be substituted?

"I think the word 'hugger-mugger' is a pretty good word, and I think that in a way Bache deserved it," Taft answered. "But I don't want to give pain where I can avoid it. . . . What word would you suggest?"

Knaebel offered "evade his obligations by a manipulation of his numerous companies" as an alternative and the Chief Justice said he did not mind the change.[12] For some reason, however, it was not made.

The howl from labor over the Coronado decision was immediate, but not unanimous. President Gompers of the A. F. of L. said that the court had annulled the protections of the Clayton act. The United Mine Workers, however, hailed with joy the remission of the staggering damage award.

If the Coronado case was really a death blow against labor, why were the voices of Justices Brandeis and Holmes silent? An answer is to be found in an article, concurrently published, by Professor Frankfurter, who was close to both those jurists. He

[11] 259 U.S. 344. [12] Knaebel to Taft, Oct. 27, 1922; Taft to Knaebel, Oct. 28, Nov. 2, 1922.

agreed that labor, generally, regarded the decision as "a great set-back for labor." But the United Mine Workers or any other union, he pointed out, had the right to incur debts and could, therefore, be sued for them. It would, he thought, have been "a distinct departure from reality" for the court to have held other-wise in this case. He thought it might well constitute, in the end, "a source of gain to labor." The real problem, he added, was "not to deny the fact" of what a trade union was, "but to work out the legal scope of its activities." [13]

The Chief Justice, about to sail for England in July, 1922, an-ticipated the attacks which would be made because of the Coronado decision and was complacent under them. The ruling, he reported later, "seems to have called forth great denunciation by Gompers and LaFollette and other demagogues, and to have suggested a movement to deprive the court of the power of holding laws . . . unconstitutional." He did not know, he said, how formidable this movement was, but he consoled himself with the thought that "threats against the Court" had been just as menacing in the past. He was convinced that "the supporters of an amendment to the Constitution will find arrayed against them a conservative strength that in their blatant mouthings they do not realize the existence of." [14]

Just how close labor came to drastic restrictions under the Sher-man law was demonstrated in the United Leather Workers' Union decision in June, 1924. The union had demanded a closed shop in St. Louis in February, 1920, and had threatened to wreck the business of certain trunk and leather manufacturers unless they obtained it. The District Court and the Circuit Court of Appeals both upheld an injunction against the union. The Supreme Court reversed their ruling, however. This was another labor victory. Mere reduction in the supply of an article to be shipped in interstate commerce, the Chief Justice said, was "an indirect and remote obstruction to that commerce." It was only when the supply could be monopolized and prices controlled that the obstruction was direct. Otherwise, Taft observed, every strike could be enjoined, and he could not "think that Congress intended any such result in the enactment of the anti-trust act." [15]

[13] *New Republic,* Aug. 16, 1922. [14] Taft to R. A. Taft, July 29, 1922. [15] 265 U.S. 457.

—4—

The potentialities of the Sherman law as a weapon against unions increased, however, when the Coronado case reached the Supreme Court a second time early in 1925 and was decided on May 25. New evidence had been introduced at the trial in Arkansas. This time, taking note of the 1922 ruling of the Supreme Court, the lower federal courts had held that no damages could be assessed against the United Mine Workers and that there had been no conspiracy in restraint of trade. The Chief Justice agreed; he said again that the national organization had not been culpable in the property destruction. Regarding the question of a conspiracy, he was not so sure. The Arkansas mines involved had a productive capacity of 5,000 tons a day, not 5,000 tons a week as the 1922 evidence had indicated. Witnesses had declared that officers of the local union sought to prevent possible competition from lower coal prices in nonunion mines and this was "relevant evidence" for a jury to consider. The case, ordered the Supreme Court, must be tried a third time. The Chief Justice repeated his earlier declarations that mere reduction in supply did not transgress the law, but when prices were directly affected in the interstate movement of a product by a strike, the strike was illegal. In this case, he thought, there was "substantial evidence" showing that the purpose of destroying the mines "was to stop the production of nonunion coal." [16]

Two years later labor's jeopardy under the Sherman law was increased again. The Journeymen Stone Cutters' Association of North America had declined to work on limestone quarried by the Bedford Cut Stone Company and twenty-three other companies, all in Indiana. The companies shipped annually some $15,000,000 in stone to contractors all over the country and these contractors, of course, were damaged by the union's orders. The Bedford Cut Stone Company had sought an injunction under the Sherman law, but had been denied it by the district court and the Circuit Court of Appeals. The fight of the union, naturally, was on the open-shop policy of the Bedford company. Chief Justice Taft, although he did not write the opinion, was greatly interested in the case. He

[16] 268 U.S. 295.

saw in it a parallel to *Moores & Co.* v. *Bricklayers' Union* which he had decided so many years before as judge of the Superior Court of Ohio and in which he had declared this to be an illegal form of boycott. As chief justice of the United States he now affirmed Judge Taft of Hamilton County, Ohio.

"If we were to hold," he wrote Justice Sanford privately, "that 5,000 men constituting the great bulk of all the stonecutters of the United States may, by refusing to work material shipped to the great centers of building throughout the country, compel the shipper either to give up his sales or to subject himself to the control of the union, we should be imposing on interstate trade a burden that would be intolerable, and every national labor union could at once adopt it as a means of establishing a closed shop . . . in every center of business activity in the country." [17]

The opinion by Justice Sutherland so held and an injunction was granted. It did not matter, said a majority of the court, that physical movement of the stone in interstate commerce had ended before the stonecutters refused to work upon it. Justice Harlan Fiske Stone, who was beginning to annoy the Chief Justice by his dissents, could not agree. Taft tried to swing Stone to his side, but without avail. Justice Brandeis also dissented. He observed that only "unreasonable restraints" were prohibited by the cases interpreting the Sherman law. He could not agree that the action of the stone-cutters had constituted unreasonable restraint. With this view, Justice Holmes concurred.[18]

Justice Stone had been elevated by President Coolidge in March, 1925, and the Chief Justice had then observed with satisfaction "that I rather forced the President into his appointment. The President was loath to let him go, because he knew his worth as attorney general, but I told him . . . that he was the strongest man that he could secure in New York that was entitled to the place." [19] The new member was still in favor that fall; he was often one of the Van Devanter-Sutherland-Sanford-Butler group who were invited to the home of the Chief Justice for a Sunday afternoon, faintly extracurricular conference at which, it may safely be as-

[17] Taft to Sanford, Jan. 25, 1927. [18] 274 U.S. 37; Taft to Stone, Jan. 26, 27, 1927. [19] Taft to R. A. Taft, July 2, 1925.

sumed, plans were made to block the liberal machinations of Holmes and Brandeis.[20]

The approbation had vanished by the spring of 1929. It was widely known that Taft's health was not too good and rumors occasionally arose that he might retire. In May of that year the Chief Justice was asked whether this was true and whether Stone might then be moved over to the post of chief justice. Taft said nothing publicly, of course. To his younger son, he expressed his emphatic disagreement:

Hoover's attachment for Stone is very great. . . . I have no doubt that if I were to retire or die, the President would appoint Stone as the head of the court. I think in doing so he would make a great mistake, for the reason that Stone is not a leader and would have a great deal of trouble *in massing the court.* . . . I don't think there is anybody on the court, except Stone, who would think that he was fitted for chief justice. . . . He is a learned lawyer in many ways, but his judgments I do not altogether consider safe. . . . He definitely has ranged himself with Brandeis and with Holmes in a good many of our constitutional differences.[21]

Safety and the preservation of a conservative majority in the court became an obsession with Taft as the final days approached. The most that could be hoped for, he wrote Justice Butler in the fall of 1929, "is continued life of enough of the present membership . . . to prevent disastrous reversals of our present attitude. With Van [Van Devanter] and Mac [McReynolds] and Sutherland and you and Sanford, there will be five to steady the boat . . . we must not give up at once." [22] The gloom of the Chief Justice increased. "Brandeis is of course hopeless," he observed in December, "as Holmes is, and as Stone is." The President was well-nigh so; "I don't think Hoover knows as much as he thinks he does, and that it is just as well for him to remember the warning in the Scriptures about removing landmarks." [23]

[20] Taft to Butler, Nov. 7, 1925. [21] Taft to C. P. Taft, II, May 12, 1929. (Italics mine.) [22] Taft to Butler, Sept. 14, 1929. [23] Taft to Horace Taft, Dec. 1, 1929.

—5—

No Magna Carta for labor was written during the decade of the Taft court although the statement of the Chief Justice that unions were organized because a "single employee was helpless in dealing with an employer" would often be cited by those who fought its battles. Labor had its champions. One of them was Senator Norris of Nebraska, so often distrusted by Taft. In August, 1929, the senator demanded an end of injunctions in labor disputes and said they crushed any hope of the worker to fight effectively for his rights. That fall, in collaboration with Representative F. H. LaGuardia of New York, he drafted his anti-injunction bill. It was finally passed, finally signed by President Hoover. The authority of the federal courts in the granting of injunctions was somewhat curbed.[24]

Yet Chief Justice Taft, in two opinions on disputes between the Pennsylvania Railroad and its employees, paved the way for the Supreme Court to uphold the Wagner-Connery Act of 1935 which created a National Labor Relations Board to prevent unfair practices by employers. In the first case, decided in February, 1923, Taft held that the United States Railway Labor Board, authorized by Congress to pass on labor issues between the railroads and their workers, could determine who the proper representatives of the workers were.

"If the board has jurisdiction to hear representatives of the employees," he said, "it must of necessity have power to determine who are proper representatives of the employees."

The Pennsylvania Railroad's management, in common with most employers, had no taste for such a doctrine. It might spell— as indeed it did in due time— an end of company unions controlled by management. So the Chief Justice, to his annoyance, found himself confronted with a second Pennsylvania case two years later. He pointed out, sharply, that the Pennsylvania "is using every endeavor to avoid compliance with the judgment and principles of the Labor Board as to the proper method of securing

[24] Neuberger, R. L., and Kahn, S. B., *Integrity, the Life Story of George W. Norris*, pp. 253-256.

representatives of the whole body of its employees . . . and is thus defeating the purpose of Congress."

The Railway Labor Board had no mandatory function, the Chief Justice then observed. It could merely rely on public opinion to enforce its decrees. But Taft implied, although he did not say so outright, that Congress might have decreed that the rulings of the board were enforceable at law.[25]

Senator Robert F. Wagner of New York so provided in the Wagner-Connery Act of 1935 and the National Association of Manufacturers promptly ordered its members to defeat the bill in Congress. True, there seemed to be every probability that the Supreme Court would rule against the bill. But as one broadside of the association pointed out, labor would have "a great advantage to use *before* it is declared unconstitutional. Invalidation by the Supreme Court . . . two years hence, could not undo the harm which would occur in the meantime." [26] So the National Labor Relations Board was swamped with injunctions. A group of fifty-eight distinguished attorneys, apparently deluded that they were members of the Supreme Court, publicly declared the measure unconstitutional.[27]

It is certain that Taft, had he lived, would have reacted with hot anger toward their arrogance. Nor is there much doubt that his wrath would have been comparable when prominent lawyers, who called themselves the friends of law and order and the foes of anarchy, told their clients to ignore the Wagner law while it was being tested in the courts. One of these was Earl F. Reed, counsel for the Weirton Steel Company.

"I feel perfectly free," he said, "to advise a client not to be bound by a law that I consider unconstitutional." [28]

The Supreme Court, Chief Justice Hughes presiding, overruled the fifty-eight prominent lawyers as well as Mr. Reed, however. In a five-to-four decision which leaned heavily on Taft precedents, it sustained the validity of the act. The connection between manufacturing and commerce was obvious, said the Chief Justice.

[25] 261 U.S. 72; 267 U.S. 203. [26] Morison, S. E., and Commager, H. S., *The Growth of the American Republic*, Vol. II, pp. 575-577; Ross, Malcolm, *Death of a Yale Man*, pp. 167-170. [27] Gellhorn, Walter, and Linfield, S. L., "Politics and Labor Relations, N.L.R.B. Procedure," *Columbia Law Review*, March, 1939. [28] Ross, Malcolmn, *op. cit.,* p. 174.

Protection of the right of labor to organize had an intimate relation to interstate commerce because industrial strife had a "serious effect" on its freedom.[29]

—6—

During five of his years as chief justice, while the Sacco-Vanzetti case was arousing interest and protests throughout the world, Taft paid little or no attention to the question of whether the shoe worker and the fish peddler were guilty of the murder at South Braintree, Massachusetts, for which they were condemned to die. The Chief Justice was, of course, aware of the agitation on their behalf and he disapproved of it.

"I don't know anything about this criminal prosecution of two Italians, as I think they are," he wrote in May, 1927. Nonetheless, he thought it highly improper for the faculty of the Yale Law School, in particular Acting Dean Robert M. Hutchins, to intervene on behalf of the doomed men. Taft noted that Professor Frankfurter of the Harvard Law School was active, but Frankfurter "seems to be closely in touch with every Bolshevist, Communist movement in this country." The Chief Justice expressed wonder that Sacco and Vanzetti had been able to escape punishment for so long and "to rouse in their behalf a great deal of money . . . and the active manipulation of bomb throwers throughout the world." He urged President Angell of Yale to clamp down on the Law School staff who were embroiling themselves in the case.[30]

It is obvious that the Chief Justice, despite his ignorance of the facts, had his own opinion regarding the Italian radicals. At two o'clock on the morning of August 22, 1927— the men were to be executed the following night— the case came directly to Taft. He was asleep at his home in Murray Bay when a car arrived from the nearby Manoir Richelieu. The telegraph company had dispatched two operators with a message from the defense lawyers. This asked for a stay of execution pending an appeal to the Supreme Court. The Chief Justice, being on foreign soil, would have to cross the border to grant it. The request had already been

[29] Morison, S. E., and Commager, H. S., *op. cit.*, Vol. II, p. 577. [30] Taft to J. R. Angell, May 1, 1937.

denied by Associate Justice Holmes and Taft was somewhat indignant that he had been asked, as he described it to his brother, "to take a full, long day" and leave Canada. He refused to do so, pointing out that he would undoubtedly follow the ruling of Holmes in any event. Besides, no federal question was involved.[31]

So Sacco and Vanzetti died, protesting their innocence, and the Canadian government posted guards around the country home of the Chief Justice so that radical desires for vengeance could be thwarted. No attempt to injure Taft was made, however. It is not clear whether the Chief Justice familiarized himself with the case or not. But in October, having returned to Washington, he wrote a fulsome letter to President Lowell of Harvard, who had served on the committee of citizens affirming the Italians' guilt. Until the men had been "properly executed," Taft said, it had been impossible for him to write. The propaganda for Sacco and Vanzetti "had been created by large contributions of female and male fools and had been circulated through all the communistic and criminal classes the world over. . . . The quiet that has now followed is an evidence of how artificial and perverse the promoters of the propaganda were." By upholding the convictions, he added, Dr. Lowell had "pricked the bubble as it now proves itself to have been." [32]

[31] Taft to M. A. Musmano, Aug. 22, 1927; to Horace Taft, Aug. 25, 1927. [32] Taft to A. L. Lowell, Oct. 30, 1937.

CHAPTER LVI

. . . NOR SHALL ANY STATE

CHIEF JUSTICE TAFT's dislike toward dissenting opinions went deeper than his dislike toward the liberal ones of Justices Holmes, Brandeis and Stone. He shrank from all dissents, including his own. A major standard by which he judged potential jurists was whether, if appointed, they would agree with their fellows. Thus he was dubious regarding Judge Cuthbert W. Pound of the New York Court of Appeals— suggested as a successor to Justice Pitney in 1922— because of reports that "he is rather an off-horse and dissents a good deal." It would, the Chief Justice added, "be too bad if we had another on the bench who would herd with Brandeis." [1] He reminded Justice Stone that "the continuity and weight of our opinions on important questions of law should not be broken any more than we can help by dissents." [2]

"I would not think of opposing the views of my brethren," he said in the fall of 1927, "if there was a majority against my own."

Dissents by the Chief Justice were, then, extremely rare although the court, itself, was constantly torn by them. In nine years Taft's came to about twenty, and it was even more unusual for him to write a minority opinion.[3] The most important dissenting opinion by Taft was in the famous District of Columbia minimum-wage case, *Adkins* v. *Children's Hospital*. Here, the Chief Justice stood squarely for a liberal interpretation of the police powers of the states— it was one of the few times that he did so. And it should be noted that the majority opinion to which he took exception was so reactionary as to be archaic, replete with outworn observations on "liberty of contract," confused in thought and based on a fallacious understanding of the law. The vote was five to three; Justice Brandeis would not sit because his daughter

---

[1] Taft to Hilles, Dec. 1, 1922. [2] Taft to Stone, Jan. 26, 1927. [3] Ragan, A. E., *Chief Justice Taft*, p. 38.

was secretary to the Minimum Wage Board of the District of Columbia, the appellant in the case.

Mr. Justice Sutherland wrote the verbose and sometimes ornate majority opinion in which McKenna, McReynolds, Van Devanter and Butler concurred. The question at issue was whether a minimum-wage law passed by Congress for the District of Columbia in 1918 violated the Fifth Amendment. A board was to fix and enforce wages for women and children. The obvious purpose of the measure was to protect the health and morals of the women and children of the district. The Children's Hospital of Washington was, curiously enough, the first employer to challenge the higher wages fixed. Its plea that the law was unconstitutional was upheld by the district court of appeals and permanent injunctions against the wage board were granted.

Also protesting against the law was one of those strange figures who so often appear when laws limiting hours, fixing wages or elevating other conditions of the worker are attacked in the courts. This was a twenty-one-year-old girl named Willie A. Lyons, who had been an elevator operator in a Washington hotel and of whom Justice Sutherland took judicial cognizance. The learned justice pointed out that Willie had been employed at $35 a month plus two meals a day and averred in her brief that, as he phrased it, "the work was light and healthful, the hours short, with surroundings clean and moral," that she had been anxious to work for $35 a month and insisted that "she did not earn more." But the hotel had declined to meet the wage increase, so Willie lost her job.

Justice Sutherland apparently realized that the majority view of the court would be severely criticized.

"The judicial duty of passing upon the constitutionality of an act of Congress," he wrote, "is one of great gravity and delicacy. . . . This court . . . has steadily adhered to the rule that every possible presumption is in favor of the validity of an act of Congress until overcome by rational doubt."

No rational doubt existed, though, that the minimum-wage law transgressed "the right to contract about one's affairs" guaranteed by the Fifth Amendment. Thereupon, Justice Sutherland called to his aid those ghostly voices so dear to the hearts of jurists when they write opinions— the voices of departed jurists who

agree with them. One voice was that of Mr. Justice Rufus W. Peckham who, in *Lochner* v. *New York,* had held it illegal to limit
the working hours of bakers. Such statutes, said Justice Peckham,
"limiting the hours in which grown and intelligent men may labor"
were "mere meddlesome interferences with the rights of the individual." Justice Sutherland then brushed away a later decision of
the Supreme Court, *Bunting* v. *Oregon,* in which an Oregon law
establishing a ten-hour day in mills and factories was upheld. A
third case, *Muller* v. *Oregon* concerned another Oregon statute in
which the ten-hour day for women was approved by the court.

How, then, could the District of Columbia minimum-wage
law be upset? Justice Sutherland admitted, first, the structural differences between men and women "especially in respect to the
maternal functions." He indicated his belief, however, that these
differences had been nullified by the woman suffrage amendment.
In view of the changes in "the contractual, political and civil status
of women, culminating in the Nineteenth Amendment," he said,
"it is not unreasonable to say that these differences have now come
almost, if not quite, to the vanishing point." The law under discussion differed from the limitation of hours law which the court
had affirmed, he said, because it was "simply and exclusively a
price-fixing law." There could be "no difference between the case
of selling labor and the case of selling goods."

Chief Justice Taft, for the minority, opened with an expression
of regret that he was forced to dissent. Beneath the surface of his
urbane disagreement, however, more than a touch of irritability
may be discerned. He was "not sure from a reading of the opinion,"
he said, "whether the Court thinks the authority of *Muller* v. *Oregon* is shaken by the adoption of the Nineteenth Amendment" and
he added that the suffrage amendment "did not change the physical
strength or limitations of women" upon which that decision rested.
The Chief Justice said he could not understand, either, whether the
court was departing from its position on the Oregon hours law
or not. How could that decision be reconciled with the earlier
one invalidating the New York bakery hour law? Had *Lochner* v.
New York been overruled or not?

"I have always supposed," Taft observed, "that the Lochner
case was . . . overruled *sub silentio.*"

The Chief Justice could find no validity in the apparent contention that it was legal to limit hours and illegal to fix minimum wages for in "absolute freedom of contract the one term is as important as the other. . . .

"I do not feel," he said, "that, either on the basis of reason, experience or authority, the boundary of the police power should be drawn to include maximum hours or exclude a minimum wage."

Taft paid his respects, also, to the idea that sanctity of contracts forbade such a law:

Legislatures, in limiting freedom of contract between employee and employer by a minimum wage, proceed on the assumption that employees in the class receiving least pay are not upon a full level of equality of choice with their employer, and in their necessitous circumstances are prone to accept pretty much anything that is offered. They are peculiarly subject to the overreaching of the harsh and greedy employer. The evils of the sweating system and of the long hours and low wages which are characteristic of it are well known.[4]

It was a fine dissent. Chief Justice Taft might, had he chosen, have made of himself a fine, dissenting member of the court and might have swung the court along the path of his own, inner convictions on major issues— when certain five-to-four decisions came up— in subsequent years. Thereafter, in important cases, he suppressed his own disagreements, however. *Adkins* v. *Children's Hospital* gravely damaged the prestige of the Supreme Court. It was called a "slaughtering of social legislation on the altar of the dogma of 'liberty of contract.' " Gompers said that "in practically every case of importance involving employment relations and the protection of humanity, the court ranges itself on the side of property and against humanity. . . ."[5]

—2—

The Fifth Amendment was a limitation on the powers of the federal government. The Fourteenth, in which those sanctified

[4] 261 U.S. 525. [5] Ragan, A. E., *op. cit.*, p. 41.

words, "due process of law," were repeated, was ratified in July, 1868, so that the Negro would have all the privileges of liberty. Such, in any event, was the theory and the amendment's ostensible purpose, although it may be suspected that Thaddeus Stevens had no objection to strengthening the central government at the expense of the states. To the Supreme Court was given the power to say whether a state law transgressed the Fourteenth Amendment or not. Sometimes the court said that it did. Sometimes it sanctioned the enactment. And there is precious little logic in the history of its rulings.

"No state shall make or enforce any law," declares the first section of the Fourteenth Amendment, "which shall abridge the privileges or immunities of citizens of the United States; nor shall any state deprive any person of life, liberty or property, without due process of law; nor deny to any person within its jurisdiction the equal protection of all laws."

And what did this mean in so far as the corporate interests of the nation were concerned? A "person" could mean a corporation, of course, and the phrase "due process," which was to be so pregnant with meaning to lawyers and to jurists and so vague to the layman, had specific implications. "Due process" protected fundamental rights: that the property owner was entitled to a fair return on a fair valuation of his property, that liberty of contract must be preserved. Before long, however, the states were limiting these rights. Certain forms of business— the railroads, water companies, gas and electric companies among them— were patently public in their nature and could be regulated by the states under certain conditions. Other forms were private. Could they be regulated at all? Yes, would be the ultimate position of the Supreme Court, but not unless they were "affected with a public interest." Even then, prices could not be fixed.

At first, as Professor Corwin has observed, the court was "genuinely reluctant to enter upon its new legacy of power." When Louisiana established a centralized slaughterhouse in 1873, a five-to-four decision declared this to be within the police powers of the state. Four years later, the Supreme Court said that Illinois could limit grain elevator charges. But a change came with the growth of the railroads, the increasing power of public utilities, experimental legislation demanding control of industry and attempts by the states to regulate business and working conditions. The dissents which had been voiced in earlier cases were being quoted frequently in the eighties. Judicial warnings were voiced that the court would decide when the police powers of a state were permissible under the Fourteenth Amendment and when they were not. Between 1896 and 1905 the Supreme Court was flooded with due process cases. What was the reason for this? Professor Corwin has asked.

"In the main," he thereupon answered, "it is to be found in the Court's ratification of the idea, following a period of vacillation, that the term *liberty* of the 'due process' clause was intended to annex the principles of laissez faire capitalism to the Constitution and put them beyond reach of state legislative power." [6]

The District of Columbia minimum-wage decision was not the only ruling of the Taft years which confused the issue of due process. Due process, whether relating to laws passed by Congress or by the states, was to be further complicated by the question of the degree to which the public interest was involved. The doctrine of "affectation with the public interest" was, naturally, a departure from laissez faire. Like all innovations, it would be accepted with reluctance by the Supreme Court. An important case came up for argument in April, 1923. Was the Kansas Court of Industrial Relations constitutional or did it violate the guaranties of the Fourteenth Amendment? The verdict, by a unanimous Supreme Court, would be that it did.

In 1920, owing to the economic unrest which followed the war, the Kansas legislature established five classifications in business and industry which were affected with a public interest: first, manufacture and preparation of food for human consumption; second, manufacture of clothing for human wear; third, production of any substance in common use as fuel; fourth, transportation of any of these products; fifth, public utilities and common carriers. An industrial court of three judges was created which could fix the wages in any of these industries or adjudicate conditions of employment. The industrial court was empowered to act when it found the peace and health of the public imperiled by a controversy in the business concerned. Its rulings were reviewable by the

[6] Corwin, E. S., *The Twilight of the Supreme Court*, pp. 71-78.

Supreme Court of Kansas and were also to be enforced by that tribunal.

The act was tested when the Charles Wolff Packing Company refused to meet wage increases decreed by the industrial court. It was ordered to do so by the Kansas Supreme Court and thus the case reached Chief Justice Taft and his brethren. The Chief Justice wrote the opinion and frankly admitted the complexities involved.

"It is very difficult under the cases to lay down a working rule by which readily to determine when a business has become 'clothed with the public interest,' " he said.

The railroads, other common carriers and public utilities were so affected, he thought. So were the keepers of hotels, the operators of cabs and the proprietors of gristmills. The Chief Justice granted that circumstances had changed and possibly had enlarged these traditional classifications, but "a mere declaration by a legislature" was not sufficient to clothe a business with public interest. A shortage of food, clothing and fuel, Taft agreed, might endanger the public health under certain conditions. But here was no proof that a shortage in Kansas could not be remedied by obtaining these commodities from other states.

"It has never been supposed, since the adoption of the Constitution," the Chief Justice said, "that the business of the butcher, or the baker, the tailor, the wood chopper, the mining operator, or the miner was clothed with such a public interest that the price of his product or his wages could be fixed by state regulation." [7]

Almost three years later, the court invalidated a New York law which forbade theater ticket brokers to collect more than fifty cents above the box-office rates. The law, again, violated the Fourteenth Amendment. A theater, wrote Associate Justice Sutherland, was not affected with the public interest. This time, however, Justices Holmes, Brandeis, Stone and Sanford all dissented. The tide was beginning to turn.

". . . if we are to yield to fashionable conventions," wrote Justice Holmes, "it seems to me that theaters are as much devoted to public use as anything well can be. . . . I am far from saying that I think this particular law a wise and rational provision. That is not my affair. But if the people of the state of New York speaking

[7] 262 U.S. 522.

by their authorized voice say that they want it, I see nothing in the Constitution of the United States to prevent their having their will." [8]

The Chief Justice, by his vote against the New York law, created the majority of five. He told Justice Sutherland that he had written "a fine opinion." [9]

So the Supreme Court was able by its involutions on due process, as Professor Corwin has described it, to approach the question "from either of two opposed angles, according as it wishes to sustain a statute or to overturn it, and is able to cite an ample array of precedents in justification of either approach." In a word, he added, "what 'due process of law' . . . means in relation to state legislative power is the approval of the Supreme Court."

The decisive change would come with the opinion written by Mr. Justice Owen J. Roberts in the New York Milk case. The Supreme Court then rejected the idea that there was anything "peculiarly sacrosanct about the price one may charge for what he sells or makes." It said that a state was free to adopt whatever economic policy "may reasonably be deemed to promote public welfare. . . ." [10]

And thereby the phrase, "affectation with a public interest," was read out of constitutional law. It was even more dead than that honored, fictitious character of the law, John Doe, whose name had been called by so many criers in so many courtrooms throughout the centuries. Chief Justice Taft had slain John Doe during an argument before him in the spring of 1922 and was more than a little astonished by the attention he aroused. John Doe was a device long used by district attorneys in bringing prosecutions against unidentified criminals. The case which reached the Supreme Court and resulted in his demise was an involved suit on the part of Massachusetts for title to some land in Rochester, New York, claimed under a treaty of 1786. John Doe was, this time, named together with Massachusetts as the plaintiff. The members of the court, it appears, were in a jovial humor.

"Is John Doe in court?" demanded Justice Van Devanter while

---

[8] 273 U.S. 418. [9] Taft to Sutherland, Jan. 31, 1926. [10] *Nebbia* v. *New York,* 291 U.S. 502; Corwin, E. S., *op. cit.,* pp. 87-89, 99.

all the many lawyers in the room laughed both tactfully and heartily.

Justice McReynolds also expressed objection to the fiction. A hurried conference resulted in an order by the Chief Justice to have John Doe eliminated and a proceeding in equity substituted for the action.[11] In due course Taft received a communication in his morning mail enclosing a poem written by Joseph B. Gilder, a brother of Richard Watson Gilder, editor of the *Century Magazine:*

> Who killed John Doe?
> "I," said Judge Taft;
> "With my little shaft
> I killed John Doe.
> I saw him come and seized my bow;
> I pulled the string and laid him low."

"I didn't know that in burying John Doe I was going to attract so much comment as his demise seems to have brought out," answered the Chief Justice, "but nothing has been more graceful or touching than your epitaph." [12]

—3—

Four justices would resign or be retired during Taft's period as chief justice and the changes added to his problems. ". . . the truth is," he wrote in November, 1922, "the court has been shot to pieces." Justice Day "has been doing no work" and would shortly retire. Van Devanter "has had trouble with his eyes, and Judge McReynolds has the gout." Pitney, to make it still worse, "is ill at home." [13] Associate Justice Clarke had announced in August that the burden of work on the court was too great, although he was only sixty-five years old, and that he desired to withdraw.

The Chief Justice did not believe that he was estopped from suggesting worthy successors. In "a general way," that spring, he had urged President Harding to name Governor Nathan L. Miller of New York. Among the other aspirants, he thought, would be James M. Beck "and the President could hardly make a weaker

[11] New York *Times,* April 25, 26, 1922. [12] Taft to J. B. Gilder, May 14, 1922. [13] Taft to Judge Learned Hand, Nov. 9, 1922.

appointment." Another was Frank B. Kellogg. All in all, Taft favored Governor Miller.[14] Harding's choice, however, was former Senator George Sutherland of Utah whom he had been seeking to elevate prior to Taft's own appointment. The Chief Justice thought that Sutherland would be "a very excellent appointment." [15]

Day was the next to go. He retired in November, 1922, under the Congressional provision for a pension at seventy. This time the Chief Justice took an active part and told the President that he favored Pierce Butler of Minnesota, a corporation lawyer of wide experience, or John W. Davis of New York. Taft told Harding that he had known Butler "for a number of years very well indeed." He was a Democrat, a Catholic and a self-made man.[16] Inasmuch as seven Republicans were now on the court, it was wise to name a Democrat and one "with the sound views of Davis . . . would please the country very much and would help the court." [17] Davis, however, declined to serve and Butler took Day's seat in January, 1923. The third to leave was Justice Pitney who, Taft heard in September, 1922, was suffering from a nervous breakdown.[18] A few weeks later Pitney— like Day— applied for a pension on the ground that he had served ten years, and this was granted by Congress.

Taft was irritated by reports that he was influencing the White House unduly in these important judicial appointments. He denied that Judge Edward T. Sanford of the Circuit Court of Appeals, who would take Pitney's place in February, 1923, was his selection. Attorney General Daugherty had been back of Sanford, he said. To one New York attorney, who protested that men of higher caliber might have been found, the Chief Justice replied good-naturedly that the problem was complicated, that there were "sidelights that don't strike you when you are sitting up in an apple tree and view the process from there."

If you people in New York were not so eager for money and would be content to live on a reasonable salary (and the same thing is true of Pennsylvania) you might have some representatives on the bench, but you are all after the almighty dollar. Now put that in your pipe and smoke it.[19]

---

[14] Taft to Justice Van Devanter, Aug. 31, 1922. [15] Taft to Daugherty, Aug. 21, 1922. [16] Taft to Harding, Oct. 30, 1922. [17] Taft to Hilles, Oct. 9, 1922. [18] Taft to Horace Taft, Sept. 17, 1922. [19] Taft to C. C. Burlingham, Jan. 16, 1923.

Taft's dislike for attorneys whose chief interest was the "almighty dollar" was an echo of his father's comparable dislike. More than eighty years before, the youthful Alphonso Taft had been seeking a city in which to practice law and had rejected the "notorious selfishness and dishonesty" of New York's industrialists and lawyers. The son, from his eminence as chief justice, was sharply critical of attorneys who demanded fees which were excessive. This was particularly true in receivership cases.

"The wolfish character of the members of the bar in respect to unreasonable allowances staggers one," he wrote in January, 1926.[20]

In May, 1922, the Supreme Court had drastically cut the fees granted to a special master in a gas company rate case in New York. Speaking for the court, Justice McReynolds said that A. S. Gilbert, the special master, had rendered "excellent services" but the allowances of $118,000 were wholly disproportionate. They were, he said, fifteen times greater than the compensation of the trial judge and eight times as much as the salaries of members of the Supreme Court. A fair compensation was $49,250, and this was thereupon fixed by the court. More than five years later, the case came up again. Gilbert had not returned the excess allowances and Chief Justice Taft ordered him to do so forthwith, including interest at six per cent, or be cited for contempt.[21]

The most disturbing example of a failing member which faced the Supreme Court was Justice McKenna, over whom Taft had worried from his first weeks as chief justice. He had reached seventy-nine in August, 1922, and Taft felt that he should have retired several years earlier. The aged jurist was, however, clinging to his post and was pointing to the fact that Holmes was his senior by two years.

"He says," the Chief Justice reported, "that when a man retires, he disappears and nobody cares for him." [22]

It was a situation touched with pathos and one which had been too frequent in the history of the Supreme Court. McKenna continued to sit through all of 1923. In the summer of 1924, the Chief Justice faced the repugnant task of attempting again to convince his brother jurist that he should withdraw. A final conference

[20] Taft to Judge A. N. Hand, Jan. 1, 1926. [21] 259 U.S. 101; 276 U.S. 6. [22] Taft to Hilles, Sept. 9, 1922.

with Justice McKenna was held on November 10, 1924, and Taft dictated a memorandum describing it. The associate justice was inclined to argue and said that he had handled every case assigned to him. Thereupon the Chief Justice was forced to say that only cases of the simplest variety had been placed in his hands. In the end, he consented to leave in January. Taft noted:

I want to say that while the attitude of the justice was in some respects that of questioning the soundness of our judgment and the opinion that we had of his work, he was very manly and just as knightly in his way of doing things as one might expect, and I told him so, and thanked him most cordially for making the conference as little painful as such a conference could be.[23]

The new member, this time, would be Attorney General Stone, whom Taft at first viewed with approval and then, because of his dissents and his liberal leanings, with extreme distaste. Of the four Supreme Court appointments of Taft's incumbency, however, that of Stone would be criticized publicly the least.

Conservative decisions by the court— notably the overthrowing of the child labor laws, the minimum-wage ruling and the others which limited the powers of the states— were joined in the public mind with the fact that some of them had been by the narrow margin of five justices to four. Nor did there seem much hope that Sutherland, Butler or Sanford would be a liberal influence on the court. In June, 1922, Senator LaFollette urged a constitutional amendment allowing Congress to repass any law declared invalid by the Supreme Court. The following year Senator Borah proposed that the votes of seven justices be needed before a Congressional enactment could be set aside. LaFollette injected the issue into the 1924 campaign when he ran independently for the presidency. His party platform called for Congressional power to re-enact invalidated laws and for popular election of all federal judges.[24] The indignation of Chief Justice Taft toward LaFollette and his suggestions was, of course, extreme. By April, 1924, he had concluded "that the welfare of the country is critically dependent upon the success of President Coolidge. The Republican party has no

[23] Memorandum by the Chief Justice, Nov. 10, 1924. [24] Ragan, A. E., *op. cit.*, pp. 98-101.

chance without him. I don't remember a case in which a party is so dependent on a man." [25]

The memory of the Chief Justice was not too clear. He forgot that as president, pressed by the perils of a forthcoming campaign, he had bowed to the greed of the G.A.R. and had increased their pension allowances. Now, he prayed that Coolidge would veto the pension raids of the World War veterans, the increased appropriations for the army and navy, the larger salaries for postal workers. Every such measure vetoed, Taft was confident, would make Coolidge "stand out in the landscape against these groveling demagogues of both Republicans and Democrats that have no conception of the welfare of the country." [26]

—4—

Once again, the Supreme Court was something less than a retreat from the world. Taft called for "war to the knife" on all Republicans who dared to side with LaFollette; they should be "thrown off the Republican ticket." [27] The Chief Justice was able to relax somewhat, however, after the Democrats had assembled for their long and tortured convention in New York and had, at last, selected the stanchly conservative Davis as their nominee. Taft attended five of the sessions, the first national convention he had ever seen, and "enjoyed every minute of it." [28] He had no doubt that Davis would make a fine president. He was sure that his judicial appointments would be made "with the utmost care." [29] Even a Davis, of course was not so desirable as a Republican in the White House.

"The truth is," the Chief Justice reassured himself, "that John Davis is too good a candidate for the Democracy to succeed with." [30]

But, after all, to use a Rooseveltian phrase which never fell from the lips of Taft, John Davis was a man of his own type. Late in October, the newspapers carried reports that the Chief Justice had been ill and Candidate Davis sent a message of concern. Replying, Taft recalled the indecencies of a presidential canvass:

[25] Taft to Andrew Mellon, April 28, 1924. [26] Taft to Horace Taft, April 28, 1924. [27] Taft to Hilles, June 5, 1925. [28] Taft to (?) Green, Aug. 22, 1924. [29] Taft to May E. Patten, July 16, 1924. [30] Taft to H. W. Taft, Aug. 19, 1924.

You have my sincere sympathy in the experience through which you are going. . . . It is a wonder that people can live through it. The strain, the worry, the craving for mere opportunity to sleep without interruption, the flabbiness of one's vocal cords . . . the necessity for always being in a good humor, and the obligation to smile when one would like to swear all come back to me.[31]

The nation was saved from the great hazard of LaFollette as well as the lesser one of a conservative Democracy, and Taft rejoiced. He saw, apparently, no significance in the fact that LaFollette received close to 5,000,000 votes, although the electoral votes of Wisconsin alone. The Chief Justice would watch but one more presidential campaign. He had observed fourteen of them, more or less closely, since that far-off day in 1876 when he had delivered, at Yale, his oration on the "vitality of the Democratic party." It is to be wondered that Taft did not grow weary of politics and campaigns, but he never did. Nor did he ever again fall into the heresy of extolling the Democrats.

The Chief Justice grew disillusioned, to a degree, with the cautious New England politician who had saved the nation and the Supreme Court from LaFollette in 1924. By spring he was confiding that he was "going to keep out of judicial selections hereafter" because Coolidge regarded him as "too insistent on having good men and . . . not sufficiently sympathetic with his trials with senators." [32] He thought that the President "does not consult enough people with reference to what he is going to do, and he often consults the wrong people." [33] Taft's conclusion, by 1926, was that Coolidge's chief weakness was with respect to appointments of all kinds. "He hasn't good judgment . . . and he yields too much to senators and congressmen in their demands for patronage," the Chief Justice said.[34]

And yet "it would be very satisfactory" if Coolidge were to run for a third term. Taft could see no parallel with the yearnings of Theodore Roosevelt in 1912. The third term tradition did not apply "except to two elective terms— certainly not where a president

[31] Taft to J. W. Davis, Oct. 20, 1924. [32] Taft to R. A. Taft, March 15, 1924. [33] Taft to Hilles, March 21, 1925. [34] *Idem*, July 7, 1926.

who dies has been long enough in office to have made the appointments which give color and character to his administration." [35]

Meanwhile the star of Herbert Hoover, who had never been
quite certain whether he was a Democrat or a Republican, was
beginning to glow and his supporters were pondering 1928. The
Chief Justice's first impressions of Hoover were not favorable. He
did not often see the secretary of commerce, he said, but had
found him "not particularly suggestive and not interesting, unless
you find a subject in which you are interested and he is, and then
he can tell you a great deal more about it than you ever knew."

He is a curious man. He has the reputation of being anxious to
absorb credit in matters in which he is interested. I presume he has
a good opinion of what he does in a particular enterprise where he
shares it with others, but I don't know that he exaggerates his particular share. He is not communicative, and he has a capacity for
cutting off inquiry if he does not wish to be inquired of. But I think
he is doing good work.[36]

But Taft soon started to swing toward Hoover, as he would
have swung toward any safe Republican with a good chance for
the nomination. Toward Alfred E. Smith of New York, virtually
certain to be the Democratic nominee, he was characteristically
suspicious. He remembered the statements by Root and Wickersham
praising Smith's intelligent labors in the 1915 Constitutional Convention in New York. Root had called him the "best informed on
the business of the state" among all the delegates. Wickersham had
said that he was "the most useful man in the convention." There
was no real reason, of course, why Taft should have known much
about the 1915 assemblage for the revision of New York's basic
law. He was not aware that the Republican machine had included,
among certain excellent changes, a grossly unfair reapportionment
clause which could not with docility be accepted by the residents of
New York City. Then, in an attempt to force reapportionment
through, the Republicans had decreed that the new constitution
must be accepted or rejected as a whole. So Smith had been among
the leaders who had demanded its defeat.[37] All this, Taft did not

[35] Taft to Sutherland, July 7, 1925. [36] Taft to Horace Taft, Oct. 11, 1925. [37] Pringle,
H. F., *Alfred E. Smith, a Critical Study*, pp. 186-187, 198-201.

know and he wondered about Smith and his reported capacity for good government. He had never been able, he told Root, "to reconcile his course, after he had united with you all in support of the new constitutional draft, in knifing it thereafter at the behest of Tammany."

I like Al Smith from what I have heard of him, but the Tammany tiger generally does not bring out and elevate anything but Tammany kittens. Still, if we have to have him, I am very hopeful he will respect our court and not put anybody on it who will be a serious menace, if he has the opportunity.[38]

For the bigots who objected to Smith's religion, the Chief Justice had deep contempt. When the candidate explained his views, in the famous letter to Charles C. Marshall on April 17, 1927, Taft called it "an admirably written document" which exactly met the situation.

I have never had any concern about the loyalty of American Catholics. They are just as loyal as any other denomination, and indeed the influence that their church associations have upon them stiffens that loyalty. So far as I know, and I have known a great deal about it, the Catholic Church has never affected detrimentally the Americanism and loyalty of its communicants in this country. . . . The usefulness of the Roman Catholic Church in our community is so great that I am most grateful for its presence. Were Al Smith to be elected president, his defects would not appear in his Catholicism but they would grow out of his origin in Tammany Hall and in the most vulgar and coarse political atmosphere of lower New York.[39]

Although Hoover "would make a very excellent president," Taft had decided by August, 1927, that re-election of Coolidge was the only hope and that the nomination should be forced upon him.[40] But Coolidge did not "choose to run" and, with possible prophetic vision of the economic debacle ahead, he meant what he said. So Taft, because he had no other choice, came to the conclusion after the conventions and as the 1928 campaign was almost

[38] Taft to Root, Sept. 17, 1926. [39] Taft to R. A. Taft, April 24, 1927. [40] Taft to I. M. Ullman, Aug. 25, 1927.

ended, that Hoover was "really one of our great men." An interview
with the nominee, he reported, "made me long for him to be given
an opportunity of leadership. . . . He has the highest ideals and . . .
the courage to follow them when they seem to imperil his success."
As a father and as a sensible citizen, however, Taft was greatly
grieved that his son-in-law, Frederick Manning, and probably his
daughter too, would be outwardly for the Democratic candidate.

I observe that Fred Manning has come out and announced for
Smith, and that Julia [Mrs. Henry W. Taft] has. Helen wrote that
she was not going . . . to announce, but I rather think she cannot
avoid it. I am very much disappointed that a child of mine should
manifest such blindness . . . and should wish to welcome into
power a product of Tammany who has shown himself so lacking in
dignity or in real honesty as Smith has in the conduct of this canvass. I can only hope that experience will convince them that mere
youth and the fact that older people have reached a different conclusion does not furnish a basis for . . . political fantasies.[41]

The result of the voting was "overwhelming" and the "breaking of the Solid South . . . a great achievement." [42] Yet the Chief
Justice would, in due course, have his misgivings about Hoover.
"Some of his appointments are very queer," he wrote soon after the
inauguration.[43] He thought in the fall that the President was
"getting along all right, but I am intensely disappointed in the
failure of himself and his attorney general to keep out of office two
or three utterly incompetent judges." [44]

Among the burdensome cases on which the Supreme Court had
to pass—burdensome because the questions involved were financial
and economic and complicated in the extreme— were those which
involved the rates charged by public utilities and the railroads and
a fair valuation for those properties.

[41] Taft to R. A. Taft, Nov. 4, 1928. [42] *Idem,* Nov. 11, 1928. [43] Taft to C. P. Taft,
II, March 31, 1929. [44] Taft to Helen Manning, Oct. 20, 1929.

"I dislike them extremely and don't feel competent in them," the Chief Justice said in October, 1928. "We have some experts on our court. One is Pierce Butler, the other is Brandeis." [45]

In a broad sense, the problem was simple enough. How could the Interstate Commerce Commission or regulatory bodies in the states arrive at schedules just to both the investor and the consumer without knowing what the property concerned was worth? The difficulty lay in the radically divergent theories of how true worth could be determined. It was correct, as Taft said, that Associate Justices Butler and Brandeis both were competent in the field. They represented, however, two utterly different schools. Justice Butler believed that cost of reproduction should be a determining factor and this meant, in a time of rising prices, higher rates. Justice Brandeis stood for a doctrine which came to be known as "prudent investment," an attempt to determine the exact value. The Supreme Court, with Taft in agreement, would hold to the former theory, favored by most conservatives.

When he was president, Taft had forced through Congress a law authorizing the Interstate Commerce Commission to make physical valuation of railroad properties and to fix tariffs. The act did not, however, specify the method of determining the value. Twenty years before, the Supreme Court had decided that the reasonableness of railroad rates was a proper subject for judicial investigation and had assumed thereby, as Professor Edwin C. Goddard of the University of Michigan has observed, an undertaking of vast magnitude, one "for which judges had so little training and knowledge." Ill-fitted for the undertaking or not, the nation's jurists proceeded to pass on rates and to offer their varying conceptions of how a proper valuation was to be determined. [46]

Meanwhile, in the Middle West and the Far West, the railroads had failed to bring happiness. Behind all the learned briefs of expensive lawyers, behind the speeches of the politicians and the statistical tables of the experts, lies the emotional fact that the gleaming rails which had been pushed westward across the prairies did not bring prosperity. They did not assure higher prices for wheat. They did not, in the main, lower the cost of the essentials which the wheatgrower needed. The politicians who had scrambled to grant

[45] Taft to R. A. Taft, Oct. 21, 1928. [46] *Selected Essays*, Vol. II, p. 554.

subsidies in land or bonds were changing their tunes as the century ended. Most of the politicians, or many of them, were as insincere as they had been venal in their greed for railway promoters' bribes. One, William Jennings Bryan, was neither insincere nor dishonest, though, and his voice carried far when he showed in 1898 that the railroads which crossed Nebraska could have been built for $20,000 a mile. Instead, the stocks and bonds issued by the Union Pacific totaled $103,000 per mile, those of the Missouri Pacific $93,000, those of the Northwestern $42,000. It was the unanimous view of the railroad men and the bankers that a fair rate was one which returned adequate earnings on all these securities. In 1897, the Minnesota Supreme Court— no doubt with due recognition of the lean years which followed 1893— had said that the rule for determining value was not what the road cost originally but the cost of reproduction. The Supreme Court straddled the issue in 1898 by deciding that original cost, plus permanent improvements, plus the market value of the securities, plus "the probable earning capacity of the property under the particular rates prescribed" all were to be considered. Nobody, naturally, had the training or the knowledge to do all that.[47]

There was a trick to the whole matter of "reproduction cost." In the slump after 1893 and until a long period of rising prices began, it was the doctrine of the consumer and was violently opposed by the carriers. But when the price level rose above the mark at which the railroads had been built, "reproduction cost" was the gospel of the railroads and was damned by those who used them. So confusion, politically and judicially, would rule for twenty-five years. The confusion persisted when the Taft court faced its first major rate case. This was an appeal from the decision of the Supreme Court of Missouri upholding rate reductions decreed by the Public Service Commission of Missouri for the Southwestern Bell Telephone Company. Justice McReynolds, the Chief Justice agreeing, said that "a fair return on properties devoted to public service" could not be ascertained "without giving consideration to the cost of labor, supplies, etc., at the time the investigation was made. . . . Estimates for tomorrow cannot ignore prices of today." In other words, a rate which did not give due consideration to current cost

[47] *Ibid.,* Vol. II, pp. 559-561.

of reproduction was in violation of the Fourteenth Amendment and would not receive the sanction of the Supreme Court. The importance of the case did not lie so much in the words of Justice McReynolds, however, as in the dissenting opinion written by Justice Brandeis, with which Justice Holmes agreed.

"I differ fundamentally from my brethren concerning the rule to be applied in determining whether a prescribed rate is confiscatory. . . ." Justice Brandeis wrote. He rejected the method prescribed by the court in 1898, the famous rule of *Smyth* v. *Ames*— whence much of the confusion had arisen— as "legally and economically unsound." Justice Brandeis did not, on the other hand, believe that the rates fixed in Missouri were legal. They were not, because they prevented the company from "earning a fair return on the amount prudently invested in it."

The Brandeis doctrine of "prudent investment" was relatively new. He explained that its purpose was to exclude from the fair valuation such capital as might be found to have been dishonestly invested and also wasteful or imprudent expenditures. He added that "insuperable obstacles" had made it impossible to determine rates as suggested by the Supreme Court in 1898.[48]

The Supreme Court would not follow Justice Brandeis's rule of prudent investment. It has not done so yet. Until the O'Fallon case in 1929 there had been some hope that the court would endorse the less flexible method of valuation determination. The Transportation Act of 1920 had authorized the Interstate Commerce Commission to evaluate the nation's railroads. This was vital if the recapture clause of the law, transferring to the weaker lines half of all earnings over six per cent piled up by the stronger, was to mean anything. It was an obviously impossible task to fix a value for all the nation's railroads; years would have been needed and an enormous appropriation.

The I.C.C. sensibly concluded that its first objective was to work out a method which could be used for valuations and which would end the confusion of decades. So it selected a little nine-mile spur railroad in Illinois called the St. Louis & O'Fallon Railway. By a majority of seven to four, the I.C.C. rejected cost of reproduction as upheld by the Supreme Court. Commissioner Joseph B. East-

[48] 262 U.S. 276.

man, speaking for the majority, said that "acceptance of the current cost of reproduction doctrine would in its ultimate results be disastrous to private operation of railroads and public utilities, not only in periods of low prices but in high price periods as well." [49] The commission issued an order requiring the little railroad to turn over, in accordance with the Transportation Act of 1920, half of its earnings above six per cent. The case reached the Supreme Court on appeal.

Every railroad in the land was vitally interested in the outcome and distinguished attorneys appeared before the court. They included two former members of President Taft's Cabinet: Charles Nagel, who had been secretary of commerce and labor and who appeared for the railroad, and George W. Wickersham, who argued the case as special counsel for the government. The hopes of those who thought that a more modern system of public utility valuation might be sanctioned were dashed soon after Justice McReynolds began reading the opinion of the Supreme Court on May 20, 1929. He held to the established rule.[50]

Thereby, the purpose of the Transportation Act of 1920 to evaluate the railroads was nullified. The I.C.C. abandoned further attempts to do so. But in all of this, if his letters are a sound indication, Chief Justice Taft played a minor part. As he had said, he did not feel "competent" in rate and valuation cases.

[49] *Selected Essays*, Vol. II, pp. 571-572. [50] 279 U.S. 461.

CHAPTER LVII

A GLASS TO THE DEAD ALREADY

SOMETIMES, during the last half decade of his life, the Chief Justice of the United States would remember a song. He did not recall the words accurately. Perhaps he did not remember the melody at all. But the connotations of the song were clear enough.

It is safe to say that William Howard Taft had listened many and many a time to "Stand By Your Glasses." It had been written in India during a cholera epidemic and it was familiar wherever white men gathered in all the endless, sultry stretches of the Far East. They would sing it when they grew a little melancholy with alcohol, and so Taft must have heard it drifting out from the clubs and bars of Manila during his years in the Philippines.

The song had spread from the islands of the Pacific. It had reached, as the United States started to dig a canal, the swamps of Panama. Then yellow fever, not cholera so much, had been the terror of the engineers and the laborers who arrived on army transports and dingy tramps to do the work or, for all they knew, to die. American genius conquered yellow fever and that peril ended. But the song still rose, sometimes, from windows yellow with lamplight at night on the isthmus. Again Secretary of War Taft, charged with building the canal, must have listened on his trips of inspection in Panama.

The words came back to him, in any event, on a morning in February, 1926, when news reached him that another of the Yale familiars was dead. Sorrowfully, he dictated a note to his classmate, George Burton.

"We have reached a time when the dead among our friends are in the majority," the Chief Justice wrote. "It is hard to get used to it but it is so, and you feel like drinking the toast they drank . . . in India, 'Here's a health for the dead already, and here's for the next man that dies.'" [1]

[1] Taft to G. W. Burton, Feb. 21, 1926.

Yet Taft was not really old. He was but sixty-nine. Almost three years later, he again wrote about the song. For Otto Bannard, whom he had known through all his adult years and with whom he had corresponded as much as with any person except members of his family, was also gone.

"It seems as if there will be nobody left alive," Taft said. ". . . I grieved especially about Ban. . . . I had a great warmth of affection for him, and we shall miss him in New Haven. You remember that old song . . .

> 'Then stand by your glasses steady,
>   And look to your comrade's eyes,
> Here's a glass to the dead already,
>   And here's to the next man that dies.' " [2]

It is a gloomy occupation of men advanced in years to read the obituary columns. Few young men do so, for the names are names of strangers. To men advanced in years the listing is a daily reminder that little time remains; it was so with Taft.

"One of my constant duties," he said, "is to look over the necrology of the morning papers, and I am sorry to find in almost every issue the account of the death of some friend of mine." [3]

Among them were the men who had been so close to him in the Philippine Islands. ". . . the old actors in the Philippines are dropping off," he mourned. "Worcester is gone, Luke Wright is gone, Ide is gone, Moses is still living, but poor fellow, he is blind. . . ." [4] Among them, too, were the men and women who had been boys and girls with young Will Taft so long ago in Cincinnati.

"I would like to go back to the old town, but if I did the city would be peopled with ghosts for me," he wrote.[5]

The moments of sadness, far from frequent for on the whole he was still a happy man, were partly due to his failing health. In the summer of 1927, at Murray Bay, he said he was not disposed "to question the general accuracy" of the adage that three score years and ten constituted the allotted span.

"I have had a serious warning of the hard use to which I have

[2] Taft to Horace Taft, Jan. 24, 1929. [3] Taft to Helen Manning, May 27, 1928. [4] Taft to F. S. Bourns, March 25, 1926. [5] Taft to S. H. Wilder, Jan. 28, 1929.

put my body," he said, "and am now obliged to take great care of myself to enable me to compass the judicial duties I have assumed. My heart has a great burden to carry and has given symptoms that I hearken to." [6]

—2—

The Chief Justice had reason to be concerned about his health. Like all men whose weight is excessive, he lacked a normal resistance to organic diseases and his heart, pumping blood through his mountainous body, had been gravely strained for many years. Taft was a temperate man in all ways but one. He did not use alcohol. He did not smoke. He did not stay up late and sacrifice sleep. His only dissipation was food and surely, in so big a man, this was a human fault. At times he conquered even that. Returning to the United States early in 1904 to become secretary of war, he had weighed 326 pounds. By dieting and exercise, he had cut this to 250 pounds in somewhat over two years.[7] He fell from virtue in the White House, though; he had too many other problems to bother with weight. Indeed, it is almost possible to plot relating curves on Taft's weight and happiness. When he was contented, his weight went down because he paid attention to it. When he was bothered, his bulk increased. Thus he dieted after leaving the presidency and its worries in 1913. He was careful again when he was chief justice. He congratulated himself, a year before he died, that he weighed just 244 pounds. On graduating from Yale in 1878, he noted, the figure had been 243 and his doctors thought that 240 to 250 pounds was about right.[8]

It may be that the reformation had come too late. It is also possible that the ills he was heir to had no very direct connection with obesity. In any event, Taft was troubled during most of his service as chief justice with attacks in one form or another. In a curious way, he found a measure of satisfaction in them, for he had always been fascinated by his ailments and would describe them with minute detail. This was not hypochondria. It was merely that Taft, interested himself, was aware that the members of his family

[6] Taft to Mrs. Bellamy Storer, Aug. 8, 1927. [7] See pp. 286-288. [8] Taft to C. P. Taft, II, March 10, 1929.

were also interested in his health. His tendency to consult doctors and tell what he learned was emphasized by Mrs. Taft's flat refusal to do so. She would rarely admit that anything was the matter with her.

In December, 1922, the Chief Justice told his relatives and friends about a brief period of hospitalization in which gravel had been removed from his bladder.[9] The following spring he suffered from an internal inflammation and thought it was due to "the hard work I have been doing."[10]

Far worse were digestive disturbances a year later which affected his heart and made it impossible, in February, 1924, for him to attend the funeral of President Wilson. "The truth is," he wrote, "I have had a pretty close call to a breakdown. . . . I cannot do all the work there is to do. I was treating myself as I might have . . . thirty years ago. There is no fool like an old fool."[11] The Chief Justice was inclined to berate himself for not having taken care in time. Looking back over life, he said, "I think I have been just what I have been— a damn fool in many ways. . . . I have thought . . . that my strength was equal to anything, and I found that it was not."[12]

It was all enormously irritating. The Chief Justice greatly desired to round out ten years of service on the Supreme Court, retire on the allowance provided by law and review, perhaps, his correspondence so as to fill in "lapses in the continuous story" and make easier whatever method his children might adopt "to make clear the facts in the fields in which I have humbly participated."[13] But this was not to be granted him. The heart attacks continued and he reluctantly concluded, as the court adjourned in May, 1924, that a projected trip to England would have to be canceled, that he could not even go to commencement at Yale.[14] Instead, he went to Murray Bay, where the calm and peace were healing influences. That winter he subjected himself to a rigid discipline which forbade dinner engagements, which transferred his principal meal to the middle of the day and limited supper to toast and an apple.[15]

[9] Taft to J. C. C. Black, Dec. 25, 1922. [10] Taft to Horace Taft, April 27, 1923. [11] Taft to H. W. Taft, Feb. 6, 1924; to Dr. J. E. Gregg, Feb. 15, 1924. [12] Taft to C. C. Jobes, Dec. 27, 1924. [13] Taft to Mrs. Bellamy Storer, Aug. 8, 1927. [14] Taft to H. W. Taft, May 29, 1924. [15] Taft to I. M. Ullman, Jan. 6, 1925.

It was, he said, "a very critical year, and doubtless all the years that are coming will be critical." [16]

Nor did the mind of the Chief Justice wholly escape the creeping shadow of old age. "It doesn't seem to me that I write as rapidly as I used to. . . . I am more leisurely in my methods of application," he complained in February, 1925. Three years later, in response to a request for information regarding some person he had known, Taft said that he could not remember. "My memory is growing poorer and poorer," he said.[17] ". . . The truth is that my mind does not work as well as it did, and I scatter," he added.[18] Proof of it came at the inauguration of President Hoover in March, 1929. The Chief Justice administered the oath and the proceedings were, for the first time, broadcast by radio. Taft made a minor variation, of no importance at all, in the words, and a small girl in New York wrote to say that she had listened and to correct him.

". . . you may attribute the variation," the Chief Justice answered, "to the defect of an old man's memory." [19]

On September 15, 1927, he celebrated his seventieth birthday, and his friends and neighbors gathered at Murray Bay in his honor. First, however, came a message from the man who had once been his foe and so bitterly hated.

"To you of Eternal Youth— it must be permissible to tell that Mrs. Brandeis and I send best wishes for the birthday on which we congratulate ourselves," wrote Justice Brandeis.[20]

More than one hundred were present at the function and it was inevitable that the Chief Justice of the United States, surrounded by these old friends, his children and his ten grandchildren, should speak in that vein of reminiscence to which his new estate of septuagenarian entitled him. He remembered that first summer, thirty-five years before, when the Taft clan had first come to Murray Bay, when "we thought we would stay a week. . . .

"I feel gratitude to God that I am permitted to stand here and in this company welcome so many warm friends," he said, "and that at this time it has been given me to gather here all my children

---

[16] Taft to A. P. Stokes, Jan. 24, 1925. [17] Taft to R. A. Taft, Feb. 15, 1925; to Horace Taft, May 30, 1928. [18] Taft to J. M. Dickinson, Dec. 12, 1928. [19] Taft to Helen Terwilliger, March 8, 1929. [20] Brandeis to Taft, Sept. 13, 1927.

THE CHIEF JUSTICE, HIS CHILDREN AND GRANDCHILDREN

See page 1074]

THE FOUR FAMOUS TAFT BROTHERS: HENRY W. TAFT, WILLIAM H. TAFT, CHARLES P. TAFT AND HORACE D. TAFT

See page 1077]

and their consorts, and my ten grandchildren. . . . I appreciate what a blessing that is. . . .

"I come now to a more personal statement. I admit that I am seventy years old today. I realize as I look about that those who have had relations with me in the past are a little bit sensitive as to when my relations with them began. . . . I have fallen into the habit to celebrate the coming of this birthday . . . it seemed to be necessary on the same principle that my aunt [Delia Torrey] pursued who lived in Millbury, Massachusetts. She lived to be ninety-two, and she gave a dinner on her seventieth birthday in order that people might not think she was eighty. Then she gave a dinner on her eightieth birthday to prevent them assuming that she was ninety. . . . It was on that principle that I have fallen into this habit. . . .

". . . one struggles along, and though it is borrowed time beyond seventy, I am going to struggle and try to enjoy it in spite of the fact that the Good Book, which we should hearken to, indicates that possibly it is just as well to show *nunc dimittis* now rather than to wait. But still I am going to hold on if I can." [21]

—3—

The closing years of life were quiet and tranquil save for worries about dissents in the court and the problem of prohibition enforcement. He had always been a sociable man, but being a recluse did not disturb him. He had small leisure in which to be lonely. Other duties were added to the pressure of court work. One of these was a new building for the Supreme Court; the marble temple which now graces Washington may be criticized architecturally but there is no doubt that it was needed. Chief Justice Taft hastened its erection. In December, 1922, he said that he was in favor of it although some of his associates opposed a move from the chamber in the Capitol, so long the scene of the court's deliberations.[22] By May, 1925, he appears to have persuaded the reluctant members that a new Supreme Court structure did

21 Manuscript Address, Taft papers, Library of Congress, Sept. 15, 1927. 22 Taft to Joseph Guerin, Dec. 21, 1922.

not mean a radical departure from sacred precedents.[23] Ultimately Senator Reed Smoot of Utah led the Congressional fight for the new building and said he would include it in an appropriation of $50,000,000 for new buildings.[24] The Chief Justice did some gentle lobbying in its behalf.

"We ought to have a building by ourselves and one under our control, as the chief body at the head of the judiciary branch of the government," he told Senator Charles Curtis of Kansas.[25]

Minor details of life kept Taft busy, too. He was reading a good deal, particularly in the summers at Murray Bay, and he found history and biography most to his liking "with some detective stories mixed in between." [26] A source of amusement, faintly touched by disapproval, while he was Chief Justice was Mrs. Taft's somewhat calloused policy of using the innumerable presents of their Silver Wedding anniversary for wedding presents. A silver and glass basket was dispatched to a Washington jeweler in April, 1922, to have the Taft monogram erased and the initials "M.R." substituted. The jeweler thought that it could be done, but pointed out that the Tafts must take the risk of having the dish spoiled.[27] He did not mention the risk of detection.

In May, 1925, the Cincinnati Commercial Club presented the Chief Justice with, as Taft described it to his daughter, "a very beautiful and very heavily solid silver fruit bowl which your mother will now promptly annex." However, "it is marked with a circular dedication, so that my claim is established, and it cannot be parted with as a substitute wedding present." [28] Actually, Taft co-operated with his wife's practical and sensible method for getting rid, at a profit, of some of the silver for which they had no conceivable use. He accepted $1,000 from the Berry & Whitmore Company of Washington.

"I am sure you fully understand . . . that . . . if you conclude to dispose of them as they are, you will before doing so erase all initials, dates and marks of identification," he said, in acknowledging the check.[29]

In age as well as in his youth, Taft found it almost impossible

[23] Taft to Stone, May 28, 1925. [24] Smoot to Taft, July 6, 1925. [25] Taft to Curtis, Sept. 4, 1925. [26] Taft to Root, Sept. 19, 1924. [27] Berry & Whitmore Co. to Mrs. Taft, April 28, 1922. [28] Taft to Helen Manning, May 31, 1925. [29] Taft to C. E. Berry, Feb. 2, 1926.

to differ with the girl who had been the enchanting Nellie Herron of Cincinnati— their only major difference in life, as we have seen, was on prohibition and its enforcement. In April, 1924, she went abroad and he was desolate.

"It is hard to realize that she is gone for four months," he told his younger son. "It will come on me with more and more force as I live all alone in this house. We have had our sitting rooms next to one another, and I don't remember that we have ever been absent from one another for four months since we were married. It is easy to agree to such an arrangement, but it is hard to bear it." [30]

His health grew worse, not better. "I am really in an invalid state," he reported in the spring of 1928.[31] His blood pressure was high. The possibility that his arteries were hardening alarmed him.[32] Ominous signs in the summer of 1929 pointed to the danger that the end was not far off or that, at best, he could not continue with his work on the court. For Taft would never be one of those jurists who cling to their high posts in the face of physical or mental disability. When it became clear that he could no longer "pull his weight in the boat," as he liked to phrase it, his resignation was prompt. He had been in the hospital for a time before leaving for Murray Bay that summer, and then was confined to the house most of the time.[33] The Chief Justice was tired as well as ill.

"You were good enough to say you would take over that patent case for me . . ." he wrote Justice Sanford, "and I thought I ought to take it myself; but the truth is that I have been sick for nearly a month and I haven't been able to do any work." [34]

The grains of sand still left were pitifully few, were running fast. The Chief Justice was back in his old place when the Supreme Court convened for its October, 1929, term. But those who saw him could not doubt that he would not be there long. On November 25, he gave the opinion in *General Insurance Company* v. *Northern Pacific Railway Company,* a case involving a warehouse fire. But on January 6, 1930, Associate Justice Van Devanter read two opinions of which the Chief Justice had made a draft but was unable

[30] Taft to C. P. Taft, II, April 1, 1924. [31] Taft to R. W. Moore, April 19, 1928. [32] Taft to R. A. Taft, Nov. 20, 1927. [33] Taft to C. P. Taft, June 7, 1929; W. W. Mischler to Hilles, June 7, 1929. [34] Taft to Sanford, July 4, 1929.

to finish or deliver.[35] For he was, in actuality, desperately ill. On December 31, Charles P. Taft had died in Cincinnati. The Chief Justice found it quite out of the question not to lay his wreath of affection and gratitude on the grave of the man who had helped him all his life with advice and with financial support and whom he had never regarded as a half brother. So he went to the funeral and the strain aggravated his condition. He slept badly. The doctors told him as the new year began that he must put aside, for seven or eight weeks, the work of the court. The Chief Justice had not abandoned hope. He told his associates that he would return on February 24 and would, in the meanwhile, rest at Asheville, North Carolina. Before leaving, he would go to the hospital for treatment.[36] Horace Taft saw his brother on the morning after the funeral and he seemed as alert as ever. The younger brother could not recall ever seeing him that way again.[37]

No letters were brought to Chief Justice Taft before he left Washington and his only visitors were the physicians and Justice Van Devanter. Yet he stood the journey to North Carolina well, was able to take an occasional automobile trip with Mrs. Taft in the warm sunshine. Their rooms at the Grove Park Inn looked out over the golf links and toward the blue shadows of the Smoky Mountains. Toward the end of January, however, the situation grew worse. The Chief Justice kept insisting that he wished to return to Washington; he suffered from hallucinations that he was going at once.[38] On February 3, his resignation went to the President of the United States and the Chief Justice went home to die. For Washington, where he had joined the "bigwigs" in the dim decades of his past, was truly his home now. Mischler, his secretary, watched in agony when he was lifted off the train at the Union Station. The big-boned, heavy man was helpless now. He was wheeled to an automobile and all that came from his lips was an occasional "darling" when Mrs. Taft was near.

"Welcome home, Mr. Chief Justice," said the maids at the Wyoming Avenue house. "You will now get well." He seemed

---

[35] 280 U.S. 71, 173, 183. [36] Taft to Horace Taft, to Holmes, Jan. 6, 1930. [37] Horace Taft to author, July 12, 1933. [38] Mischler to Horace Taft, Jan. 11, 1930; Helen Manning to R. A. Taft, Jan. 16, 25, 1930.

pleased and was put to bed. But no chance of life remained. The doctors told Mrs. Taft that it was a question of time, alone.

"It is like some sturdy oak tottering," wrote Mischler, in his grief, as he looked back across the associations of twenty-six years.[39]

Taft could take little nourishment. He recognized hardly anybody. But a fragment of life would linger for a month. On February 11, Secretary Mischler came into the bedroom with the draft of a letter which must, if conceivably possible, be signed. It was to the justices of the Supreme Court and it was in answer to a final, moving tribute.

"We call you Chief Justice still— for we cannot give up the title by which we have known you all these later years and which you have made dear to us," wrote Justice Holmes, and all the members signed it. "We cannot let you leave us without trying to tell you how dear you have made it. You came to us from achievement in other fields and with the prestige of the illustrious place that you lately had held and you showed us in new form your voluminous capacity for getting work done, your humor that smoothed the tough places, your golden heart that brought you love from every side and most of all from your brethren whose tasks you have made happy and light. We grieve at your illness, but your spirit has given life an impulse that will abide whether you are with us or away." [40]

With difficulty, the former Chief Justice scratched his signature to the reply which had been drafted for him. The phrases were conventional. He could not "adequately say how deeply I am touched." His chief regret in leaving the court had been "the ending of those pleasant associations with each and all of you, which during the past nine years have been so dear to me. Only the advice of my doctors and my own conviction that I would be unable to continue adequately the great work of the court, forced me to leave you. That work, in your hands, will go on well without me." [41]

He died on Saturday night, March 8, 1930.

[39] Mischler to Hilles, Feb. 5, 1930. [40] Holmes *et al.* to Taft, Feb. 10, 1930. [41] Taft to Holmes *et al.*, Feb. 12, 1930.

THE END

APPENDIX

THE ENORMOUS collection of private and official papers of William Howard Taft, on deposit in the Library of Congress, constitutes the principal source for this biography. At a conservative estimate, there are nearly 500,000 letters and documents, and they cover all periods of Taft's life. The executors of the Taft estate agreed, when the author undertook the biography, to have the papers sorted and roughly classified. For that purpose they engaged Dr. Paul Lewinson and Val Lorwin. Without the intelligent and painstaking work of those two scholars, this life of Taft could not have been written without at least another year of work. The debt of the author to them is profound.

Letters and documents, however valuable and complete, cannot be the sole source for a biography of a man who lived so recently as Taft. Many of his contemporaries are still alive and they gave freely of their time and searched in the storehouses of their memories. To all these, also, the author is heavily in debt. Biographers at work in other vineyards were also of great help. To cite all these voluntary assistants would be impossible. To name but a few may be unfair. And yet it is imperative that some of them should be mentioned— absolved of responsibility, of course.

Horace D. Taft was ever willing to be consulted and to give advice. So were Henry W. Taft and the late George W. Wickersham. Among the others I must name are: surviving members of the class of 1878 at Yale, W. W. Mischler, Chief Justice Charles E. Hughes, Miss Maria Herron of Cincinnati, Dr. Nicholas Murray Butler, Fred W. Carpenter, Charles Nagel, Senators William E. Borah and Charles W. Norris, Charles D. Hilles, Arthur Krock, the late Frank P. Walsh, W. Jett Lauck and Professor Philip C. Jessup, the author of *Elihu Root,* who generously watched for Taft items among the Root papers and invariably called my attention to them.

I am indebted to the staffs of the libraries at Swarthmore and Bryn Mawr Colleges, and at Columbia University, and to the staff of the Library of Congress; at the last, in particular, to Dr. Herbert Putnam, the late Dr. John Franklin Jameson, Dr. St. George Leakin Sioussat, Dr. M. A. Roberts, and Dr. Martin. Dr. Curtis D. Garrison, formerly at the Library of Congress, assisted me in using the Taft papers. Certain theses written by the students of Professor Frederick J. Manning at Swarthmore were of great value. Among them were the studies of John H. Powell on the Payne-Aldrich tariff, Martha Willard on Alphonso Taft and Elizabeth Ward Chaney on the 1906 outbreak in Cuba. Miss Eleanor Polland of Radcliffe College wrote a thesis in 1932 on the history of tariff reciprocity which I used and from which I have quoted extensively.

BIBLIOGRAPHY

ABBOTT, LAWRENCE F., *The Letters of Archie Butt*. Doubleday, Page, 1924.

ALLEN, FREDERICK L., *Only Yesterday*. Harper, 1931.

ASSOCIATION OF AMERICAN LAW SCHOOLS, *Selected Essays on Constitutional Law*. Foundation Press, 1938.

BAKER, RAY STANNARD, *Woodrow Wilson, Life and Letters,* Vols. III and IV. Doubleday, Doran, 1931.

BEER, THOMAS, *Mark Hanna*. Knopf, 1929.

BEMIS, SAMUEL F., *The American Secretaries of State and Their Diplomacy,* Vol. IX. Knopf, 1929.

BISHOP, JOSEPH B., *Presidential Nominations and Elections*. Scribner, 1916.

———, *Theodore Roosevelt and His Time*. Scribner, 1920.

BISHOP, JOSEPH BUCKLIN, and BISHOP, FARNHAM, *Goethals, Genius of the Panama Canal*. Harper, 1930.

BLOUNT, JAMES H., *The American Occupation of the Philippines, 1898-1912*. Putnam, 1912.

BOWEN, HERBERT W., *Recollections Diplomatic and Undiplomatic*. Hitchcock, 1926.

BOWERS, CLAUDE G., *Beveridge and the Progressive Era*. Houghton Mifflin, 1932.

BRYCE, JAMES, *The American Commonwealth*. Macmillan, 1888.

BUSBY, L. WHITE, *Uncle Joe Cannon*. Holt, 1927.

BUTT, ARCHIE, *Taft and Roosevelt, the Intimate Letters of Archie Butt, Military Aide*. Doubleday, Doran, 1930.

CHAMBRUN, CLARA LONGWORTH DE, *The Making of Nicholas Longworth*. Long & Smith, 1933.

CORWIN, E. S., *The Commerce Power Versus States Rights*. Princeton University Press, 1936.

———, *The Twilight of the Supreme Court*. Yale University Press, 1934.

CROLY, HERBERT, *The Promise of American Life*. Macmillan, 1912.

———, *Willard Straight*. Macmillan, 1924.

DARLING, ARTHUR B., *The Public Papers of Francis G. Newlands*. Houghton Mifflin, 1932.

DAVIS, OSCAR KING, *Released for Publication*. Houghton Mifflin, 1925.

DENNETT, TYLER, *John Hay, from Poetry to Politics*. Dodd, Mead, 1933.

———, *Roosevelt and the Russo-Japanese War*. Doubleday, Page, 1925.

DUMOND, DWIGHT, *Roosevelt to Roosevelt*. Holt. 1937.

DUNN, ARTHUR WALLACE, *Gridiron Nights*. Stokes, 1915.

——, *From Harrison to Harding*. Putnam, 1922.

FAY, SIDNEY B., *The Origins of the World War*. Macmillan, 1928.

FISHER, H. A. L., *James Bryce*. Macmillan, 1927.

FLYNN, JOHN T., *God's Gold, the Story of Rockefeller and His Times*. Harcourt, Brace, 1932.

FORAKER, JOSEPH B., *Notes of a Busy Life*. Appleton, 1916.

FORAKER, JULIA B., *I Would Live It Again*. Harper, 1932.

FORBES, W. CAMERON, *The Philippine Islands*. Houghton Mifflin, 1928.

FRANKFURTER, FELIX, and LANDIS, JAMES M., *The Business of the Supreme Court*. Macmillan, 1928.

GLASSON, E. W., *Federal Military Pensions in the United States*. Oxford University Press, 1918.

GWYNN, STEPHEN, *The Letters and Friendships of Sir Cecil Spring Rice*. Houghton Mifflin, 1929.

HAMMOND, JOHN HAYS, *The Autobiography of John Hays Hammond*. Farrar & Rinehart, 1935.

HAPGOOD, NORMAN, *The Changing Years, Reminiscences of Norman Hapgood*. Farrar & Rinehart, 1930.

HARVEY, GEORGE, *Henry Clay Frick, the Man*. Scribner, 1928.

HENDRICK, BURTON J., *The Life of Andrew Carnegie*. Doubleday, Doran, 1932.

HIBBARD, BENJAMIN H., *A History of the Public Lands*. Macmillan, 1924.

HIBBEN, PAXTON, *The Peerless Leader*. Farrar & Rinehart, 1929.

HILL, HOWARD C., *Roosevelt and the Caribbean*. University of Chicago Press, 1927.

HOLTHUSEN, HENRY F., *James W. Wadsworth, Jr*. Putnam, 1926.

HOOVER, IRWIN H. (Ike), *Forty-two Years in the White House*. Houghton Mifflin, 1934.

HOWLAND, HAROLD, *Theodore Roosevelt and His Times*. Yale University Press, 1921.

HUGHES, CHARLES E., *The Supreme Court of the United States*. Columbia University Press, 1928.

JESSUP, PHILIP C., *Elihu Root*. Dodd, Mead, 1938.

JOHNSON, CLAUDIUS O., *Borah of Idaho*. Longmans, Green, 1936.

KEMMERER, EDWIN W., *Postal Savings*. Princeton University Press, 1917.

KOHLSAAT, H. H., *From McKinley to Harding*. Scribner, 1923.

LATANÉ, JOHN H., *Development of the League of Nations Idea*. Macmillan, 1932.

LEARY, JOHN J. JR., *Talks with T. R. from the Diaries of John J. Leary, Jr.* Houghton Mifflin, 1920.

LODGE, HENRY CABOT, *Selections from the Correspondence of Theodore Roosevelt and Henry Cabot Lodge.* Scribner, 1916.

MARBURG, THEODORE, *Taft Papers and the League of Nations.* Macmillan, 1920.

McELROY, ROBERT M., *Grover Cleveland, the Man and the Statesman.* Harper, 1923.

MORISON, S. E., and COMMAGER, H. S., *The Growth of the American Republic.* Oxford University Press, 1937.

NEUBERGER, RICHARD L., and KAHN, STEPHEN B., *Integrity, the Life Story of George W. Norris.* Vanguard, 1937.

NEVINS, ALLAN, *Grover Cleveland, a Study in Courage.* Dodd, Mead, 1932.

———, *Henry White, Thirty Years of American Diplomacy.* Harper, 1930.

POWELL, TALCOTT, *Tattered Banners.* Harcourt, Brace, 1933.

PRINGLE, HENRY F., *Alfred E. Smith, a Critical Study.* Macy-Masius, 1927.

———, *Big Frogs.* Macy-Masius, 1928.

———, *Theodore Roosevelt, a Biography.* Harcourt, Brace, 1931.

RAGAN, ALLEN E., *Chief Justice Taft.* Ohio State Archaeological and Historical Society, 1938.

RHODES, JAMES FORD, *The McKinley and Roosevelt Administrations, 1897-1909.* Macmillan, 1927.

ROOSEVELT, NICHOLAS, *The Philippines, a Treasure and a Problem.* Sears, 1933.

ROOSEVELT, THEODORE, *An Autobiography.* Scribner, 1926.

———, *Presidential Addresses and State Papers,* Homeward Bound Edition. Review of Reviews Company, 1910.

———, *Works,* National Edition. Scribner, 1925.

ROSS, MALCOLM, *Death of a Yale Man.* Farrar & Rinehart, 1939.

SCHURMAN, JACOB GOULD, *Philippine Affairs, a Retrospect and Outlook.* Scribner, 1902.

SEYMOUR, CHARLES, *The Intimate Papers of Colonel House.* Houghton Mifflin, 1926.

STEPHENSON, N. W., *Nelson W. Aldrich.* Scribner, 1930.

STODDARD, HENRY L., *As I Knew Them.* Harper, 1927.

TAFT, WILLIAM HOWARD, *Ethics in Service.* Yale University Press, 1915.

———, *Our Chief Magistrate and His Powers.* Columbia University Press, 1925.

TAFT, WILLIAM HOWARD, *The Anti-Trust Act and the Supreme Court.* Harper, 1914.

———, *The Presidency.* Scribner, 1916.

———, *The United States and Peace.* Scribner, 1914.

TAFT, MRS. WILLIAM HOWARD, *Recollections of Full Years.* Dodd, Mead, 1914.

TAUSSIG, F. W., *The Tariff History of the United States,* Fifth Edition. Putnam, 1910.

THAYER, WILLIAM ROSCOE, *Life and Letters of John Hay.* Houghton Mifflin, 1915.

TUMULTY, JOSEPH J., *Woodrow Wilson as I Knew Him.* Doubleday, Page, 1921.

WASHBURN, MABEL T. R., *Ancestry of William Howard Taft.* Frank Allaben Genealogical Co., 1908.

WILEY, HARVEY W., *An Autobiography.* Bobbs, Merrill, 1930.

WINKLER, JOHN K., *Hearst, an American Phenomenon.* Simon & Schuster, 1928.

WISTER, OWEN, *Roosevelt, the Story of a Friendship, 1880-1919.* Macmillan, 1930.

WORCESTER, DEAN C., *The Philippines, Past and Present.* Macmillan, 1921.

ZIMMERN, ALFRED, *The League of Nations and the Rule of Law.* Macmillan, 1936.

INDEX

Vol. I: pages 1-555
Vol. II: pages 557-1086

Saratoga, 577; Ohio bosses, 59; Old Guard opposition to T. R., 563; opposition to League of Nations, 946; opposition to monopoly, 824; outlook in 1916, 884; patronage, 321, 424, 613; presidential campaigns, 311, 318, 320, 343-557, 646, 827-837; presidential nomination in 1912, 611; progressives in, 354; Roosevelt break with, 771, 783, 801, 805; Royalists, 59; seating of T. R. delegates, 806; status in 1884, 65-68; strength of candidates in 1912 convention, 809, 813; strife within, 369; tariff stand, 411-414, 426, 438
Review of Reviews, 625, 930
Reynolds, G. M., 718
Reynolds, J. B., 457
Rhodes, James Ford, 590
Rice, Sir Cecil Spring (*see* Spring Rice)
Richards, W. A., 486
Ripley, Alfred L., 36, 719
Rivers and Harbors bill, 528
Rizal, José, 157
Roberts, Owen J., 1056
Robinson, Mrs. Douglas, 673
Rockefeller, John D., 355, 659-667
Rockefeller, John D., Jr., 413
Rockefeller Foundation, 662
Rockhill, W. W., 689
Roman Catholic Church, 833, 1064; charges against friars, 221; in Mexico, 705; in Philippines, 158, 173, 220-236
Rome, Taft in, 177
Roosevelt, Alice (*see* Longworth, Alice Roosevelt)
Roosevelt, Archie, 914
Roosevelt, Franklin D., 368, 533, 571, 880, 1007, 1027
Roosevelt, Quentin, 912
Roosevelt, Theodore, 31, 55, 66, 93, 639; African hunting trip, 380, 399; Ananias Club, 416; ancestry, 17; and Bryan, 152; and Supreme Court, 238; article on Taft, 199; at Harvard, 41; attack on Taft, 751; banking policy, 717; belief in capitalism, 655; birth, 41; bolt from party, 552, 771, 783, 801, 805; California-Japan controversy, 300, 684; campaign vs. Bull Moose, 834; campaign funds, 789; character, 296, 312, 339, 830; charges against Lorimer, 614; Civil Service Commission, 112; college paper, 41; Columbus speech, 765, 769; confusion in party caused by, 578; conservation crusade, 472; conservation quarrel, 513; criticism of, 410; criticism

of Wilson, 869; crusades of, 112, 472; death, 913; dislike of Hughes, 331; dismissal of Negro soldiers, 323; early political opinions, 44; end of administration, 387-398; Far Eastern policy, 256, 686, 712; friendship with Taft, 153, 243, 379; ill-health, 912; in Cuba, 154; indictment of Taft, 570; in 1908 campaign, 358-378; in 1910 campaign, 759; intervention in Russia approved, 909; Japanese immigration question, 300, 684; labor and, 99; libel action, 858; meeting with Taft at Beverly, 554; military command demanded by, 904; Nobel Peace Prize, 738; opinion of McKinley, 149; opinions of Taft, 138, 361, 369; opposed to Peace League, 931; Osawatomie speech, 570, 578; party confusion caused by, 515; peace attitude, 747, 750; political cunning, 337; political demise, 892; political doctrines, 425; political objectives in 1912, 825; political plagiarism charged, 345; political visitors at Oyster Bay, 561; presidential election, 121, 210, 272; progressives praise, 563; quarrel with Taft, 576, 673, 758-771, 859; radicalism, 339, 569; reception for, 542, 548; reconciliation with Taft, 891, 897, 911; reforms demanded, 1012; renomination suggested, 318; return from Africa, 538, 758; return to politics, 551, 560, 645, 756, 767, 888; Rough Riders, 46; Russo-Japanese peace conference, 297; shot by lunatic, 836; simplified spelling crusade, 273; South American visit, 888; Storers' opinion of, 250; success in 1912 primaries, 797; succession difficulties, 330; support of Taft, 311; surrender to conservatism, 825; tactlessness toward Taft, 211; Taft's opinion of, 858; temporary retirement, 579; truculence of, 154; trust-busting activities, 248, 260, 272, 523, 670, 790, 997; vice-presidential nomination, 190; warlikeness, 295, 702, 873-882; western trips, 569-579
Roosevelt, Mrs. Theodore, 113, 541, 546, 913
Roosevelt, Theodore, Jr., 1021
Root, Elihu, 173, 204, 226, 296, 393, 644, 651, 686, 785, 793, 863; advice on Supreme Court, 534; antiprohibition arguments, 981; at 1912 convention, 801-804, 809, 811; at state convention, 517; enmity of Roosevelt, 274; in tariff debate, 422; Nobel Peace Prize, 885; notification

speech, 832; on Philippine imposts, 266; opinion of Al Smith, 1063; opposed to Brandeis, 953; personality, 275; presidential possibility, 311, 316; reconciliation between Taft and T. R. attempted, 897; re Philippine problem, 159; report on conservation quarrel, 508; report to T. R., 545; resignation from Cabinet, 380, 384; retirement from War Department, 256; secretary of state, 204, 274, 311; secretary of war, 173

Rosario, Tomaso G. de, 246

Rose, newspaper publisher, 74

Rosewater, Victor, 798, 803

Ross, Major, 976

Rusby, Dr. H. H., 729

Russia, 296, 332, 683, 871; American sympathy for political experiment in, 909; friction with Japan, 256; military collapse, 908; U. S. intervention suggested, 909

Russo-Japanese War, 296, 681, 687, 738; peace conference, 297

Sacco-Vanzetti case, 1047

Safety Appliance act, 997

St. Lawrence River, 123

Sanford, Edward T., 1043, 1058

San Francisco earthquake, 285

San Salvador, 697, 864

Santo Domingo, 694-699; debt problem, 273; revolution, 274; U.S. takes a hand, 274

Saturday Evening Post, 856

Saunders, Alvin H., 457, 599

Schurman, Jacob Gould, 158, 166, 177

Schurz, Carl, 66, 737

Schwab, Charles M., 681

Schwartz, H. H., 487

Scott, Nathan B., 294

Second Philippine Commission, 165, 338; instructions from McKinley, 182; legislative powers granted, 192; plan for governing islands, 204; religious troubles in islands, 220-236

Seibold, Louis, 757, 761, 781, 837

Serbia, 871

Sewall, William W., 387

Shaffer, Frank, 51

Shaw, A. C., 490, 492, 497

Shaw, A. F., 85

Shaw, Albert, 625, 930

Shaw, Leslie M., 259

Sheldon, George R., 362, 829

Sherman, James S., 577, 617; death, 837; vice-presidential nominee, 350, 354, 564

Sherman, John, 61, 113, 122

Sherman, William T., 249

Sherman Antitrust act, 143, 524, 654-677, 790, 824, 887, 1038; weapon against unions, 1041, 1042

Sherman Silver Purchase act, 150

Sherwood, Isaac R., 643

Sherwood bill, 644

Shipping Board, U. S., 924, 936

Shiras, George, Jr., 240, 244

Shoe Machinery case, 669

Short, W. H., 928, 934

Shrank, John, 836

Sibley, J. C., 654

Silver (*see* Money)

Sinclair, Harry F., 1020

Sixth Circuit Court, 122, 958

Sloan, Jimmy, 554

Smith, Adam, 920

Smith, Alfred E., 982, 1063, 1064

Smith, Charles J., 501

Smith, George Otis, 482, 493

Smith, Herbert Knox, 790

Smith, James F., 226

Smith, Jess, 1021

Smith, Rufus B., 29, 77, 92, 100

Smith, Sallie, 29

Smith, Walter I., 410

Smith & Wesson Arms Co., 921, 923

Smoot, Reed, 892, 1076; apostle of beet-sugar interests, 414; reciprocity stand, 582, 594; tariff views, 459

Socialism, 655, 828, 858

Socialist party, 367

Societe Anonyme de la Distillerie de la Benedictine v. *Micalovitch, Fletcher & Co.*, 100

Solid South, 1065

South America, 693

Spain, 273

Spanish-American War, 112, 154; outcome, 156; peace treaty, 187, 223

Speyer, James, 363

Spring Rice, Sir Cecil, 112, 874-879, 902

Standard Oil Co., 93, 98, 147, 323, 355, 361, 654, 830; Supreme Court decision, 658-667

Stanford, Leland, 98

Star, Kansas City, 354, 883, 932

Star, Montreal, 597

States' rights, 1049-1069

Steel strikes, 1032, 1046

Steffens, Lincoln, 522

Sternberg, Speck von, 277, 300